W9-BMK-542

A WORD FITLY SPOKEN

SUNY Series in Religious Studies
Harold Coward, Editor

A WORD FITLY SPOKEN

CONTEXT, TRANSMISSION, AND ADOPTION OF THE PARABLES OF JESUS

PHILIP L. CULBERTSON

STATE UNIVERSITY OF NEW YORK PRESS

Published by
State University of New York Press, Albany

© 1995 State University of New York

All rights reserved

Printed in the United States of America

No part of this book may be used or reproduced
in any manner whatsoever without written permission
except in the case of brief quotations embodied in
critical articles and reviews.

For information, address State University of New York
Press, State University Plaza, Albany, N.Y. 12246

Production by Diane Ganeles
Marketing by Nancy Farrell

Library of Congress Cataloging-in-Publication Data

Culbertson, Philip Leroy, 1944–
    A word fitly spoken : context, transmission, and adoption of the
parables of Jesus / Philip L. Culbertson.
        p.   cm. — (SUNY series in religious studies)
    Includes bibliographical references and index.
    ISBN 0-7914-2311-5 (alk. paper). — ISBN 0-7914-2312-3 (pbk. :
alk. paper)
        1. Jesus Christ—Parables.   2. Bible. N.T. Matthew—Criticism,
interpretation, etc.   I. Title.   II. Series.
    BT375.2.C85   1995
    226.8′066—dc20   94-9989
                                                                            CIP

10 9 8 7 6 5 4 3 2 1

To Zev and Miriam
LeRoy and Wanda

Contents

Introduction ix

1. Contextuality (Matthew 7:29) 1

2. The Hermeneutical Location of Paradise 25

3. Halakhic Midrash as Parable (Deuteronomy 23:19) 53

4. The Impact of Cumulative Parables: Strings of Pearls
   (Matthew 13:3–53) 85

5. Pancultural Adaptations: He Who Never Lifts His Gaze Will
   Never Know the Truth (Matthew 25:1–12) 119

6. Unexpected Literary Forms: The Fish Who Paid Taxes
   (Matthew 17:24–27 and 22:15–21) 149

7. Shifts in Transmission: Mites, Motes, and Mistakes
   (Matthew 7:1–5) 187

8. Parables with a Foreign Nimshal: A Skeleton in the King's Closet
   (Matthew 21:42–44) 219

9. Listener Response: Wedding Feasts and Wineskins
   (Matthew 9:14–17) 257

Epilogue 283

Appendix I: Proverbs 25:11: A Word Fitly Spoken 285

Appendix II: Selections from Haim bar Bezalel's
Iggeret ha-Tiyyul 293

viii   *Contents*

Appendix III: The Half-Sheqel Offering in the Second Temple
Period   297

Bibliography   309

Name Index   363

Subject Index   371

Biblical and Apocryphal Citations   375

Classical and Early Christian References   383

Rabbinic References   385

Introduction

Many great teachings have been given to us through the Torah and the Prophets and the other books that followed them. For these we should commend Israel for instruction and wisdom. Now, those who read the scriptures must not only themselves understand them, but must also as lovers of learning be able through the spoken and written word to benefit others. . . . It seemed highly necessary that I should myself devote some diligence and labor to this book. During that time I have applied my skill day and night to complete and publish this book for aficionados of studies, even of a different cultural frame of reference, who are predisposed by their training to pursue a life according to the Torah.[1]

Although I have been a committed student of the New Testament and Christianity for my entire life, I began to study rabbinics only in 1984. A whole new world opened up for me, and I have continued to commit myself to this avocation which so nourishes my primary work as a pastoral theologian. This book is the product of nine years of steady research, under the tutelage of various teachers in Israel who have helped me understand the complexities of both the Christian and Jewish traditions in ways that continue to surprise and delight me. Setting texts from both monotheistic traditions side by side has helped me see messages and themes that I would never have seen had I followed the more traditional academic line of staying within the narrower limitations of my own professional discipline.

Any book about parables will of necessity deal with texts—texts that continue to be the source of profound faith as well as the cause of heated academic debate. In the course of this book, examples chosen will be treated in a holistic manner that respects the historical fictions inherent in the received texts of both the New Testament and rabbinic literature. Since the rise of nineteenth-century German scholarship, it has become normative to address scriptural texts through the eyes of higher criticism: form, source, redaction, and, more recently, literary criticism—to name but a

---

1. Prologue to Ben Sirah.

few. Without devaluing the insights of these various analytical methodologies, the intention of this book is to address Christian and Jewish texts as we have received them, while recognizing the merits of variant textual readings as well.

The reasons for this approach of respect are several. There is as yet little overall unanimity within the academic community about the results of the critical analysis of Scripture. For example, the Jesus Seminar has reduced the actual words of Jesus as recorded in the Gospels to a mere handful, thereby creating a storm of controversy. The two-source theory is repeatedly under attack from both conservative and liberal academic circles. Various attempts have been made to reconstruct the Q source, but again there is no consensus on its contents.

Second, much less critical work has been done on rabbinic materials than on New Testament materials. In order to keep them on a par for purposes of comparison, it is simpler to treat both sets of texts as though they carried an inherent integrity, rather than being more critical of one set and less critical of another. Even the dating of rabbinic pericopes is in its infancy; we are aware that parables and midrashim sometimes circulate orally for many centuries before suddenly appearing in a written compendium ascribed to a specific tradent, but their history is nearly impossible to track. Jacob Neusner and those he has trained have capably pointed out the possibility that attributions in such cases may be pseudepigraphical. This type of pioneering work is a praiseworthy first step in the application of higher criticism to rabbinic sources, but needs another generation or two of development before it reaches the level of dialogue typical to the analysis of Scripture.

Third, and in a quite different vein, parables and stories are ultimately the product both of the audience and of the transmitter. Thus, to destroy the text is to destroy the story or parable itself and, even more important, to jeopardize whatever memory lies behind the received text that might give us some clue as to its messages originally spoken and originally received. Further, to overanalyze a text raises the specter of destroying its authority, for the arguments which then proceed from such analyses often render the authority of the text ultimately relativistic, subjective, and individualistic.

In dealing with New Testament texts, then, the assumption will be that we have received an intentional record of the early Christian traditions about Jesus, including the written record of what the hearers remembered hearing. Within the text lies the memory of what the teacher said, though possibly not the most accurate record of what was said. The written New Testament texts that we have received are the memory of individuals or communities that transcribed their oral traditions because these oral traditions nourished them. The record may not be complete or verbatim, nor does it necessarily encompass all traditions, but these texts are all we have. Whatever memory of Jesus is contained within those texts is ephemeral and must not be jeopardized by overly aggressive criticism. In dealing with rabbinic texts, it will be assumed again that the community remembered, and ultimately transcribed, parables and sayings by various teachers for a specific purpose. It is not my task to criticize either community for the way it chose to remember but rather to accept that memory and then to look behind it for the messages inherent within the text.

A related issue is the role of revelation and interpretation in our comprehension of the various received texts. Sanctity is attributed to texts when they are assumed to reveal something of the nature of God and God's relationship to humanity. But without doubt, various texts have become obscure over the course of their transmission, and so we must take into account the trajectory of interpretation that has attempted to keep the meaning of these texts alive even in their obscurity as one method of making the texts dynamic again in each generation. Certain questions may be raised about some subsequent interpretations of texts deemed sacred, for even community consensus does not carry the same weight of authority as the hearers' original revelation. But the value of the interpretations offered by subsequent tradents is indisputable for the comprehension of many difficult texts.

It is my sincere hope that this book will contribute to engaging my colleagues in even more serious study of rabbinical background materials to the New Testament. The rather detailed footnotes to references in ancient, medieval, and modern rabbinic literature are intended to serve as a guide in the pursuit of such studies to those who have the ready skills, or are willing to seek a teacher to instruct them "to swim the sea of the Talmud."

It is impossible at this moment for me personally to resolve the heated scholarly debate over the relationship between rabbinic parables and the writings of the New Testament. I can only confess my biases and then apply scholarly criteria to the examples I cite to the best of my present ability. The debates within Christianity, correctly generated by form and text criticism, have continued for a great deal longer and yet leave many issues unresolved, so one can hardly expect a clear consensus concerning rabbinic literature. My own current position is that Judaism's sense of tradition and continuity argue in favor of giving a fair amount of credence to certain concepts and attributions as dating from the early and middle Second Temple period, in spite of their initial inclusion in collections that can be dated only to the second century at the earliest.

In his fascinating article "A Rabbinic Guide to the Gospels," William Braude argues that the New Testament reflects a knowledge on the part of some redactors, though not necessarily the final ones, of rabbinic oral tradition, particularly as that same oral tradition shows up later in *Pesiqta Rabbati* (and to a lesser degree *Tanḥuma* and *Shoḥer Tov*). Braude's argument echoes the theories of Geza Vermes that the New Testament and rabbinic literature share a common source in Jewish tradition, passing along a common oral tradition though in variant forms.[2] This idea is not new, having been put forth by Fiebig in *Die Gleichnisreden Jesu* in 1912. I also see no reason to be as skeptical as Jacob Neusner is concerning attributions in every instance, although I appreciate the strong words of caution that permeate his many writings. In the end I can only applaud the statement of P. S. Alexander: "Doubtless there are some academic hardliners who would argue that until the Rabbinic experts have solved some of the problems . . . New Testament scholars had best keep their hands off Rabbinic literature. That is not my opinion. I believe that we have to do the best we can under the circumstances, and that only good can come from New Testament scholars studying Rabbinic literature . . ."[3]

The field of the comparative study of texts between the New Testament and rabbinics was pioneered some one hundred years ago. The scholars of that generation and their successors, including Claude Montefiore, Herbert Danby, R. Travers Herford, Charles Taylor, George Foote Moore, W. H. Loewe, Israel Abrahams, Hermann L. Strack, C. C. Torrey and Joseph Klausner, today are names regrettably unfamiliar in much of the religious world. This earlier body of work has been more recently honed through the writings of Geza Vermes, Lloyd Gaston, William Braude, James Charlesworth, David Daube, E. P. Sanders, David Flusser, W. D. Davies, Morton Smith, and Jacob Neusner, to name but a few. It is in continuity with this chain of scholars that I offer my own observations herein. One value of this historical body of work lies in helping us to recover oral traditions preceding or in dialogue with the written text— traditions now often murky or lost for the simple reason that they were oral and could not be sustained in their original form over the course of so many subsequent generations.

One method for recovering an oral tradition is the reconstruction of earlier sayings on the basis of insights gained from later sources, assuming that the writing down of a text does not immediately or thoroughly cancel out the memorized oral tradition. A more specific technique for recapturing lost oral traditions is etymological studies, which play an important part in this book and at times go so far as to "backtranslate," that is, to try to clarify the meaning of a presumed original semitic text behind the (re-

---

2. See Vermes, "Jewish Literature and New Testament Exegesis," 374. Vermes's thesis is similar to the scholarly theory that holds a common source for the Doctrine of the Two Ways (see Chapter 5), which then appears in variant form in the Didache and in the Epistle of Barnabas. Neither copied from the other, but used their common source variantly; see Quasten, 1.91.

3. Alexander, 238. For additional arguments, see in particular Lachs, "Rabbinic Sources"; Parsons; Kister; Harrington, "The Jewishness of Jesus"; Vermes, "Jewish Studies and New Testament Interpretation"; Townsend, "How Can Late Rabbinic Texts Inform?"; and Brad Young.

ceived) translation.[4] Backtranslating will often uncover the source of an error when one language is translated into another. For example, the Hebrew words for political authority (*moshel*) and parabolist (*moshel*) are homonyms. Hence, one translating into Greek without a full comprehension of the particularities of Hebrew can easily make the mistake of translating *moshel* into Greek as *exousia* ("political dominion") rather than *parabletes* ("teller of parables").[5]

Our task is complicated by the fact that we have no Hebrew or Aramaic source documents for the Greek texts of the Gospels. Without such sources (if they ever existed!), our search for the semitisms that lie behind the Greek is necessarily conjectural. We are aided by a simple though often overlooked fact that although New Testament Greek is a hellenistic idiom, it does not reflect a hellenistic culture but rather a semitic culture, however influenced by hellenism. Therefore we must look to semitic sources to understand the Greek text, rather than to the philosophical, methodological, and literary sources of hellenistic culture. Such a methodology assumes that there is a cultural trajectory that transcends the change in language, though a change in language necessarily introduces both ambiguity and new connotations. Our task is to trace the trajectory in spite of the ambiguity that results from difference in mentality between the semitic languages and Greek, and the fact that no two languages directly parallel each other. This trajectory, then, is traceable from Jewish sources into early Christian sources, developing simultaneously in a parallel but variant manner in the early rabbinic sources. The work of Vermes is particularly helpful here in pointing out that a common semitic matrix produced early rabbinism and early Christianity as "sisters" but not "identical twins," not unlike the linguistic theory termed "monogenesis."

The structure of the book is designed to make the assimilation of unfamiliar theory and literature more comfortable for the Christian reader, and perhaps for the Jewish reader as well. The book includes many theoretical or basic topographical discussions; I have avoided putting all these into one chapter or into one place so as not to discourage readers with too much theory at once. This structure means that occasionally material seems to double back on itself, and even to repeat, but the generally abstract rules of criticism or guidelines for analysis appear more plausible when directly applied to text analysis one small piece at a time.

Nor do I have any intention for this book to be exhaustive in covering all the recorded parables and stories of Jesus. Rather, specific examples are used to illustrate more general theories and to prove the value of a listener-response analysis of gospel texts. A dozen parables or aphorisms are

---

4. For convincing attempts, see Young 209, 212, 255.
5. Further examples can be found in the articles by Harrelson and Cronbach.

engaged specifically in detail. Chapter 1 addresses the foundational issue of contextuality, arguing that no parable can be understood correctly if divorced from the context in which it was originally heard. Chapter 2 explores the tradition common to Judaism and Christianity that oral and written texts have a multiplexity of simultaneous meanings, variously intended either for the general public or the most intimate initiates. Chapter 3 analyzes a "lost" teaching of Jesus, in an effort to show that parables are not simply stories, but also contain halakhic behavioral expectation. Next, the string of parables about the kingdom in Matthew 13:3–53 is used in chapter 4 to illustrate how parables build upon each other to drive home a point, particularly in the literary form known as *catena* (Latin: "a series of links in a chain"). Chapter 5 employs the parable of the Wise and Foolish Maidens (Matt. 25:1–12) to reaffirm the point that meshalim appear in various forms panculturally but are adapted to the specific concerns of the culture in which they are told. The aphorism Render unto Caesar (Matt. 22:15–21) and the miracle story of the Coin in the Fish's Mouth (Matt. 17:24–27) in chapter 6 illuminate both how historio-political conditions shape the analysis of a parable and how parables do not always take the expected literary form. In chapter 7 the parable from Matthew 7:1–5 about the Splinter and the Beam illustrates how parables lose their message when their wording is altered in the course of textual transmission. The famous saying about the Stone that the Builders Rejected (Matt. 21:42–44) is used in chapter 8 to show how a familiar nimshal changes its meaning when we treat it as a nuclear parable within itself, rather than the moral of the parable to which it has been appended. Finally, chapter 9 uses the parable of New Wine in Old Wineskins (Matt. 9:14–17) to argue that our inherited traditions of interpretation are enlightened significantly through the new possibilities of exegesis presented by listener-response theory.

The Prologue to Ben Sirah contains a remarkably contemporary observation about the perils of translating from one language to the next:

> You are invited therefore to read [this] with goodwill and attention, and to be indulgent in cases where, despite our diligent labor in translating, we may seem to have rendered some phrases imperfectly. For what was originally expressed in Hebrew does not have exactly the same sense when translated into another language. Not only this book, but even the Torah itself, the Prophecies, and the rest of the books differ not a little when read in the original.[6]

---

6. The prologue is the composition of Ben Sirah's grandson, who also translated the grandfather's Hebrew edition into Greek. At Hebrew Ben Sirah 7:17, we find the text "Be exceedingly humble, for the hope of mortal humanity is the worm" (*Sefer Ben-Sirah*, 9). When the grandson translated it into Greek, he not only

Most of the cited texts from the Bible conform to the new Jewish Publication Society translation for the Hebrew Bible or to the New Revised Standard Version for the New Testament. Rabbinic and later Jewish texts are in my own translation unless otherwise indicated. In this latter case, I am convinced of the propriety of what Mena<u>h</u>em Banitt calls "metaphrasis"— choosing to translate in a manner that clarifies as opposed to a wooden literalism, even when the metaphrasis involves paraphrasing texts or adding words to them.[7]

There is as yet no standardized method by which Hebrew and Aramaic are transliterated into English characters. The method often used by scholars of the Old Testament renders Hebrew words virtually unrecognizable even to those fluent in Hebrew. Spellings vary: for instance, one can find the same collection of works spelled Tosephta, Tosefta, Tosephtah, Toseftah, and Tosepta. I have chosen to modify the system of transliteration recommended in 1936 by representatives of the Jewish Theological Seminary of America, the Hebrew Union College, the Central Conference of American Rabbis, and the National Council for Jewish Education. This plan was published in *Jewish Education* 8:2 (April–June 1936), page 89. For common biblical names, I generally follow the transliteration of the Jewish Publication Society translation of the Holy Scriptures. Similarly,

א	בּ	ב	ג	ד	ה	ו
a	b	v	g	d	h	v

ז	ח	ט	י	כ	כּ	ל
z	<u>h</u>	t	y	k	kh	l

מ	נ	ס	ע	פ	פּ	צ
m	n	s	a	f	p	tz

ק	ר	שׁ	שׂ	ת		
q	r	sh	s	t		

---

changed the language, he also changed the theology, adding the fear of Hades: "the hope of mortal humanity is fire and worms" (Charles, 1.340). When Ben Sirah's grandson writes of "differ not a little when read in the original," he seems to include more far-reaching changes than just from one language to another. Interestingly, when the phrase is quoted three hundred years later by R. Levitas in Pirqei Avot (Herford, *Ethics*, 98), the grandfather's terminology appears rather than the grandson's. This reversion to the original stands as an example that a later text or a later tradent does not always convey a later version or reading; in this case, the later text (and tradent) recaptures the earliest reading.

7. See Banitt, "Exegesis or Metaphrasis?"

for ordinary nonscientific purposes, I use the spellings of common names and terms that have gained currency.

Finally, particular thanks are due to those who have assisted me over the past nine years in a variety of ways as this book took shape in my heart: Shraga Abramson, Sue Armentrout, Peter Atkins, Lewis Barth, Almut Sh. Bruckstein, Christopher Bryan, Ed Camp, Naomi Cohen, Mara Donaldson, Wayne Floyd, David Flusser, Robert Giannini, the late Miriam Gotthold, Zev Gotthold, Daniel Harrington, Lyndon Harris, David Hartman, Marion J. Hatchett, Esther Janas, Marshall Johnson, the late Kalman Kahana, Steve Lipscomb, Ed Lovelady, Malcolm Lowe, Hananel Mack, Tzvi Marx, Yaakov Meshorer, Eric Meyers, Aaron Milavec, Adam Newton, John Pawlikowski, James Hill Pritchett, Shemuel Safrai, Rob Schwarz, Arthur Bradford Shippee, Daniel Sperber, David Stern, Steve Smith, Emanuel Tov, the late Ephraim E. Urbach, Charles van Heck, Minnie Warburton, Michael West, Clark Williamson, Rebecca Abts Wright; the University Grants Committee of the University of the South, Sewanee, Tennessee; the Shalom Hartman Institute, Jerusalem; the Christian Study Group on Judaism and the Jewish People; and, finally, my editors at SUNY Press, William Eastman, Diane Ganeles, and Jessica Hornik Evans, without whose sage counsel and eye for detail this book would not be in your hands.

Chapter 1

Contextuality

(Matthew 7:29)

In the fifth century B.C.E, the Athenian politician and military commander Alcibiades testified to Socrates' charisma in public discourse:

> If I were to describe for you what an extraordinary effect his words have always had on me (I can feel it this moment even as I'm speaking), you might actually suspect that I'm drunk! Still, I swear to you, the moment he starts to speak, I am beside myself: my heart starts leaping in my chest, the tears come streaming down my face. . . . I have heard Pericles and many other great orators, and I have admired their speeches. But nothing like this ever happened to me: they never upset me so deeply that my very own soul started protesting that my life—my life!—was no better than the most miserable slave's. And yet that is exactly how this [fellow] here at my side makes me feel all the time; he makes it seem that my life isn't worth living! . . . He always traps me, you see, and he makes me admit that my political career is a waste of time, while all that matters is just what I most neglect: my personal shortcomings, which cry out for the closest attention. So I refuse to listen to him; I stop my ears and tear myself away from him, for, like the Sirens, he could make me stay by his side till I die.[1]

According to Matthew 7:29 (parallel Mark 1:22), Jesus taught after the manner of a charismatic teller of parables and not in the method of direct teaching as was customary in halakhic style.[2] The collected testimony of the Gospels points to Jesus' skill as an evocative storyteller; his facility

---

1. Plato, *Symposium* 215–216 (Nehamas and Woodruff, 67; also in Lamb, 5.221).
2. The claim of Matthew concerning Jesus' skill—"he taught them as a parabolist and not as a scribe"—comes at the end of the Sermon on the Mount in Matthew, a section particularly packed with picturesque metaphor and parable. It must thus be interpreted to make it fit its preceding context.

1

with metaphor and his resourcefulness with picturesque speech were sources of his attraction for the general population. It is not so much his stories that were unique, for many of them echo the religious insights of his general culture. Rather, we are told that what made Jesus so compelling was his novel talent for drawing his listeners into his parables and stories as active participants with him. In this manner, his listeners became his partners in the adventure of illuminating new meanings in these simple tales of human encounter and human behavior, a didacticism uncommon in the more "frontal" styles of teaching typical of many educators. For Jesus' listeners, this inspiring and seductive partnership served to acknowledge their individual dignity and intellectual creativity. When a teacher encourages listeners to be partners in the creative process of elucidation, no longer patronizing them, the disciples rise from the role of passive recipients to that of active participants in the pursuit of edification. As Jesus' listeners moved deeper into the revelatory character of each tale, their responses and conclusions became as important as both the tale and its teller.

This mutuality of participation provided an opportunity for each listener to feel secure in the lessons or truths discovered in the details of the story. In common, the listeners brought to the task of listening the symbols, assumptions, and popular wisdom of their Jewish culture. They listened as a faithful community gathered around a charismatic teacher, sharing the same political oppression, the same sense that the various sects of Judaism were competing for their loyalty, and the same cultural heritage and presuppositions. Some listeners were engaged in the fishing trades, others in agriculture; some were single, many others were set in extended families of young and old—all shared associations, references, and allusions.

At the same time the overtones of these parables transported the listeners into a dimension transcending their generally grim daily lives. True enough, each listener differed one from the other. Just as each storyteller is unique, so each listener hears uniquely. Each brings a particular life experience, a particular preparation or need for insight, a particular understanding of the role of faith in everyday life, an individualized way of combining inherited symbols to form whatever perceptual grid by which religious and moral standards are measured.

Listener-response theory seeks to identify both the specific culture in which a story is told and the various meanings that can be heard within that story, based on our knowledge derived from other external sources of the people who lived in that culture. The stories, tales, references, and parables of Jesus were uttered in the complex context of the Second Temple Judaism of Galilee and Judea. Over the past several decades, an increasing amount of information about the inhabitants of those territories—their values and worries, hopes and fears—has become available to students of Scripture. As we know more and more about the mentality of those who listened to the tales of Jesus, we can begin to assess the impact that Jesus' parables had on his listeners, and thereby also hear them freshly in our time.

The Historical Context of the Jewish Jesus

Who is this historical Jesus who attracted crowds with his innovative methods of telling simple tales? As with all questions of ultimate human import, the scholarly community finds itself internally at odds over this question. Scholars as well often find themselves in a very different place from the masses of the faithful. Because the Gospels give us so little information to work with, any specific identification of the personal identity of Jesus will always be highly conjectural.

The shortage of historical details within the Gospels has not prevented repeated searches over the past century to find the historical Jesus. The "quest of the historical Jesus" began some one hundred years ago with Ernest Renan and Albert Schweitzer, but its career may be described as checkered at best. The work of Rudolf Bultmann and his school in demythologizing biblical texts dealt a threatening blow to the scholarly search for records of the earthly Christ. The next generations of scholars had to learn to work around Bultmann's profound criticisms, and to this task an increasing number of both theologians and Bible scholars are rededicating themselves. The latest round of such inquiries includes John Dominic Crossan's *The Historical Jesus: The Life of a Mediterranean Jewish Peasant*; A. Roy Eckardt's *Reclaiming the Jesus of History*; John P. Meier's *A Marginal Jew: Rethinking the Historical Jesus*; and E. P. Sanders's *Jewish Law from Jesus to the Mishnah*, to name a handful among the recent flood of books on the subject.[3] The Jesus Seminar, a much publicized attempt begun in the mid-1980s to identify the *ipsissima verba* of Jesus, continues to draw both support (attributable to the intellectual weight of its participants) and extremely heated detraction. What the Jesus Seminar and each of the books mentioned above hold in common is their grounding of Jesus and his ministry of teachings firmly within the Judaisms of the late Second Temple period.

As was typical of other itinerant teachers of the time, including those within the Pharisaic movement, Jesus gathered around himself a group of

---

3. For additional resources, see my "What's Left to Believe in Jesus."

students,[4] men from small villages on the northern shore of the Sea of Galilee. To these disciples, he imparted certain esoteric interpretations of faith and halakhah, and on occasion imparted to larger crowds of people a more public, exoteric set of teachings. Like certain other itinerant teachers, especially from that subsect of the Pharisees known as Hassidim,[5] he was perceived by his followers as performing healings and miracles, thereby confirming his particularly close relationship with God, whom certain types of Pharisees designated by the honorific "abba," meaning both "daddy" and "father," indicating both intimacy and tremendum.[6]

---

4. For further information on the classical and rabbinic models of the relationship between a teacher and his pupils, see Milavec, *To Empower*, 105–150, and Lee Levine, chap. 2 and the extensive bibliography there. On the antiquity of "learning under the trees," see for example BT Pesahim 50b, and in novel form, Steinberg. To learn in a shady place is a synonym for studying intensely, as is the Hebrew *tiyyul* in the sense of the Greek *peripateo*; see BT Sukkah 18b, Shabbat 40b; Tos. Shabbat 3:3 (Lieberman, 12) and 16:18 (Lieberman, 79); Tos. Betzah 2:10; Kohut, 3.367 and 4.28, 34; Banitt, *Rashi* to the word "esbanoyer"; Ginzberg, *Palestinian*, 3.27 n32; Lewis and Short, 1927 to *umbra* and *umbraculum*.

5. See Vermes, *Jesus the Jew*, 80ff.; Safrai, "Hassidim ve-Anshei Maaseh."

6. See Mark 14:36, Rom. 8:15, and Gal. 4:6. The phrase "Father who is in heaven" appears in Matt. 6:9 and elsewhere in the New Testament. We must reject the claim of Schillebeeckx (266–68) and many others, who assume that the relationship of intimacy that led Jesus to call God "abba" was a unique revelation unprecedented in earlier Judaism. When we speak of the Church *Fathers* and of Pirqei *Avot*, we are speaking with this same combined sense of intimacy and awe, just as when we call the Bishop of Rome *Il Papa*. For the rabbinic phrase "father in heaven," see M. Kelayim 9:8, Yoma 8:9, Rosh ha-Shanah 3:8, Sotah 9:15, Sanhedrin 7:10; JT Maaserot 3.2,50c; Shabbat 16.1,15c; Sanhedrin 10.1,28d; Qiddushin 1.7; Tos. Hagigah 2:1 (Lieberman, 380, lines 10–13); BT Taanit 23b; *Mekhilta de Rabbi Ishmael* (Horowitz and Rabin, 7, line 15; 156, line 13; 227, line 10; 244, line 17); *Bereshit Rabbah* 71 (Theodor and Albeck, 2825); *va-Yiqra Rabbah* (M. Margulies, 42, line 5; 735, line 8); *Midrash Tannaim* (Hoffman, 2.164, beginning line 3); *Mekhilta de Rabbi Shimeon Bar Yohai* (Epstein and Melamed, 104, line 15; 157, line 2); *Sifrei ba-Midbar* (Horowitz, 90, line 13); *Sifrei Devarim* 48 (Finkelstein, 113), 232 (Finkelstein, 265), 306 (Finkelstein, 341), 352 (Finkelstein, 409); *Sifra* Qedoshim 8, perekh 11:6 (Weiss, ed., 95a), Qedoshim 2, perekh 4 to Lev. 19:19, perekh 10 to Lev. 20:16; *Seder Eliyahu Rabbah* (Friedman intro. 80–82, pp. 17, 46, 61, 84, 91, 110, 112, 115, 121, 128, 173). For further information on the subject, see Lerner; "Abba" in Kutscher, *Milim*, 1–7 (where it is clear that *avinu* carries every bit of the sense of intimacy that *abba* does in Aramaic); Sadan; Barr, "Abba Isn't Daddy"; D'Angelo; and on a related subject, see R. Brown, "Does the New Testament Call Jesus God?" Eckardt, 19–20, provides enough documentation for me to suggest that the centurion's cry at Mark 15:39 should be translated "Truly this man [Jesus] was a good Jew."

Most of the teachings of Jesus are surely lost to us, though those retained in the Gospels are generally within the broad spectrum of interpretation that has come to be identified as Pharisaism. Specific interpretations within this broader Pharisaic tradition appear to be peculiar to Jesus.[7] For example, his saying about two masters, that no one can serve both God and Mammon, seems to reflect a Pharisaic philosophy expressed in Essene terminology.[8] But for the most part the teachings attributed to Jesus are clearly within the complicated and diverse Pharisaic tradition known to us from Pirqei Avot and elsewhere in the early rabbinic literature, emphasizing the intent and motivation compelling halakhic observance, rather than dry external obligations.[9] About one-third of Jesus' teachings have to do with a human being's relationship with material goods, about one-third have to do with a human being's relationship with other human beings or with God, and about one-third have to do with the kingdom of God, though the specific definition and location of that kingdom is not clear in Jesus' teachings as they have been received.

Although the point can be argued, it seems Jesus was more egalitarian in his teachings than were some other Pharisaic teachers. He emphasized more strongly the plight of the suffering, the disenfranchised, and the social outcast, and he consistently called for a radical focus on allegiance to God, unsullied by any earthly political allegiance or by inauthenticity of human character and behavior.[10] Some of his teachings are halakhic in nature, concerning the specific ways in which Jews are called to respond to God's grace, and many of his teachings are aggadic in nature, often delivered in the form of parable, or mashal, so important to many other teachers in the Pharisaic tradition.[11] These parables proved quite memorable, and were much loved by his disciples as his esoteric message and by the larger crowds as his exoteric message. He was at times misunderstood by his disciples, teaching in a provocative manner calculated to

---

7. A summary of attempts to identify Jesus as a Pharisee can be found in my "Reclaiming the Matthean Vineyard Parables."

8. See Flusser, *JOC*, 173–85, on these Essene influences.

9. See Flusser, ibid., 469–508. On the competition between kerygma and halakhah within the earliest church, see Koester, especially chap. 2, and on the lost halakhic content of the sayings of Jesus, see Pines.

10. See, for example, J. Sanders, *From Sacred Story to Sacred Text*, 175–91.

11. I have also addressed this subject in my "The Pharisaic Jesus and His Gospel Parables"; see also Thoma and Wyschogrod; Young; and Flusser, *JOC*, esp. chap. 9. The volume of recent work in this field of New Testament parable criticism is enormous, and the majority of it remains ignorant of Judaism. Even the classics, such as Jeremias's *The Parables of Jesus*, exhibit now-indefensible errors; see for example the exchange of opinion between Meyer and E. P. Sanders in *JBL*, 1991.

confuse his hearers even further. Our earliest extent reference to the parables in Jesus—Mark 4:33—sets forth how few of Jesus' listeners understood what he was conveying to them. But throughout his teachings, it is
undeniably clear that he held Jewish tradition and halakhah in the highest
respect and never questioned the continuing relationship of the Jewish
people to the God of the ancestral covenants nor questioned the sacred
character of the land of his birth as a continuing sign of God's special love
for the Jewish people.[12]

The value of summarizing such research is to place Jesus within a
quite specific historical context. But no such summary can capture whatever may have been unique about Jesus nor explain what was so urgent
about his life, teaching, and death that would compel the writing of more
than four different gospels and ultimately affect the course of world history. What has been handed down to us is a collection of some of the
sayings in the name of Jesus, however sketchy and contradictory even this
minimal record might be. At least from that record we can claim that
Jesus was an unusually effective storyteller, or aggadist, whose parables
also have sufficient halakhic reference to suggest valuable behaviorist
norms to his listeners. To grasp the import of such a claim, we must first
understand both the simple character and the complicated function of the
literary form called parable.

Parable: Form and Symbol

The considerable influence of literary criticism on our present readings of the New Testament parables—compelling us to focus on the written text—seems at times to obscure the contextually complex responses by
those who were listening to Jesus' oral stories. In addition, the homiletic
and exegetical traditions of the church have accumulated as a burdensome
interpretive weight that makes it difficult to hear the parables in a fresh
manner. An exaggerated emphasis on Jesus' divine nature or his own intentions as a teacher,[13] including the contention that he spoke allegorically, have sidetracked our appreciation of his skill as a rhetor—one who

---

12. On covenant, see my "New Christian Theologies of Covenant." On Jesus and the
Land, see Davies, *The Gospel and the Land*, and Brueggemann.

13. Psychoanalyzing Jesus is the quickest way to fulfill the apocryphal saying of
Albert Schweitzer, that "we look down the well of history and see our own faces
reflected." Schubert Ogden (49–59) is correct to caution those seeking the historical Jesus to avoid the temptations of psycho-history; we can conclude nothing
more about Jesus' emotional or psychological health than the Gospel records provide, including whether Jesus was *homo authenticus*.

uses words not simply to tell, but to "do," to change the values and responses of his listeners. A fresh appreciation of the parables necessitates our understanding them as a complicated emotive genre.

Few of the parables of Jesus are easy to understand, and Scripture indicates that they are often intentionally obscure: "To you has been given the secret of the kingdom of God, but for those outside, everything comes in parables, so that 'they may indeed look but not perceive, and may indeed listen but not understand'" (Mark 4:11–12a, quoting Isa. 6:9–10 LXX). Even the disciples seem not to have understood all that Jesus was teaching them. It may be that the parables were taught in an obscure form; it may be that they are made obscure by the historical process of transmission; it may be that the disciples were quite humanly obtuse.

Whatever the explanation, it is also certain that parables are made obscure when alien or universalized categories are applied to them. For example, Jacob Neusner has defined the literary genre of parable as follows:

> A parable is different from a story in that its author presents a totally abstract tale, not mentioning specific authorities nor placing the action in concrete time and setting nor invoking an authoritative text (for example, a prooftext of Scripture). Like a story, a parable does not prove a point of law or supply a precedent. But while a story centers on a sage's exemplary actions as the point of tension and resolution, a parable ordinarily focuses on wisdom or morality, which the parable's narrator proposes to illustrate. A parable teaches its lessons explicitly; a story about a sage is rarely explicit in specifying its lesson, and the implicit lesson is always the exemplary character of the sage and what he does—whatever it is, whatever its verbal formulation as a lesson. . . . The parable in its narrative traits is the opposite of a historical story, such as we find told about the sages. The one is general, universal, pertinent to humanity wherever and whenever the narrated event takes place. The other is specific, particular, relevant to a concrete circumstance and situation and person.[14]

Neusner has failed to analyze correctly the philosophy of the genre, as supported repeatedly through biblical and postbiblical sources. He attempts to distinguish "parable" so severely from "story" that he destroys the meaning of "parable" altogether. If a parable is so abstract, listeners cannot identify with it; it is the parable's concreteness that reminds the empathic listener of his or her own experience.[15] Parables do cite scriptural

---

14. Neusner, *Invitation to Midrash*, 191–93.
15. Compare BT Sanhedrin 92b, in which R. Judah speaks of *emmet mashal hayah*, that is, "truth in the form of a parable." And see R. Loewe, 173–74.

texts on occasion, or at least use scriptural verses as a "package" before and after the body of the mashal (one obvious example from the New Testament is the use of prooftexts in Matt. 13). In claiming that "a parable does not prove a point of law or supply a precedent," Neusner thereby dismisses altogether the important category of midrash halakhah, particularly as I develop it in chapter 3. More important, Neusner insists that a "parable teaches its lesson explicitly," yet it is at the same time "general, universal, pertinent to humanity wherever and whenever the narrated event takes place." The fact that parables need morals or nimshalim to direct the listener's attention to their meaning proves both that they do not teach explicitly but rather implicitly, and that their meaning is not universally applicable.[16] Because the component parts of his premise are incorrect, the conclusion he reaches in the final two quoted sentences is de facto incorrect.

The parable is a universal literary genre. Parables are known in many cultures and in many religions, frequently in a parallel form. But within the larger and universal framework of the parable, there are identifiable cultural differences, contexts, and purposes behind the telling of parables. For instance, "fox" is a concept that may be understood even by those who have never actually seen a fox; but the relation of a fox to a vineyard—in that a fox raids a vineyard for food—is known only to those who are closely tied to viticulture, such as Israelite society. When Jesus used parables, he used them from within the Jewish localized experience, rather than from within some universalized pancultural tradition. His facility with parables was such that he earned the reputation of an expert: "And when Jesus finished these sayings, the crowds were astonished at his teaching, for he taught them as a parabolist, rather than as a scribe."[17]

Apples of Gold in Silver Settings

For decades scholars have tried to apply hellenistic forms of analysis and structure to the parables of Jesus, failing to recognize that Jesus' para-

---

16. See for example Ezek. 17:3–10; 20:45–48 [Heb. 21:1–4], and 24:3–5. In each case, the prophet attaches a nimshal in order to direct the recipient's reception of the prophet's intended point. Without the nimshal, Ezekiel cannot be sure his message will be understood correctly. And see Landes, 145–46.

17. Matt. 7:29. In Ezek. 20:49 [Heb. 21:5], we find the term "maker of meshalim" [parabolist]; see also Landes, 141, 150, 155 n60. According to Klausner, 264–65, the first source for this interpretation is Hirsch Peretz Chajes in *Markus Studien*, 10–12; yet cf. Schechter, *Studies in Judaism*, 117, 123, and Lapide, 30; see also the panel discussion appended to Petuchowski, 148. The term should also be compared with *logopoios*; see Perry, *Babrius and Phaedrus*, Intro., xxxv; and Beavis, 45.

bles are conditioned by the Arameo-Hebraic religion and culture out of which they proceed and thus cannot be forced into Greek categories of mentation. To understand the parables of Jesus, we must also appreciate the philosophy of parables unique to Judaism, as opposed simply to grasping the more universal function of the parable as a literary genre. Though written many centuries later, perhaps the most skillful articulation of Judaism's particular philosophy of parables comes from Maimonides' *Guide of the Perplexed*:

> "The Wisest of All Men" [King Solomon; vide 1 Kgs. 4:31] has said: *A word fitly spoken is like apples of gold in settings* [maskiyyot] *of silver* (Prov. 25:11).[18] Let us try to understand what he is saying here! *Maskiyyot* denotes latticework openings, that is, a covering pierced with extremely tiny holes, like the filigree work of a silversmith. They are so called because they admit scrutiny, just as the targum indicates when it translates (Gen. 26:8) *and [Avimelekh] looked [out of the window]* as "and he espied."[19] Solomon thus likened *a word fitly spoken*[20] to an apple of gold overlaid with particularly fine silver filigree. See how marvelous is this dictum in its description of a sagacious parable! For in this manner he indicates that a saying offers ambiguous meaning—its exoteric sense (*peshat*) and its esoteric sense (*sod*).[21] The exoteric meaning should be as becoming as silver, thereby magnifying the even more beautiful character of the esoteric meaning, as is the case when gold is compared to silver. It also should be obvious that the exoteric meaning is constructed in such a way as to point to its esoteric implication, as would a silver overlay of fine filigree molded around an apple of gold. When seen from a distance or with a clouded comprehension, it would be possible to assume it to be an apple of silver, but to a perspicuous observer looking with trained com-

---

18. The phrase is popular with Maimonides, who uses it in four places—*Sefer ha-Mitzvot* 179 (Kafiḥ, 269 n3); Commentary to M. Miqvaot 4:3 end (Kafiḥ 1957, 346); *Moreh Nebukhim*, preface (Pines, 11–12); and the opening of Epistle to Yemen (*la-Am*, 10.16 n55, where the editor claims, "By this phrase, Maimonides wants to indicate a clear statement," that is, its fullest depth and significance).

19. See Jastrow, 989, *sekhi*. On the meaning of the Hebrew behind Prov. 25:11, see Appendix 1.

20. According to Kafiḥ, "Here Maimonides uses an Arabic translation of a Biblical word indicating a double meaning, i.e., that a parable and its moral should interweave skillfully. He understands *ofenav* either as two meanings or two facets, after ibn-Janah. In his *Sefer ha-Mitzvot*, Injunction 179 [Kafiḥ, 269 n3] and in his *Perush ha-Mishnah* to Miqvaot 4:3 it appears to refer to "someone's grasp of a speaker's exact intention." See Appendix 1.

21. According to Kafiḥ, "Here ibn-Tibbon added the words 'both overt and covert,' upon which David Qimhi built his analysis of the root alef-pey-nun [see Qimhi's *Sefer ha-Shorashim*, 25, and his compendium *Mikhlol*, 151b, under *poel*]."

prehension, its contents are obvious: he recognizes it as an apple of gold. Similar are the parables of the prophets, peace be upon them. Their wisdom is efficacious in so many ways, including the amendment of human social intercourse, as is shown by the exoteric sense of the Book of Proverbs and similar wisdom literature. Yet within them lies wisdom even more efficacious for one's spiritual formation in accordance with their inherent [esoteric] truth.[22]

Maimonides goes on to say that turning a parable into an allegory, by seeking parallel meanings for each word, tends frequently to obscure further the meaning of the parable, for parables are ordinarily not meant to be allegories.

You should not inquire into all the details occurring in the parable, nor should you wish to find significations corresponding to them. For doing so would lead you into one of two ways: either into turning aside from the parable's intended subject, or into assuming an obligation to interpret things not susceptible of interpretation and that have not been inserted with a view to interpretation. The assumption of such an obligation would result in extravagant fantasies such as are entertained and written about in our time by most of the sects of the world, since each of these sects desires to find certain significations for words whose author in no wise had in mind the significations wished by them. Your purpose, rather, should always be to know, regarding most parables, the whole that was intended to be known.[23]

Allegorization of a parable often leads one farther away from the "apple of gold," the truth that lies inside the parable. If Maimonides' philosophy of parables is an accurate extension of Second Temple Jewish thought, we can assume that to seek an allegorical meaning to the parables of Jesus is generally a violation of the spirit of those parables.[24]

22. Maimonides, *Moreh Nebukhim* 6b–7a. Pines's translation modified by the author; compare Kafih̲, 10.
23. Maimonides at 8b, trans. Pines, 14. Rose (392) claims that the first Greek philosopher to use the term "allegory" was Kleanthes, a Stoic of the third century B.C.E. Among useful works on the history of allegory in Greek philosophy and early rabbinics are Wolfson's *Philo*, esp. vol. 1, chap. 2; Edmond Stein, *Philo*, 162–85; Heinemann, "Scientific Allegorization"; and ibn-Parh̲on, 2b–c on metaphor.
24. The dilemma of the early church is obvious here. The Epistle of Barnabas, approximately contemporaneous with Matthew and Luke, admits that Christians can see Christ in the Old Testament only if they have been given a special gnosis, an esoteric secret knowledge (6:9; 9:8; 10:10; 13:7 in Lake, 1.361, 373, 377). The same thought is typical of Clement of Alexandria, who claimed that Christianity is

The Radical Character of a Parable

The Hebrew word *mashal* means "to compare," and evolves from an ancient semitic stem.[25] The nuances of the word suggest the equation of two things that are alike enough that a lesson can be learned by setting them side by side and then using the similarities and differences between the two to define the distinct character of each. Our English word "parable," from the Greek prefix *para* plus the stem *bol-*, does not carry nuances identical to the semitic root. To define the Greek word *para-bole* is complicated. It may be a story; it may be the deposit made to a court when lodging an appeal; some sources suggest that it can mean to teach "through deceit" (*para-bolos*).[26] It is perhaps kinder and gentler to explain the meaning applicable here as to "throw down a decoy near someone whom you wish to catch," or to "lay down a fiction as a foundation upon which to build." When the term "parable" is used in English, even in its narrowest definition it carries a certain sense of surprising reversal, even entrapment. A parable is often intended to topple expectations and norms. Unlike the word "parable" as it is usually understood in English, the

---

primarily a collection of secret gnosis, not intended to be obvious to the public; see R. Brown, *Sensus Plenior*, 39–40. Theodore of Mopsuestia was convinced that only four psalms had anything to do with Christ—surprisingly, they were not ones common to our present liturgical tradition, but rather 2, 8, 45, and 110 (Zaharopoulos, 100 n28). For many patristic writers, the fatal error of the Jews (Barnabas 4:7 in Lake, 1.351) was to read their own Scriptures as though they meant what they said. See Bennett and Edwards, 51; also Hellwig, 175; and Kelly, 32, 65–66. In other words, Christ could not be found in scripture unless it was read allegorically; such a reading at the same time violated the spirit of the "plain" meaning of Christ's words.

25. See "New Akkadian Witnesses," by Chaim Cohen, where he explores the etymological history of the word, concentrating in particular on its confusion with a similar word meaning "to exercise political dominion." See McKane 1970, 22–33, and Landes, 137–58. On parable and analogy, see Frank, esp. 148–82, and Fromm, *The Heart of Man*; see also Haran in *Biblical Encyclopedia*, 5.548–554. Clearly neither God nor revelation can be known without the use of parabolic comparisons, given our limited human capacities for perception.

26. In this sense, the Greek is perhaps more closely related to the Hebrew *ḥiddah*, or enigma, as it is used in Ps. 78:2. Landes (154 n32, 156 n63) observes that *ḥiddah* and *mashal* are often found in combination in the Hebrew Bible, underlining the intentionally enigmatic character of a *mashal*; see e.g. Hab. 2:6–19. For the sake of simplicity in this chapter and elsewhere, however, I will use *mashal* and parable as though they were synonymous, though any number of articles point out that the parallel is not exact.

Hebrew word *mashal* carries a larger definition than simply an illustrative story or fable; it can also mean any kind of enigmatic, mystical, or dark saying, as well as a proverb, a maxim, or an ancient saw. A mashal, then, is any comparison in which an abstract idea and a real-life (whether fictional or not) situation are set side by side. The "decoy" occurs in the minds of the listeners, as they discover new truths illuminated by the activity of side-by-side comparison. Such side-by-side, or whole-to-whole, abstract comparison differentiates a parable from an allegory, at least as the latter form became a technical term for one-to-one comparisons in medieval exegesis.

Parables generally have a specific form—the body of the story, which in Hebrew is called the mashal, and a stated application or point or moral, which is called the nimshal. Even when the body of the parable, the mashal, is the same between parables originating in two different cultures, the nimshal may vary. This variation can be illustrated by two examples, the first from the fables of Aesop, and the second from a rabbinic commentary on Qohelet (Ecclesiastes):

> A half-starved fox, who saw in the hollow of an oak tree some bread and meat left there by shepherds, crept in and ate it. With his stomach distended he could not get out again. Another fox, passing by and hearing his cries and lamentations, came up and asked what was the matter. On being told, he said: "Well, stay there till you are as thin as you were when you went in; then you'll get out quite easily."
>
> This tale shows how time solves difficult problems.[27]

> It is like a fox who found a vineyard which was fenced in on all sides. There was one hole through which he wanted to enter, but he was unable to do so. What did he do? He fasted for three days until he became lean and frail, and so got through the hole. Then he ate [of the grapes] and became fat again, so that when he wished to go out he could not pass through at all. He again fasted another three days until he became lean and frail, returning to his former condition, and went out. When he was

---

27. *Fables of Aesop*, in Handford, 3. Another parallel is found in *Babrius and Phaedrus*, Perry, 107 #86, though his nimshal is, "You'll not get out of here until your belly is the same size as when you entered," and thus more like that of the second example. The same parable exists in various forms in the folk literature of the world; for example, in classical Indian literature it takes the form of a jackal trapped inside the hide of a dead elephant. In the sixth-century Christian collection *Historia Francorum* by Gregory of Tours, it is a snake trapped in a bottle of wine. For another example of a mashal with two different nimshalim (one by Phaedrus, one by R. Itzhak Nafha), see Schwarzbaum, "Talmudic-Midrashic Affinities," 441.

outside, he turned his face and gazing at the vineyard, said, "O vineyard, O vineyard, how good are you and the fruits inside! All that is inside is beautiful and commendable, but what enjoyment has one from you?"

As he had come naked from his mother's womb, so will he return as he came (Qoh. 5:14).[28]

The mashal in Aesop's "The Swollen Fox" and in the parable of the fox from *Qohelet Rabbah* are the same: the hungry fox eats too much in the vineyard (or oak tree) and cannot get out again without fasting. But each has a different nimshal: For Aesop, the point of the parable is that "time solves difficult problems."[29] For the author of *Qohelet Rabbah*, the nimshal is quite different—"As one enters (this world at birth) so one leaves (this world at death)—you can't take it with you!"

Contextual Determination of the Nimshal

That nimshalim vary from culture to culture and from situation to situation, even in relation to the same basic mashal, is of extreme significance. According to listener-response theory, a listener's application of a

---

28. Qohelet Rabbah 5.14, 1. Schwarzbaum ("Talmudic-Midrashic Affinities," 430) points out how familiar the rabbinic sages were with the Aesopic tradition. On 433, he suggests that the biblical nimshal led the sages to add the Aesopic mashal, rather than vice versa. For an extensive and fascinating history of this parable, see Scharzbaum, *Mishlei Shu'alim*, 210–218. On the influence of Greek literature and thought on rabbinic literature in general, see Mack, *Aggadic*, 84–87.

29. It should be noted that this almost trite aphorism appears here as a nimshal, but often stands on its own, as it does in Philo, *On Joseph* 10–11 (Colson, 6.145–146 to Gen. 37:9), and in Shakespeare's *Macbeth*, Act I, Scene 3, line 146; and see Davidson, *Otzar*, 119 #1924 and Savar, 1215. However, the nimshal here attached by *Qohelet Rabbah* is nicely nuanced by comparing this mashal with a very similar text in Semahot 3.3 (Higger, 221–22), and see Ps. 49, esp. v18. Another nimshal added on occasion to this mashal, particularly by medieval Jewish writers, is "rebuke thy lust that it persuade thee not, and guard thee from diseases occasioned by changes of habit" (see, for example, ibn-Zabara). R. Nissim gives the far-fetched nimshal, "In a similar way the wicked will not cease repenting of their past deeds, without securing any good acts. Their penitence will, however, be of no avail!" ; in a Spanish version, the nimshal is given: "If your sense were as long as your beard, you would look for exits as well as entrances." For other examples of Qoh. 5:15 as a nimshal, see Abramson in ibn-Shu'eib intro p. 9; ben Yatzliah 53a–b (105–106); Duran to Avot 4.21; *Sefer ha-SMa"Q* of Isaac of Corbail, 20, Mitzvah 19 to "Do not covet."

parable to one's own life generates in turn an emotional reaction unique to that person. Such individualized applications are themselves variant nimshalim, particularly when the teller of parables does not provide the listeners with a ready-made nimshal. In this sense, a nimshal is the concretization of a listener's emotional response to the mashal. The range of emotional responses to a given mashal is determined by the manner in which a mashal is narrated. A parabolist chooses carefully the details in the crafting of each mashal, so that the elicitation of a variety of responses functions as an exhibition of the skill and agenda of the teller (though is not intended to focus attention on the teller). A parable used for illustration will generate a response different from one used for concretization. A parable that has a human situation will generate a response different from a fable about animals, even though the two may have identical structures. A parable about a king will generate a response different from a parable about a beggar. A parable about a king will be told and will be heard differently in a kingdom, a conquered land, or a democracy.

Among the theorists of catharsis as the generative power by which an individual produces a personalized nimshal are Aristotle, Friedrich Schiller, and Erich Auerbach. For Aristotle (*de Poetica* 1448b), the pleasure of tragedy is that it teaches us to imitate the ultimate good, and then to experience the reward of self-respect when we recognize the results of that good within ourselves. This imitation becomes possible only through the clear depiction of the tragedy that has befallen another, such as "the forms of the lowest animals, and dead bodies." To the insightful, such depictions yield catharsis as opposed to pride, that is, a firmer resolve to rededicate oneself to higher values. Friedrich Schiller, in his essay "Of the Cause of the Pleasure We Derive from Tragic Objects," observes that we continue to attend tragedies in the theater because of the affirmative catharsis we experience when we reflect back upon the moral triumph of the suffering, no matter how bitter their end. For example, "When Timeleon of Corinth puts to death his beloved but ambitious brother Timophanes, he does it because his idea of duty to his country bids him to do so. The act here inspires horror and repulsion as against nature and the moral sense, but this feeling is soon succeeded by the highest admiration for his heroic virtue, pronouncing, in a tumultuous conflict of emotions, freely and calmly, with perfect rectitude." In other words, the personal nimshal which a viewer derives from seeing a tragedy well presented is the product of the viewer's subsequent reflection upon what was earlier witnessed. The tragedy itself may present no nimshal, but if it has been effective, it will of necessity produce a nimshal post facto among those whose sense of moral propriety has been affected. To this end, claims Schiller, we do not attend the theater to enjoy the plot of a tragedy but rather to individualize and digest the moral point of the drama, then to use it to affirm again our own optimism that life has a higher meaning, thus leaving the theater more pure and more focused than we were when first viewing the tragedy. Auerbach's seminal essay "Odysseus' Scar" explores the difference between classical and biblical narratives. Homer's *Odyssey* is full of ever-present detail ("of the foreground"), while the Sacrifice of Isaac narrative speaks powerfully in its silences and in the vast number of details ignored by the writer ("fraught with background"). In the biblical narrative it is the silences, the absence of specificity, that force the listener to provide the interpretation, and ultimately to frame the nimshal as a way of staking a claim to the authoritative truth of the story.[30]

We must also hold out the possibility of a "pseudo-nimshal" in certain instances. As Mary Ann Beavis points out in her comments on the parable collection known as *Babrius and Phaedrus*, compiled at approximately the same time as the canonical gospels, "According to Babrius (Prologue), Aesop told stories so that his hearers might 'learn and understand'; however, Phaedrus (3, Prologue) explains that the fable is an obscure form of speech that allowed the slave [Aesop] to escape punishment for his opinions."[31] In other words, if the slave Aesop told a certain mashal, omitting the nimshal, and his master through the process of listener response added his own nimshal, the result could be the death of the slave in that the master reached an insulting conclusion from his own associations with the figures of the mashal. In this sense, a storyteller might even attach a certain nimshal to a mashal to confuse or deceive the hearer, or to mask the point more intended by the parabolist. Clever Aesop could make his own personal point in telling an acerbic mashal, but then mask that very point with a nimshal that saved his life by confusing his master. We can designate that masking process as a "pseudo-nimshal," the true nimshal remaining implied but unstated within the directionality of the mashal.

Given the vast variety of the world's literature, not every mashal is followed by a nimshal, as the following familiar quotation illustrates:

"Well, goodbye, if you're sure you won't have any more."

"Is there any more?" asked Pooh quickly.

Rabbit took the covers off the dishes, and said, "No, there wasn't."

"I thought not," said Pooh, nodding to himself. "Well, good-bye. I must be going on."

---

30. On the importance of silences in shaping the meaning of a text, see also Bergson, 187–89; Williams, 65.
31. Beavis, 45 n57.

So he started to climb out of the hole. He pulled with his front paws, and pushed with his back paws, and in a little while his nose was out in the open again . . . and then his ears . . . and then his front paws . . . and then his shoulders . . . and then—

"Oh, help!" said Pooh. "I'd better go back."

"Oh, bother!" said Pooh. "I shall have to go on."

"I can't do either!" said Pooh. "Oh, help *and* bother!"

Now, by this time Rabbit wanted to go for a walk too, and finding the front door full, he went out by the back door, and came round to Pooh, and looked at him.

"It all comes," said Rabbit sternly, "of eating too much. I thought at the time," said Rabbit, "only I didn't like to say anything," said Rabbit, "that one of us was eating too much," said Rabbit, "and I knew it wasn't *me*," he said. "Well, well, I shall go and fetch Christopher Robin." . . .

Christopher Robin nodded.

"Then there's only one thing to be done," he said. "We shall have to wait for you to get thin again."

"How long does getting thin take?" asked Pooh anxiously.

"About a week, I should think." . . .

And at the end of the week Christopher Robin said, "*Now!*"

So he took hold of Pooh's front paws and Rabbit took hold of Christopher Robin, and all Rabbit's friends and relations took hold of Rabbit, and they all pulled together . . . .

And for a long time Pooh only said "Ow!" . . .

And "Oh!"

And then, all of a sudden, he said "Pop!" just as if a cork were coming out of a bottle.

And then Christopher Robin and Rabbit and all Rabbit's friends and relations went head-over-heels backwards . . . and on top of them came Winnie-the-Pooh—free![32]

Here the same basic motif as we have seen in previous meshalim has no explicit moral appended.

---

32. Milne, *The World of Pooh*, 37–43. Accordingly, we read in Lewis Carroll (*More*, 110): "Perhaps it hasn't one," Alice ventured to remark. "Tut, tut, child!" said the Duchess. "Everything's got a moral, if only you can find it."

Some rabbinic parables have nimshalim and some do not; some of the parables of Jesus have nimshalim and some do not. It is then obvious why early Jewish Scripture commentaries forbid the "veneration" of any given nimshal; the point of a parable is the mashal, the narrative story itself. The nimshal must of necessity be left up to each listener to determine, unless, or even when, the teller specifically attaches a nimshal so as to clarify unequivocally the teller's point in relating the mashal. The existence of a nimshal underlines the contextual relativity of the mashal's usage; even if the body of the mashal may seem at first to be universal, the nimshal proves that more than a universalized human problem is being addressed here. Even a preexisting mashal is particularized in its application to the aspirations and disappointments of a specific time, a specific culture, or a specific person by the addition of an explicit or implicit nimshal. Because, as in the examples above, some of the gospel parables of Jesus have nimshalim and some do not, and some meshalim appear in more than one gospel but with variant nimshalim,[33] we are forced to ask in relation to each parable: who attached the nimshal extant in the gospel text to the mashal? Did Jesus? the gospeller? Christian tradition? or is it accidentally misplaced from a different mashal?

Combinations of Agglutinate Symbols

Parables ordinarily draw on a repertoire of stock figures.[34] They are short and have no time for extensive character development. Rather, they rely on the cultural associations brought by the hearers to the evocation of these stock figures. In this sense, the figures in a parable are archetypes or symbols, particularly in the Jungian sense,[35] though as has been stated, the allegorization of parables is not generally an accepted part of the rabbinic tradition. With the passage of centuries, we have lost our grasp of the cultural definitions automatically associated with the stock figures common to first-century Jewish parables. For example, the parable of the fox from *Qohelet Rabbah* contains three stock figures or clues in the first sentence: fox, vineyard, and fence. Each of these words has strong associations in the literature of the Second Temple and early rabbinism; their

33. See for example the Parable of the Rich Fool in Luke 12:16–20; some manuscripts include v21 as a mashal, and some (such as the Gospel of Thomas #63) omit the verse altogether. And see Fitzmyer, 2.971.
34. Scott, *Jesus*, 49–50; Goulder, 55.
35. For an exercise in the application of archetype and symbol to Scripture, see Fromm, *The Forgotten Language*, esp. chaps. 2 and 6.

very mention, particularly in combination, would dredge up associations, other traditional tales, stereotypes, mind-pictures, and expectations for the outcome of the story.

The fox is a very common figure in rabbinic parables, and even more fox stories were known than have survived: "Rabbi Meir had three hundred parables of foxes, and we have only three left."[36] The image of the fox suggests craftiness and danger of exploitation. A fence is also a common figure in both rabbinic parables and sayings; for example, "Be deliberate in judging, and raise up many disciples, and make a fence for the Torah."[37] The fence suggests a safeguard, and particularly in relation to Torah, suggests safeguards of behavior. Vineyard is a word with a long and unquestionable association in Hebrew Scripture, the best example of which is also one of the finest parables in Scripture, Isaiah 5:1–7. Vineyard suggests the house of Israel, the people Israel. Foxes and vineyards are connected with each other in the traditional literature, such as Song of Songs 2:15 (the little foxes that spoil the vineyards) and *ba-Midbar Rabbah* 20.14 (shall the vineyards be sold like foxes?). Thus in three simple words—fox, vineyard, fence—a whole set of associations emerges in the minds of the listener.

These associations would be quite different from the associations brought by Aesop's contemporaries to his version of the mashal. To illustrate: A combination of bear, honeypot, and stuck-in-a-hole automatically conjures up associations with Winnie the Pooh, but only for those listeners who have been raised in a family or culture in which Pooh is a familiar figure. For listeners from another culture, one may wind up with the same story, but without the richness of our associations with Winnie the Pooh as a developed character. Nearly 150 years ago, Anglican linguist R. C. Trench recognized the indispensability of contextuality in reading parables:

> The proverbs are so frequently [a culture's] highest bloom and flower, while yet so much of their beauty consists often in curious felicities of

---

36. The reference at Sanhedrin 39a is to only three of Rabbi Meir's since there are many fox parables scattered throughout the Talmud and Midrash. *Ad loc.*, Rashi tells the three parables. The literature of "fox fables" became a highly developed populist form, the most famous collections of which can be found in the thirteenth-century *Mishlei Shu'alim* of R. Berekhiah ha-Naqdan (the introduction by Schwarzbaum to the English translation is itself a treasure); the twelfth-century *Sefer ha-Sha'ashuim* (The Book of Delights) of R. Joseph ben Meir ibn-Zabara; and the eleventh-century *Ḥibbur Yafe* of R. Nissim Gaon. See also Baba Batra 134a, in which it is recorded that the study of the fox fables was an integral part of the education of Yoḥanan ben Zakkai, along with Scripture and Halakhah. See also *va-Yiqra Rabbah* 28.2 (M. Margulies, 3.56 n4). On the claim of 300 parables, see Musafia, 4–5 and 13 at *lamed*; Harkavy, 183 and 371; Ḥazzan, 6a–b.

37. M. Avot 1.1. See also Isa. 5:1–7 in relation to a vineyard, and Siegfried Stein.

diction pertaining exclusively to some single language, either in a rapid conciseness to which nothing tantamount exists elsewhere, or in rhymes which it is hard to reproduce, or in alliterations which do not easily find their equivalents, or in other verbal happiness such as these—[there] lies the difficulty which is often felt . . . of transferring them without serious loss, nay, sometimes the impossibility of transferring them at all from one language to another.[38]

So for the rabbinic audience, the combination of fox, vineyard, and fence, while telling a story on the "silver filigree" level, at the same time (without allegorization and without needing interpretation) tells a story about Israel and the Torah being endangered by an intruder. The two stories are told simultaneously, rather than sequentially, though the hearer may at first be conscious only of the primary level. Unless we can recapture the associations, taken for granted by the author of *Qohelet Rabbah*, we can hear only the "silver filigree" story; the "golden apple" story will be lost to us completely. So too with the parables of Jesus; if we cannot grasp the associations that were automatic to the original hearers, we cannot grasp the full richness of those parables. They remain for us one-dimensional, seeming to offer little beyond the level of popular entertainment.

The problem remains of identifying the associations with stock figures that would have been common to Jesus and his hearers. In a provocative article, C. H. Cave claims that "the 'original context' of the parables was always a sermon, and that we have lost the point which the parable was originally intended to enforce because we have lost the sermon."[39] On the basis of Cave's hypothesis, if we cannot rediscover the original sermons of Jesus, which were the contextual settings of the parables, then we cannot ever hope to understand what Jesus was teaching in his parables. The only other possible source for definition, it would seem, is Jewish literature of the period as close in time as possible to the life of Jesus: the parables contained in the Mishnah, Midrash, and Talmud. There remain serious problems for the scholar, for without extensive form and text criticism of rabbinic materials, we are on shaky ground in deciding what associations belong to what period. But we do have evidence supporting the tenacity of oral tradition in Judaism, and it is quite possible that the rabbinic parables shed important light on the parables of Jesus simply because oral tradition

---

38. Trench, 31, writing in 1858. He cites as an example of an untranslatable proverb the German "Stultus und Stolz/Wachset aus Einem Holz." A similarly cryptic epigram, to any but an American in the 1970s, would be "Only Nixon could go to China." One untranslatable phrase is *ve'ahavta le-reikha kamokha*; "you shall love your neighbor as you love yourself" is not a truly accurate translation (see chaps. 3 and 8 of this book).
39. Cave, 376.

would have kept stock figures and automatic associations alive for several generations.[40] It therefore seems appropriate in a search for meanings in the parables of Jesus to seek out whatever illumination is possible from the rabbinic parables retained in traditional Jewish literature.

Attempts have been made by Christian exegetes to prove that Jesus did not draw on this common Jewish repertoire but that he used stock figures to mean something very different from what his contemporaries did. The obvious problem with this reasoning, usually offered in an attempt to prove the uniqueness of Jesus, is that his listeners would never have understood his parables had he altered the meaning of the stock figures, for the listeners would have brought such contrary associations. Furthermore, the attempt by some Christian scholars to shift the symbolism of stock figures is unconvincing because there is so little literary support for their contention.

Listener Response and Historical Specificity

In principle, it is not surprising that Christians have found alternative meanings in their inherited Jewish texts. Augustine praised joyfully the diverse meanings heard by Christians within the same texts foundational to the Christian faith. For him, this was an integral part of the great richness of Scripture:

> For as a fountain within a narrow compass is more plentiful, and supplies a tide for more streams over larger spaces than any one of those streams which, after a wide interval, is derived from the same fountain; so the relation of [Moses] that dispenser of Thine, which was to benefit many who were to discourse thereon, does out of a narrow scantling of language, overflow into streams of clearest truth whence every man may draw out for himself such truth as he can upon these subjects, one, one truth, another, another, by larger circumlocutions of discourse. . . . So when one says, "Moses meant as I do"; and another, "Nay, but as I do," I suppose that I speak more reverently, "Why not rather as both, if both be true?" And if there be a third, or a fourth, yea if any other seeth any other truth in those words, why may not he be believed to have seen all these, through whom the One God hath tempered the holy Scriptures to the sense of many, who should see therein things true but divers? For I certainly (and fearlessly I speak it from my heart), that were I to indite

---

40. Perry Dane refers to the Oral Torah as "a textless text," thereby emphasizing that oral tradition has cadence, structure, and intention, a specific content, and internal methods to protect its own integrity.

any thing to have supreme authority, I should prefer so to write, that
whatever truth any could apprehend on those matters might be conveyed
in my words, rather than set down my own meaning so clearly as to
exclude the rest, which not being false, could not offend me.[41]

A very early tradition understands that texts, including those of Scripture, have a number of valid meanings in addition to the obvious "literal"
meaning. Not only does a parable usually have a number of simultaneous
meanings, it is not always clear whether a parable is intended to entertain,
form attitudes, or teach norms of behavior. These issues will be explored
in detail in the following chapters; suffice it here to say that in Judaism
the distinction between midrash and halakhah is not always clear. Moreover, parables sometimes masquerade as another literary form. In the New
Testament, it is possible to read certain "real-life" stories as parables, including certain miracle stories such as the Coin in the Fish's Mouth (Matt.
17:24–27). Therefore each story or parable presented in the pages that
follow must be analyzed carefully to determine whether and how it falls
into the general category of parable, or some other identifiable literary
form by which wisdom teaching is passed from one generation to another.
The line between literary types is not always clear; even less clear is the
"literal" reading of any parable as opposed to the "situational."

A parable is most alive when it is oral; once written, the text is only a
generalized indicator, pointing to meanings in various directions. Ortega y
Gasset observes: "A dictionary furnishes, at best, a general scheme in
which the manifold actual significations a word admits of may be inserted.
But the real meaning of a word appears when the word is uttered and
functions in the human activity called speech. Hence we must know who
says it to whom, when and where. Which indicates that meaning, like all
things human, depends on circumstance."[42] The value of a listener-response analysis is to clarify what varieties of meaning might have been
available to the original followers of Jesus, rather than concentrating upon
textual analysis.

Sometimes it is assumed that a word or saying can be understood by
anyone, without regard for the context of its utterance and reception, and

---

41. Augustine, *Confessions* 12.27, 31, in Pusey, 294, 299.
42. Ortega y Gasset, 12. Judah ha-Levi, at *Sefer ha-Kuzari* 2.72 (Hirschfeld, 126),
adds that to grasp the meaning we even need to know the movement of the
speaker's eyes and eyebrows of his whole head and hands. In ancient rhetoric, there
was a whole panoply of physical actions, taught and drilled, that were clearly part
of the "meaning" of a text. Of course, in antiquity, all texts were oral—either never
written down at all, or if written, read aloud.

this presumed understanding is referred to as the text's literal meaning. In the twelfth century, Maimonides addressed the same issue of literal readings of the biblical text that has continued to plague Christianity and Judaism subsequently. He divides those who would interpret Scripture into three distinct groups. The first group might be called "the simple literalists," who never bring even so much as a question to the text of Scripture. Maimonides informs his readers that the literalistic approach, which leads to intellectual isolation, "destroys the glory of the Torah and extinguishes its light, for they make the Torah of God say the opposite of what it intended." A second group, "the rejectionists," even more emotionally impoverished than the first, accepts a surface reading of Scripture that does not lead them to submission but rather into derision and rejection of the religious tradition itself.

There is a third group. Its members are so few in number that it is hardly appropriate to call them a group, except in the sense in which one speaks of the sun as a group (or species) of which it is the only member. This group consists of those to whom the greatness of our sages is clear. They recognize the superiority of their intelligence from their words which point to exceedingly profound truths. Even though this group is few and scattered, their books teach the perfection which was achieved by the authors and the high level of truth which they had attained. The members of this group understand that the sages knew as clearly as we do the difference between the impossibility of the impossible and the existence of that which must exist. They know that the sages did not speak nonsense, and it is clear to them that the words of the sages contain both an obvious and a hidden meaning. Thus, whenever the sages spoke of things that seem impossible, they were employing the style of riddle and parable which is the method of truly great thinkers. For example, "The Wisest of All Men" began his book by saying, *To understand a parable and a saying, the words of the wise and their riddles* (Prov. 1:6).[43] All students of rhetoric know the real concern of a riddle is with its hidden meaning and not with its obvious meaning, as: *Let me now put a riddle to you* (Jdgs. 14:12). Since the words of the sages all deal with supernatural matters which are ultimate, they must be expressed in riddles and analogies.[44]

---

43. R. Judah Loew Shapira, in his commentary on Gen. 42:23, interprets "saying" (*melitzah*) as meaning the nimshal, in that a nimshal is an interpretation, or translation, which "solves" the riddle of the mashal, just as a dragoman makes accessible a "barbarian" text.
44. Maimonides, Introduction to Pereq Ḥeleq, near the end of section 2, in *la-Am*, 10.121–123; trans. Arnold J. Wolf; modified by PLC. See also Shilat, *Haqdamot*, 134, 155; the trans. of Abelson, 34–35; and as cited in D. Hartman, *Torah and Philosophic Quest*, 36–37 (paper 33–35); notes, 218–19. And see Talmage, "Apples

Our search for meaning within the parables and stories of Jesus necessitates our recognition of the truth and value of particularism and contextuality, as opposed to the abstract or universal. Any parable or story
originates in a particular situation from the mouth of a particular teacher,
but comes to us only through the memory of a particular hearer as recorded in a particular text. It is subsequently interpreted for us by particular individuals with particular agendas, shaped by the particular historical
and religious culture within which they speak. To seek universal truth in
parables is an exercise in frustration, for the various messages of any given
parable are in its particulars. One key to unlocking the complexities of
these particulars, and thus recapturing the lessons and values of an ancient teacher, is the application of listener-response theory. Only by recon-
structing what might have been heard by those who sat at the feet of the
sages do we then have the ability to access the participatory adventure of
applying these original truths to the hopes and fears of our own generation, just as Jesus' listeners did to their own.

---

of Gold," 334–37. Much of Maimonides' thought here is prefigured in Origen and
Gregory.

Chapter 2

The Hermeneutical Location of Paradise

Few of the communications that cross my desk evoke an emotional response. In the day's mail (which are the texts I most frequently encounter), there are descriptive matters, factual materials, advertising notices, minutes of meetings, and routine bills and charitable appeals, all of which are merely informative or declaratory, but without involving my own self or my ego. However, emotive communications do exist that draw a personal response of varying degrees, to the point that I may laugh out loud, or break into tears, merely by absorbing the words of the message. Perhaps these are letters from old friends, or the Scripture readings appointed for the day, some long-anticipated academic treatise, a new murder mystery, or even a political cartoon. Because these materials affect me on a different level than do the routine arrivals of the day, they must be recognized as being of a different literary genre, one calculated to evoke a response (a performative) rather than simply to inform (a constative).

Parables, too, intend to evoke a response. The failure to recognize them as a literary genre that tends to excite emotion and with meanings that are contextually defined, is not the only factor preventing our appreciation of their rhetorical multiplexity. Our task of message-reception is also complicated by (1) the layers of "creative" exegesis within the church over the course of centuries, often claimed as the "literal" reading; (2) the presumed sacrality of the received biblical text; (3) the chronological distance between our culture and the culture of the first century C.E.; and (4) a Christian tendency to distinguish descriptive narrative ("story") from normative prescription ("law") and then dismiss the latter as irrelevant to the Christian revelation.

Numerous contemporary studies have argued the problem of how we relate to the gospel texts. May we justifiably read them like any other text whose language is familiar, or must we impose upon ourselves a certain respectful distance because of the revelatory or sacral character of the words presented? The answer is not simple. From the beginning, New Testament texts were not interpreted literally, even in the earliest patristic

25

church.[1] Early Christian exegetes in Antioch often interpreted texts typologically, whereas Christian exegetes in Alexandria at times interpreted allegorically.[2] Both the Antiochene and Alexandrine schools of exegesis believed they had discovered and clarified the accurate meaning of a text, but differed from each other significantly. The church has struggled throughout the centuries with such competitive interpretations of the same texts, as one century faded into the next. With the advent of the Reformation, and the translation of the Bible into the vernacular, believers assumed they could handle the text directly even though they read only a translation, and so the predicament of interpretation took on a new urgency. As Haran observes, "from the time of the conclusion of the canon, biblical exegesis has been incessantly augmented in a never-ending volume, resulting in a multifarious, enormous literature, which attempts to throw light on the biblical texts from every possible point of view. . . . Any mode of thought that ever existed through the ages, has ensconced itself in this literature." Over and over, clergy and laity have sought a "literal" authority in the words of Jesus, yearning for the New Testament text to speak plainly and unequivocally, and even to function as a guide to the specific details of daily living.

As if this complication were not enough, a second threat clouds our comprehension in that we tend to set apart the scriptural text as "holier" than other texts with which we come into contact. With the advent of modern biblical criticism in the eighteenth century, the scholarly world was relatively quick to apply such tools to the Old Testament, perhaps encouraged by the admission of the patristic exegetes that even they could not find Jesus adumbrated in the plain meaning of the received Hebrew texts. Through "scientific analysis" of the biblical text, allegory could be distinguished from typology, source influences from form influences, ur-texts from subsequent layers of editing. For decades, however, the New Testament was held aloof from critical analysis on the assumption that, as Christian revelation, it was a special category of text to which "normal" literary rules or observations were neither applicable nor appropriate.[3]

---

1. See von Campenhausen; Kugel and Greer; Haran, 19–21; for additional references, see notes to my "Known, Knower, Knowing."
2. A great deal of material is available on this distinction between allegory and typology in the early church; a classic is Grant, *The Bible in the Church*; see also Quasten, 2.2–4, 121–23, and Hanson, esp. chap. 6 on the belief by early patristic writers that already by the third century c.e., the text of Scripture had been corrupted and so demanded exegetical explanation to clarify. On allegory and typology in early rabbinic writings, see notes 23 and 24 in the previous chapter.
3. The modern application of scientific methodology to the study of scripture began in the 1770s with the work of Semler, Michaelis, and Griesbach; for an excellent

A third complication preventing our understanding of the complexity of parables is the chronological distance between the Second Temple period and our present time. Without a concerted effort to suspend, at least temporarily, our own values, questions, and agendas, we have no chance to appreciate fully the importance of Jewish literary sources contemporaneous with the early church. Nor can we recapture the import of the earliest Jesus tradition within its particular cultural and religious context without similar suspension. Any attempt to read the New Testament texts otherwise is to risk destroying the incarnational value of God's revelation through individual human beings in specific historical settings.

A further significant confusion is created by the Christian tendency to divide both Hebrew and Christian scriptures into the false oppositional categories of "narrative" (aggadah) and "law" (halakhah), then refusing to recognize the possibility that Jesus spoke at least as much as a halakhist as he did an aggadist.[4] A quick survey of Christian seminarians will reveal that the books of Leviticus and Numbers are dismissed as irrelevant to the Christian faith, although they were foundational to the Judaism in the midst of which Jesus lived and taught, and remain foundational in our own time.[5] Such dismissal eviscerates the halakhic tradition within which Jesus firmly stood, and it is repeatedly fueled by centuries of insistence that Jesus was but a charismatic teller of simple stories, disinterested in behavioral norms. Jewish tradition generally does not recognize such a thing as a "simple story"; simple stories are intended only for the entertainment of those who are too ignorant to hear the sophisticated subtexts

---

survey, see Fuller in Borsch, 145; Kümmel; and on the "protected sanctity" of the New Testament, see Gavin, especially the chapters by Simpson and Grant.

4. The terms are defined carefully in Bialik's essay "Halachah and Aggadah," and see Ginzberg, *Law and Lore*, 77–124. In fact, "descriptive" and "normative" are false oppositional categories; the line between them is no more clear than the line between "law" and "grace." The same question may be raised about the distinction between apodictic and casuistic law; is there any such thing as an apodictic law unaffected by context?

5. See Article Seven of "The Thirty Nine Articles of Religion" in the Episcopal prayerbook. Another classic example is the *Third Jubilee Bible of the British and Foreign Bible Society*, 1954, wherein all legal material is printed in type of an unreadable size, suggesting thereby its lack of relevancy to Christians. On p. vii of the preface, the editors pride themselves on this innovation. Such distinction is at least as old as the Christian Gnostic Ptolemy who, in his late-second-century *Letter to Flora*, divided Mosaic law into three parts: the pure law (the ten commandments), the law adulterated with injustice but now suspended by Christ, and ceremonial law now spiritualized by Christ. The letter is preserved in Epiphanius, *Haer.* 33, 3–7 (Quasten, 1.261).

of attitudinal reorientation that are always present, for frequently literary messages overlap, existing simultaneously within a single but multifaceted text.

Halakhah as Aggadah

A parable does not always look like a parable at first glance. It may be preserved as a text fragment, a partial memory, or even condensed into a metaphor. If parts of the parable are missing, it may appear within a text as a proverb, or even as a mere historical description. At other times, a single text can be both a parable and an extended proverb, and at the same time convey a significant legal or behavioral implication. This compression of literary categories can be illustrated by a parabolic fable that begins with a proverb and concludes with another proverb derived from known halakhic expectations. According to BT Sanhedrin 38b–39a:[6]

> R. Yoḥanan said: When Rabbi Meir taught his students, his lesson-plan would include three halakhot, three aggadot, and three meshalim.
>
> R. Yoḥanan said: Rabbi Meir had three hundred fox-parables, but we have left only one. [Let me tell it to you]:
>
> *Parents have eaten sour grapes, and children's teeth are blunted* (Jer. 31:29; compare Ezek. 18:2).
>
> Once a fox said to a [hungry] wolf: "Go into the yard of a Jewish family on the eve of Sabbath and help them prepare everything they need for a festive meal, and then eat it with them." When [the wolf] went in the yard, [the family] fell upon him and beat him with sticks. [Escaping], he came looking for the fox to kill him.
>
> [The fox] said "This wouldn't have befallen you except on account of your father, who one time was sharing a meal [with a Jewish family] and ate all the best portions of everything."
>
> [The wolf] was puzzled: "On account of my father, I am punished?!"
>
> [The fox] said: "Indeed—*parents have eaten sour grapes and children's teeth are blunted*. But come with me and I will show you a place to eat to your heart's content."
>
> He took him to a well. At the edge of the well grew a tree, and a rope hung from one of its branches. At each end of the rope was a bucket. The

---

6. BT Sanhedrin 38b–39a, and Rashi thereto; Taubes, 343 #758; Harkavy, 371 and 183 #362; Musafia, 13 #30; R. Hai Gaon in Ḥazzan, 6a resp. 13 and commentary *Iyei ha-Yam*, ad loc.

fox jumped into the upper bucket, thus weighing it down, and descended down into the well, while the bucket on the other end of the rope ascended.

The wolf said to him: "Why are you going down there?"

[The fox] replied: "There is meat and cheese down here to eat to your heart's content."

He pointed out to him the reflection of the moon in the water, which to the wolf looked like a huge round of cheese.

[The wolf] said to him: "How can I get down there?"

He answered: "Get into that upper bucket."

So the wolf got into the upper bucket, weighing it down, and descended, while the bucket with the fox in it ascended.

[The wolf] cried out: "How will I get back up?"

[The fox] replied: "*The righteousness of the upright saves them, but the wicked is felled by his own wickedness* (Prov. 11:5). Is it not said (Lev. 19:36): *You shall have an honest balance, honest weights. . . .*"

Here, the "aesopic"[7] double parable about the fox concludes with a nimshal that is itself an independent wisdom saying from the Proverbs, and is then reinforced by a metaphorical interpretation of the Levitical injunction concerning accurate scales in the marketplace (here suggesting the balance of the two buckets in the well).

In a similar manner, a historical narrative may be employed as a parable. As an example, the following parable is structured around the metaphorical interpretation of established halakhic expectations concerning the repayment of a depositor's money held in trust. According to *Midrash Mishlei* 31:[8]

---

7. The primary difference between such fables in Aesop and the rabbinic material is that for Aesop they are classical wisdom literature, whereas in the rabbinic materials their purpose is interpretive. This parable (without the biblical nimshal) can also be found in *Babrius and Phaedrus*, Perry, 538 #593, and in similar form on 315 #9; see also Odo of Chariton, 89; Thompson, *Motif-Index*, K651; Schwarzbaum, "Talmudic-Midrashic"; and A. Solomon.

8. See *Midrash Mishlei* (Buber, 108; Visotzky, 190–91); *Yalqut Shimeoni* to Prov. 31:10 and *Yalqut ha-Makhiri* on Mishlei (Greenhut, 97b). For related Jewish sources concerning children as *piqadon* ("deposit"), see ARN-A 14 (Schechter 59, parallel Goldin, *Fathers*, 77); al-Naqawa, 4.585; Gaster, Heb., 105; Nissim Gaon, 53–54; Kirchan, 41; *Midrash Tanḥuma* vulgar to Gen. 7; al-Ḥarizi, 340 Gate 45; and references to *pidyon ha-bekhor* ("redemption of the firstborn"; Num. 18:15) such as Singer, *ADPB*, 308–9 and explanatory notes. A *bekhor* is *pars pro toto*, the

A woman of valor who can find? (Prov. 31:10).

It is told of R. Meir that once while he was sitting and teaching in the Bet Midrash on Shabbat at the hour of eventide, his two sons died. What did their mother [Beruria] do? She laid both of them out on the bed and spread a sheet over them.

When the Sabbath was over, R. Meir came home from the Bet Midrash.

He asked: "Where are my two sons?"

She answered: "They went to the Bet Midrash."

He said: "I waited for them but I didn't see them."

She gave him the Havdalah cup [proclaiming the distinction between Sabbath holiness and the coming workaday week], and he recited Havdalah.

When he was finished, he again said to her: "Where are my two sons?"

She answered: "They went somewhere and will be back soon."

She sat down with him to dinner.

After he had eaten, she said to him: "Some time ago, a man came and gave me something to keep on deposit for him, and now he has come to take it back. Shall I give it to him or not?"[9]

He said to her: "My dear woman, is whoever holds a deposit for someone not obliged to return it on demand?"[10]

She said to him: "So—I acted with your consent when I returned it."[11]

---

part which represents the whole, and is also *primus inter pares*. Though such children are biologically the products of their parents, they must still be redeemed from God's representative, the kohen, because they are simply "on loan." This story has many parallels in Greek sources, including those listed in note 9. It therefore cannot necessarily be considered historical, in spite of Beruria's heroic attempts.

9. The idea of children as a deposit on loan from God is an ancient one. For Greek sources on *parathēkē*, see Epictetus (Oldfather, 2.491 #11; here the development of a proverb to a parable is well illustrated); Josephus, *Wars* 3.372 (Thackeray, 2.681); Philo, *On Abraham* (Colson, 6.127, and 598–99 for more references). Kierkegaard (*Fear and Trembling*, esp. Problemata 2) develops the same idea, arguing that God demanded the "sacrifice" of Isaac to remind Abraham that Isaac was only "on loan." And see Boswell on the history of the mistreatment of children.

10. Compare Ex. 22:7; for New Testament parallels, see Matt. 25:14–30, Luke 19:11–27.

11. Beruria here says to her husband "You are the man!" in the same manner that

> Thereupon she took him by the hand, and walked him upstairs to the room, and led him over to the bed. She pulled back the sheets, and he saw the two of them dead, stretched out upon the mattress.
>
> He began to cry, saying "My sons, my sons! My masters, my masters! My sons as my natural offspring; my teachers in opening my eyes with their Torah wisdom!"
>
> At that moment, she said to him: "Rabbi, did you not just say to me that we are obligated to return a deposit to its rightful owner? For thus is it said, *The Lord has given, and the Lord has taken away; blessed be the name of the Lord* (Job 1:21)."

Here a "real-life" situation illustrates the nonliteral interpretation of halakhic legislation concerning entrusted funds, which is in turn reinforced by a theological principle from the hagiographa concerning God's sovereignty. In both cases, it is clear that halakhah can function as the starting point for aggadic amplification.[12] However, this amplification of a halakhic foundation yields in turn a reaffirmation of the society's norms for acceptable social intercourse. As Bialik observes: "The value of *Aggadah* is that it issues in *Halachah*. *Aggadah* that does not bring *Halachah* in its train is ineffective. Useless itself, it will end by incapacitating its author for action. . . . *Aggadah* gives us air to breathe; *Halachah* gives us solid ground to stand on."[13] Without norms, our social life would be chaos, but norms become infinitely more palatable when taught through stories than by way of endless rulebooks.

The same ideational evolution is typical to the teachings of Jesus. Beginning with a halakhic point, he could then present his listeners with a

---

Nathan responds to David in 2 Sam. 12:7. The use of parable to elicit self-indictment further enriches our understanding of its multiplex character. And see Lasine.

12. The following articles provide the literary and philosophic foundation for the relationship between these two types of literature: Bialik, *Halachah and Aggadah*; Ehrentreu, "Millah be-Sela Mishtuqa be-Terein," in *Talmudic Studies*; Ginzberg, "The Significance of the Halakhah for Jewish History," in *On Jewish Law and Lore*; Kahana, "Aggadah she-Hi Halakhah," in *Heqer ve-Iyyun*, vol. 5; Lieberman, "How Much Greek in Jewish Palestine?" in *Texts and Studies* and "Halakhah she-be-Aggadah" in *Mekhkarim*, 116–17; Mirsky, "Meqorot ha-Halakhah be-Midrashim," in *Talpiot*; Sperber, "Tehumai Halakhah ve-Aggadah," in *Maamarot*; Einhorn's introduction to his *Baraita*; Weiss, "Halakhah, Midrash, Aggadah," in *Dor Dor ve-Dorshav* 2. On Midrash Halakhah, see Urbach, "Ha-Derashah ki-Yesod ha-Halakhah." There he distinguishes between two forms: (1) biblical citation to legal formulation (A–B) and (2) legal formulation to biblical citation (B–A).

13. Bialik, *Halachah and Aggadah*, 26.

homily built upon a familiar rationale, yet without ever mentioning the rationale itself. To illustrate briefly: According to Matthew 5:27–28, "You have heard it said, 'You shall not commit adultery.' But I say to you that everyone who even looks at a woman lecherously has already committed adultery with her in his heart."[14] The unstated source of Jesus' teaching is Job 31:1, interpreted halakhically: "I have made a covenant concerning [the use of] my eyes; why then should I look at [any] young virgin?"[15] Indeed, the entire Sermon on the Mount is a long oral discourse upon a series of halakhic dialectics, generally interpreted in line with the rabbinic dictum, "Keep away from what is hideous, and all that resembles it."[16] The sermon is comprehensible only as a reaffirmation and extension of recognized halakhic norms, delivered aggadically with the purpose of intensifying devotion to the Torah on the part of Jesus' followers.[17] Since behavioral

---

14. On the typical halakhic formula "you have heard it said," see Daube, *New Testament*, 55–62; Lachs, *Commentary*, 95–98. Sanders, *Jesus and Judaism*, 260–64 deems the antitheses in Matt. 5–6 inauthentic.
15. Compare BT Shabbat 20b; *va-Yiqra Rabbah* 23:2 (M. Margulies, 527–28); Hertz Pentateuch to Num. 15:39, 634; Agnon, 114; compare also T. Iss. 7:2, T. Isaac 4:53.
16. The rabbinic saying is an extension of Lev. 18:6; compare Num. 32:22, Deut. 22:5, and Prov. 5:5. See Tos. Yevamot 4.7 (Lieberman, 12; Zuckermandel, 245); BT Hullin 44b; Tos. Hullin 2.24 (Zuckermandel, 503); ARN-A 2.9, 12 (Schechter, 5a and 7a–b; Goldin, *Fathers*, 17); ARN-B 3 (Schechter, 7a); Derekh Eretz 1.12 (Higger, Heb. 63, Eng. 35), 1.26 (Heb. 78, Eng. 38), 7.2 (Heb. 126, Eng. 50); Derekh Eretz Zuta 4 (Higger, *Zeirot*, 90); Yir'at Het 1 (Higger, *Zeirot*, 75), and 2 (83); *Midrash Tannaim* to Deut. 22:5 (Hoffman, 134); *Midrash ha-Gadol Devarim* (Fish, 488, line 9); Kallah Rabbati 3.21; *ba-Midbar Rabbah* 10.8; R. Isaac Berlin, *Omer ha-Shikhehah*, par. 93; S. Luria, *Yam shel Shelomo* to Hullin 3.8–9 and Yev. 2.20; Yehiel min ha-Anavim, 304–5; Talmidei R. Yonah Gerondi to Berakhot 1 (Vilna edition, 6); Shabbatai Kohen, "Siftei Kohen" in Shulhan Arukh, part 2, Yoreh Deah, par 152 #2. And see Alon, *Studies*, 1.282; Yalon, 211; Ehrentreu, *Studies*, 56 n1; E. E. HaLevi; *ha-Historit*, 19; and Flusser, *JOC*, 494–508. On "mishnat hassidim," see JT Terumot 8.1, 46b; Duran, 2.8; Bialik, *Sefer ha-Aggadah*, 214 #392. Comparison with the phrase *viyitem neqiyim* (Num. 32:22) in Tos. Sheqalim 2.2 (Lieberman, 205) and Mishnayot 3.2 (Kehati, 420–21) suggests the interpretation that one must appear manifestly innocent not only in the eyes of God, but also in the eyes of suspicious Israel; see M. Sheqalim 3.2, Avot 2.1 and 6.1, and notes in Taylor, 2.134. The rabbinic phrase is often connected to a proverb, "Go, go by a roundabout route; we shall not approach the vineyard." For an explanation of how the proverb develops out of Jdgs. 14:5, see Jacob Fidanki in Abravanel to loc. cit.
17. Compare Rom. 12:9–10 and 1 Thess. 5:21–22. Classical sources include Solon 1.60 in Diogenes Laertius (Hicks, 1.61); Demosthenes 20, "Against Leptines" 135 (Vince, 581); and Plutarch, *Moralia*, 5.528 (DeLacy and Einarson, 7.47). The rabbinic dictum about "fleeing from the hideous" enters early Christian thought via the Didache 3:1 (Lake, 1.313), and ultimately develops into a particularized Chris-

expectations are the product of attitudinal orientation, the pedagogically astute recognize that attitudes are fairly easily formed, and thus behavior modified, through the use of an engaging story that inculcates the desired norm in a memorable way.

Aggadah as Halakhah

Of equal importance in understanding the issue of behavioral expectations within the story-teachings of Jesus is the opposite question: can aggadah function as halakhah? Can legal principles, by which Christians would be expected to behave, be derived from the parables and quasi-historical teachings of Jesus? An illustration of such movement from aggadah to halakhah is found in the history of the relationship between Deuteronomy 24:1–4 and Jeremiah 3:1–5, a history that also gives us a clear example of how not only parables, but also halakhic norms, contain the simultaneous possibility of multileveled meanings.[18]

Deuteronomy 24:1–4	*Jeremiah 3:1–5*
	The word of the Lord came to me as follows:
A man takes a wife and possesses her. She fails to please him because he finds something obnoxious about her, and he writes her	
a bill of divorcement,	*If a man divorces his wife*
hands it to her, and sends her away from his house;	

---

tian "holiness code," including the whole struggle with human sexuality which Brown has so dramatically traced in *Body and Society*. Compare Clement of Alexandria, *Stromateis*, 1:20, 2:23, 4:21 (ANF 2.323, 377, 433). The Syriac Rite of Antioch interprets the phrase in the Lord's Prayer, "Deliver us from evil," as meaning "Deliver us from evil, and from all that resembles it." The liturgy thus witnesses to the early interpretation of the seventh petition of the Lord's Prayer that we be delivered from all that is either morally or aesthetically repugnant (as correct a translation of *kiʾur* as is "hideous" or "murky"; see Yalon, 211–12).

18. The process by which these two passages relate to each other is made particularly clear in Luzzato to Jer. 3:1–5. For another example of a halakhah that becomes a mashal, see Tzemed Lo Matʾim ("An Incompatible Match") in *Sefer ha-Ḥinnuk*, commandment 570 (Chavel, 697–98).

she leaves his household and becomes the *wife of another man*; then the latter rejects her, writes her a bill of divorce, hands it to her, and sends her away from his house; or the man who married her last dies. Then the first husband who divorced her shall *not take her to wife again.* since she is *disqualified* for him— for that would be abhorrent to the Lord. You must not bring sin upon the land that the Lord your God is giving you as an inheritance	*she leaves him* *and marries another man,* can he ever *go back to her?* Would not [the society of] the land be *polluted?* [cf. Num. 35:31–33] Now you have whored with many lovers; Can you return to Me?—says the Lord. Look up to the bare heights and see: Where have they not lain with you? You waited for them on the roadside like a bandit in the wilderness. You defiled the land with your whorings and your promiscuity. And when the showers were witheld and the late rains did not come, you had the brazenness of a streetwalker. You refused to be ashamed. Just now you called to Me, "Husband! You are the companion of my youth. Does One hate for all time? Does One rage forever?"

In the Deuteronomic text, the husband is forbidden under any circumstance to take back the wife who has disqualified herself by her subsequent marriage to another man. Yet in the Jeremiah text, God the metaphorical husband seems to forgive Israel the wife for her promiscuity, and to take her back. The Jeremiah text seems antithetical to the Deuteronomy text, for a prohibitive injunction has been promulgated in the Torah: a man may not take back his "wandering" wife, in any circumstance. The answer to the question at the end of the Jeremiah passage should be God's reply: "I'm sorry, but I am bound by my own rules; if you have broken the covenant with me, I cannot take you back." The logic of ethical monotheism dictates that if the Torah is binding upon humanity, it is also binding upon God the giver, for justice would demand that giver and recipient be bound by the same set of norms.[19] Such a thought is hinted at in *Aikhah Rabbah*: "[Upon seeing the massacres that accompanied the destruction of the Temple], Moses said to the Holy One, Blessed be He, 'Master of the Universe, did you not write in your Torah *No animal from the herd or from the flock shall be slaughtered on the same day with its young* (Lev. 22:28)? Yet here so very many children have been killed alongside their mothers, and you remain silent?' "[20]

However, during the subsequent historical exploration of the juxtaposition of Deuteronomy 24 and Jeremiah 3, commentators discovered other, more felicitous, levels already inherent in the original meaning. For these interpreters, the tension between the two texts makes it clear that the prophetic text not only contradicts the Mosaic prohibition, but ultimately overrides it, for in history, Israel *has* been forgiven and taken back into God's favor. In BT Yoma 86b, Rabbi Yoḥanan explains this specific contradiction with a sweeping theological principle: "Great is repentance,

---

19. In classical philosophy, this topic of discussion was referred to as *para basileōs ho nomos agraphos*—"Law issues from a king in unwritten form," or in more modern English, "The king's word is law." See Lieberman, *Greek in Jewish Palestine*, 37–38 and n51; *Texts and Studies*, 222. Special thanks to Dr. Naomi G. Cohen of Haifa, for pointing out that this phrase is clarified by Porphyry (third century C.E.), as "The fool and the king pay no attention to the written law." Her research on the subject will appear in her forthcoming book on Philo. Philo, *On the Special Laws* 4.150 (Colson, 8.101–3 and n149 on p. 435), and see *On the Virtues* 194 (Colson, 8.283), however, refused such an interpretation, agreeing more with JT Rosh ha-Shanah 3:1,57a, that God has the power to be above the law, but chooses to observe it. According to an apocryphal story, Louis XIV made the philosophy famous by saying "L'Etat c'est moi." However, this sort of absolutist corruption has no place in rabbinic thought; here the midrash holds out an ethical nomism in which God is seen as a *model* for observing halakhah; see Weinfeld on "the king as the servant of the people" (1 Kgs. 12:7). For a related thought, see *naeh doresh*, ref. Yevamot 63b, which is in turn derived from Hagigah 14b. In ethical monotheism one desires a God who acts according to the same demands placed upon others; see Tos. Hagigah 2:1 (Lieberman, 380; Neusner, *Tos. Moed*, 312); Heinemann, "Die Lehre."

20. Buber midrash, 14b (28), Petikhta 24:23. The thought of God being bound by the same standards as humanity is found with frequency; for example, the whole thirtieth chapter of *Shemot Rabbah* is about this subject. See also Bacher, *Aggadot ha-Tannaim* part 1.159; Jacobson, 294–96. In Targum Jonathan ben Uzziel, the unusual rendering of Lev. 22:28 is the vocative "My people Israel, as I am merciful in heaven, you should be merciful on earth" (Ginsburger, 212; Clarke, 145).

for it supersedes a prohibition of the Torah." From the Deuteronomy/Jeremiah and similar contradictions[21] is derived the principle *asseh doheh lota'asseh*, "a directive injunction overrides a prohibitive injunction" in a situation where they are in conflict with each other. In order to arrive at such a possibility, R. Yoḥanan has to posit that the relationship between God and Israel is not exactly analogous to Deuteronomic marriage and divorce. Were it literally analogous, no reconciliation, even after repentance, would be possible according to the plain reading (*peshat*). But since reconciliation is obviously possible, then the covenantal relationship between God and Israel must transcend the limitations of the human marital relationship, marriage being only a partial analogy.

The halakhic principle derived from the juxtaposition of the two texts, then, is one based on the understanding that Jeremiah is a homiletic extension (*derash*) of Deuteronomy with the express intention of proving how much more comprehensive is God's relationship to Israel than is a marital relationship between two human beings. In such a reading, the Deuteronomy text becomes the mashal, and God's forgiveness the surprise nimshal, since such a nimshal should be impossible according to the halakhic logic of the mashal. One must further conclude that the Jeremiah passage would be impossible if it were not understood from the beginning that the Deuteronomy passage has more than one meaning—pointing out concurrently how like and unlike human marriage is God's relationship to Israel.

Though texts had been understood in a variety of ways from the beginning of the biblical period, at some point in history four different levels of interpretation were systematized as standard. By the thirteenth century these were known in Christianity as the literal, the allegorical, the tropological, and the anagogical.[22] In medieval Judaism a similar schema of

---

21. See, for example, Lev. 18:6, where one is prohibited from having intercourse with one's sister-in-law, in comparison with Deut. 25:5–10, where one is duty bound to have intercourse with one's sister-in-law and take her as his wife (levirate marriage); or see Deut. 22:11, where it is enjoined that one may not wear a garment (including a tallit) of mixed wool and linen, and yet the headgear or kefiye described at Num. 15:38ff. allows just such a mixture. Some commentators attempt to explain away the conflict by theorizing that God revealed the contradictory items simultaneously (*be-dibbur eḥad*) rather than sequentially; see Kasher, 16.65; Bacher, *Erkei*, 13; E. Z. Melamed in B. Z. Segal, 147–63; Mack, "Seventy Aspects," 450–52. The prooftext cited for simultaneous utterance is usually Ps. 62:12, itself the subject of many fascinating commentaries. On the tallit as originally being a kefiye (not a prayer shawl), see BT Moed Qatan 24a; *Shulḥan Arukh* 1, Orah Ḥayyim sec. 8 par. 2; Jastrow, 1063, *atifa*; W. H. Loewe, 75, notes; R. Margulies, *Mekhkarim*, 61ff.

22. The traditional Christian formulation was *Littera gesta docet, quid credas Alle-*

four interpretations—the plain, the allusive, the homiletical, and the secret (*peshat, remez, derash, sod*)—were referred to by the acronym PRDS, or "Paradise." The origin of this rabbinic systemization is unclear; there appears to be little evidence of it before the thirteenth century, though the Christian schema existed by the midpatristic period. Indeed, Chrysostom refers to "The Paradise of Scripture."[23] Nor is it clear, in the complicated back and forth of history, whether Christianity borrowed its various systems of codification from Judaism, or vice versa.[24] But one prooftext supporting codification is an ancient one, possibly contemporaneous with the end of the New Testament period. This now-famous text illustrates that the multiple layers of meaning within Scripture are available only to those who have been properly initiated into the varieties of listening to multiple levels simultaneously.[25]

---

goria; Moralia quid agas, quo tendas Anagogia ("The literal text as it stands teaches the events; allegory, what you are to believe; the moral [tropological] sense, what you are to do; the anagogue, what you are to expect at the end of life"). Quoted from the *Postillae perpetuae in universam S. Scripturam* 1.3E by Nicholas of Lyra (c1330); for historical background, see Hailperin. Compare Dante, *Epistle to Can Grande*, on Ps. 114:1–2.

23. John Chrysostom, *In principium Actorum* 3.1, Montfaucon 3.71C (unpublished translation by Arthur B. Shippee) speaks of "the Paradise of Scripture" as a walled garden with an abundant fountain and trees inside. A very similar reference can be found in the Gospel of Truth (Layton, 262), where paradise is God's perfection of thought, and the plants therein are God's verbal expressions of that thought-perfection. On the wall around this garden, see Clement of Alexandria, *Stromateis*, 1.20 (ANF 2.323).

24. Haran claims (33 n20) that no one systematized exegesis existed until Scholasticism. But Saadya Gaon was making clear distinctions in the tenth century between peshat and derash (see *Sefer ha-Emunot ve-ha-Deot*, 7). That the systematization of the concept does not develop fully until the medieval period cannot be seen as a counter-indication of its early origins; there is simply too much evidence to the contrary, as van der Heide has argued effectively; see also summaries by Morray-Jones; Dan, "The Religious"; Himmelfarb; and Flusser, "Scholem," 61–63. Angus Fletcher (313n) also makes the point that the four categories here directly parallel Aristotle's Four Causes (*Physics*, Book 2, chapter 2, 194b–195a): literal = material; allegorical = formal; tropological = efficient; anagogical = final. The relationship needs to be explored further. And see Gruenwald, "Esoteric," 44; Feldman, 98; and Donski, *Shir ha-Shirim*, 27 n2. For other essays on the relationship between the Christian and Jewish exegetical systems, see the excellent articles by Sandler, Bacher ("Das Merkwort"), and Talmage ("Christian Exegesis" and "Apples of Gold").

25. This theory is known in music as "contrapuntal syntax," a type of ambiguity in which two variant forms of the same theme are developed simultaneously in counterpoint; see Bernstein, 109. Multiplex texts also function like a diminished seventh

The Intended Esotericism of Communication

Repeatedly in the Gospels Jesus takes his disciples aside to offer them acroamatic teachings not intended for the mass of listeners or to explain a secret meaning to some parable with which he has entertained the larger crowd. The obvious examples are the Sermon on the Mount and the Lord's Prayer, neither of which is intended to be shared with those outside the circle of initiates. According to the gospel redactors, Jesus explains an esoteric meaning of Scripture (Luke 24:44ff) on the road to Emmaus. Those reading on their own were unable to perceive from the "plain" meaning that Jesus was the fulfillment of Hebrew prophecy without an exegete to "open their eyes" to less-than-obvious meanings. The same idea—that Scripture has levels of meaning inaccessible to the simple and uninitiated—is familiar to patristic writers as well. Witness John Chrysostom:

> Let those who can walk faster wait for their slower fellows; after all, they can wait, while the weaker don't have the strength to keep up with them. For this reason, Paul said that we ought not compel the weak prematurely, as they may not have the strength to extend themselves as completely as the strong. . . . The clearer [ideas] are useful for the simpler folk, while the deeper are for the more quickly observant. It is necessary for the fare to be varied and different, since the yearnings of those called are different.

He describes this gradual education from exotericism to esotericism as "guiding from the sensible to the intelligible."[26]

Esotericism has been a part of Judaism since at least the early Second Temple period,[27] and of Christianity since at least the writing of the Gos-

---

chord, which is capable of at least four different resolutions, perpetuating "a four-way ambiguity"; see Bernstein, 233.

26. John Chrysostom, *In principium Actorum* III.74B–D, Shippee translation. Origen, *De principiis* (praef. 8, in Quasten, 2.92) writes: "Scriptures were composed through the Spirit of God and . . . they have not only that meaning which is obvious, but also another *which is hidden from the majority of readers*" (emphasis added). See also his *In Matth. comm.* 11, 4 (Quasten, 2.95), in which Origen argues that only the initiates into the esoteric meanings are truly disciples; the rest of Jesus' hearers are simply "the multitudes," and are by inference inferior to the cognoscenti.

27. See, for example, the Wisdom of Solomon 6:21–25 (Charles, 1.545 and notes); compare Philo, *Special Laws*, 1.320: "Tell me, you initiates, if these things are good and profitable, why do you shut yourselves up in profound darkness and

pels, in which Jesus is portrayed as teaching in parables so as to confound his listeners.[28] The esoteric tradition—gnosis if you will—has been more openly discussed at certain times in both Judaism and Christianity than it usually is today, but at no time has the idea been absent from either tradition. In every religious tradition, sacred scriptures have been seen as the repository for an intentionally complex and rich revelation behind the simplicity of the written text. Even classical poetic texts were treated in this manner by subsequent philosophers and critics, who would quote directly from those texts and then add an interpretation whose logic or intention was not readily apparent from the plain meaning of the quoted text.[29] All such systems of exposition, whether from the religious or the philosophical tradition, were based on the assumption that communication is not limited to plain prose. Metaphor, simile, parable, allegory, proverb, synecdoche, paradigm, rhetoric, fable, and poetry would all be impossible forms of communication were we strictly to limit ourselves to the plain meaning of the words we use. These highly valued forms of communication have in common the assumption that communication happens simultaneously on more than one level. Each level is as intended as the other, but not every level is equally accessible to the listener or the reader. To grasp levels beyond the plain and immediately accessible level (the "sensible"), the creative mind of the hearer must have already been filled with a repertoire of symbols and associations, many of which are culturally bound, and some

---

reserve their benefits for three or four only, when by producing them in the midst of the market-place you might extend them to every one and thus enable all to share in security a better and happier life?" (Colson, 8.284–87). On early Jewish esotericism, see also Ben Sirah 47:17 in Charles, 1.498; M. Z. Segal, 328 n23; Wolfson, *Philo*, 1.24–26.

28. Matt. 13:10–23; Mark 4:10–13; Luke 8:9–10, 18:34, and elsewhere. Many commentators have attempted to explain away these secret teachings of Jesus, but the intention of the texts seems incontrovertible. See also the use of the word *mystērion* at Matt. 13:11, Rom. 11:25, Eph. 3:9 and 5:32, Col. 1:26 and 4:3, 1 Tim. 3:16, Rev. 1:20, and see the clear reference to multiple meanings of texts at Gal. 4:24. Most patristic writers posit a gnosis not obvious in the written biblical text without further exegesis; the trend begins as early as the Epistle of Barnabas (Quasten, 1.85). Compare Perotti's Appendix to *Babrius and Phaedrus* (Perry, 380): *consulto involvit veritatem antiquitas ut sapiens intellegeret, erraret rudis* ("It was by design that antiquity wrapped up truth in symbols, that the wise might understand, the ignorant go astray").

29. As one of many possible examples, see "Longinus," *On the Sublime* 9.9 (Fyfe, 148–49), where the first century C.E. philosopher quotes the Hebrew Bible and then adds an interpretation not obvious from the text itself. See also M. Stern, 1.361–65; and Weiler, esp. chaps. 1 and 2.

of which are limited to hearers already privy to carefully guarded philosophical or religious mysteries (the "intelligible").

Thus it is that communication functions simultaneously on various levels of exoteric and esoteric gradation. The power of the human intellect and the creativity of human communication dictate that we speak and write constantly in words that convey more than their plain meaning. Further, the distinction between exoteric (Hebrew: *nigleh*) and esoteric (*nistar*) need not imply value-judgment. Exotericism and esotericism are no more than two different ways to convey two different messages in the same set of words. Some messages are intended for the general listener; other messages are intended for the initiate. But every message is as intended as the other, and no one message takes away from the immediate inherent value of the others. The danger in communication comes when the hearer seeks to transfer from one type of message, for example, the exoteric, to another, for example, the esoteric, without having been sufficiently prepared for such an application. It is this danger that has led both Jewish and Christian traditions repeatedly to caution their adherents not to seek the esoteric meaning of their sacred writings, yet never denying the existence and validity of such hidden meanings within the very same scriptures.[30]

Various levels of communication were common stock in trade during the late Second Temple Period, as attested by Josephus in his *Antiquities* 1.24:[31]

> I therefore entreat my readers to examine my work from this point of view. For, studying it in this spirit, nothing will appear to them unreasonable, nothing incongruous with the majesty of God and His love for [humanity]; everything, indeed, is here set forth in keeping with the nature of the universe; some things the lawgiver shrewdly veils in enigmas,

---

30. Ben Sirah 3:21–25 cautions, "Seek not out the things that are too hard for you, neither search the things that transcend your strength. Reflect upon what has been assigned to you, for you do not need what is hidden. Do not meddle in what is beyond your tasks, for matters too great for human understanding have been shown you. For their hasty judgment has led many astray, and wrong opinion has caused their thoughts to slip. If you have no eyes you will be without light; if you lack knowledge, do not profess to have it." (But cf. Ps. 131:1, where the refusal to stretch one's comprehension of esoterica is seen as a childlike virtue.) This is cited in the Talmud; see M. Segal, 17, notes; see also Charles, 1.326 and notes; and 2 Esdras 4, Deut. 29:29, 2 Thess. 2:11, 1 Cor. 2:9, and James 3:1. *Seder Eliyahu Rabbah* (Friedman, intro. 46 and 86) contains a similar warning, actually in the form of a parable.

31. Josephus, *Antiquities* 1.24 (Thackeray, 4.13).

others he sets forth in solemn allegory; but wherever straightforward speech was expedient, there he makes his meaning absolutely plain. Should any further desire to consider the reasons for every article in our creed [of Judaism], he would find the inquiry profound and highly philosophical.

Josephus's encouragement to his listeners to explore deeper meanings is unusual. For the most part in Jewish and early Christian tradition, plumbing the depth of a text's many meanings was considered a hazardous occupation.

Paradise as a Hermeneutical Location

Two themes—the multiplexity of scriptural texts, and the terrors of the uninitiated's seeking the esoteric meaning of these texts—are illustrated in a famous rabbinic parable:[32]

> Four entered "Paradise": Ben Azzai and Ben Zoma, ʿAḥer and Rabbi Aqiba. Ben Azzai peered and died; of him scripture says *Precious in the sight of the Lord is the death of his saints* (Ps. 116:15). Ben Zoma peered and went mad; of him scripture says *Have you found honey? Eat so much as is sufficient for you* (Prov. 25:16). ʿAḥer looked and hacked down the plantation; of him scripture says *Let not your mouth lead you into sin* (Qoh. 5:6). Rabbi Aqiba entered in peace and went out in peace; of him scripture says *Draw me after you; let us run* (Song 1:4).

The tradition out of which this story proceeds is an ancient one known as "merkabah mysticism." The pericope cannot be given a more specific date than is suggested by the characters in the story itself: the late first to early second centuries.[33] The tradition of merkabah mysticism has

---

32. The following translation is a composite of four texts in six versions: Tos. Hagigah 2:3–4 (Zuckermandel, 234, and Lieberman, *Moed*, 381 and commentary); JT Hagigah 2.77b; *Shir ha-Shirim Rabbah* 1.4,1; BT Hagigah 14b (including Steinsaltz); compare also Eisenstein, 2.505. Although the differences between the four texts are fascinating, their complication makes them beyond the scope of this study.

33. The Midrash Rabbah and BT texts are introduced with the phrase "Our rabbis taught . . ." According to Mielziner (201), the phrase indicates material of the category *baraita*, that is, from before 200 C.E.; see also Strack, 3–4. The names of the four rabbis connected with the story, possibly contemporaries of St. Paul, do not vary in the tradition, and the broader tradition supports the personal charac-

influenced Christianity and has been extensively developed in Judaism. Paul's reference in 2 Corinthians 12:1–7 proceeds out of this same mystical tradition, as do numerous references in the Mishnah.[34] Merkabah mysticism receives further articulation in certain forms of medieval Christian spirituality and its fullest articulation in Jewish qabbalism, but the roots of the tradition can be traced back at least as far as the late Second Temple period.

The clue to understanding the parable, and the purpose of bringing it into our discussion at this stage, is the word "paradise."[35] The word "paradise" is originally from Avestan, the oldest attested group in the Indo-Iranian branch of the Indo-European language, and means "a garden, field, vineyard or plantation enclosed by a wall made of clay or mud bricks." The word is intended to convey privacy and inaccessibility, a rich and fertile place closed off to the general public. The word enters Greek as *paradeisos* (introduced by Xenophon[36]); Aramaic as *pardisa*; and Hebrew as *pardes*. The Septuagint uses the Greek form to translate *gan* ("garden"), while the Hebrew form *pardes* appears only three times in the Hebrew Scriptures. Nehemiah 2:8 speaks of a *pardes* owned by a king. Qohelet 2:5 describes a *pardes*, similar to a garden, in which trees are planted. Song of Songs 4:13 refers to a *pardes* of pomegranates.[37] All three of these references carry a

---

teristics of the four individual rabbis portrayed here. Finkelstein ("Pirke Avot," 22; *Akiba*, 70, 163) certainly does not doubt the authenticity of the figures involved or the date of their story; he suggests that early in their scholarly activity these four formed a private "philosophical society," which Finkelstein names "The Society of the Orchard (Pardes)"; see Higger's *Masekhet Kallah*, 343, for one such lesson taught under an olive tree; Strashun, 86–87; and Büchler, "Learning and Teaching." The same model is familiar from classical Greek literature; see, e.g., Cicero, "Laelius on Friendship" 1.2 (Falconer, *De Amicitia*, 108–9).

34. See Scholem, *Jewish Gnosticism*, 14–19, and *Major Trends*, 52–54 and 361 n45; Charlesworth, *Pseudepigrapha*, 1.230–31; Steinsaltz, *Essential Talmud*, 216; Gruenwald, "Esoteric"; Idel, 153 n8; and Origen, *Contra Celsum* 6:33 (Chadwick, 349). On the varieties of interpretation given to the parable in history, see Halperin; A. Segal; Fischel's *Rabbinic Literature*, chap. 1; and Tabor.

35. For a fascinating pan-religious history of the term "paradise," see Manuel.

36. Liddell and Scott, 1308.

37. All three biblical references can as easily be interpreted mystically as they can be read literally. For example, rabbinic interpretation of the world "pomegranate" supports the mystical sense of PaRDeS which I am developing here. At BT H̲agigah 15b: "Rabbi Meir found a pomegranate; he ate the fruit within it, and the peel he threw away!" Tradition has understood the pomegranate as a metaphor for a parable's multilayered meaning—hence the "peel" (exoteric) and the "fruit" (esoteric) levels of a parable, in the same sense as Maimonides' image of a golden apple in

certain poetic quality, even in English; an enchanting image is conjured up by the phrase "a paradise of pomegranates." However, the Hebrew word *pardes* carries opportunities for rich mystical interpretation that neither the Greek nor English words can support.

Because the earliest meaning (in Avestan) of the word paradise is "circumvallation," it is natural that subsequent development of the term focused on its characteristic of being fenced or hedged in. When dealing with the combination of *pardes* and a fence, we discover a symbol agglutination that conveys multiple layers of message in the same rabbinic tradition that informed Jesus' teachings. For example, at Proverbs 25:28 we find counsel to self-control as a metaphorical fence: "Like an open city without walls is one without a curbed temper."[38] At Ben Sirah 36:30 we discover another early use of the fence metaphor: "Where there is no fence, the property will be plundered; where there is no wife, a man will become a fugitive and a wanderer." The fence metaphor implied in these biblical and rabbinic texts has roots in the earlier classical Greek philosophies. Somewhere about 500 B.C.E., the Greek sage Heraclitus of Ephesus wrote: "The people must fight for the law [*nomos*] as for the wall of their city."[39] In his article "The Concept of the 'Fence',"" Siegfried Stein traces the manner in which this connection between disciplined human behavior and the symbol of the wall enters rabbinic thought by the turn of the millennium. Strongly influenced by Stoicism, the early rabbis believed that the function of *nomos*—in this case both Torah and halakhah—was to protect humanity from itself, from its tendencies to turn away from obedience to the Creator. Disciplined obedience and the diligent observance of halakhic ordinances were the wall defending the commitment of the Jewish people to God, just as the teeth can be interpreted as a wall

---

silver filigree. An inherent controversy is obvious here, in that R. Meir's peel seems discardable, whereas Maimonides' silver filigree is beautiful and worth retaining. See also Feldman, 118, though he misunderstands the saying about Rabbi Meir; and *Zohar Ḥadash*, Midrash Ruth (R. Margulies, 83a).

38. See Delitzsch, *Proverbs*, 2.173: "As such a city can be plundered and laid waste without trouble, so a man who knows not to hold in check his desires and affections is in constant danger of blindly following the impulse of his unbridled sensuality." Clement, *Stromateis* 1.20 (ANF 2.323), understands philosophy as the fence that guards the vineyard of Christianity; see Quasten, 2.20.

39. Diels, 1.154 #12; Heraclitus in Diogenes Laertius (Hicks, 2.409); and see S. Stein, 306–7. A related rabbinic midrash, based on Ex. 15:22–26, can be found in *Shemot Rabbah* 25:5; see also Kasher, loc. cit., 162 and important notes (esp. Luzzato); and Stein, 315, 328 n76. On "builders of the wall" (*bonei ḥayitz*) as a (derogatory!) synonym for Pharisees in the Dead Sea Scrolls, see the Damascus Covenant 4:19, 8:12, 18 in Ginzberg, *Unknown*, 272; and Schiffman, 32.

protecting the tongue from verbal error.[40] To assure that the halakhah was safe-guarded from transgression, the generations of early rabbis began to devise walls around the "wall," that is, ordinances designed to prevent even the temptation to transgress. This is the halakhic philosophy within which Jesus could observe: "You have heard it said. . . . But I say to you." Jesus's halakhic ordinances are comprehensible as an "extension of the fence," an attempt to remove humanity even further from the temptation to violate divinely revealed norms of human behavior.[41]

The question was raised earlier in this chapter, in a discussion of Deuteronomy 24 and Jeremiah 3, whether legislator and recipient are not bound by the same set of norms. Not only would Jesus have assumed that he was bound by the same halakhic expectations as the rest of the Jews to whom he spoke, but rabbinic thought too soon came to understand that God was bound by his own expectations of humanity, and even bound by the words of the Torah. Although there are times when we might choose to quarrel with the New Testament formula "this was to fulfill the words," the concept is no different from God's having to fulfill the words of the Torah, for God had therewith fenced himself in. Without such a fence, the actions of God could only be interpreted as arbitrary; with such a fence, God is seen as being as faithful to the Torah as humanity is expected to be. God's faithfulness and God's "fence" are discussed at the beginning of the *Avot de Rabbi Nathan*, commenting on Pirqei Avot 1.1:[42]

> *And make a hedge about the Torah.* [This means]: and make a hedge about your words the way the Holy One, blessed be He, made a hedge about His words, and Adam made a hedge about his words. The Torah

40. On this image, see the delightful mashal of R. Yossi ben Zimra at BT Arakhin 15b; compare Philo, *De Confusione Linguarum* 44–48 (Colson, 4.33–36).

41. Both versions of the *Avot de Rabbi Nathan* discuss various aspects of "the fence" in their first chapters, based on Song of Songs 7:3, there connecting with the idea of fleeing evil. The rabbinic dictum to flee from *ki'ur* (see note 17 above) is usually extended with the words, "and everything which resembles *ki'ur*." See *ba-Midbar Rabbah* 10:8—"How can a man make a fence around his words in the way that the Torah made a fence around her words? . . . one should refrain from what is ugly and from anything resembling the ugly." However, on the danger of "building the fence taller than the object it is intended to protect," see *Bereshit Rabbah* 19:3, where R. Hiyya observes, "Don't add to God's words, lest God prove you to be a liar."

42. ARN-A1 (Goldin, *Fathers*, 8 to Schechter, 2a–b esp. n37); and see E. E. HaLevi, *ha-Historit*, 19, and S. Stein, 302. Herford, Avot 6:2 (*Ethics*, 151), discusses the idea that one can be free only after voluntarily accepting a yoke of discipline. According to Kant, "True freedom is in the autonomous acceptance of the law."

made a hedge about its words. Moses made a hedge about his words. So too Job, and also the prophets, the holy writings, and the sages—all of them made a hedge about their words. What is the hedge which the Holy One, blessed be He, made about His words? Lo, it says, *And all the nations shall say: Wherefore hath the Lord done thus unto this land?* (Deut. 29:24). This teaches that it was manifest to Him-that-spoke-and-the-world-came-into-being that future generations were to speak in this manner. Therefore the Holy One, blessed be He, said to Moses, "Moses, write down the following and leave it for the coming generations: *Then people shall say: Because they forsook the covenant of the Lord . . . and went and served other gods and worshipped them, gods that they knew not, and that He had not allotted unto them* (Deut. 29:25–26). Thus you learn that the Holy One, blessed be He, meted out the reward of His creatures to the letter [of that biblical text which was delivered in advance].

Extensions to the fence were to originate only from authoritative sources—first and foremost from God, and then from the tradition, and finally from scholars to whom the community granted authority (it is in this last category that Jesus would have been empowered, as in Matt. 5:27–28). Version B of the *Avot de Rabbi Nathan* includes this warning: "A vineyard which is surrounded by a fence is unlike a vineyard not surrounded by a fence. [This also means] that no one should make the fence more important than what is to be fenced in—for if the fence falls down, then he will cut down the plants."[43] Because our text under consideration here deals with a hedged orchard, the ears of the initiate are already alert to listen for something within the text that addresses the halakhic expectations characterizing God's relationship to humanity.

It will be noted that nowhere in the *original* meaning of "paradise" is found a hint of the Garden of Eden, the afterlife, or the heavenly kingdom. Nor is this the case in the parable under consideration. Here Ben Azzai peeked and died; certainly if this is paradise in terms of an afterlife or heaven, Ben Azzai already would have been dead before looking. Ben Zoma lost his mind, again an event that we do not usually associate with any existence after death.[44] ʿAḥer, the derisive nickname for Rabbi Elisha ben

43. ARN-B1 (Saldarini, 29, parallel Schechter, 2a); and see S. Stein, 320 n31a; Maimon, 86 n6. The relationship to "hacked down the plantation" is obvious; cf. Isa. 5:5, Prov. 24:31, 25:28.
44. The Hebrew word "peered" carries the same sense of indiscretion as the English term "peeping Tom." The Hebrew *nifga* ("lost his mind") implies a sudden attack of dementia; see Abrahams, 50. For the same image of "eating honey," see the poem "On Sacred Scripture" by George Herbert. On the danger in general, see Maimonides, *The Book of Knowledge* 39b.13, in Hyamson.

Abuyah,[45] is said to have hacked down the plantation; whatever happened to ʿA̲ḥer upon entering paradise caused him to destroy his own cultural heritage, in the sense that he became a heretic.[46] Only Rabbi Aqiba entered safely and came out safely.[47]

The symbols of "orchard" and "Torah" are specifically linked by a parable in *Shemot Rabbah* 30:9:

> R. Abbahu, in the name of R. Jose b. Ḥanina, said:
>
> It can be compared to a king who had an orchard (*pardes*) in which he planted all kinds of trees and where only he entered, because he was its keeper. When his children became of age, he said: "My children, hitherto I guarded this orchard, not allowing any to enter it. I want you now to look after it as I did." This is what God said to Israel: "Prior to My creation of the world, I prepared the Torah. . . ."

By at least the thirteenth century, rabbinic tradition had come to understand "paradise" as a metaphor for scriptural multiplexity, though this medieval understanding remained rooted in the ancient tradition of merkabah mysticism. Our parable was interpreted as an adventure by the untutored into the realm of Scripture's many meanings, PaRDeS being a notarikon[48] for Peshat, Remez, Derash, and Sod:

---

45. The nickname ʿA̲ḥer may be translated "that other guy"; see Yalon, 303–4, and Lieberman, *Texts and Studies*, 190–99; see also W. Green, 59–69. Maimonides, *Guide* chap. 32 (Pines, 69), connects ʿA̲ḥer's gluttony for knowledge with Ps. 131:2 and Ben Sirah 3:21–22.

46. The same phrase, "hacked down the plantation," is used to describe Adam's fall. See Theodor and Albeck, 1.172, and Scholem, *Gnosticism*, 16 n6. For interpretations of what this mysterious accusation might mean, see *Shir ha-Shirim Rabbah* 1.28; JT Ḥag. 2,77b; Donski, *Shir ha-Shirim*, 27; Scholem, *Gnosticism*, 127 note to 16; and Steinsaltz, *Essential Talmud*, 216.

47. The meaning of *be-shalom* is "in safety," "in peace," "composed," but not "whole" as Neusner translates it (Tos. Ḥagigah, 313); the same phrase is used in *Bereshit Rabbah* 36 to describe Noah's deliverance by the Ark (Theodor and Albeck, 1.336; parallel Y. Shapira to Isaiah 43:13, 141), the deliverance of Daniel and his three companions, and other heroic survivals in the early aggadic midrash literature. The point is that Aqiba and Noah were properly prepared in advance, and so survived their ordeal "in one peace."

48. According to Scholem (*On the Kabbalah*, 52–57), the first person to use PRDS in this manner was Moses de Leon (compiler of the Zohar) in 1290, probably as a reaction against Christian allegorical and figurative commentaries; see Haran, 33–34, and Scholem, *Major Trends*, 210. However, R. Hai Gaon (Musafia, 34b #115) and R. Ḥananel to Berakhot (B. M. Lewin, in "Additions," 3) both refer to PRDS as

Peshat—The simple, the "literal," the plain meaning of the text, usually accessible to the uninitiated, and having its own inherent value as memory, instruction, and entertainment.

Remez—The allusive, the intimated meaning, the metaphor hinted at, though always based on a rational and concrete form of logic, such as a notarikon, tachygraphy, mnemonic, gematria; this form of exegesis became popular in both Judaism and Christian as a sort of puzzle.[49]

Derash—The homiletical meaning, more a synthetic attribution than an analytic clarification of meaning, an excursus by which moral and ethical applications are drawn.

Sod—The secret meaning, the mystical message accessible only to the select few initiated, and often having to do with the very nature of God.[50]

Thus we see that in this exegetical principle, scriptural texts speak simultaneously (as opposed to sequentially or hierarchically) on these four levels. One approaches the complexity of Scripture, particularly in seeking

---

a place in one's heart, surely the seat of esoteric exegesis. On notarikon, see Mode 30 of the 32 Modes of Exegesis, *Mishnat Rabbi Eliezer* (Enelow, 11); see also *Midrash ha-Gadol Bereshit* (M. Margulies, intro. pp. 23, 38); and Bacher, *Erkei*, 86.
49. On gematria, see Jastrow, 239; Enelow, 11; Dan, "Midrash," 139 n4; and Gruenwald, "Gematria." Gematria appears in the New Testament text at Rev. 13:17–18, where "the beast" is to be identified by the way in which the letters in his name add up to the number 666; on gematria in the Matthean genealogy see Davies and Allison, 1.163–65. Christianity has a legitimate tradition of understanding *remez* as forms of mathematical "games" and as notarikons. Clear examples can be found in the Epistle to Barnabas 9.8 (Lake, 1.372–73); the Venerable Bede, *Hexameron* PL91 78C as cited in McNally, 26–27; and Enelow, 38 nL7f. On *sod* in the Christian tradition, see Origen, *Contra Celsum* 4.87 (Chadwick, 253); Odo of Chariton, 68. On multiplexity of interpretation, see Augustinus of Dakia's (c1260) *Rotulus Pugiliaris* (Haran, 33 n2); see also St. Bernard, St. Basil, and Cardinal Hugo to Song of Songs 1:4 in Pope, 307; Pico della Mirandola in Kutscher, *History*, 175 and Scholem, *On the Kabbalah*, 2 n1; Nicholas de Lyra in Scholem, *On the Kabbalah*, 61; Heinemann, "Scientific," 251; and my "Known, Knower, Knowing."
50. The tradition of secret meanings to Biblical texts, available only to the cognoscenti, is strong throughout Christian history. Two examples: Clement of Alexandria, "The Rich Man's Salvation" 4–5 (Butterworth, 278–83; Quasten, 2.15–16), and Augustine of Hippo, Letter 137 (Cunningham, 193). For an essay applying the principles to specific texts, see my "Multiplexity in Biblical Exegesis." The question should be allowed whether there is such a thing as a text with only a *sod* meaning but no *peshat*. What do we do, for example, with "'Twas brillig, and the slithy toves Did gyre and gimble in the wabe" ("Jabberwocky," in Carroll, *More*, 176)?

the mystical meaning of a text, at the risk of physical (Ben Azzai), mental (Ben Zoma), or spiritual (ʿAḥer) health. Only those best fit, disciplined, and already initiated can enter scripture to its fullest complexity of meaning, and like Aqiba, emerge "in peace."

In the case of parables and stories, the "plain" meaning may at times reside in the entertainment value of the text. But there are other instances, particularly in Scripture's passages of theological discourse, in which even the "plain" meaning can be grasped only by those with prior tutoring, or perhaps the intended "plain" meaning is the opposite of what the words appear at first to mean. As Erasmus asked five centuries ago, "if it is all so plain, why have so many excellent men for so many centuries walked in darkness?" Frank Kermode, in his essay "The Plain Sense of Things," points out that three factors obscure forever our ability to identify a plain meaning of a scriptural text, or at least one that will hold true through successive centuries:

> 1. that the human mind has an almost overwhelming temptation to interpret things metaphorically;
>
> 2. that we are never immune to the pressures of the present context in which we read or hear a text;
>
> 3. that no scriptural text is ever free in its presentation from the weight of authoritative tradition.

Kermode's observation should be balanced in turn by the theory of George Lindbeck and others that the *consensus fidelium*, the way in which most of the faithful understand a text at any given period, *is* its "plain" meaning, even if this is a field of meaning as opposed to a sharp definition.

We note a sharp contrast between Kermode's third point, the authority of tradition (including, one would assume, the *magisterium*), and Lindbeck's point concerning the consensus of the faithful in whatever present tense. Once either point is conceded, then it is clear that no such thing as a "plain" meaning of a text is recoverable in the sense of authorial intention, but rather that the plain meaning is fluid to the degree to which it is determined by an outside authority (tradition or "majority vote") rather than by the author or by the text itself. For example, should the church so desire, it could declare that the allegorical interpretation of a text is its "plain" meaning; indeed this has been the case repeatedly throughout the history of scriptural exegesis.[51] However, once the tradition is at log-

---

51. See Raphael Loewe (a bibliography of older references on *peshat* is found on 178 n189); and see Rabinowitz, "Talmudic Meaning"; R. Margulies, *Ha-Miqra*, 56–59; Tanner; and Lindbeck.

gerheads with the consensus, or once a difference of opinion over the meaning of a text is apparent among the faithful themselves, then it must be conceded that texts properly have multiple meanings, meanings as much created by their interpreters as by their authors.

It is not always possible to reconcile the various meanings of a biblical text with each other. The *pashtan*, who concentrates on the peshat, will find himself at odds with the *darshan*, who concentrates on the allegorical or homiletic meaning. As Uri Simon remarks insightfully:

> The *pashtan*, attentively listening to the text and striving for objectivity, is bewildered at what he sees as the confident subjectivism of the *darshan*. He is inclined to thrust at him the words of Rabbi Ishmael to his colleague Rabbi Eliezer: "You are saying to scripture, 'Be silent, while I make a derash!'" The *darshan*, on the other hand, seeking to give voice to the verses out of an intimate relationship with them, fears that there is nothing in the *pashtan*'s objectivism but spiritual indifference and lack of creativity. . . . Yet, woe to the *pashtan* who completely effaces himself before the text, and woe to the *darshan* who completely silences it. The former would deplete his *peshat* interpretations of all living meaning, and the latter would drain his *derashot* of their status as an interpretation of scripture.[52]

I wish to offer the hypothesis that Jesus was well aware of Scripture's "walled garden," however that may have been comprehended in the Second Temple period, and that he purposefully taught his own parables and memras with an eye to multiple interpretation. Any parable of Jesus may be read on the plain (*peshat*) level, but no parable of Jesus may be limited to the peshat, any more than it may be limited to the metaphorical or homiletical level. Above all, we must understand that the parables of Jesus can be expected to carry a secret meaning (*sod*) intended only for those already initiated into mystical communication, just as they carry a plain meaning intended to instruct and entertain ordinary people.

A Text for Reading, or the Record of a Dialogue?

The meaning of a biblical text can never be limited to a particular understanding of the written words. Behind those words lies a series of messages from their tradent, and in front of them lie the various meanings apprehended by the listeners. Written texts are but codes through which

---

52. Simon, "The Religious Significance," 41–42, quoting *Sifra*, Tazria, parasha 13.2.

greater meanings are conveyed and assimilated, doorways through which pass communication between speaker and listener, each suffering human limitation. Truly to understand a text is to live in the middle of it, hearing with our own ears the voice of revelation and education. Paradise is a not so much a geographical location as it is a sensory location of hermeneutic. As Shalom Spiegel has observed, "The letter is too feeble to imprison the spirit. It is useless to try to freeze the tides of spiritual life into permanent retrospection. Ancient meanings cannot be perpetuated through the ages. At best, sounds may be reproduced, or perhaps only the symbols of script, but a new spirit will transfigure them in each age."[53] The function of written texts as a bridge between speaker and listener is well summed up in a ninth-century Egyptian text entitled *The Book of Elements*:[54]

> Whenever God wants to communicate a message to humanity, He appoints a prophet to deliver it—not a message as a text. For God knows the intellectual differences of His creatures. A written text will be enlightening to some and obscure to others. Some will absorb only what can be perceived by sensory perception, whereas others are trained and gifted to perceive conceptually. And between these two extremes are many intermediate groups. . . . Therefore God does not communicate prophecy through some univocal text, because a book or text presents the message in the form of a single literary model which will appeal with a variety of meanings to different people. Even textual communications, letters or books may sometimes create difficulties for those addressed with a message. They will look for an interpreter who is competent to explain it. The interpreter will then employ analogies and parables suitable for the intellectual level of his inquirers until he succeeds in making the essence plain to them. Then he will proceed to raise the level of their grasp again by analogous methods and trains of thought familiar to them, till he has made them comprehend in their way the entire message. This method has been employed by all good teachers and philosophers. For the live word of the narrator communicates what a dead text fails to convey.[55]

---

53. Spiegel, 92–93.

54. *Sefer ha-Yesodot* by Isaak b. Salomon Israeli (Egypt 854–955), translated from Arabic into Hebrew by Abraham b. Samuel ha-Levi ibn Ḥasdai in the early thirteenth century, ed. Salomon Fried; English translation a conflation of variant sources.

55. The slogan *mi-Pi Soferim ve-lo mi-Pi Sefarim* ("From the mouth of tradents and not from the mouth of texts"), that is at least the philosophy behind this claim if not an even more overt reference, is probably an adaptation of an Arabic saying (generated by the compilation of the Isnad) that enters Hebrew literary theory in the ninth century, probably via Anan the Kara'ite. The phrase emphasizes the reliability of the chain of oral tradition over the reliability of written texts. See Aris-

There is an anecdote reported about Plato and his disciples. When the philosopher had a premonition that his end was approaching, he convened his disciples and asked them to sum up his teaching. They paraded before him their achievement in absorbing his doctrines. However, he told them: "You have left me greatly disappointed. The profound truth has not penetrated to your minds." The disciples stood there confounded and ashamed. They entreated him to be kind enough and reveal the profound truth to them. But Plato was adamant:

"Go away and make more of an effort,
Think and search, investigate and probe,
And then come back in three days.
However, do not enter here without my express permission."

They went away and diligently attended to their difficult assignment. When the three days expired, they sent a messenger to obtain Plato's permission to enter his study. At the gate the messenger asked the guard to announce him to his master, stating that he had a mission from Plato's disciples. The guard went in, and upon his return indicated to the messenger to enter. The messenger found Plato turning his back to him. He waited and watched for a sign to be noticed. When no such sign was forthcoming, he addressed the master: "Sir, I am the messenger of your disciples. They respectfully ask for your kind permission to be admitted to your presence." Plato paid no attention to him. He repeated his mission, but elicited no response. Again he restated his charge in a louder voice. Thereupon Plato turned to him with a grim face and dismissed him with a weary and laconic: "Let them come already!" The messenger hurried away and reported to the disciples with consternation. They made haste to appear before their master, worried about his resentment. When they

---

totle, *Rhetoric* 1.10, 6, 1368b (Freese, 22.107–8); 1.13, 2, 1373b (Freese, 22.139–40); Diogenes in *Lives* 6.48 (Hicks, 2.51); Quintilian, *Institutio oratoria* 11.3, 1–9 (Butler, 4.242–47); Cicero, *Tusculan Disputations*, Book 2 (King, 147–223); Pliny the Younger, *Letters* 2.3, 9 (Radice, 61); Seneca, *Ad Lucilium* 6.5 (Gummere, 1.26–29); Hillel in Shabbat 31a (see Ben-Amos, 19–29, and Gerhardsson, *Memory*, 131–36); Eusebius, *HE* 3.39, 3–4 (Quasten, 1.83); and Erasmus, Adage 1.2,17 in *Coll. Works*, 31.161–62. St. Jerome, *Letters* 53.2 (NPNF2, 6.97), argues, "Spoken words possess an indefinable hidden power, and teaching that passed directly from the mouth of the speaker into the ears of the disciples is more impressive than any other." The phrase in various wordings becomes a kind of "battle cry" in medieval Jewish literature, quoted by Moses and Abraham ibn-Ezra, Yehudah ha-Levi, Shelomo ibn-Parhon, Maimonides (*Teshuvot*, Blau, 721 esp. n9), Joseph ibn-Kaspi, Bahye ibn-Halawi, Samuel di Ozida, Joseph Ya'avets he-Hassid, and Joseph ben Harran ha-Azovi, to name but a few. And see *Torah Temimah* 2.481–82 to Ex. 34:27; Wolfson, *Crescas' Critique*, 24–28.

entered his study, Plato rose and greeted them with a friendly smile. Somehow the disciples felt relieved, yet angry with their messenger. Plato advised them: "Do not fret at your messenger. He carried out his mission and bears no blame. He reported precisely his impressions as he saw them. It is this very lesson that I had in mind to teach you yet. The conflicting data originates from one source, but according to their circumstances, vary their meaning. Live direct face-to-face contact with a teacher is better than reading a voiceless text!"[56]

---

56. The text that approximates this exclamation is Plato's *Phaedrus* 274c–277a (Fowler, 1.561–71).

Chapter 3

Halakhic Midrash as Parable

(Deuteronomy 23:19)

St. Paul's dictum that "The letter is dead but the spirit gives life" (2 Cor. 3:6) is often interpreted by Christian commentators to mean that halakhah holds out no hope of God's grace to the believer, since human nature determines that everyone will transgress such weighty and impossible expectations and, by this failure, will condemn themselves to damnation. However, there is strong precedent in classical Greek literature for a different interpretation of Paul's phrase, one which precedes historically the exegesis usually given it by those reading Paul through the eyes of Augustine and Luther.

Study of the development of languages reveals a trajectory from pictograph to consonant to the present stage of most Western writing, which has vowels sprinkled among the consonants to indicate how the consonants are to be sounded out. Consonants without vowels do not by themselves impart enough information for a reader to know how to articulate them. The point can be illustrated by using my own initials, P-L-C. Only by adding a variety of vowels to these "lifeless" letters can words be created, but the vowels chosen make all the difference in the meaning finally assigned to each word:

Feluca	Flack	Fleck	Fleece
Flick	Flock	Phallic	Plaque
Pluck	Police	Folk	Pollack

In this manner, vowels animate consonants, or as the metaphor widely known in classical Greek expressed it, spirits (*pneumata*) animate dead bodies. This then is one possible meaning which precedes Paul's dictum that "The letter is dead but the spirit gives life."

However, Paul's dictum can be understood in yet another manner. In

53

the previous two chapters, we have seen that associations agglutinate around symbols, thus making a symbol come alive most fully in the cultural context in which it is employed. As I have pointed out, a combination of bear, honeypot, and stuck-in-a-hole automatically conjures up associations with Winnie the Pooh, but only for those readers who have been raised in a family or culture in which Winnie the Pooh is a familiar figure; for readers from another culture, one may wind up with the same story but without the richness of our association with Winnie the Pooh as a developed character. In three other short words—fox, vineyard, fence—a whole set of associations is put in motion in the mind of an informed hearer through the process of agglutination, and this in turn provides the opportunity for multiplexity of meanings within a given text, including the literal, the allegorical, the tropological, and the anagogical. St. Francis of Assisi applied Paul's dictum about the letter and the spirit to Christians who read the biblical text as if it had only one literal meaning: "Those are killed by the letter who merely wish to know the words alone, so that they may be esteemed as wiser than others and be able to acquire great riches to give to their relatives and friends."[1]

Yet a third interpretation is possible, for Paul's dictum can be applied not only to the way in which vowels animate consonants, or the way in which associations animate a story. The dictum applies as well to the way in which an accurate knowledge of *historical* context unravels obscure texts to reveal Jesus as a teacher who expounded orally upon the received halakhic tradition. In this manner, he was in line with the Pharisaic heritage to which he was indebted for his education and cultural context. As important as the beloved parables of Jesus may seem, we do not grasp their full import unless we reconstruct the frames of reference in which they were taught, and elucidate the social, ethical, and legal issues they were intended to resolve.

Scholars have known for decades that certain sayings of Jesus are found in patristic literature such as Clement of Alexandria, but not found in the New Testament. Such sayings are called "agrapha." Also known to some scholars is a peculiar story about Jesus contained in the midrashic literature. The story has often been dismissed as spurious, even by scholars who are ordinarily sensitive to the noncanonical literary materials pertaining to Jesus' ministry.[2] Yet a reconstruction of the context and intent of Jesus' words in the early rabbinic text helps us appreciate the plausibility that the pericope may well reflect a dominical origin.

---

1. Francis of Assisi, "The Admonitions," in Vaughn, 30.
2. Meier, *Marginal Jew*, 97–98., rejects this text as spurious.

A "Lost" Teaching of Jesus?

The text as we have it is set one generation after Jesus, in the Lower Galilee, where Rabbi Eliezer ben Hyrkanos has been arrested by the local Roman police:[3]

> When Rabbi Eliezer was arrested for heresy [*minut*], they hauled him to the civil tribunal for judgment.
>
> The consul said to him: Is it befitting for a venerable scholar like you to occupy himself with such futile things?
>
> He answered: I have full confidence in the judge.[4]
>
> The consul assumed that R. Eliezer was referring to the consul himself, though he was not, but to his Father who is in Heaven.
>
> [Flattered, the consul] said to him: Since you are so trusting of me, I order your dismissal [that is, you are acquitted].[5]

---

3. The text can be found in Tos. Ḥullin 2:24 (Zuckermandel, 503), Qohelet Rabbah 1.8, 3, and in BT Avodah Zarah 16b–17a (parallel Abramson, *Avodah Zarah*, 28; see also *Midrash ha-Gadol Devarim* to 23:19 in Fish, 528); Maimonides, *Iggeret ha-Shemad* (la-Am, 10(2).39–40; Kafiḥ, ed., *Iggerot*, 111; Shilat, 1.37–41); *Yalqut Shimeoni* to Mic. 1 and to Prov. 5:8, #937; *Yalqut ha-Makhiri* to Micah, 5–6; *Moshav Zeqenim* to Deut. 23:19, 509; and *Pugio Fidei*, 361. Lieberman, in his recent posthumous book (*Mekhkarim*, 62–63) accepts this story as historically true. Loewe, *Fragment*, 69f., overly Christianizes even his translation. On the legal details of the story, see Lieberman, *Texts and Studies*, 76–80; there he also pokes fun at Herford's translation of the passage. Bacher ("Le Mot 'Minim'") is highly critical of M. Friedlander's failure to understand this story, but Neusner, *Eliezer*, 199 and 366, also repeatedly misses the point. Young (97, 122, and elsewhere) makes the critical error of confusing the stories about R. Eliezer with those about R. Eleazar (or, as the name is spelled in the New Testament, Lazarus). Part of the general scholarly confusion is that some texts describe this Jesus as "ben Patera," though this reference to Jesus' origins as being through illicit intercourse has been proven purely polemical (see, for example, Patterson; Klausner, 20–24; Rokeah, 9–18; Meier, *Marginal Jew*, 96, 223). It was, however, oddly attractive to certain theologians in Nazi Germany; see Alfred Rosenberg (6, 37, 379, 382–83) who describes Jesus as Aryan, of Nordic stock (fathered by a British conscript with the Roman occupation legions), his "pure" Christian message having been "bastardized" by the Jew, Paul.

4. On this interesting phrase, see E. E. HaLevi, *ha-Historit*, 350. There are parallels in Tertullian, Dio Cassius, the Martyrdom of Polycarp, and elsewhere in the early literature. W. H. Loewe (70) compares this to 1 Peter 2:23.

5. The Hebrew word is *dimus*. The pertinent question is whether it means par-

When Eliezer arrived home, [he was depressed by the ordeal]. His disciples came to comfort him, but he refused their encouragement.

Rabbi Aqiba said to him: Teacher, allow me to remind you of something you yourself once taught me.

[Eliezer] said: Speak!

[Aqiba] said: Teacher, could it be that you heard a heretical exegesis which pleased you, and your arrest came upon you in retribution for this pleasure?

[Eliezer] said to him: Indeed, Aqiba, you've reminded me of such an incident. Once I was walking through the upper market of Sepphoris, and there I ran across one of the disciples of Jesus the Nazarene, whose name was Jacob, from the village Sakhnin.

This Jacob said to me: "It is written in your Torah, *You shall not bring the fee of a whore or the pay of a dog into the house of the Lord your God in fulfillment of any vow; for both are abhorrent to the Lord your God* (Deut. 23:18). Yet if the whore insists upon donating her wages to the Temple, what is to be done with them?"

I reminded him that it was forbidden to accept them in any circumstance.

He said to me: Just because they are prohibited to be received as an offering at the altar, does that necessarily mean that they are doomed to go to waste?

[Intrigued, I asked]: So what can be done with them?

[He answered]: You may use them to build a toilet for the high priest, for he has to leave his own home during the week preceding Yom Kippur and to reside in the Palhedrin chamber, outside the Temple precincts, where all his various needs must be provided for.

I nodded in tacit approval.

He then said to me: This is the solution that Jesus the Nazarene taught me, on the basis of the prophetic dictum: *For they were amassed from fees for harlotry, and they shall become harlots' fees again* (Mic. 1:7), [that] *"since they have come from a place of filth, they should go to a place of filth."*

I was delighted with [the cleverness of] the saying, but this obviously brought down upon me my arrest for heresy. For I have transgressed

---

doned (guilty but forgiven) or acquitted (released on the grounds of insufficient evidence). Neusner (77) to BT Avodah Zarah translates "acquitted." D. Sperber prefers "pardoned" (*Dictionary*, 86–87), confirming in a personal conversation with the author that guilt may even be a possibility here, at least in the eyes of the Roman government.

what is written in the Torah (Prov. 5:8), *Keep yourself far from her*—this means heresy—*Do not come near the doorway of her house*—this means the political authority.[6]

The question under discussion between Rabbi Eliezer and Jacob of Sakhnin is a point of halakhah: if a promiscuous woman wishes to donate money, earned by accommodating a lover, to the services of the Temple, but the Temple authorities are forbidden by biblical law to accept it, how might such a situation be resolved to the ultimate benefit of all parties involved? The rabbinic text has a great deal to teach us as we reconstruct the historical and religious circumstances of the period from approximately 30 to 90 c.e., including:

1. that Jesus' disciples seem to have remembered stories about him that were not ultimately included in the gospels;

2. that even the memories we have may be only partial, such as this one in which the story Jesus told is missing, and only the nimshal ("since they have come from a place of filth, they should go to a place of filth") remains;

3. that Jesus was very concerned to support the authority of Jewish law, even in cases that struck a sentimental chord, yet he also sought a compassionate resolution;

4. that Jesus, like many of his Pharisaic contemporaries, was concerned with maintaining and enriching the traditional Jewish mode of living;

5. that well after the destruction of the Jerusalem temple in 70, Jews who attributed a messianic character to Jesus continued to enjoy warm relations with Jews who did not.

Each of these points has long-term importance to the Christian tradition and is addressed in this chapter.

James the Brother of Jesus

The characters in the rabbinic story are identifiable historically because they are so well-known in the literature. Klausner and many others identify this Jacob of Sakhnin as being James, the brother of Jesus (see

---

6. Alternative manuscripts (e.g., Avot de Rabbi Nathan A, Schechter, 14) read "this means prostitution" (see W. H. Loewe, 70–71, on prostitution as an early-church heretical practice). The tradition for the reading of "political authority" is both textually and contextually stronger, and fits more neatly with the general Pharisaic suspicion of government; see Chapter 6.

Matt. 13:55 and Mark 6:3; Gal. 1:19). James, though originally from a Lower Galilean village,[7] and perhaps still living there part of the time, is identified in Acts 21 and Galatians 2 as the head of the church in Jerusalem, the "mother congregation" of Christianity in the earliest decades when the followers of Jesus were still a sect within Judaism. These Jewish-Christians vigorously defended themselves against Paul's claims that halakhic demands such as circumcision and dietary restrictions had been abrogated (Acts 11 and 15). Ultimately the sect asserted the importance for Jews to continue their commitment to halakhic tradition as the way to remain faithful practitioners of Jesus' teachings.

It was nearly impossible for many members of this Jerusalem sect to accept the idea that non-Jews could be Christians without first becoming Jews.[8] Such a firmly held belief would have placed James in an ideological position close to the Pharisees; indeed, Josephus relates how the Pharisees rescued "James the brother of Jesus" from a certain death sentence.[9] Whether we can claim with certainty that this James of Sakhnin is the same as the brother of Jesus, we at least can identify him as a follower of Jesus, for he is familiar enough with Jesus' teachings to quote their intricacies to an inquirer. James also appears elsewhere in rabbinic literature, at *Qohelet Rabbah* 1.8, 3 as one who heals through touch and whose exegesis of Torah passages is refuted by the School of Rabbi Ishmael.

Of particular interest is James' reference to "your" Torah when quoting Deuteronomy. It appears only where he is speaking for himself, but

---

7. Sakhnin is also spelled Sikhnin, Siknaya, and Sikhna. In Greek it is Zoganeh, appearing in Josephus, *Life*, 188 and 265 (Thackeray, 71 and 99); *Wars* 2.573 (Thackeray, 543). See Bagatti, 302–4.

8. E. P. Sanders, *Jewish Law from Jesus to the Mishnah*, 284 and notes.

9. *Antiquities* 20.9, 1. Elsewhere on James, see Acts 1:13, 12:17, 15:13, 21:18, and Gal. 2:9. He figures prominently in Josephus, *Antiquities* 20.200 (Feldman, 497–99); and Eusebius, *History* 2.12, 4ff (Lake, 171–79; DeFerrari, 104–5). The Epistle of James and other apocryphal literature connected with his name often portray him as zealous for his brother's halakhic legacy, as does Eusebius in *History* 2.23 (DeFerrari, 124–30), quoting Hegesippus. See Klausner, 41–42, and van Voorst. Cohen's notes (in Soncino Ecclesiastes Rabbah, Freedman/Simon, 27; also Soncino Avodah Zarah, Epstein, 85) claim he is either James the son of Alphaeus (Mark 3:18) or James the Less (Mark 15:40). Herford (*Christianity*, 106) rejects the identification with James the brother of Jesus, whom he says was martyred in 44 c.e., and so too early for our story here; he traces this story to third-generation Christianity, not second. On the contact between Jews and Christians at that time, see Urbach, *Sages*, 294–97 and notes, 817–18. Bacher, *Aggadot ha-Tannaim*, part 1, 81–82 discusses the unusually extensive contacts between Eliezer and various "gerim," as does Neusner, *Eliezer* 330ff. and 365ff.

not where he is quoting Jesus. Yet this same phrase appears as dominical in John 10:34, and at John 15:25 the phrase "their Torah" appears. At John 10:34, Jesus quotes Psalm 82:6 as "your Torah";[10] at 15:25 he quotes Psalms 36:19 and 69:4 as "their Torah." In the case of Jesus' usage of the peculiar phrase, although the overt reference is to "Torah," the quotations are not from the Pentateuch as would be expected, but from the Hagiographa. Here we must understand that neither Jesus nor Jacob of Sakhnin were distancing themselves from the Pentateuch by referring to it as "your Torah," nor are their references intended to reflect the tensions already developing among the various sectarian interpreters of biblical tradition.[11] At Deuteronomy 26:3, when one brings a basket of firstling fruits to the Temple in Jerusalem, one offers it before the priest to be dedicated to "the Lord your [the priest's] God," and a similar example is found at 1 Kings 13:6. The noninclusive pronoun does not necessarily mean exclusion; "your" God does not mean that God is not "my" God. Rather, the use of a third-person reference serves as a call to conscience and commitment. This is Rashi's point when he comments on the use of *torato* ("his Torah") in Psalm 1:2: "At first it is called the Torah of God, but once one has invested oneself in it, he also calls it his own Torah."[12] James's words to Eliezer—"your Torah"—remind Eliezer of his commitment to the received scriptural tradition.

Eliezer's Meeting in the Market

The market is a symbolic setting in stories from classical, rabbinic, and early Christian literature. Many of St. Paul's most famous sermons took place in marketplaces, or in similar public squares, and still today the Middle Eastern market is the site of extensive public intercourse. A humorous story about biblical exegesis in the marketplace is attributed to eighteenth-century R. Jonathan Eybeshuetz:[13]

---

10. On Ps. 82:6, see Fromm, *You Shall be as Gods*; Hakham, *Tehillim*, 2.88; and the various targumim: the meaning is not "God" but "Judge."

11. There is a tradition for such distancing, as in the Passover haggadah where the "wicked" son answers *lakhem* (second person) instead of *lanu* (first person); see Ex. 12:26; *Mekhilta de Rabbi Ishmael* (Horowitz and Rabin, 66) and *Mekhilta de Rabbi Shimeon* (Epstein and Melamed, 26). However, that tradition is not applicable here.

12. See also *Tanhuma* Devarim (Buber, 10a) and *Midrash Tehillim*, Ps. 1:2, sec. 16 (Buber, 15 n213).

13. Tzintz, 2.82; for a similar story, see *va-Yiqra Rabbah* 4:6 (M. Margulies, 92);

Once a certain priest asked our rabbi the following question:

"What does scripture mean when it says: *You shall follow a major-ity*" (Ex. 23:2)?[14]

Our rabbi said: "Come back on the third day from now, and I will give you an answer."

Now it so happened that on the third day, the priest was walking through the marketplace, and he chanced upon our rabbi. The rabbi was standing, staring up into the heavens in wonderment, and the priest asked him: "Whatever are you looking at?"

The rabbi answered him: "I see angels up there, flying through the celestial heights, and each one of them is holding a harp in his hand."

The priest was too embarrassed to admit that he didn't see a thing.

So to save face, he allowed as how he saw the very same thing, and stood in the very same spot as the rabbi and lifted his own eyes heavenward.

It wasn't long before a crowd of people had gathered, all of them insisting that they too saw the phenomenon. Of course, everyone of them was embarrassed to admit that actually he didn't see a thing, particularly after the priest announced that *not* seeing any angels in the heaven was a sign that the onlooker was in a state of sin.

The longer this went on, the greater swelled the number of the crowd, all of them goyim, and all with their eyes turned expectantly upward.

After some time, the rabbi pulled the priest off to one corner, and admitted to him, "Truthfully, I couldn't see a damn thing. I was only doing that to make a fool out of you."

The priest answered: "Well, actually I didn't see anything either. I was only saying I did so that you wouldn't make fun of me!"

The rabbi said to the priest: "Now, however, you can see with your own eyes how that crowd is standing, gawking up at the sky, every one of

---

see Acts 1:11—"Men of Galilee, why do you stand looking up to heaven?" But well into our own era, the marketplace retains its power as a setting for dramatic stories. For some, the marketplace is closely connected with Nietzsche, *The Joyful Wisdom*, Book 3, par. 125 (Common, 167–68). Ref. Diogenes Laertius 6.41 (Hicks, 2.43), "I am looking for a man" [*ecce homo*?]), and *Babrius and Phaedrus*, Perry, 291 #19.

14. At times this passage is translated in the negative: "you shall *not* follow." The Hebrew text here resembles a "zeugma," two nouns yoked to one adjective. In this case, the question is whether "follow" is linked to the negative repeated twice earlier in the same verse, or whether this clause should be translated exactly as it reads, without the negative. Rabbinic tradition usually opts in this case for the latter. And see BT Ketubot 14b–15a.

them insisting that they see something which you and I know damn well is an outright lie. The Torah rule that the majority should be followed does not apply in situations where there is no doubt to be resolved. In those situations, one should be guided by one's own clear and certain conviction."

"Truer words were never spoken," responded the priest, and went on about his way.

Rabbi Eliezer is one of the most important figures of the middle-Tannaitic period, coinciding with the period in which the New Testament gospels were written. He was a member of a circle of men and women, based for a short time in Yavneh (Jamnia), who were known for their liberalism and for their dedication to social reform and the uprooting of corruption. The same circle included, among others, Eliezer's wife Imma-Shalom and her brother Rabban Gamliel II.[15] Eliezer, from the city of Lod (Lydda) in the south, and Jacob, from the village of Sakhnin in the north, must have been already acquainted with each other, since they recognized each other in the marketplace of a town far from where either of them lived. One explanation for the location of their chance encounter might be that, because of heavy taxation and cruel exploitation by the Roman oppressors, Jews and sectarian Jewish-Christians moved about frequently to avoid being caught; so their meeting was serendipitous.[16] But a second explanation is perhaps more plausible: At the time of the story, the Sanhedrin, having been chased out of Yavneh, met in Zippori (Sepphoris). Though all marketplaces were socially important meeting places, the one in Zippori was particularly so. Both great scholars may even have been in Zippori on business related to the Sanhedrin, as the primitive Jewish-Christians still recognized its authority.

Rabban Gamliel and Imma-Shalom

Eliezer's circle of colleagues also included Rabban Gamliel. A number of parables are attributed to him, at least some of which have the ring of

15. The title Rabban, wherever used, indicates that the bearer was the head of the Sanhedrin. The name Imma-Shalom is intriguing. Imma is probably parallel to the title "Abba," given to those within Pharisaism who practiced Hassidic piety (*mishnat hassidim*) and their successors. See Herzog, 1.384–85 and notes; Jastrow, 50 and 144; Betz; E. E. HaLevi, *Shaarei ha-Aggadah*, 169ff, 173ff, and 176ff; A. Epstein, 119–20; Safrai, "Hassidim."

16. S. Klein, *Eretz*, 59–61. Klein also reminds readers that Sakhnin was the site of the famous Beit Din of Rabbi Hanina ben Teradion (Sanhedrin 32b) and that the village was also the source of a certain pure wine used in Temple worship prior to 70 C.E.

gospel parables. One of these, from Tractate Semahot, about a king who gave a banquet for a number of guests, is dealt with in chapter 5. Gamliel was the brother of Imma-Shalom, wife of Eliezer. Like her husband and brother, Imma-Shalom was part of the sophisticated urban circle of faithful Jews in Yavneh, yet a delightful story is told (at her expense!) concerning her contact in Yavneh with a certain "philosopher" who was clearly a follower of Jesus. The story, like that from Eybeshuetz, attests to the ongoing contact between Jews and Christians and their mutual temptations to play tricks on each other:[17]

> There was a "philosopher" in the neighborhood,[18] who had earned a reputation for himself of not taking a bribe. [When Imma-Shalom and Rabban Gamliel had to go to court concerning their father's estate, they] decided to have some fun testing his reputation, so Imma-Shalom sent him a lamp of gold.
>
> When she came before him to plead her case, she said: "I desire that my father's inheritance be divided in such a way as to include me."
>
> He said to her, "It will be so divided."
>
> But R. Gamliel said to him [in protest]: "In our tradition it is written that a daughter may not inherit as long as there is a son" [see Num. 27:8, 36:8].
>
> [The "philosopher"] said to him: "Beginning the day that you went out of your land into exile, the Law of Moses was annulled, and another Law has been given, wherein it is written: 'The son and the daughter shall inherit equally'."[19]
>
> The next day it was R. Gamliel's turn to plead, and he sent [the "philosopher"] a Libyan ass.
>
> [The "philosopher"] said to him: "I skipped ahead further in the scroll, and there I found it written: 'I came not to abolish the Law of

17. See BT Shabbat 116a (Steinsaltz, 511–12). Klausner (45) and others date this story c.73 C.E., but the judge's citation of New Testament sources makes this date impossible. On the other hand, as we shall see, even if Eliezer was excommunicated as late as c.100, it does little to solve the historical anachronism here.

18. An intellectual of some sort, but most certainly a Jewish-Christian; see Wallach, 410–11. Herford's claim that he was a monk or bishop cannot be taken seriously. But see W. H. Loewe, 68 (and note, in which he mentions the early Jewish folk etymology that a "philosoph" meant "an old elephant"; see Kohut, 6.355, and tosafot to BT Shabbat 116a, Steinsaltz, 511), and see Rabbinowicz, *Diqduqei Soferim* to Shabbat 116a, 54a letter p. On early Christian theologians as "philosophers," see Berner, 132–33.

19. Rom. 8:16–17? Gal. 3:28? At Luke 12:13–14, Jesus refuses to decide such cases.

Moses, but I came to maintain[20] the Law of Moses' [Matt. 5:17]. And it is written in that Law [of Moses], 'where there is a son, a daughter shall not inherit'."

Imma-Shalom cried out [to the "philosopher"]: "May your light shine forth like a 'lamp'! [that is, don't forget the bribe I sent you!]"

Rabban Gamliel responded: "The ass has come and kicked over the lamp! [that is, my bribe has superseded yours, Imma-Shalom!]"

The setting of the passage again affirms that there was significant contact between Jews and the new sectarians, at least among the sophisticated Galilean circles.[21] The story does not make the motivation of Imma-Shalom and Gamliel entirely clear, but a knowledge of the larger circumstances suggests that they may have attempted to trick the "Christian" philosopher to prove to R. Eliezer that these sectarians, of whom he was so enamored, were as capable of corruption as anyone else.

The preceding passage has a number of peculiar components, though these do not warrant its dismissal as fictional, as Travers Herford argues (*Christianity*, 146ff). First of all, the "philosopher" seems to refer to some text written on a scroll and containing sayings that subsequently appear in the Gospels. It appears to be some sort of sayings source which the judge takes quite seriously and uses like responsa. Secondly, anyone familiar with what became the New Testament knows that there is no overt statement that sons and daughters inherit equally. At most it could be derived from Romans 8 and Galatians 3; it may also reflect the situation described in Acts 4:32–37, that members of the early church held all things communally. But we cannot imagine that at such an early date a sayings gospel and a Pauline epistle would have appeared in the same scroll, for the idea of a New Testament canon was not yet conceived. The third odd reference is suggested by the statement "I came not to abolish . . . but to maintain." The philosopher cites it as being farther into the scroll, though in the Gospels the statement's sole appearance is near the beginning of Matthew, well before Acts, Romans, or Galatians in our present canonical order—yet which the philosopher refers to as preceding Matthew in the written scroll. Herford hypothesizes that the philosopher was quoting from some collection of *logia* that antedated the Gospels and was in a different order. His

---

20. The [Hebrew/Aramaic] original here is surely either *leqayyem* or *leyased*, though certain received texts use *lehosif*. See Mena<u>h</u>ot 99a–b and Rashi thereto. For discussion see Jastrow, 160; Albright and Mann, 57–59; W. H. Loewe, 69 n2; Flusser, *JOC*, 378–79, 497, 504 n40; Flusser, *Yahadut*, 229–30; Flusser, "Ten Commandments," 234; and Pines. See also Rom. 3:31; Bacher, *Erkei*, 116–117. Ben Sirah 3:8(9) offers yet a different alternative; see Segal, 13.
21. See the several articles by Eric Meyers.

theory is nothing more than wild speculation; on the other hand, we cannot understand what document the philosopher was reading from.[22]

The story contains an even more oblique reference to the theological claims of the new sect. The witticism "the ass has kicked over the lamp" became a slogan with a broad usage. Whether it is original to Rabban Gamliel is impossible to determine. It appears elsewhere in rabbinic literature, usually associated with one bribe superseding another.[23] But because the ass is a messianic symbol (Zech. 9:9) quickly connected with Jesus following his "triumphal" entry into Jerusalem on Palm Sunday (Matt. 21:1–9 and parallels), the implied meaning of the witticism could as well be that "the messianic symbol of Christianity has kicked over the Torah light (compare Matt. 5:14–16) of Judaism," for here associations agglutinated to the symbols lead us to a different level of meaning.[24]

We can suggest, based on the above, at least four meanings to the *bon mot*, "the ass has kicked over the lamp":

1. its plain meaning, referring to a donkey and a candelabrum;

2. its allusive meaning, that Gamliel's bribe has superseded Imma-Shalom's;

3. its homiletic meaning, that the two seeking to make an ass out of a philosopher have managed to kick over his lamp of justice; and

4. its secret meaning, that the Christian "Messiah" claims to have abrogated the Torah.

These four possible meanings serve to illustrate well how the PaRDeS of meaning could apply to the sayings of Jesus. Removing the artificial limitation of the number four, a fifth and sixth meaning can be identified:

---

22. Wallach (408) argues that "the end of the scroll" refers to Deut. 27:26, but the only support he can muster for his argument is Epiphanius, *Haer.* 29:8. He believes the entire passage to be anti-Ebionite.

23. *Pesiqta de Rav Kahana* 122b (Mandelbaum, 260 line 8; Buber, 123a); JT Yoma 1.1,38c; *va-Yiqra Rabbah* 21.9 (M. Margulies, 489 and n3); *Yalqut Shimeoni* to Isaiah, sec. 391. On the ass in connection with Christianity, see *Qohelet Rabbah* 1.8, 4.

24. On agglutinate symbols leading in different directions, see Derrett, *Studies,* 2.165–83. The slogan appears in a highly allegorical form in a sixth-century prayer by Yannai (Zulai, 189 line 21). Lamenting the growing eclipse of Judaism by Christianity, Yannai wrote, "The lamps of Byzantium shine forth in honor and beauty; the lamps of Zion are captured and kicked over." The slogan also appears in *Sifrei ba-Midbar* (Horowitz, 173), *Pesiqta de Rav Kahane* (Buber, 123a; Mandelbaum, 261 and notes), and in Tertullian, *Apol.* 8.1 (*eversores luminum canes*).

Eliezer was a teacher/scholar of extreme personal integrity, whose rulings so often contradicted the majority opinion that he was ultimately unwelcome in the rest of the religious community. An examination of mishnaic texts such as Temurah 3 or Taanit 1 shows how often the formula occurs that R. Eliezer said "x," and the sages said "y."[31] Eliezer re-presents only those opinions that he holds on the authority of his teachers, without innovation on his own. Hence he fought violently for the faithful perpetuation of his particular tradition, being quite intractable about it. Apparently he also held strictly to the advice in Avot 4:1—"Who is wise? He who learns from every man," a maxim derived from Psalm 119:99.[32]

Given that Eliezer's excommunication was due to a long-standing tension over halakhic development, it apparently had nothing to do with his contacts with Christians. His first contacts with them seem to have been about the year 60, before the First Revolt and the Temple's destruction, and these contacts continued afterward.[33] His excommunication, however, came later in life; certainly after his embassy to Rome, c.96, and probably around the turn of the century. The difficulty in pinning down the accuracy of the many stories attributed to R. Eliezer is that so little critical work has been done in coordinating and synchronizing the scattered rabbinic materials, and thus whatever consensus about dates in his life presently exists in the scholarly community is also based on uncritical use of sources. Eliezer's meeting in the marketplace seems to occur in the few

---

31. See BT Baba Metzia 49b; JT Moed Qatan 3.1,81c–d; see R. Margulies, *Mekhkarim*, 34ff; and Aberbach and Grossfeld.

32. English translations of the Psalm verse are frequently misleading. The *mem* of *Mikkol* is the originative rather than the comparative sense. The correct translation is "I learned *from* anyone who would teach me" (originative), not "more *than* my teachers" (comparative). Eliezer too seems to have learned from anyone who would teach him. The LXX and the Vulgate incorrectly choose the comparative *mem*, which leads to an incorrect English translation of Ps. 119:99. See R. Ḥanina in BT Taanit 7a and Rabina in Makkot 10a. Also compare JT Ḥagigah 2.1,7b; *Qohelet Rabbah* to Qoh. 7:8; and Tobia ben Eliezer to Qoh. loc. cit. (Feinberg, 33).

33. Eliezer was a student of Rabban Yoḥanan ben Zakkai (c.1–c.80 c.e.) and the teacher of Aqiba (c.50–135). He seems to have been born slightly before 40 c.e., and Klausner believes that the encounter with James took place sometime around 60, about thirty years after Jesus' death. After the destruction of the Temple in 70, Eliezer founded a famous academy in Lod (Lydda), to which students came from all over the country. In c.95–96, Eliezer and Rabban Gamliel undertook a mission to Rome on behalf of the Jews of Judea, so he can hardly have been excommunicated before then. Lieberman, Klausner, and Chajes all put his excommunication in the very late 90s. Eliezer is said to have lived the rest of his life in Caesarea, where his "heresy trial" took place, and to have died excommunicate in 117 c.e. during the persecution of Lucius.

decades between the writing of the synoptics and the writing of John's Gospel.

We cannot deduce that Eliezer's excommunication indicates the severance of ties with Christians by the rabbinic community, in spite of the increasing tensions. The gradual parting of the ways between Christians and Jews began before the Bar-Kokhba rebellion in 135 C.E., but even then developed only slowly over the next several centuries. Eliezer's arrest does, however, suggest the extent of Roman suspicion toward Christianity. Though the "heresy" charge in the story is confusing (the word *minut* is also used by various sects within Judaism about each other), it is possible that Eliezer was arrested because the government was suspicious of his overly friendly attitude toward Christians. Nothing in the tradition suggests that Eliezer actually was a believer in Jesus, but apparently he took great delight throughout his life in debating textual exegesis and halakhic interpretation with Jesus' followers. At issue in the arrest, then, is the cost of talking to sectarians whom the government viewed as subversive. Christians were persecuted under both Domitian (c.96) and Trajan (c.109), though in neither case does the persecution appear to have extended to Jews.[34] The Roman overlords of Judea, Samaria, and the Galilee were distrustful of Judaism, but having worked out an uneasy truce over a period of decades, granted it a licit status. Christianity, on the other hand, was viewed with grave suspicion, as a popular sectarianism, which with its "regal" acronym INRI threatened to undermine the uneasy truce. Such suspicion explains both the political reasons for Jesus' arrest and crucifixion and the continuing persecution of Christians throughout the first three decades of the church. From the beginning, the claim that Christianity is dangerous to political authority has been correct.[35]

Parable as Halakhic Midrash

To the modern mind, Christianity is viewed as having the character of a creed but not of a sophisticated system of halakhic and behaviorist demands, for that legacy seems to have been intentionally downsized with the growing attraction to the faith by non-Jews.[36] In order to grasp, there-

---

34. See the First Apology of Justin Martyr (Quasten, 1.199–200) for a historical document from the period of persecutions; and see Pagels, 70–101, on the general history.

35. Lieberman, *Texts and Studies*, 75–88.

36. See Safrai, "Ḥassidim ve-Anshei Maaseh," 152[20]; E. P. Sanders, *Jewish Law*, 90–96. For this reason, Jesus' halakhah was not preserved in traditional Christian sources, for it served no purpose for the developing Christology in the Roman

fore, the full import that the discussion between Jacob the Christian and Eliezer the Jew was completely of a halakhic nature, passing along Jesus' skill as a teacher of innovative halakhic interpretation, we must clarify the distinction between mashal, midrash, and halakhah—categories no longer familiar to most Christians.

A mashal is an imaginative and seductive way to illustrate how one arrives at a midrash, or the rhetorical extrapolation of a new moral or ethical lesson from a scriptural text. Once the new lesson emerges, the halakhic application seems to be a stringent result of the new insight. The nuances of these definitions will develop as the next several chapters unfold. For the time being, the summary can be offered that a mashal is a literary form that may express an imaginary, fictional, or *real-life* event. Mashal, from the semitic root meaning "analogy" or "likeness," is a life-situation or even a text that bears within it the possibility of comparison with another life-situation or even another text. Midrash is the method by which any text is hermeneutically reinterpreted to draw forth an explanation of an inner meaning of that text.[37] Often the explication of an implicit meaning reveals a new ethical or moral lesson. Once midrash has been used to identify an inner meaning, the significance or effect of that inner meaning can be stated as a topic for spiritual, mental, or behavioral guidance, all of which come under the heading of halakhah.

Halakhah proceeds out of mashal by way of midrashic methodology.[38] Perhaps an example will clarify. Biblical legislation is traditionally divided

---

Empire. See also Grintz, 186–87, *Ruth Rabbah* Proem 2, and *Shir ha-Shirim Rabbah* 4.22 (Donski, 118–19) on the principle of selective retention: "All prophecy which was pertinent as well as for future generations was preserved. And all prophesy which was pertinent for the contemporary situation but which was inapplicable to future generations was not preserved. But in the future, the Holy One, blessed Be He, will restore and preserve all their prophecies, as it is said [Zech. 14:5], *and the Lord my God, with all the holy beings, shall come to you.*" It is interesting that Christianity (*notzrut*) "preserved" (*N-Tz-R*) for Judaism the writing of Philo, the Pseudepigrapha, and much of the Apocrypha, whereas Judaism preserved for Christianity certain memories of Jesus that might otherwise have been lost.

37. The word *midrash* occurs twice in the Hebrew Bible, at 2 Chron. 13:22 and 24:27. In both cases, it appears to be a reference to a type of collected materials. Mack, *Aggadic*, 39 and 49, points out that the midrash methodology proceeds out of the targumic commentaries known from the time of Ezra and Nehemiah. According to both Strack and Mielziner, the collections of midrashim that are tannaitic (i.e., that predate the Mishnah, c.200) include the Yelammedenu fragments preserved in sections of *Tanḥuma* and elsewhere; *Mekhilta de Rabbi Ishmael* and *Mekhilta de Rabbi Shimeon bar Yoḥai*; *Sifra*, also called *Torat Kohanim*; *Sifrei ba-Midbar*, *Sifrei Devarim*, and *Sifrei Zutta*.

38. See note 12 in the previous chapter for supportive references.

into apodictic and casuistic law.[39] Apodictic laws are pithy, terse, and categorical in character. For example, Exodus 20:13—You shall not murder— is an apodictic law. Casuistic law is situational: if such and such happens, then it should be handled in such and such a manner.[40] For example, Deuteronomy 22:23—"In the case of a virgin who is engaged to a man—*if* a man comes upon her in town and lies with her, *then* you shall take the two of them out to the gate of that town and stone them to death." The laws in both verses fall into the category of halakhah, that is, regula, model, or example. However, an apodictic law, like that in Exodus 20:13, can also function as a mashal or associative analogy in the further midrashic development of halakhah, particularly if the apodictic law is treated midrashically as a narrative. In contrast to Deuteronomy 22:23, which is concerned with consensual cohabitation, we read at Deuteronomy 22:25: "But *if* the man comes upon the engaged girl in the open country, and the man lies with her by force, *then* only the man who lay with her shall die, but you shall do nothing to the girl. The girl did not incur the death penalty, for this case *is like that* of a man attacking another and murdering him." In other words, the penalty for murder is death, hence the penalty for rape is also death, for by explicit analogy, *rape is like murder*. The situation is explained in the legal sense by a comparison (mashal) that arouses more indignation through the analogic process of reframing apodictic law as casuistic.

On the same subject area, a similar move from apodictic to casuistic—by turning the apodictic into a mashal—can be found in the relationship between Exodus 21 and Deuteronomy 19. According to Exodus 21:12– 13: (apodictic) "Whoever fatally strikes a person shall be put to death. (casuistic) *If* it was not premeditated, but came about by an act of God,

---

39. On *apodictic* and *casuistic* (a concept whose definition is presently in flux), see the summary in *IDB*, 3.82 and Suppl. vol, 534; *ABD* 4.252–53; Fishbane, *Biblical Interpretation*, 101–4; Daube, *Studies*, chap. 1; Sellin and Fohrer, 67–70, 174; Childs, chap. 5; Eichrodt, vol. 1, chap. 3; von Rad, 1.33, 72, 433, 2.136. The Hebrew version of Cassuto to Exodus 21:1 also addresses the issue, but the English translation omits the discussion.

40. *Casus*, as in case law, means a situation that has occurred and demands legal judgment. Case law is what we know today as common (Anglo-Saxon) law, and etymologically implies casualty. A legal "case" is by definition "an unexpected disaster" (see Lewis and Short, 299–300), and is by nature inductive. The antonym is statutory (apodictic) law, which is typical to the Julian Code and Continental law; it is by nature deductive. Casuistry is *not* a nasty word for rabbinic or jesuitical hairsplitting; it is a perfectly respectable word defining a method of legal thinking and procedure. And see Yalon, 89–93, on *pilpel*, which has nothing to do with "pepper," but rather means to look at a word circumspectively, from all aspects.

then I will appoint for you a place to which the killer can flee." Deuteronomy 19:4–13 shows even more extensive development on the issue of how murderers are to be dealt with, there shifting back and forth between apodictic and casuistic. In this midrashic process, an apodictic law is given (one who kills must die); a mashal is then constructed (but what if he killed in an accidental manner?); and a new halakhah is thus derived (he shall be sent to a city of refuge rather than being put to death). As we shall see, the apodictic statement at Deuteronomy 23:18—You shall not bring the fee of a whore—is dealt with casuistically by Jesus in his teaching to Jacob of Sakhnin by turning it into a mashal, matching like with like.

Sometimes halakhah is derived from a mashal by the listener her- or himself, by process of the maieutic method. Such is the case in the famous interchange between Nathan and David in 2 Samuel 12:1–15. Once Nathan has told David the story of the rich man who took the poor man's ewe, "David flew into a rage . . . and said to Nathan, 'As the Lord lives, the man who did this deserves to die! He shall pay for the lamb four times over, because he did such a thing and showed no pity.'" From the parabolic story, David makes a legal and behavioral judgment, of course never realizing until too late that he is judging himself. Once Nathan has pointed out to David, "You are the man," the legal case becomes a mashal for David and he derives a personal application, or nimshal, which functions as a halakhic judgment upon himself.

Telling a parable, then, can be a manner of teaching, in addition to a form of entertainment.[41] A situation is presented, and the listener is encouraged to draw her own conclusions, some of which may take the form of halakhic behaviorist commitment. Maieutic teaching, so integral to the Socratic method, may begin with a question, just as Aqiba asks R. Eliezer a question, or Jesus asks his disciples "What do you think?"[42] The methodol-

---

41. Rofe, *Prophetical Stories*, 140–41, points out that in some parable texts, it is not always possible to distinguish between historical elements and imaginary incidents. Some parables are constructed, then, when actual historical incidents do not serve sufficient purpose and something more ambiguous and transcendent is needed to make the point. Such parables may still be couched, however, in seemingly historical language, such as the parable of the Good Samaritan. Is the story of the rich man and the poor man's ewe a historical court case or a useful fiction?

42. On the maieutic method in Socrates, see references at Liddell and Scott, 1072, *maieutikos*, literally, "skilled in midwifery," but metaphorically, "the Socratic method of eliciting from others information which was in their minds but of which they were not yet aware." See also Daube, *New Testament*, 151–57, and Kierkegaard, *Philosophical Fragments*, esp. chap. 1. Maieutic methodology seeks to stimulate thaumatic thinking; see Plato, *Theatetus* 148D–155D and 161E (Fowler, 2.28–55, 76–77), wherein wonder and query are the beginnings of philosophy.

ogy was useful to Eliezer's teacher, Rabban Yoḥanan ben Zakkai: in the *Avot de-Rabbi Nathan* A, chap. 14, Yoḥanan sends his students out of the academy to learn experientially, in answer to a number of questions that begin "Go out and see . . ."[43]

The Fee of a Whore

According to the rabbinic text, Jesus bases his teaching on an apodictic statement from Deuteronomy 23:18—"You shall not bring the fee of a whore or the pay of a dog into the house of the Lord your God in fulfillment for any vow; for both are abhorrent to the Lord your God." The fee of a whore (*etnan zonah*) need not be money; it could also be animal stock (Latin: *pecunia*), which is, in fact, at least as likely. For instance, at Genesis 38:17, Judah attempts to pay a whore (actually his daughter-in-law Tamar in disguise) with a baby goat.[44]

Over the course of the halakhic development interpreting the *etnan zonah*, its application became more and more restricted. Well before the destruction of the Temple in 70, the biblical law had been interpreted quite restrictively. According to M. Temurah 2:1 and elsewhere, the injunction applies only to the direct income from services rendered. The "fee" of the whore was understood not to apply to any gifts given her voluntarily (*matanah*), but only to whatever she received conventionally as a direct payment for services rendered (*etnan*). By extension to Ezekiel 16:33, *etnan* was also applicable to anything given by a prostitute to a man in return for his services rendered to her; also by extension to Exodus 21, *etnan* was applicable to any fee paid by one owner to another in order to hire the copulative services of a male Hebrew slave with a female Canaanite slave.[45] However, were she to purchase something else with the income, and then donate the new purchase, such a gift was acceptable. Whereas the fee—the *etnan*—is summarily rejected, the prostitute herself is not judged. Rabbinic literature is careful to make sure that the words

---

43. Herford, *Ethics*, 54, misunderstands the formula "Go and see"; it is a charge for students to leave the academy and learn from social engagement with the world. On Yoḥanan ben Zakkai, see Neusner's lengthy study, but compare the acid critiques of Neusner's scholarship by Lieberman, Zeitlin, and Shaye Cohen.
44. On the use of animals as payment, see the etymologies of both "chattel" and "pecuniary" in Pokorny (*pecu-*), and the OED, 386, 2110. A kid is not a small gift, but a substantial one, fit for a king; see 1 Sam. 16:20. On Judah's paying Tamar with a kid (and ultimately becoming an antecedent of the Messiah), see Chap. 8 of this volume, and Ginzberg, *Legends*, 5.335 n87.
45. See M. Temurah 6:2; Kehati, 10.114; Tos. Temurah 4:6 (Zuckermandel, 555); BT Temurah 29a–30b. The *etnan zonah* is also referred to in M. Parah 2:3.

"both are abhorrent" are understood as applying to the fee and the pay, rather than to the prostitute and the dog. The critical distinction that Jesus makes, consistent with the Pharisaic literature, is that between *in rem* and *in personam*; blame or discrimination can attach to an act or an object without affecting the person involved.[46] Nor was her very urge to donate something condemned.[47] The desire to make an offering was never condemned in even the greatest of sinners, as long as the gift could not be interpreted as a bribe (see Mal. 1:6–10) or any attempt to justify the harlot's sexual activity.

The Purity of the Temple and the High Priest

It is not surprising to find Jesus concerned with the holy character of the Temple in Jerusalem, for Temple purity was a subject of grave concern to virtually every trend among the Judaisms of the late Second Temple period. In 161 B.C.E., Judah Maccabee had come to the Temple and, seeing the desolation there, rent his garments in distress (1 Macc. 4:36–40). Twenty years later, Simeon combined the office of high priest with that of ethnarch, and all traces of the previous Hasmonean sensitivity disappeared into a cloud of controversy (1 Macc. 7:33–42, 14:47, 15:1–2).[48] In the opinion of many (Pharisees and Essenes in particular), Hasmonean administration of the Temple in Jerusalem was marked by simony and corruption. Although Deuteronomy 17:14–20 mandates a clear separation of powers between the throne and the temple, the Hasmonean dynasty had confused the powers of the two, corrupting the priesthood in a manner that continued its decadence until the destruction in 70.

---

46. The rabbinic concept is called *Heftsa ve-Gavra* (*in rem, in personam*); see N. Solomon, 123–26; and Herzog, 1.49ff. According to the New Testament account, Jesus got himself in trouble by being so careful to make this distinction that he was too often seen in the company of "sinners." However, since the distinction is itself Pharisaic, one can hardly accept testimony that the Pharisees were angered with Jesus for carrying out their own analytic system. See also Schüssler Fiorenza, who points out that there is little evidence that Jesus ever actually spent so much time in the company of notorious sinners, though the Gospels record that others so accused him.

47. On the urge to donate (*koah nedivah*), see Tos. Yoma 1:23; 2:2–3 (Lieberman, 228, 230). Gifts were accepted from a wide variety of people, and they were "remembered with honor." See also Lieberman, *Texts and Studies*, 212, where he shows that the Greek *entolē* is parallel to *mitzvah*, both coming to suggest a particular emphasis on charitable alms.

48. The tragedy is the melding of the "three crowns"; see Avot 4:13 (17) in Herford, *Ethics*, 112. See also Josephus, *Antiquities* 13.213–215, 299–300, 333–335 (Marcus, 7.333–34, 377–78, 395, and notes); and *Wars* 1.69 (Thackeray, 2.35).

High priests followed on each other's heels, changing annually. According to Tos. Yoma 1.7: "When the kings multiplied, they enacted that ordinary priests should be appointed (to the high priesthood) and displaced each year." No longer was the high priesthood hereditary (see Lev. 16:32) or of extended tenure, both of which had been the case in the First Temple. Often the office was purchased through bribe and benefaction, so that the most powerful held the office rather than the most worthy.[49] Gospel evidence confirms that such practices continued through the period in which Jesus lived: "Caiaphas, who was the high priest that year" (John 11:49); "He did not say this of his own accord, but being the high priest that year" (John 11:51); "Annas, for he was the father-in-law of Caiaphas, who was high priest that year" (John 18:13).[50] As has been noted, in a number of places rabbinic literature uses the witticism "The ass has kicked over the menorah" to signal the general distress and disgust by the population (including the Pharisaic party) with the corruption of the high priesthood.[51] Hence the rekindled poignancy of the ancient cry in the postexilic book of Malachi (1:10): "If only you would lock My doors, and not kindle fire on My altar to no purpose! I take no pleasure in you—said the Lord of Hosts—and I will accept no offering from you."

In spite of the corruption, regular worship life of the Temple continued in accordance with the details of the received tradition, including the annual observance of Yom Kippur, the Day of Atonement, as mandated in Leviticus 16. In order to effect atonement for the community's sin, the high priest was to conduct the entire day-long service alone and in a state of total purity. Both to insure such purity and to be present for the necessary dress-rehearsals, he left his home one week before the date of Yom Kippur to move into assigned quarters adjacent to the Temple environs. There an appointed staff met his every need, that he might not only be pure but also completely relaxed and focused on the task that lay ahead.[52] So, according to JT Yoma 1, 38c: "Seven days before the Day of Atonement, the High Priest was removed from his house to the Chamber of the Palhedrin. . . . At first they used to call it the Chamber of the Bouleutin

49. Excellent summaries of these developments can be found in Alon, *Jews, Judaism*, 48–87; M. Stern in Avi-Yonah, *World History*, 7.124–79; Greene; and E. P. Sanders, *Judaism*.

50. See also Eusebius, *Ecclesiastical History* 1.3, 10 (DeFerrari, 46–51); and Chrysostom, "In ins. alt.," homily 1 of *In principium Actorum* in Migne, PG 51.74, discussing John 11:49.

51. See *Sifrei*, Balak par. 131 to Num. 25:12 (Horowitz, 173); *va-Yiqra Rabbah* par. 21 (M. Margulies, 488, notes); *Pesiqta de Rav Kahana*, Aḥare Mot (Buber, 177a); JT Yoma 1, 38c.

52. See Maimonides, Hilkhot Yom ha-Kippurim 2:5 in *la-Am*, 6.591.

('where the elders debate'), but now it has become known popularly as the Chamber of Palhedrin ('where the usurpers debate')." As Maimonides, Lieberman, Alon, and others have shown,[53] the palhedrin was simply the apartment in which the high priest lived for this week prior to Yom Kippur. As witnessed by BT Yoma 10b, it was outside, but adjacent to, the Temple precincts;[54] from his apartment, the high priest could enter the Temple through a corridor, without the risk of any contamination from going outside. According to BT Yoma 9b–10a, each successive high priest had the right to refurbish, or even remodel, the palhedrin to his taste and convenience, so that over the course of years it became more and more splendid, even decadent.

At any given time, a large number of priests were confined to the Temple to conduct the requisite sacrifices; as is well known, they took turns according to a specified rotation.[55] For the most part, the scholarly literature has ignored the delicate problem of where these hundreds of men went to the toilet during their period of service, or for that matter, where the high priest went to relieve himself during the week when he resided in the palhedrin. A careful reading of the rabbinic literature answers at least some of these questions.

According to M. Yoma 3:2,[56] 3:3, and 4:5, among the physical needs of the members of the priesthood were a place to bathe, a toilet, and a place to perform their post-toilet ablutions.[57] Numerous references to the word

---

53. On *palhedrin*, see Jastrow, 1216; Kehati, vol. 10, intro to Tractate Middot; BT Yoma 10a; Tos. Yoma 1:1–2 (Lieberman, *ki-Feshutah*, 230 and notes on 717); Kohut, 6.84, 407 and 414; Liddell and Scott, 1704, *sunhedra*, and 1332, *parhedreia*; Zeitlin, "Bouleuterion"; Alon, *Jews, Judaism*, 48–88, and *Mekhkarim*, 1.48–51.

54. The Temple, of course, was not a residence, and so the palhedrin had no mezuza. Mezuzot could be affixed only in legitimate residential accommodations, according to Tractate Yoma. The residence also had to be of one's own choosing, so a prison had no mezuzot. At BT Yoma 10b, the question is raised whether the high priest is a prisoner in the palhedrin, as it is not a residence of his own choosing. And see Maimonides, Hilkhot Mezuzot 6:1–6 in *la-Am*, 2.181–83.

55. See Maimonides, Hilkhot Klei ha-Miqdash 3.9–11 (*la-Am*, 6.70–71; Lewittes, 52–53).

56. In this Mishnah passage, "covering his feet" is a euphemism for defecation, and "making water" a euphemism for urination. And see also Kehati, 4.22 and 40.

57. The Bible tells of wilderness toilets (Deut. 23:13; 1 Sam. 24:3) and urban toilets such as the private outhouse on the roof that belonged to Eglon the king of Moab (Jdgs. 3:20 and 24); this latter room is called a *meqeirah* (roofed place), and the toilet inside it called a *kisseh* (seat; throne?). Ginzberg (*Unknown*, 284) calls it the *sella familiarica*. In the Temple Scroll (col. 46, lines 13–16), the toilet is called a *meqom yad* ("designated place"). There it is written: "And you shall make for them

mehilah (cave, passageway) suggest that there were a series of subterranean latrines under the Temple compound, in nonconsecrated areas, for
the general use of the priests. The sages clearly distinguished between
Levitical impurity (*tamé*) and filth (*tzoah*); according to JT Pesahim 7.12,
35b, the presence of a latrine in the basement of the Temple does not
prove that this part of the Temple may be entered in a state of Levitical
impurity, for "excrement is not impurity, but merely filth." The high
priest, however, had separate facilities, attached to his private quarters.[58]
His purification pool (*miqve*) was known generically as the *bet parvah*, and
his toilet was known generically as the *bet kisseh*, literally "the house of
the seat." One would presume that just as the palhedrin chamber became
increasingly more elaborate with the succession of new high priests, so did
these private facilities. From other archaeological evidence, we know of
the existence of golden toilets from this period, and it is not difficult to
imagine the desirability of such splendor.

　　A final note on toilets: the siege and conquest of Jerusalem by Vespasian was exhaustingly expensive. When he became emperor, his coffers
were depleted. Needing to raise massive amounts of money quickly, virtually nothing was left untaxed, including public toilets. According to the
Roman historian Dio Cassius, Vespasian had no scruples about the ways in
which he procured financial support:

---

a *meqom yad* outside of the city, to which they shall go out, to the northwest of
the city—small houses, furnished with beams and with pits in them, through
which the excrement may fall down and [not] remain visible, [and] with a mini-
mum distance from the city of three thousand cubits." See Yadin, *Temple Scroll*,
1.294–304 and 2.199; J. Maier, 41, 117; also ref. 1QM 7.6; *Sifrei Devarim* 257
(Finkelstein, 281). General regulations for keeping military camps clean are found
at Deut. 23:10–14; these did not apply to the Temple or to the city of Jerusalem,
and even the requirement of the Temple Scroll was but a future vision of the
Essenes. For various mention of toilets and related ablutions in rabbinic literature,
see Jastrow, 761; M. Tamid 1:1; M. Middot 5:3–4 and Kehati's intro. to Middot; M.
Yoma 3:3 and 6, 7:4 and Kehati, Yoma, 5, 22 and 40; Tos. Yoma 1:20 (Lieberman,
228, line 95 and notes in *ki-Feshutah*, 747–48); Tos. Kelim (BQ) 1, 11 (Zuckermandel, 570 line 8); BT Tamid 27b–28a; Berakhot 55a and 62b (Steinsaltz, 272);
Maimonides, Hilkhot Talmud Torah 6:1, in *la-Am*, 2.109; *Enc. Talmudit*, 3.206–
10.
58. See Maimonides, Hilkhot Avodat Yom ha-Kippurim 2:2–3 (*la-Am* 6.589–90,
notes; Lewittes, 390–92). And see BT Shabbat 25b: "Who is the rich man? He who
has a toilet near his dining table"; Greek parallels to this saying can be found in E.
E. HaLevi, *Erkei*, 4.143.

When some persons voted to erect to him a statue costing a million, he held out his hand and said: "Give me the money; this [cupped hand] is its pedestal." And to Titus, who expressed his indignation at the tax placed upon public urinals . . . he said as he picked up some gold pieces that had been realized from this source and showed them to him: "See, my son, if they have any smell."[59]

Sarcastically, then, the urinal tax became known as the *pecunia non olet* (the tax that has no smell). Titus, who succeeded his father Vespasian as emperor, abolished this tax upon his return to Rome.

Jesus' Innovation and Historical Parallels

The New Testament is clear that Jesus' parables were often composed spontaneously, using examples at hand. One can imagine him, then, walking past the magnificent Temple in Jerusalem, perhaps below the Mount, in the Tyropean Valley where the poor lived. As he walked, he met a crowd of people arguing in the narrow street, including one very outraged woman of ill repute. Like all good semites in the Middle East even today, he rushed toward the crowd rather than away from it to see what was going on and to offer his advice. Someone turned to him and explained: Sir, we know it is written in our Torah that the priests may not accept the fee of a whore. But this woman here wishes to make an offering to the Temple. What shall we do? Isn't there some way her gift can be put to use? Jesus immediately sees the situation as a living parable, a mashal, proceeding out of the biblical text (Deuteronomy), and he offers them a nimshal based upon another biblical text (Micah): because the hire came from filth, it should be returned to filth. Then, looking up at the Temple towering over his head on the Mount, he proceeds to offer a halakhic application of the nimshal: Let her wages be accepted for use on something outside the consecrated precincts of the Temple. Let them be used to buy a golden toilet for the comfort of the high priest when he is living in his apartment before Yom Kippur.

In this halakhic resolution, Jesus at one and the same time manages to resolve a difficulty, to offer something compensatory to the prostitute, and to slam the corruption of the office of high priesthood. In his attitude toward the prostitute we see again his distinction between *in rem* and *in*

---

59. Dio Cassius, *Roman History*, Epitome of Book 65, 14 (Camp, 8.288–89); see also Suetonius, *de vita Caesarum* 8.23, 3 (Rolfe, 2.319); Elkoshi, 321 #1174.

personam. It was characteristic of Jesus' ministry not to condemn sinners, but to address the halakhic demands upon his people. Whereas the donation could not be used inside the consecrated precincts of the Temple, it could be used just next to them, and for the purpose of easing the life of the one upon whom the annual atonement of the community depended. Jesus' skill as a teacher of halakhah is exhibited by the midrashic manner in which he extracts a justifiable affirmation from the blanket injunction of Deuteronomy.

Perhaps one of the reasons that Jesus' teaching proved so memorable to Jacob of Sakhnin is the dramatic character of the mashal. By its nature, a mashal is an indirect image that staggers the imagination in such a manner that each listener conjures up a personal application. The more lively and creative the mashal, the stronger effect it has on the listener, and the more it encourages the listener to process his or her own life situation. Hence even those meshalim that have some rootedness in reality must at the same time transcend the details of that reality so as to exaggerate their impact. One such exaggeration is the combination of a whore and the holiest site in the religion.

We know of certain other ancient writers who explored the implications of the Deuteronomic exclusion of *etnan zonah*. In an attempt to extract an ethical lesson from the halakhic regulation, the historian Flavius Josephus wrote in *Antiquities* 4.205–9 (9) [Thackeray, 4.575]: "From the wages of a prostitute let no sacrifices be paid; for the Deity has pleasure in naught that proceeds from outrage, and no shame could be worse than the degradation of the body. Likewise, if one has received payment for the mating of a dog,[60] whether hound of the chase or guardian of the flocks, he must not use thereof to sacrifice to God." Before him, Philo, the noted exegete of Alexandria, uses the biblical passage in a more metaphorical manner in his *Special Laws* 1.280–81 [Colson, 263]:

> There is a very excellent ordinance inscribed in the sacred tablets of the law, that the wages of a harlot should not be brought into the temple; the hire, that is, of one who has sold her personal charms and chosen a scandalous life for the sake of the wages of shame. But if the gifts of one who has played the harlot are unholy, surely more unholy still are the gifts of the soul which has committed whoredom, which has thrown itself

---

60. Josephus understands "dog" literally. The JPS translation of the Hebrew Bible understands it metaphorically, as "a male prostitute" (presumably on the basis of the verse immediately preceding), illustrating again the multiple interpretations of a single text. The JPS translation contradicts the literal understanding at M. Temurah 6:3.

away into ignominy and the lowest depths of outrageous conduct, into wine-bibbing and gluttony,[61] into the love of money, of reputation, of pleasure, and numberless other forms of passion and soul-sickness and vice.

Philo's exegesis is constructed through the typical rabbinic pattern of argumentation called *kal va-homer*[62] (in Latin, *a fortiori*): if God despises the gifts of a whore of mere flesh, then *kal va-homer* how much more will God despise the gifts of a whore of the spirit.

Jesus' practice was not to allegorize, but rather to leave the application of his meshalim to his listeners. Jesus was a homilist, a teacher, and an expositor of halakhot.[63] His memory is retained in the Babylonian Talmud out of respect for his innovative contribution to solving halakhic complications. He addresses halakhah not by abolishing or abrogating it, but by upholding its value and then extracting from within it an unnoticed inherent meaning. Jesus is remembered in Jewish tradition, both for better and for worse, as one skilled in *hiddush*—the extraction of new meanings and applications from within the received halakhah.[64]

That Jesus is within the purview of the Pharisaism of his time can be seen by comparing his *hiddush* with other stories from rabbinic literature that echo a similar methodology. For example, in the application of the process by which a *sotah*, or suspected adulteress, is tried (Num. 5), the rabbis asked why the suspect should be given unrefined grain as a meal offering for the altar, rather than the usual sifted flour (see M. Sotah 2:1). Rabban Gamaliel understands the unusual action as a parable:

> It has been taught: Rabban Gamaliel said to the Sages: "Learned men, permit me to explain this (*ke-min homer*) 'allegorically'."

> He had heard R. Meir say, "She fed [his animal appetites] with the

61. One cannot help noting again the reference here to Matt. 11:19, in which Jesus seems rather to enjoy his reputation as "a wine-bibber and glutton."
62. Originally two nouns: *qol* and *homer*; on their present erratic adjectival form, see Strack, 94 and 285 n2; Bacher, *Erkei*, 118. On rabbinic methods of argumentation, see Mielziner as well as Rabinowich's translation. Later sources often used the Deuteronomic passage allegorically as well. See for example, Avraham ibn-Ezra's extended allegory on Isa. 23, in which he employs the *etnan zonah* as an allegory for illegal profits gained by the city of Tyre (Friedländer, 107).
63. Flusser, *JOC*, 494 and notes; Daube, *New Testament*, 158–69, on "Four Types of Questions." On the sermons of Jesus, see Pool, 6.
64. On *hiddush*, see Daube, *New Testament*, 205–23.

dainties of the world [that is, her pampered body]; therefore she offers animal's fodder."

[Gamaliel] then said to [Meir], "You may be right about [the delights of] a rich woman, but what of a poor woman [who hasn't a pampered body to offer]? [You have not drawn the correct nimshal from the mashal. The emphasis is on the deed, not the physical attributes of the *sotah*.] Rather [you should reason like to like]: As her *actions* were the action of an animal, so she is given animal fodder for her act of offering [and thereby we refrain from judgment upon her personal worth]."[65]

One is tempted to draw the distinction between a humane *hiddush* (a novel insight and elucidation) and an inhumane one.[66] Jesus' halakhic *hiddush* retained in Tractate Avodah Zarah and parallels is consonant with other New Testament evidence concerning Jesus' consistently humanitarian application of halakhah.[67] In the parable of the Widow's Mite (Mark 12:41–44), he affirms the importance of motivation over circumstance. In the story of the Woman Caught in Adultery (John 7:53–8:11), he concerns himself with alleviating the woman's public humiliation rather than condemning her for past behavior. The Pharisaic tradition valued the same humanitarian leniency: for example, according to M. Makkot 1:10, "A Sanhedrin which administers the death sentence even once in seven years is called a murderous court. Elezar ben Azariyah says 'Even once in seventy years.' R. Tarfon and R. Aqiba say 'Even were the Sanhedrin empowered to administer the death sentence, it should never do so'." Jesus was able to balance his loyalty to the halakhic tradition, while never compromising his overriding interest in helping highly motivated and well-meaning people to learn to conform their wills again to God. At the same time that he confronted the corruption of the Temple priesthood in Jerusalem, he never questioned the Temple's centrality to his own faith and the faith of those who followed him.

The Greatest Principle of the Torah

One further "lost" tradition concerning Jesus affirms the conclusion just set forth. In a somewhat confusing passage at Mark 12:28–34, we read:

---

65. BT Sotah 15a–b. Here again we have a distinction between *in personam* and *in rem*.
66. The same distinction is made by Bialik, in *Halachah and Aggadah*, 19; see also Fromm, *The Forgotten Language*, 254, on the distinction between the "authoritarian conscience" and the "humanistic conscience."
67. See Matt. 7:1; Mark 4:24; Luke 6:37; John 8:11 and 8:15; Rom. 2:1 and 14:10.

One of the scribes came near and heard them disputing with one another, and, seeing that [Jesus] answered them well, he asked him, "Which commandment is the first of all?" Jesus answered, "The first is, 'Hear, O Israel: The Lord our God, the Lord is one; you shall love the Lord your God with all your heart, and with all your soul, and with all your mind, and with all your strength.' The second is this, 'You shall love your neighbor as yourself.' There is no other commandment greater than these." Then the scribe said to him, "You are right, Teacher; you have truly said that 'he is one, and besides him there is no other'; and 'to love him with all the heart, and with all the understanding, and with all the strength,' and 'to love one's neighbor as oneself'—this is much more than all *wholly-burnt offerings and sacrifices*" (compare Lev. 6; Deut. 33:10). And when Jesus saw that he answered wisely, he said to him, "You are not far from the kingdom of God."

Why does the scribe conduct a conversation with Jesus that combines the value of the traditional Temple offerings and sacrifices with a question about the "greatest principle" of the Torah? Many Christian interpreters have assumed that Jesus here abolishes the need for his loyal followers to maintain the requisites of Temple offerings and sacrifices, thereby setting himself at odds with rabbinic tradition. But such a conclusion is overturned by a fascinating midrash, though garbled in the course of rabbinic transmission:[68]

> *In the day that God created Adam, in the likeness of God he made him* (Gen. 5:1)
>
> Ben Azzai asked: What is the greatest principle in the Torah?[69]
>
> Rabbi Aqiba said: *Love your neighbor as yourself* (Lev. 19:18)—this is a great principle in the Torah.[70]

---

68. The text here is conflated, but based on Yaakov ibn-Ḥabib's introduction to *Ain Yaaqov* (Romm's, viiib); in a less complete form it appears in JT Nedarim 9, 4; *Sifra*, Parashat Qiddushin 4:12; *Bereshit Rabbah* 24 (Theodor and Albeck, 1.236–37 and extensive notes); Finkelstein, *Assemani #66*, 400; Zohar 1.129a; Kasher, 1.345 and notes, 2.16 and 2.22 and notes; Jacobson, 179. Compare 1 Cor. 3:16—"Do you not know that *you* are God's temple, and that God's Spirit dwells within you?"

69. Such a basic or all-embracing rule is called a *kephalaion*; see Fischel ("Story and history," 72–73), who claims this means the Golden Rule, though he also understands the Golden Rule as derived from Lev. 19:18.

70. So also says Paul in Rom. 13:8—"the one who loves another has fulfilled the law." On Lev. 19:18, see Samuel, 96–104; Reines, 206–27; Roth, 20–30; Theodor and Albeck, 1.236–37 esp. notes; E. E. HaLevi, *Shaarei*, 200–201; Jacobson, 174–

Ben Azzai said: . . . *in the likeness of God He made him.* This is a greater principle than yours, so that you may not say [by an overly literalist application of "as yourself"]: if I don't mind being offended, neither should my neighbor; if I don't mind being disgraced, neither should my neighbor.[71]

R. Tanhum responded: [Aqiba], if you should act like this, know [that it is God] whom you offend—*in the likeness of God He made them* [for "as yourself" means that your neighbor, like yourself, is created in the image of God].

Ben Zoma said: I have found a greater principle—*Hear O Israel, the Lord our God is One; and you shall love the Lord your God with all your heart, and with all your soul, and with all your might* (Deut. 6:4–5) [which teaches us that God's sphere and our neighbor's sphere are coterminous; we cannot love one and neglect the other].

Shimeon ben Pazzi said: I have found a still greater principle—*The one lamb you shall offer in the morning, and the other lamb you shall offer at evening* (Num. 28:4). [The lamb-sacrifice is there called the Tamid, and since *tamid* means "constantly," we know we are to love God and neighbor ever without ceasing.]

R. "X" jumped to his feet and said: The halakhah is according to ben Pazzi, for—*Let them make me a sanctuary [and offer offerings there], that I may dwell inside of them* (Ex. 25:8).[72]

80; Petuchowski, 84–85; Ernst Simon; Kasher to Genesis 5:1, 1.345 esp. notes; ibid. to Exodus 25, 2.21–22; Bacher, *Aggadot ha-Tannaim*, part 3.34–35, 131; Urbach, *Pitron Torah*, 79 and notes. And see Maimonides, Hilkhot Evel 14:1 in *la-Am*, 9.345–46 (Twersky, *Reader*, 214).

71. According to Protagoras the Sophist (481–411 B.C.E.): "Man is the measure of all things, of those which are that they are, and of those which are not that they are not," in Plato, *Theatetus* 160D (Fowler, 2.72–73). The issue is the fallacious temptation to use one's subjective and personal norms as the appropriate measure in the exercise of *as yourself*. Other classical references include Sextus Empiricus, *Adversus Mathematicos* 1.14 (Bury, 1.25–93); and Plato, *Theatetus*, 152 and 166–68 (Fowler, 2.40–45 and 92–101). R. Tanhum rejects Aqiba's argument, asserting that an objective referent must be used: the image of God (as opposed to myself) in the other person. See E. E. HaLevi, *Historit*, 391–94; Safrai, "The Correct," 40–42; Kahler, esp. 72–126; and see Burckhardt, 358.

72. Urbach's discussion of "The Summary of the Law" in his notes to *Pitron Torah* (79–80) is confused; he curtly glosses over the issue of the interplay between directive and injunctive mitzvot, nor is it clear why he describes this exchange in *Ain Yaaqov* as a polemic. Rashi to Shabbat 31a is more helpful, as is Roth, chap. 2, but

I am not the first to suggest that the R. "X" whose anonymous memory is preserved here is none other than Jesus. In conjunction with his fellow rabbis, the discussion affirms the humanitarian application of the over-arching principle of halakhah, that where the will of God is followed, as revealed in the tradition, there will God choose to reside in people's hearts and to write God's law therein.[73] As the Temple offerings are made constantly, so one is to love one's neighbor constantly, regardless of human whim or temperament. It is this principle of constancy that brings Rabbi "X" to his feet in acclamation.

And so we see that St. Paul's famous dictum (2 Cor. 3:6) that "The letter is dead but the spirit gives life" applies not only to the way in which the vowels animate consonants, or the way in which associations animate a story. The dictum applies as well to the way in which an accurate knowledge of historical context unravels obscure texts to reveal Jesus as a teacher who expounded upon traditional Jewish law. At least to some degree, the halakhic content of Jesus' teaching can be reconstructed from a careful reading of historical and rabbinic sources, thus revealing a teacher who managed to balance carefully his received tradition with a deep and nonjudgmental humanitarian social conscience.

One does not have to be a great person to say no to others. To be great, one has to see the special hardships of others and respond to them with a yes. Those who live in the midst of any particularist religious revelation often need constructive solutions to the many seeming no's that the revelation presents to them. The late Rabbi Joseph B. Soloveitchik once commented upon the difference between an electrician and a physicist: "The electrician is immersed in his vocational material, and knows mechanically how to apply the technical principles of operation to various appliances. But it takes the physicist, who stands above the physical aspects of electricity and masters its theory, to discover creative new applications of the known principles, based on his expert insight." A true master is one who is skilled in constructive solutions which affirm God's revelation and the ordering of creation. Such dual loyalty to God and neighbor is

the entire subject needs more thorough investigation. And see Flusser, "Ten Commandments," 227, 241–42.

73. Kasher to Exodus 25:8 insists there is no rabbinic discussion of the discrepancy in that verse between the *reisha* (build a house for God) and the *seifa* (God dwells in people, not the house), claiming that the exegesis suggested here is only about three hundred years old, entering rabbinic thought from Christian influences. But Jer. 31:33 seems to contradict Kasher's claim, for there the heart is the seat in which God is known.

the truth behind the ancient teaching: "You shall love the Lord your God with all your heart and your soul and your mind and your strength; and your neighbor as yourself. There is no greater commandment than these."[74]

---

74. Mark 12:29–31. On this dual loyalty, see Rashi to Shabbat 31a (Steinsaltz, 127) and to Prov. 27:10. In both places, Rashi bases his remarks on the Proverbs passage, "your friend who is also your father's friend, do not abandon." Accordingly (and perhaps defending Aqiba), when we refer to our friends and neighbors, God is included, for God is not only our neighbor but also our *habib* who loved our parents and therefore must love us too (see D. Stern, 115–16). In the same vein, the first five commandments and the second five are yoked to show the inseparable character of the responsibility to God and to neighbor, and the responsibility of the individual and of the community (see Jacobson, 97–98).

Chapter 4

The Impact of Cumulative Parables: Strings of Pearls

(Matthew 13:3–53)

Each spring I take a small group of Episcopalian tourists to Israel in search of "the many faces of holiness." The tour itinerary includes the study of the varieties of Judaism practiced in Israel and, of course, the varieties of Christianity. I can predict a certain reaction each time: Upon encountering Orthodox Christianity as practiced at the Church of the Holy Sepulchre in Jerusalem, the group as a whole will have a reaction of rejection—"That's not Christianity!" The unfamiliar languages, the cacophonous chanting, the hostility and mistrust from one denomination to the next sharing the space, the jangle of visual and olfactory stimuli, the aesthetics of a foreign iconography—all these make many Western Christians uncomfortable. They struggle desperately to find there something that looks vaguely like Western Protestantism. The final judgment often is that if it does not look like the Christianity we know, then it does not merit being called Christianity. "If only these people would understand Christianity as we do, they could straighten themselves out." This reaction is age-old: the Crusaders said the same thing upon encountering semitic Christians resident in the Holy Land. When the native Christians refused to adopt Western ways, the Crusaders killed them, rather than address the difference of faith.[1]

On occasion, some members of my tour groups are able to move from their initial reaction of aversion to a stage of wonderment, a broadening of their frame of reference, and once they do, they have begun an encounter with the Other. Those more sensitive grasp a hint that the truth of revelation is larger than their enculturated perception, and begin to wonder at what they do not know. Sometimes they also encounter a different Chris-

---

1. See, for example, Setton 1.374, 620; 2.187–99 (on the sack of Constantinople).

tian reading of familiar texts or even a different New Testament canon. As their sense of wonderment grows, they begin to ask questions, to analyze these differences and weigh them. As their knowledge accumulates they begin to systematize it, and so stand on the threshold of a more philosophical comprehension of religion.

Without knowing it, they have recapitulated in microcosm a process described by Plato in his *Theatetus*: wonderment as the beginning of philosophy.[2] Philosophy, then, begins with a critical challenge to one's cherished beliefs, followed by the willingness to overcome self-righteousness and the courage to view things differently than originally expected—in sympathy and appreciation. The function of wonderment has been debated by philosophers for centuries, including an extensive discussion by Søren Kierkegaard in the "Pars Prima" of his *Philosophical Fragments*.[3]

The Development of the Alphabet

Wonder can also be applied to the history of written language, leading us to a philosophical approach to the value and intention of the written word: How do we form these funny lines? how is it that the eye can see such odd squiggles and know how to pronounce them? We take it for granted that we can read, and yet suddenly it is a wonderment which we wish to analyze, and then to explain, and then to philosophize. How do people comprehend, and why do modes of comprehension differ so from one culture to the next? How does a sign conjure up associations and meanings, and how culturally bound are these associations and meanings, even to the same combination of letters, from one culture to the next?

Each language uses combinations of consonants and vowels. In some languages, one is emphasized over the other. For example, in English we have twenty-one consonants, and (ignoring diphthongs) only five vowels—a mixture, but hardly an equal ratio. In written Hebrew, Aramaic, and Arabic, usually there are only consonants, with no vowels at all. Of course, our earliest known forms of written communication, such as Egyptian hieroglyphics, have no vowels—they are only pictographs. Eventually, these pictographs evolved into more abstract strokes of the stylus, brush, or pen, representing consonant-vowel combinations (syllabaries), and then eventu-

---

2. Plato, *Theaetetus* 155D (Fowler, 2.54–55); see also Aristotle, *Metaphysics* 1.2 (Tredennick, 1.8–17), and compare Clement of Alexandria, *Stromateis* 2.9, 45 and 3.4, 26 (Quasten, 1.126), that wonder leads to philosophy which in turn leads to faith.
3. Kierkegaard, *Philosophical Fragments*, Hong, 132, 133–56, 239–40.

ally into separate letters.[4] When these individual letters were combined in various ways, the manner in which they were to be pronounced was not always readily apparent, particularly in semitic languages with consonants alone, so small signs were added, usually as superscript, to indicate the shape into which the mouth needed to be formed for pronouncing that combination of strokes correctly.[5] Eventually, in most alphabets these superscripts were drawn down onto the line amid the strokes, becoming vowels.

The consonant strokes also needed to be ordered so that they might be taught and memorized. A rabbinic midrash plays with the necessity of each generation's being taught by the previous generation how to order the alphabet and how to pronounce the letters:

> Our rabbis taught: A certain heathen once came before Shammai and asked him, "How many Torahs have you?"
>
> "Two," he replied, "the written Torah and the oral Torah."
>
> "I believe you with respect to the written, but not with respect to the oral Torah; convert me on condition that you teach me the written Torah [only]."
>
> [Shammai] scolded and threw him out in anger. When the heathen went before Hillel, he was accepted as a proselyte. On the first day Hillel pointed to the sequence of signs and taught him to read them as alef, bet, gimmel, dalet. . . . On the following day he pointed to the same sequence but taught him to read the names in reverse.
>
> "That's not how you taught them to me yesterday!" the proselyte protested.
>
> Hillel replied: "Mustn't you then rely upon my oral instruction? Then rely too upon the oral Torah."[6]

---

4. For a concise history of the development of Indo-European languages, see Watkins.

5. Some early biblical scrolls are written in Hebrew (consonant) characters, with the pronunciation indicated by Greek vowels in superscript. This method of indicating pronunciation preceded the present Hebrew system of vowel-pointing (*niqud*). Eventually, the distinction is made in rabbinic texts between the Babylonian method of indicating pronunciation and the Tiberian method, for even the pronunciation of vowel indicators had to be taught from generation to generation. See for example Sperber, *Jonathan to Former Prophets*, Prefatory Remarks, viii; and Kahle.

6. BT Shabbat 31a; see also Bialik, *Sefer ha-Aggadah*, 158 #15, and T. Marx, 65–66.

One point of this story is that the order of the letters of the alphabet is a matter of conventional transmission rather than an expression of some natural law or organic development. Nonetheless, the consonants are the primary elements of which articulate sounds consist, and the function of the vowels is simply to teach the reader or the speaker how to put the consonant sounds together in a manner that is contextually appropriate.[7]

The Culture of the Ear and the Culture of the Eye

The development of writing produced two distinct types of culture—the culture of the ear and the culture of the eye, or the culture in which tradition is transmitted orally versus that in which it is transmitted in writing. Until the introduction of vowels, the culture of the eye was one in which the curious could learn only by being taught, for the meaning of any combination of strokes was not clear. The oral culture preceded the written culture, and ultimately has never been replaced by the written, for still children must be taught carefully that certain strokes are to be pronounced in one way and not in another. One need think only of the difficulty that most Christians have in recognizing the characters of the Hebrew alphabet: unless they have been taught, the strokes themselves make no sense. One is taught orally, and hence the oral culture retains power over the written. Listener response is situated firmly within the culture of the ear.

Rabbinic tradition attributes to Moses the handing down of the oral tradition concerning the vocalization and cantillation of the biblical text, under the technical name *massora* (transmission). The original biblical text is unvocalized. Over the course of time, certain traditional markings enter the biblical text, though it is true that we do not always understand what they mean. Even these markings—some obscure, some more clear—have become the basis of rabbinic hermeneutic.[8] The purpose of the received tradition of vocalization (*massora*) is to guide the reader's interpretation by providing "proto-vowels" which dictate the vocalization of the given consonants.

If such vocalizations are a type of proto-vowel, then we can say that the early alphabets were divided into consonants and breaths, or perhaps

---

7. See Aristotle, *Poetics* 20.1–5 (Fyfe, 74–75 at #20), or his *Metaphysics* 3.3 (Tredennick, 1.116–17). On *stoicheia* as both "letters" (elements) and the foundational principles of creation and philosophy in Plato, see Frank, 165 n1.

8. See, for example, BT Shabbat 115b–116a or *Minḥat Shai* of Yedidiya Shelomo of Nortzi to Num. 10:35.

"letters and spirits." According to tradition, the entire Torah is written without vocalizations, yet the angels can read it easily. However, so that we limited human beings might be able to read Torah, God revealed neumes (biblical phrasing units and other forms of cantillation) to assure that those who read the Torah would not misunderstand its intention as a guide to correct living and a shaper of human hearts. The early midrash assumes that the Torah itself has a double meaning: that which can be read by angels (without neumes) and that which can be read by human beings (with neumes added, most often orally).[9]

Alphabetical Metaphors

Medieval Jewish commentators were profoundly concerned whether the written biblical text (the culture of the eye) might be overly limited through the addition of neumes inscribed on the parchment, thus preventing people from hearing a variety of meanings in the text (the culture of the ear). According to a responsum of R. David Abu-Zimra, in mid-fifteenth century Egypt:[10]

> You asked my opinion on why the inclusion of written vocalization aids would disqualify a Torah scroll. Since Moses our teacher (may he rest in peace!) received the Torah at Sinai orally, surely he received also the correct pronunciation of the words. If this is true, why are they not written down in the scroll, in order that a reader might articulate the text without error, and so that sense can be made out of those verses made more difficult due to the lack of neumes. . . .
>
> In all humility, this is how I would answer you. Something I found in the margins [of a scroll] seems to have been written by one of our early sages, though I do not know his name. He wrote:
>
> "Know that the vocalization is the form and soul of the letters. Therefore a Torah scroll may not be written with the vocalizations, in order that no option for interpretation might be excluded, nor any of its

---

9. See *Avot de Rabbi Nathan* A, 2 (Schechter, 5b at n39; Goldin, *Fathers*, 20). On neumes and related topics, see Werner, 110 and 125 n30; on the vocalizations as limiters to interpretation, see Scholem, *On the Qabbalah*, chap. 2. Plutarch, *Quaestiones Convivales* 1.1, 613 (Babbitt, *Moralia*, 8.13), describes ignorant persons in the company of intellectuals as "mute consonants among sonant vowels."

10. Abu-Zimra, Responsum #1068 (643), in 3.132–33; the text is also in Mack, "Seventy Aspects," 461–62. For related texts, see R. Jacob ben Sheshet and ibn-Gikatilia in Idel, 146 and 150.

infinite depth be neglected. Thus the Torah can be interpreted letter by letter, facet by facet (see Ezek. 20:35), aspect by aspect, secret by secret— indeed, the possibilities are limitless, as it is written, *Even the depths are inexhaustible* (Job 28:14). Were we to include vocalization in the Torah scroll, these rich exegetical possibilities would be restricted, just as when matter takes on a concrete form and so limits the imagination. We would no longer be able to exegete the Torah except within the confines determined by the pre-existing neumes. On the other hand, because the Torah is enhanced with all kinds of perfection, including the squiggles and curliques of cantillation and decoration, even these open up new horizons of exegetical possibility, as long as the text remains unvocalized. In this manner we can find ourselves instructed to sound out a text according to a specified but variant vocalization (*al tiqre kakh ella kakh*).[11] Had some vocalization been already affixed to the text, we would not have been free to read otherwise than the text allowed. But in this creative manner, our sages (of blessed memory!) became alert to excellent midrashic interpretations in a number of instances. To illustrate: 'Bar Qappara expounded: [What is the meaning of the verse] *And you shall have a peg* [yataid] *among your implements* [azenekha] (Deut. 23:13)? Do not read *azenekha*, but *oznekha* [your ear]. This teaches us that whenever a man hears something reprehensible [about someone else], he should plug his finger into his ear.'[12] This serves as an example of how the sages revealed an enigmatic meaning which is accessible only on the basis of an unpointed text, thereby offering simultaneously coarse food to the uninitiated, and celestial manna (compare Pss. 78:25, 105:40) to the cognoscenti. All of this is extractable from the "plain reading" of the unvocalized text, and the entire Torah is subject to such interpretation, for as our sages pointed out, 'The Torah has seventy faces.'"[13] So get your mind working!

---

11. Paronomasia is the derivation of an alternative reading from the one indicated, often signified in Hebrew by the rubric *al tiqre*. The word is Latin, from the Greek, meaning either "to call something by a different name," or "to name something beside." Pei (43) posits that "paroimia" means "by the roadside," meaning that these are sayings that have grown up "along the road." And see Banitt, *Rashi*, 36.
12. BT Ketubot 5a; Maimonides, *Guide* 3:43, 97a (Pines, 573). The word *azenekha* includes a prefixed alef, but in the word *oznekha* the alef is a radical. On the prefixed alef, see Deut. 23:13; and ibn-Parhon, 3a in the middle.
13. On the 70 faces of the Torah (*shiv'im panim*) as opportunities for exegesis and interpretation, see, for example, appendix to 3 Enoch in Charlesworth, *Pseudepigrapha*, 1.314; "Otiyot de Rabbi Aqiba" in Wertheimer, 2.354; A. ibn-Ezra, "Intro. to Commentary on the Torah" (Levin, 144; Weisser, 1.10); Bahye Halawi to Ex. 19:17 (Chavel, 2.172); Zohar 1.26a, 47b, 54a, 3.160a, 216a, 223a, 239a; *Raayah Mehemna* 3.20a, and many places in Geonic literature, including ibn-Tibbon and ibn-Parhon as cited in chap. 7 text, this volume. And see Ps. 25:14: "The mystery [*sod*] of the Lord is for those who fear him." In gematria, sod = 70 as in 70 faces, though here the sod is a remez! Mack's "Seventy Aspects" is an excellent summary.

Traditionally, then, letters/consonants have been connected with the culture of the eye (the written text), and breaths/vowels with the culture of the ear (the *massora*, or the way the text is to be spoken aloud regardless of what it seems to read). This consonant/vowel distinction has given rise to a number of analogies, each illustrating the point that consonants without vowels have no defined meaning, though neither can vowels stand on their own. For example, consonants may be compared to bodies and vowels to souls: "In their relation to the consonants, [the vowel signs of Moses' Torah] are like the soul in a human body: the body cannot survive and function if the soul is not within it."[14] In another metaphor, consonants are like witnesses in a court: they just give the facts, ma'am. Vowels are like judges, in that they give the interpretation.[15] In still another anal-

---

14. Eliyahu Gaon, *Sefer Bahir* #113; see also R. Margulies, *Bahir*, 60–62; Scholem, *Das Buch Bahir*, 87; Kaplan, 43–44. The same soul/vowel analogy is common to Abraham ibn-Ezra, in his *Yesod Diqduq*, intro., 85 and n5; "Sefer Yesod Mora ve-Yesod Torah" in Levin, *Reader*, 316; and his commentary to Ex. 20:1 (Weisser, 1.137) and Deut. 5:5 (3.330); Luzzato in his *Betulat Bat Yehuda* (S.VII); Judah ha-Levi in his *Kuzari* 4.3 (Hirschfeld, 201–2); and ibn-Gikatilia in his *Ginat Egoz*, 413. On the "soft" consonants of *alef, hey, vav,* and *yod* as being "like souls, and the rest of the letters are like bodies," see *Sefer ha-Kuzari* 4.3 (Hirschfeld, 201–2); see also ibn-Ezra, intro. to Ex. 20 in Weisser, 1.127; Responsa 157 of Solomon Adret, 1.59; Saadya Gaon, *Sefer Yetzirah*, 48–49. An important survey of related classical sources can be found in Frank, chap. 6 on "Letter and Spirit."

15. See Aristotle, *Rhetoric*, 1.15, 13–17 (Freese, 155–59): "Witnesses are of two kinds, ancient and recent; of the latter some share the risk of the trial, others are outside it. By ancient I meant the poets and those of repute whose judgments are known to all. . . . Further, proverbs (*paroimia*) are, as it were, evidence (*martyria*); for instance, if someone advises another not to make a friend of an old man, he can appeal to the proverb, 'Never do good to an old man.' And if he advises another to kill the children, after having killed the fathers, he can say, 'Foolish is he who, having killed the father, suffers the children to live.' Ancient witnesses are the most trustworthy of all, for they cannot be corrupted." In others words, proverbs (and presumably the sorts of nimshalim attached to parables) have an authority as witnesses in court that is almost unchallengable, particularly when they are conveyed in a manner that makes them directly applicable to the present. One's evidence presented in a trial is of greater weight when supported by such wise sayings than when limited to mere personal observation or experience. The same thought can be found in Quintilian, *Institutio oratoria* 5.11, 37 and 41 (Butler, 2.293, 295), 6.3, 8–10 (Butler, 2.443); Cicero, *Pro L. Flacco* 65 (Macdonald, 513); and see BT Megillah 9a, and Rashi thereto. According to Rabbinowicz, *Diqduqei Soferim* to Megillah 9a, p. 8, all manuscripts to this passage read *goofan*, or "body." Hence Rashi understands a *goof* as "a written letter," not unlike a font character.

ogy, vowels are compared to mothers and consonants to fathers. Quite early in the literature, vowels are called *matres lectiones* (Hebrew: *aim ha-miqra*), the mothers who help us read. R. Izhak Alfasi contrasts the "freedom" of vowels to the "rules" of the consonants.[16] In a fairly sophisticated philosophy of linguistics, he argues that the consonants are a prototype from which other models can be derived; a vowel is not a prototype since it inspires but does not generate. However, though the building blocks of language (Hebrew: *binyan av*; archetype) are the consonants, to be arranged in a variety of combinations, they remain meaningless until they are given life by the "mothers," the vowels.

The arbitrary conventions by which vowels are supplied is just one of the ways in which the reader attempts to grasp the meaning of a Hebrew saying by choosing a concrete context (see my play on the initials P-L-C in the previous chapter). Listener-response theory suggests that meaning is also supplied by the context in which a speaker speaks a message vis-à-vis the context in which a listener hears that message. The meaning of any given message, then, is extremely context-specific, but even the context in which the saying lives is itself so multifaceted that the message of a text can be grasped only by detailed contextual analysis of all parties involved: the author, the listener, and the potential inherent in the specific words chosen. For example, a parable may be intended to convey one certain meaning according to the context in which it is spoken, but may be heard as meaning something altogether different according to the context in which it is heard by someone else.

Hearing Voices that Aren't There

These discussions of philosophical wonder and inspired alphabets highlight further aspects of listener response. Wonderment is a response, of course, triggered not only when we encounter those who are so different from us in belief or liturgy, but also when we hear a surprising new message jump out of a comfortable old text or a speaker's words. Vocalizing texts in a given manner is a reader's response to what has been heard throughout the reader's life. We pronounce words in a certain way because we have heard them that way from someone else. As we are taught to hear the sound of various combinations of consonants and vowels, so we are

---

16. Alfasi, Responsa #1; see also Bacher on *binyan av* in *Erkei*, 7 and 82–83; Kohut, 1.109, second definition of *em*; ibn-Janah to the radix ʿA-Q-R, 383 and related; BT Qiddushin 30b, BT Niddah 31a; *Midrash va-Yiqra Rabbah* to 18:1 (M. Margulies, 390–91, esp. note to line 4); and Gesenius to *av* and *em*. And see Har-Zahav and Aminah.

also taught to hear specific messages within familiar combinations of words. The *massora* enlightens us as to how the reader should read so that the listener gets a clear and particular message. Listener response addresses how one hears messages beyond the massora, spirits beyond the letter.

Recent research by James Bell, professor of continuum physics at Johns Hopkins University, attempts to trace how those who listen to music hear notes that are not being played. The mysterious effect that Bell is researching is known as "Tartini's beats." When two tones are sounded together, the human ear "hears"—adds in, really—the sound of the numerical difference between their pitches. For example, if one plays both middle C and the G above it, one's ear will discern something more than just the two notes. Middle C has a pitch of 261 cycles per second, and G has 392; $392 - 261 = 130$, which happens to be the pitch of C below middle C. That lower C is heard as a "difference tone"—because it is produced by the difference between two others. The C below middle C is not being played; nonetheless, the listener hears it as clearly as if it were. Neither the culture of the eye nor even the exact science of physics can explain why people hear what they do. Music is a product of the culture of the ear, transcending concrete analysis and categorization.

One of a teacher's roles is to teach people to hear, yet without infantilizing them. The parabolist's problem is to teach people to hear in a specific way—to teach them to hear the point of a story without spelling it out for them. Often a parabolic teacher will opt for a way of teaching best characterized as poetic. Poetry's appeal throughout the cultures of the world is that it conveys feelings and truths too big to be expressed in concrete language. A parabolist, then, will often teach by drawing people into an emotional process that transcends concretization. For the same reason, rather than stating a nimshal a parabolist will often simply tell another mashal, thereby encouraging people to derive their own nimshal. Parabolic methodology leaves room for listeners to draw the nimshal most appropriate to their needs and context.

The Parable of the Sower

The decisive importance of contextuality is illustrated by the famous parable of the sower (Matt. 13:3–9):

And [Jesus] told them many things in parables, saying:

Listen! A sower went out to sow.

And as he sowed, some seeds fell on the path, and the birds came and ate them up.

Other seeds fell on rocky ground, where they did not have much
soil, and they sprang up quickly, since they had no depth of soil. But
when the sun rose, they were scorched; and since they had no root, they
withered away. Other seeds fell among thorns, and the thorns grew up
and choked them. Other seeds fell on good soil and brought forth grain,
some a hundredfold, some sixty, some thirty.

Let anyone with ears to hear listen!

The parable is about the hearing of different messages in a text, depending upon the context within which the message is heard by a listener,
"sowing" being a metaphor for "disseminating information." To some, the
message is of no avail; these are suggested by the metaphor of a path from
which the birds eat the seed before it has time even to take root. To
others, the message is interpreted so superficially that the effect of the
message is "scorched" in the glaring light of day. Others hear the message
as intended by the teller, but are so unable to sort it out from the many
other possible messages that ultimately the teller's intentions are "choked
out" by the thorny competition. Only to a select few is the teller's message
available, and in the context of this good soil, tilled and cultivated well in
advance, the message is received as intended.

Obviously a number of interpretations of the parable are possible. In
Matthew 13:18–23, the parable of the sower is interpreted as a parable
about evangelism and eschatology:[17]

Hear then the [meaning of the] parable of the sower:

When anyone hears the word of the kingdom and does not understand it, the evil one comes and snatches away what is sown in the heart;
this is what was sown on the path. As for what was sown on rocky
ground, this is the one who hears the word and immediately receives it
with joy; yet such a person has no root, but endures only for a while, and
when trouble or persecution arises on account of the word, that person
immediately falls away. As for what was sown among thorns, this is the
one who hears the word, but the cares of the world and the lure of wealth
choke the word, and it yields nothing. But as for what was sown on good
soil, this is the one who hears the word and understands it, who indeed
bears fruit. . . .

---

17. Cave (380) points out that no "harvest" is ever mentioned in the parable, so it
cannot really pertain to evangelism. A very similar metaphor of seeds planted in
good soil to insure a harvest can be found in Plato's *Phaedrus* 276B–D (Fowler,
1.567–69). Jülicher (1.110) believes the parable's lesson to be that the expenditure
of effort cannot everywhere count on the same success.

Daniel Harrington observes: "Even the most learned and persistent champion of the authentic words of Jesus attributed this [portion of the] text to the early Church. Thus Joachim Jeremias confessed: 'I have long held out against the conclusion that this interpretation must be ascribed to the primitive church; but on linguistic grounds alone it is unavoidable.'"[18] The concerns of the provided interpretation are the concerns of the early church, which had no qualms about claiming its own interpretations as dominical. The challenge attached to the end of the original parable is confirmed by another early-church interpretation which is also apparently added to the text (Matt. 13:10–17). Here the challenge "Let anyone with ears to hear listen!" appears to function as a *kakh* nimshal, for the followers of Jesus are assured that they are the good seed which brings forth fruit: they have seen and heard correctly. Unfortunately, we have no way of knowing what nimshal the members of the early church felt so assured they had heard. Some would claim that the heard nimshal was Matthew 13:18–23, but if they had already understood the nimshal at verse 17, why would it need to be spelled out in the verses following?

> Then the disciples came and asked him, "Why do you speak to them in parables?"
>
> He answered, "To you it has been given to know the mysteries of the kingdom of heaven, but to them it has not been given. For to those who have, more will be given, and they will have an abundance; but from those who have nothing, even what they have will be taken away. The reason I speak to them in parables is that 'seeing they do not perceive, and hearing they do not listen, nor do they understand.'
>
> With them indeed is fulfilled the prophecy of Isaiah that says: *You will indeed listen, but never understand, and you will indeed look but never perceive. For this people's heart has grown dull,*[19] *and their ears are hard of hearing, and they have shut their eyes, so that they might not look with their eyes, and listen with their ears, and understand with their heart, and turn—and I would heal them* (Isa. 6:9–10, LXX).
>
> But blessed are your eyes, for they see, and your ears, for they hear. Truly I tell you, many prophets and righteous people longed to see what you see but did not see it, and to hear what you hear but did not hear it."

---

18. Harrington, *Matthew*, 200–201, citing Jeremias, *Parables*, 77.
19. Though the NRSV here gives the translation "dull," it is less accurate than the KJV's "waxed gross." The referents in choosing a translation should be Deut. 32:15, Ps. 73:7 (and see Hatch and Redpath, 1112, *pachunein*). The sense is "grown fat and insensitive due to complacency."

By such words—the most complete setting forth of a philosophy of parables in the Gospels—the esoteric circle of initiates find themselves affirmed in that they have grasped the author's intended meaning.

Is What Is Heard the Same as What Was Meant?

Revelation is inherently relational; it demands eyes and ears to perceive that which is being revealed. The question (though trite) about whether a tree falling in a forest makes any noise if there is no human ear to hear it applies here as well. At Sinai, when God wished to reveal the Torah to Moses, he first asked Moses to go down to the people to ask whether they were willing to receive it. Only after God had received the people's answer, by way of their agent Moses, that "We will do and we will obey,"[20] did God give the Torah (Ex. 24:7). They were willing to receive the Torah because they had already come to know God through a variety of ways and in a variety of contexts, and had grown to trust God enough to commit themselves to do God's will.

The complex interpretive questions of intention and contextuality lead us logically to explore further that subset of literary criticism known as listener-response theory. Though much of the literature of critical analysis deals with readers as opposed to listeners, the theories derived from the dynamism within a written text have applicability by extension to an analysis of oral tradition. Listener-response theory concerns itself with the impact upon the listener of what is said; there are also three different attitudes that precede listening, and thus mold the manner in which what is said will be heard.

First, some listen eagerly, trustingly, and appreciatively. To these a valuable though naive message is available, but if the text contains a more complicated or esoteric message, they might miss it.

---

20. The Hebrew at Exodus 24:7 for "obey" is *nishm'ah*, a complex word that, according to Qimhi's *Shorashim* (395), has three possible meanings: (a) the acoustic, "to hear"; (b) the receptive, "to obey"; and (c) the cognitive, "to comprehend." BT Shabbat 178a observes that the phrase seems backward; it should read "we will hear and [then] we will do." The rabbis conclude that the proper way to understand the biblical text is "do now, and study later," but do it anyway, whether or not one's study leads to comprehension. "Obey" and "hear" overlap in meaning, in that one cannot obey what one does not hear. If one hears correctly, it is assumed that obedience will follow. The Greek verb *akouo* has a similar range of meaning: hear; hear and obey; hear and understand. For further commentary, see Rashi to Ex. 12:28; bar-Hayya, 146–47; ha-Nasi, 41a; Gotthold, "Opvoeding," 10.

Second, some listen critically, argumentatively, or analytically. To these, more complicated messages are available, though as well in their desire to critique, argue with, or analyze what is being said, they too might miss the message altogether.

Third, reminiscent of Ricoeur's "second naiveté," some of those listening know in advance that the wise sages will mean more than the mere words convey. This third group would include not only the cognoscenti of the moment, who listen with a "third ear" to the words of a sage, but also those in our own generation as well who listen to the covert messages behind our received texts. Every culture has aspects that are inaccessible to those who do not know it, such as the culture's unique sense of humor. Only with extreme familiarity can a listener of today understand the textual report and frame of reference of something said in past centuries. Whether addressing the written or the oral biblical tradition, we have too consistently been oblivious to the contextuality of what we have received, perhaps seduced by certain theories of inspiration and infallibility, perhaps inured by sloppy reading habits, or perhaps through reading texts only to confirm our particular predetermined suppositions.

Leviticus Rabbah brings the following story of a famous preacher named Rabbi Levi:[21]

> *Before the sun and the light and the moon and the stars are darkened* (Qoh. 12:2). ["The sun"] refers to the appearance of the face. "The light" refers to the forehead. "The moon" refers to the nose. "The stars" refers to the protruding cheek bones. *And the clouds return after the rain.* R. Levi made two statements on this matter in a single utterance, one directed to colleagues, one directed to the ignorant. The one directed to colleagues: "When one comes to weep, his eyes will overflow with tears." The one directed to the ignorant: "When one comes to urinate, turds will come out first [for one will not control his natural functions]."

A clear distinction here is made here between an attuned esoteric circle of disciples, or colleagues, and the exoteric multitude. The disciples are able to understand an esoteric message within the scriptural text, whereas hoi polloi receive only a crudely comic message. There is no indication that R. Levi taught the same parable twice but rather that in a single utterance he was able to teach (at least) two different lessons simultaneously, depending upon the identity and prior initiation of the hearer.[22]

---

21. *Va-Yiqra Rabbah* to Lev. 18:1 (M. Margulies, 391); see also Neusner, *Judaism and Scripture*, 350. On this biblical passage as metaphor for the body, see Gordis, *Koheleth*, 338–49.

22. See Neusner, *Invitation to Midrash*, vii–ix. On "Intended Equivocality," see

According to an ancient proverb: "To the wise, a hint is enough; to the fool, a stick is enough."[23] Again the point is made that a single utterance can have multiple meanings, even a *pardes* of meanings, but these meanings are discoverable by encompassing the multiplicity of listeners' responses rather than by a sole exegete.[24] In other words, the various meanings of a single utterance can be identified only after the character of the hearers has been identified.

Contextuality is aptly illustrated by the philosopher J. L. Austin in his book *How to Do Things with Words*. He distinguishes between constative language and performative language. Constatives describe and objectify; performatives *do*. As responsible statements of reality, constatives are appropriate candidates for true/false evaluation, though performatives are not. Performatives are context-specific; their truth or falsity depends upon the conditions in which they are spoken and what they ultimately effect, rather than upon their objectifiable relationship to objectifiable reality. A performative approach to the statement, "We will do and we will obey," focuses our attention not upon God, but upon those who "hear." "Hearing" is not visible to the naked eye, and thus the impact of any given statement must be measured performatively, not constatively. Respecting the "authority of the listener" (that is, one who nurtures or teases a meaning out of any message received), we must then evaluate declarative and interrogative statements not by asking "What does that mean?" but rather "What does that do?"[25] Meaning is not a function of utterance, but ultimately a

---

Yellin, 2.86–106, also "metaphor" on 2.41–66. That a word can apparently have a double meaning, see Jacobson, 221–22, ref. to Yellin, *Biblical Phraseology*, 20, 124.

23. *Dictum sapienti sat est (Oxford Dictionary of Quotations*, 374 #14); in Elkoshi, #518; attributed to Terence, *Persa* 729, and Plautus; quoted also in *Midrash Mishlei* to Prov. 22:8 (Buber, 46a; Visotsky, 152). John Chrysostom, *In principium Actorum* III at Montfaucon 3.3, 74D observes: "The clearer [arguments] are useful for the simpler folk, while the deeper are for the more quickly observant. It is necessary for the fare to be varied and different, since the yearnings of those called are different." And see Alpha Beta of Ben Sirah at Lamed (Eisenstein, 1.40); Savar, 2.1049; Cohen, *Proverbs*, 72; Jastrow, 625, *kormiza*. The Italians have a similar proverb: *Ad un uomo dabbene avanza la meta del cer cervello; ad un tristo non basta ne anche tutto* ("For an honest man, half his wits is enough; the whole is too little for a knave."). According to Pei (49), the Czechs say, "To a wise man, just whisper; but to a fool you must spell out everything." In English we usually say "A word to the wise is sufficient."

24. According to Plautus (*Miles Gloriosus* Act 3, scene 3): "No one is wise enough by himself."

25. Fish, 28. The theory, of course, is ancient; see any of the classical works on rhetoric, including Aristotle.

function of listener response. The meaning of a given declaration or inter-
rogation is seated not in the intention of the author (though that is where
the provenance originates), but rather in the perception and subsequent
assimilation by those who hear: "We will obey that which we hear."

In the same manner, authority is contextual. Only what is heard in
context carries the authority to effect obedient behavior. The fluid, life-
giving word "Torah" has so long been translated "law" that we mistake it
for the abstract authoritarianism typical to abusive human regimes.[26] A
more accurate definition of the Torah's authority would be *mitzvah*, or
"that which is commanded," in the persuasive sense of "I need you to do
this for me if we are going to have a good relationship." Such definition
emphasizes the volitional nature of a covenant relationship, in which both
parties agree to please each other so as not to call into question their
mutual loyalty. From the human end, Judaism understands this responsiveness to be embodied in the halakhah, and in describing the value of
halakhah, Bialik captures poetically the truth of listener receptivity:[27]

> Every form of life whilst it is still in process of creation is so much
> definite content for its creator; but when once it is finished, and passes
> out into the world as a thing apart, it sinks to the condition of a mere
> vessel; it has no definite content of its own, and everybody finds in it just

---

26. "Torah" is an organismic concept, literally derived from the complex Hebrew
root *Y-R-H* meaning "to shoot," and hence, "to inseminate." This sense of the root
is illustrated in *Shemot Rabbah* 3.15 to Ex. 19:13: *"And I will be with thy mouth*
[Ex. 4:12]. What is the meaning of *And I will teach thee* [horetika] *what thou shalt
speak?* R. Abahu said: I will throw [*moreh*] My words into thy mouth as with an
arrow, as it says: *or shot through—yaroh* [Ex. 19:13]." YRH ultimately devolves
into a second meaning, built upon "to inseminate," or "to in-spire, to reveal something which causes life." This sense is indicated at Job 3:3—*Oh that the day had
perished wherein I was born, and the night which said, 'There a man has shot*
[HoRaH] *[his semen].'* Grammatically, "Torah" is a *hifil* form of YRH with the formative *taf*. According to the commentary of Hirsch (*Pentateuch*, 1.232, 286, 368,
431–32; 2.43–44, 190–91, 254–55, 432–33 and 486–87), examples of its use as
"shoot/inseminate" include Gen. 16:5 (*haratah*, I was inseminated); 22:2 (Moriah,
meaning the land which will yield revelation/increase); 26:5 (*toratai*, my "teachings"); Ex. 4:12 (*horeitikha*, I will instruct/shoot into your mouth); 15:4 (*yarah*,
hurl); 19:13 (*yaroh yeyareh*, shot through); 25:10 (*aron* as a receptacle for what is
"shot'); Num. 21:30 (*niram*, we have shot at them). Often the tension is further
heightened by the interplay between YRH and YRA ("to be seen"), both in the sense
of making something previously invisible suddenly visible.
27. Bialik, *Halachah and Aggadah*, 21. This paragraph is actually a midrash on
Deuteronomy 32:47. According to *Midrash ha-Gadol Devarim* (Fish, 337), if a
reader cannot understand a scriptural passage, the problem is with the reader, not
the scripture; compare JT Peah 1.1 (Steinsaltz, 10).

what he himself puts into it whenever he handles it. It owes everything to the man, and to the spirit of the man, who finds it ownerless and uses it as his own. Put gold in it—you find gold; fill it with dust—you have dust for your pains. Have you nothing to put in it? Then you may leave it empty till it rusts. But if such is your case, do not say that the vessel is useless, and should be thrown on the scrap-heap; rather blame your own poverty.

Catena: A String of Pearls

Hearing is intensified when images pile one on top of another, each somewhat sufficient unto itself, but more important, combining to form a message from speaker to hearer. The combination is itself a context—that of oral intensification. By oral intensification, a context is simultaneously narrowed, broadened, and circumscribed—narrowed in that more examples make the focus more pregnant; broadened in that more examples give more flexibility to multiplex interpretation; circumscribed in that the central idea might be sharper in outline.

Chains of multiple images or associations are called catenae, from the Latin word for "chain."[28] Catenae are often formed by stringing biblical verses together so as to support or argue a specific point, though petitionary chains such as the Lord's Prayer are also familiar. The catena was a popular literary form in the patristic period. For example, in his *Confessions*, Augustine employs a catena to argue the nurturing character of God:

> O house most lightsome and delightsome! I have loved thy beauty, and the place of the habitation of the glory of my Lord, thy builder and possessor. Let my wayfaring sigh after thee; and I say to Him that made thee, let Him take possession of me also in thee, seeing He hath made me likewise. I have gone astray like a lost sheep: yet upon the shoulders of my Shepherd, thy builder, hope I to be brought back to thee.[29]

The catenic form is not, however, original to the patristic literature.[30] In early rabbinic literature, the constructing of a catena is referred to as

---

28. The Hebrew *terminus technicus* is *shirshur*; see Rivlin, *Munaḥon*, 64.

29. Augustine, *Confessions*, chap. 12 (Outler, 282). Although Augustine paraphrases Scripture on occasion here, his sources are identifiable. In order they are: Ps. 26:8; Gen. 14:19; Ps. 79:11; Ps. 139:15; Prov. 8:22; Isa. 53:6/Ps. 119:176; Ps. 23:1; Jer. 31:4; all to set the stage for the final and only New Testament citation, Luke 15:5.

30. Contra the suggestion of Danker, 142 and 144, who confuses the catena with

"stringing pearls," for just as each pearl is unique, so when strung together they form a necklace that is even more beautiful than the individual pearls themselves. The inspiration for the image of "stringing pearls" comes from Song of Songs:

> *Thy cheeks are comely with circlets*: (Song 1:10) when they explore the halakhah with one another, as did R. Abba b. Mimi and his colleagues.

> *Thy neck with pearls.* When they were "stringing pearls,"[131] the words in the Pentateuch with those of the prophets, and the prophets with the writings, the fire flashed around them and the words rejoiced as on the day when they were delivered from Sinai. For was not the original delivery from Mount Sinai with fire, as it says, *And the mountain burned with fire unto the heart of heaven* (Deut. 4:11)?

> Once as Ben Azzai sat and expounded, a fire played round him.

> They went and told R. Aqiba, saying, "Sir, as Ben Azzai sits and expounds, the fire is flashing round him."

> [R. Aqiba] went to [Ben Azzai] and said: "I hear that as you were expounding, the fire flashed round you."

> [Ben Azzai] replied: "That is so."

> [Aqiba] said to him, "Were you perhaps treating of the [mystical] secrets of the Divine Chariot [the first chapters of Ezekiel]?"

> "No," he replied, "I was only 'stringing' the words of the Torah with one another, then with the words of the prophets, and the prophets with the writings, and the words rejoiced as when they were delivered from Sinai, and they were sweet as their original utterance."

> As R. Abbahu sat and expounded, the fire floated around him. He said, "Am I perhaps 'stringing' together the words of the Torah in an improper way?"

> For R. Levi had said, "Some are able to 'string' together but not to penetrate [to the real difficulties raised by the text], and some are able to

---

the *opus musivum* (see Ginzberg, *Unknown Jewish*, 366–68, for a clear example of the latter). The catena is known in the Dead Sea literature; see Flusser, *JOC*, 248, on 4QFlorilegium, and see Brooke.

31. *Yoshevin ve-horezin*, a *terminus technicus* for catena in both the *kal* and *hifil* forms. The copyist in JT Hagigah 2.1,77b, which parallels this text, seems not to understand the radix *haraz*, and changes it to *hazar*; see Bacher, *Aggadot ha-Tannaim*, part 1.92 n3.

penetrate but not to 'string' together. But I am an expert both at stringing and penetrating."[32]

To "string pearls" is to link verses from disparate parts of Scripture in
such a manner as to argue a point that might not otherwise be obvious.

Rashi grasps both the aesthetic value of the catena by comparing it to
a string of pearls,[33] and the practical value by comparing it to a button that
holds one's clothing closed.[34] However, he tends to conflate two different
types of literature, the rhetorical genre known as catena and the homiletic
genre known as *ke-min homer*. A catena often makes use of scriptural
passages in a typological manner, whereas a *ke-min homer* makes use of
them in an analogical manner. The two literary genres are distinct enough
to merit not being conflated.

In addition to the simultaneous narrowing and broadening of an image, catenae serve several purposes. First, they allow one to become oriented to the unfamiliar by being reminded of comfortable picturesque images. The purpose of stringing together a series of images is that listeners
presented with new images are then allowed the choice of connecting the
images presented with their individual Sitz-im-Leben. In addition, each
image presented complements those previously presented, for no single
metaphor is adequate to meet the needs of the message conveyed or of the

---

32. *Shir ha-Shirim Rabbah* (Donski, 41 at 52). See also *va-Yiqra Rabbah* 16:4 (M.
Margulies, 354); JT Hagigah 2.1,77b; al-Naqawa, 4.104–5 (ref. "Epistle on Sanctity"
attributed to Nahmanides, in Chavel, Hebrew 2.315); Neusner, *Eliezer*, 1.429–30;
Taylor, 65; and see Ben-Yehuda, 1753–54, *haraz*; Kohut, 5.240–41; Urbach, *Sages*,
300 and 820–49. For an example of the harm done by an overly enthusiastic catena, see BT Berakhot 33b (Steinsaltz, 147), and with this compare *Midrash Tehillim* to 19:2 in Braude, 272, and Berakhot 12a on the benediction *emet ve-yatziv*,
itself a catena (and see tosaphist Moshe of Evreux thereto).

33. At Qiddushin 22b, "pearls," in relation to *homer*. Rashi's suggested conflation
there, that a *homer* is a string of berry-buds and a bundle of perfume, clarifies
nothing. He also uses *homer* at Shabbat 148a to describe a collection (string?) of
baraitot (Avineri, 2.382). Banitt, 114 (ref. Moshe Qatan, *Otzar ha-La'azim*, 82
#1229 to Sotah 15a) explains that in using the Old French *boton* as a synonym for
homer, Rashi is making the point either that (1) there is here a linkage of two
things, the mashal and the nimshal, just as a button links the two sides of a
garment, or (2) this symbol is pleasant to the ear and the heart in the same way
that a gold button decorates a shawl. But in general, Rashi seems not to be helpful
on the subject.

34. Lieberman is correct (*ki-Feshutah* Baba Qamma, 65–67) in saying that we do
not understand *ke-min homer*. The author is presently at work on a paper explaining *ke-min homer* as a homiletic genre of *doreshei hamurot* pertaining both to the
New Testament and to rabbinic literature.

listener seeking understanding. Illustrations of this literary method appear later in this chapter.

Second, catenae are designed to provide self-justification for the innovative interpretations of the specific community out of which they proceed. In a kaleidoscope, the same pieces are used over and over again, but even the most minor change in contiguity creates a new pattern and presents to the observer new moments of perception. Flusser points out that the catena was particularly helpful to the Essenes, for it allowed them to retain continuity with cherished sources and yet provide a contemporary exegesis that justified their own ideological position.[35] Such "dissident" groups (including Essenism and Christianity) must accept a selection of religious and doctrinal motifs from the mother-religion and at the same time reinterpret their meaning.

Third, catenae seduce the listener with their attractiveness, thus increasing the likelihood that the listener will be attentive as opposed to critical. As new wine is poured into the old wineskins, the emotional impact of intrinsic development is highlighted. It is this novelty which grips the human heart. This is a basic law of aesthetics in all brands of art: to mix the familiar with the novelty of surprise.

Little systematic study of the catena's variant forms has been done. Because most scholars gloss over the distinctions in form, the subtleties of how a decontextualized text is reemployed have escaped notice. By literary analysis, the catena can be subdivided into five types of classification, depending on the purpose for which the material is strung together.

1. THE TOPICAL CATENA

The topical catena links biblical verses from disparate and related sources to form a composite ideogram. The verses are usually taken out of biblical context, but when linked together take on a new nuancing that in turn results in a new insight, often related to "salvation history." An illustration can be found by examining a series of topical catenae built upon Deuteronomy 6:4: "Hear [*Shema*] O Israel, the Lord our God, the Lord is One." According to *Sifrei Devarim*, the intention of the Shema is to emphasize the universalist character of God's dominion over all creation, an interpretation based upon the relationship between Deuteronomy 6:4 and Zechariah 14:9:

> Another interpretation: *The Lord our God*, over us [the children of Israel]; *the Lord is one*, over all the creatures of the world. *The Lord, our God*, in this world; *the Lord is one*, in the world to come, as it is said,

---

35. Flusser, *JOC*, 248–49.

> *The Lord shall be king over all the earth. In that day shall the Lord be one and His name one* (Zech. 14:9).[36]

If *our* God is taken as a possessive pronoun, then God is Israel's exclusively. Those excluded by the possessive pronoun must then have (a) another God, or (b) no God at all. Rashi adds a link to this catena by inserting Zephaniah 3:9 to help resolve the conceptual tension between *our* God and God's *one*ness—the two halves of Deuteronomy 6:4. He first explains that *our* is not a possessive but a relational pronoun. He then goes on to argue that Deuteronomy 6:4 refers to a dynamic, ongoing process throughout history, wherein pure monotheism is gradually realized.[37] God is ruler at present but will reign in the future as God acknowledged by all. By means of the Zephaniah addition, he shifts the emphasis in the Deuteronomy verse from particularity ("over us") to universality ("over all the creatures of the world"):

> *The Lord will reign for ever and ever* (Ex. 15:18). The Lord who is now our God and not the God of the other peoples of the world, will at some future time be the One sole Yah, as it is said, *For then I will turn to the peoples a pure language that they may all call upon the name of the Lord* (Zeph. 3:9), and it is further said, *In that day shall the Lord be One and His name One* (Zech. 14:9).[38]

This conceptual dimension is obvious also in an ancient *piyyut* (hymn), apparently derived from an even earlier *piyyut* for Rosh ha-Shanah known as the *Aleinu le-Shabeaḥ*, but now incorporated into the daily morning service.[39] It combines a Psalm verse with Obadiah and Zechariah (as did *Sifrei*) to form a catena on Deuteronomy 6:4. Something appears to have been lost in the transmission of the prayer to its present form in the daily service, for M. Rosh ha-Shanah 4:6 suggests that the original *piyyut* upon which this prayer is based contained ten prooftexts. In present form, the prayer may date from the third century C.E; but according to Israel Abrahams, its source, the *Aleinu le-Shabeaḥ*, is pre-

---

36. Hammer, 59; *Sifrei Devarim*, Pisqa 31 (Finkelstein, 54).
37. Maimonides also asserted the gradual realization of God's reign, for Christianity and Islam were methods by which non-Jews were prepared ultimately to receive God's fullest revelation; see Twersky, *Introduction*, 452.
38. Rashi to Deut. 6:4, in Silbermann, 37.
39. Singer, *ADPB*, xxxviii, lxxxvii, cxcviii, compare 76, 247–48; see also Scholem, *Jewish Gnosticism*, 27–29, 105–6; Flusser, "Scholem's recent book," 61. If Singer is correct in dating this prayer as pre-Christian, it may be parodied at Luke 18:11.

Christian, suggesting that the catena is already a developed art form by the beginning of the millennium:

> *For the kingdom is the Lord's and he is ruler over the nations* [Ki l'Adonai ha-Melukhah u-Moshel ba-Goyim] (Ps. 22:28). And saviors shall come up on mount Zion to judge the mount of Esau; and the kingdom shall be the Lord's (Obad. 21). And the Lord shall be King over all the earth; in that day shall the Lord be One, and his name One (Zech. 14:9). And in thy Torah it is written, saying, Hear, O Israel: the Lord our God, the Lord is One (Deut. 6:4).[40]

Addressing the tension between the present kingdom and a future kingdom, this *piyyut* links isolated verses from the Writings, the Prophets, and the Torah. In rabbinic thought, any such a triple citation gives the expressed thought a greater authority.[41] None of the verses quoted reflects its original context, but together they form a new context, positing that although God is presently recognized by the Jews as king over all the earth, the day will come when all the nations of the world recognize God as such. God is the king of the world, but since gentiles do not recognize this, he governs them without reigning. God will come to punish the rebellious ("to judge the mount of Esau"). In so doing, God will be recognized by the whole world. On that day. . . .

2. THE AUTHENTICATING CATENA

In the topical catena, a theological truism is embellished. The authenticating catena differs in that a "novel" idea is immediately set forth by the writer. Then a "string of pearls"—isolated Scripture verses from other contexts—is brought to justify the idea as not at all "novel" but indeed rooted directly in the heritage of biblical theology. By sheer weight of amassed biblical quotations, an argument is granted significant additional authority. Each successive reference therefore demands a conceptual scrutiny to discover the relevancy of the citation to the essence of the argument as a whole. For example, a pre-Christian *piyyut* in the "Additional

---

40. Singer *ADPB*, 36; Baer, 74. It should be noted that the ordering of the citations in the *Ki l'Adonai* is a mirror reversal of the usual canonical order Torah, Neviim, Ketuvim (TaNaKh).

41. Singer, *ADPB*, cxcviii, and see the story of Ben Azzai from *Shir ha-Shirim Rabbah* presented earlier, that "stringing" always includes a verse from each of the three-fold divisions of the Tanakh. Only one verse appears in all three divisions: *The Lord is my strength and my might, and he has become my salvation* (Ex. 15:2; Isa. 12:2b; Ps. 118:14).

Prayers for Rosh ha-Shanah" reads: "It is our duty to praise the Lord of all things, to ascribe greatness to him who formed the world in the beginning, since he has not made us like the nations of other lands, and has not placed us like other families of the earth, since he has not assigned unto us a portion as unto them, nor a lot as unto all their multitude."[42] In this case, the authenticating catena is constructed to justify a xenophobic view of God's care and protection, a literary mode that Harrington points out is employed to build up the identity of the "insiders" at the expense of the "outsiders."[43] To make its point, this *piyyut* attaches a catena of nine proof-texts to justify the claim of Israel's privileged position in God's eyes:

> As it is written in thy *Torah*, The Lord will reign for ever and ever. (Ex. 15:18)

> And it is said, He has not beheld iniquity in Jacob, neither has he seen perverseness in Israel: the Lord his God is with him, and the trumpet shout of a King is among them. (Num. 23:21)

> And it is said, And he became King in Jeshurun, when the heads of the people were gathered, the tribes of Israel together. (Deut. 33:5)

> And in your Holy Words [*Ketuwim*] it is written, saying, For the kingdom is the Lord's, and he is ruler over the nations. (Ps. 22:28)

---

42. Singer, *ADPB*, 247–48; and see Baer, 397–404, footnotes for sources and dating. Abrahams (Singer, lxxxvii) argues that this is the source for the *piyyut* cited above from the daily service. For another early example of an authenticating catena, see Zulai, 22: the author, Yannai, wrote c.550 C.E.; his disciple is said to be Eleazar ha-Kallir, generally referred to as the earliest *paytan* (writer of *piyyutim*) whose works are complete enough for continued liturgical usage. Here most of the *piyyut* is missing in our manuscripts, but the proof-texts remain: "For thus it is written: *Now, when King Amraphel of Shinar, King Arioch of Ellasar, King Chedorlaomer of Elam, and King Tidah of Goiim. . . .*" (Gen. 14:1) "And it is said: The wicked draw their swords, bend their bows, to bring down the lowly and needy, to slaughter those whose way is upright." (Ps. 37:14) "And it is said: When the wicked sprout like grass, and when all the workers of iniquity flourish, it is only that they may be destroyed forever. But you are exalted (for all time, O Lord). Surely, Your enemies, O Lord, surely, Your enemies perish; all evildoers are scattered." (Ps. 92:7–9) "And it is said: Nation was crushed by nation and city by city, for God threw them into panic with every kind of trouble." (2 Chron. 15:6)
43. Harrington, *Matthew*, 202; he also understands Matt. 13:1–23 as a similar "insider-outsider" polemic. Rudyard Kipling's poem "The Stranger" (*Kipling's Verse*, 549–50) is an excellent example of the human fear of those whose ways and beliefs we do not understand.

And it is said, The Lord reigns; he has robed him in majesty; the Lord has robed him, yea, he has girded himself with strength: the world also is set firm, that it cannot be moved. (Ps. 93:1)

And it is said, Lift up your heads, O you gates, and be lifted up, you everlasting doors, that the King of glory may come in. . . . (Ps. 24:7)

And by the hands of your servants, the prophets [Neviim], saying, Thus says the Lord the King of Israel and his Redeemer, the Lord of hosts: I am the first, and I am the last; and beside me there is no God. (Isa. 44:6)

And it is said, And saviors shall come up on Mount Zion to judge the mount of Esau, and the kingdom shall be the Lord's. (Obad. 21)

And it is said, And the Lord shall be King over all the earth: in that day shall the Lord be One and his name One. (Zech. 14:9)

Perhaps the authenticating catena should be adjudged audacious or arrogant, for it is a form in which the author presumes to bring proofs from outside the purview of the audience's ordinary connections, as if to say: "Now I have caused you, by using a string of seemingly unrelated proof-texts, to understand what the primary text intended to mean. You would not have understood had I not strung them together for you." A standard rabbinic formula for introducing such innovative reinterpretation is *hada hu dekativ*, "this is what is *meant* when it is written. . . . " But both Christian and Jewish traditions suggest that this form of novel reinterpretation is a normative part of human communication with God, and perhaps even that God is not beyond such innovative reinterpretation in reply.

3. THE METAPHORICAL CATENA

In this literary variation, isolated figures of speech are strung together, each in itself alluding to a complex of agglutinate thought, but in their new combination creating a particularly beautiful "string of pearls" to adorn the spirituality of those who worship. As example, again a hymnal *piyyut*:

Verily, Thou as Creator knowest the nature of man, for he is but flesh and blood. Man's origin is dust and he returns to the dust (Qoh. 3:20). He obtains his bread at the peril of his life (Lam. 5:9); he is like a fragile potsherd (cmp. Ps. 22:15), as the grass that withers, as the flower that fades (Isa. 40:6–7; Ps. 103:15), as the fleeting shadow (Job 14:2; Ps. 144:4), as a passing cloud (Job 7:9), as the wind that blows (Ps. 1:4; Isa.

40:7), as the floating dust (cmp. Isa. 5:24), yea, and as a dream that vanishes (cmp. Job 20:8).[44]

All three of the catenic types cited above imply a particular approach to the revelatory character of Scripture. Not only is revelation contained within the scriptural corpus as a whole, but each isolated verse is itself an authoritative revelation. Even when one rearranges the verses, bringing them as proof isolated from the thought they were originally intended to convey, they retain their authority. Revelation is assumed to be as authoritative in isolated verses as in the canon itself.

4. The Forensic Catena

In the rhetoric of the courtroom, both the prosecution and the defense array their arguments in a series or chain, structured according to an accepted pattern and including a summary at its conclusion. This conclusion usually consists of an appeal to the jurors or to the judge to accept the data presented and the arguments drawn from them for favorable consideration. This form of rhetoric has been transferred and applied to a style of private and nonobligatory prayer in which the petitioner "argues" with God, concluding with an appeal to the reputation and prestige of the Judge, as if to say: I argued this because it is in keeping with your own principles. Favor me for your own sake and prestige![45]

In his important analysis of religious rhetoric, Eduard Norden arrived at the conclusion that in Greek religious addresses one never finds an appeal to the deity: "For indeed Thou art such and such!"[46] Arthur Spanier advanced Norden's observation by pointing to the often recurring, peculiar introductory word *ki* ("for") prior to the concluding eulogy in a composite prayer of blessing or petition.[47] This characterization of the indicator *ki* has led Joseph Heinemann to the comparison of forensic rhetoric with prayer.[48]

---

44. *Mussaf le-Rosh ha-Shanah*, trans. Silverman, *High Holiday Prayer Book*, 148; and see Davidson, *Thesaurus of Mediaeval Hebrew Poetry*, 2.199–200 #451; Goldschmidt, 1.171–72 and notes.
45. Biblical precedents are found with Abraham (Gen. 18:25), Moses (Ex. 32:12, Num. 14:15, Deut. 9:28), Joshua (7:9), and even Ezekiel (36:19–23); see Jacobson, 118–19.
46. Norden, 183.
47. Spanier, 339ff; compare Lieberman, *Tos. ki-Feshutah* Berakhot, 1.5, line 26.
48. Heinemann, *Prayer*, 193–217. The *ki* (Greek: *hoti*) possesses a particular force in all these cases of the concluding plea. Traditionally *ki* may have four connotations: for, that, when, and because; see Rashi to BT Rosh ha-Shanah 3b and on Gen. 18:15. *Ki* here is an indicator in the same sense that *kakh* indicates the beginning of a nimshal.

Heinemann did not take note of the catenic form of this rhetoric. In keeping with the main topic of the blessing or petitionary prayers, God's actional attributes most applicable to the petitioner's needs are spelled out, blunting the request as if trying to avoid the horns of a dilemma: "If I believe that God is omniscient, God does not have to be reminded of my needs; if I believe that God is omnipotent, yet has not provided my need, it is impertinent on my part to request it." This dilemma caused Franz Rosenzweig to define petitionary prayer as "tempting God" (Deut. 6:16).[49] Hence the only request by which a petitionary prayer ought to be concluded is "Thy will be done!" It is God's decision whether to withhold my need, but I appeal to God in his attribute as such-and-such to revise the decision. Though my deserts seem not to warrant the granting of my request, I have full confidence in the judge (see R. Eliezer's arrest in the preceding chapter).

The Hebrew word for "to pray" is *lehitpallel*, built upon the root *p-l-l*, meaning to be judged in a courtroom; the reflexive form, *lehit-*, indicates that prayer is a way in which one judges one's self—one's ego, one's relationship to God and the world, and of God and the world to oneself.[50] Forensic rhetoric is observable not only in the "clinching line" at the conclusion of an argument, but also at the opening appeal to a pertinent divine attribute, prior to the argumentative or petitionary catena.[51] The Lord's Prayer (Matt. 6:9–13, Luke 11:2–4) provides an apt illustration of forensic prayer, particularly because it contains the word *peirasmos*, often translated "temptation" but having as well the meanings of "a testing of the faith under persecution or duress" and of "a court trial." The opening address, "Our Father in Heaven," is an appeal to God's attribute of caring omniscience. This opening address "to the court" is followed by a catena of several petitions, including "Your kingdom come." Then, in its traditional liturgical form, the prayer closes with the words "*For* the kingdom . . . is

---

49. Rosenzweig, 265–67, argues that when one prays "Lead us not into temptation," God is "accused of a twofold denial of his providence as well as his paternal love." Do we really wish God to limit our freedom so much that we are never led into temptation? On the actional attributes of God as shaping the manner in which humans pray, see Jacobson, 294–96; and Bruckstein, 5–18. Both Thomas Aquinas and Maimonides discuss God's actional attributes at length.

50. Hirsch, *Horeb*, 2.472. On the same subject, see his *Pentateuch* to Gen. 11:7, 20:7, 24:63, 48:11, Deut. 6:8, 32:31.

51. In rabbinic thought, knowing in advance which attribute of God the petitioner will invoke is termed as *yode'ai shemkha*. Compare Didache 8.2 (Lake, 1.321), and see Singer, *ADPB*, 4; Spanier 343; Hoffman, *Va-Yiqra* 1.71ff. It should be noted that most Christian liturgies would also fall into the category of forensic catena.

yours."[52] The two phrases are not contradictory, as some have assumed. The closing phrase of the prayer, beginning with the word *ki*, recapitulates the opening acknowledgment of God's omniscience.

Arguing for a forensic definition of the Lord's Prayer is supported by the use of the word *paraclete* in 1 John 2:1.[53] A paraclete is an advocate, a counselor in the legal sense, one who defends the accused through skilled argumentation. At the end of a complex string of legal arguments, the advocate entrusts the accused to the mercy of the court or the judge. Similarly, the formal structure of petitionary prayers concludes with a re-capitulation of God's attribute appropriate to the requests offered. Examples from the Jewish prayerbook include such closing *ki* statements as "For [*ki*] the kingdom is yours and you will reign in glory for ever"; "For you are a faithful and merciful physician"; "For you nourish and sustain all beings, and do good unto all, and provide food [daily bread?] for all creatures whom you have created"; "For you give light to the apple of your eye."[54]

Although the opinion of the vast majority of scholars is that the ending of the Lord's Prayer "For the kingdom . . . is yours" is not dominical, because it is missing in the Lukan and earliest Matthean texts, an understanding of the catenic structure of the prayer, combined with the function of a closing *ki* statement, seems to argue for reopening the case. In this instance, an argument based on the final phrase's omission in earlier Matthean texts is not conclusive, as text criticism now shows that later texts sometimes retain earlier memories or earlier readings than do intervening texts.[55] Rather, the catenic *ki* structure argues that the Lord's Prayer was originally taught with the liturgically traditional ending attached, because it bespeaks the divine attribute honored (God's omnis-

---

52. On the classical structure of forensic prayer, see Heinemann, *Prayer*, 194. He calls it "law-court prayer," and points out that it is found in rabbinic literature most often in situations of impending political crisis or oppressive subjection by foreign powers. He contrasts forensic prayer with the normal pattern of petitionary prayer known from the Eighteen Benedictions and elsewhere, in that a) thanksgiving and "court etiquette" are absent from forensic prayer; and b) petitionary prayer seeks divine favors whereas forensic prayer seems somewhat impertinent in reminding God what is due the petitioner.

53. Compare Avot 4.13 (Herford, 108; Taylor 1.83 n18). *Avot de Rabbi Nathan* B-35 reads *sunegoros* instead of *parakletos* (Saldarini, 207 n10; compare D. Sperber, 165).

54. Singer, *ADPB*, 248, 47, 280, 293.

55. According to Houlden, 357, the closing phrase is tacked on to the Lord's Prayer in the fourth or fifth century. See Nestle-Aland for textual evidence in support of the closing phrase.

cience) and the petitioner's "clinching argument" from humility ("I have full confidence in the Judge").[56] The controverted ending is not an appended doxology as many assume, but a forensic signature, the inclusion of which restores the Lord's Catena to a form consistent with the Jewish tradition of petition. The forensic signature creates no tension between the kingdom to come and the present, but serves to safeguard against the human tendency to tempt God by recognizing God's prior history of faithful response.

5. THE PARABOLIC CATENA

At times in the literature, whole parables are strung together *ad seriatum*. The editor of a midrash (or a rabbinical decree as well) usually proceeds through the string by progressive degrees of difficulty. Each parable complements or corrects the one before, and adds to the process of building a powerful cumulative picture, a sort of *gradus ad parnassum*, a trajectory of correction and recorrection, ever rising, ever plumbing new depths. For example, according to Psalm 92:13, "The righteous shall spring up like a palm-tree; he shall grow taller than a cedar." Commenting on the verse, the *Midrash Tehillim* asks why one righteous person needs to be defined by two trees so obviously different from each other.[57] The text then explains several comparisons, including that whereas a palm produces fruit, it provides no shelter, but whereas a cedar provides shelter, it produces no fruit. Because the righteous produce both the fruits of their endeavors as well as shelter from the storms of life, both metaphors are necessary to correct each other's deficiencies. In their mutual complementation, each strengthens and honors the other.

A parabolic catena is like a journey toward truth, the dance of two steps forward, one step back. According to *Shir ha-Shirim Rabbah* 1, 8: "Our Rabbis say: Let not the parable be lightly esteemed in your eyes, since by means of the parable one can master the words of the Torah. If a king loses gold from his house or a precious pearl, does he not find it by

---

56. Idelson (308) and Houlden (357) attempt to argue that the closing phrase of the Lord's Prayer is simply a reference to 1 Chron. 29:11, but the biblical passage is missing the word *ki*, which as I have now shown, is the critical indicator.

57. Buber, 205b. The principle applied here is #21 of the 32 Exegetical Rules of Rabbi Eliezer: "Something is compared with two things and so only the good properties of both are attributed to it" (Strack, 97 and 293–94 n25; Enelow, 33; M. Margulies, *Midrash ha-Gadol Bereshit*, 34; Einhorn, 38a–39a; Katzenellenbogen, 76a). See also *Tanḥuma* Lekh Lekha 5 (Buber, 67); Shemini 3 (Buber, 24); *Midrash Tehillim* 92 (Buber, 409); *Bereshit Rabbah* (Theodor and Albeck, 1.186–87); ba-*Midbar Rabbah* 3.1; *Pirqei de Rabbi Eliezer* 19 (Luria, 45b).

means of a wick worth a pittance? So the parable should not be lightly esteemed in your eyes, for by means of the parable one arrives at the true meaning of the words of the Torah. Here is a proof that it is so: Solomon, by means of the parable, penetrated to the finest nuances of the Torah." By stringing together five progressive metaphors, each of which corrects and complements the previous one (as suggested by my parenthetical interludes), an imaginative parabolic catena from the midrash on Song of Songs addresses the difficulties in comprehending biblical texts:[58]

> *Not only was Qohelet a sage himself, but he also taught people knowledge, weighing and searching and fashioning many parables* (Qoh. 12:9).
>
> Rabbi Naḥman told two examples. He said:
>
> It is like a great palace, in which there were many doors. Everyone who entered there would get lost in the maze, and never find his way back. Along came a resourceful person who took a rope and hung it up to mark the way back to the gate; then everyone came in and out by way of the rope.[59] So it was with Solomon: Until his day, no one could grasp fully the Torah, but when he came along and taught with illustrations and parables, everyone could comprehend the Torah.

[The process of correction and recorrection can occur because every metaphor is inherently inadequate to grasp the fullness of its subject. A catena is a cumulative effort to compensate for the accidental deficiencies of its individual parts. Here the problem is that the metaphor wishes to address how one enters the mysteries of scripture, but instead describes a manner of getting *out* (ex-egesis?). In that the metaphor portrays Scripture as a labyrinth in which the reader may become lost or trapped, it begs complementation by another metaphor.]

> Rabbi Naḥman taught a different version:
>
> [It is like] a thicket of reeds, and no one could pass through to the other side. Along came a resourceful person and took a sickle and hacked

---

58. Donski, *Shir ha-Shirim* 1, 8, pp. 5–6. Gordis, *Koheleth*, 339, brings several biblical examples of such strings of metaphors, including Pss. 23, 48, 126, and 133, but he is simplistic. See Pei, chap. 5, on parallel proverbs.
59. This is plainly Ariadne's Thread that led Theseus from the Minotaur's lair, another example of rabbinic parallels to classical sources. Compare *Bereshit Rabbah* 12:1 (Theodor and Albeck, 98), and *Shir ha-Shirim Rabbah* 1, 8 for similar catenae, including this delightful one: R. Naḥman said: "If a mortal king builds a palace and sets its waterspout at its entrance, it is unbecoming. Yet the supreme King of Kings, the Holy One, blessed be He, created man and set his spout [sc. the nose] over his entrance [mouth], and that constitutes his beauty and his pride."

a passage through it. Everyone began to go in and out by way of the passage. Thus it was with Solomon.[60]

[Here the defect is that Scripture is pictured as innately inaccessible, its comprehension a goal that cannot be reached without strenuous, even violent, activity on the part of some predecessor.]

> Rabbi Yossi said:
>
> [It *is like*] a huge basket which was full of fruit, but it had no handle [*izzen*],[61] so no one could move it. Along came a resourceful person who put handles on it, and made it possible for people to move it around. So it was with Solomon: until his days, no one could grasp fully the Torah, but when he resorted to teaching with illustrations and parables, everyone could comprehend the Torah.

[Here scripture is pictured metaphorically as something to be handled, controlled, something even to be "carried around in one's pocket," thereby seeming to deny the mystery, the unpredictability, the uncontainability of God's revelation.]

> R. Shella said:
>
> [It is like] a huge pitcher full of boiling water, but without a handle [*izzen*] to carry it. Someone came along and made a handle, and so made it possible to move it.

[The metaphor seems "too hot to handle"; thus Scripture appears dangerous, even potentially fatal.[62]]

> R. Ḥanina said:
>
> [It is like] a deep well full of water, which was cool and sweet and tasty, but no one could [get down to the water to] drink from it. One man came along and provided rope, string, and twine, and drew water from it to drink; thus he made it possible for everyone to draw water from the well. So are the teaching aids of Solomon: saying to saying, parable to

---

60. Perhaps the classical reference is to the Gordian Knot. Augustine, *Confessions* 12.38, also compares Scripture to a dense thicket; within is fruit to be picked, but it is difficult to penetrate.

61. The *piel* form of *leha'azin* functioning like a *hif'il*. Because *izzen* is a *hapax* (Qoh. 12:9), it is prone to a variety of possible interpretations, as is explained after the final metaphor in this catena.

62. Again we are reminded of the Four who entered Paradise. For Ben Zoma the venture was fatal; only Aqiba emerged in one "peace."

parable, Solomon unfolded the secrets of the Torah, as it is said, *These are the parables of Solomon the son of David, King of Israel* (Prov. 1:1). By the aid of his parables, Solomon unlocked the words of the Torah.

Several times in this catena, the word *izzen* is at times interpreted to mean "handles," but can also be interpreted as an intensive verb form of *ozen*, "ear," some causative form of the verb *leha'azin*. Thus, in a clever pun, handleless objects suddenly have handles, while the listener is cautioned to "ear" intensively.[63] In this manner, a material solution to a problem suggests simultaneously a spiritual demand upon the initiate, throwing out the challenge that what is to be "eared" in the biblical text are the messages that lie deep below the surface message. At the same time that the handle appears to "tame" the metaphorical object, the careful listener is reminded of the untamed and untamable power of scriptural revelation, particularly within the literary form of the parable.

The Catena of the Kingdom: Matthew 13:24–53

Stephen Mitchell writes of the powerful role of metaphor and parable in renewing our comprehension of the life and teachings of Jesus:

> We can use different metaphors to describe the experience that changed Jesus [at the baptism in the Jordan]. It is the kind of experience that all the great spiritual Masters have had, and want us to have as well. Jesus called this experience "entering the kingdom of God." We can also call it "rebirth" or "enlightenment" or "awakening." The images implicit in these words come from experiences that we all know: the birth of a child, the light of the sun, the passage from sleep to what we ordinarily call consciousness. Any of these images can be helpful in pointing to a realm of being which most people have forgotten. It *is* like being born into true life, or like the sun streaming into a room that has remained dark for a long time, or like waking up from a dream, or, as Jesus must have felt, like returning home to the Father [Luke 15:11ff]. And each of these images contains a further truth, if we follow it attentively. Being reborn is only the first stage of a new life, and doesn't mean coming into full spiritual maturity: the infant has a lot of growing up to do before it is self-sufficient. Awakening doesn't necessarily mean arriving at full con-

---

63. Kohut (1.301) speaks of "receiving a heart to hear," and see other references there. See Jastrow, 109, *afarkeset*, paralleled in BT Ḥullin 89a. See also Liddell and Scott, 246, but Even-Shoshan, *Millon*, 541, is implausible; and see Feinberg, 54–55.

sciousness: the dreams are gone, but we may still be sleepy, and not truly alert. Or, to return to the image of sunlight passing through a window: the area that has been suddenly wiped clean of selfishness and self-protection—desires, fears, rules, concepts—may be the whole windowpane, or it may be a spot the size of a dime. The sunlight that shines through the small transparent spot is the same light that can shine through a whole windowpane, but there is much less of it, and if someone stands with his nose pressed to one of the other, opaque spots, he will hardly see any light at all.[64]

Mitchell has presented us with a chain of metaphors that the reader now can recognize as a classical catena. The fullest employment of a parabolic catena in the Gospels can be found at Matthew 13:24–53. At last we are in a position to appreciate fully its literary characteristics and its emotional power:

> The kingdom of heaven is like someone who sowed good seed in his field; but while everybody was asleep, an enemy came and sowed weeds among the wheat, and then went away. So when the plants came up and bore grain, then the weeds appeared as well. And the slaves of the householder came and said to him, "Master, did you not sow good seed in your field? Where, then, did these weeds come from?" He answered, "A saboteur has done this." The slaves said to him, "Then do you want us to go and gather them?" But he replied, "No: for in gathering the weeds you would uproot the wheat along with them. Let both of them grow together until the harvest: and at harvest time I will tell the reapers, Collect the weeds first and bind them in bundles to be burned, but gather the wheat into my barn."

[The metaphor stands in need of complementation. The reader understands the kingdom to be inseparable from not-the-kingdom, as wheat is inseparable from tares. If only God can separate them at the harvest, the faithful are destined to live a life of perpetual tension, ever threatened with being choked out by not-the-kingdom forces, yet which appear to be a given part of our presently groaning creation.]

> The kingdom of heaven is like a mustard seed that someone took and sowed in his field; it is the smallest of all the seeds, but when it has grown it is the greatest of shrubs and becomes a tree, so that the birds of the air come and make nests in its branches.

---

64. Mitchell, 40.

[Here the kingdom seems to be the property of the landowner, one who sowed the seed in his field, just as one who plants an olive on his own farm then owns the tree. It does not appear to be either a state of mind or a geographical location, but an object intended for the enjoyment of someone other than the landowner.]

> The kingdom of heaven is like yeast which a woman took and mixed in with three measures of flour until all of it was leavened.

[We are confronted by the disbelief which comes with hyperbole. No one would work with such a massive quantity of raw materials (Jeremias, 147, suggests this would make a loaf of bread to feed one hundred people), and so the reader can hardly take the metaphor literally.[65]]

> Jesus told the crowds all these things in parables; without a parable he told them nothing. This was to fulfill what had been spoken through the prophet: *I will open my mouth to speak in parables; I will proclaim what has been hidden from the foundation of the world* (Ps. 78:2; LXX?)

> The kingdom of heaven is like treasure hidden in a field, which someone found and hid; and from joy over it he goes and sells all that he has, and buys that field. Again. . .

[This particularly problematic parable is often approached as though it were obvious; the nimshal seems clear, but the mashal is so truncated that it no longer makes sense.[66] However, the Jerusalem Talmud aids us with the following story:[67] R. Shimeon ben Shataḥ purchased a donkey, and

---

65. For "three measures" as a traditional metaphor for a large quantity, see Gen. 18:6 and 1 Sam. 1:24.
66. Newman and Stine, 448–49, admit that it cannot be understood without adding a lot of details not in the original text. The mashal version in Thomas, Logion 109, is significantly clearer than the Matthean, though with a different story line (see Funk, Scott, and Butts, 37); Jeremias (*Parables*, 32–33, 198–201), calls the Thomas version "degenerated." Young (212–25) attempts to clarify through rabbinic parables, but manages to avoid the nagging problems. Mitchell, 142, claims that under normal circumstances in Jewish law the owner would have been entitled to half the treasure. This is patently false. The dispute continues: see Crossan, *Historical*, 281–82; and his earlier extensive exegesis in his *Finding Is the First Act: Trove Folktales and Jesus' Treasure Parable* (Philadelphia: Fortress, 1979).
67. JT Baba Metzia 2.5. The critical text can be found in Rosenthal, 48, with Lieberman's notes on 135 #44; a parallel text is in *Devarim Rabbah* 3:3 (Lieberman, 85). See also Bialik, *Sefer ha-Aggadah*, 155 #4, and E. E. HaLevi, *Olamah*, 179. A similar parable that is actually about a treasure buried in a field can be found in BT Tamid 32a (parallel *Bereshit Rabbah* 33, Theodor and Albeck, 1.301; Bialik, *Sefer ha-Aggadah*, 126 #35).

later discovered that it had a valuable pearl tangled in its mane. His disciples exclaimed over his good fortune, that God had blessed him with riches. He replied, "I paid for a donkey, not a pearl," and returned the jewel to the seller of the donkey. The seller responded, "Blessed be the God of Shimeon ben Shatah!" Thus R. Shimeon ben Shatah taught his disciples that a deed which causes God's name to be magnified (*qiddush ha-shem*) is greater than the sum of all worldly riches. Here, the nimshal introduces the idea that the kingdom of heaven is worth sacrificing everything for, a theme particularly important to the Matthean community as well. The emphasis in the parable is the buyer's response to the value of the treasure.]

> The kingdom of heaven is like a merchant in search of fine pearls; on finding one pearl of great value, he went and sold all that he had and bought it.[68] Again. . .

[Here we see a strengthening of the emphasis upon the value of the kingdom, at the same time that the parable corrects any sense of hiddenness, as in a mustard seed or leaven.]

> The kingdom of heaven is like a net which was thrown into the sea and caught fish of every kind; when it was full, they drew it ashore, sat down, and sorted the good into baskets but threw out the bad. So it will be at the end of the age. The angels will come out and separate the evil from the righteous, and throw them into the furnace of fire, where there will be weeping and gnashing of teeth.

[Mitchell points out that the "metaphor is amusingly inaccurate, since from the fish's (= the human's?) viewpoint, being chosen for the basket is death, while being thrown back is life. Or if the fish are being thrown not into the sea but onto a heap on the shore, it doesn't matter whether they are chosen or thrown away."[69]]

> Have you understood all this?

> They answered, Yes. And he said to them, Therefore every scribe who has been trained for the kingdom of heaven is like the master of a household who brings out of his treasure what is new and what is old.

> When Jesus had finished these parables, he left that place.

---

68. Compare al-Naqawa, 3.283.
69. Mitchell, 67.

Though it may seem incomprehensible to us that the disciples answered "yes" to the question, "Have you understood all this?", the final metaphor about old and new indicates the intentionality of the correction-recorrection process of the catena, for the new corrects the old and the old corrects the new. Each metaphor presented is in itself deficient in that it contains "the seeds of its own destruction." Yet the cumulative effect is a powerful emotional encouragement to the audience to seek those values of God which transcend human limitation. In Matthew 13, the catena of parables narrows, broadens, and circumscribes Jesus's teaching about the kingdom. Parable answers parable in circles, and the text's nimshal—"Thus every scribe . . ."—seems as cryptic as the meshalim it follows. The true nimshal is left to the individual listeners. The life of the catena lies beyond its "dead" surface, in the meaning infused by the animating perceptions that each recipient brings to the catena, in part and in whole. It is this emotional impact upon the hearers that leads them to wonder, from wonder to philosophy, from philosophy to faith, and then on to the mysteries of the kingdom of God.

Chapter 5

Pancultural Adaptations:
He Who Never Lifts
His Gaze Will Never Know the Truth

(Matthew 25:1–12)

The mashal gives each listener an opportunity to project himself into the story. That is why listener-response theory is so critical to the appreciation of a parable's message—the listener's response creates the message. Any subsequent allegorical interpretation of a parable may close off those opportunities for projection, in that it identifies the allegorizer's perceptions of the parable's meaning, but not the other meanings necessarily apparent to the variety of listeners present. One of the primary ways in which the message of any parable is grasped by the listener is through the listener's own personal experience and associations. Indeed, the listener's own person becomes a parable, as he or she responds to a parabolic teaching. According to the Secret Book of James, Jesus said to his disciples: "At first I spoke with you in parables, but you did not understand; now I speak with you openly, and you (still) do not perceive. Yet it was you who served me as a parable in parables, and as that which is open in the (words) that are open."[1]

Capturing the sense of comparison inherent in the word *mashal*, certain introductory formulae have become common indicators of parables.

---

1. Robinson, 32–33; Meyer, 7; Schneemelcher, 1.293; and see Flusser, *Die rabbinischen*, 261 n40. A person or people are treated as a "mashal" at 1 Kgs. 9:7; also 2 Chron. 7:20; Deut. 28:37; Jer. 24:9; Pss. 44:14, 69:11; Ezek. 14:8; Job 17:6; and Isa. 14:4b–21; see Landes, 139–42 and notes; Frank, 163–64. See also Ralph Waldo Emerson: "Time and space are but psychological colors, which the eye makes, but the soul is light; where it is, is day; where it was, is night; and history is an impertinence and an injury, if it be any thing more than a cheerful apologue or parable of my being and becoming" ("Self-Reliance," 40).

As a matter of transmission, many parables lack an introductory formula, while yet other parables survive only in nuclear form, such as certain aphorisms, metaphors, or logia. In addition to the common introductory formula *Mashal: le-mah ha-davar domeh?* (A parable: to what may this be compared?), other stock yet seductive phrases of comparison are also known from Jewish literature. For example, in a famous Sabbath morning hymn, we find the phrase "Who is *like* you, who is *equal* to you, who can be *compared* to you, O God, great, mighty, and awful, most high God, Possessor of heaven and earth?"[2] The question remains whether these three words—like, equal, compare—are synonyms.

For clarity, the issue must be raised whether the Bible speaks in synonyms, or whether what at first appear to be synonyms are actually separate categories.[3] In a discussion of this question in *Sifrei ba-Midbar* 23, we read:

> . . . *he shall separate himself from wine and strong drink* (Num. 6:3):

> Wine is a synonym for strong drink, and strong drink is a synonym for wine.

> It's just that the Torah makes use of two words for the same thing.

> Along these same lines, an act of slaughter is the same as an act of sacrifice, and vice versa, an act of taking up a handful is the same as an act of raising up and vice versa, low is the same as depressed and vice versa, a sign and a signal are synonyms, so the Torah makes use of synonyms.

> So too here: Wine is the same thing as strong drink, and strong drink is the same thing as wine. . . .

> [Rejecting the former view,] R. Eleazar ha-Qappar says,

> "Wine refers to mixed wine, while strong drink refers to wine that is not diluted.

> "You maintain that wine refers to mixed wine, while strong drink refers to wine that is not diluted.

---

2. In the end of the hymn *Nishmat Kol Ḥai*, Singer, *ADPB*, 126; compare M. Pesaḥim 10.7.

3. Actually, most languages do not have real synonyms. In Hebrew, words that first appear to be synonyms reveal, when simplified to a radix, distinct and unique nuances in each. Antonyms also need careful examination. For example, we say in English, "All creatures great and small," but great is not a true antonym to "small"; the phrase should read "large and small."

"But perhaps it is, to the contrary, that wine refers to wine that is undiluted, and strong drink refers to mixed wine.

"Scripture states, *And the accompanying libation-offering, a quarter of a hin for a single ram; you are to pour out this strong drink in the holy place as an offering to the Lord* (Num. 28:7). Now it is undiluted wine that you pour out as a libation offering, and it is not diluted wine that you pour out.

"Therefore you have to state matters in accord not with the latter but with the former of the two propositions: wine refers to diluted wine and strong drink to undiluted wine."[4]

This discussion of synonyms raises in turn the issue of contextuality. The majority opinion expressed in this tannaitic passage is that the application of such biblical doublets should emphasize the similarity between synonyms rather than their distinction. However, R. Eleazar ha-Qappar holds the firm (but minority) opinion that words which may appear at first to be synonyms must in actuality be carefully analyzed according to the specific context in which they are used, lest, among other things, sacrificial offerings become invalidated. Medieval exegete Abraham ibn-Ezra sides with the majority opinion expressed above, belittling distinctions between synonyms:

Scholars of biblical linguistics adjudge that the text speaks at times *in plene*, and at other times *in defectivo*, assuming that it is enough for the listener merely to grasp the intended sense. I am reminded of the aphorism that "words are like bodies, and meanings are like souls." This body-soul analogy provides us with a kind of "tool," whereby we can comprehend the preference of the experts to grasp a meaning as opposed to focusing too narrowly on the words. They are not so obsessed with distinguishing between synonyms, but rather seek the mutual sense behind such words. Let me give you an example. God said to Cain, *Cursed are you from the soil. . . . If you till the soil, it shall no longer yield its strength to you. You shall become a ceaseless wanderer on earth* (Gen. 4:11–12). Cain replied, *Since you have banished me this day from the soil . . .* (Gen. 4:14). Who could have such an uncomprehending heart as to wish to make a strong distinction here between "soil" and "earth"? Another example: in one place, Eliezer says, *Let me sip a little water from your jar* (Gen. 24:17); later he is reported to have said, *Let me drink a little water from your jar* (Gen. 24:43). . . . From such examples, we may derive the principle that though the words may differ, the meaning behind them remains the same.[5]

---

4. Trans. Neusner, *Sifrei* 23, 135–36; the Hebrew text is in *Sifrei de Be Rab* (Horowitz, 27).

5. Abraham ibn-Ezra, Introduction to the Decalogue, Exodus 20, in Weisser, 127.

A careful analysis of the arguments above confirms, however, that there is no clear agreement on the issue of synonyms, but rather that exegetes at times side with the argument of R. Eleazar, and at times with the argument of ibn-Ezra. We must conclude that in texts employing the phrase "likened or compared," things are sometimes alike or comparable (soil is the same as earth), and sometimes not alike or comparable (wine is not the same as strong drink), depending on both the intention of the author and the needs of the listener. Even in cases of conflicting interpretation of the same analogy, Scripture may be brought as a proof in support of either point of view.

The Piper and the Fish

"To be alike" is a constative whereas "to be comparable" is a performative, in the scheme of J. L. Austin discussed in the previous chapter. The combination of the terms *liken* and *compare* appears in the New Testament at Luke 7:31–35, though its parallel at Matthew 11:16–19 fails to make the distinction. According to Luke:

> To what then will I *compare* the people of this generation, and what are they *like*?[6] They are like children sitting in the marketplace and calling to one another,
>
> "We played the flute for you, and you did not dance;
>
> we wailed, and you did not weep."

In Responsa 157 of Solomon Adret, 1.59–60, the Rashba applies ibn-Ezra's principle in a strictly Halakhic manner, though without crediting his source. David Qimḥi articulates the principle as "It is the manner of language to employ synonyms in order to strengthen the central idea" (Melamed, *Mifareshei*, 2.833 esp. #16 and 19), and see Saadya Gaon, *Sefer Yetzirah*, 48–49 on the interplay of homonyms. For an amplification of these same principles, see ibn-Ezra's "Introduction" to his commentary on the Torah, in Levin, 141–45; and Kugel's essay, "The Ox Knows His Master" in *The Idea*, 9–10. Pei (44) would be likely to translate "many minds with but a single thought." The sages sometimes argued that the difference between synonyms was insignificant, under the rubric *dibrah torah bileshon benei adam* ("the Torah speaks in human language"), indicating a humanizing colloquialism in the biblical diction. On this rubric and its historical interpretations, see Bacher, *Erkei* 13; Steinsaltz to BT Berakhot, 138 n6; and Twersky, "Joseph ibn Kaspi," 239 and 253 n27–28.

6. It seems that this passage is associatively related to Isa. 40:25, where two different roots, *D-M-H* and *Sh-V-H*, appear in verbal form; see Gotthold, "Moses our Teacher," 39 n21.

For John the Baptist has come eating no bread and drinking no wine, and you say, "He has a demon"; the Son of Man has come, eating and drinking, and you say, "Look, a glutton and a drunkard, a friend of tax collectors and sinners!" Nevertheless, wisdom is vindicated by all her children.

Both the Lukan and Matthean sayings make reference to what seems to be a children's song, perhaps in the mood of a playful taunt. The whole pericope is complicated by the insertion, between the mashal ("They are like children . . .") and the nimshal ("wisdom is vindicated. . . ."), of certain descriptive remarks concerning John the Baptist and Jesus. The theme of the children's taunt to each other appears to be that one group of children has failed to respond to the leadership or example of another group of children, and each group believes that the other is at fault. Each group accuses the other of following its own self-interests, rather than modeling their behavior on that of the other group. Only in this sense can the nimshal be connected to the mashal: "The wise choice is vindicated by the outcome for those who have made it."

Perhaps Luke and Matthew intend the citing of the children's song to be a condemnation of those who, rather than following Jesus or John the Baptist, have leveled highly condemnatory charges against them. Again, however, we discover a relatively common nimshal, applicable in a number of situations. The Lukan nimshal conveys the same message as M. Avot 5:23: "According to the labor is the reward." The end-result of any action or choice is determined by one's initial investment.

The parable in the two gospels bears a striking similarity to a certain fable from Aesop's collection. It is impossible to tell whether the children's song quoted within the parable predated Aesop or vice versa.

A fisherman skilled in music took his flute and his nets to the seashore. Standing on a projecting rock, he played several tunes in the hope that the fish, attracted by his melody, would of their own accord dance into his net, which he had placed below. At last, having long waited in vain, he laid aside his flute, and casting his net into the sea, made an excellent haul of fish. When he saw them leaping about in the net upon the rock he said: "O you most perverse creatures, when I piped you would not dance, but now that I have ceased, you do so merrily."[7]

---

7. The source of this fable is Herodotus 1.141 (Rawlinson, 78); see Perry, *Aesopica* no. 11 and Thompson, *Motif* J1909. The fable is echoed at BT Avodah Zarah 3b on Hab. 1:14, as cited in the next chapter. On the rabbis' knowledge of Greek proverbs and fables, see Schwarzbaum, "Talmudic-Midrashic," 430, and Lieberman, *Greek in Jewish Palestine*, 144–60.

This mashal has a nimshal appended in some versions of Aesop and not in others. According to George Fyler Townsend's version of Aesop's parable, there is no nimshal. According to Salomon Span's, the nimshal is "Thus it is with people: they will always have the tendency to do the right thing at the wrong time." When the same parable appears in *Babrius and Phaedrus*, it has the nimshal "It's not possible for you to gain anything by lounging around and making no effort; but when you get what you want by working for it, then with propriety you may indulge in banter and idle play."[8] The latter nimshal seems to put the emphasis on the fisherman, whereas Span's appears to put the emphasis on the fish by addressing them. The gospel version seems to pick up the theme of timing and commitment in the children's taunt: in life, one has a choice whether to respond voluntarily, or to suffer the consequences of turning one's back on revealed truth. The fable raises issues of both one's response and the timing of that response—what is the right response and what is the right time? Translated into biblical terms, it asks the question: What is one's purpose in this world: commitment to visible standards of indulgence or to the more challenging standards of the transcendent?

Choosing Between Competing Values

This combination of the words "liken" and "compare," and the necessity in life of choosing between competing values, appears in Scripture in Isaiah 40:21–26. There Isaiah speaks words of comfort to Israel in exile, and yet chides those who had interpreted the exile as the triumph of political regimes over God's influence in history as creator and redeemer:

> Do you not know?
> Have you not heard?
> Have you not been told from the very first?
> Have you not discerned how the earth was founded?
> It is God who is enthroned above the vault of the earth,
> So that its inhabitants seem as grasshoppers;
> Who spread out the skies like gauze,
> Stretched them out like a tent to dwell in.
> God brings potentates to naught,
> Makes rulers of the earth as nothing.
> Hardly are they planted, hardly are they sown,

---

8. Townsend, *Aesop's Fables*, 47; Span, *The Fables of Aesop*, 129 #268; *Babrius and Phaedrus*, Perry, 15–17.

Hardly has their stem taken root in earth,
When God blows upon them and they dry up,
And the storm bears them off like chaff.

"To whom, then, can you *liken* Me,
To whom can I be *compared?*"

Lift high your eyes [*se'u marom aineikhem*] and see:
Who created these?
He who sends out their host by count, who calls them each by
    name;
Because of God's great might and vast power, not one fails to
    appear.

Again the theme is sounded: Isaiah calls upon humanity to choose
whether it will focus on its own self-interests and perceptions of ultimate
power, or whether God will be recognized as creator and lord of history as
evidenced in the transcendent power and creativity of natural phenomenon. True recognition will come only to those faithful who choose "to lift
heavenward their eyes and see."[9] The challenge is to be taken not literally
but metaphorically; indeed, later commentators noticed the acronym
formed by the first letters of *Se'u Marom Aineikhem*, or SheMA, the central commitment of Judaism. One is to lift up the eyes of one's heart,
choosing the transcendence of God over the concrete materiality of this
world. The separated clauses in the midst of Isaiah's challenge—"To
whom, then, can you *liken* Me, To whom can I be *compared?*"—are God's
own challenge to those who are quick to grant ultimate authority to temporal political regimes over and against God's transcendent dominion.
They are echoed again in Job 38 and Psalms 92:8 and 104.

As in the Isaiah passage, so in parables it is common that a story
illustrates the necessity of making a choice between competing values, of
lifting up one's eyes. Typically such a contest is couched in the contrast
between human values and values divine.[10] In a particularly familiar illus-

---

9. Gregory of Nazianzus, in "Concerning His Own Affairs," 467–546, connects this
phrase with the doctrine of the Two Ways (Meehan, 40–41). Minucius Felix also
develops the imagery in his *Octavius*, 14–19 (see Quasten, 2.157).
10. As Kee points out (Charlesworth, *Pseudepigrapha*, 1.816), this ethical tradition known as the doctrine of "The Two Ways" has biblical precedent in Deut.
11:26–28 and 30:15, Josh. 24:15, Jer. 21:8–14, Ben Sirah 15:11–20, and 2 Enoch
30:15. For Greek sources, see Xenophon's *Memorabilia* 2.1, 21ff (Marchant, 94–
95); Hesiod, *Works and Days* 288–93 (Loeb, 24–25); Perry, *Aesopica* #94; Pinax of

tration from Matthew 6:24 (paralleled in Luke 16:13), we read this nuclear parable:

> No one can serve two masters; for a slave will either hate the one and love the other, or be devoted to the one and despise the other. You cannot serve God and mammon.[11]

In a brilliant article, Shemuel Safrai and David Flusser have shown how Jesus allowed the context of his teachings to dictate a change from the original parable to this one we have in the Matthean text. The generally accepted rabbinic parallel reads: R. Shimeon ben Pazzi said "*And the slave is free from his master*" (Job 3:19). Man, while he lives, is the slave of two masters: the slave of his creator and the slave of his urges. When he does the will of his creator, he angers his human urges, and when he does the will of his urges, he angers his creator. When he dies, he is freed, a slave free from his master."[12] Safrai and Flusser note that whereas the

---

Cebes in *Scripta Minora* 1, 140f.; *Babrius and Phaedrus*, Perry, 490 n383; Theognis, Maxims 893–917 (Banks, 267); for early church sources, see T. Asher 1:3; Didache 1:1–2 (Lake, 308–9; Richardson, 161–67, 171; Quasten, 1.29–39); Barnabas 18–20 (Lake, 1.401–7), Apostolic Constitutions 7:1 (ANF 7.465), Pseudo-Clementine Homilies 7:7 (ANF 8.269); Clement of Alexandria, *Stromateis* 5:5 (ANF 2.451); Gregory of Nazianzus, "Concerning His Own Affairs," 37–62 (Meehan, 26–27); Erasmus, Adage 1.2, 48 in *Coll. Works*, 31.190 ("In trivio sum"). For rabbinic sources, see *Midrash Tehillim* (Buber 5a); M. Avot 2:1; *Mekhilta* Beshallah 7 (Lauterbach, 248); BT Berakhot 28b; ARN-A 25:2 (Schechter, 40a; Neusner, 154); Tos. Hagigah 2 (Lieberman Moed, 381 and *ki-Feshutah* 1291); JT Hagigah 2:1,77a; *Tanhuma* vulgar, Reah, 3; *Aikhah Rabbati* (Buber, 55 at 157); *Derekh Eretz* (Higger, 70 and 205); *Midrash Aggadah* (Buber, 164–65); Bialik, *Sefer ha-Aggadah*, 174 #114. And see Jaeger, 8–9 and notes; Milavec, "Didache," 106; and Flusser, *JOC*, 499–506. On the parts of the body as parable, see 1 Cor. 12:12–26; Livy, Book 2.32,8–12 (Foster, 322–25); W. Nestle in *Philologus* 7 (1911), 45ff.; Handford, 150; 1 Clement 37:5 (Lake, 1.73); Jaeger, 14–15, 22.

11. George Bernard Shaw, a confirmed bachelor, parodied this saying in *Androcles and the Lion* (Preface, 51): "Get rid of your family entanglements. Every mother you meet is as much your mother as the woman who bore you. Every man you meet is as much your brother as the man she bore after you. Don't waste your time at family funerals grieving for your relatives: attend to life, not to death: there are as good fish in the sea as ever came out of it, and better. In the kingdom of heaven, which, as aforesaid, is within you, there is no marriage nor giving in marriage, because you cannot devote your life to two divinities: God and the person you are married to." Compare Matt. 10:37 and 19:29, and see Flusser, *JOC*, 153.

12. *Ruth Rabbah* 3.1; see Safrai and Flusser's detailed notes, "The Slave of Two Masters," 30–31. On mammon in the Qumran scrolls, see Kosmala.

usual Pharisaic dichotomy is between one's human urges or tendencies (*yetzer*) and the creator (*yotzer*), Jesus' parable speaks of the dichotomy between mammon and God. That alternative imagery is in fact more common to the Essene literature, illustrating how Jesus took a Pharisaic saying and substituted within it a typical Essene dualism. The context of Jesus' concern with social purity and detachment from the woes of an oppressive economic structure (as is shown in the following chapter), dictated the alteration of the parable, without losing its impact.

The Two Ways, the choice between one's human tendencies and the will of God, is a contest that engages every individual, then and now. R. Shimeon ben Pazzi (the same one referred to by Safrai and Flusser) expressed the struggle in a particularly terse manner: "Woe to me on account of my creator (*yotzer*); woe to me on account of my urges (*yetzer*)!"[13] Amoraic texts also combine the struggle between one's human urges or tendencies against God, with the conflicting dichotomy of God versus mammon. This dilemma is illustrated by the story of R. Yohanan ben Zakkai in BT Baba Batra 89b:

> Our rabbis taught: "[A merchant] shall not make the stick by which he levels a dry measure wide at one end and narrow at the other [so that a portion of the measure can be scraped off without the buyer's knowledge]. Neither shall he level a dry measure with one quick swipe of the stick, for this favors the buyer, but not the seller. Nor shall he level a dry measure bit by bit, for this will favor the seller, but not the buyer."
>
> R. Yohanan ben Zakkai recognized an ethical dilemma in the midst of this teaching. He said: "Woe to me if I tell them this ruling, and woe to me if I don't. If I teach them, some will get the idea in their heads how they ought to cheat. If I do not teach them, the cheaters will say, 'Haven't all these smart guys caught on yet to what we're doing?'"
>
> They asked: "So nu! did he teach it or not?"
>
> Shemuel bar R. Izhak said: "He did teach it, and he based it on the verse: *For the paths of the Lord are straight. The righteous shall walk in them, but the transgressors shall stumble in them* (Hos. 14:9).[14]

13. BT Berakhot 61a (Steinsaltz, 266 at alef); Rashi loc. cit. comments: "If I follow my urges, woe to me from my Creator; if I do not follow my Creator, woe to me from my urges which bother me with [lustful] fancy." Shimeon's statement is a *remez* derived from the unorthographic spelling in Gen. 2:7 of "and he created," *vi-yetze*, which can then be read either "Woe, Creator" or "Woe, urges"; see also BT Eruvin 18a; *Leqah Tov* at Gen. 2:6 (Buber, 10a). On the expression *oy li* ("woe is me"), see Fishbane, "The Holy One."

14. BT Baba Batra 89b; see Tos. Neziqin Baba Batra 5 (Lieberman, 145, and *ki-Feshutah* 387 #23 and 24). The text is also in Bialik, *Sefer ha-Aggadah*, 512 #173.

The choice between conflicting values—those of God versus those of humanity—is a theme repeated with frequency in rabbinic and early Christian literature. Tractate Baba Qamma 79b sets forth a parable which echoes that theme in an aggadic vocabulary consistent with the gospel accounts of Jesus' own articulation of the Two Ways:

> A parable transmitted in the name of R. Gamliel:
>
> > To what may the matter be compared? To two men who lived in the same city, each of whom decided to host a banquet. One issued a blanket invitation to all the inhabitants of the city but did not invite the royal family, while the other neither issued a blanket invitation nor invited the royal family. [Since neither of them invited the royal family], how can we determine which of the two behaved more egregiously? The one who insulted the royal family by purposely not including them in the blanket invitation extended to the inhabitants of the city.

This parable nuances further the choice between God's values and human values, indicating that to choose human values is never simply one of two alternatives but will always register with God as a blatant slap in the face. To choose a self-serving system of values is automatically to reject God, to flaunt one's refusal to recognize God's authority as the source of creation and life. Like so many other decisions, the decision to commit to a specific system of values has extended ramifications that are apparent only when the larger context of the choice has been fully comprehended.

Translating Culture as Context

As we have seen, a parable needs to be context-sensitive in order to communicate anything to its listeners. Contextuality has been too long ignored by subsequent readers of the New Testament texts—those who were not present when the teachings were spoken and who understand little or nothing of the original cultural setting. On the basis of predetermined evidence in the manner Stanley Fish has identified,[15] Christian response to the gospel texts has tended both to universalize the message of the parables and other teachings of Jesus, and to emphasize Jesus' uniqueness to the point that he is divorced from his indispensable historical setting. In either case, the resultant Jesus is not human, and if not human, has no manner to identify with humanity or humanity with him. The point can be illustrated by reference to Christian attempts to isolate Jesus' use of the word "abba" from its Second Temple Jewish context. Much is made of

---

15. Fish, for example on John Milton's "Samson Agonistes," 274.

Jesus' "unique" use of it. Jesus' use of the *abba* address is of course partic-
ular, but is unique only in that it is so very different from our address to
God, which tends to be so much more formal and distanced. Stephen
Mitchell observes:

> Few of us . . . can feel the intensity of what Jesus meant when he said
> *abba*. Actually, we don't have a word for it. Our word *father* reflects a
> personal and social reality which is a much diluted version of the reality a
> first-century Jewish father had for his children: a position of absolute
> power, for both good and evil, which commanded a fear or a respect that
> we can barely conceive of. To really translate the word, we would have to
> translate the culture.[16]

The term "abba" implies both extreme formality (for such was the
almost unlimited power of the adult Jewish male in Second Temple society), at the same time that it conveys an intimacy foreign to many contemporary men. The Jewish abba was both *pater potestas* and *pater familias*,
and yet extremely intimate and warm with his sons, inviting them to accompany and imitate him in all aspects of life. According to C. H. Dodd:
"There is a parable about a son learning his trade by watching his father at
work: 'A son can do nothing on his own account, but only what he sees his
father doing. What the father does, the son does in the same manner. For
the father loves his son and shows him everything that he does himself (all
the secrets of the craft).'"[17] "Abba" and, for that matter, "amen," so long
identified by New Testament scholars as characteristic of Jesus, gain their
full power as simultaneously unique and common only when their accepted usage within Jesus' historical context is addressed.[18]

"To really translate . . . we would have to translate the culture." Students of languages and scholars of biblical translation know that words do
not translate easily or directly from one language to another. "Abba" in
Aramaic and Hebrew carries a different set of emotive nuances than does
"daddy" or "father" in English. *Q-R-A* (to read, to call out) in Hebrew
carries a nuance of exaggerated audibility that cannot easily be conveyed
by the simple English "read."[19] Nor do ideas easily translate from one culture to the other. For example, the Hebrew phrase "with an upraised

---

16. Mitchell, 29. On "abba," see chap. 11. See Bernstein, 123–40, on "metaphor."
17. John 5:19–20a, rewritten as though it were a received parable, by Dodd,
Founder, 120.
18. On cultural particularity as a clue to understanding common biblical expressions, see Lindsey, "Verily or Amen," and the fine response by Zev Gotthold appended to Lindsey's article.
19. For the theological import of such a concept, see Martin Buber, *Israel and the
World*, 89–102.

hand," in Exodus 14:8 and Numbers 33:3, meaning "brazenly displayed," is rendered in both Targum Onqelos and Pseudo-Jonathan as "with a bare head." Neither do symbols translate easily, either from culture to culture or even individual to individual, such as in the case of dream analysis. Sigmund Freud devoted an entire book, *The Interpretation of Dreams*, to the problem of how people dream in individualized "code," thereby eluding ready analysis. Explaining Carl Jung's theories of dream interpretation, Robert Hopcke writes:

> Jung's idea of the dream is that it is an accurate representation of the current unconscious situation of the dreamer, a kind of photograph of the dreamer's psyche. Jung found that dreams do indeed have meaning but only after that meaning is created through the sometimes laborious task of familiarizing oneself with the language that dreams speak. . . . To familiarize oneself with the language of dreams, therefore, is in actuality to familiarize oneself with the peculiar private symbolic language spoken by the inner lives of each individual counselee.[20]

Dreams, then, are an extreme form of the context-specific. They appear in a highly individualized and encoded symbolism. A dream's message is addressed to the dreamer alone, and yet is accessible only when the code is cracked. The same encoding symbolism in another person's dream would carry a different message and need a different set of decoding tools.

The Individual Style of the Speaker

When analyzing biblical texts, two forms of contextuality must be distinguished: (1) an individual speaker's style and (2) the individual listener's context within the particular social, cultural, and religious environment.

Don Isaac Abravanel is among the traditional writers who called our attention to the stylistic differences between prophets. In the introduction to his commentary on Jeremiah, Abravanel is troubled by the stylistic discrepancies between Isaiah and Jeremiah:

---

20. Hopcke, 122–38; Fromm, *Forgotten Language*, chap. 2. See also the role of dreams in Thomas's *The White Hotel* and Broner's *A Weave of Women*; and Heschel, *Man's Quest for God*, 132–44, on symbolism. In Fromm, the further puzzle of dreams is that symbols are not always intelligible. Fromm distinguishes between consensus symbols (e.g., a traffic light); emotive symbols (e.g., a national flag); and personal symbols (e. g., the language of dreams). The personal language of dream codes corresponds to the particularity and contextuality of listener response.

I am of the opinion that Jeremiah was not very expert either at composition or rhetoric, as was Isaiah or other prophets. Hence you find in his speeches many verses . . . missing a word or two . . . very, very frequent use of *'al* [properly "on"] for *el* [properly "to"], masculine for feminine . . . singular for plural and vice versa, past for future and vice versa, and shifts of second to third person in a single sentence. Moreover, there is chronological disorder in his speeches.

I believe that the cause of this was the youth of Jeremiah when he was called to prophesy. . . . Indeed he protested, *I do not know how to speak, for I am but a youth* (1:6). Isaiah, of royal blood, urbane and raised in the court of the king, spoke with eloquence; the other prophets were called after they attained maturity in worldly matters and gained experience in dealing with people, so they knew how to arrange their sermons. Jeremiah, on the other hand, was of the priests of Anatot (a class apart and a villager to boot); while still young, being called to prophesy . . . he was constrained to proclaim what the Lord commanded in language he was accustomed to.[21]

For Abravanel, the stylistic differences between prophets are of significance, in keeping with the concept that things which are described as "like or comparable" need careful examination to discern their dissimilarities. On the other hand, a delightful midrash from BT Sanhedrin 89a argues that prophetic style (*signon*) differs according to both the ability of the particular prophet and the context in which the prophecy is delivered:

> Ahab the king of Israel invited his ally King Jehoshaphat to come up with him and to wage war in Ramot-gilead [against the Arameans].
>
> Jehoshaphat agreed in principle, but first requested: *Please, first inquire of the Lord* [1 Kgs. 22:5] about our prospects.
>
> Ahab brought in four hundred "prophets" and inquired of them, *Shall I march upon Ramot-gilead for battle, or shall I not?*
>
> They answered *in unison, March, and the lord will deliver [it] into your hands!*
>
> Jehoshaphat was not convinced by this answer, and asked *Isn't there another prophet of the Lord here through whom we can inquire?*

---

21. Trans. Moshe Greenberg; see his "Jewish Conceptions," 159. The later commentator MaLBYM (preface to Jeremiah) was shocked by Abravanel's harsh judgment of Jeremiah; see also Gotthold, "Moshe our Teacher," 22–23.

Ahab snarled, *There is one more man through whom we can inquire of the Lord; but I hate him, because he never prophesies anything favorable to me, but only misfortune—Micaiah son of Imlah.*

But Jehoshaphat was not convinced by this rebuke. On the contrary, he immediately defended the pessimistic prophet: *Don't say that, Your Majesty!*

Ahab sent an officer to bring Micaiah. This eunuch, educated in Ahab's court, wished to fulfill his agency in a manner pleasing to Ahab, and so he warned Micaiah, *Look, the words of the prophets are with one accord favorable to the king. Let your word be like that of the rest of them; speak a favorable word.*

Micaiah found the two kings sitting, each on his own throne, and all the prophets prophesying before them. It would seem that one of them perceived that Jehoshaphat's suspicion was aroused by the unanimity of their prophesy. Thereupon Zedekiah the son of Chenaanah provided himself with iron horns, and cried out, *Thus says the Lord; With these you shall gore the Arameans till you make an end of them.*

Micaiah came before Ahab. The king demanded of him, *Micaiah, shall we march upon Ramot-gilead for battle, or shall we not?*

Micaiah answered him, *March and triumph! The Lord will deliver [it] into Your Majesty's hands.*

Was Ahab overjoyed, now that even Micaiah the pessimist had prophesied something good for him? No! Ahab grew furious with him: *How many times must I adjure you to tell me nothing but the truth in the name of the Lord?*

So [Micaiah] prophesied [again], saying, *I saw all Israel scattered over the hills like sheep without a shepherd; and the Lord said, "These have no master; let everyone return to his home in safety."*

How did Ahab respond to this [new] prophecy? He turned to the suspicious Jehoshaphat and cried out, *Didn't I tell you that he would not prophesy good fortune for me, but only misfortune?*

The sages ask: What caused Jehoshaphat to distrust the prophecy which he heard from four hundred unison voices? And what disturbed Ahab about Micaiah's first prophecy, and then about his second prophecy?

When Jehoshaphat requested "Isn't there another prophet of the Lord," Ahab said to him, "But here are all these standing here in front of you!"

Jehoshaphat answered, "This saying was passed down to me through my grandfather's family: Though the same divine oracle [*signon*] is passed to many prophets, no two prophets express themselves in the same style [*signon*].[22]

The Individual Context of the Listener

We now turn our focus to the importance of contextuality in understanding the message of four parables, each having to do with the same theme: the choosing of values and the importance of discipline and attention to the transcendent divine. Each of the four parables is concerned with the choice between the self-serving hedonistic values of the world and the values of God, which by their very nature demand that the human being suppress his quest for self-gratification. The chapter ends with the offering of a new parable.

In addition to the theme of choosing between values, the act of eating and drinking appears as a common theme tying the four parables together. Often in Jewish and Christian tradition, a banquet is a metaphor for God's kingdom. But other times, a banquet can be a metaphor for the human temptation to short-sighted hedonism. The negative use of the banquet metaphor is as biblical as its positive use, for the metaphorical comparison must be adapted to fit the context and message (*signon*). Isaiah 22:12–14 speaks to those who mistake historical calamity for a victory justifying celebration:

> My Lord God of Hosts summoned on that day
> To weeping and lamenting,
> To tonsuring and girding with sackcloth.
> Instead, there was rejoicing and merriment,
> Killing of cattle and slaughtering of sheep,
> Eating of meat and drinking of wine:
> "Eat and drink, for tomorrow we die!"
> Then the Lord of Hosts revealed Himself to my ears:
> "This iniquity shall never be forgiven you
> Until you die," said my Lord of Hosts.

Those who are duly attuned recognize God at work in history according to divine values and the divine plan, and the concomitant need to be ever-disciplined and prepared. Those who are not attuned suffer the consequences of their negligence: "this iniquity shall never be forgiven you." To

---

22. BT Sanhedrin 89a, based on 1 Kgs. 22; compare 2 Chron. 18. On *signon* from the Latin for "watchword," see standard dictionaries under "ensign," "insignia."

be attuned, to pay attention, is what it means to be truly religious; the opposite of being religious is then being negligent, particularly in the sense of self-indulgent. In *Concord and Liberty*, José Ortega y Gasset argues:

> To live not wantonly but warily—wary of a transcendental reality—is the strict meaning of the Latin word *religiosus*, and indeed the essential meaning of all religion. . . . *Religio* does not derive from *religare*, to bind—that is, man to God. The adjective, as is often the case, has preserved the original meaning of the noun, and *religiosus* stands for scrupulous, not trifling, conscientious. The opposite of religion thus would be negligence, carelessness, indifference, laxity. Over against *re-ligo* we have *nec-lego*; *religens* (*religiosus*) is contrasted with *neglegens*.[23]

To be faithful then carries no sense of involuntary obligation or dry legalism, but of the directing of one's focus and attention to the generous source of all life.

THE PARABLE OF THE TEN MAIDENS

The first of our four examples comes from Matthew 25:1–12:

> Then the kingdom of heaven will be like this: Ten maidens took their lamps and went to meet the bridegroom. Five of them were foolish, and five were wise. When the foolish took their lamps, they took no oil with them; but the wise took flasks of oil with their lamps. As the bridegroom was delayed, all of them became drowsy and slept. But at midnight there was a shout, "Look! Here is the bridegroom! Come out to meet him." Then all those maidens got up and trimmed their lamps. The foolish said to the wise, "Give us some of your oil, for our lamps are going out." But the wise replied, "No! there will not be enough for you and for us; you had better go to the dealers and buy some for yourselves." And while they went to buy it the bridegroom came. Those who were ready went in with him to the wedding banquet, and the door was shut. Later the other

23. Ortega y Gasset, 22; he refers the reader to Aulus Gellius, *Noctium atticarum libri* 20, 4.9 (mid-second century C.E.). The etymology of the word "religion" is obscure. Some define it from *relegere*, "to attribute" (not as the OED, "to read over again"); others define it from *religare*, "to bind" (Lewis and Short, 1556). Ortega y Gasset offers a third possibility. I understand Ortega y Gasset's point to be the contrast between scrupulous conscientiousness (exaggerated attention to detail, reputation, the "fences around the Torah") and trifling conscientiousness (an oxymoron suggesting inattention, complacency, and failure to hold oneself alert and prepared). Compare Abba Poemen #43 (Ward, 145): "The beginning of evil is heedlessness."

maidens came also, saying "Lord, lord, open to us." But he replied, "Truly I tell you, I do not know you."

[Nimshal] Keep awake therefore, for you know neither the day nor the hour.

The parable is much more complicated than it appears at first, and has been misunderstood by many Christian commentators in their desire to allegorize the bridegroom as Christ, the Son of Man.[24] Here is no place to bog down in the "silver filigree" level of the parable by trying to explain the specific details of the story, for, given the total absence of the bride, among other reasons, the story makes no sense as the description of a wedding. Rather, the parable is a "warning parable," employing the vehicle of a happy public occasion to which half the participants arrived unprepared. (The nimshal should, therefore, read "Be prepared" rather than "stay awake," since all ten maidens fell asleep but five are later ushered in anyway.) Though early Jewish tradition generally eschews detailed allegorization of parables,[25] nevertheless this parable is clearly intended to cause

---

24. Though a great deal of insight is available by reading M. Ketubot 4:5, which describes the role of young maidens who accompany a bride. On the number "ten" (a *minyan*), see Ruth 4:2; acc. to BT Ketubot 7b, ten are required at a wedding to represent the general public. In any case, contemporary American romantic customs about bridesmaids and weddings should never be read back into this parable. Such customs are culture-specific, just as the customs portrayed in Matthew's parable are specific to a completely unrelated culture.

25. The tendency to allegorize this parable develops early; see for example the parable's treatment by St. Methodius, in Quasten, 2.130–32. But see my article "The Pharisaic Jesus and His Gospel Parables," particularly on the obvious fact that the bride is missing from this story. (One of the few versions to include the bride is Pusey's *Tetraevangelium*, and there the inclusion appears spurious.) Even such a sensitive and reliable commentator as D. Harrington misunderstands this parable in his commentary on Matthew, 347–51. He is certainly correct in rejecting allegorical interpretation of the parable, contra Jeremias, *Parables*, 51–53, 175. But his most egregious error is his failure to understand that engagement (*erusin*) and marriage (*nissuin*) are two very different occasions in Judaism. He attempts to explain the bridegroom's delay as a last-minute haggling with the bride's father over the details of the marriage contract. Such explanation is impossible, since the contract would have been negotiated fully and finally at the *erusin*. He also reads into the parable a number of details that simply are not in the text, including that a bride is present. For more correct information, see Mordecai Friedman, esp. 1.194 n9; Falk, 38–43; Büchler, *Studies*, 145–59, but check his notes carefully. Harrington's explanation on 347–49 contradicts his own previous explanation on 37. He suggests seeing de Vaux, 1.24–38, and Argyle, but the former contradicts Harrington's explanation of the bridegroom's delay, and the latter is too ignorant of tannaitic material to be authoritative.

the listeners to remember that God (the obvious metaphorical parallel to the bridegroom, given Isa. 54:5 and 62:5, Jer. 31:32, and Hos. 2:16, among others)[26] will summon the faithful on his schedule rather than according to any human timetable. The foolish maidens (the Greek text does not identify them as bridesmaids, but simply as the young women of the town) are unprepared because they cannot imagine having to wait. Their focus is on the party about to happen, rather than allowing for any unforeseen complications in the publicly announced schedule. Hence they have no oil, and by the time they awake to their error, it is too late: no oil-dealer in a local Middle Eastern village would be open for business at midnight. To those so foolishly inattentive, so absorbed in the imagined delights of the feast-to-come, "this iniquity shall never be forgiven you."[27]

THE PARABLE OF THE SURPRISE BANQUET

Our second example comes from Babylonian Talmud, Tractate Shabbat 153a:

> R. Eliezer said: "Repent one day before your death" (Avot 2:10).[28]
>
> His disciples asked him, "Does then one know on what day he will die, that he should know when to repent?"
>
> "All the more reason that one repent today," he replied, "lest he die tomorrow; let him repent on the morrow lest he die the day after: and thus his whole life is spent in repentance."
>
> And Solomon too said in his wisdom, *Let your clothes always be white; and your head never lack ointment* (Qoh. 9:8).
>
> R. Yohanan ben Zakkai said:

---

26. And see for example *Pirqei de Rabbi Eliezer* chap. 41 (Friedlander, 322), in which Moses awakens Israel with the metaphorical warning that "the Bridegroom" is coming. Hill (326) points out that there is no connection between "bridegroom" and "Messiah" in the Hebrew Bible or the literature of late Second Temple Judaism, though the claim is simplistic in light of Isa. 61:10, 62:5.

27. Hence Schweizer (468), who says the parable is about a long waiting-period in which the church is called to be patient, is incorrect to claim that the nimshal has nothing to do with the parable. However, it seems obvious to me that the nimshal here is appropriate, as the whole parable is about readiness and paying attention. And see Didache 16:1 (Lake, 333). The point is reinforced by the Gospel of Thomas #75 (Layton, 393), where only the "solitaries" enter, that is, those without distraction, à la George Bernard Shaw in note 11?

28. Herford, *Ethics*, 55. See also ARN-A 15 (Goldin, *Fathers*, 82); ARN-B 29 (Schechter, 62; Saldarini, 175). The talmudic text can also be found in Steinsaltz, *Shabbat*, 2.674.

This may be compared to a king who summoned his servants to a banquet without appointing a time.

The wise ones adorned themselves and went to sit near the door of the palace, ["for,"] they said, "is anything lacking in a royal palace?"

The fools carried on with their work, saying, "can there be a banquet without someone going to a lot of trouble?"

Without warning, the king demanded [the presence of] his servants: the wise entered adorned, while the fools entered soiled. The king rejoiced at the wise but was angry with the fools:

"Those who adorned themselves for the banquet," he ordered, "let them sit, eat and drink. But those who did not adorn themselves for the banquet, let them stand and watch."

R. Meir's son-in-law [objected] in R. Meir's name: "Then [those standing] too would look as though they were in attendance. Rather, both should sit, the former eating while the latter hungers; the former drinking while the latter thirsts, for it is said: *Assuredly, thus said the Lord God: My servants shall eat, and you shall hunger; My servants shall drink, and you shall thirst; My servants shall rejoice, and you shall be ashamed; My servants shall shout in gladness, and you shall cry out in anguish, howling in heartbreak* (Isa. 65:13–14).[29]

Again we find the image of a banquet, the anticipation of gala eating and drinking, such as at a sumptuous table fitting to royalty. Some were ready, dressed in proper clothing; others did not dress for the occasion,[30] assuming they would have plenty of time to change once they saw the king's courtiers begin to cook and to set the table. The issue of clothing seems to be critical to an interpretation of this parable, improper clothing being a metaphor for not taking the invitation seriously enough. Ortega y Gasset's definition of *religio* would suggest that being ever alert and attentive is the clothing metaphor's referent. The juxtaposition of the sayings of R. Eliezer

---

29. The theme of this nimshal should be compared to 2 Esdras (4 Ezra) 8:3 and 2 Baruch 44:15 (Charlesworth, *Pseudepigrapha*, 1.542 and 635).

30. One is obviously reminded of the parable of the Wedding Feast in Matt. 22:1–14; on that parable, see, for example, Harrington, *Matthew*, 305–9, and compare *Qohelet Rabbah* 9:8. However, the Matthean nimshal is "Many are called but few are chosen" (this nimshal is suspect, as it seems to "freefloat" in the Gospels, becoming attached to other parables as well, and indeed could be just as applicable to the Ten Maidens). In the parable from Shabbat, all remain in the dining hall, though not everyone gets to partake of the sumptuous food. Harrington observes that Matt. 22:1–14 is about "invitation and ejection"; in the Shabbat parable, there is no ejection. Because such a central theme is missing, a comparison of the two parables should be avoided.

and R. Yoḥanan ben Zakkai suggests a strong connection between constant preparedness and an attitude of repentance.[31] Those who through attention, discipline, and conversion of heart have kept their focus on the king's banquet, rather than upon their private concerns, are those who actually get to eat the food that the "unadorned" had so eagerly anticipated.

THE PARABLE OF THE ALL-DAY PARTY

The third example comes from the minor Talmudic tractate Semaḥot 8:10:[32]

> Rabbi Meir used to tell the parable of the king who threw a great banquet, to which he invited many guests, but he neglected to tell them what time they would be expected to go home. The prudent of them arrived early in the morning, stayed until the ninth hour of the day, and went home to their beds while the sun was still up. Others of them stayed until the sun had set, when the bars were opening, and candles had been lit. They went home in the dark, and had to go to bed with only a candle to light their way. Others stayed until the wee hours of the morning, and went to bed still groping in the dark. The remaining guests at the party got so drunk that they began to fight with each other, and finally to kill each other, as it is said: *I saw the Lord standing by the altar, and He said "Strike the capitals so that the thresholds quake, and shatter them on the heads of all the people; and I will slay the last of them with the sword; not one of them shall escape, and not one of them shall survive"* (Amos 9:1).[33]

---

31. See Büchler, *Sin and Atonement*, 237–41, 319–27, 357–66 on *levanim*, the white garments of repentance; cf. Zech. 3:3–6.

32. Higger, *Semaḥot*, 156 line 70ff.; also trans. in Dov Zlotnick, 61.

33. I have not appended the nimshal here because of the problems it presents. The nimshal in Semaḥot reads: "As for the remaining servants of the king, the greatest were punished because of the least of them, as it is said: *That is why I have hewn down the prophets, I have slain them with the words of My mouth. Does your judgment go forth in light?*" (Hos. 6:5). The nimshal presumes a piece of action not conveyed in the body of the mashal, but conveyed in the authenticator from Amos 9:1. The words "not one of them shall survive" suggest that the king was so angry over the behavior of the brawling group that he punished everyone who had attended, even those who went home early—hence the nimshal, that the greatest were punished because of the least. Rashi then reads the last clause of the quotation from Hosea 6:5 as a question, based on the shift from first person ("I have hewn") to second person ("your judgment"): "If you are going to slay the prophets because some of those to whom they spoke disobeyed, then how am I to believe in your quality of justice (*middat ha-din*), O God?"; see Maarsen, 11. The parable in Semaḥot appears in the literary context of the Roman occupiers' murder of Israel's

This parable may be interpreted as being somewhat more lenient than the previous two. Here at least, everyone gets a taste of the king's banquet, and each gets to taste according to his or her own sense of discipline and propriety. Some are quite disciplined: they arrive in the daylight, and leave after only a few hours, before nightfall. Those who have no sense of discipline engorge themselves, winding up in a drunken and ultimately fatal brawl. The message is that all those invited, who had equal opportunity for discipline and reward, are expected to maintain that discipline and to comprehend the limits of the king's hospitality. Again, it is those distracted by the prospect of an unlimited supply of delicious food and fine aged wine who suffer the disastrous consequences. To the undisciplined comes the warning: "this iniquity shall never be forgiven you."

THE PARABLE OF THE VOYAGERS

The fourth example has its roots in classical Greek literature. According to *The Enchiridion*, by the first-century philosopher Epictetus:

> When you are on a voyage, and your ship is at anchorage, and you disembark to get fresh water, you may pick up a small shellfish or a truffle by the way, but you must keep your attention fixed on the ship, and keep looking towards it constantly to see if the Helmsman calls you; and if he does, you have to leave everything, or be bundled on board with your legs tied up like sheep. So it is in life: If you have a dear wife or child given you, they are like the shellfish or the truffle; they are very well in their way. Only if the Helmsman call, run back to your ship, leave all else, and do not look behind you. And if you are old, never even go far from the ship, for fear that when He calls you may be missing.[34]

The parallel we consider here is taken from a collection of aggadic homilies entitled *Menorat ha-Maor* ("The Lamp of Illumination") by R. Israel al-Naqawa, who lived in fourteenth-century Spain:[35]

---

great leaders because the common people would not cease their revolt in 132–35 C.E. In this context the nimshal makes sense, but still does not complement the mashal, which reports no punitive action by the king. Flusser, *rabbinischen Gleichnisse*, 24–25, understands the historical context but analyzes the nimshal incorrectly.

34. Arrian's Discourses of Epictetus, *The Enchiridion*, #7 (Oldfather, 489–91; P. E. Matheson in Murphy et al., 640–41).

35. al-Naqawa, 3.88, beginning at line 18. A famous composer of *piyyutim* (hymns for worship) as well as an essayist, al-Naqawa lived in Toledo. According to Enelow, he died in 1391, committing suicide rather than be killed by a violent crowd of Christians.

A parable: To what may this be compared?

To a group of people who went a-sailing on the sea. Days passed and they began to despair of reaching their destination. One day a strong wind arose on the sea, driving their ship towards an island. Now there were on that island incredibly tall trees, groaning with all sorts of fruit which was both beautiful to look at and delicious to eat. The island also had perpetually flowing springs, so many that every field was verdant, full of herbs and blossoms and flowers. Beautiful birds twittered in the trees, singing ethereal songs. It was such an exquisite place to rest, next to the springs in the shade of the trees.

In their reaction to running ashore to the island, the passengers fell into five groups.

The first group did not wish to leave the ship to explore the island, for, they said, if we leave board, a strong wind might come up, blow the ship back out to sea, and we would be stranded on the island. For only an hour's refreshment, even with the delight of the luscious fruit, it is not worth taking the risk that the ship will leave without us, and we will die. So we will stay here and wait it out until the voyage resumes.

The second group left the ship to explore the island, but they did not tarry there. They strolled around a bit, tasted a bit of the fruit, but soon hurried back to the ship. When they got back, they found enough space to sit in comfort, and were none the worse off for having taken their brief excursion to the island.

The third group left the ship to explore the island, ate some of the fruit, and strolled around, stopping here and there, until the winds came up again and they heard the captain of the ship sound the whistle that it was about to sail, just as captains are wont to do. The moment they heard the whistle they rushed back to the ship and found that the others were sitting comfortably spread out, and they had to make do only with the space that was left.

The fourth group enjoyed the island immensely, immersing themselves in its rich fruits, exploring every possible corner. When they heard the whistle blow, they said to themselves, "That's OK, we still have time; he won't be able to leave until he's raised the mast, or until he has unfurled the sail." When they saw that he had raised the mast, they decided that they could stay even longer until he raised the anchor. But by then they had lost their sense of direction, their eyes were blind from looking at such riches, they were drunk on their own indulgence and turned from the will of their Creator to the exercise of their own will. Then the captain raised the anchor and set out to sea. They said to each other, "You know, we'd better get a move on or we're liable to be stranded!" They raced back to the shore, jumped into the water, and began madly swimming toward the ship. They could barely find any room for themselves and had to crowd in with the others.

The fifth group settled in, abandoning themselves to the pleasures of the island without giving a single thought that they ultimately had to return to the ship, even when they saw it sail away. They passed the days of the summer in comfort. But winter came, and the trees shed their fruit and the leaves withered, and they suffered from both hunger and exposure. Wild animals appeared from another part of the island and began to attack and kill them. The people wept bitterly that they had not returned to the ship, but now there was no one to save them. And there they remained, until everyone of them perished, and no trace of them remained, either on the ship or on the island.

[Nimshal] So it is with humanity. If they are true to their own hearts, and remain alert to the reverent adoration of their Creator and do not give in to their inclination to pursue the pleasures of the flesh and all its woes, they will enter in peace and come out in peace.

The first group, which did not wish at all to explore the island, are the pious ones, who have never tasted the pleasures of sin and have disciplined their human nature. Rather than pursuing the pleasures of the flesh, they have remained alert to the reverent adoration of their creator. They do not embark on to that island, which so resembles the woes of this temporal world and which would seduce them into the pursuit of "happiness," but have succeeded in holding themselves apart in discipline and purity.

The second group, which explored the island briefly but then left immediately, are like those who have sinned in their youth, tasting the pleasures of this world, but repenting immediately while they were yet young. This is the highest form of repentance.

The third group, who chose not to leave the island until they heard the sound of the ship's whistle, are like those who do not repent before reaching their golden years. Suddenly, they are worried that their end is near, and so they repent just before dying in a state of dissolution. Though they do have a place on account of their repentance, their position is not as advantageous as that of the first two groups.

The fourth group, who refused to leave the island until the ship had begun to sail, pushing their delay to the limits of absurdity, are like those who do not repent until they are about to breathe their final breath. As they teeter on the brink between life and death, they look ahead to see that without repentance they have no promise of life in the world to come, and so they repent hastily. Even so, they repent only because they fear death. Though their repentance improves their lot, they do not attain to the position even of the third group.

The fifth group, who remained on the island until it was too late, and whose weeping and mourning was ultimately to no avail, are like those who are completely absorbed in their own worldly error, following their base inclinations, failing to care for their souls by repenting. When they die in their dissolution, they are lost and they go to doom and perdition, where their reveling in the pleasures of this world is turned into obliteration. The worms devour their flesh and fire consumes their spirits, until their memory is erased forever, just as the fifth group's pleasure in the island became their own judgment. They suffered scorching heat by day, and bitter cold by night, and ultimately the sea washed them away, where snakes and moray eels and scorpions made a feast of them till there was no trace left of them.

Automaton or Providence?

In each of these four parables, the theme identified has been whether one will lift one's head from the distractions of this world to focus one's gaze upon the values of God, in both discipline and self-control. Such a question assumes, of course, that there is a caring God, rather than the world's being an automaton, a theological position sometimes ascribed by the rabbis to the Greek philosopher Epicurus.[36] Such a view—that the world runs by itself, as if set in motion by a divine clockmaker and then abandoned—was held by the rabbis to be a weighty heresy. Salvation history was a generally unquestioned truism; human responsibility was to hold oneself in a state of readiness and attention for whatever plan God might choose to play out on history's stage according to some inscrutable schedule. The midrash on Psalms addresses the "heresy" of thinking that the world can run itself without its creator's involvement:

> *Therefore* (al ken) *the wicked will not survive judgment* (Ps. 1:5). This is just as the Torah informs us: *The lips of the wise disseminate knowledge; not so the minds of dullards* (Prov. 15:7). *The lips of the wise disseminate knowledge*: these are the faithful disciples of the sages, who study Torah. *The dullards*: these are the heretics, and they do not enjoy the *dolce vita* of the Torah. R. Ḥizkiya says: this refers to people who view the Torah as external to them, as opposed to those who have Torah written in their hearts. "A single coin in a small box will make a tinkling sound like 'kish-kish,' but if the box is full, it makes no noise when shaken" (BT Baba Metzia 85b). Another reading: *the lips of the wise disseminate knowledge*: these are they who acknowledge God's reign daily in prayer, and who

---

36. Patristic writers also argued hard against Epicurianism; see for example Lactantius, *De ira dei* (summary and bibliography in Quasten, 2.399–400).

confess God's oneness [by reciting the Shema] three times every day. However, those who say that the universe is an automaton [Hebrew: *atomom*] are heretics.[37]

The clue to understanding the midrash is in the Hebrew phrase *al ken*. Commonly it is translated as "therefore"; however, *al ken* can also be understood by the cognoscenti as "pedestal" or "support stand" (see Ex. 30:18), conjuring up an image such as a top spinning of its own momentum "upon a pedestal" (*al ken*). The question of whether the world runs by itself or is the arena of a more providential and immediate *heilsgeschichte* has been raised repeatedly by those who have challenged biblical revelation. For example, Voltaire scandalized the intellectual world of eighteenth-century France by claiming that the daily rising of the sun was proof that God is merely mechanistic. Such a claim was grievously offensive to the faithful, and thus deemed heretical. *Therefore* [alternatively, Those who believe it runs on a pedestal are] *the wicked* [who] *will not survive judgment.*

In the rabbinic period, the view that the world ran by itself was attractive to certain educated Jews under the influence of the Epicurian philosophy. The question was debated among the Greek philosophers themselves long before it was raised in the rabbinic literature. In the course of just such a debate, Plato suggested a nuclear parable:

> Those who have no experience of wisdom and virtue but are ever devoted to feastings and that sort of thing are swept downward, it seems, and back again to the centre, and so sway and roam to and fro throughout their lives, but they have never transcended all this and turned their eyes to the true upper region nor been wafted there, nor ever been really filled with real things, nor ever tasted stable and pure pleasure, but with eyes ever bent upon the earth and heads bowed down over their tables they feast like cattle, grazing and copulating, ever greedy for more of these delights; and in their greed kicking and butting one another with horns and hooves of iron they slay one another in sateless avidity.[38]

---

37. *Midrash Tehillim Shoḥer Tov* (Buber, 11b and notes), and in Cohen, *Parables*, 72. According to Lieberman, *Texts and Studies*, 223, this is the only time the word is found in rabbinic literature, perhaps having heard that the Epicurians say: *ton kosmon automaton einai*. There is no evidence that the sages' knowledge of Epicurianism was anything more than hearsay; see M. Stein, *Bin Tarbut*, 122–24. On the mechanistic image of God, see the parable of Judah HaLevi, *Kuzari* 3, 11 (107). Gregory of Nazianzus uses the image of a rattling coin in "Concerning Himself and the Bishops" 371–94 (Meehan, 61).
38. Plato, *The Republic* 9, 586A–C (Shorey, 2.390–93); "Longinus" quotes this

The mystical world of qabbalistic Judaism found God even in inscrutability. The qabbalists' esoteric interpretations claimed interrogatives as denominatives, and questions as among the many names of God. The identity of questioner and question became merged in the quest for union with God, so that even the equality of God and humanity could be proven through *gematria*, or mystical mathematics. According to the *Zohar* 1.1b:

> *In the beginning God.* . . . (Gen. 1:1)
>
> R. Eleazar began his discourse with the text: *Lift up your eyes on high and see: who* (mi) *has created these?* (Isa. 40:26). *Lift up your eyes on high:* to which place? To that place to which all eyes are turned, to wit, *Petah 'Enayim* ("eye-opener").[39] By doing so, you will know that it is the mysterious Ancient One (Dan. 7:9), whose essence can be sought but not found, that created these: to wit, *Mi* (Who?), the same who is called *from* (mi)[40] *one end of the heavens to the other* (Deut. 4:32), because everything is in God's power, and because God is ever to be sought, though mysterious and unfathomable, since further we cannot inquire. That extremity of heaven is called *Mi.* But there is another lower extremity which is called *Mah* (What?). The difference between the two is this: The first is the real subject of inquiry; but, after someone by means of inquiry and reflection has reached the utmost limit of cognition, he stops at *Mah* (What?), as if to say, "what" (*mah*) knowest thou? "what" have your searchings achieved? Everything is as baffling as at the beginning.
>
> In *allusion* to this, it is written, *What,* mah, *can I* compare *or* liken *to you, O Fair Jerusalem? I,* Mah, *testify against you.* . . . (Lam. 2:13). When the Temple was destroyed a voice went forth and said, I, Mah, have testified against you day by day from the days of old, as it is written, *I called heaven and earth to witness against you* (Deut. 30:19). Further I, *Mah, likened* myself to you: I crowned you with holy crowns, and made

---

same passage in *On the Sublime* 13.1 (Fyfe, 165–67) and an identical image can be found in *Mekhilta* Beshallah 7 (Lauterbach, 248). Compare these with Aesop's fable of the man who tried to sell a statue of Hermes, in Handford, 151. Odo of Chariton (thirteenth century) tells a similar fable, though about an eagle. To his fable (80–81) he appends this comment: "Those who know God, and know as well the divine matters we need to contemplate, *those* He nurtures and saves. But those too ignorant to look on any except earthly things, those He casts into outer darkness."
39. Gen. 38:14; compare *Bereshit Rabbah* 85:7 (Theodor and Albeck, 1041); Ginzberg, *Legends,* 5.334 n84.
40. The Hebrew *mi* can mean who, which, or from. The Zohar text plays constantly with alternative readings of the word. Here the word "from" is reread as the originative Mi ("Who," a question which is one of God's names). On the Divine ego, see Altmann.

you ruler over the earth, as it is written, *Is this the city that is called the perfection of beauty?* (Lam. 2:15), and again, *I called you Jerusalem that is builded as a city compact together* (Ps. 122:3). Further, I, *Mah*, am *equal* to you; in the same plight in which you, Jerusalem, are here, so I am, as it were, above; just as the holy people does not go up to you any more in sacred array, so I swear to you, I will not ascend on high until the day when your throngs will again stream to you here below. And this may be your consolation, inasmuch as to this extent I am *sharing* with you in all things. But now that you are in your present state, *your breach is great like the sea* (Lam. 2:13). And lest you say there is for you no abiding and no healing, *Mi will heal you* (Lam. 2:13). Be assured that the veiled one, the most High, the sum of all existence will heal you and uphold you—Mi, the extremity of heaven above, *Mah*, as far as the extremity of heaven below. And this is the inheritance of Jacob, he being the *bolt that passes from extremity to extremity* (Ex. 26:28), that is, from the higher, *identical* with *Mi*, to the lower, *identical* with *Mah*, as he occupies a position in the middle. Hence, *Mi* (Who, the Originator) *created these* (Isa. 40:26).[41]

In this passage, one sees by using gematria that the Hebrew characters for *Mi* (mem = 40, yod = 10) add up to 50, as do the Hebrew characters for *you* (lamed = 30, kaf = 20). Thus, "I am equal to you." Then, playing on the formula of "liken and compare," which we have already seen at Isaiah 40:26, Matthew 11:16–19, and elsewhere, qabbalists could claim, in mystical prefigurement of contemporary relationship-theology, that *Mi* is to be likened to *you* (a gematria is a constative)—God is to be likened to humanity—for each bears the numerical value of 50. Humanity may be compared to a cow focused on its food, but it also may be likened to God. The descriptive likeness can defuse the power of the metaphorical comparison when human attention is redirected properly. The God whom the faithful choose to acknowledge is not an object in the third person (*nistar*). Rather, the Ineffable Inscrutable (*nigleh*) is the same God with whom humanity has a "Thou" relationship, to echo Buber. The insecurity that results when human beings attempt to relate to third person objects leads only to further questions and problems. When the inscrutable God is confronted by humanity through parable and analogy as a knowable Thou, the result will be the certainty of faith. The transcendence of God must always be corrected by a prior engagement with God's immanence.[42] This is a

---

41. *Zohar* 1.1b, from Sperling and Simon, 1.4–5; translation modified by the author.
42. In such qabbalistic thought surely lies one of Judaism's closest parallels to the Christian doctrine of Incarnationalism.

function of parable and analogy: to teach humanity the power of God's immanent love. As the ancient rabbinic homilists said, "If you wish to recognize The-One [*mi*]-Who-Spoke-and-the-World-Came-Into-Being, study the aggadah, for thus you will recognize Him . . . and cleave to His ways."[43]

Jacob Burckhardt, the nineteenth-century art historian and student of the history of philosophy, recognized the problems inherent in human allegiance. The survival of the human race would depend upon our transcending the limitation of human perceptions of good and evil, necessitating rather a focus upon a knowledge of the Ultimate, and a commitment to its realization within the over-arching course of human history.

> Imperceptibly we have passed from the question of good and evil fortune to that of the survival of the human spirit, which in the end presents itself to us as the life of *one* human being. That life, as it becomes self-conscious *in* and *through* history, cannot fail in time so to fascinate the gaze of the thinking man, and the study of it so to engage his power, that the ideas of fortune and misfortune inevitably fade. . . . Instead of happiness, the able mind will, *nolens volens*, take knowledge as its goal. Nor does that happen from indifference to a wretchedness that may befall us too—whereby we are guarded against all pretense of cool detachment—but because we realize the blindness of our desires, since the desires of peoples and of individuals neutralize each other. If we could shake off our individuality and contemplate the history of the immediate future with exactly the same detachment and agitation as we bring to a spectacle of nature—for instance, a storm at sea seen from land—we should perhaps experience in full consciousness one of the greatest chapters in the history of the human mind.[44]

The Enduring Consequences of Human Choice

In Chapter 1, a story of Winnie the Pooh was used to illustrate cross-cultural parallelism of literary themes. It serves here again as an example. Pooh got stuck in a hole when he organized his world around his private preoccupations with eating and drinking. His gaze was focused upon his own "I" as opposed to the competing values of the transcendent. His sense of discipline was rendered fragile through this focus on his own baser

---

43. *Sifrei Devarim* 49 to Deut. 11:22 (Finkelstein, 115); compare *Midrash ha-Gadol Shemot* (M. Margulies, 91); Urbach, *Pitron Torah*, 251. On this phrase in tension with the commitment to halakhah as the source of knowing God's will, see Goldin, "Freedom and Restraint."
44. Burckhardt, 369.

values. Though the character Winnie the Pooh is clearly a culturally specific image, it makes immediate a larger theme that runs from classical literature to the present: those who never lift their gaze to the Ultimate will never know the truth about their own existence. Each age needs to repeat this fact, but in its own words and images for its own people; the fact must be immediate, that is, without mediation, immediately clear to this people. Yet however it is manifested, whatever shape a culture gives to it, this basic universal fact can be recognized beneath the particular formulation, and those who can recognize it will always do so.

Therefore (*al ken*), having now come full circle in our review of the tension between Two Masters, I would suggest a new parable, drawing together the many themes of this chapter:

> A parable: To what can this be likened and to what may this be compared? Two deer, lured from safety deep within the forest, were grazing in an open meadow of lush green grass, oblivious to anything except the delicious herbage that was unexpectedly available to them. Unseen, a hunter approached from behind, with his gun at ready. Suddenly, the first deer felt a slight stirring of the wind and, raising his head, spied a beautiful butterfly floating by on the breeze. Smitten with the creature's ethereal beauty and serenity, the deer gamboled off back into the woods, in pursuit of this unexpected vision. The second deer, absorbed in a seemingly endless supply of tender fodder, never heard the sharp report of the hunter's rifle.
>
> [Nimshal] He who never lifts his gaze will never know the truth.

Chapter 6

Unexpected Literary Forms:
The Fish Who Paid Taxes

(Matthew 17:24–27 and 22:15–21)

Matthew 17:24–27 is one of the most frequently misunderstood gospel pericopes. In 1706 the British scholar John Arbuthnot understood this story to be about civil taxation; in English bibles today, however, it is traditionally entitled "Jesus and the Temple Tax," as if it concerned a religious obligation.[1] An extended discussion of this puzzling pericope about a coin in the mouth of a fish will provide the opportunity to discuss certain associative symbols of the Second Temple and mishnaic periods, types and methods of civil taxation, the iconographic function of imperial coinage, and the concept of covert (as opposed to overt) civil disobedience. All this to conclude that Jesus taught, in esoteric symbolism, that those who would walk in the paths of his teaching must maintain the overt posture of compliant loyalty to whatever political government they live under. However, while maintaining such an appearance, Jesus' followers were to hold fast to a higher allegiance which recognized earthly forms of government to be exploitative, idolatrous, and deluded, until such time as God would establish that long-anticipated reign on earth. John 18:36 confirms this early philosophy, as Jesus retorts to his accusers: "My kingship is not of this world; if my kingship were of this world, my servants would fight." At a later point in history, the two commitments in tension were pictured by Augustine as the City of Man and the City of God.

---

1. The OED, under "tribute," quotes Arbuthnot (*Misc. Works* 1751, 3.185) as saying: "Let down your Nets, and you may fetch your tribute money [that is, secular taxes] out of your Fishes." In 1705 Arbuthnot also wrote an essay on Greek, Roman, and Jewish coins and taxation. A number of scholars, including Cassidy, have pointed out how erroneous such a heading is, but Bible translations persist in misleading the readers.

Jesus' encouragement of covert civil disobedience is not readily apparent in the plain reading of the New Testament texts. As usual, it is taught to the initiates by the clever use of agglutinate symbols, allowing stories to speak on several levels simultaneously and encouraging a complex spectrum of listener response. To grasp the levels embedded within the gospel texts, the symbols inherent in several related stories must be examined closely.

According to the *Oxford English Dictionary*, a symbol is "something that stands for, represents or denotes something else (not by exact resemblance, but by vague suggestion, or by accidental or conventional relation); a material object representing or taken to represent something immaterial or abstract, as a being, idea, quality, or condition." The word comes originally from the Greek meaning "thrown together." Around every symbol, other concepts, assumptions, and perceptions agglutinate. The concepts, assumptions and perceptions that agglutinate around a specific symbol will vary from person to person, culture to culture, and to a lesser degree from period to period. For the sake of simplicity, I will argue that "fish" is an agglutinate concept, certain of whose associations remain relatively constant throughout the Second Temple and early rabbinic period. The fish as symbol refers to humanity and its conditions, as well as to the behavior of human beings among and toward each other.

The Fish as a Symbol for Exploited Humanity

Over the course of Second Temple and rabbinic literature, the fish develops as an associative symbol for the fate of the Jewish people themselves. This development does not occur through necessarily clear and successive stages, but certainly by the beginning of the talmudic period the "fish" has moved from being a symbol of oppressed humanity (see Qoh. 9:12) to a symbol of vulnerability (Hab. 1:14–15) to a symbol of the ultimate and future triumph of God's will for those who are faithful (see Ezek. 47:8–10). The fish, a religious symbol antedating Christianity, is held jointly as a common indicator by Judaism and Christianity for several centuries, and is ultimately taken over within Christian art as a symbol connected to the eucharist.[2] The fish symbol was scratched into the walls of

---

2. The understanding of *ichthys* as a notarikon for *Iesous Christos Theou Huios Soter*, or "Jesus Christ, Son of God, Savior," does not appear in Christianity until Optatus, Bishop of Milevis (N. Africa) in the late fourth century, possibly even then with Gnostic origins (see *Oxford Dictionary of the Christian Church* under "fish"). Tertullian's use of "fish" as a symbol of Christ in his homily *On Baptism* does not

both Christian and Jewish catacombs, for under first-century Roman persecution both groups felt strongly the vulnerability that a fish symbolized.
In certain instances, the fish symbolizes humanity as a whole, in its
fertility and its teemingness. In *Bereshit Rabbah* 36.2 to Gen.
48:16, as Jacob bestows his deathbed blessing upon his children, we read: *"These
three were the sons of Noah, and from these the whole earth branched out*
[Gen. 9:19], as by a huge fish that spawned its eggs and filled the earth."
Even more definitive is the use of fish in the *Testament of Judah* 21
to signify those who are victimized politically by their own brothers and
sisters. Predicting a coming time of apocalyptic catastrophe, the author
writes:[3]

> Those who rule shall be like sea monsters, swallowing up human beings
> like fish. Free sons and daughters they shall enslave; houses, fields,
> flocks, goods they shall seize. With the flesh of many persons they shall
> wickedly gorge crows and cranes. They shall make progress in evil; they
> shall be exalted in avarice. Like a whirlwind shall be the false prophets:[4]
> they shall harass the righteous.

In this passage, the coming tribulation is pictured as a time when the
Jewish people would be ruled over by wicked Jewish rulers, though eventually by God's intervention the true kingship would pass back to Judah. Of
particular note in this pre–New Testament passage are: (1) the image of a
fish being swallowed ("swallowing up" appears in a number of Jewish and
Christian parables about fish); (2) the contrast between free sons and
daughters and the enslaved; and (3) the belief that rulers will always ex-
ploit the common people out of avarice and covetousness. Here the fish
suggests not simply all of humanity, as in the previous example, but rather
those who are persecuted by the government as it pursues its own greed.
The horror of the story is that these avaricious rulers are the people's own
kind, now elevated to the role of "false" kings, linked to false prophets, as

---

reflect a notarikonic usage (see n23, this chap.; see also Morrey, and Doelger).
Goodenough (5.3–11) makes clear that the fish was a special symbol in Judaism
and paganism long before Christianity found a unique use for it, as for example
Gen. 48:16 (the cross was also originally a Jewish symbol; see Barnard). On the fish
as Gnostic symbol, see Layton, 120.
3. T. Judah 21:7–9, in Charlesworth, *Pseudepigrapha*, 1.800–801; see also his
Pseudepigrapha and the New Testament, 38–41; M. DeJonge, *Twelve Patriarchs: A
Study*, 91ff; and *Twelve Patriarchs: A Critical History*, 77.
4. On false prophets, see Matt. 7:15; 24:11, 24; Mark 13:22; Luke 6:26; Acts 13:6; 2
Peter 2:1; 1 John 4:1; Rev. 16:13, 19:20, 20:10.

opposed to kings and prophets who rule and speak in accordance with God's will. The rulers seem to have crossed some identity boundary from fish to sea monsters, even reverting to the antediluvian horrors imagined to live under the waters, and finding their political power secured by a religious establishment, likened to a whirlwind.

Sea monsters are not the only ones who swallow fish. Sometimes fish swallow each other, and woe to those who would involve themselves in this cycle of viciousness. *Esther Rabbah* 7 tells of Haman's explorations into the meaning of the zodiac:[5]

> On reaching the sign of Pisces, which shines in the month of Addar, [Haman] found no merit in it and rejoiced, saying "Addar has no merit and its sign has no merit, and what is more, in Addar Moses their master died." He did not know, however, that on the first of Addar Moses died and on the first of Addar Moses was born. [Haman] said: "Just as the fishes swallow one another, so I will swallow them." Said the Holy One, blessed be He, to [Haman]: "Wretch! Fishes sometimes swallow and sometimes are swallowed, and now it is you who will be swallowed."

The story teaches a "theology of reversal" reminiscent of (though more simplistic than) the Song of Hannah (1 Sam. 2:1–10), the Magnificat (Luke 1:46–55), and the Beatitudes (Matt. 5:3–11): in the reign of God, the mighty fall and the oppressed are exalted.[6] Just as powerful Haman, the devious political schemer, threatens to swallow the Jews, so God replies with the promise that in the end it is Haman who will be swallowed. The resolution in this sense appears similar to the previous one: those who prey upon the fish will themselves eventually be destroyed.

The Fish as a Symbol of Vulnerability

The fish was also used as a symbol by the Dead Sea sect in reference to itself, particularly in persecution. Though an initial reading of the following text might suggest that fish symbolize all disenfranchised or per-

---

5. *Midrash Esther Rabbah* 7.11 (Horeb, 757a; Donski, 165).
6. On the theology of reversal, see J. Sanders, *Sacred Story*, chap. 9; see also Robert McAfee Brown, 43: "God does not enlighten the powerful but empowers the powerless. That is very good news to the powerless. And it is very bad news to the powerful." In other words, the good news for someone is quite often bad news for someone else. See also R. M. Brown, 93ff and 157. Compare the *lex talionis*, whose foundational principle also addresses retribution.

secuted humanity, the continuing context makes it clear that the reference is to the specific political oppression of the Jews by the Romans (*Kittim*). The Dead Sea sect's pesher on Habakkuk begins by quoting Hab. 1:14–16:[7]

> *You have made humankind like the fish of the sea, like creeping things "over which to rule." He has fished them all up with a line, pulled them up in a trawl, and gathered them in [his] n[et]. That is why he sacrifices to his trawl, and makes offerings to his net. For [through them] his portion is [ri]ch [and his nourishment fat].* . . . . Its prophetic meaning concerns the rulers of the Kittim[8] who will tread down peoples and subdue them; and their cities will be given to the power of the army of the Kittim, who will gather their wealth with all their loot as from the fish of the sea. And as for what it says, *That is why he sacrifices to his trawl and makes offerings to his net*, its prophetic meaning is that they sacrifice to their standards and [that] their weapons of war are their objects of veneration. *For through them his portion is rich and his nourishment fat.* The prophetic meaning is that they will distribute their yoke and their tax burden, their food, upon all the peoples, year by year, in order to lay waste many lands.

The pesher draws a picture of a defenseless group of people ("fish") who are humiliated and exploited by idolatrous conquerors with military strength and then burdened with excessive taxes that threaten to destroy

---

7. English translation modified from the restoration of Brownlee, 99. At 101, Brownlee, quoting Ethelbert Stauffer, connects the passage with the T. Judah 21:7 (as quoted previously). For an alternative translation, with less hypothetical reconstruction, see Vermes, *Dead Sea Scrolls*, 238. There are many references in the literature in which Jews are portrayed as "fish." For example, BT Pesahim 119a uses the phrase, attributed to Shimeon b. Laqish, "like a pond without fish" to describe Egypt after the Israelites had departed, taking with them hoards of gold and silver. Shimeon b. Laqish's quote is a play on words in the line immediately before. A similar image is set forth in the *Mekhilta de Rabbi Ishmael*, Beshallah to Exodus 14:5 (Lauterbach, 1.195). In *Aikhah Rabbah*, Proem 34, R. Huna answers the question of R. Hanina: "How did the fish go into Babylonian exile with the Israelites?" by saying, in the name of R. Jose, "They went into exile by way of the subterranean and returned by the same way." This speculative hyperbole is based on Gen. 7:22, where it says that everyone *on dry land* died. Since this obviously exempts the fish, they must have gone somewhere; the sages conclude that they went into exile (see Rashi loc. cit., and BT Sanhedrin 108a).

8. On the identity of the *kittim*, see Burrows, 123–142. On fish escaping the net, see Thompson, *Motif*, L330 and 331, Babrius no. 4 (Perry, 8–11), Aarne and Thompson, *Type* 253.

them all.[9] Several items within the pesher quotation are of particular interest. Whereas the masoretic text of Hab. 1:14 says that God has created humankind as fish of the sea that have no ruler, the pesher, in requoting Habakkuk, appears to alter significantly the quotation to read that God has created humankind as fish of the sea over whom it is appropriate for someone to rule. The possible reference justifying such a change in the pesher is Gen. 1:26, 28, in which humans are given dominion over the rest of the animal life. But there are obvious limits to dominion: it should never cross over into exploitation. Though taxation itself here seems not to be opposed, the pesher does seem to oppose taxation at such point that it becomes a "yoke" by which people are humiliated and cities laid waste. This exploitation is made even more vexing by the idolatry of the exploiters: they have made military weapons and "standards," or imperial insignia,[10] into objects of worship. From the point of view of the Dead Sea community, taxation by the imperial power had become synonymous with idolatry.[11]

In such a situation of vulnerability—both to political exploitation and the compulsory support of idolatry—the image of the fish can easily take on associative emotions of despair and hopelessness, as suggested in BT Moed Qatan 25b. Rav Ashi (by tradition the ultimate editor of the Babylonian Talmud) asks Bar Kippok, a noted eulogist, what Bar Kippok might say as a funeral oration over Rav Ashi. Bar Kippok takes advantage of the situation to present a hypothetical eulogy laced with political despair:[12]

---

9. Brownlee misunderstands the image of the fish. The Masoretic text of Habakkuk states clearly that humankind is created as the fishes of the sea. He misunderstands line vi.2: "It is clear that the fish are interpreted as 'wealth' and 'loot'" (101). The fish are not themselves the wealth or loot, but the source of the wealth; through annual ("year by year") exploitative taxation, the military overlords have a constant and seemingly limitless source of revenues. The distinction is a crucial one.

10. Hebrew: *otatam*. The Hebrew word *ot* carries a special significance with it, for a covenant relationship is marked by some sort of *ot* in the Hebrew Scriptures. To venerate an *ot* is to acknowledge the covenant it betokens. Thus, to venerate an imperial military insignia is to acknowledge a "covenantal" relationship with the governmental power the insignia represents. See also Krauss, 260; Gotthold, "Tarbut," 74–76.

11. Taxation here is *masam*, a secular term that stands in opposition to any requisite religious contribution, including the Half-Sheqel Tax; Brownlee (102) claims this phrase means the corvee or forced-labor tax. The Dead Sea sect also opposed annual payment of the temple tax.

12. For emendation of corrupt Talmudic text, see Rabbinowicz to Moed Qatan 18b, note (p); see also Brody and Wiener, 1.14–15, and Bialik, *Sefer ha-Aggadah*, 253 #747.

If even the cedars have been set ablaze,
What can avail the lichen on the wall?
If even Leviathan has been caught in the net,
What hope is left for the fish in the marsh?
If rushing streams have been hit by drought,
What fate might await stagnant waters?

Bar Abin, another noted orator, responds to the speech of Bar Kippok with the words: "God forfend that I should talk of 'hook' or 'flame' in connection with righteousness."[13] Vulnerability and powerlessness lead easily to a despair that to its victims feels worse than death. In such a situation, reliance upon the will and the promised triumph of God often become the sole source of hope for the afflicted.

The connection between vulnerability or despair, fish, and the power of political authority is a strong and early tradition. In general, governments were viewed as idolatrous and not to be trusted or supported, yet paradoxically for the present time they seemed to be the only guarantor against complete social disintegration. According to M. Avot 3.2: "R. Hanina, the deputy of the priests, said: 'Pray for the peace of the government; but for the fear of [the government], we should have swallowed each other alive.'"[14] The metaphor that inspired this saying, though it is not made so explicit in this early source, could well be one of fish swallowing

13. In Hebrew, both hook (*hakah*) and fishing (*dug*) are words which can have positive or negative reference, depending on context. The term "fishers of men" (Matt. 4:19) is not always a compliment, since it can also convey those who entrap or ensnare others who are vulnerable; see Lachs, *Commentary*, 59 and "Sources," 163. The sense of Bar Kippok's words is that if even our leaders are vulnerable (to death, though Bar Kippok's words can carry another tone of political persecution, for those who need to hear), what hope have the common people? The mention together of Leviathan (Jastrow, 698) and Raqaq ("diluvium," Jastrow, 1498; "marsh," Ben-Yehuda, 6740; Kohut, 7.299 n4) returns the reference again to the natural order of creation, of which it would seem that political exploitation is at least as much a violation as is death.

14. Taylor, 1.43, connects (implausibly) this passage with Jer. 29:7 via the Mahzor Vitry (Horowitz, 505), as do Goldin (*Living Talmud*, 190) and Albeck (*Sha'S Neziqin*, 363n). (Taylor gets carried away and connects it with 1 Tim. 2:1–2.) Herford dates Hanina's birth at approximately 20 c.e., and Strack (109 and 304 n18) says that he was the last to hold this office as deputy of the priests, thereby being a survivor of the destruction of the Temple in 70. *Avot de Rabbi Nathan* Version B (Schechter, 68; Saldarini, 186) brings this quote in the name of R. Nehunya, but Saldarini and others suggest that Hanina is more likely. The saying does not appear in *Avot de Rabbi Nathan* Version A.

and being swallowed, particularly if the passage is compared with Ps. 124:2–3: "Were it not for the Lord, who was on our side when others assailed us, they would have swallowed us alive."[15] This connection with the fish is made even more explicit in a subsequent rearticulation of the previous passage at BT Avodah Zarah 4a:

> As among the fish of the sea, the greater swallow up the smaller ones, so with people: were it not for the fear of the government, people would swallow each other alive. R. Ḥanina, the deputy of the priests, said: "Pray for the peace of the government; but for the fear of it, each one would have swallowed his neighbor."[16]

Fear of the oppressive foreign government was justified in the Second Temple period and the following few centuries, for the lot of both the Jewish people and the early church was not an easy one. To avoid being swallowed alive one should remain outside the pale of government attention. Quoting Hillel, Avot 1.13 begins: "A name made great is a name destroyed," bearing a remarkable similarity to Luke 14:11, "Everyone who exalts oneself will be humbled." *Avot de Rabbi Nathan* (A-12) comments upon Hillel's saying: "This teaches that one's name should not come to the attention of the government. For once one's name comes to the attention of the government, the end is that it casts its eye upon him, slays him, and

---

15. Given the political turmoil of the late Second Temple period (the attributed date of the saying), "we" in Avot 3:2 is a perfectly logical reading rather than "they," as in the reading here. R. Yosef ibn-Aqnin, a disciple of Maimonides, in his *Sefer Mussar* (86) comments: "Were it not for the fear that the masses have of the king, men would try to get power over one another, would kill each other, oppress each other, rob each other—they would be like the fish where the bigger one is always swallowing the smaller one, and there is none to prevent it." The continuing currency of the expression was proven when in 1989 Ibrahim Yazdi, former Foreign Minister of Iran, commented on the internal political struggles in his country: "There is no big fish capable of eating all the other fish" (see Ibrahim).

16. A number of scholars have pointed out the similarity between the saying of R. Ḥanina and the speech of Marcius in Shakespeare's *Coriolanus*, Act I, Scene I: "What's the matter, That in these several places of the city You cry against the noble senate, who, Under the gods, keep you in awe, which else Would feed on one another?" The suggestion has been made (Kelner in *Devir*, Berlin 1923, 1.287) that Shakespeare deliberately echoed Ḥanina, having become familiar with *Avot* through the Latin translation by Paulus Fagius, published in 1541. The editors of Soncino (BT Avodah Zarah, 12 n2) prefer to explain Shakespeare as mimicking Ps. 124:2–3, though in fact it seems that Shakespeare's speech is indeed significantly closer to that of R. Ḥanina than to Ps. 124.

takes away all his wealth."[17] The safest way to remain unrecognized, to avoid being swallowed alive, was to make sure that one's name never came to the government's attention. Once one had become known, the consequences appeared to be grave (taxation) or fatal (death)! Perhaps this explains the saying attributed to Hillel's teacher Shemaiah at Avot 1:10: "Love work and hate authority, and do not make yourself conspicuous to the government."

Powerless against governmental persecution, legal discrimination, and financial oppression—already in place in the Second Temple period and continuing long after—the community was encouraged by its leadership to remain constant to God's revelation, to place therein its hope, and to remain "faceless" by channeling its energies into the study of sacred writings. Total immersion in the ways of God was the only source of hope available to the persecuted community, and thereby the wellspring of a power that could not be deprived. BT Berakhot 61b tells a story about commitment to the Torah, set in the chaotic aftermath of the Bar Kokhba revolt in 132–135 C.E.:

> Once the wicked [Roman] government issued a decree forbidding Jews to busy themselves with the Torah. Pappus ben Judah came and found Rabbi Aqiba organizing study circles to engage in the pursuit of Torah.[18]
>
> Pappus said to him: "Aqiba, are you not afraid of the Government?"
>
> Aqiba said, "Are you Pappus, of whom it is said that you are so wise? You are not wise, but foolish! I will explain with a parable. A fox was once walking on the bank of a river, and he saw fishes racing in swarms from one place to another. He said to them: "From what are you fleeing?" They replied: "From the nets and seines which are cast upon us by humans." He said to them: "Would you like to come up on dry land so that you and I can live together in the way that my ancestors lived with your ancestors?" [compare 1 Macc. 1:11] They replied: "Are you the one of whom it is said you are the cleverest of all animals? You are not clever but foolish.

---

17. Compare the themes here with those in Pesher Habakkuk cited earlier. Saldarini, 163, argues that the same theme appears in ARN-B toward the end of chap. 22, but the argument is not convincing (see Saldarini, 139 n21); ARN-B has the person well-known to the government being robbed by robbers, not by the government itself. The principle remains the same today in any totalitarian government: you are fine as long as the government hasn't opened a file on you.

18. Not only was Aqiba violating the restrictions on religious practice, but he was also violating the banning of public assemblies (see Lieberman, *Texts and Studies*, 361); Alon, *Jews, Judaism*, 46, and *Jews in Their Land*, 2.499, 634).

If we are afraid in the element which is our natural habitat, how much more in the element in which we would surely die?"

[Nimshal] So it is with us. If such is our condition when we busy ourselves in Torah, of which it is written, *For thereby you shall have life and shall long endure* [Deut. 30:20], we are afraid that if we neglect the words of the Torah how much worse off we will be![19]

The parable is pertinent on several counts. Not only does it mention images and people already familiar to us—Rabbi Aqiba, fear of the government, Torah, and fish[20]—but it also gives an indication of what it means to remain "faceless" to the government. Anonymity is not to be understood literally here, though of course there is a certain inconspicuousness that comes simply from holding one's private and religious life far apart from scrutiny by those perceived to be hostile. Rather, anonymity should here be understood figuratively, in that one's personal values remain pure from and unwarped by the seductive and coercive values of the political realm, particularly when that political realm is also oppressive and exploitative. Out the waters, or above the waters, fish come immediately to the attention of predators, and that attention can only result in death, whether spiritual or physical. Keeping one's values focused on God and promoting the solidarity of the community protects the faithful from predators and preserves the only commitment in this world that can truly give life.

Such was the understanding of much of both Christianity and Judaism in the first few centuries C.E. Within Judaism, this approach generally meant to keep oneself outside the reach of the government, with its exploitative interests, corrupting idolatry, and life-threatening power. In

---

19. Compare Gaster #20 (Heb. 16–17, Eng. 189); al-Naqawa, 3.243–44; Thompson, *Motif* J758.3; Schwarzbaum, "Talmudic-Midrashic," 474–75 (433–34). A similar image is presented in BT Avodah Zarah 3b–4a.

20. See *Bereshit Rabbah* 973 to Gen. 48:16 (Theodor and Albeck, 1246–47): "Just as fish live in the water, yet when a drop falls from above they catch it thirstily as though they had never tasted water in their lives; so are Israel brought up in the waters of the Torah, yet when they hear a new exposition of the Torah, they receive it thirstily as though they had never heard a Torah teaching in their lives." The same passage adds an attribution to R. Zakkai the Elder, who said, "And the son of him whose name was as the fish would lead them into the land, *Nun his son, Joshua his son*" (1 Chron. 7:27). *Nun*, a proper name in Hebrew, is spelled the same as *nun*, the word for "fish" in Aramaic (Jastrow, 888). Joshua is of course at root the same name as Jesus. In the Galilean fishing culture, where both Aramaic and Hebrew were spoken, is it not possible that the connection between "Yeshua" and "fish" would have been apparent to the followers of Jesus? See also M. Margulies, *Midrash ha-Gadol Bereshit*, 825.

Christianity's early centuries, the fish image retained the same message of safety, with an added caution to avoid heresy. In his early third-century homily on baptism, Tertullian writes:[21]

> This discussion of the sacred significance of that water of ours in which the sins of our original blindness are washed away and we are set at liberty unto life eternal, will not be without purpose if it provides equipment for those who are at present under instruction, as well as those others who, content to have believed in simplicity, have not examined the reasons for what has been conferred upon them, and because of inexperience are burned with a faith which is open to temptation. And in fact a certain female "viper" from the Cainite sect, who recently spent some time here, carried off a goodly number with her exceptionally pestilential doctrine, making a pernicious point of demolishing baptism. Evidently in this according to nature: for vipers and asps as a rule, and even basilisks,[22] frequent dry and waterless places. But we, being little fishes, as Jesus Christ is our great Fish, begin our life in the water, and only while we abide in the water are we safe and sound. Thus it was that that portent of a woman, who had no right to teach even correctly, knew very well how to kill the little fishes by taking them out of the water.[23]

With this illustration, we see that Christianity and Judaism, at least in the past, have drawn upon a common stock of imagery, metaphor, and simile. In neither case is the expression of the shared heritage limited to canonical Scripture, but in both cases continues to develop from this common stock through the first several centuries. Safety from both spiritual and physical death is found by retaining one's commitment to the received

---

21. Trans. by Evans, *Tertullian's Homily on Baptism*, 4–5 and n45–49; see also Quasten, 2.278–81. Thales, the first-known Greek philosopher, speaks in the *Pre-Socratic Fragments* about the origins of life in water, or moisture. Lubrication and fluids are necessary for a sperm to swim to an ovum. All such symbols are deeply ingrained in the human psyche.

22. Legendary dragons with lethal breath; compare Prov. 23:32 (JPS).

23. See also the famous epitaph of Abercius Marcellus, Bishop of Hieropolis in Phrygia, c.161–180: "For I had Paul in my carriage, and everywhere Faith led me. And she served up everywhere food; a fish [*ichthyn*] from a fountain, mighty, pure, which a pure virgin grasped; and [Faith] gave this to her friends to eat always, having good wine, giving the mixed cup with the bread." Quoted in Wischmeyer, 24–25; see also Quasten, 1.171–73. According to E. Evans (48), this is the earliest historical reference to ICTHUS as a notarikon for Christ, but he is surely mistaken, for here the use is symbolic but not a notarikon; the idea is more fully developed in Augustine, *The City of God* 18.23 (Walsh and Honan, 114–17), and in the Inscription of Pectorius, c.400 C.E. (Quasten, 1.173–75). And see n2, this chap.

revelation in its purity, or as the Desert Fathers expressed it: "As fish can live only in the sea, so we must run back to our cells. Perhaps, if we dallied outside, we might lose our inner guard."[24]

The Fish as Agent of Providence

A final story concerning fish, from BT Shabbat 119a, needs to be explored, for it parallels the strange pericope of the coin in the fish's mouth (Matthew 17:24–27). In both traditions, the fish appears as an agent of divine providence by which a faithful person is both rewarded for having been faithful and protected from further danger. In these surprise encounters with a fish, the faithful receive a foretaste of God's ultimate victory over mundane political regimes.[25]

> Joseph-who-honors-the-Sabbaths had in his vicinity a certain gentile who owned much property. "Soothsayers" told [the gentile]: "Joseph-who-honors-the-Sabbaths will consume all your property." So he went, sold all his property, and bought a priceless pearl[26] with the proceeds, which he wrapped carefully in his kefiyeh.[27] As he was crossing the river on a ferry, a blast of wind blew off his kefiyeh and it fell into the water where a fish swallowed it. [Subsequently] the fish was hauled up and brought to market on the eve of Sabbath as it was already getting dark. "Who will buy so

---

24. Sayings of the Fathers 2.1, in Chadwick, 40, and compare Athanasius, *The Life of Anthony*, 85 (DeFerrari, 209) for a similar image.

25. BT Shabbat 119a; *Yalqut Shimeoni* to Gen. 2, par. 16, p. 5b, and to Isa. 58–59, par. 496, p. 104a; Rabbi Loew (MaHaRaL) *loc. cit*, 105–7. This is a much-loved story in subsequent rabbinic development, and among other things is the source of a beautiful Shabbat glee; see Naphtali ben Menahem, 31. Montefiore, 66, butchers both this tale as well as *Midrash Bereshit Rabbah* 11.4, getting the point behind both stories wrong. For the custom of Jews eating fish on Friday, see M. Stern, 1.437.

26. The word *marganita* here is the same word used to denote the "priceless pearls" strung together by the sages, as explained in the previous chapter; see Jastrow, 836, *margalit* and *marganita*.

27. Both versions in Yalqut say *sadiniye*; however, Jastrow (957) is convincing that this is "a bedsheet," clearly a scribal error; Rashi rejects the reading. MaHaRaL and Steinsaltz say *saiyana*, which Jastrow (978) defines as "a felt cap with a visor" (a baseball cap?). Surely here Jastrow misses the point as well. He wrapped it in a kefiyeh, a scarf that wraps around the head; modern-day Arabs still have the custom of tying small valuables in one corner of their kefiyeh, where they are secure but hidden while the kefiyeh is worn. See a specific illustration of this custom in *Qohelet Rabbah* 1.10, 1.

late?" cried the fishermen. "Go and take it to Joseph-who-honors-the-Sabbaths," they were told, "as he is accustomed to buy [this late on Sabbath eve]." So they took [the fish] to him. He bought it, opened it, found the pearl therein, and sold it for thirteen containers of gold denarii.

[Nimshal] A certain old man met him and said "He who lends to the Sabbath, the Sabbath repays him."[28]

Through a fish, God rewards Joseph for having kept scrupulously his commitment to the practice of his religious values. The story here is a fable in the same way as it is presented in the version in Matt. 17:24–27, "the Coin in the Fish's Mouth." In both cases, the common stock of symbols is brought to life through story in order to entertain and to teach. But it is brought on a simultaneous level as a theological observation on the nature of God: a tenacious faith effects the providence of God, so that the faithful continue to be supplied with whatever is needed to sustain them and protect them from further harm.

Taxation in the Second Temple Period

Taxation in the biblical world was heavy and, as is the nature of taxes, seemed to escalate as years progressed. The burden became heavy in the Persian period, increased through the Hasmonean period, and became particularly onerous during the Roman period, both before and after the fall of the Temple in 70 C.E. A significant innovation of the Roman government was the awarding of governorships, satrapies, and senatorial seats as rewards for political favors. With these awards came the understanding that a certain amount of the taxes collected had to go back to Rome, but whatever the governor could squeeze out in addition could go directly into his pocket.

The study of taxation during the Second Temple and Mishnaic periods is complicated by three factors: (1) sources are not always as complete as we would like; (2) reasons, rates, and even names of taxes seemed to have fluctuated alarmingly; and (3) it is difficult to coordinate the names of

---

28. Norman Cohen (167 n27) understands the nimshal to mean: "He who expends money to honor the Sabbath will be rewarded for it," but on 174 shows that the same Hebrew phrase can be reconstructed to mean "He who falsifies (profanes) the Sabbath will be punished." See Mark 2:27 and parallels: "The Sabbath was made for humankind, not humankind for the Sabbath." Compare *Mekhilta* on Ex. 31:16 (Horowitz and Rabin, 341); JT Yoma 8, 5; BT Yoma 85b; Betzah 17a; Kasher, 21.63 n53.

taxes in the languages of various sources: Hebrew, Aramaic, Greek, Latin, and English.[29] Among the regular taxes mentioned in the sources are the head or capitation tax; the salt tax; the corvee; the coronation or crown tax; the tax of one-third of the grain produced in a field; the tax of one-half of the fruit of a tree; the estate tax; the revenues tax; the tax on moveable property; the imperial gifts tax; the buying and selling tax; the crafts tax; the tax on dwellings in Jerusalem; the change of domain tax; the military defense tax; and numerous port duties, road and bridge tolls, not to mention fines and bribes.[30] It is estimated that the sum of these taxes ate up between forty and fifty percent of a citizen's income. These civil taxes are to be distinguished from the obligatory religious gifts and offerings such as the tithes, the redemption of the firstborn, festival offerings, and the annual half-sheqel tax due the temple. These religious obligations required in the neighborhood of twenty percent of one's income. No wonder, then, that when Korah wanted to incite the Israelites to rebel against Moses (Num. 16), rabbinic literature claims that he used the religious obligations as his source of complaint. To drive home his point, he told the Israelites the following story (the story is only pseudobiographical, of course, for it is taught by a nomad in the wilderness, long before the application of halakhah in relation to harvests and domesticated animals):[31]

> There lived in my vicinity a widow with her two unmarried daughters, who owned for their support one field whose yield was barely sufficient for their needs. When [the widow] set out to plow her field, Moses appeared and said, *You shall not plow with an ox and an ass together* (Deut. 22:10). When she began to sow, Moses appeared and said, *You*

---

29. The story of taxation in the Second Temple period is further complicated by the amount of misinformation repeated from one source to the next. One reliable source is Schalit, 137–54 and 437–451, though he does not understand well the coinage of the period. Most Christian sources consulted were patently in error, apparently attempting to draw all their information from the scanty materials of the New Testament, and ignoring or misunderstanding information available from other sources in the Second Temple and mishnaic periods.

30. Josephus mentions most frequently the land tax payable in money or in kind; the capitation tax and the accompanying tax on personal property; export and import customs; and in Jerusalem, a house tax. For a summary of recent research on taxation in Egypt and Judea and Samaria, see Cassidy, 576–79.

31. *Midrash Tehillim* to Psalm 1.15 (Buber, 14–15); compare BT Sanhedrin 109b–110a; *Midrash Aggadah* Korah (Buber, 116–17). See also Ginzburg, *Legends*, 3.290–91 and 6.101 n567, and for a delightful defense of Moses in this instance, see Derrett, "The Case." Compare Matt. 23:14.

shall not sow your field with mingled seed (Lev. 19:19). When the first fruits showed, Moses appeared and bade her bring it to the priests, for to them are due *the first of all the firstfruits of the earth* (Ex. 23:19); and when at length the time came for her to cut it down, Moses appeared and ordered her *not [to] reap all the way to the edges of your field, or gather the gleanings of your harvest, . . . but you shall leave them for the poor and stranger* (Lev. 19:9–10). When she was about to thresh the grain, Moses appeared once more, and said: *Give me the heave offering, the first and the second tithes to the priests* (see Num. 18). She accepted God's inscrutable will in humility and submitted herself to Moses's demands [but despaired of the hardship created for her].

So what did she decide to do? She sold the field and [with the proceeds] purchased two ewes in the hope that she might be able to clothe her family with their wool, as well as benefit in various ways from their offspring. [However], when the firstling sheep was born, Aaron appeared and said, "Give me all your firstborn lambs, for the Holy One blessed be He said to me: *All the firstling males that come from your herd and from your flock you shall consecrate to the Lord*" (Deut. 15:19). She acted righteously, handing them over. At shearing time Aaron reappeared and said, "Give me the first of your fleece, for the Holy One Blessed be He said to me: *The first of the fleece of your sheep shall you give [to the priest]*" (Deut. 18:4). Not content with this, Aaron reappeared later and demanded one sheep out of every ten as a tithe (see Lev. 27:32), to which again, according to the Torah, he had a claim. This, however, was too much for the long-suffering woman. She said: "I haven't the strength to defy this man, so I will slaughter [the ewes] and eat them. [At least I can benefit from their meat in peace.]" No sooner had she slaughtered them but Aaron appeared, and said: Give me *the shoulder, the two cheeks, and the stomach* (Deut. 18:3). "Oy!" exclaimed the widow, "Even slaughtering the sheep did not deliver me out of his hands! So let this meat then be consecrated to the sanctuary!" [Refusing to pass up this last opportunity,] Aaron appeared and said: "Then the meat shall be mine, for thus said the Holy One blessed be He to me: *Everything that has been proscribed in Israel shall be Yours*" (Num. 18:14). He picked up the meat and departed, whereupon the widow and her daughters began to weep bitterly.

It is imperative to keep the two systems—civil taxation and religious contribution—separate from each other in any discussion. They were levied by two separate systems of authority, collected by separate categories of officials, had separate types of enforcement connected in case of failure to pay, were due from different types of people (the religious contributions were not due from non-Jews, of course), and above all symbolized very distinct types of loyalty and privilege to the exploited people of the Roman-occupied Levant. Some of the civil taxes were more bitterly resented than others, but in general it can be stated that the civil taxation burden was a primary source of those tensions which fed the revolts of 70 and 132,[32] while the obligatory religious gifts produced far less controversy within the Jewish community.

The two most hated and burdensome civil taxes in the Second Temple period were the capitation tax (*mas gulgolet*)[33] and the estate tax (*mas qarqa'ot*). The capitation tax was an annual tax, possibly paid monthly. The calculation of the tax was based upon the Roman census taken approximately every six years, in which every resident of Judea and Samaria— man, woman, and child, slave or free—was registered along with complete information about their occupations and property holdings. The penalty for failing to register in the census or for giving false information was death. The capitation tax due from every resident between ages fourteen and sixty-one was the primary source of income for the Roman administration, and Herod applied every ounce of his duly notorious efficiency and ruthlessness to make sure the capitation tax was collected in full. Administrative tax districts were established throughout the country, headed by non-Jewish employees of the government called *architelōnai*, or in the New Testament, publicans.[34] These *architelōnai* in turn hired out the actual collection of taxes to a complex system of local Jewish clerks and Jewish tax-farmers—called in the New Testament "tax-collectors" (*telōnai*)—who were given quotas to meet and charged with the right to collect that quota by whatever coercive and underhanded means necessary.[35] They were further given the right to make a profit on their collections without being questioned about the amount of the "commission" or the means by which it was obtained.

Civil taxation felt to the residents of Palestine as though it were end-

---

32. Josephus, *Antiquities* 18.4–10 (Feldman, 9.5–9) details an earlier revolt for the same reasons, as he also does at 17.32, explored later; and at *Wars* 2.117–18 (Thackeray, 2.366–69).

33. In Aramaic, *mas reisha*, or *kesef reisha*. *Gulgolet* means "skull" as in the New Testament explanation of Golgotha (see John 19:17). The tax is a capitation tax or head tax (as both Hebrew and Aramaic names imply), but not a poll tax, for poll tax in its modern usage implies the power to vote, a power not available to conquered people of the Roman Empire.

34. They were also known as *katholikoi*; see Liddell and Scott, 855; Krauss, 268; Kohut, 3.229.

35. Jews did not always make the best tax-collectors; sometimes their sense of community loyalty overruled their civil obligations. See for example the story of R. Zera's father at BT Sanhedrin 25b–26a, who used his office as a local tax-collector to undermine the regional administrator.

less, arbitrary, and strangling. According to the *Avot de Rabbi Nathan* (A.20):

> Rabbi H̲ananiah, deputy of the priests, commenting on Deut. 28:46f— *therefore you shall have to serve—in hunger and in thirst, naked and lacking everything—the enemies whom the Lord will let loose against you*—says: *In hunger*: for example, at a time when one craves food and cannot find even coarse bread, the heathen nations demand from him white bread and choice meat.[36] And *in thirst*: for example, at a time when one longs for drink and cannot find even a drop of vinegar or a drop of bitters, the heathen nations demand from him the finest wine in the world.

The same sentiment concerning the crushing burden of Roman taxation is expressed in *Sifrei* to Deut. 33:19: *"For they shall suck the abundance of the seas.* Two take away abundantly and give abundantly, and these are the sea and the [Roman] government. The sea gives abundantly and takes away abundantly. The government gives abundantly and takes away abundantly."[37]

The leadership and teachers of the community did not quarrel over the necessity of civil taxation; in fact they encouraged the faithful to pray for the peace of the government, for political structures, including taxation, were necessary for the proper regulation of society. But not all taxes were equally respected, nor did the community's teachers feel the same about each tax. Bridge tolls and port duties were not opposed with the same vehemence as the capitation tax.[38] As we shall see, it is also the capitation tax to which Jesus specifically refers in both Matthew 17 and 22. In general, the religious leadership of the community objected to the capitation and certain other taxes on three grounds: they were excessive; they caused people to worry so that they were constantly distracted from their religious and ethical obligations; and above all, the capitation tax was interpreted theologically as a form of idolatry in its implied recognition of the authority of those royal emperors who adopted the ascription of *divus*.

---

36. Here, as in the earlier Pesher Habakkuk, food becomes a metaphor for taxation. The metaphorical use of "bread" for livelihood, and then derivatively as slang for "money," enters very early into the English language.

37. *Sifrei Devarim* 354 (Finkelstein, 416; Hammer, 371). See also *Aikhah Rabbah* 3.5–8, 3 (Buber, 63a, 125) and *Ruth Rabbah*, Proem 3. On the inevitability of taxes, see *va-Yiqra Rabbah* 29.2 (M. Margulies, 671 and var. lect. 8–9) on Lev. 23:24.

38. Though see BT Shabbat 33b, on why R. Shimeon bar Yoh̲ai went into hiding.

Pharisaic Opposition to the Capitation Tax

The capitation tax apparently was administered according to community quota, rather than individual assessment. Annually a fixed amount of money needed from each community was determined by the Roman authorities, and district collectors were assigned to produce that amount within the year. In turn, the collectors divided the amount of money by the number of eligible taxpayers according to the most current census, and this was each taxpayer's due amount regardless of income. The tax collector then went to each taxpayer to extract the individual amount by whatever means. However, the community's forced assessment did not take into account that some of those eligible might have moved away or fled the region, or might attempt to hide their eligibility.[39] When taxes could not be collected from these shirkers, other members of the community had to make up the difference by increasing their own amounts paid. Further, certain members of the community claimed exemption, most often on theological grounds.

The capitation tax was particularly onerous to the Pharisees, and they were divided on the appropriate response to the tax, whether it should be paid or not. They were not divided, however, on the fact that the capitation tax functioned as a form of idolatry; on this particular issue, the Pharisees seem to have been in total agreement with each other.[40] Josephus, in *Antiquities* 17.32–45, tells the story of an open revolt by some of the Pharisees over payment of the capitation tax: Herod, plagued by escalating troubles in his kingdom, had turned over a certain amount of authority to his son Antipater. Sensing this young man's growing power, Pheroras (Herod's brother and Antipater's uncle) began to conspire with Antipater to take over the throne, and this conspiracy was secured by the cooperation of Pheroras's wife, her mother and sister, and Doris the mother of Antipater (one of Herod's wives). Herod's sister (and the sister of Pheroras) Salome got wind of the plot and attempted to warn Herod, but he did not trust her enough to heed her warning. In the meantime, the four women in the plot had developed a relationship with a group of Pharisees. When

---

39. According to Mandel (60–61), from 70–132 c.e., some Jews did not circumcise their sons in order to avoid being identified as Jews who would have to pay taxes to the Roman government. See Tos. Shabbat 15.9 (Zuckermandel, 133; Neusner, *Moed*, 59–60), that during the Bar-Kokhba revolt, there were mass circumcisions to make up for having neglected the commandment.

40. See Urbach, *Sages*, 608–20, on the Pharisaic opposition to the capitation tax, and Krauss, 260. Tertullian's *Apology* 13:6 (Arbesmann, 43–44) clearly identifies the capitation tax as a sign of subjugation to a ruling authority.

Herod attempted to test the loyalty of these Pharisees by some sort of "oath of allegiance"—and here I would claim that this "oath" is in fact whether or not the Pharisees would pay the capitation tax—more than six thousand Pharisees refused this loyalty test, and their capitation taxes were paid for them by the wife of Pheroras (Herod's sister-in-law). Enraged at what seemed to be an open revolt by the Pharisees against his authority, and seeming to prove the plot of which Salome had attempted to warn him, Herod had the principally accused Pharisees slaughtered along with several members of his own family and other members of the court.

This incident took place somewhere within approximately twenty-five years of the life of Jesus. No revolt of six thousand prominent Jews could go unnoticed in such a small country, nor would their martyrdom soon be forgotten. We may assume that the issue of taxation was therefore a highly loaded subject for most of the citizens of the period, including Jesus. The purpose of the relationship between the four royal women and the Pharisees is not clear. It may be that some members of Herod's family sought to study the Pharisaic approach to Judaism, or perhaps they were simply attracted to this group which, as Josephus says, "made others believe they were highly favored by God." It would certainly not be the first time in history that religion and politics have made strange bedfellows. Nor is it clear who courted whom: whether the relationship was initiated by the Pharisees themselves, or by the royal court (which is more likely, given the Pharisees' general mistrust of all whose practices differed from their own).

Josephus writes: "When all the people of the Jews gave assurance of their goodwill to Caesar, and to the king's government, these very men [the Pharisees] did not swear, being above six thousand; and when the king imposed a fine upon them, Pheroras's wife paid their fine for them."[41] To grasp the interpretation that Herod's loyalty test took the form of taxation, and the capitation tax in particular, one must turn to a midrashic interpretation of Deuteronomy 33:3 that is brought as proof of the correctness of Jewish refusal to pay the capitation tax:

> Moses said to the Holy One, blessed be He: "You have decreed that your children bear two yokes: the yoke of the Torah, and the yoke of the government."
>
> [The Holy One] answered [by citing the Torah]: *Although he loves the peoples, all his saints* [qedoshav] *are in your hand* [Deut. 33:3].

---

41. Josephus, *Antiquities* (Thackeray, 8.387–93). See also *Antiquities*, 15.1–4 in 8.2–5; there, the Greek text names the leaders of the Pharisees as Pollio and Sameas, but the reference is surely to Hillel and Shammai.

On account of this passage, when the disciples of the sages died due to the yoke of the government, and even when they died because they could not meet their basic needs for food and shelter, they did not sever themselves from the One who gave them the yoke of the Torah that they might rejoice day and night. For as it is said: "Because they are pious, their Torah is preserved and their work is blessed" [BT Berakhot 32b]. It is also said: "The earlier generations made the study of the Torah their main concern and their ordinary work subsidiary to it, and both prospered in their hands" [Berakhot 35b].[42]

It is clear that the "yoke" is already a developed symbol before the redaction of the above rabbinic passage. Apocryphal literature treats the yoke as at times a joy, at times a source of despair, depending upon whether it is adopted voluntarily or imposed from without. For example, at Ben Sirah 6:30, 51:17, and 51:26 the faithful are urged to put on the yoke of Wisdom with rejoicing, whereas at Ben Sirah 40:1 the burdensome yoke of daily living is enough to break a person, as it has been imposed involuntarily from birth. In the passage just quoted the yoke of the government (perhaps even more burdensome than the yoke of daily living) is connected directly with Deut. 33:3. The connection is even clearer in another related passage, from BT Baba Batra 8a, which connects the government, the capitation tax, and the sanctity that proceeds from commitment to the yoke of the Torah:

> R. Naḥman ben R. Ḥisda informed the rabbis of their due share of the capitation tax.
>
> Said R. Naḥman ben Isaac to him: "You have transgressed against the Torah, the prophets, and the holy writings. Against the Torah, where it says, *Although he loves the peoples, all his saints* [qedoshav] *are in your hand* [Deut. 33:3].

Interpreting "saints" (*qedoshav*) as a synonym for "Pharisees,"[43] the traditional reading of the Deuteronomic text sets up a dichotomy between the

---

42. Text as presented by R. Shimeon ben Tzemaḥ Duran (RaSHBaTz, 1361–1444) in *Magen Avot* 3:5, which is probably, according to Flusser, the original version. See also *Sifrei Devarim* to Deuteronomy 33:3 (Finkelstein, 400–402; Hammer, 356–57), as well as the commentary of the Vilna Gaon thereto; Rashi to *loc. cit.* (Silbermann, 5.171); compare Gal. 4:8–9.

43. The connection between *qedoshim* ("saints") and *perushim* ("Pharisees") is based upon the exegesis of Lev. 19:2; see Rashi thereto; Avot 2:5 (see esp. Herford, *Ethics*, 45); *Sifra* 86a; Tos. Berakhot 4:25 (Lieberman, 18 line 96 and *ki-Feshutah*, 53); *Midrash ha-Gadol va-Yiqra* (Steinsaltz, 584 line 5, particularly in relation to *melekhet borer*). Other pertinent texts include Flusser, *JOC*, 639–43; Finkelstein,

yoke of loyalty to the government versus the yoke of loyalty to God. Those who would be "holy" or "saints" were obligated to choose between one yoke and the other, though fear of divine punishment was never to be a factor in the choice of God's yoke. One's choice of either yoke was to be completely voluntary. The clarity and consequences of the choice are articulated in a saying from M. Avot 3.5: R. Nehunyah ben ha-Qanah said, "Every one who takes upon himself the yoke of the Torah, they remove from him the yoke of the government and the yoke of worldly occupation. But every one who breaks off from him the yoke of the Torah, they lay upon him the yoke of the government and the yoke of worldly occupation."[44] According to this tradition, to recognize the yoke of the government (ol ha-malkhut) is to submit to it, thereby denying the larger and more urgent authority of the yoke of the Torah (ol ha-Torah) or of the kingdom of God (ol malkhut ha-shemayim).[45] For some significant portion of the Pharisaic movement, submission to paying the capitation tax was a form of idolatry, the resistance to which justified martyrdom (qiddush ha-Shem).

Coins as Icons of Authority

For "saints," the capitation tax symbolized not only submission to the pagan government, but also seemed an idolatrous act because the coins

---

Pharisaism, 175–86; Lauterbach, "The Sadducees and Pharisees"; Schechter, Aspects, chap. 13; Berkovits, Man and God, chap. 4; Ullendorf; Roth. The word perushim, commonly translated "Pharisees," means simply "separatist, secessionist," and can as often be an encomium as it can a derogative. Nor is the term limited to that group we now call Pharisees; for example, the Essenes at times referred to themselves as perushim; see Ginzberg, Unknown, chap. 7; Qimron and Strugnell, 10. This distinction between perushim (those who have separated themselves) and paroshim (those who have been separated involuntarily) makes an enormous difference in the way JT Sotah 3, 4 (the seven types of Pharisees) is read, especially by Christians. On the morphological problem, see Gordis, "Studies," 193–95.

44. Herford, Ethics, 69–70; Taylor, 45–46 (where one will also find a good definition of derekh eretz, "worldly occupation"). At ARN-A 20 (Goldin, Fathers, 95), R. Nehunjah's comment is connected with taxation, in the name of Haniniah.

45. Matt. 11:29–30: "Come to me, all who labor and are heavy-burdened, for my yoke is easy and my burden is light." See also Taylor, 46; ARN-A.20 (Goldin, Fathers, 94); Maimonides on Avot 3.6 (la-Am, 1.77 and notes). The connection between taxation and Caesar's yoke is also made by Gregory of Nazianzus in "Concerning his Own Affairs" 145–60 (Meehan, 30). On the modern existential tension between the two yokes, see Soloveitchik; and David Hartman, Joy and Responsibility, 146–50.

with which taxes were paid carried the image of human beings which the surrounding cultures treated as divine. Up until approximately 100 B.C.E., Roman coins carried only images of pagan deities, and to infringe upon this tradition by minting coins with human images on them was scandalous even to the Romans.[46] Many kinds of coins, bearing many different images, were in circulation during the Second Temple and mishnaic periods. Governments and municipalities near and far minted their own currency under various sorts of official license. "In addition to the procurators, the cities of Caesarea and Ascalon minted bronze, and the coins of the Phoenician cities (mostly Tyre and Sidon) were brought through the trade routes. Additionally, Roman copper and silver coins flooded the country, through troop movements and commerce; and further, there was the imperial coinage of the region, which was minted in Antiochia. Accordingly we meet (in the first century C.E.) with bronze coins from various parts of the Empire, and silver (and gold) coins from Rome, Antiochia, Tyre, Alexandria and Caesarea in Cappadocia."[47] This explains in part why three different varieties of coin—the dinar, the didrachma, and the stater—are mentioned in the few short verses of Matt. 17:24–27.

Because coinage was in such a constant state of disarray, literature of the period shows frequent concern that coins used to pay debts according to contract or agreement be designated as the coinage current in the country at the time of repayment.[48] One manner in which coinage was shown to be current was that it carried the image of the ruler of the moment. Each caesar minted his own coinage, frequently bearing his likeness as well as an inscription. In this manner, coins served to inform the provinces who was in power, and so were a form of political propaganda. Coins also functioned as graphic representations for those who could not read. As each successive emperor changed, the coinage changed with him. The value of a coin was determined by its percentage of metal alloy, that is, by its weight, but whether it was legal tender in every realm was usually determined by whose image the coin bore. JT Sanhedrin 2, 3 tells this charming story:[49]

---

46. Mattingly, 71ff.

47. *Interpreter's Dictionary of the Bible*, 3.428. See also Tos. Sheqalim 2.13: "Every kind of coin circulates in Jerusalem" (Lieberman, *Tos. Moed*, 210). See also Kohut, 1.207–8; 3.148–49; 5.198; 8, index 128; and *Enc. Miqrait*, 4.808–25, esp. 811.

48. See M. Ketubot 13.11, and the gemara thereto, BT Ketubot 110b.

49. Compare Midrash Shemuel 23:12 (Buber, 59a). A variant reading, with less punch, is found in BT Megillah 14a–b. See also JT Sanhedrin 2, 20b, BT Baba Qamma 97b, and Shemot Rabbah 15 on coins losing their currency; BT Pesaḥim

When Abigail saw David, she quickly dismounted from the ass and threw herself face down before David, bowing to the ground (1 Sam. 25:23).

She said to him, "My lord David, as to me, what have I done? And my children, what have they done? My cattle, what have they done?"

He said, "It is because [Nabal] has cursed the kingdom of David."

She asked, "And are you [now] a king?"

He replied, "And has not Samuel [already] anointed me as king?"

She said to him, "[But] our lord Saul's coinage is still in circulation!"

Thus coins carried an implicit, but powerful, recognition of the authority of a government over those who used the coins, and the use of coins implied the user's consent and loyalty to that political authority. Rabbinic literature occasionally portrays God as a minter of coins (BT Sanhedrin 38a), as a king who mints coins (*Bereshit Rabbah* 36.7), or as a king who collects tolls and duties (BT Sukkah 30a, *Qohelet Rabbah* 9.7, 1). In a word play on the Hebrew root *a-v-d*, the sages point out the confusion between service to God the King in the form of worship, and service to Caesar the king in the form of paying taxes, particularly in coins that bore the word *divus*. Commenting on the situation in which Nebuchadnezzar confronted Daniel and his three companions with the demand to worship idols, *va-Yiqra Rabbah* 33.6 reads:[50]

Nebuchadnezzar said to them: "Did not in fact Moses write down for you in the Torah, *There you will serve* [avadatem] *man-made gods* (Deut. 4:28)?

They replied: "Your majesty! This service [*avodah*] does not mean worship, but 'service'—in taxes, produce assessments, fines, and capitation taxes."

54b, that coins are part of God's plan for creation; and BT Shabbat 33b. And see Kohut, 4.11; BT Shevuot 6b (ref. Dan. 7:23); BT Baba Qamma 97b. Dictionaries indicate that "moneta" is synonymous with "fame."
50. M. Margulies, 768; the reference is to Dan. 3:14. See also Masnut (thirteenth century), *Midrash Daniel and Midrash Ezra*, 34. On the Second Temple source of this philosophy, see Josephus, *Antiquities* 18.1–10 (Feldman, 9.3–9). Krauss (260) brings an interesting targumic variation on Hab. 3:17: "But the government of Babylon will not endure, nor will it hold any power over Israel; the kings of Media will be killed, and the idolaters and soothsayers will go down in defeat; the Romans will perish and they shall not delight in the destruction of Jerusalem."

For Samuel ben Naḥman explained that [in Babylon] kings were called "gods."

The understanding of kings as "gods" was too uncomfortable for the Pharisees' successors. When combined with the fact that many taxes, particularly the capitation tax, had to be paid in coins that bore a human image and the word *divus*, the sages could *only* connect this with idolatry. The most pious of the Jewish community leaders refused even to look at such coins. JT Avodah Zarah 3.1 asks: "Why was [Naḥum bar Simai] called 'Naḥum the most holy'? Because he never gazed upon a minted coin in his entire life [to avoid seeing the 'idol' imprinted thereon]."[51] But although the Pharisees and their successors disagreed among themselves over whether this idolatry was serious enough to justify martyrdom, they apparently did agree that for most of the religious community there was no choice. The only expedient option was to pay the requisite civil taxes so that they could continue to live, all the while focusing on the truth that life belongs only to God, and that the internal commitment of the pious should be to the yoke of God alone, writing God's law in their hearts. According to *va-Yiqra Rabbah* 23.5:[52]

> *Like a lily among thorns, so is my darling among the maidens* (Song 2:2).
>
> R. Ḥanina ben R. Idi interpreted this verse as applying to contemporary events. *Like a lily among thorns.* How is it with the lily? When a north wind blows, she bends to the south and a thorn pricks her, and when a south wind blows, she bends to the north and a thorn pricks her; yet in spite of that, her heart remains directed upwards.
>
> [Nimshal] So it is with Israel. Though Israel is enslaved among the nations by corvee and capitation taxes and state confiscations, their hearts point upwards toward their Father who is in heaven.

To stamp the world and all that is in it, even its currency, with the effigy of a ruler, or any symbol which suggests that human power has a claim equal to or greater than God's, is to deface the image of God stamped upon creation and actively to promote idolatry. The commitment of the faithful, even while paying capitation tax, is to "Give unto God of that which is God's, for you and what you have are God's, as we find it

---

51. Similar stories are found in the BT at Pesaḥim 104a, Avodah Zarah 50a, and Moed Qatan 25b.
52. M. Margulies, 532 and notes. A similar story is found in *Shir ha-Shirim Rabbah* 2.2, 4. On the "lilies of the field," see Matt. 6:28.

expressed in the case of David, who said, *All things come of thee, and of thine own have we given thee*" (1 Chron. 29:14).[53]

Render Unto Caesar

Jesus spoke and taught within this climate of frustration, fear of the government, and the burdensome character of civil taxation near the end of the Second Temple period. Without this identification of the social, political, and religious backgrounds in which Jesus cried out, his two parables concerning civil taxation—Matt. 17:24–27 and 22:15–21—are easily misinterpreted. Seen in their proper context, these two parables take their place alongside the sayings of other sages and authorities, communicating through the codes and the symbols of the time. Teaching simultaneously on several levels, Jesus conveys to his initiates the esoteric message of the empty power of idolatrous political authority, and the real hope of liberation for the oppressed and exploited in both the present and the future.

Matt. 22:15–21 reports an attempt by an unusual political bloc to elicit from Jesus his halakhic opinion concerning the permissibility of Jews paying the capitation tax (and by inference other civil taxes). Jesus delivers the requested halakhic opinion, with its multiple layers of meaning, the deepest of which is an affirmation that his followers need do nothing beyond the minimal placation of the political authority, for indeed the true power is already in the hands of his initiates. The story goes as follows:

> Then "the Pharisees" went and formed a plan how they might trick [Jesus] through discussion. And they sent to him their students, with the Herodians, who said: "Teacher, we know that you can be believed, and that you teach truthfully the way of God, that you are not afraid of anyone in particular, for you are not swayed by human opinion. Tell us, then, your opinion: Is it permitted for us to pay the capitation tax to Caesar or not?"

> But Jesus, aware of their malice, said: "Why are you testing me in this manner, masking your faces with sincerity? Show me the coin with which you must pay the capitation tax!"

> And they brought to him a dinar.

---

53. Translated literally, the Chronicles passage reads: "For from you is everything, and from your hand we give to you." See Avot 3:7, on Eliezar Ish Bartota, where the same proof-text is brought to support an interesting philosophy of communal property.

And he said to them, "Whose image and ascription is here?"

They said, "Caesar's!"

[Nimshal] He said to them, "Then return what is due Caesar to Caesar, and what is due God to God."[54]

This story is paralleled in Mark 12:13–16 and Luke 20:20–25, but among the three versions the introductory verse concerning the identity of the inquirers contains great discrepancies. Matthew describes them as being the students of the Pharisees, along with the Herodians, whereas Mark describes the inquirers as some of the Pharisees themselves (not their students) along with some of the Herodians. Though scholars have no firm idea who the Herodians were, it is possible that any number of groups could have been curious to discover where Jesus stood on the controversial issue of the capitation tax—the Pharisees to see where he stood within the broad range of argument inside the movement itself concerning the tax,[55] and others to double-check Jesus' identity as a Pharisee (and a potential subversive) based on his answer. Luke identifies the inquirers neither as Pharisees nor Herodians; rather, he leaves the identification vague, noting only that spies "who pretended to be sincere" were sent, seeking to find some reason to turn Jesus over to the local governor. David Flusser suggests that these anonymous people—probably Jews, as there would be no reason to send non-Jews to Jesus were a serious answer desired—were *agents provocateurs* at the hire of the government, a scene set up by Luke to justify charges at the trial of Jesus that he had encouraged a tax rebellion (Luke 23:2).[56] Flusser's suggestion is initially attractive, for it helps point out three fallacies in the Matthean and Markan versions: (1) if Mat-

54. The Gospel of Thomas 50:12 (Layton, 397 #100) gives the nimshal as "Give unto Caesar the things that are Caesar's, give unto God the things that are God's, and give unto me that which is mine." Compare Qoh. 8:2–5—"Keep the king's command because of your sacred oath. . . . Whoever obeys a [king's] command will meet no harm, and the wise mind will know the time and way."
55. Pharisaism was no more monolithic than any other large scale group such as Democrats or Presbyterians. Practices of piety and opinions about revolt against the government varied within the Pharisaic movement (commentators such as Hill, Lightfoot, Klausner, and the Interpreter's Bible draw too strong a line between the Zealots and the Pharisees), and such an inquiry by the sages of Jerusalem to a relatively unknown Galilean who showed up claiming the authority of a teacher would be possible. On the "students" of the Pharisees, see Milavec, *To Empower*, chap. 5.
56. Flusser, *Yahadut*, 41.

thew is correct, the Pharisees did not care enough to come themselves but only sent their students; (2) if Mark (and to a lesser extent Matthew) is correct, we have here only a request for clarification, one Pharisee to another, about a controversial issue inside the movement, for the Pharisees would not seek a ruling from someone outside their own movement on an issue that had been under discussion for several years by their own most learned teachers; and (3) if Luke is correct that this was "a trick," particularly for the purposes of handing Jesus over to the government, then Pharisees would not have been sent at all, as their opinions were already widely known in society and Jesus could not have been expected to fall for such a blatant ruse.[57] At any rate, the English word "trick" is misleading; what we have here is nothing more than the sort of "trick" typical to rabbinic argument, that is, a clever learned argument in which equally matched opponents try to cause each other to falter in their logic. Jesus uses exactly such devices on his opponents as often as they do on him because it was a way in which the "academics"(!) of the period behaved with each other.[58] Indeed, in spite of the curious Latinism in Matthew's version,[59] the Matthean and Markan versions may be closest to the truth in that we have here a request for clarification. That Pharisees would inquire of Jesus suggests that he had prior credentials inside the Pharisaic movement.

The flattering phrases used to describe Jesus in the Greek text do not suggest a semitic language syntax, probably as a result of heavy Matthean redaction. Of special interest in this verse is the phrase "the way of God." The Peshitta brings an alternative reading, which possibility restores a semitic original: "the way of God in truth" (*urha de-elaha be-qushta*), suggesting that Jesus' petitioners sought to affirm his understanding of oral Torah, altogether an appropriate way to address someone whose halakhic opinion is sought sincerely. That the Pharisees were the proponents of oral Torah, as differentiated from the other known groups in Judaism of the period, again supports an identification of Jesus with the Pharisaic movement itself.

In Matt. 22:17 comes the question to which the introduction has been leading. A halakhic opinion is requested: Is it permitted for us as Jews to pay the capitation tax to Caesar or not? The word "permitted" is in line with a request for a halakhic opinion; the standard English translation,

---

57. See Peake to Matt. 22:15, 791.
58. Thus the phrase carries no sense of value judgment. See Matt. 21:24–27, Mark 4:29–33, Luke 20:3–8. See also Daube, *New Testament*, 159–60.
59. See Beare, *Matthew*, 2.438.

"lawful," is misleading, for halakhic opinion is open to minority and majority disagreement whereas "law" suggests an incontrovertible rule.[60] The question itself carries multiple layers of meaning, ranging from simple opinion to theological principle.[61] Flusser holds that the original text, now retained only in Luke, referred to all taxes in general. However, Matthew and Mark both specifically read *kēnson*,[62] the Greek name for the capitation tax, and further the Peshitta actually reads "capitation tax" (*kesef resha*). The witness of the Hebrew Scriptures that taxation based on a census implies ownership and authority is patent,[63] and as we have seen, the theological issue was clearly in the mind of the Jewish community of the Roman-occupied Levant. The implication of the inquirer's question is: Are we permitted halakhically to pay the capitation tax, given that it implies that we have chosen the yoke of the government over against the yoke of God?

The issue of the questioners' malicious intent is raised at Matthew 22:18, and Flusser uses this verse to justify his reading of *agents provocateurs*. The verse on the whole is troubling, but one must resist the temptation simply to ignore it. Many biblical scholars agree that "hypocrites," at least as it has come to be understood in modern English, is not the correct equivalent to the Greek *hypokritai*.[64] Even respected dictionaries contradict each other on the root meaning of the word.[65] The Peshitta to this verse offers *nasbei b'apa*, one possible translation of which

---

60. We have seen that the Pharisees had a disagreement over the issue of the payment of capitation tax, yet even a minority opinion had halakhic status. On the continued recording of majority and minority opinions, and their respective halakhic status, see M. Eduyoth 1, 4–6 (Albeck *Sha"S*, 4.282–83, 475–76); BT Ḥullin 11a–b; Hirsch, *Horeb*, 352–56 and his commentary on Ex. 23:2 (*Pentateuch*, 388–90).

61. See Hill, 303–4.

62. See Kohut, 7.137–38; Jastrow, 1393–94; Ben-Yehudah, 6035–37, esp. 6037a n1; Kassovsky, *Otzar Lashon ha-Mishnah*, 1594.

63. On the census bringing death, see Ex. 30:11–16. There the half-sheqel functions as a form of atonement (*kofer*). See 2 Sam. 24; Kasher, 21.161–68; M. Margulies, *Midrash ha-Gadol Shemot*, 649–50, with ample references; Liver, 174–77.

64. For scholarly interpretations of *hypokritēs*, see Garland, chap. 4. Albright and Mann (273) translate this as "casuists," but this does not solve the problem in any significant way.

65. See, for example, the contradiction between *The American Heritage Dictionary* and Liddell and Scott. Both agree that the Greek word hypocrite is built on *kreinein*. According to *The American Heritage Dictionary*, 648, citing Pokorney *skeri-* (sec. 2, 946), *kreinein* means to "cut" a judgment, to differentiate, to decide, and therefore ultimately, "to exercise partiality." According to Liddell and Scott, 1886, supported by *OED* 509, *kreinein* means "to act a part on a stage."

is "those who lift up their faces."[66] Cueing off the Peshitta reading, etymological study indicates three possible connotations:

1. In Deut. 28:50, one possible parallel Hebrew phrase, *yisa panim*, means "someone respected in society, an elder to whom others look up." Such a definition of "hypocrites" is consistent with the Peshitta above, but certainly casts a different twist than is usually assumed on the verbal exchange between Jesus and the Pharisees.

2. In Deut. 10:17, the Hebrew *yisa panim* means "impartiality" (in the positive sense) or "arbitrariness" (in the negative). The same sense of impartiality/arbitrariness is found in the "Priestly Benediction" (Num. 6:24–26) familiar to many Christians, there usually translated "the Lord lift up his countenance upon you," but meaning "May God treat you impartially, being neither unduly biased in your favor nor prejudiced against you."[67]

3. In Aristotle's *Nicomachean Ethics*,[68] the term "hypocrites" is used to signify "children who mouth grown-up words innocently without understanding their true meaning." David Garland argues that hypocrites are what we would today call biblical literalists, that is, those who concentrate on the exoteric to such intensity that they miss altogether the existence of the esoteric, much less its message and power. Hypocrites in this classical usage are "those who seek simplistic answers," preferring to ignore anything that would necessitate intellectual labor or which would challenge emotionally one's comfortable assumptions.

I would suggest that Jesus here senses the danger of being drawn too deeply into internal Pharisaic politico-halakhic controversies, which he has avoided for most of his ministry. He is willing to explain his halakhic opinion, but does not wish to be lured into showing partiality toward one side of the controversy to prove its numerical superiority in a majority decision. Again we are reminded of Jesus' retort to his accusers in John 18:36: "My kingship is not of this world; if my kingship were of this world,

---

66. *Apa* (*nasbei b'apa*) suggests "faces," which is reminiscent of images on coins, a provocative wordplay, but one that cannot be translated into Greek. See Jastrow, 915; Kassovsky, *Targum Onkelos*, 1.307–11, where *N-S-B* = *N-Sh-A*. The Old Syriac as preserved in the Mt. Sinai Palimpsest (Agnes Smith, 21) reads "for thou regardest not the faces of men," which would then connect with the Peshitta interpretation of *hypokritēs*. What Jesus meant to say according to the Peshitta was: "Why pick on me, you bastards?"; see Gen. 40:13, 19:20; Deut. 10:17. Ps. 4 of the Psalms of Solomon describes these people as "sycophants."

67. See Mal. 2:9, and compare BT Berakhot 20b (Steinsaltz, 91), *Tanḥuma* to Num. 6:26 (Buber, 17a–b).

68. Aristotle, *Nicomachean Ethics* 1147a 23 (Rackham, 390–91). See also Garland, 96–117, esp. n20; and Barr, "Hypocrisy," on definitions of "hypocrite" that have nothing to do with "acting a role."

my servants would fight." Delivering a halakhic judgment in this case would entrap Jesus in yokes and political issues that apparently were of no consequence to him. However, he does answer his inquirers.

Repeatedly through the Gospels we find Jesus using items at hand to illustrate his parables and halakhic opinions. Here Jesus requests to see the coinage with which the capitation tax is to be paid, in this case apparently the Roman denarius, which during the reign of Tiberias (14–37 C.E.) carried the image of the head of the emperor, and the inscription *divus et pontifex maximus*.[69] Some scholars have suggested that this verse proves that the normal taxation rate for the capitation tax was one dinar per person, but the only source cited as evidence is this Matthean verse, and as has been shown, the capitation tax varied greatly from one year to the next depending both on the amount demanded by the government and the number of people in the community who stayed around long enough to pay their share. Other scholars have made a great deal out of Jesus' not having such a coin on his own person.[70] The point here is not that Jesus, like Mena<u>h</u>em ben Simai, refused all contact with Roman money (even visual), or that Jesus was under strict vows of poverty, but simply that the discussion "trick" is being turned back on the inquirers, typical to the sort of gamesmanship that characterized this very Jewish form of debate.

Jesus asks whose image is on the coin. The Greek text reads *eikōn*; the Peshitta translates *tzalma*, cognate of the Hebrew *tzelem*. Jastrow (1284) points out that *tzalma* can mean "image,"[71] but in many places in the targumim and the midrash rabbah it also means "idol."[72] Physical images easily become idols, just as caesars become Gods. Given the readily available Aramaic wordplay between "image" and "idol," Jesus's listeners could easily receive the message that the coinage of Tiberias Caesar was the currency of idolatry.

Harrington argues that Matthew 22:21 is not to be understood as a political philosophy but as a display of Jesus' skill at argument and illustration, not unlike the rabbinic delight in the beauty of argumentation. However, to gloss over the passage so lightly is to leave its more tragic inter-

---

69. See Hill, 304; Beare, *Matthew*, 2.439; Peake (791) to Matt. 22:20. Beare quotes the inscription as *Ti Caesar Aug F Augustus*: "Tiberias Caesar, Son of the Deified Augustus, Augustus." The dinar was a particularly hated coin; see M. Sheqalim 2:4 (Albeck, 2.192); JT ibid. 46d. Denarii were not acceptable in the Temple Sanctuary; see Kohut, 3.99; M. Margulies, *Midrash ha-Gadol Shemot*, 655.

70. See Meier, *Matthew*, 251; *Interpreter's Bible*, 12.519.

71. As in the Aramaic targumim to Genesis 1:27 and Gen. 9:6; see also Avot 3:15 (Albeck, *Sha"S*, 366 and 497, Taylor 1.56).

72. Both *tzelem* and *tzalma* can mean "idol"; see for example Num. 31:52; 1 Sam. 6:5; Ps. 73:20; and all uses in the book of Daniel.

pretations unchallenged. The "render unto Caesar" answer has been twisted in Christian history to the point that one commentator suggests that the Nazis believed themselves to be "rendering unto Caesar" what was legitimately his.[73] Jesus' answer makes sense only in light of the choice between the yoke of government and the yoke of God, no one being able to live bearing both (Matt. 6:24). In other words, the initiate to whom the correct esoteric association is available realizes that what is due Caesar is nothing, for to recognize anything as Caesar's due is to give credence to idolatry. Out of expedient prudence, the tax must be paid, for the "way of God" is the way of life and not of death.[74] But all that Caesar believes to be his is no more than Caesar's illusion, for the faithful initiate knows that neither the idolatrous coins nor the oppressive government have any power or authority at all. Authority comes only from God who offers the joy of his own yoke. Roman political authority is empty, futile, and effete, and the loyalty suggested by the use of Roman coins is hollow. Covert civil disobedience here takes the form of dramatic illusion: a coin with neither power nor authority is returned to a government with neither power nor authority. The public appearance of obedience is to be maintained only so that the faithful remain free to serve the true source of power and authority.

The Coin in the Fish's Mouth

The Gospel of Matthew includes another story about taxation that has no apparent parallel in Mark or Luke. The story—Matt. 17:24–27—seems

---

73. Simcox, 239. Davies (*Jewish and Pauline Studies*, 285) addresses the mentality that could lead to such a twisted interpretation of Matt. 22:21: "For certain elements in the early Church, the commandments of Jesus in their absolute form were guides for conduct. But under inevitable pressures it became necessary for the Church to apply these absolutes to life. There began that process which tended to transform the absolutes into practical rules of conduct—Christian casuistry." In the same vein see BT Ketubot 50b: "R. Eleazar intended to allow maintenance out of movable property. Said R. Simeon b. Eliakim to him, 'Master, I know that in your decision you are not acting on the line of justice [*middat ha-din*] but on the line of mercy [*middat ha-rahamim*], but [the possibility ought to be considered that] the students might observe this ruling and fix it as an halakhah for future generations.'"

74. On the understanding of mitzvot as bringing life, rather than encouraging death, or even martyrdom, see Tos. Shabbat 15:17 (Lieberman, *Moed*, 75 with notes and *ki-Feshuta*, 262 n83–84); Sifra 85b at #14 to Lev. 18:5; *va-Yiqra Rabbah* 23; and Steinsaltz, *Midrash ha-Gadol va-Yiqra*, 519.

confusing in the Greek text and almost unintelligible in English. Only four verses long, it appears to break into three distinct, nearly unrelated parts when it is exegeted as a story about "the half-sheqel," the annual tax that the Jewish community imposed upon itself for the Jerusalem temple. But when exegeted as a story about civil taxation, it makes sense at last.

In order to comprehend the difficulties, the RSV text must first be presented:

The Temple Tax

When they came to Capernaum, the collectors of the half-sheqel tax 2[Greek: *didrachma*] went up to Peter and said, "Does not your teacher pay the tax?"

He said, "Yes."

And when he came home, Jesus spoke to him first, saying: "What do you think, Simon? From whom do the kings of the earth take toll or tribute? From their sons or from others?"

And when he said, "From others,"

Jesus said to him, "Then the sons are free. However, not to give offense to them, go to the sea and cast a hook, and take the first fish that comes up, and when you open its mouth you will find a sheqel [Greek: *statera*]; take that and give it to them for me and for yourself."

As read in English, the text presents an extraordinary number of problems, which may be listed as follows:

1. *The tax seems to have been demanded.* The text says the tax collectors came to Peter's home. Those who collected secular taxes roamed town and country to meet their quotas. Those who "collected" the half-sheqel donation for the temple did not go out to townspeople to collect it; the townspeople came to them at special collection centers, even in the provinces.[75] Further, "collect" is not a verb used in the literature in relation to the half-sheqel, for the donation was completely voluntary.[76]

---

75. See M. Sheqalim 1:1 and 3 (Albeck, *Sha"S*, 187–88). The pre-70 early date of this tractate is unquestioned by most scholars. According to the text, tables were set up in the provinces, to which the local citizens came to pay their temple tax. The taxes were collected at these tables by *benei ha-ir*, that is, local citizens without official capacity to collect payment forcibly (Bar-Droma, 46).

76. Compare the Greek for "collect" at Matt. 17:24 with the word for "seize" at Matt. 5:40; the Greek does not bear a sense of voluntary giving. The distinction in Hebrew must be kept clear between *gabbah*, to collect, and *natan*, to give. Civil taxes were "collected"; religious taxes were "given"; see Cassidy, 574. The verb *lishqol* ("to sheqel," to weigh) is used in a number of different contexts, and cannot be limited to the payment of the half-sheqel.

2. *The drachma is not the same as the sheqel*. The Greek text reads that the collectors came for "the didrachma" (a half-drachma). There is no known Jewish source that specifically nominates "the didrachma" as an official translation into Greek of "the half-sheqel" donation. In fact, the didrachma was used more often for everyday purposes than for religious donations, as is obvious from Clement's *Stromateis* 1.20.[77]

3. *The collectors are not identified clearly*. The Greek text does not identify "the collectors." The Peshitta identifies them as "those who collect the two zuzin of the capitation tax" (*de nasbin train zuzin de-khesef raisha hinnun*). In other words, the Peshitta identifies them as civil tax-collectors come to collect a civil tax.[78]

4. *The royal metaphor has insufficient precedent*. The image that Jesus uses in his question is "the kings of the earth." The English text makes it appear that a religious predicament is being addressed by a quiz about mundane authority. If indeed the half-sheqel is under discussion, we are presented as well with the complication that there is no precedent in the literature of the period for "kings of the earth" as a metaphor for the Temple authorities.

5. *Conflicting coins are named*. The Greek text says "there you will find a stater." English texts, stuck in the assumption that this story is about the half-sheqel, usually substitute the word "sheqel" for the Greek "stater." In fact, the stater had not been legal coinage in Palestine since the time of Alexander the Great.[79] The word "stater" continued in Aramaic as a generic term for a small worthless coin, but would not have been used, even generically, in reference to a sheqel.[80] Staters, as Greek coinage, could not be used to pay the half-sheqel donation; only Tyrian sheqels could be used.

6. *The coin delivered is an insufficient sum*. Even had the stater been a legal coin equivalent to a sheqel, it would not have been enough to pay the

---

77. Clement, *Stromateis* 1.20 (ANF, 2.323). It cannot be assumed that the didrachma was the direct equivalent of the Tyrian sheqel. Nor can it be assumed that the word "didrachma" is to be taken literally, as will be seen in verse 27; see Schalit, 444 n427a–428. Didrachma is used as a sort of generic term for civil taxes.
78. Even Israeli scholar Samuel Safrai fails to catch this point! (Avi-Yonah, *World History*, 319).
79. According to Meshorer, personal interview.
80. Aramaic: *istira* (Jastrow, 57). The understanding of a stater as a small useless coin is found in *Midrash Tehillim Shoḥer Tov*, 1.21 (Buber, 22), Jastrow, 637, *kish*, and BT Baba Metzia 85b: "One single coin in a crock makes much noise, but if the crock is full of coins, it is silent. Similarly, the scholar who is the son of a scholar is modest; but the scholar who is the son of a yokel trumpets his knowledge all around." The same image was referred to in the previous chapter.

half-sheqel donation for two people since an eight percent surcharge was added for changing "secular" coins into the appropriate temple coinage.[81]

Virtually every one of these problems is created by the assumption that the tax under discussion in the story is the voluntary half-sheqel annual donation to the Temple. Tricked by the incorrect identification, Schweizer points out that the miraculous coin in the fish's mouth is anticlimactic, as the point about taxes has been made already.[82] Once the incorrect identification of the tax is untangled, the story falls neatly into line with Matthew 22:15–21 and the coin in the fish's mouth can be seen as a theological statement integral to the story line.

Kefar Nahum (Capernaum) was a fishing port on the northern shore of the Sea of Galilee. As the coin was a convenience already at hand in the previous pericope, so here it is logical to hear a fish story in a fishing port. By Christian tradition, Capernaum was also the adult home of Jesus and the hometown of Peter, and the story suggests that it takes place just outside, and then just inside, Peter's house, where Jesus is apparently a guest. As indicated above, we can only assume that the provocative questioners who came to Peter were local collectors of the civil capitation tax. Given the size and location of Kefar Nahum in the period, it would have been a logical center for the civil taxation of the entire region.[83]

The tax collectors want to know whether Jesus has paid his annual capitation tax, to which Peter answers that he has.[84] On going inside the house, he finds that Jesus has already turned the situation into an opportunity for teaching.[85] The question Jesus asks should be read as a straight-

---

81. Meshorer, personal interview; see also M. Sheqalim 1.

82. Schweizer, 356.

83. See Schalit, 153. Archaeologists have uncovered a collection-house in Kefar Nahum (vide Matt. 9:9). Harrington (*Matthew*, 261) mixes up the office of Matthew the tax collector (*telonion*), who collects *telonai* on fish being exported, with the office for collecting the Temple tax. Fish were taxable produce, as was the buying and selling of fish; as there were lots of fish in the fishing city of Kefar Nahum, we can also assume there were lots of taxes and lots of tax-collectors. As well, taxes from Trans-Jordan and the Golan Heights seem to have been brought to Kefar Nahum for centralization. See Meyers and Strange, 58–61, and Tsaferis et al.

84. Derrett ("Peter's Penny") identifies the rumor that prompts the inquiry as being that Jesus was a Samaritan. Samaritans (and non-Jews) were forbidden to pay the half-sheqel (see M. Sheqalim 1:5), so were he a Samaritan, to receive the half-sheqel from Jesus would cause the tax-collectors to have committed a sin! The idea is interesting, among other reasons because it is such a flight of fancy for which there is no plausible evidence at all.

85. Beare (*Matthew*, 2.371) wishes to argue here that Jesus had "super-natural powers," by which he can hear conversations out of earshot. The idea should be rejected.

forward one, rather than an introduction to a parable: "From whom do earthly kings collect tolls [Greek: *telē*; Peshitta Aramaic: *maksa*] and capitation tax [Greek: *kēnson*; Peshitta Aramaic: *kesef resha*]?"

The point of the story must be identified in the dichotomy between "sons" and "strangers,"[86] rather than seeking an explanation connected to the payment of the half-sheqel. Sons are those who carry out the will of God, and strangers (or at times "servants, slaves, aliens") are those who do not.[87] The apparent political question about who carries the heaviest burden of taxation has as well a hidden theological message: those who have accepted the yoke of the Torah are like God's own children and those who have not accepted that yoke remain strangers to God.[88] The irony, as will be shown, is that in the eyes of the Roman government the true "sons" look like "strangers," and vice versa.

The line between "son" and "stranger" can be a delicate one, as the following story from *Shemot Rabbah* 46 illustrates:

Said the Holy One, blessed be He, to Israel:
"Now you [have the audacity to] call me Father?
When you find yourselves in trouble, you call out to Me 'Our Father'!"
They replied: "Yes, for is it not written *In my time of distress I turn to the Lord*" (Ps. 77:2)?
To what can this be compared?
To the son of an eminent physician who happened across a quack, and began to inquire after his health,
addressing him as "my master, my lord, my father."[89]

---

86. *Banim ve-nokhrim*, a parallelism retained also in the Peshitta text as *beneihon* and *nokhraiya*. See also Deut. 29:22 and Mal. 1:6. See also Schechter, *Aspects*, 51–56. Many ancient prayers express this dual relationship. See also *allotrios* in Hatch and Redpath, 57; Gen. 31:15, where *nokhri* is a relative term; and Isa. 61:5 and 56:3–6 on the in-group vs. the out-group. In the Ashkenazic service for Rosh ha-Shanah see the hymns *Avinu Malkeinu* and *HaYom Harat Olam*. And see Weinfeld; Beavis; Lindars; and Lauren, 6.

87. BT Baba Batra 10a, attributed to R. Aqiba (c.50–135 C.E.), and even more interestingly, connected to tax collectors (Soncino, 45 n8). Schweizer (357) is obviously misinformed on the whole subject: "The contrast between the son, who is free, and the servant, who is not, is almost without parallel in Judaism but is peculiar to all of primitive Christianity." Harrington's mistaken exegesis (262) is based on the assumption that civil tax words become loose generalizations, making room for the inclusion of Temple tax.

88. In the sense of "ignorant" rather than "unloved." See Flusser, "Hillel's Self-Awareness."

89. *Avi, mari, kuri*. This latter term is of course a loan word from the Greek "kyrie."

When his father heard this, he was angry with his son, saying,
"Let him no longer see my face, since he calls that quack his
'father.'"
Some time later, the son became ill.
He said, "Please call my father, that he may come to see me."
When the father was informed of his son's request,
His mercy was immediately stirred toward his son and he went
to him without delay.
The son said: "Please, my father, will you examine me?"
The father said: "Now I am your father?
Only yesterday you called that quack 'my father'!
Now, however, that you are in trouble, you call *me* 'father.'"
[Nimshal] This is what God said to Israel:
"Now you call out to me, 'You are our Father,'
though yesterday you worshipped idols, addressing them as
'father.'"
This is why it says:
For they have turned their backs to me, and not their faces.
But in the time of their trouble, they say "Come and save us!"
(Jer. 2:27)
And this is why it says:
Yet now, O Lord, you are our Father. (Isa. 64:8)[90]

The "sons" in Matt. 17: 25–27 are those who have accepted the yoke of the Torah. Their "citizenship" in the Kingdom is not apparent to temporal authorities, including those who collect taxes. Like fish, their life is below the water, away from public view. The sons of the earthly king view themselves as free and the strangers as enslaved, but the secret sense of hope in Jesus' story is that "they" have it all upsidedown.[91] Those who appear to be enslaved are in fact the ones who are truly free, free by virtue of having put on the yoke of God. The strangers to the political kingdom are actually the children of God's kingdom; the political sons are in fact strangers to the true Kingdom, though they cannot yet see it.

---

90. *Shemot Rabbah* 46:4; compare Isa. 33:22 and 63:16; BT Taanit 25b and R. Samuel Edels thereto (plus Rabbinowicz, *Varie Lectiones*); Berkovits, *God, Man and History*, 73.
91. See BT Pesaḥim 50a (Steinsaltz, 206); Sanhedrin 104b, Baba Batra 10b; *Yalqut Shimeoni* to Prov. 22, all on the phrase *Olam hafookh raiti: eliyonim lamattah ve'taḥtonim lema'alah* ("I saw a topsy-turvy world: the upperclass on the bottom, and the underdog elevated to power!"). Compare Matt. 23:12 and Luke 14:11, "he who exalts himself will be humbled." And see Flusser, *JOC*, 512.

This is the hope offered by Jesus in the midst of his own oppressed and exploited people: to realize that you have already won, and how much sweeter the victory because the political powers do not recognize it. To emphasize the rewards of the faithful, Jesus reminds Peter of a myth about the miraculous deliverance through the agency of a fish. The fish story is a myth, just like the stories of Jonah and of Joseph-who-honors-the-Sabbath. Myths and parables carry comforting truths to the faithful that transcend the concreteness of nature miracles.[92]

For the time being, until God's "realized" victory is apparent to the nations of the world, the semblance of obedience is to be maintained. Civil taxes are to be paid, in the knowledge that this money which disappears will return to the true children in abundance.[93]

To those whose manner of life is pure and who are skilled in the true understanding of the Torah comes the opportunity "to enter in peace and go out in peace." To them come the true riches, the true victory, the offer of hope in the face of political oppression. True civil disobedience is to fulfill only enough of the minimal obligation that the government never finds out that its coinage has no currency, that God's children have already won. For, in the words of *va-Yiqra Rabbah* 23.5:

> Though Israel is enslaved among the nations by corvee and capitation taxes and state confiscations, their hearts point upwards toward their Father who is in heaven. What is the proof? *My eyes are ever toward the Lord, for He will loose my feet from the net* (Ps. 25:15).

---

92. This part of the story is not to be taken literally (though Albright and Mann, 213, struggle hard to do so!), nor do we have any indication that the payment ever took place. At any rate, if a stater equaled a sheqel (as we have already shown that it did not), it would not have been enough to pay for two, for the surcharge would be required to change the found coin into Tyrian sheqels. For details see M. Sheqalim 1:6 and elsewhere. There may well be an implied joke here, for in this case the "head" (the image on the coin) contributes the *tributum capitis*! Obviously the reason for ending the pericope in this manner can only be to refer listeners back to the same common source from which proceeds the story of Joseph-who-honors-the-Sabbaths. The story itself as it appears in the Talmud probably would not have been known to Jesus, but the common ground from which both the Matthean story and the Talmudic story derive would have been.

93. The Hebrew expression *yarad le-timeon* means that something got lost, never to be found again. The origin of the expression is that money in the form of the capitolina tax was sent away to the *timeah*, the Roman treasury, and never seen in the country again. On the antiquity of the phrase, see Kohut, 4.42–43 (Greek loanword *tameion*).

Chapter 7

Shifts in Transmission:
Mites, Motes, and Mistakes

(Matthew 7:1–5)

One essential function of parables is that they are employed to illuminate—to make abstract or vague concepts clear and distinct, to enlighten rather than obscure. The parable describes a situation with which the listener can readily identify; its purpose is doomed if the parable contains elements that confound intelligibility. The imagery of any parable—particularly when used to clarify dogma or norms of conduct—must be clear and distinct, though not necessarily transparent, for its telling to be justified.

The time-honored children's game of telephone illustrates perfectly the problems in transmission of any oral tradition. After the message has passed all around the circle, the last child announces it in a comically garbled form. We bring less ready humor when messages to which we wish to grant grave authority have also become garbled in transmission.

Any believing person, even the most rational, will admit that in contradistinction to knowledge and opinion (Greek: *epistēmē* and *doxa*), belief will always include a nonrational element. Even this claim contains a problematic kernel that illustrates the point of this chapter. A certain hyperbolic formulation is often attributed to Tertullian: *credo quia absurdum est*—I believe because it is absurd (otherwise it would be rational knowledge). However, what Tertullian actually wrote is *et mortuus est Dei Filius; prorsus credibile—quiea ineptum est*: "The Son of God has died; this is absolutely credible—because it is inept."[1] The difference between these two terms—"absurd" and "inept"—consists of delicate nuances,

---

1. Tertullian, *de carne Christi* 5 (Evans, 19; Migne, PL 2.806). According to the OED, "inept" means "not suited for the intended purpose," but in a more positive sense, it means "folly"; "absurd" means "tasteless, insufferable to the ear."

187

making ineptitude an awkwardness and absurdity a defiance of reason and common sense.

At times we are beset by both absurdities and ineptitudes in our English translations of the Bible. Christological claims such as the Virgin Birth, the Atonement, and the Resurrection are inept, in the best sense of the word, but are not necessarily absurd. However, certain sayings in our English bibles are patently absurd. As we shall see, in some instances this absurdity can be explained by errors in transmission, just like the children's game of telephone. In other instances, the absurdity is due to the living character of language, in that words change meaning from the usage in previous English translations. In yet other instances, the syntax and grammar in one language prevent capturing the sense of a phrase in its original language. Any translator is faced with the complicated problem of how to translate a metaphor from one culture to another and still have it make sense.[2]

The Translator's Dilemma

In the twelfth century, R. Yehuda ibn-Tibbon was well aware of translation's pitfalls when he set out to translate the classical book on spirituality, now known as "The Duties of the Heart," by R. Baḥye ben Yosef ibn-Paquda. Ibn-Paquda, a friend of Maimonides' father in Cordoba, had written his book in the literary Arabic of the eleventh century, a language known for its extensive use of metaphor and simile, and ibn-Tibbon wanted to make it more broadly available by translating it into Hebrew. Because this was the first book translated from Arabic into Hebrew, ibn-Tibbon was faced with a pioneering set of problems and no precedent to draw upon. He found his task so difficult that he began his Hebrew translation of ibn-Paquda's work with a lengthy essay on the difficulties of translation. Among the problems he identified was that a metaphor in one language may make no sense when translated literally into another, and thus a translator is compelled to take certain limited liberties in the course of working. Ibn-Tibbon wrote:[3]

---

2. According to a famous Italian proverb, *Traduttori, traditori* ("Translators, traitors"). John Ciardi has observed: "Translation is the art of the best possible failure." 3. Ibn-Tibbon's introduction to Baḥye ibn-Paquda, *Duties of the Heart* (Tzifroni, 60–61); compare Maimonides' advice on translation to Samuel ibn-Tibbon, son of Yehuda (*Iggerot*, Shilat, 2.530ff.; Marx in HUCA). Ibn-Tibbon's essay is surely the source of Elias Levita's identical comments near the end of his introduction to his sixteenth-century *Lexicon Chaldaicum*. A philosophy similar to ibn-Tibbon's here

At times a translator will need to transfer an idiomatic expression which presents itself in one language, into a compatible idiom which resembles or approximates it in the language into which he is translating. At other times he will need to alter a mashal or a nimshal[4] which does not fit the cultural frame of reference in the second language, into a mashal or a nimshal which is similar and which performs in the same manner.

The most important principle is that he understand the idiomatic character both of the language from which he is translating and the language into which he is translating, and that thereby he understand the author's intentions in an accurate and fitting manner,[5] so that the translation will reflect accurately both the author's emotional tenor and the concept he intends to convey. Once the translator has digested this basic principle, he can exercise some creativity in his manner of translation and his choice of parallelisms, as long as he is faithful to capture the intent of the author.

We find this to be the case with the early translators of scripture, that is, those skilled translators were obviously adept at the principle of substituting one figurative idiom for another which was idiomatic in the language to which they were translating. Onqelos, for example, translated the Hebrew idiom "they went out with a raised hand" [be-yad ramah] into a compatible imagery in Aramaic as "with a bared head" [be-reish galei], for this was the way to express in Aramaic "one who refuses to take flight."[6] Indeed we discover that any number of translators and exe-

---

stated can be found in Moses ibn-Ezra, *Iyyunim ve-Diyyunim*, 225–27, including a whole list of biblical metaphors that could be abbreviated parables. Goldin in *Midrash*, 240–52, also has an excellent essay on translation and aggadah.

4. *Mashal u-melitzah*, quoting Prov. 1:6. Zer-Kavod's commentary to the Proverbs passage (2 n14) begins correctly that the root of *melitzah* is *malatz*. However, his translation of the word as "pleasant" (ref. Prov. 3:17) is mistaken, for the dragoman by translating is not making a text more "pleasant." Rather, I accept the interpretation of Judah Shapira (Frankfurter) to Gen. 42:23, that *melitzah* is the translation or explication of a mashal, simply borne out by the *parallelismus verborum* that the sages presented their ideas in figurative speech (like parables) that to the uninitiated sounds like enigma (see Pseudo ibn-Ezra to Prov. 1:6). Such an interpretation, that *mashal u-melitzah* refers to a mashal and its nimshal, is supported by Yonah Gerondi ad loc.; Joseph and David Qimhi in Talmage, 4 and 332; Saadya Gaon and ibn-Nahmias ad loc. See Zer-Kavod's additional explication of Prov. 1:6 in "Hiddot."

5. The word here is *ofen*; see appendix 1 on Prov. 25:11.

6. Ex. 14:8; Num. 33:3. Ibn-Tibbon errs in suggesting "one who refuses to take flight"; compare the same expression at Num. 15:30, where it is obvious that no one is trying to flee; and see Onqelos to Deut. 32:27 and Targum Jonathan to

getes have translated the Bible, Mishnah, and Talmud into various languages, and yet we see that there is no consensus or uniformity in their translations. One says a passage means so-and-so; another says the passage means such-and-such!

Any translation, then, is always both a work of art and an emphatic craft of interpretive commentary. Done well, it sustains the meaning of the original but in words both familiar and comprehensible to the reader of the second language. Done poorly, idioms are awkward or obscure, thereby casting the text's original meaning into doubt. Furthermore, in making adaptations to the second language, any translator must necessarily inject his or her personal opinion into the choice of words, for no language parallels another exactly, yet once such a choice is made all nuancing in the original language is lost and a "foreign" nuancing or even new voices are added from the repertoire of the new language.

The problems of exegesis and lost nuancing were addressed by Shelomo ibn-Parḥon in his twelfth-century work entitled *Maḥberet ha-Arukh*:[7]

> "Know this, that I have been dealing so far with the plain meaning [*peshat*], and not with the midrashic [*derash*]. I need to emphasize this, since you may note that some of my explanations do not conform to the words of our sages. Do not assume that my explanation conflicts with

---

Judges 5:9 (Sperber, 2.55). This transformation of idiom is not unique to Onqelos. We find the same transformation between "with a raised hand" and "with a bared head" in tannaitic literature; see M. Avot 3:12 (Taylor, 51 n28–29); *Sifrei ba-Midbar* (Horowitz, 120–21). In keeping with Num. 15:30, BT Sanhedrin 101b and Rashi thereto explain that to remove one's tefillin in the presence of one's teacher is an act of baring one's head, and therefore of defiance and disrespect. Phylacteries are a symbol of subordination, and doffing them is the opposite; see BT Sanhedrin 101b on 1 Kgs. 11:27; and Hildesheimer, 1.494 (playing on the distinction between spatial *befanav* and temporal *lefanav*). Rashi to Ex. 14:8 (Silbermann, 70) and Adler's *Netinah la-Ger* to loc. cit., like ibn-Tibbon, seem not quite to get the point. To tie this discussion to appendix 1, it may be claimed that *megalei panim ba-Torah* means "to reveal a facet of the Torah which is not among the 70 facets," and thereby to act in brazen defiance of tradition; see Eruvin 54b; *Mekhilta* (Horowitz and Rabin, 15 lines 15–16); Avot 3:14 (Herford, *Ethics*, 80; Taylor, 65); Bacher, *Erkei*, part 1, 101–2, esp. n2; and Lieberman, *Mekhkarim*, 545–46. However, according to *Sifrei ba-Midbar* to Num. 15:22 (Horowitz, 120), *megalei panim ba-Torah* means "twisting the meaning of the Torah."

7. Page 11b, at the very end of Ḥeleq ha-Diqduq. The text printed in the Stern edition has been censored by Christian overseers. This text is restored, based on an early manuscript at Hebrew University, Jerusalem.

theirs, for the method of plain reading is one thing and homiletic exegesis is another [so we must approach them as complementary in their difference, rather than contradictory]. Now when the gentiles—who use all sorts of translations of the Bible, each claiming to have captured the plain meaning of the text—ask you to explain to them some of the midrashic interpretations which originated with our sages, they will then refute you, saying: "You are twisting what we know to be written in scripture, and you are trying to explain it in a way that we do not recognize." They will refute you in this manner because they have a text which [because it is a translation] has erased the "seventy faces of the Torah" in which we discover multiplex meanings, nor do they comprehend the thirteen hermeneutical rules which traditionally are applicable to the Torah.[8] The rules and methods at the beginning of this book are written out so that when you get into a debate with the gentiles over the meaning of scripture, you may remember the words of our sages, "Be diligent in the study of the Torah, and know how to answer a heretic" (Avot 2:14).[9]

Ibn-Parhon's point is that Scripture cannot be discussed using any language except its original as the basis of the discussion. He is objecting most obviously to the Septuagint and the Vulgate, recognizing that once the Hebrew Bible is translated into Greek or Latin, it no longer says what the original says, for so many voices have been wiped out of the text. Without those original voices, meanings of the text that seemed so apparent to the rabbis are no longer recognizable.

STRAIGHTJACKETS OF SYNTAX

Certain idioms simply cannot translate directly into another language because the second language is not equipped to deal with the particular subtleties endemic to the first. For example, toward the end of Chapter 3, reference was made to the *kelal gadol ba-Torah*, "You shall love your neighbor as yourself" (Lev. 19:18). But this principle, subject to controversy concerning its all-comprehensive character, is not as transparent as it might first appear. In Hebrew, as a result of the technicalities of syntax, it can have two possible meanings: either (1) You shall love your neighbor as you love yourself (structured adverbially), or (2) You shall love your neighbor because you recognize that he or she is a person like you, that is, bearing the image of God just as you also bear that image (structured adjectivally). However, the Greek language cannot carry the simul-

---

8. The thirteen rules are listed at the beginning of the halakhic midrash on Leviticus, *Sifra, Torat Kohanim*; cf. Singer, *ADPB*, xxv and 13. They are summarized in English in Strack, 93–98.
9. On this passage from Avot, see Herford, *Ethics*, 61; Taylor, 1.40 n45.

taneously doubled meaning of the Hebrew and thus renders a version limited to the first meaning, the misunderstanding of which has haunted preaching ever since the rise of social psychology. Read in Greek translation, Lev. 19:18 seems to say "You shall love your neighbor as much as you love yourself." The second meaning disappears altogether as soon as the phrase is translated into the Septuagint. The limited though popular Greek reading begins with a Self which must undergo a process of assessment and acceptance before offering love to the Other. The meaning of the Hebrew original just as correctly begins with the Other and then works backward to Self. This inversion of meaning is possible only because Greek syntax cannot nuance in the same way as Hebrew syntax, and thus the complex doubled meaning of the original is obscured at the moment it is translated out of Hebrew.[10]

THE LIVING CHARACTER OF LANGUAGE

When I was in seminary in the late 1960s, with a certain sacrilegious humor typical to Episcopal seminarians we used to smirk each time John 6:10 was read in chapel: "Jesus said, 'Make the people sit down.' Now there was a great deal of grass in the place; so they sat down, about five thousand in all." For our generation, "grass" was slang for marijuana and, in an urban situation with virtually no lawns, the slang definition had quickly superseded the one intended. Many other words have changed meaning or association between the time of the standard English translations and our contemporary linguistic idiom. A "mite" is now a small bug rather than an insignificant coin; a "minstrel" (Matt. 9:23) is a Southern banjo-player rather than a funeral musician; "scrip" (Matt. 10:10) is a redeemable coupon rather than cash. Language lives, and the individual words and details of any biblical text must be claimed and reclaimed anew in every generation.

THE PROBLEM OF ERRORS IN TRANSMISSION

The primary focus of the rest of this chapter is a pericope from the Sermon on the Mount (Matt. 7:1–5, paralleled in Luke 6:37–38, 41–42) on what it means to judge another person. The King James version is perhaps most familiar:

---

10. See Jacobson, 175, especially in relation to Naḥmanides' exegesis here; and see additional notes near the end of chap. 3. Conversely, the simple definition of Zeno (Diogenes Laertius 7.23 in Hicks, 2.134) that a friend is an alter ego (*állos egó*) cannot be translated into Hebrew. Scores of Hebraists and Arabists have tried and failed; see, e.g., Maimonides to M. Avot 1.6 and Kafiḥ's note 36, and Elkoshi, 38. In semitic languages, ego is exclusively a personal pronoun, not a noun as in Indo-European languages.

(1) Judge not, that ye be not judged, (2) for with what judgment ye judge, ye shall be judged; and with what measure ye mete, it shall be measured to you in turn. (3) And why beholdest thou the mote that is in thy brother's eye, but considerest not the beam that is in thine own eye? (4) Or how wilt thou say to thy brother, Let me pull out the mote out of thine eye, and behold, a beam is in thine own eye? (5) Thou hypocrite, first cast out the beam out of thine own eye; and then shalt thou see clearly to cast out the mote out of thy brother's eye.

The plainest reading of this parable renders it incomprehensible. Structurally, a nimshal (vs. 1, "Do not judge") precedes the mashal, in this case then predetermining how we comprehend the parable that follows. Taking literally the "judgment" referred to in the nimshal, the parable that follows seems to introduce two people, one a judge and the other a defendant. In the metaphor of the parable, each is afflicted with a foreign body in his eye. The judge is holding in his eye a large wooden beam, while chiding some defendant suffering an invisible mote or a speck of sawdust in his eye. This sounds not merely inept, but downright absurd. Luther's German Bible exaggerates the imagery further by translating the Greek *karfos* (mote?) as *Splitter* (splinter), from which derives the German derogative *Splitterrichter* (splinter-judge), that is, "one who is corrupt." In Luther's "absurd" translation, the pointed metaphor feels even more harmful to the eye, and a splinter is hardly an object one could suffer for any length of time without noticing.

The Eye as the Seat of Punishment

In biblical diction, we do find an ocular metaphor for punishment with dire consequences: "Those whom you allow to remain [in the land] shall be *stings in your eyes* and thorns in your side" (Num. 33:55).[11] At first glance, the Numbers and Matthean sayings seem related, as both are about stings in the eye. However, the point of the Matthean imagery is altogether different from that of Numbers. In the Numbers metaphor, the sting is caused involuntarily by an external force, and there is no suggestion of trying to hide something in the sensitive oculum. In the Matthean parable, the judge accuses the defendant of retaining the evidence of his guilt—a stolen splinter or sawdust as corpus delicti—in his eye where

---

11. The second half is also preserved in the New Testament, at 2 Cor. 12:7: "And to keep me from being too elated by the abundance of revelations, a thorn was given me in the flesh [*skolops tē sarki*], a messenger of Satan, to harass me, to keep me from being too elated."

everyone might notice. Even a lesser foreign body would cause a person to squint, squirm, or close the eye until it was removed, as the eye is highly sensitive to any intrusion by a foreign body. The judge's accusation of the defendant's brazen flaunting seems hardly credible.

The parable goes on to imply that the defendant tried to get away with his theft, yet his crime is evident to the eye of the beholder. The beholder seems to be a judge who, though charging a defendant as a thief by detecting the stolen goods in the guilty eye, harbors a beam or a plank in his own eye! With that ungainly load, he appears in court (perhaps the *reductio ad absurdum* of "blind justice"). Even granted that we are dealing here with inflated hyperbole, the absurdity of the situation portrayed makes it incompatible with most other parables attributed to Jesus. This parable is surely intended to illuminate or visualize the evils of self-righteous critics. Instead it evokes our compassion for both the sufferers rather than arousing indignation and establishing the guilt of either. Anyone who keeps either a mote or a beam in his eye is more a fool than a scandal (compare 1 Cor. 1:23). What are we to learn from a parable comparing the pain of two fools?

The Case of the Inept Mashal

One characteristic attraction of any parable is the clever relationship between the mashal and the nimshal. Ordinarily, the mashal is designed to serve the nimshal, for the nimshal is both the more difficult lesson as well as the message justifying telling the mashal. When instead of cleverness we find an absurdity, or even an ineptitude, between the mashal and the nimshal, we may begin to unravel the puzzle by questioning the fidelity of textual transmission. Throughout this book, such questions have been raised about the complementary character of various meshalim and nimshalim attached to each other in the received texts. These are not questions about the body of the mashal or of the nimshal, but about how aptly the two fit together.

However, when we find an absurdity within the body of the mashal itself, we can be fairly certain that the text has become corrupt in the historical process of transmission. Such is the case in the parable under consideration. The precedent nimshal—"Judge not, lest you be judged"— is in itself seemingly transparent, but the mashal is confused and ultimately confounds the nimshal. The listener is prevented from identifying with the story line of the mashal because the condition of both the accuser and the accused defies the realm of physical possibility. An absurd mashal will not draw a listener into active reception of its nimshal, instead leaving the listener puzzling over the infelicitous connection between the two.

Surely Matthew's Jesus is attempting to convey to his listeners that delivering judgment upon other people, whether formally (forensically) or informally (socially), carries an inherent price: judging is likely to boomerang, wreaking worse judgment upon the critic himself than he intended to dish out. Of course such behavioral lessons are more easily learned through illustrations than through laconic statements. Jesus faced the dilemma of selecting an illustration from among several popular maxims that might best convey his particular message about the dangers of judging.

Three likely choices of the day would have been (1) the aphorism "Doctor, cure yourself," (2) the aphorism "Judge yourself first and only afterwards judge others," or (3) an extant nuclear story that has come down to us as "the mote and the beam." Any of these three might have been apt illustrations, though each differs from the others in emphasizing a particular approach to the responsibilities and dangers of judging or criticizing others. Jesus' choice of illustration from among the alternatives conveys to us the particular way in which he wished to have his listeners understand his charge that we not judge others, in order that we may not be judged in turn. Familiarity with parallel materials from classical sources affords us a more profound appreciation of the illustration chosen.

1. DOCTOR, CURE YOURSELF

A first choice might have been the popular aphorism, "Doctor, doctor, cure yourself!" The antiquity of the charge is indisputable. Apparently it was current in cultures besides the semitic, for we find this Greek fable in the ancient collection now known as *Babrius and Phaedrus*:[12]

> That denizen of the swamps who likes the shade, the frog, who lives beside the ditches, once came forth on dry land and bragged to all the creatures: "I'm a physician, skilled in the use of drugs such as no one, doubtless, knows, not even Paean who lives on Olympus, physician to the gods."
>
> "And how," said a fox, "can you cure someone else, when you can't save yourself from being so deathly pale?"

Evidence for the popularity of this proverb in rabbinic literature comes from an early midrash based on the story of Lamekh and his wives 'Adda and Zilla (Gen. 4:23–25). According to *Bereshit Rabbah* 23:4:[13]

---

12. Perry, 157 #120; see also 480 #289 and references there.
13. Theodor and Albeck, 1.224–26; Rashi to Gen. 4:24–25; Tanhuma Bereshit 1:26, 10a; *Yalqut Shimeoni* to Gen 4, ib. 38 variant; and see Kamin, 215–16.

And Lamekh said to his wives: "Adda and Zilla, hear my voice O wives of Lamekh, give ear to my speech. I have slain a man for wounding me, and a lad for bruising me. If Cain is avenged sevenfold, then Lamekh seventy and sevenfold. And Adam knew his wife again. . . ." (Gen. 4:23–25a)

R. Yossi the son of R. Hanina said,

[Just as Cain's descendants experienced death at the hand of Lamekh, so Lamekh expected his descendants to experience death, yet he wished to go on procreating.]

Lamekh asked his two wives to cohabit with him.

'Adda and Zillah said to him, "But the deluge is coming tomorrow! . . . How can we procreate at a time like this?"

Lamekh said to them, "Let us go ask Adam to arbitrate between us [whether we should be fulfilling the commandment to be fruitful (Genesis 1:28) or be worrying about the coming destruction]."

And so they went.

Adam said to [the women], "You take care of your responsibilities and God will take care of God's responsibilities [that is, go back and have intercourse with your husband; it is up to God whether you survive the flood or not]."

They replied to [Adam], *"Doctor, doctor, cure your own limp!*[14] For you have held yourself apart from Eve for the past 130 years [since the death of Abel] and have not brought her any sort of sexual gratification."

We know that Jesus was aware of this ancient aphorism about the physician's cure. Apparently the aphorism was originally a doublet: "No prophet is accepted in the prophet's hometown, and a doctor cannot cure a member of his own household."[15] Jesus quotes the second half in the synagogue at Nazareth, and then answers his own challenge with the first half

---

14. On this aphorism, see Ben Sirah 18:20; Theodor and Albeck, 1.225 n28; Elkoshi, 274 #992; *Midrash Aggadah Bereshit* 4.25 (Buber, 14); Vulgar *Tanhuma* Genesis, 11; Kohut, 1.163; Span, 88–89; M. Margulies, *Midrash ha-Gadol Bereshit*, 126; Ginzberg, *Legends*, 1.118 and notes (though he misunderstands), and sources in previous note.

15. At both POxyl 6 and GThom 31, we find the two phrases connected as though they were a single saying. At Luke 4:23 the connection between the mashal and the nimshal is not clear in the Greek text. A paroimia, like a proverb, is a nuclear parable, and therefore we might not comprehend its referent. The saying about the dishonored prophet appears in later rabbinic literature, but not from the sages, in spite of Moses Schreiber in his *Hoshen Mishpat*, Responsa 22 (5.13c) and 196 (5.74d). Ibn-Zabara (Davidson, *Sha'ashuim*, 16–17) develops it extensively. Kasher, to Ex. 2 (8.73) cites ibn-Ezra, Joseph Yavetz to Avot 3:15, and Midrash Shemuel (di Ozida); and see Elkoshi #1056 and 1106 for additional parallels. For bibliography on "the honorless prophet," see J. L. Zlotnik, 44–45, and Siker, 75, n9–10.

of the aphorism. By reversing the two halves of the doublet, he recasts it as an internal dialogue:

> And he said to them, "You will surely quote unto me the proverb, 'Physician, heal yourself.' What we have heard that you did in Capernaum, do now in your own country. In response, I quote to you, 'No prophet is accepted in that prophet's hometown'" (Luke 4:23).

Elsewhere, at Mark 2:17, Jesus is reported to have used the analogy of a doctor curing the sick to describe himself. That image is surely meant to inspire confidence. However, in the Lukan text, a physician who is ill would seem not to inspire others' confidence in his competence,[16] any more than a local boy could command authority or a corrupt judge inspire others' respect for his sense of justice. Thus "Doctor, cure yourself" does not seem to be an appropriate mashal for Jesus to use in illustrating his nimshal "Judge not," for the miserable condition of the hypocritical doctor gives the listeners reason to refuse to see themselves in the parable. Instead of conveying an image of ineptitude on the part of one who calls others to accountability, the nimshal to "Judge not" demands an illustration that promotes mutual responsibility between individuals and within the community.

2. Judge Yourself First

A second popular aphorism that Jesus might have chosen, one quite similar in tone to the nimshal at Matthew 7:1, is "Judge yourself first and only after that judge others." Again we find a parallel Greek fable in *Babrius and Phaedrus*:

> "Don't walk aslant!" said a mother crab to her young one. "Don't drag yourself crosswise over the wet rock."
>
> "Dear mother and teacher," replied the young crab, "first you walk straight yourself, then I'll do so by watching you."[17]

---

16. See *va-Yiqra Rabbah* 5.6 (M. Margulies, 118 and notes; Neusner, *Judaism and Scripture*, 203): Said R. Levi, "Pity the town whose physician has gout [and cannot walk to visit the sick], whose governor has one eye, and whose public defender plays the prosecutor in capital cases." The phrase is brought to illustrate the problem of a high priest who cannot prevent himself from sinning; he is equally ill-suited if he cannot keep his wife from sinning! For other rabbinic parallels on our inability to identify our own sins and blemishes, see Davidson, *Otzar ha-Meshalim*, 121 #1972, 150 #2465, 151 #2466, 2481, 2494.
17. Perry, 143 #109; Handford, 135, appends the nimshal "Fault-finders ought to

This philosophy that self-correction must precede any attempt to correct others appears in the midrash on 1 Samuel 25:18–31, concerning Abigail's attempts to defend her husband Nabal's refusal of hospitality to David and his troops. According to the setting, David has interpreted Nabal's refusal as a point of honor, and decides to teach Nabal the ultimate lesson: he will kill him. Realizing the long-term consequences to David if he follows through on that threat, Abigail sacrifices her pride to persuade David not to act. She goes out to meet the young warrior:

> Abigail said to David:
>
> My Lord David, [you will ultimately reign over Israel]. If the following case were to come before you then for arbitration, what would you do?:
>
> A poor man went [to his landlord] and said: "Grant me your charity by giving me one pita."
>
> The landlord coldly pretended not to hear the poor man's request. [Enraged], the poor man fell upon [the landlord] and murdered him.
>
> Now if [the family of the provoked murderer] were to come before you demanding a judgment in this case, how would you decide: [guilty, or not guilty?] You'd be put on the spot; you might hesitate, fumble, and not be able to get the words out of your mouth.
>
> But [the man's family] would say: "You, David, did you not do the same thing to Nabal when he refused you hospitality?"
>
> For is it not written [that previously Abigail argued with him]: *[David], do not let this be a reason to stumble, bumble and fumble* (1 Sam. 25:25)?
>
> Nor should you say "Since I am king, no one will dare to reprove me for my actions!"[18]
>
> Rebuke yourself in your own heart now; do not let this issue be a source of hesitation in judgment. Are you not the one appointed to appease? Are you not the judge?

---

walk straight and live straight before they set about instructing others." The idea seems to parallel the common expression in classical Greek: "Rule, but after first learning to be ruled"; see Solon 1.60 in Diogenes Laertius (Hicks, 1.61); and compare Plato, *Laws* 6.762e (Bury, 10.431); Plutarch, *Moralia* 780b (Fowler, 10.54–57); Seneca, "On Anger" 2.10, 6 (Basore, 187).

18. This is a perfect example of *para basileōs ho nomos agraphos*, as referred to in Chap. 2, n19.

David answered, It is written: *You shall certainly rebuke your neighbor* (Lev. 19:17).

But it is also written: *Straighten out yourself, and then straighten out others* (Zeph. 2:1).

[Nimshal] *If you wish to rebuke, first rebuke yourself, and afterwards rebuke others.*[19]

Interestingly, Rashi, in his commentary on the story of Lamekh and his wives at Gen. 4:25, substitutes this aphorism on rebuking for the one cited previously, "Doctor, cure yourself":[20]

Lamekh [and his wives] came to see Adam, and Lamekh complained about them.

Adam pronounced the judgment [on the women]: "Is it for you to be overly particular regarding the edicts of God? You do your wifely duties and God will take care of his duties."

[The women replied] to [Adam]: "*Judge yourself first!* Have you not refused your wife these past 130 years ever since, through you, death was decreed as a punishment?"

Whereas *Bereshit Rabbah* to Genesis 4:25 (cited above) has "Doctor, cure yourself," Rashi to the same verse in Genesis brings "Judge yourself first." The two phrases certainly do not mean the same thing, and one must wonder at Rashi's reason for altering the midrash. It is possible that Rashi was using a different text of the midrash, though no such alternative text is presently known to scholars. It is more likely that Rashi wished to alter the emphasis of the midrash. "Doctor, cure yourself," delivered from 'Adda and Zilla to Adam, sounds harsh and disrespectful, as though they were accusing him of hypocrisy, and of failure to inspire confidence in them. On the other hand, "Judge yourself first" sounds more like a plea for equity and equality: why should the women be ordered to comply with the mitzvot when Adam, in his grief over Cain and Abel, seems unable to observe the husbandly behavioral norms?

---

19. *Midrash Shemuel* (Buber, 59a), corrected according to *Midrash Tehillim Shoher Tov* 53:10 (Buber, 287–88 and notes); see also *Yalqut ha-Makhiri* to Zeph. 2:1 (Greenup, 13), and Ginzberg, *Legends*, 4.117 and 6.275. On the medieval Islamic use of Lev. 19:17, see Lazarus-Yafeh, 145–46.
20. Rashi in Silbermann, 1.21; compare *Bereshit Rabbah* 23:4. It should be noted that Theodor and Albeck, 1.225, also conflate the two sayings in their note. Kamin (*Rashi*, 215–16) pays no attention to Rashi's deviation.

The foundational text for the wordplay in the aphorism on rebuking is Zephaniah 2:1. The KJV translates: "Come together and hold assembly [*hitqoshashu va-qoshu*], O shameless nation, before you are driven way like the drifting chaff." The Hebrew phrase is a language doublet, combining reflexive *hitpael* and simple *kal* plural imperatives. The unusual phrase has been dealt with repeatedly in the rabbinic literature but without consonance of opinion. The standard translation, "Come together and hold assembly," seems at first glance to have no apparent relation to Jesus' charge to "Judge not," but we shall see that their connection in Hebrew is less inept than in English. Talmudic and rabbinic opinions over the meaning of this obscure doublet, *hitqoshashu va-qoshu*, can be divided into six categories:

1. *Gather chaff or sticks*. The Targum Pseudo-Jonathan, the Peshitta, Symmachos, and Rashi to Zephaniah 2:1 all seem to understand the doublet in the sense of Ex. 5:12, to gather stubble (*qash*) for straw.[21]

2. *Assemble, gather together*. The earliest known Jewish biblical commentary, by the ninth-century Persian Karaite Daniel al-Qumsi, renders Zephaniah 2:1 as "Foregather and cause others to gather unto God in order to hear the reproof of the prophets."[22] The Septuagint interprets the doublet in a similar manner and thus informs most English translations.

3. *Adorn*. A third understanding, based on the Hebrew word *qishut* (a piece of jewelry that beautifies the wearer), accepts the phrase as meaning "Adorn yourself before adorning others."[23] This exegesis bears close resemblance to the first meaning of Leviticus 19:18 referred to above, "Love your neighbor as yourself": one first "adorns" oneself with self-appreciation and self-confidence, and only afterward turns outward to others.

4. *Compare, analogize*. Rashi to BT Baba Metzia 107b understands the doublet's origin as *heqesh*, "to make an analogy or a comparison."[24] Accordingly, the phrase should be translated deontologically: "Compare how you are to what you should be, before you compare others to what you think they should be."[25] Elsewhere, at 2 Samuel 19:43–44, Rashi again

---

21. R. Shemuel ben Meir to Baba Batra 60b also understands it this way. See also Bacher, *Palestinische Amoräer*, 3.599; Moses ibn-Gikatilia as cited in ibn-Ezra to Zeph. 2:1 also prefers this reading, based on the radix *qavatz*. BDB, 905, admits that the Zephaniah doublet is not related to *qashash*, in the sense of straw, but does not know how to understand it, conjecturing that it should be emended to read *hitbosheshu ve-voshu*. Max Margolis ("Tzephaniya" in Kahane, *Perush Madda'i*, 103) allows this emendation as a second choice.

22. This interpretation is supported by Urbach, *Pitron Torah*, 229.

23. See *Aikhah Rabbah* 3.41 (Buber, 136); Bacher, *Palestinische Amoräer*, 1.357.

24. The reading is missing from Maarsen, 1.80 and notes, but is found in Rashi to *Miqraot Gedolot* to Zeph. 2:1 and in parallel sources.

25. Compare *Yalqut Shimeoni* to Jer. 21. See Erasmus: *quod alliis vitio vertas ipse*

offers this as the preferred interpretation, suggesting that one first measures oneself according to a given norm or set of standards and only afterward measures others according to the same standards. David Qimhi attempts to draw two meanings closer, relating the phrase to Numbers
15:32, the story of the man who gathered sticks on the Sabbath (me-
qoshesh) and so blemished its sanctity. He interprets the phrase to mean
"First search out your own blemishes, and then search out the blemishes
of others afterwards."[26] Ibn-Janah understands the meaning as moqesh, to
ensnare, based on Isaiah 29:21; hence "Ensnare yourself before you set out
to ensnare others."[27]

   5. *Get wise, become mature.* Ibn-Ezra and others connect the phrase,
by way of 1 Samuel 12:2, to *qashish*, to be mature or wise; hence, "Make
sure you yourself are mature before drawing conclusions about the maturity of others."[28] Ibn-Ezra may well have been drawing upon Ben Sirah
18:19(20) as his source of inspiration: "Before judgment, examine yourself,
and in the hour of visitation, you shall find forgiveness."

   6. *Shoot straight, straighten out.* The most useful understanding for
our purposes seems to be that of Reformation-period grammarian Elias
Levita, as offered in his *Lexicon Chaldaicum.* Arguing from an interpretation of Ex. 19:13, he understands the root of the Zephaniah phrase to be
qashat, "to go straight," as an arrow goes straight to its target. Hence he
interprets, "Set yourself straight before setting others straight."[29] BT Baba
Batra 60b understands the radix Q-Sh-T in the same manner: "*I will in-*

---

ne feceris, "do not project onto others the faults from which you yourself suffer"
(Erasmus, Proverb 33, *Opera Omnia*, 2.926); and see Baba Metzia 59b. Erasmus
may have been influenced by Rashi.
26. Trans. by King, 402–3; compare *Aikhah Rabbah* to Lam. 3:40 (Buber, 68a).
Ginzei Schechter, 1.128 line 8, 130 line 24, argues that a judge must be without
blemish and above reproach. Elkoshi #927 suggests *Loripedem rectus derideat,
Aethiopem albus*, "Let the straight-legged man laugh at the club-footed, the white
man at the blackamoor" (Juvenal, *Satires* 2.23 [Ramsay, 18–19]). Cf. BT Qiddushin
70a.
27. Ibn-Janah, *Shorashim*, 446, radix Q-V-Sh; but read the whole entry carefully.
28. Max Margolis in Kahane, 103, rejects any sense that sagacity is synonymous
with age, because not all elderly people are mature or wise. A member of the
Sanhedrin was called a *zaken*, and like a senator could be young or old. See *sen-
atus* in Lewis and Short, 1668, versus *senectus* on 1669; and *yashish* in Even-Shoshan's *Millon*; Job 12:12; Prov. 8; *Sifra* to Lev. 19:32 (Weiss, Jer. reprint, 92a); BT
Qiddushin 32b; *Bereshit Rabbah* 59 (Theodor and Albeck, 635); *Tanhuma*, Chayye
Sarah (Buber, 60a); Ginzberg, *Unknown*, 332 n42.
29. He cites as support BT Sanhedrin 18a and 19b, and JT Taanit 2, 65a; see also
Jastrow, 1429; Ben-Yehudah, 6240 and 6243 n1; *Midrash Tehillim* 91.3 (Buber,
199a n22) and 53.1–2 (144a note); D. Qimhi to Zeph. 2:1.

struct you and teach you in the way you should go (Ps. 32:8). I will lead you back *straight* [qoshetkha] to the good path."[30] Having laid out an exegesis, ibn-Ezra proceeds to connect *qosh* with the radix *Y-Kh-H̱* ("reprove") in Leviticus 19:17, and so translates the doublet "Reprove yourself, and only afterwards reprove others." It is this last understanding which connects most closely with the opening charge in Matt. 7:1, "Do not judge, so that you may not be judged."

Given the length of explanation above, it should be obvious that the wordplay in Zephaniah 2:1 is a sophisticated and complicated pun.[31] It can in fact be claimed to be a PRDS structured around the variety of meanings possible in the doublet, depending upon which radix is chosen to define *hitqoshashu va-qoshu*. It may well be a pun so complex as to be inappropriate for the rough Galilean Aramites to whom Jesus addressed his Sermon on the Mount, and hence, like "Doctor, cure yourself," an inappropriate choice.

3. The Judge or the Critic?

The third possibility, ultimately chosen to illustrate Jesus' point about withholding judgment, seems to be a preexisting proverb now come down to us as "the mote and the beam." Again, the antiquity of the nuclear thought is apparent from classical sources. *Babrius and Phaedrus* records a related etiological tale, though without a judicatory setting:

> Prometheus was a god, but of the first dynasty. He it was, they say, that fashioned man from earth, to be the master of the beasts. On man he hung, the story goes, two wallets filled with the faults of humankind: the one in front contained the faults of others, the one behind the bearer's own [faults], and this was the larger wallet. That's why, it seems to me, people see the failings of each other very clearly, while unaware of those which are their own.[32]

30. See also *Tanḥuma* Lekh Lekha [4], Buber, 31b and va-Yera [45], 57a; Rashi to Mishlei 15:24; *Midrash Tehillim Shoḥer Tov* (Buber, 122a [18]); *Pesiqta Rabbati* (Friedman, 170a [54]); *Yalqut ha-Makhiri* Psalms (Buber, 207 #12).
31. Additional sources that further nuance the complexity are BT Baba Metzia 107b; Baba Batra 60b; Sanhedrin 18a and 19a; Rashi to Gen. 4:25 and 2 Sam. 19:44; Abramson "Divrei HaZa"L," 275.
32. Trans. Perry, 83 #66. Handford, 179 gives the nimshal: "This story satirizes the busybody who, blind as regards his own affairs, concerns himself about other men's." There is a similar version on Perry, 317 #10; for parallels see Catullus 22.21 (Cornish, 27); Persius, *Satires* 4.23–24 (Ramsay, 361); Horace, *Satires* 2.3.299 (Passage, 71); St. Jerome, *Letters* 102.2.1 (*Epistulae*, 2.235); "Verba Seniorum" in *PL* 73.1014 #18; and Erasmus, Adage 1.6, 90 in *Coll. Works*, 32.59

The same theme appears twice in the Talmud and with two different settings:[33] The first setting is a forensic setting, creating a word picture of a judge in a courtroom, followed by the picture of two men arguing in the marketplace. The second setting concerns the ethics of social intercourse. Both settings make creative use of supportive biblical texts, though in either case the texts are read in an unorthographic manner. According to BT Baba Batra 15b:[34]

> Rabbi Yoḥanan said:
>
> *And it came to pass in the days of the judges' judging* (Ruth 1:1).
>
> [What is the meaning of "judges' judging"? Woe to a generation which judges its judges!]
>
> [A courtroom scene:]
>
> The judge says to the defendant: "Take that toothpick from out of your teeth!"
>
> [This charge provokes the indignant retort of the accused]: "Take that beam from off your forehead."
>
> [Just as in the marketplace:]
>
> One says to the other: *Your silver has become dross!* (Isa. 1:22) [that is, you have cheated me in the market place by paying me with adulterine silver coins!].
>
> The other replies: *Your wine is adulterated with water!* (Isa. 1:22) [that is, you have cheated me in your own home by serving me watered-down drinks!]

The talmudic saying about "judges' judging" is a pun upon the opening of the Book of Ruth, which could be rendered in pedantic literalism

---

("Non videmus manticae quod in tergo est"). E. E. HaLevi (*Erkei*, 48 and 51) suggests further parallels in Cicero, Seneca, and Plato. This fable seems to be the source for the mysterious saying in BT Yoma 22b, *quppah shel sheratzim* ("a can of worms"); see also Bialik, *Sefer ha-Aggadah*, 566 #52, and C. White, 141 and 169. And see M. Negaim 2:5, "The high priest sees the blemishes of everyone, but he does not see his own."

33. For notes and variant texts, see *Ruth Rabbah* 1; *Yalqut Shimeoni* to loc. cit.; Bialik, *Sefer ha-Aggadah*, 81 #13. See also *Sefer ha-Aggadah*, 541 #34 and 542 #45, and parallels to BT Arakhin 16b; M. Stein, *Bin Tarbut*, 217–25.

34. See also Bialik, *Sefer ha-Aggadah*, 81 #13; Hakham, Isaiah, 15; Rabbinowicz, *Diqduqei* to Baba Batra 15b and Arakhin 16b; Saul Katz; and Joseph Cohn.

"In the days of judging the judges." Although the plain meaning (*peshat*) is obviously that the judges were judging, the gerund form may also be taken in the objective sense, that the judges were being judged by others. In this latter sense it is interpreted in the same general manner that Jesus seems to use in Matthew 7:1–2, "Do not judge, so that you may not be judged. For with the judgment you make you will be judged, and the measure you give will be the measure you get." In other words, do not charge and chide others when you yourself are prone to charges. Woe to the generation in which judges have lost the prerequisite respect of their authority and have forfeited the moral force of their office.[35]

Also of interest in the preceding parable is the manner in which the indirect discourse of the prophetic text has been turned into direct discourse. Isaiah 1:22a ("silver to dross") is treated as an accusation, and 1:22b ("adulterated wine") as a retort, a clever method by which a received text is made applicable to a contemporary situation. Here is an apt illustration of the point that axioms and metaphors can be foreshortened versions of parables or stories. As we shall see, even our saying in Matthew 7 is in fact a foreshortened parable, though most of the standard lists of gospel parables by Christian scholars do not include it.

The second talmudic setting, other than the forensic, deals with the implementation of Leviticus 19:17 by asking for the credentials and qualifications of the person who undertakes to rebuke and correct others. As opposed to a forensic setting, here the same story is set within a commentary on the ethics of social intercourse. According to BT Arakhin 16b:

> From whence do we learn that
>   when one sees his comrades doing something improper,
>   he is obligated to rebuke him?
>   It is said, *You shall rebuke your neighbor* (Lev. 19:17).
>   Rebuke, without ceasing!
> From whence do we learn that [if the first rebuke was ineffective]
>   he shall return and rebuke him again?
>   [Because] the text states: 'surely rebuke' all ways.[36]

---

35. Hence Rabbeinu Gershom paraphrases the Baba Batra passage, "If the judge said to a man, Remove the splinter which you have acquired by theft, he would reply to the judge, Remove the beam which is larger than this splinter." RaLBaG thus understands the splinter-beam proverb as referring to a theft, as does Samuel Edels, ad loc.

36. Like *hitqosheshu va-qoshu*, the Hebrew phrase here translated "surely rebuke" is actually a language doublet, combining a causative *hif'il* and simple *kal* plural imperatives.

Shall one continue even to the point where the comrade blanches?[37]
[No, for] it is written, *you shall not suffer sin on his account* (Lev. ad loc.).

It is taught in a baraita:

Rabbi Tarfon said, "I wonder if there is anyone in this present generation who will readily accept reproof when delivered.[38] If someone says to
another, 'Take that toothpick from between your teeth!'

The other will respond back to him, 'Take that beam from between
your eyes!'"

R. Eleazar b. Azariah [was skeptical]: "I wonder if there is anyone in
this generation who even knows how to rebuke?"

R. Yohanan b. Nuri said, "I call heaven and earth to witness for myself
that often was Aqiba rebuked through me because I used to complain
against him before our Rabban Gamaliel, and all the more [Aqiba] showered
love upon me, to fulfill what has been said: *Reprove not a scorner, lest he
hate thee; reprove a wise man and he will love thee* (Prov. 9:8).[39]

A parallel version from *Sifrei Devarim* is even more terse. It will be noted
that the specific parable of the toothpick and the beam is missing from
this earlier version:[40]

These are the words that Moses addressed to all of Israel (Deut. 1:1).

Hence we learn that all of them were deserving of rebuke and able to
stand up under rebuke.

---

37. According to Cicero *De Amicitia* 24.89 (Falconer, 197), advice and rebuke will
be received properly only when given in a spirit of kindness.
38. Compare Anthony, #23, in Ward, *Sayings*, 5: Abba Anthony said, "God does
not allow the same warfare and temptations to this generation as he did formerly,
for men are weaker now and cannot bear so much." This Tarfon is assumed by
some to be the same person addressed in Justin Martyr's *Dialogue with Trypho*.
39. See Finkelstein, *Aqiba*, 112–14 for an account of Aqiba's being rebuked. Moses
ibn-Ezra (*Iyyunim ve-Diyyunim*, 227) connects the phrase "Remove the beam"
with the interruption of prophecy. On the verb *Y-Kh-H* taking the direct or the
indirect object, see Hirsch, *Pentateuch* to Leviticus, 523 .
40. *Sifrei Devarim* 1 (Finkelstein, 3–4; Hammer, 24), and compare *Sifra* to Lev.
19:17 (Weiss, 89b); see also Bialik, *Sefer ha-Aggadah*, 542 #45; Bacher, *Aggadot
ha-Tannaim* part 2.87 notes. Zunz (*Gesammelte Schriften*, 3.294) points out that
the parable of the toothpick is often quoted here right after the Tarfon section, and
attributed to Tarfon, but that the original sources seem not to contain the parable.
On these three sages together, see M. Makkot 1.10.

R. Tarfon said, "I swear by the Temple service, I doubt if there is anyone in this generation who is fit to rebuke others."

R. Eleazer b. Azariah said, "I swear by the Temple service, I doubt if there is anyone in this generation who is able to receive rebuke."

R. Aqiba said, "I swear by the Temple service, I doubt if there is anyone in this generation who knows how to rebuke."

To clarify whether Jesus' use of "the mote and the beam" was intended as a commentary upon the judicial system of his day or upon social ethics, the details of the parable itself will need to be examined, with a particular concentration on the manner in which words and idioms are translated from one language to the next.

The Toothpick and the Beam

We return to the texts from BT Baba Batra 15b and BT Arakhin 16b to compare their Hebrew and Aramaic vocabulary with the Greek vocabulary of Matthew 7:3–5 and its Latin translation in the Vulgate. According to the talmudic texts:

> Take that toothpick [*qisam*] from between your teeth [*bain shenekha*]!

> Take that beam [*korah*] from between your eyes [*bain 'ainekha*]!

The Hebrew *korah* (beam) appears in Greek in the Matthean version of the parable as *dokos*, a joist, a bearing or main beam especially of a floor or a roof. The Vulgate chooses *trabem*, so that all three of the languages carry the same meaning: a large wooden beam used to bear heavy weight in the construction of buildings. The only correct English translation, then, is "beam"; "plank," also used in some English translations, is too modest.

Karphos is used in the Greek text of to translate the Aramaic *qisam*.[41] From antiquity, the Greek *karphos* has included the meaning of toothpick, though it has more frequently meant twig or sprig.[42] The more specialized

---

41. The word *qisam* is nearly a technical term for a woodchip used as a toothpick; see M. Betzah 4:6 and BT Betzah 33a–b; targums Pseudo-Jonathan and ben Uzziel to Num. 15:32 (Clarke, 176; Ginsberger, 255) and 25:3 (Clarke, 191; Ginsberger, 277); M. Shabbat 6:6, M. Hullin 9:4; M. Yadaim 2:2.

42. For *karphos* as toothpick, see Alciphron, *Epistolographus* 1:22 (Benner and Fobes, 241 #39); as twig, see the LXX to Gen. 8:11 (unless the dove returned to the ark with a toothpick in its mouth!).

meaning of *karphos* apparently escaped Jerome in his Vulgate translation, for he chose the Latin *festucam*, meaning a piece of straw.[43] Once the meaning had become fuzzy subsequent to Jerome, further translations read as conjecture, leading ultimately to the use of obscure terms to avoid the confusion. The English words ordinarily chosen for the Matthean parable are either "a mote," an obsolete Middle Dutch word meaning damp dust or sawdust,[44] or the even more inappropriate "speck," meaning a spot of discoloration. Once the confusion occurred between "eyes" and "teeth," translators had no idea what to do with the object that caused the discomfort and so offered ad hoc conjectures that only further confused the parable. It well may be that *karphos* is a guess even on the part of the Greek authors or translators, for it is possible that the shift from "teeth" to "eyes" had already occurred in a sayings source at some point between the time of Jesus and the writing of the inherited Greek text, so that even the gospellers were not quite sure what to do with the parable.[45]

Where Is "Between Your Eyes"?

The idiom by which the location of the judge's beam is described— *bain ʿainekha* (literally, "between your eyes")—possesses its own history in Hebraic tradition.[46] In four places in the Pentateuch (Ex. 13:9, Ex. 13:16, Deut. 6:8, Deut. 11:18) we find the commandment of wearing phylacteries (*tefillin* in Aramaic[47]) on the head and on the arm, by tradition

---

43. *Festucam ex alterius oculo ejicere*; and see also Jerome, *Adversus Rufinum* 1.31 (NPNF2, 3.499); compare Horace, *Satires* 1.3.25–27, 3.73–74 (Passage, 23–25); and Erasmus, Adage 1.6, 91, *Coll. Works*, 32.59–60.
44. According to King, the first translator to use "mote" was Wycliff in 1380. Mite and mote, both derived from Middle Dutch, have stayed associated with their particular New Testament contexts, though according to the OED they have no significant venue in English outside the biblical text.
45. The Arabic New Testament destroys the analogy even further: "Take the wood out of your eye first, and then the dust out of your neighbor's." According to Goldziher ("Zwischen"), the splinter-beam proverb is common to Islamic tradition, cited by the Moslem commentator Meidani as "How glaring is the dust in your brother's eye, while you ignore the splinter in your own." Ibn-Merwan al-Jaziri exegetes the phrase in the sense of "the blind leading the blind" (see Matt. 15:14).
46. On the complexity of the preposition *bain*, see Orlinsky, 278–81.
47. The word "phylacteries," at times used as a synonym for tefillin, is in fact a misnomer, for a phylactery (Matt. 23:5) is an amulet, connoting a "magical charm," but not a ritual device. The word phylactery comes from the Greek for "guard-post," further emphasizing its apotropaic sense. See M. Shabbat 6:2 and

requesting the binding by leather thongs of a cubic capsule of leather containing the four pericopes of this commandment inscribed on parchment, one pericope in each of the capsule's four compartments. When the commandment is given concerning the phylacteries, one is told that "It shall be to you as a sign on your hand and as a memorial *between your eyes.*" The literalism of this translation stands in glaring contrast to the anatomical locus for the capsules as practiced by twenty centuries of observant Jews: "between your eyes" would indicate the bridge of one's nose—thus obscuring sight—whereas all the tradition of praxis indicates that the normative placement of the tefillin is somewhere on the forehead or higher. Here is a clear example of the oral tradition's remarkable deviation from the plain reading of the biblical text.

Certain sectarians who rejected the binding validity of the oral tradition found here a welcome opportunity to demonstrate the literal fundamentalism of the text's plain reading over against the adherents of the oral tradition. Sectarians insisted upon placing their phylacteries on their hand and on the bridge of their nose respectively—literally "between their eyes." We find the Pharisaic response to this sectarian practice in M. Megillah 4:8: "He who places his tefillin on his lower forehead [*mitzho*] or on his palm—follows heretical doctrine." According to Chanok Albeck, wearing the tefillin low between the eyes was the practice of the Sadducees and related fundamentalist sects, though such point of disagreement does not show up in any of the usual lists of controversy between the Pharisees and Sadducees.[48] Rashi to Megillah 24b attempts a resolution of the contention by invoking the weight of oral tradition to explain the physical geography:

> The sectarians, who hold the interpretation of the sages in contempt, prefer to follow a literalist interpretation of the text: "between thine eyes"—verbatim, "upon thy hand"—verbatim;
>
> > our sages, however, handed down an interpretation based on textual analogies which reads "between thine eyes" as a reference to the pate, the

Kelim 23:1, where tefillin and amulets are clearly distinguished from one another. Tigay attempts to minimize the distinction, but I could not find a Jewish source that agreed with him. Because the misnomer "phylacteries" is more familiar to Christian readers than *tefillin*, I will continue to use it here.

48. M. Megillah 4:8–9 in Albeck, *Moed*, 367 notes. According to Naomi Cohen (202–3), Philo seems to be most familiar with the wearing of four tiny tefillin, fastened at the top by a cord and dangling so low on the forehead that the wearer could see them with his own eyes, a description matching the tefillin found at Qumran (see Yadin).

fontanel of the infant skull, and "upon thy hand" to the biceps muscle uppermost on the arm, opposite the heart.

At issue here is the anatomical geography implied in the term *bain 'ainekha*. Where exactly is "between one's eyes"? Rashi knows that his tradition teaches one not to bind the phylactery between the eyeballs, but then can understand its received placement only as a matter of authoritative interpretation of the biblical text, opposing the "sectarian" fundamentalist interpretation. A historical study of the placement of the phylactery shows that it has been worn variously on the bridge of the nose, in the middle of the forehead, at the hairline, and even square-up on the pate. The variance of practice proves the complex definition of the phrase *bain 'ainekha*. Tannaitic evidence suggests that the specific anatomical reference point of *bain 'ainekha* is the longitudinal (vertical) line between the eyes rather than the latitudinal (horizontal). The specific placement point along this longitudinal line is indicated at M. Negaim 10:10: it is one's *qodqod*, or pate, the highest point on the top of the vertical line that runs straight down between one's eyes through one's groin to the floor. In other words, *bain 'ainekha* is an idiom in Hebrew that does not admit a verbatim translation into another language, including the Greek of the New Testament or the Septuagint. In Jesus' parable, the location of the offending object on the judge's head is not in the eye or between the eyes, but high atop the fontanel.

The meaning of this idiomatic term is not conjecture or a peculiar eccentricity of the oral tradition cherished by the tannaim. It dates back to a usage preceding the era of the Patriarchs. More than fifty years ago, a French expedition digging in Syria at Ras Shamra exposed an ancient semitic culture known as Ugaritic. Among the texts discovered there was a description of the annual contest of natural forces in the Near East, where vegetation flourishes in early spring and withers in early summer during the Hebrew month of Tammuz (see Ezek. 8:14). During the verdant season, the wadis teem with spring and rain waters streaming toward the sea (see Qoh. 1:7). This is the very season during which the mythological personage Judge Nahar is the proud supplier of his bounty, on which the insatiable sea, Prince Yamm, is dependent. However, the latter resents the condescending arrogance of his supplier. In the month of Tammuz (approximately mid-June), they meet for an extended duel, in which Judge Nahar is killed and mourned. In Ugaritic, the blow-by-blow account of this fight goes as follows:[49]

---

49. The Ugaritic text can be found in Gordon, Text #137; English translations can be found in Pritchard, *ANET*, 130–31 and Albright, "Zabul Yam."

> Strike the back [*katef*] of Prince Yamm!
> Between the arms [*bain yadayim*] Judge Nahar!
> Strike the pate [*qodqod*] of Prince Yamm!
> Between the eyes [*bain 'ainayim*] Judge Nahar!

The parallel idioms leave us no doubt that *yad* (hand, arm) is close to the *katef* (shoulder, upper back), and that *bain 'ainayim* has as its anatomical locus the *qodqod* (pate, vertex). Thus the oral tradition for locating the spot on which the tefillin are to be worn, high atop the head in line with the nose, may be vindicated by reference to a prebiblical idiom from documents that had been buried under ruins even in the days of the Patriarchs.

Social Mores of Defiance

An additional idiomatic usage pertains to our parable under consideration, for it is closely related to *bain 'ainekha* (literally: between eyes). The Hebrew *le'ainav* (literally: before his eyes) is a tautology for "brazenly displayed" in Deuteronomy 6:22. We find the same expression—*le'ainav* or related variants—used frequently in the biblical text, including Psalm 79:10, "Let the avenging of the blood of your servants which is shed be brazenly displayed [*le'ainenu*] among the nations."[50] The phrase *le'ainav* is synonymous with another, "with an upraised hand" (*be-yad ramah*), at Exodus 14:8 and Numbers 15:30, 33:3, in that both phrases signal a defiant gesture. One need only consider the sense of defiance conveyed by the raised hands of the followers of Hitler, or the confrontational salute of the Black Power movement, to grasp the ability of a hand gesture to astonish. Interestingly, and as already suggested in the excerpt given earlier by ibn-Tibbon, Targums Onqelos and Pseudo-Jonathan translate *be-yad ramah*, with a raised hand, as *resh galei*, bare-headed, that is, with your most visible part exposed. Two phrases combine at Numbers 33:3, when the children of Israel begin their exodus "with a high hand [*be-yad ramah*] before the eyes [*le'ainai*, brazenly] of the Egyptians."[51] The sense of defi-

---

50. Other typical references would include Num. 19:5, 2 Sam. 13:8, Jer. 39:6 and 52:10, Deut. 6:25, Josh. 24:17, and 2 Kings 25:7. The phrase *neged ainav* appears to carry the same sense of blatancy; see 2 Sam. 22:25, Pss. 5:5, 18:24, 26:3, 36:2, 101:3 and 7, and Job 4:16; Pseudo-Jonathan to Ex. 14:8 and Num. 33:3 (Clarke, 82 and 203).

51. See also Num. 15:30, one who acts *be-yad ramah* dishonors the Lord; compare *Sifrei ba-Midbar* 112, 120; BT Sanhedrin 99b; *Midrash ha-Gadol ba-Midbar* (Rab-

ance in all these is identical but the parts of the body used to structure the metaphor change. In this sense, they too are biblical synonyms that strengthen a single concept. Thus to carry a beam on top of one's head is doubly defiant: not only is it "between one's eyes," it is also displayed on that part of one's body is most visible, properly kept covered with a hat rather than a timber.

The Confusion of Eyes and Teeth

One further mix-up is significant in unraveling Matthew 7:1–5. *Bain shenekha*, "between your teeth," is easily confused with *bain ainekha*, "between your eyes," by a simple scribal confusion of the Hebrew letter *shin* with the Hebrew letter *ayin*, which look extremely similar if formed carelessly. Such an explanation presumes that Matthew was working with a Hebrew or Aramaic sayings source, as this could be a confusion only of the eye but not of the ear. The mix-up can work either in Hebrew or in Aramaic, at any point when a *shin* becomes spotty and faded so that the left-hand stroke of the *shin* is broken, and the single letter then appears to be two: *yod* and *ayin*. The phrase "between your teeth" has biblical precedent. According to Zechariah 9:7, "I will take away his blood out of his mouth, and his detestable things from between his teeth." Early lexicographers attest to the *bain shenekha* reading of the proverb about the splinter and the beam.[52] Ultimately, some editions of the Talmud seem to have adjusted the texts in Baba Batra and Arakhin to match the New Testament text; according to King, the earliest such adjustments began in the mid-fourteenth century.[53]

---

binowicz, 253); JT Peah 1.1 in Steinsaltz, 33; JT Pesaḥim 6.2. It should be noted that "bare-footed" is not an act of defiance, but of humility; see Ex. 3:5 and Josh. 5:15. Yet another related phrase meaning "defiance" is *gilui panim*, open-faced; see Avot 3.12, Herford, *Ethics*, 80–82; Ben-Yehudah 5002 n2 and 775; Taylor, 1.51 and 2.150; ibn-Aqnin, 96; Eruvin 69a; and Rashi thereto, where he defines "impudently, publicly." Bacher, *Erkei*, 102 n2, traces *be-rish gilui* to describe the rabbis who dared to teach Torah during the Roman ban on all such activities. *Gilui panim* is related etymologically to the name Goliath at 1 Sam. 17:8; see Sotah 42b; Kohut, 2.296; and see Cowley #37, lines 7–8; and Porten and Greenfield, 80–81.

52. Kohut, 7.147 under *qisam*; *Yalqut Shimeoni* to Ruth 1:1; *Ain Yaaqov* to Baba Batra 15b, Arakhin 16b.

53. King, 396–97, dates the beginning of this change to the Munich Codex Hebraicus 95, written in 1343. Abramson, *Baba Batra*, 26, identifies *ainekha* as the reading in regular editions of the Talmud, and at n22 insists it not be changed to *shenekha*.

As it stands originally in BT Baba Batra 15b and BT Arakhin 16b, the proverb about the splinter and the beam is a mixture of Hebrew and Aramaic. Such mixtures are not unusual for the period: the Bar-Kokhba letters, simultaneous with the New Testament period, are regularly a mixture of Greek, Aramaic, and Hebrew. In either semitic language, the *ayin–shin* confusion is pertinent. Once we understand this, it is apparent that the original form of the popular parable that Jesus seems to have chosen was not about a mote in someone's eye but a toothpick between someone's teeth, nor about a beam in someone else's eye but a figurative rafter sitting high up on his pate. The sting of the parable is felt in the contrast between two things of the same kind though not of the same size. Thus, in the saying the metaphorical toothpick represents a slight sin or a small fault of which one is guilty, whereas the beam represents a serious sin or fault that can escape the notice of no one. To those who bear the beam, Matthew 7:1–5 cautions "Judge not, lest you be judged." Such a conclusion suggests that the Matthean parable is about social ethics, rather than the judicial system of the day, for the bearing of sins and faults is a universal human condition that transcends the forensic venue.

What the Listeners Heard

Neither judging nor rebuking is a pleasant task; neither being judged nor rebuked feels good. Nonetheless, the biblical commandment envisions internal community discipline through mutual reproval: *You shall certainly rebuke your neighbor* (Lev. 19:17). Rebuking and judging are such unpleasant tasks for many people that they will avoid them whenever possible. According to Proverbs 15:12, "A scorner does not like to be reproved, nor will he go to the wise."[54] Although the scorner may not like to be reproved, it is very human to give in to the temptation to stand in judgment upon each other. The Matthean mashal under consideration reminds its listeners that before they succumb too quickly to the temptation to criticize one standing before them with a toothpick between his teeth, those who judge should first be aware of their personal vulnerability, in that a bearing-beam sits brazenly displayed on top of their own heads. One

---

54. See also Prov. 9:7–8. According to Haberman, *Miv̲ḥar ha-Pininim*, Shaar Horot, Derekh Yesharah, 53: "He who reproves one who does not wish to be reproved/ He who teaches one who does not wish to learn/ Is like one who fiddles among the dead/ Or one who screams at idols." Immanuel HaRomi, 47 to Prov. 9:7–8, points out that if one reproaches another who is unreceptive, the unwilling recipient is likely to spread gossip about the awful character of the reproacher.

can no more easily see what sits on top of one's head than one can see what hangs in a purse behind one's back. However, until one has cast a critical eye upon one's own glaring faults and sins, one has no right to evaluate the performance of others. Communal responsibility does demand that members of a community of faith support and correct each other from time to time. The sort of rugged individualism typical to American society, as well as the philosophy of "live and let live," are foreign to biblical and rabbinic Judaism and to primitive and patristic Christianity. But rebuke, criticism, and evaluation must be carried on responsibly and in a manner designed to build up the individual within the community, so that the community as a whole is strengthened. Even Jesus did not hold himself above the rebuke of others, as is obvious from story of the Samaritan woman at John 4:7 and the Canaanite woman at Matthew 15:27. The gospel accounts do not indicate that he was quick to rebuke, criticize, or even evaluate others: according to Luke 12:14, Jesus charged an antagonist, "who made me judge over you?"[55] Jesus appears to have opted instead to emphasize the individual's future potential for repentance and altered responsible behavior.

The listeners of Jesus certainly understood what he had in mind; the problem is that once the words were severed from their semitic context and translated into another language, they became not only inept but absurd. As a teacher of halakhah, Jesus enters into the conversation among Tarfon, Eliezer ben Azariya, and Aqiba. With them, he discusses the meaning and applicability of Leviticus 19:17, always within the context of loving one's neighbor. Every human being is painfully aware both of what it feels like to be unjustly accused and of the temptation to jump hastily to judgment about the behavior or values of another person.[56] The halakhic opinion delivered by Jesus, in the Matthean nimshal, suggests that judging, criticizing, reproving another person is so risky that it should be avoided except in instances where rebuke serves the good of the greater community.

The exaggerated tone of reproach and harsh criticism of the "other" typical to certain types of Christianity today has little precedent in the Gospels, and even less precedent in early Christian ascetical spirituality. In spite of the power in rabbinic Judaism of the biblical mandate "to reprove," by the fourth century c.e., the Desert Fathers and Mothers taught as well the complementary virtue of refusing to judge, seeing our temptation to evaluate others as a cardinal human sin. A number of stories are retained

---

55. Luke there echoes Ex. 2:14, clearly a social setting rather than a forensic.
56. For a poignant story on hasty judgment, see 1 Sam. 1:14–15, and BT Berakhot 31a–b (also in Bialik, Sefer ha-Aggadah, 541 #28–31).

in the tradition, attributed to various early Christian teachers of spirituality, which prove that not judging others was a foundational principle for their own continued spiritual health:

> The old men used to say, "There is nothing worse than passing judgment."[57]

> Whenever his thoughts urged him to pass judgment on something he saw, he would say to himself, "Agathon, it is not your business to do that." Thus his spirit was always recollected.[58]

> Abba Poemen said, "If a man has sinned and denies it saying 'I have not sinned,' do not reprimand him, for that will discourage him. But say to him, 'Do not lose heart, brother, but be on your guard in the future,' and you will stir his heart to repentance."[59]

> One day Abba Isaac went to a monastery. He saw a brother committing a sin and he reproved him. When he returned to the desert, an angel of the Lord came and stood in front of the door of his cell and said, "I will not let you enter." But he persisted, saying, "What is the matter?" The angel replied, "God has sent me to ask you where you want to cast the guilty brother whom you have condemned." Immediately he repented and said, "I have sinned; forgive me." Then the angel said, "Get up, God has forgiven you. But from now on, be careful not to judge someone before God has done so."[60]

John 8:7

Reference was made in Chapter 3 to the pericope from John's Gospel about the woman caught in adultery. She is brought to Jesus by the crowd and they ask his opinion on the method by which she should be punished. Jesus' answer—"Let anyone among you who is without sin be the first to throw a stone at her" (John 8:7)—emphasizes the same message as the parable of the toothpick and the beam. This text, as well as all other texts concerning capital punishment, must be read in light of the controversy detailed at M. Makkot 1:10: a synhedrion (criminal court) that carries out the death sentence, even only once in seven years, is termed "murderous." There, it is the opinion of R. Gamaliel that punishments were legislated for

---

57. Anthony #10 in Ward, *Desert of the Heart*, 2; and see Bondi, *To Love as God Loves Us*.
58. Agathon, #18 in Ward, *Sayings*, 20.
59. Poemen, #23, in Ward, *Sayings*, 143.
60. Isaac the Theban, #1, in Ward, *Sayings*, 93.

the protection of society; if one interfered with the administration of capital punishment, one exposed society to extensive criminal risk. Tarfon and Aqiba, however, held for leniency whenever possible, seeking arguments by which capital punishment could be avoided. Leniency is their intention when they insist that had they been members of the synhedrion, they would have questioned witnesses to such an extent that ultimately each one would have been disqualified, thereby terminating the proceedings for capital punishment.

Witnesses could be disqualified on a number of technical grounds, including personal shortcomings (*resha'im*).[61] The context of John 8:7 presumes the prior halakhic context of Deuteronomy 17:7, that the witnesses against an adulteress must themselves stone her to death. The "Pharisees" come to Jesus, asking if there is any way in which the witnesses can be exempted from the legal obligation to stone the woman caught in adultery. Jesus stalls for time, and then writes something in the sand—perhaps the word *resha'im*, referring to witnesses disqualified on the grounds of personal shortcomings.[62] Turning to the crowd, he asks if everyone present is of such integrity of character as to function as a kosher witness. If there is any one present who so qualifies, let him be the one to cast the first stone. Because all quickly realized their personal shortcomings (including the "judges" themselves), thus disqualifying them as witnesses who could perform the stoning, all those present drifted quietly away.[63] Then,

---

61. See Maimonides, Hilkhot Edut, *la-Am*, 9.142ff, esp. chap. 4 and source references.
62. See Ex. 23:1, and Horowitz and Rabin, *Mekhilta*, 322; however, according to Miller, 425 note, "a tenth century manuscript fills in the detail by having Jesus writing the [specific] sins of the accusers." The legal term for one who is qualified to give testimony in such a case is *Neqi ha-Daat*. However, according to Maimonides, Hilkhot Edut 10:1 (*la-Am*, 9.178): Transgressors (for example, those who have violated any injunctive commandment) are ineligible to testify as witnesses (see Ex. 23:1), nor may they give witness in the company of anyone else who is a transgressor, lest they give credence by association to the transgressor's testimony. In other words, even had there been someone present who was "without sin," he or she would have been prevented from casting the stone as long as there was anyone else present who was not "without sin." For a summary of scholarly opinion about what was written on the ground, see O'Day, 635–36.
63. On the avoidance of the death penalty, see Makkot 1.10 in Kehati, Neziqin, 2.20–21. The question of whether the Sanhedrin could execute is almost impossible to resolve on the basis of our present evidence, though most scholars seem to concur that beginning with the reign of Herod, that power had been removed from them. In John 18:31, the crowd reminds Pilate, "We are not permitted to put anyone to death." See also JT Sanhedrin 1:1 (Neusner *TLI*, 12); BT Shabbat 15a

Jesus was left alone with the woman standing before him.

He looked up and said to her, "Woman, where are they? Has no one condemned you?"

She said, "No one, lord."

And Jesus said, *"Neither do I condemn you.* Go, and do not sin again."

A Faithful Response to the Demand to Rebuke

An obvious tension exists among the epigrams "You shall surely rebuke" and "Judge not, lest you be judged." Is the religious community called to an internal policing of each other or not? "You shall surely rebuke" would suggest that there is a mutual obligation to reinforce norms and values among those who profess to have taken upon themselves the yoke of God. And yet, the dangers in such rebuke are obvious, given the human tendency to elevate oneself as judge over others whether entrusted with that responsibility or not. Christian tradition has not developed the demand to rebuke within the religious community to any significant extent. Perhaps this is because of the prominence within the gospel texts of Matthew 7:1–2 ("Judge not"), 7:3–5 ("remove your own beam first"), and John 8:7 ("Let whoever is without sin cast the first stone"). Although the traditional "Protestant" emphasis on the individual's relationship with God certainly has its lamentable dark side, it might also be argued that such rugged individualism is consistent with the gospel insistence that when we go sin-hunting, we had better start with ourselves.

Confronted with human sinfulness, both Judaism and Christianity call their faithful to begin with self-examination, and if they are not found

---

(Steinsaltz, 59); Avodah Zarah 8b; and Sanhedrin 41a (Steinsaltz, 178–79); see also R. Brown, *John*, 1.2848–50; Haim Cohn, 346–50; Sherwin-White, 35–47; E. P. Sanders, *Jesus and Judaism*, 309–18; Mantel, 268–90, 307–16; Rosenblatt; and Brandon. From these and other sources, we must conclude that a) the Sanhedrin had powers to execute only on paper, but was not actually allowed to do so during the life of Jesus, because of Herod's fear that it would use such a power against Roman collaborators; b) these powers were at any rate restricted to violations against Jewish law; c) Jesus was not charged with blasphemy or any other such "theological" crime, as only stoning would have fulfilled the required punishment; d) only those Jews who were not particularly scrupulous in the keeping of the halakhah would have been complicitous in Jesus' arrest; and e) those who were complicitous were so because they feared the Roman government's reaction to Jesus' political agitation.

worthy through their own fearless inventory, to avoid the temptation to judge others. We live in a contemporary society in which self-evaluation and self-absorption are at a premium, and yet the fundamental injunction to avoid judging others goes unheeded most of the time, both within the Church and outside it. Two stories give us a renewed focus on the dangers of succumbing to the temptation to criticize the toothpick in our neighbor's teeth while ignoring the timbers we so brazenly display above our own foreheads. The first is from Jewish literature:

> Truly just men
>   do not complain about wickedness
>   but increase justice;
> They do not complain about heresy
>   but increase faith;
> they do not complain about ignorance
>   but increase wisdom.[64]

The second is from Christian literature:

Abba Anthony predicted that this Abba Ammonas would make progress in the fear of God. He led him outside his cell and, showing him a stone, said to him, "Hurt this stone, and beat it."

[Ammonas] did so.

Then Anthony asked him, "Has the stone said anything?"

He replied, "No."

Then Anthony said, "You too will be able to do that," and that is what happened.

Abba Ammonas advanced to the point where his goodness was so great, he took no notice of wickedness.

Thus having become bishop, someone brought a young girl who was pregnant to him, saying, "See what this unhappy wretch has done; give her a penance."

But he, having marked the young girl's womb with the sign of the cross, commanded that six pairs of fine linen bedsheets[65] should be given her, saying, "It is for fear that, when she comes to birth, she may die, she or the child, and have nothing for the burial."

---

64. From "Arfilai Tohar," by R. Abraham Isaac ha-Kohen Kook, cited in Yaron, 9. English translation by Miriam Gotthold.
65. See Judges 14:12–14, as referred to in chaps. 1 and 7.

But her accusers resumed, "Why did you do that? Give her a punishment."

But he said to them, "Look, brothers, she is near death; what am I to do?"

Then he sent her away, and no old man dared accuse anyone any more.[66]

---

66. Ammonas, #8, in Ward, *Sayings*, 23.

Chapter 8

Parables with a Foreign Nimshal:
A Skeleton in the King's Closet

(Matthew 21:42–44)

The previous chapter focused on an absurdity in textual transmission that was created by a redactor's failure to understand its Jewish background. This chapter offers one theory to explain what it may mean when the images presented in a mashal and its attached nimshal, or even nimshalim, contradict each other. In this particular instance, two competing images are pasted together as though they were a mashal and a nimshal. Both are based on stock figures in the associative repertoire of Second Temple Judaism, but when juxtaposed with each other, their combination kills the effectiveness of both. The second subject of concentration is how a supposed nimshal might actually be a mashal in its own right, though truncated. Building on this truncated mashal masquerading as a nimshal, the final section of the chapter examines the difference in the messages received when a text is interpreted typologically rather than allegorically.

From time to time, certain Christian exegetes have claimed that Jesus did not draw upon the common repertoire of associative symbols in Second Temple Judaism, but rather that he used stock figures to mean something very different from what his contemporaries put forth. The obvious problem with this reasoning, usually offered in an attempt to prove the "uniqueness" of Jesus, is that had he altered the meaning of the stock figures his listeners would never have understood his parables, for the listeners would have brought such contrary associations to the words spoken. Furthermore, that there is so little literary support for this iconoclastic method of story-telling renders the attempt by some Christian scholars to shift the symbolism of stock figures unconvincing. For example, Jewish associations with the figure of "the vineyard" are so strong in Scripture that it is very difficult to imagine Jesus using that figure in any way other than as a metaphor for the people Israel, the House of Israel. The specific association is stated most clearly in a parable of Isaiah 5:1–7:

> Let me sing for my beloved a song of my lover about his vineyard:
>
> My beloved had a vineyard on a fruitful hill.[1]
>
> He broke the ground, cleared it of stones, and planted it with choice vines. He built a watchtower inside it, he hewed out a wine press in it; and he hoped it would yield good grapes.
>
> Instead, it yielded putrid [grapes].
>
> Now, then, dwellers of Jerusalem and people of Judah, you be the judges between me and my vineyard:
>
> What more could have been done for my vineyard, that I failed to do in it? Why, when I hoped it would yield good grapes, did it yield putrid?
>
> Now I am going to tell you what I will do to my vineyard:
>
> I will uproot its hedge, that it may be ravaged; I will break down its wall, that it may be trampled;
>
> And I will make it a desolation. It shall not be pruned nor hoed; and it shall be overgrown with briers and thistles. And I will command the clouds to drop no rain upon it.
>
> For *the vineyard of the Lord of hosts is the house of Israel* [*bet Israel*], and the seedlings he lovingly tended are the people of Judah.
>
> He hoped for fairness, but behold, disease;
>
> justice, but behold, a wail.

The association between vineyard and *bet Israel* is strongly established in both the Hebrew Scriptures and early rabbinic literature. This scriptural association, supported by rabbinic continuation, is the logical meaning to attach to Jesus' use of such a stock figure. There is no con-

---

1. According to ibn-Ezra (Friedläender, 26–27), the verses before this are the mashal, and the next verse is the nimshal because it describes the land of Israel. Thus, for ibn-Ezra the vineyard is a metaphor for the land of Israel, but the land of Israel is in turn a representative symbol for the people Israel. See also Hakham, *Isaiah*, 49; the Silverman *mahzor* for Yom Kippur, 294; and Mirsky, *Mahatzavtan*, 12, for a piyyut based on *va-Yiqra Rabbah* 36:2; *Yalqut Shimeoni* to Ps. 80, at sign 829; and *Ginzei Schechter*, 1.91–94 ("Midrash al Parashat ba-Midbar"). A fuller discussion of this material can be found in my "Reclaiming the Matthean Vineyard Parables."

vincing reason to shift the meaning of vineyard to "the world," or to "the Torah," or to neutralize it of any parabolic meaning at all. Nor is vineyard to be interpreted as "inheritance," as certain Christian exegetes attempt to do, particularly subsequently in Matthew 21:33–41. *Bet Israel*, the covenanted people itself, is the vineyard. The house of Israel is the recipient, not the gift, of God. Inheritance implies something that can be given or withheld. Whatever Israel's troubled relationship with God at times may appear to be, there is no scriptural witness that the relationship was dissolved—that is, that Israel has been disinherited.[2]

Matthew 21:33–43

The Wicked Tenants in the Vineyard is one of the most troubling of the Matthean vineyard parables because it has been used historically to argue that Israel has indeed been disinherited. The focus of this chapter is one of the three nimshalim attached to the Matthean parable, but the disjuncture between the mashal and the nimshalim cannot be comprehended without a cursory look at the mashal itself. Although a great deal of attention has been paid to this mashal by Christian commentators,[3] few have addressed the mashal/nimshalim disjuncture. According to Matthew 21:33–43:

> There was a landowner who planted a vineyard: put a fence around it, dug a winepress in it, and built a watchtower.[4] Then he leased it to tenants and went abroad.

---

2. The point is here belabored because the idea of the vineyard as an inheritance that can be taken away from a partner in covenant with God is an argument that plays a major role in the subsequent Christian exegesis of this and other Matthean vineyard parables, but that has no significant literary precedent in Judaism. On the permanence of God's covenant with Israel, particularly in light of Jer. 31:31–34, see Lohfink, *The Covenant Never Revoked*.

3. For historical summaries of Christian interpretations of the parable, see M. Lowe, "From the Parable of the Vineyard"; Milavec in Thoma and Wyschogrod; Derrett, *Studies*, 2.92–98; and Young, 282–316. For Jewish views on the parable itself, see David Stern in Thoma and Wyschogrod, including 79 n60; Flusser *JOC*, 558–60.

4. Beare (*Records*, 209) argues that these details are irrelevant to the parable as a whole and were surely added later by the early church once the standard interpretation of this parable had become allegorical. However, removal of these details removes much of the parallelism to Isaiah 5:1–7.

When the harvest time had come, he sent his slaves to the tenants to collect his produce.

But the tenants seized his slaves and thrashed one, killed another, and stoned a third. Again, he sent other slaves, this time a larger number; and they treated them in the same way.

Finally he sent his son to them, saying, "They will respect my son."[5]

But when the tenants saw the son, they said to one another, "This is the heir; come on, let us kill him and get his inheritance."

So they seized him, flung him out of the vineyard, and killed him.

[Listener response solicited] When the owner of the vineyard comes, how do you think he will deal with those tenants?

[Listener response reported = nimshal A] They said: "He will bring those wretches to a miserable end, and lease the vineyard to other tenants, who will let him have his share of the produce at harvest time."[6]

[Nimshal B] Jesus said to them: "Have you never read in the Scriptures, *The stone that the builders rejected has become the chief corner stone. This is the Lord's doing; it is marvelous in our sight?*" (Ps. 118:22–23)

[Nimshal C] Therefore I tell you, the kingdom of God will be taken away from you and given to a people that produces the fruits of the kingdom.

The structural relationship between the Isaianic and Matthean parables is clarified by charting them together. Matthew 21:33 parallels Isaiah 5:1–2 in a manner that would have been unmistakable to a Second Temple Jewish audience.

---

5. The parable logically concludes here. Perhaps this is the form in which Jesus narrated it. The next two verses ("But when the tenants . . . and killed him") may be either a dominical addition or the addition of one of the Matthean redactors. The same two verses are included in the Gospel of Thomas #65 as part of the parable, but the nimshalim attached to the Matthean version are a separate pericope in Thomas, subsequent but not attached to the Wicked Tenants.
6. The intervention here of a specific listener response (Transition + "They said . . .") seems to confirm that the parable ended earlier, either at "respect my son" (which would leave it in its simplest classical form) or at "and killed him." If Jesus were going to add a nimshal, logically it would be attached to the end of the mashal without the intervening listener response.

Isaiah 5	Matthew 21
My beloved had a vineyard. . . .	There was a landowner who planted a vineyard;
he tilled . . . cleared . . . planted	he put a fence around it
and built a watchtower in it	hewed out a winepress
and also hewed out a wine press . . .	and built a watchtower
	then he leased it to tenants and went abroad.
and he expected that it should yield good grapes, but it yielded putrid	

This Matthean parable, the Wicked Tenants in the Vineyard, is certainly one of the most controversial parables in the New Testament. Most scholars reject its dominical origin, but such a claim does not seem necessary. The key to the puzzle must lie in the definition of "vineyard." In the parable of the Laborers in the Vineyard (Matt. 20:1–16) and the parable of the Two Sons (Matt. 21:28–32),[7] a Jewish Jesus addresses a Jewish audience with parables about people within *bet Israel*, within the vineyard. In neither of these other two parables is it the case that the jealous early laborers and the disobedient son represent the Jews whereas the latecoming laborers and the obedient son represent the gentiles.

So too in the Parable of the Wicked Tenants: the tenants do not represent Jews, ultimately to be displaced by gentiles. Rather, the message is transparent once the Wicked Tenants is paralleled with another parable from *Sifrei Devarim*. With the two side by side, a case can be made that the tenants should be identified with the non-Jews, or at least with those who have turned their backs on Judaism.

---

7. One of the more interesting exegeses of the parable of the Two Sons is by Kierkegaard, *Fear and Trembling*, 253; see also the important footnote on the parable in Miller, 97, and Derrett, *Studies*, 1.76–84. The Two Sons is another parable with a strong pre-Matthean tradition; it should be compared with J. von Arnim, 1.131, the story of the two slave boys who went looking for Plato (see Flusser, *Yahadut*, 179–80).

For the Lord's portion is His people, Jacob His own allotment [Deut. 32:9].

This is like a king who owned a field and consigned it to tenant farmers. The tenant farmers began to steal [from] it.

He took it away from them and gave it to their sons. These then began to be worse than the first.

He took it from their sons and gave it to their grandsons. They, in their turn, were worse than the previous generation.

Then a son was born to the king.

The king then said to the tenants, "Go out from that which is mine; you can no longer remain in it. Give me my share, so that I may acknowledge it and care for it."

[Nimshal] In the same way, when Abraham our father came into this world, there arose from him unworthy offspring—Ishmael and all the sons of Qetura.

Isaac came into the world. There arose from him unworthy offspring—Esau and all the princes of Edom. They began to be worse than the first.

And when Jacob came, there did not arise unworthy offspring from him, but all the sons born to him were fit, like himself, as it is said, *Jacob was a mild man who stayed in camp* [Gen. 25:27].

Whence did the Omnipresent recognize that the vineyard is his share?

From Jacob, as it is said, *The Lord's portion is His people. . . .* [Deut. 32:9], *for the Lord has chosen Jacob for Himself, Israel, as His treasured possession* [Ps. 135:4].[8]

It is dangerous to allegorize too heavily either Matthew 21:33–41 or *Sifrei Devarim*. The example from *Sifrei Devarim* treats the figures typologically but not allegorically. It is not concerned with pinning down an identity for each literary reference in the mashal. If that were the case, the initial tenant farmers who began to steal would have to be identified with Abraham. Whether the parable itself is an allegory or a typology, the attached nimshal cannot tolerate too close a correlation with the mashal. Indeed, the closer one examines the match between the two, the less felici-

---

8. *Sifrei Devarim* 312 to Deut. 32.9 (Finkelstein, 353–54); compare *Shemot Rabbah* 41.4 and *va-Yiqra Rabbah* 11.7 (M. Margulies, 1.232–33). For other examples of the servant figure representing gentiles, see Weiser, 28–33.

tous it appears. Close examination reveals a similar problem with the parable of the Wicked Tenants.[9]

The first nimshal attached to the parable of the Wicked Tenants, Matthew 21:41, is presented as the message received by the listeners. The general phrasing of nimshal A erases individual responses within the audience, and therefore must be deemed a literary fiction. It is more likely that even if the majority heard the nimshal of the parable as a prediction of the downfall of Roman occupation, at least some of the listeners would have heard it as a judgment upon the Sadducees or some other sectarian group competing for power among the Judaisms of the Second Temple period. Nimshal B (Matt. 21:41) presents another serious problem: it is illogical to attach a nimshal about a building to a mashal about a vineyard, though this nimshal will also become the focus of the rest of this chapter. Nimshal C (Matt. 21:43) also has a disturbing relation to the mashal, for as we have seen, the kingdom of God is not synonymous with the vineyard. If we read the mashal alone, without the nimshalim dictating messages that pull us in various directions, its point is simple and direct: God has a tenacious sense of ownership toward the vineyard/house of Israel. Various people attempt to interfere with that relationship, particularly as it bears fruit. But God will neither tolerate such interference nor abandon the vineyard. No matter what happens, God will find a way to make sure that *bet Israel*, God's own forever, is encouraged to bear fruit. Such a message would be very comforting to a Jewish audience living in oppression and struggling with severe community tensions. There is no reason to presume an anti-Jewish intent to the mashal as it stands, once the nimshalim have been removed; even to suggest a transference of the covenant from the Jews to the gentiles would have mystified and alienated a first-century Jewish audience.

The Case of the Discrepant Nimshal

The parable of the Wicked Tenants in the Vineyard is contained in all three synoptic Gospels: Matthew 21:33–41, Mark 12:1–9, and Luke 20:9–16. To each of these three versions is attached a quotation from Psalm 118, ostensibly spoken by Jesus as a nimshal to the parable: "The stone which the builders rejected has become the head of the corner." The mashal is structured around agricultural images, but the quoted nimshal

---

9. Milavec, in Thoma and Wyschogrod, 94–99, charts the impossibility of a one-to-one allegorical correlation between the "slaves sent" and the lives of the Hebrew prophets.

pertains to architecture. The "foils" in the parable are vintners and tenant farmers, but in the nimshal are apparently stonemasons.

Four possible solutions to this seeming discrepancy between mashal and nimshal may be considered:

1. The discrepancy appeals only to our modern ears, but the combination would have been perfectly compatible to the hearers of Jesus.[10]

2. Jesus did not use Psalm 118 as a nimshal to his parable; rather, it was added at an early redactional stage as an intentional textual anticipation of the resurrection. Assuming that the parable itself is of dominical origin, it ends with Jesus' prediction of his own death: "So they seized [the son], flung him out of the vineyard, and killed him" (Matt. 21:39) Hence the parable text ends in darkness, lacking a sense of resurrection until it is appended *post cruce* by the gospellers or the early church.[11] Such an interpretation is premised upon understanding the body of the parable as a messianic allegory.

3. The passage from Psalm 118 quoted as a nimshal is dominical, but was uttered in some context other than the parable of the Wicked Tenants in the Vineyard. Its present position in the Gospel is due to an early rearrangement by an unknown redactor.[12] This explanation is possible only if a sayings source prior to the Gospels is assumed; supporters of the theory often argue from the Gospel of Thomas, which appears not to attach the psalm quotation to the parable but to treat it as a separate though textually contiguous pericope.

4. Jesus uttered the psalm quotation in Aramaic, rather than in Hebrew, and thereby conveyed a significantly different original meaning than our present text suggests. The Palestinian targum records the Aramaic text to Psalm 118:22 as *talaya she-viqu ardikhlaya havat beinei banaya deyishai va-zakha le-itmana'ah limlikh*, and presumably would have been similar in the Second Temple period. The Aramaic text of the psalm quotation contains a complex wordplay that connects it to the parable; the Greek and Hebrew do not offer the same opportunities for double entendre. By this word play, the Aramaic text can mean either "the stone

---

10. For example, Flusser, *JOC*, 558–68.

11. For example, Bultmann, 177, 205; Beare, *Records*, 209; Klosterman, 137; Fitzmyer, 2.1281–82; Oesterley, 121; Meier, *Matthew*, 244; Fuller, 118–19; Harrington, *Matthew*, 302–3; Johnson, *Luke*, 309; Young, 318; Crossan, *Parables*, 351. Meier, *Marginal Jew*, 165 n144 notes that Thomas does not introduce the quotation from Ps. 118 as having a scriptural origin (*graphē*), nor does it function there as a resurrection prophecy.

12. Goulder, 420; Dodd, *Parables*, 99–100; Jeremias, *Parables*, 70–74; Crossan, *Parables*, 352.

which the builders rejected has become the head of the corner," or "the lad which the sons of Jesse abandoned has become the chief of the leadership."[13] Matthew substituted the traditional Septuagint psalm text for the Aramaic to support his community's Christological needs, at the same time destroying an originally apparent connection between the mashal and the nimshal.

Conflating Unrelated Meshalim

Rabbinic commentators have on occasion understood the phrase "the stone the builders rejected . . ." as open to secondary interpretation as a nimshal. However, the phrase also resembles the use of "stone" in other noted rabbinic sayings, such as "If a stone falls on a pot, woe to the pot! If a pot falls on a stone, woe to the pot! In either case, woe to the pot!";[14] "Do not cast a stone into a cistern from which you have drunk"[15]; or "The stones that we sat on in our childhood wage war against us in our old age,"[16] each of which can be recognized in itself as a truncated mashal. Similarly, rabbinic tradition has more commonly recognized "the stone the builders rejected . . ." as a mashal in its own right, a literary interpretation that can be substantiated by comparing this mashal with other meshalim.[17] What we have then in the received Gospels is two meshalim

---

13. The subject of puns (paronomasia) in the Bible is complicated and generally beyond the scope of this book. However, a pertinent pun directly related to the double meaning of the Hebrew and Aramaic texts of Ps. 118:22 can be found at Isa. 54:11–13, in the interplay between *banim* (children) and *bonim* (builders); see BT Berakhot 64a; JT Nedarim, end of 89; *Bereshit Rabbah* 45:2; *Midrash ha-Gadol Bereshit* 262; *Shir ha-Shirim Rabbah* 1.5,3; Steinsaltz to Pesahim 66b (291); and Pool prayerbook, 102 ("These we apply not only to children, but to all who build the future"). The same paronomasia works also in Aramaic and in Greek (*teknon/tekton*). Similar wordplays are treated in Derrett, "The Stone." Harrington notes the possible wordplay here only in passing (*Matthew*, 303).

14. *Esther Rabbah* 7.10. On the basis of parallels in Aesop and elsewhere, Fitzmyer (2.1286) believes that this addition at Luke 20:18 is itself a nuclear fable. Pei (45) cites a Spanish proverb: "If the pitcher hits the rock, or the rock hits the pitcher, it's too bad for the pitcher." And see above, chapter five, "Woe to me on account of my Creator (*yotzer*); woe to me on account of my urges (*yetzer*)!"

15. *Ba-Midbar Rabbah* 22:4.

16. JT Betsah 1.60,3 (Neusner, *TLI*, 35). The meaning is that those upon whom we relied when we were younger abandon us and cause us great grief when we are elderly.

17. A mashal does not need to have human characters or those of fauna; see, e.g., Isaiah's Vineyard, the Trees Choose a King, and Joseph's dreams, and in the NT,

that have become woven together during transmission in an obfuscating manner. For the purposes of this chapter, Psalm 118:22 is treated as a separate mashal that in original intention was not connected to the parable of the Wicked Tenants in the Vineyard.

One current theory argues that the evangelists worked with some sort of "sayings source" in constructing their own redactions. Attempts to reconstruct a sayings source, such as Q, often use the gospel of Thomas as an example of shape, and perhaps of content.[18] In that Gospel, logion 65 ends: "that he was the heir to the vineyard, they seized him and killed him. Whoever has ears should hear"—a recognized way to close a pericope, and indeed employed to end Thomas, logion 63.[19] Logion 66 begins: "Jesus said, Show me the stone that the builders rejected: that is the cornerstone."[20] Unlike the catenic *gradus ad parnassum*, these two contiguous parables from Thomas have no apparent cumulative purpose, at least according both to their plain reading and their textual form (Logion 65 comes to a full stop before the beginning of Logion 66).[21] We may surmise, however, the logic that compelled an early redactor to link the two: because someone is *e*jected at the end of the Wicked Tenants, and someone is *re*jected in the allusion to Psalm 118, the contiguous pericopes of an early sayings source may have been conflated in the redactor's mind. There is one further complicating factor: if the Wicked Tenants is interpreted allegorically, then it is a short leap to interpreting the Stone Rejected allegorically, cementing even more strongly the imagined bond between

---

the House Built on Sand, the Wheat and the Tares, and the Barren Fig Tree, to name but a few; see Gerhardsson, "The Narrative Meshalim." On adage, aphorism, and proverb as foreshortened parables, see Erasmus, *Coll. Works*, 31.8.

18. On the relationship between Thomas and Q, see Kloppenborg et al., especially the forward by Robinson.

19. The phrase "Let him who has ears, hear," is related to *yishme'u ve-yira'u* ("hear, and stand in awe") at Deut. 17:13. The point in both phrases is: "What I have just said to you is intended as a deterrent. If you have heard my intention, you will take it to heart, and in turn you will sin no more"; see Daube, *New Testament*, 432–37.

20. The logia can be found in Layton, 392; Fitzmyer, *Luke*, 2.1290; Funk, *New Gospel*, 121; and Guillaumont et al., 39. It is often difficult in Thomas to see any connection from one saying to the next, for example, #7 and 8, #20 and 21, #63 and 64, #73–76. The contiguity of #65 and 66 could therefore be either intentional or serendipitous.

21. Note, however, that there are catenae of "stone" parables at Rom. 9:32–33 and 1 Peter 2:4–8, which are given a cumulative Messianic interpretation in reference to Jesus; compare a similar catena in *Pugio Fidei*, #428 and 637 (Flusser, *JOC*, 247–48).

them. The son is ejected, the stone is rejected, and both sayings can then be connected to Jesus' crucifixion and death.

Does History Repeat Itself?

Whereas allegorical interpretation remained suspect in rabbinic tradition, typological interpretation was an accepted midrashic method. Typological interpretation demands a comprehensive plot whose broad sweep and movement call forth associations in the listener's mind. One rabbinic slogan describing a particular subset of typological interpretation is "Whatever occurred to the ancestors is a sign to their descendants" [*ma'asei avot siman le-banim*].[22] In his commentary to Genesis 12:6, Nahmanides explains the meaning of the slogan:[23]

> I will tell you a principle by which you will understand all the long portions of Scripture concerning Abraham, Isaac and Jacob. It is indeed a great matter, though our rabbis mention it only briefly, saying "whatever has happened to the patriarchs is a sign to the children (*ma'asei avot siman le-banim*)." This explains why the verses narrate at great length the account of the journeys of the patriarchs, the digging of wells, and other events. Now some may consider this unnecessary and of no useful purpose, but in truth all these details serve as a lesson for the future: when an event happens to any one of the three patriarchs, that which is decreed to happen to his children can be understood.

Does history repeat itself? Is there really nothing new under the sun (Qoh. 1:10)? The quickest glance at the above passage would seem to suggest that history is cyclical, playing out the same limited repertoire of patterns over and over again. Yet in his *Philosophical Understanding and Religious Truth*, philosopher Erich Frank summarizes a traditional approach to history that attempts to transcend the cyclical. He writes:

---

22. The phrase can be found in Abraham ibn-Ezra to Genesis 9:18; cf. BT Ketubot 63a on Ezek 16:44; Sotah 34a; *Bereshit Rabbah* 40 (Theodor and Albeck, 3.386 and notes): *Midrash Tanhuma*, Lekh Lekha (Buber, 35b–36a) and Vayishlah (90a); R. Bahye to Gen. 12 (Chavel, 137). On the Greek philosophy of the circularity of history, see Frank, 82–83 n41, esp. the delightful quote by Eudemus, a pupil of Aristotle. The same concept must have been familiar to Origen, for he paraphrases it in his *Contra Celsum* 4.44 (Chadwick, 219–20), discussing the lives of the patriarchs. See also BT Sotah 34a, on setting up stones as a sign to future generations.

23. Chavel, English 1.168–69, Hebrew 1.77; see Nahmanides to Gen. 26:20 (334–35); 29:2 (359); intro. to 32:4 (394); 32:9 (397–98); 43:13 (521); and see Heinemann, *Darkei ha-Aggadah*, 32–34.

> Providence is a religious idea; it does not signify God's interest in political parties or social agents, but rather His concern about the ethico-religious individual and the secret of his soul. . . . The history of religion and its moral ideals may be understood as progress toward an ever more profound understanding of the true nature of God and of His relation to man and to the world. In this sense, Augustine was justified in interpreting the chronological sequence of paganism, Judaism and Christianity as a meaningful and logical development, as a manifestation of Providence.[24]

In this historico-philosophical approach, "types" in the past prefigure "types" in the present, and types in the present become the foundation of tomorrow's new types, not in simple recapitulation, but ever ascending inward toward comprehension, and ultimately imitation, of God's character. The power of the New Testament epistle known as To the Hebrews is drawn from the artistic use of this type of typological parallelism, in order to speak of the work of Christ as simultaneously something completely rooted in the past and tradition, and yet a new and unprecedented revelation. For example, at Hebrews 3:1–2, we read: "Therefore brothers and sisters, holy partners in a heavenly calling, consider that Jesus, the apostle and high priest of our confession, was faithful to the one who appointed him, just as Moses 'was faithful in all God's house' [compare Num. 12:7]." This is the same sort of historical adumbration as in the phrase "Whatever occurred to the ancestors is a sign to their descendants."[25]

Typological parallelism is actually a form of midrash; in early rabbinic literature, it is developed to an art form, just as it was also in the Book of Hebrews. No lesson needs be pointed out, either in the form of nimshal or aphorism; the typological adumbration is in itself its own lesson for the hearer steeped in religious tradition. We might illustrate the maieutic nature of this form of midrash with certain typological parallelisms from the midrashic piyyut literature, drawing upon the work of Aharon Mirsky in his book, *The Quarry Whence the Shapes of Liturgical Poetry are Hewn.*[26] Mirsky uses the word *maḥarozet* ("to string pearls"), now familiar to us, to describe the process by which these catenae of synoptic parallelisms are constructed, or by which they are recognized as poetic in character even

---

24. Frank, 129–30; see also 144 n39. However, theologian William Reed Huntington explained the same phenomenon as a natural outgrowth of one generation fading into another: "What the grand-father practices the son criticizes and the grand-son amends."

25. On the Hebrews passage, see Flusser, "Messianology and Christology in the Epistle to the Hebrews" in *JOC*, 246–79, esp. 261–62.

26. Aharon Mirsky, *Maḥatzavtan shel Tzurot ha-Piyyut*; the source of the title is Isa. 51:1.

when written in prose form. His point is that the transition back and forth from midrash to piyyut is fluid and often repetitive; our point is that adumbration is the method by which we recognize the truth of the present, that typological parallelism defines, clarifies, and criticizes the present on the basis of an indispensable past. Several examples of catenic piyyutim illustrate the power of this literary medium.

CATENIC PIYYUT A: *THE FATHER AND I ARE ONE*[27]

"The deeds of the parents are prophetic signs to the children." You find whatever is stated of David is also stated of Solomon:

David reigned forty years, as it is said: *The length of David's reign over Israel was forty years* (1 Kgs. 2:11).	Solomon reigned forty years, as it is said: *Solomon reigned forty years over all Israel in Jerusalem* (2 Chron. 9:30).
David ruled over Israel and Judah, as it is said: *The Lord the God of Israel chose me of all my ancestral house to be king over Israel forever; for He chose Judah to be ruler* (1 Chron. 28:4).	Solomon ruled over Israel and Judah, as it is said: *Judah and Israel were as numerous as the sand of the sea* (1 Kgs. 4:20).
David built the foundations, as it is said: *King David rose to his feet and said: I wanted to build a resting-place for the ark of the Covenant of the Lord, for the footstool of our God* (1 Chron. 28:2).	Solomon built the superstructure, as it is said: *I have now built for You a stately house, a place where You may dwell forever* (1 Kgs. 8:13).
David composed words, as it is said: *These are the last words of David* (2 Sam. 23:1).	Solomon composed words, as it is said: *The words of Qohelet, son of David, king in Jerusalem* (Qoh. 1:1).
David gave voice to the vanity of things, as it is said: *Truly every one at his best state is altogether vanity, Selah* (Ps. 39:6).	Solomon gave voice to the vanity of things, as it is said: *Vanity of vanities, says Qohelet, all is vanity* (Qoh. 1:2).

27. Adapted from a traditional piyyut by Mirsky, *Maḥatzavtan*, 22; compare *Shir ha-Shirim Rabbah* 1.1, 6.

David told meshalim, as it is said: *As the ancient mashal says, Out of the wicked comes forth wickedness* (1 Sam. 24:13).	Solomon told meshalim, as it is said: *The meshalim of Solomon son of David, king of Israel* (Prov. 1:1).
David wrote books, for the Psalms are attributed to him.	Solomon wrote books: Proverbs, Qohelet, Song of Songs.
David praised God in a passage beginning with "then," as it is said: *Then our mouths shall be filled with laughter, and our tongues, with songs of joy* (Ps. 126:2).	Solomon praised God in a passage beginning with "then," as it is said: *Then Solomon declared, The Lord has chosen to abide in a thick cloud* (1 Kgs. 8:12).
David brought up the ark, as it is said: *Then David and the elders of Israel who were going to bring up the Ark of the Covenant of the Lord from the house of Obed-edom were joyful* (1 Chron. 15:25).	Solomon brought up the ark, as it is said: *Then Solomon convoked the elders of Israel to bring up the Ark of the Covenant of the Lord from the city of David, that is, Zion* (1 Kgs. 8:1).
David sang songs, as it is said: *David addressed the words of this song to the Lord, after the Lord had saved him from the hand of all his enemies* (2 Sam. 22:1).	Solomon sang songs, as it is said: *The Song of Songs, by Solomon* (Song 1:1).

CATENIC PIYYUT B: *A PROPHET HONORED AMONG HIS PEOPLE*[28]

"The deeds of the parents are prophetic signs to the children." You find that whatever Moses did, David did:

Moses led Israel forth out of vassalage in Egypt.	David led Israel forth out of servitude to Goliath.
Moses fought battles with Sihon and Og.	David fought the battles of the Lord in all the regions around him, as it is said: *my lord is fighting the battles of the Lord* (1 Sam. 25:28).

---

28. Adapted from a traditional piyyut by Mirsky, *Maḥatzavtan*, 110; compare *Midrash Tehillim* to Ps. 1:2 (Buber, 2a; Braude, 5).

Moses reigned over Israel and over Judah, as it is said: *Then he became king in Jeshurun, when the heads of the people assembled* (Deut. 33:5).	David reigned over Israel and over Judah.
Moses parted the Red Sea for Israel.	David parted the rivers of Aram for Israel, as it is said: *You have made the land quake; You have torn it open* (Ps. 60:2).
Moses built an altar.	David built an altar.
Moses offered the sacrifices.	David offered the sacrifices.
Moses gave five books of the Torah to Israel.	David gave the five books of the Psalms to Israel.
Moses blessed Israel with the words: *Blessed are you, O Israel* (Deut. 33:29).	David blessed Israel with the words: *Blessed are those who delight in the Torah of God* (Ps. 1:1–2).

CATENIC PIYYUT C: *I CAME TO FULFILL THE LAW*[29]

"The deeds of the parents are prophetic signs to the children." When the clans of Israel gathered to re-inter Joseph's bones (Gen. 50:25–26; Ex. 13:19; Josh. 24:32), the nations came questioning who lay in the coffin. The Israelites responded with the following eulogy, on how Joseph had been the fulfillment of the Ten Commandments:[30] "The one lying in this coffin [aron] has fulfilled what is written on that which lies in the ark [aron]."

On the tablets of the ark it is written: *I the Lord am your God* (Ex. 20:2).	Of Joseph it is written: *Have no fear! Am I a substitute for God?* (Gen. 50:19).

---

29. Adapted from a traditional piyyut by Mirsky, *Mahatzavtan*, 110–11; compare *Mekhilta*, Lauterbach, 1.179–81.

30. During the journey through the wilderness, the children of Israel carried with them not only the Ark, but also an arklike coffin containing the bones of Joseph. The two arks set side by side made their comparison a natural human response. See Rashi to Ex. 13:19; and Ginzberg, *Legends*, 2.183 and 5.376 n442. A catena similar to this one, but about Jacob and Joseph, can be found in Ginzberg, *Legends* 2.4–5.

On the tablets in the ark it is written: *You shall have no other gods besides me* (Ex. 20:3).	Of Joseph it is written: *I am a God-fearing man* (Gen. 42:18).
You shall not swear falsely by the name of the Lord your God (Ex. 20:7).	Of Joseph it is written: *by Pharaoh!* (Gen. 42:15), that is, he did not take the Lord's name in vain.
Remember the Sabbath day (Ex. 20:8).	Of Joseph it is written: *slaughter an animal and make ready* (Gen. 43:16). Make ready for what? The Sabbath [comp. Ex. 16:5].
Honor your father and your mother (Ex. 20:12)	Of Joseph it is written: *and he answered his father, "I am ready"* (Gen. 37:13), even though his father was sending him off to trouble.
You shall not murder (Ex. 20:13).	Joseph did not murder Potiphar.
You shall not commit adultery (Ex. 20:14).	Joseph did not commit adultery with Potiphar's wife.
You shall not steal (Ex. 20:15).	Of Joseph it is written: *Joseph gathered in all the money . . . and Joseph brought the money into Pharaoh's palace* (Gen. 47:14).
You shall not bear false witness against your neighbor (Ex. 20:16).	Joseph never told his father what his brothers had done to him; how much less likely would he be to tell his father something false!
You shall not covet (Ex. 20:17).	Joseph did not covet Potiphar's wife.
You shall not hate your kinsfolk in your heart (Lev. 19:17).	Of Joseph it is written: *Thus he reassured his brothers, speaking kindly to them* (Gen. 50:21).
You shall not take vengeance or bear a grudge (Lev. 19:18).	Of Joseph it is written: *Although you intended me harm, God intended it for good* (Gen. 50:20).
Let him live by your side as your kinsman (Lev. 25:36).	Of Joseph it is written: *Joseph sustained his father, and his brothers, and all his father's household with bread, down to the little ones* (Gen. 47:12).

The Skeleton in the King's Closet

The catenic piyyut is one method by which typological parallels are highlighted and interpreted. Other forms of typological paralleling appear in the New Testament. These parallelisms are not usually spelled out, but presume significant prior knowledge on the part of the community's more learned initiates. A poignant pre-Christian melodrama strangely parallels the life of Jesus, at least as that life would have been perceived by some among the crowds who followed him. In the midrashim about the exceptional origins of King David, we find a "catena of suspicion" concerning a skeleton in the closet of the royal family. The same chain of names is eventually used by Matthew to argue the divine propriety of Jesus' most improper human origins.

At Matthew 1:2–16 we find the following names scattered among the generations of the royal bloodline from Abraham to Joseph the father of Jesus:

and Judah the father of Peretz and Zerah by *Tamar* . . .
and Salmon the father of Boaz by *Rahab* [not the harlot],
and Boaz the father of Obed by *Ruth*,
and Obed the father of Jesse, and Jesse the father of King David
[by *Nazbat*].
And David was the father of Solomon by the wife of Uriah
[*Bathsheba*],
and Solomon the father of Rehoboam [by *Naamah*], . . .
and Jacob the father of Joseph the husband of *Mary*, of whom
Jesus was born, who is called the Messiah.

Of interest (and so italicized) is Matthew's occasional inclusion of the names of the mothers of each successive generation in the midst of what is otherwise clearly a patriarchal genealogy.[31] Some are mentioned outright; others such as Nazbat, Bathsheba, and Naamah are present only by implication. Every woman in the sequence has some sort of taint of suspicion attached to her, according to the biblical narrative or the further development of tradition. To trace the skeleton in the Matthean King-Messiah's closet, we must focus momentarily on the charge of illicit sexual behavior attached to each of these women.

The catena reporting repeated blemishes on the purity of the royal bloodline begins with Tamar. Genesis 38 recounts the seduction of the

31. On the Matthean genealogy in relation to Ruth, see Campbell, 173; Amy-Jill Levine, 84 (who also comments specifically on the manner in which women disappear from biblical genealogies); and Marshall Johnson, chap. 5.

widowed Judah by his own widowed daughter-in-law Tamar, and the subsequent birth of twin sons, Peretz and Zerah.[32] Tamar was a daughter of the clans of Aram—geographically one of Israel's neighbors—and had buried two husbands, Er and Onan, yet remained childless. Disguised as a temple prostitute (*qedesha*) in the town of Timnah, Tamar offered her sexual services to her father-in-law in order that she might at last get pregnant.[33] When Tamar was later tried as an adulteress, Judah broke down to reveal that he was the father, once confronted with the "messianic" tokens he had left in Tamar's care. Joseph the father of Jesus was descended from the lineage or "house" of Peretz, son of Judah and Tamar, by way of David the King.

By aggadic tradition, the two spies who entered the Promised Land under the direction of Joshua were these same two twins, Peretz and Zerah. Rahab the harlot helped the spies by hanging a scarlet thread out the window to warn them of danger (Josh. 2). She had received this scarlet thread from Zerah, upon whom it had been tied at birth to show that he was the first to breach the womb (though Peretz pulled him back in and managed to be born first!). Joshua later married this same Rahab, though she was not a Jew by birth.[34] The Rahab mentioned in the Matthew genealogy is not this same Rahab, but a namesake some generations later. However, the mention of her name would have conjured up associations of suspicion in the minds of Matthew's readers.

The book of Ruth chronicles the tale of Naomi, the wife of Elimelech the Bethlehemite, left in her mature years as a widow and grieving mother and survived only by her two "foreign" daughters-in-law, Orpha and Ruth, both Moabite women. As Naomi is leaving Moab to return to Judea, Orpha decides to remain in Moab among "her people and her gods." But Ruth follows her mother-in-law to Judea, and there meets and marries Boaz, a wealthy relative of Naomi's deceased husband Elimelech.[35] The story is beautiful in its simple generosity, yet behind it lies the scandal that Boaz the good Israelite married a woman from Moab, a union forbidden to Israelites by halakhic judgment at Deuteronomy 23:3–6.[36] A skeleton is thus introduced into what will become the royal lineage, and the narrator is at

---

32. For rabbinic sources related to the forbidden degrees of sexual contact here, see Ginzberg, *Legends*, 2.31–37, 199, and 5.332–36 n74–94; 380 n10.

33. Judah paid Tamar's hire with a kid from among his flock of goats; see Chap. 3 on *etnan zonah*.

34. For rabbinic sources, see Ginzberg, *Legends*, 2.36–37 and 5.336. On the many progeny of Rahab, including prophets and kings, see *Legends*, 6.171 n12.

35. The greeting "The Lord be with you," so common to Christian liturgies, originates at Ruth 2:4 when Boaz meets Ruth; see Ginzberg, *Legends*, 6.191.

36. The Deuteronomic restriction is clear; for additional sources, see Ginzberg, *Legends*, 4.34 and 6.193–94.

great pains to explain the propriety of this highly irregular marriage. Hence the awkward construction of Ruth 4:12: "May your house be like the house of Peretz whom Tamar bore to Judah."

Somehow, the royal lineage must be protected from too harsh a judgment. Accordingly, an exception to the prohibition against Ammonites and Moabites becomes normative in the halakhic literature in BT Yevamot in an attempt to salvage the purity of the Davidic line:[37]

> *No Ammonite and Moabite shall be admitted into the congregation of the Lord; none of their descendants, even in the tenth generation, shall ever be admitted into the congregation of the Lord, because they did not meet you with food and water on your journey after you left Egypt, and because they hired Balaam son of Beor to curse you* (Deut. 23:3–4).

R. Yoḥanan replied with the following midrash to justify David's suspect lineage:

> Scripture stated, *When Saul saw David going out to assault Goliath, he asked his army commander Abner, "Whose son is that boy, Abner?" Abner said, "By your life, Your Majesty, I do not know"* (1 Sam. 17:55).

But did Saul really not know young David? I will tell you how the conversation went:

Doeg the Edomite said to Saul, "Instead of inquiring whether the young man is fit to be king or not, you should be inquiring instead whether he is even permitted to enter the covenantal assembly or not!"

Saul asked, "What is the reason that he might not be permitted?"

Doeg answered, "Because he is descended from Ruth, the Moabite woman."

Abner said to Doeg, "We were taught the principle: 'An Ammonite, but not an Ammonitess; a Moabite, but not a Moabitess.' But if we extended the principle logically, should we then say that a male bastard is excluded (Deut. 23:2) but a female bastard is not?"

Doeg explained, "In the scriptural text, we should not read *mamzer* ["male bastard"] but *mum zar* ["a strange blemish"], which would then imply that either sex could be objectionable."

Abner asked, "Well, does the exclusion of the Egyptian (Deut. 23:7) exclude Egyptian women as well?"

---

37. BT Yevamot 76b–77a; compare also Yevamot 69a; Qiddushin 67b; Ḥullin 62b; Ketubot 7b; *Midrash Tehillim* to Psalm 1:2 (Braude, 4); JT Yevamot 8.3; *Ruth Rabbah* 2.9; *Midrash ha-Gadol Devarim* (Fish, 514–15); Rashi to Deut. 23:4–7 (Silbermann, 113–14). And see Ginzberg, *Legends*, 4.88 and 6.252 n44; M. Johnson, 87ff on genealogical purity.

Doeg answered, "The exclusion of the Ammonite and Moabite is different, for unlike the other examples you have raised, here the reason for the exclusion is explicitly stated: *Because they did not meet you with food and water*. It is customary for men to offer hospitality to wayfaring men; it is not customary, however, for women to offer hospitality to men at all. The men should have met the men, and the women should have met the women! But since only the men would have been expected to offer hospitality in this case, but did not, then women are not included in the prohibition of the Ammonite and Moabite, because hospitality was not expected of the women in the first place!"

The sages insisted that difficulty still remains! The following interpretations illustrate the opposing points of view. *The princess is decked in her chamber* (Ps. 45:13), that is, inside her house, where she belongs. But the Palestinian tradition explains (others quote it in the name of R. Isaac) that scripture says, *Where is your wife Sarah?* (Gen. 18:9), which implies that she was expected to come out with Abraham to provide hospitality.

These parallel cycles of suspicious birth narratives continue with Ruth's grandson, Jesse, husband of Nazbat bat Adiel. This relationship and its intrigue are the focus of a repertoire of midrashim that we explore in subsequent pages, because the outcome of the union was David the Shepherd King. Many were still suspicious that David, as a descendant of a Moabitess, was not truly a birth-member of the Jewish community; the cycle seems constructed in part to justify David's position in Israel, his anointing having erased the taint of his dubious lineage.[38] However, the cycle of suspicion does not end with Jesse, Nazbat, and their son David. King David's relationship with Bathsheba yields the future heir, Solomon; that relationship is not only embarrassing, as the two had committed adultery, but also involves the deception and subsequent murder of Bathsheba's husband Uriah the Hittite (2 Sam. 11).[39] David and Bathsheba's son King Solomon repeats the cycle through his marriage to Naamah the Ammonite woman (1 Kings 14:21 and 31; 2 Chron. 12:13), a union as suspect as Boaz's marriage to Ruth.[40]

For this reason, Tractate Yevamot continues with a thanksgiving, pointing to nagging suspicion over the "skeleton in the royal closet," and leaving us somehow with the vague impression that the whole story is not yet over:

---

38. For this complicated argument, see Ginzberg, *Legends*, 6.252 n44, and M. Johnson, 133. Sources include *Ruth Rabbah* 8:1; and Josephus, *Antiquities* 5.332–37 (Thackeray, 5.148–51).

39. For rabbinic sources, see Ginzberg, *Legends*, 4.88 and 6.252 n44.

40. For rabbinic sources, see Ginzberg, *Legends*, 4.170–71 and 6.300 n89–91.

Raba made the following exposition: What was meant by *You have loosed my bonds* (Ps. 116:16)? David said to the Holy One, Blessed be He, "Master of the Universe! Two bonds were fastened on me, and you loosed them both: Ruth the Moabitess [from whom David was descended] and Naamah the Ammonitess [wife of David's son Solomon, and thus mother of David's grandson Rehoboam]."[41]

Indeed elsewhere in rabbinic literature both Ruth and Naamah are referred to as "two precious doves," on whose account both Ammon and Moab escaped destruction.[42]

This aura of suspicion hangs over the lineage—not simply the lineage of a royal family in a political sense but also the royal family in a salvific or messianic sense. Comprehending this history of scandal, the words "the stone the builders rejected" take on poignant overtones. The lineage that extends from Judah/Tamar through Boaz/Ruth through Jesse/Nazbat through David/Bathsheba through Solomon/Naamah carries on down to Joseph the father of Jesus, and to Jesus himself, as we learn from Matthew 1:1–16.[43] Although we cannot easily construct how these connections would have registered within the early Christian community, there is little doubt that Jesus' own origins were clouded with enough suspicion that his contemporaries would have been quickly reminded of the skeleton in the royal closet.

From Mashal to Midrash

Before exploring more fully the parallels with the life of Jesus hinted at above, the birth-narrative midrashim pertaining to the origins of King David must be investigated. As stated previously, Jewish sources understand Psalm 118:22 as a mashal in its own right.[44] How early such understanding develops is difficult to determine, for the sources in which such an understanding of the psalm is recorded often are themselves redactions of earlier traditions.

Psalm 118:19–29 in the original Hebrew contains frequent shifts be-

---

41. BT Yevamot 77a. Raymond Martine quotes this in his *Pugio Fidei* at 714, citing *Bereshit Rabbah* 50:10; but compare BT Yevamot 63a. See also Ginzberg, *Legends*, 5.243 n188.
42. See Ginzberg, *Legends*, 6.300 n91.
43. For an exhaustive and penetrating discussion of this suspicion as addressed in the Matthean genealogy, see Marshall Johnson, esp. chaps. 4 and 5.
44. See the Psalm commentaries of ibn-Ezra, Rashi, David Altschuler (*Metzudat Tzion*), and Amos Hakham.

tween singular and plural voice, as well as a number of words upon which both Hebrew and Aramaic wordplays are possible. In order to understand the consequent midrashim, the text of the psalm itself must be firmly in mind:

19. Open the gates of valor for me, that I may enter them and praise the Lord.

20. This is the gateway to the Lord—the valiant shall enter through it.

21. I praise you, for you have answered me, and have become my deliverance.

22. The stone that the builders rejected has become the chief cornerstone.

23. This is the Lord's doing; it is marvelous in our sight.

24. This is the day that the Lord has made—let us exult and rejoice on it [or: in Him].

25. O Lord, deliver us! O Lord, let us prosper!

26. May he who enters be blessed in the name of the Lord; we bless you from the house of the Lord.[45]

27. The Lord is God; He has given us light; bind the festal offering to the horns of the altar with cords.

28. You are my God and I will praise you; you are my God and I will extol you.

29. Praise the Lord for he is good, His steadfast love is eternal.

Seven separate midrashic traditions grow up around this eleven-verse section, each of which develops its unique exegesis of the psalm as a mashal open to interpretations that transcend the plain reading of the text.

Midrash 1. The antiquity of a pre–New Testament midrashic tradition to 118:21–29 is suggested by what is known in the Septuagint and Qumran documents as Psalm 151:[46]

---

45. Here the JPS translation illustrates vividly a syntactical discrepancy between Jewish and Christian interpretations of this particular verse. Christian liturgies commonly repeat the phrase "Blessed is he who comes in the name of the Lord," but as can be seen above, the phrase can also be translated "Blessed in the name of the Lord is he who comes," conforming to the Masoretic neumes.

46. On Psalm 151, see Charlesworth, *Pseudepigrapha*, 2.612–13; Segal, *Ben Sirah*, 357–64; Haberman, *Ketav Sefer Lashon*, 119–20; Talmon, 244–72; Wachholder. The Greek text can be found in the proper place in the LXX.

I was the smallest among my brothers
and the youngest among the sons of my father;
and he made me shepherd of his flocks
    and the ruler over his kids.
My hands made a flute,
and my fingers a lyre;
and I shall render glory to the Lord,
    I thought within myself.
The mountains cannot witness to him,
nor the hills proclaim [him];
the trees have elevated my words,
    and the flocks my deeds.[47]
For who can proclaim and who can announce,
and who can recount the deeds of the Lord?
Everything God has seen,
    everything he has heard and he has listened.
He sent his prophet to anoint me,
    Samuel to make me great;
my brothers went out to meet him,
    handsome of figure and handsome of appearance.
[Although] their stature was tall,
    [and] their hair handsome
    The Lord God did not choose them.
But he sent and took me from behind the flock,
and he anointed me with holy oil,
and he made me leader for his people
    and ruler over the sons of his covenant.

As can be seen, Psalm 151 is itself a midrash on Psalm 118:21–29, with particular reference to verse 22, "the stone the builders rejected." The smallest and the youngest has been "rejected" (*ma'as*) to a position "behind the flock," but at the inspiration of God he is elevated to become a "leader for his people and a ruler over the sons of the covenant."

Midrash 2. Yet a second source presents us with a midrash on Psalm 118, constructed through complicated Hebrew-Aramaic word plays. According to the Aramaic Palestinian targum, the preferred reading of Psalm 118:21–29 is:[48]

---

47. On the complications in rendering these few verses, see Sanders, *Dead Sea Psalms*, 93–103, and "A Multivalent Text."
48. *Miqraot Gedolot* to Psalm 118, corrected according to the text of *Kehillot Moshe*, Amsterdam 1727, 85b. The Aramaic version winds up translated into Latin

21. I will give thanks before thee because thou hast received my prayers, and brought me to redemption.

22. The lad which the builders abandoned was among the sons of Jesse, and was found deserving of appointment to reign and rule.

23. This [has been resolved] before God.
    The builders said: This is extraordinary before us, said the sons of Jesse.

24. *This is the day that the Lord has made*, said the builders.
    Let us exult and rejoice on it, he said and the sons of Jesse.

25. *O Lord, deliver us*, say the builders.
    O Lord, let us prosper, say Jesse and his wife.

26. *May he who enters be blessed in the name* of the word *of the Lord*, say the builders.
    We bless you from the holy *house of God*, says David.

27. *The Lord is God; he has given us light*, say the clans of the house of Judah.
    Bind the lad for *festal offering* of favor, *with cords* to the place of sacrifice and pour out his blood in sacrifice *upon the altar*, says Samuel the prophet.

28. *You are my God and I will praise you*;
    You are my God and I will extol You, says David.

29. Magnified is his name; and he says, Exalt him, you people of Israel.
    Praise the Lord for He is good, His steadfast love is eternal.

As can be seen, the Palestinian Targum to Psalm 118:21–29 interprets the Hebrew text of the same psalm through the eyes of Psalm 151, thus deriving a new Aramaic midrash from an extant Hebrew mashal by the process of wordplay. The *dramatis personae* in the midrash are all characters in or implied within the biblical text of 1 Samuel 16: Jesse and his wife, the sons of Jesse, Samuel, and David, as well as "the builders" and the clans of Judah. The distinction between the sons of Jesse, the builders, and the clans of Judah is not clear at this point in the historical development of the midrash. Parts are assigned to various characters in the midrash based both on the distinction in the Hebrew psalm text between singular and plural voices and on the sentiments deemed appropriate to each of the

---

in fifteenth-century Spanish Catholicism; see Marino, 301–2. The difference between the Aramaic and Latin versions of the same text is fascinating, but not relevant to our discussion here.

characters. The dramatic sense of the text is straightforward and simple, carrying some of the feeling of Hellenistic dramatic production with an accompanying chorus (the builders).[49]

Midrash 3. As with the preceding texts, it is equally difficult to date the materials contained in the Babylonian Talmud beyond its redaction c.400 C.E. Tractate Pesaḥim 119a tells a story attributed to the Palestinian teacher Yoḥanan of the second to third centuries:

> DIASh ADISh KShDK MeODeKha—a mnemonic [*siman*].[50]
>
> Said Rabbi Samuel bar Nahmani in the name of Rabbi Yoḥanan:
>
> *I will praise you for you have answered me,* said David.
>
> *The stone that the builders rejected has become the head of the corner,* said Jesse.
>
> *This is the Lord's doing,* said the brothers.
>
> *This is the day that the Lord has made,* said Samuel.
>
> *O Lord, deliver us,* said the brothers.
>
> *O Lord, let us prosper,* said David.
>
> *May he who enters be blessed in the name of the Lord,* said Jesse.
>
> *We bless you out of the house,* said Samuel.
>
> *God is the Lord who has given us light,* said everyone.
>
> *Bind the sacrifice with cords,* said Samuel.
>
> *You are my God and I will praise you,* said David.
>
> *You are my God and I will extol you,* said everyone.

In the second line, the "rejected stone" is clearly understood as David, a reading subsequently affirmed by Saadya Gaon, Rashi, Shemuel ben Meir, and *Shemot Rabbah* 37:1. This midrash, like the previous one, is based upon a distribution of the verses to various characters, depending on voice

---

49. For another example of biblical and midrashic texts presented in the manner of a Hellenistic drama, see Ezekiel the Tragedian, c.200 B.C.E., in Charlesworth, *Pseudepigrapha*, 2.803ff.

50. David Ishai Aḥim Shemuel (DIASh) = David, Jesse, Brothers, Samuel, reading down the right side; Aḥim David Ishai Shemuel (ADISh); Koolam Shemuel David Koolam (KShDeK) = Everyone, Samuel, David, Everyone; from the word *odekha*, I will give thanks. According to Soncino (615), pronounced "Diyash Adyish Kashdek, me-Odekha"; and see Steinsaltz's explanation in *BT Pesaḥim*, 509.

and appropriateness. The cast is smaller, there being only five persons or groups instead of the previous seven, and Jesse's wife (David's mother) seems to have disappeared. Though the text is simpler and more direct than the Palestinian targum's (midrash 2), no conclusion concerning comparative dating of the texts may be drawn.

Midrash 4. Yet another dramatic midrash on the Psalm text is found in the *Midrash Tehillim (Shoḥer Tov)*, with a variant text in the *Yalqut Shimeoni*.[51] The inspiration for this midrash may come from Psalm 118 itself, which reads at verse 15, "There are glad songs of victory in the tents of the righteous," and at verse 17, "I shall . . . recount the deeds of the Lord." The midrash employs the text of Psalm 118 as an antiphonal declamatory chorus:

> *This is the Lord's doing* alludes to King David, king of Israel, who at one moment was keeping his father's sheep, and in the very next moment was made king, so that everyone exclaimed: "One moment David keeps sheep, and the next he is king!"
>
> And he replied: "You wonder at me! Truly I wonder at myself more than you do!"
>
> But the Holy Spirit replies: *This is the Lord's doing. . . .*
>
> *This is the day that the Lord has made* (Ps. 118:23–24). After all the redemption that came to Israel, enslavement followed, but from now on no enslavement will follow, as is said, *Hymn the Lord, for He has done gloriously; Let this be made known in all the world. Oh shout for joy, you who dwell in Zion! For great in your midst is the Holy One of Israel* (Isa. 12:5–6).
>
> *O Lord, deliver us!* (Ps. 118:25).
>
> From INside the walls, the men of Jerusalem will say, *O Lord, deliver us!*
>
> And from the OUTside, the men of Judah will say, *O Lord, let us prosper!*
>
> From INside the men of Jerusalem will say, *May he who enters be blessed IN the name of the Lord.*
>
> And from OUTside, the men of Judah will say, *We bless you OUT of the house of the Lord.*

---

51. *Midrash Tehillim* (Buber, 244–45; Braude, 2.245); *Yalqut Shimeoni* to Ps. 118 (at 876).

From INside the men of Jerusalem will say, *The Lord is God; He has given us light.*

And from OUTside the men of Judah will say, Order the festival procession with boughs, even *unto the horns of the altar.*

From INside the men of Jerusalem will say, *You are my God and I will praise you.*

And from OUTside the men of Judah will say, *You are my God and I will extol You.*

Then the men of Jerusalem and the men of Judah, together opening their mouths in praise of the Holy One, blessed be He, will say, *Praise the Lord for He is good, His steadfast love is eternal.*

This midrashic interpretation reads even more clearly as a liturgical dramatization with two antiphonal choruses. It capitalizes on the plural voice of the original Hebrew text but takes no advantage of Hebrew or Aramaic wordplays, nor does it include the expected characters of the biblical story as in midrashim 2 and 3.

Midrash 5. A lengthier variation on the midrash develops by approximately the year 1000 C.E. but clearly echoes the pre-Christian tradition of Psalm 151 as noted previously (midrash 1). It incorporates obviously earlier elements, but also surely mixes these early elements with later interpretations; the historical strata are again virtually impossible to separate. The text is in itself so rich and so delightful that it is quoted here at some length:[52]

> Fill your horn with oil and set out; I am sending you to Jesse the Bet-Hallahamite (1 Sam. 16:1). *Happy is the man You choose and bring near to dwell in Your courts* (Ps. 65:4). Aaron was chosen—*But I have installed My king on Zion, My holy hill* (Ps. 2:6)—and I have set him as a foundation—as it is said, *and went away with the pin of the loom, and with the web* (Judges 16:14)—and I anointed him, as it is said, *I did not anoint myself* (Dan. 10:3). His anointing was the outcome of his suffering. Rav Huna said in the name of Rabbi Aha: The sufferings are divided into three parts: one to our generation and that of our fathers; one to the generation of the destruction [of the Temple]; and one to [the era of] the King-Messiah, as it is written: *He was wounded because of our sins, crushed because of our iniquities* (Isa. 53:5). They said to the King-Messiah: "Where are you looking for David?" He said: "Do you even have to ask? *On Zion, My holy hill.* For just as we are responsible to respect his environment when it is builded up, so [must we respect it] when it is laid waste."

---

52. *Midrash Shemuel*, chap. 19 (Buber, 51a–52b).

I shall be anointed with freshing oil (Ps. 92:10). Rabbi Yehudah ben
Giron and Rabbi Yehoshua of Saknin, in the name of Rabbi Levi: One said
"Saul was anointed but his shield was not anointed." And one said, "Neither he nor his shield." David said, "I was anointed with the oil of anointing which Moses made in the wilderness: *You raise my horn high like
that of a wild ox. I shall be anointed with freshing oil.*"

Go, I am sending you to Jesse the Bet-Hallaḥamite (1 Sam. 16:1).
This means that [Jesse] owned a professional bakery, since he came from
Beit Leḥem [the House of Bread] which is in Judah. Rabbi Samuel bar
Naḥman in the name of Rabbi Simeon ben Laqish said, "It means he was
a student of the Torah, in which is written, *Come eat of my bread* (Prov.
9:5).

For I have decided on one of his sons to be king (1 Sam. 16:1). Rabbi
Yehudah ha-Nassi taught a catena: *to me*—every place where it says *to
Me* is neither a part of this world nor a part of the world to come [for it
transcends chronos]. Of kohanim [priests] what does it say? *That they
serve as priests to Me* (Ex. 40:15). Of levites what does it say? *Therefore
the Levites shall be Mine* [to me] (Num. 3:12). Of the Israelites what does
it say? *For the children of Israel are Mine* (Lev. 25:55). Of the Land of
Israel what does it say? *For the land is Mine* (Lev. 25:23). And of the
heave-offering what does it say? *That they bring an offering to Me* (Ex.
25:2). Of the tithe what does it say? *And of all that You shall give to me I
shall surely give the tenth to You* (Gen. 28:22). Of the first-born what
does it say? *Sanctify to Me all the first-born* (Ex. 13:2). Of the oil of
anointing what does it say? *This shall be a holy anointing oil to Me* (Ex.
30:31). Of Jerusalem what does it say? *Jerusalem the city which I have
chosen unto Me* (1 Kgs. 11:36). Of the Temple what does it say? *And let
them make for Me a sanctuary* (Ex. 25:8). Of the altar what does it say?
An earthen altar you shall make for Me (Ex. 20:24). Of the sacrifices
what does it say? *You shall observe to offer to Me* (Num. 28:2). Of the
Sanhedrin what does it say? *Gather to Me seventy men* (Num. 11:16). Of
the reign of King David what does it say? *For I have provided for Me a
king from among his sons* (1 Sam. 16:1). Therefore everywhere that it
says *to Me* refers to something which is neither a part of this world nor a
part of the world to come. . . .

When they arrived and he saw Eliav, he thought, "Surely the Lord's
anointed stands before Him." But the Lord said to Samuel, "Pay no attention to his appearance or his stature, for I have rejected him" (1 Sam.
16:6–7). Why? Because [though Eliav appeared to have been chosen up to
this point, God found that he] was petulant [and so He rejected him].[53]

---

53. BT Pesaḥim 66b; Ginzberg, *Legends*, 4.83–84 and 6.249 n20. Eliav's rejection
is explained by his behavior at 1 Sam. 17:26–29. On petulant, see *qafdan* in
Ben-Yehudah, 6058–59; compare the word at Isa. 38:12, Ezek. 7:25. and Ben Sira
4:31.

Then Samuel asked Jesse, "Are these all the boys you have remaining?" He replied, "There is still the least important;[54] behold, he is tending the flock" (1 Sam. 16:11). Said Rabbi Levi: This [whole] verse is inspired by the Holy Spirit, as it is said: "these" in the sense of *The punishment* [tam] *of thy iniquity is accomplished* [tam], *O Daughter of Zion* (Lam. 4:22). "All the boys"—*And a little child shall herd them* (Isa. 11:6). And he said "There is still" [od] in the sense of *There shall yet* [od] *be old men and women in the squares of Jerusalem* (Zech. 8:4). "Remaining" in the sense of *Only a remnant shall return, only a remnant of Jacob* (Isa. 10:21). "The least important" in the sense of *the least one shall become a clan* (Isa. 60:22). "Behold" in the sense of *Behold on the hills the footsteps of a herald announcing good fortune* (Nahum 1:15). "Tending"—*Tend Your people with Your staff* (Mic. 7:14). "The flock"— For *you, My flock, the flock that I tend* (Ezek. 34:31).

Then Samuel said to Jesse, Send and fetch someone to bring him, for we will not sit down to eat until he gets here (1 Sam. 16:11). Said Rabbi Samuel bar Naḥman: Just as in this world, two of the great men of history, Jesse and Samuel, did not sit down [for a meal] until David came to sit between them, so in the future which is to come, there will not be any situation whatsoever of the righteous without David's being present [within it].

So they sent, and brought him, and he was ruddy *[admoni]*[55] with beautiful eyes (1 Sam. 16:12). When Samuel took a look at David, he began to tremble ever more and more, saying "Here is one who is destined to spill blood, [just] as it is said [of Esau], *and the first* [rishui] *came out ruddy* [admoni] (Gen. 25:25). The Holy One, blessed be He, said to [Samuel]: But he has *beautiful eyes*! David would kill only with the consent of the Sanhedrin, but Esau would kill on his own initiative.

And the Lord said, "Rise and anoint him; for this is he" (1 Sam. 16:12). The Holy One, blessed be He, said to [Samuel]: Stand up in his presence! Said Rabbi Samuel bar Naḥman: *This is he* in this world, and *this is he* in the world to come; therefore [David] praised the Holy One, blessed be He, with ten songs, as it is written, *I adore you, O Lord my strength; O Lord my crag, my fortress, my rescuer* (Ps. 18:2–3). Said Rabbi Sion: Also at the end of the book [of Psalms] he praises the Holy

---

54. The Hebrew word *qatan* here does not mean the youngest but rather the least important. 1 Chron. 27:18 mentions a brother of David named Elihu. This Elihu does not appear in the list of Jesse's seven sons at 1 Chron. 2:13, so rabbinic tradition holds that he was born somewhere between 1 Chron. 2 and 27, as the youngest son who came even after David. Scholarly sources generally hold that Elihu is a misspelling of Eliav, the oldest of David's brothers.

55. See note 61 for an explanation of the midrashic importance of the term *admoni*.

One, blessed be He, in ten psalms: *Hallelujah! Praise God in his sanctuary* (Ps. 150:1).

Rabbi Samuel bar Nahman spelled out to them this passage according to the signs DIA"Sh AISh'K KShD"K [as a mnemonic from the first letters in each of the following Hebrew lines]:

> David said: *I praise You, for You have answered me* (Ps. 118:21).
> Jesse said: *The stone that the builders rejected.*
> The brothers said: *This is the Lord's doing.*
> Samuel said: *This is the day that the Lord has made.*
> His brothers said: *O Lord, deliver us!*
> Jesse said: *O Lord, let us prosper!*
> Samuel said: *May he who enters be blessed in the name of the Lord.*
> Everyone said: *We bless you from the house of the Lord.*[56]
> David said: *You are my God and I will praise you.*
> Everyone said: *Praise the Lord, for He is good; his steadfast love is eternal.*

One of the attendants spoke up, "I have observed a son of Jesse the Bet-Hallahamite, [one] who is skilled in music; he is a stalwart fellow and a warrior, sensible in speech, and handsome in appearance, and the Lord is with him (1 Sam. 16:18).

> *Is skilled in music*—in [reading] Scripture [with neumes].
> *A stalwart fellow*—in Mishnah.
> *A warrior*—in Talmud.
> *Sensible in speech*—[preferring] good deeds [to pious words].
> *Handsome in appearance*—paying particular attention to halakhah.
> *And the Lord is with him*—the halakhah is like his own words.

As can be seen, by the year 1000 C.E. the entire story had been spelled out in detail, in keeping with the midrashic purpose of filling in details that are missing from the Scriptural text.

Midrash 6. But even this extensive elaboration has its early precedents, and may not be dismissed as simply a medieval flight of the imagination. The *Midrash Tannaim* is usually identified as a collection of beraitot and aggadic materials from the first two centuries C.E. Therein we read yet another variation on the story of David; though not treating of Psalm 118:21–29, this variation does fill in background materials that seem to be assumed by the treatments of Psalm 118 that we have seen may

---

56. The text is corrupt, for in order to reconstruct the KShD"K (koolam, Shemuel, David, koolam), two more speakers would have to be added here in the sequence. Compare n50.

even precede Matthew. According to *Midrash Tannaim* to Deuteronomy 1:17:[57]

> *Saul approached Samuel inside the gate, and said to him, "Tell me, please, where is the house of the seer?* (1 Sam. 9:18). [Samuel] surely must have said to [Saul] : What is it that you are seeking?" He said to him, "I seek the one who is to be appointed to rule [as prince over Israel]." [Samuel] said, "I am the seer." The Holy One, blessed be He, said to Samuel, "You boaster! You call yourself a seer? I will show you that which you cannot see, when I show you in that hour that which you cannot see until I show you!"

> *At the time that [the Lord] said to Samuel, Fill your horn with oil and set out; I am sending you to Jesse the Bet-Hallaḥamite* (1 Sam. 16:1), upon arriving at the house of Jesse they brought Eliav before [Samuel]. [Samuel] looked at [Eliav], assumed him to be the chosen one, and commenced to anoint him. He cried out, *Surely the Lord's anointed stands before him* (1 Sam. 16:6). The Holy One, blessed be He, said to [Samuel], "Are you not he who said 'I am the seer?' *Pay no attention to his appearance or his stature, for I have rejected him* (1 Sam. 16:7)."

And so all [the sons] passed before Samuel and he said "No, God has not chosen any one of these." At last Samuel said to Jesse, *Are these all the boys you have?* (1 Sam. 16:11). And Jesse said, *There is still the least significant.* And because he is the least significant, he is laboring for me. [David] was also the youngest, as it is said, *Ozem the sixth, David the seventh* (1 Chron. 2:15). Why is he [usually] referred to as the least significant [rather than as the youngest]? Because he was rejected in the eyes of his father, for when he was only a child he had prophesied [in the presence of his father]: "In the future I will lay waste the places of the Philistines, and I will kill from among them a giant man by the name of Goliath; and in the future I will erect the Temple [in Jerusalem]." What did his father do to him [in return]? He took advantage of him by sending him out to tend the sheep.

> *Then Samuel said to Jesse, "Send someone to fetch him." So they sent and brought him. He was ruddy, with beautiful eyes and a handsome appearance* (1 Sam. 16:11–12). Samuel began to disregard him [on account of his appearance]. The Holy One, blessed be He, immediately grew angry and said, *Rise and anoint him, for this is he* (1 Sam. 16:12). "Stand up," [the Lord] shouted. "Stand up before My anointed one. He is standing and you are sitting!" And when [David] became king, what did

---

57. The text is culled from Hoffman, 10, and *Midrash ha-Gadol Devarim* to Deut. 1:17 (Fish, 31–32). On the early date of the *Midrash Tannaim*, see Strack, 206–9.

he say? *The stone that the builders rejected has become the chief of the corner* (Ps. 118:22).[58] By "the builders" is meant Samuel and Jesse. By "the chief of the corner" is meant that he is the King of Kings.

Midrash 7. One final significant story, further developing the same theme, is found in a fifteenth-century Spanish collection. Its emphasis is both messianic and miraculous. According to *Yalqut ha-Makhiri* to Psalm 118:[59]

> The stone the builders rejected has become the head of the corner. *Behold I was conceived in iniquity, a sinner from my mother's womb* (Ps. 51:5). The word "iniquity" is written *in plene* with two vavs [*avvon*] indicating the discord created when the two halves of the verse are joined as one. The first half suggests that David was the son of passion; the second half that he was the son of hatred.
>
> Now Jesse was the head of the Sanhedrin, and he did not go out and come in except with a retinue of sixty-myriad [attendants]. And he had sixty[60] grown sons, and he had held himself apart [sexually] from his wife for three years.
>
> After three years, he had a comely servant girl, and he was seized with desire for her. He said to her, "My daughter, go prepare yourself, for if you will come in to [my bedchamber] tonight [and lie with me], perhaps I will give you a letter of emancipation."
>
> The chaste servant girl was shocked by the advances of this old man, and so she went and told [Jesse's] wife, Nazbat bat Adiel: "Save yourself, and my soul, and that of my master, from Gehenna."

---

58. *Yalqut Shimeoni* to Noah 10, at number 62, 17a, applies "The stone the builders rejected . . ." to Abraham, but the association here is much more usual. See also *Pirqei de Rabbi Eliezer*, 24 (Luria, 57a–b).

59. Conflated from *Yalqut ha-Makhiri* to Ps. 118 at #28 (Buber, 214) and Ginzberg, *Legends*, 6.247. See also Jacob Sicili, *Torat ha-Minhah*, be-Shallah (manuscript); Naftali Hertz Travis (FfM), *Siddur ha-Qabbalah*, at Hallel, cue word *mah ashiv*; Meir Aldabi, *Shevilei Emunah* 3.4; Shemuel Laniado, *Keli Yaqar* on 1 Sam. 16:11; Menahem Azariah of Fano, *Ten Treatises*, 96b–97a; Haim Yosef David Azzulai, *Simhat ha-Regel* on the Passover Haggadah, to Ps. 116:16, p. 82b, cue word *ana ha-shem*; ibid, to *Peh Ehad*, 12a; ibid, *Yosef Tehillot* to Pss. 69:9, 116, 118; ibid, *Midbar Qedumot* (chap. 10, #20, pp. 27b–28a) and *Yosef Tehillot* to Ps. 51:7; Biur ha-GR"A #25 on *Shulhan Arukh* 2, Yoreh Deah #157, 2, in the gloss of Isserles; Yosef Habiba, *Nimuqei Yosef* to Baba Qamma, 79–80; Ginzberg, *Legends*, 4.82 and 6.246 n11; Zunz, *Die synagogale Poesie*, 1.128–29. The plot here reads like an ur-text for Mozart's *Le Nozze di Figaro*. See a similar story at Josephus, *Antiquities*, 12.186–95 (Marcus, 7.96–101).

60. Ginzberg, *Legends*, 6.247 says to read 6 instead of 60.

Nazbat said: "What on earth are you talking about?"

The servant girl told her everything.

Nazbat said to her: "My daughter, what shall I do? As of today, it is three years since he approached me!"

The servant girl said to her: "Shall I give you some advice? Go prepare yourself, and I will not [prepare myself]. Tonight when he says, 'Close the door,' you sneak in and I will sneak out."

And that is just the way it happened.

That evening the servant girl arrived. [Jesse] extinguished the candle, [and when] she went to close the door, Nazbat, dressed just like the servant girl, snuck in and the servant girl snuck out. Nazbat was pleasured by him the whole night long and became pregnant with David.

Because of the heat of [Jesse's] passionate love for the supposed servant girl, David turned out to be the only ruddy one among his brothers. . . .[61]

After nine months, her time came to deliver, and she gave birth to David. When David was born, Nazbat the wife of Jesse said to her sons: "If word gets out in public about this baby, just say that he is a domestically born slave [compare Gen. 17:27] , in order that no suspicion be cast upon the rest of you boys that you too are the result of illicit unions." But the brothers, who all knew that Jesse held himself apart from her, were furious with their mother for having such an obviously red-haired illegitimate son. It was only Jesse's personal intervention which prevented the sons from murdering their mother as an adulteress. As for the baby, he said to his sons, "Leave him be; we will use him as a slave and a pastor of sheep." That is why David, rejected and set apart, was tending the sheep, until the prophet Samuel came along to reveal that David was the legitimate offspring of both Jesse and Nazbat, and then anointed David to be king over Israel.

The entire matter [of David's illicit birth] was kept secret for twenty-eight years, until the Holy One, Blessed be He, said to Samuel, *Go, I am sending you to the house of Jesse the Hallaḥamite* (1 Sam. 16:1). When [Samuel] arrived, Eliav came to stand before him, and [Samuel] said, *Surely the Lord's anointed stands before him. But the Lord said to him, Pay no attention to his appearance or his stature. . . .* (1 Sam. 16:6–7).

---

61. David was said to be *admoni*, which can be translated either "red-haired" or "ruddy-complected," from the word *adom*, "red." See Ben Yehudah, 70; Qimḥi, 4. The Vulgate understands it to mean "ruddy," *erat autem rufus* (1 Sam. 16:12), *ruber* being the regular color for red (Lewis and Short, 1602), and *rufus* generally indicating ruddiness of hair and skin. The LXX brings *purrakēs* (flaming red), whereas the Aramaic targum brings *samoq* (red-hued). Josephus, *Antiquities* 6.164 (Marcus, 5.248), says *xanthos men ten chroan* (red-yellowish of complexion).

Then came forward the second and third sons, until all of his sons had come forward. Samuel said to Jesse, *Are these all the boys you have?* And Jesse replied, "Yes, that is all!" Samuel said to him, "The Holy One, blessed be He, said to me, 'Go, I will send you to Jesse,' and [now] you tell me there is no other [son]?" Jesse said to Samuel, *There is one who yet remains, the youngest, and he is but a tender of sheep* (1 Sam. 16:11).

> *Samuel said, Send someone to bring him.* When [David] arrived, the oil [for anointing] began to bubble more and more. The Holy One, blessed be He, said to Samuel, "Samuel, you are here, and my anointed one is here; *rise and anoint him, for this is he!* Samuel poured the oil on [David's] head and it congealed into precious stones and pearls, yet [when he turned upright] the oil cruet, it was as full as it had been before. And the oil ran down the length of his body (cf. Ps. 133:2). Jesse and his sons stood there trembling in awe. They said, "Samuel has come not only to humiliate us, but also to announce to Israel that it has an illegitimate son." David's mother rejoiced inwardly though she maintained outwardly an appearance of mourning. [But] when [David] took the cup of salvation, all of them rejoiced. Samuel stood up and kissed [David] on the head. He opened his mouth and said, *Thou art my son* (Ps. 2:7). At the same moment, [David's] mother said, *The stone that the builders* [banim] *rejected*—"the sons" [*bonim*], as it is written. And she said, "Indeed my son whom you rejected—you his own brothers—has become the chief of the leaders and has risen up over you all. Her sons said to her, *This is the Lord's doing;* therefore *this is the day that the Lord has made; let us exult and rejoice on it* (Ps. 118:23–24).

We have here repeatedly a clear, early tradition linking the sixteenth chapter of Samuel with Psalm 118:21–29. The tradition is developed, collected, and redeveloped over a number of centuries, but its repeated attribution to Samuel bar Naḥman (a Palestinian amora of the late third century) and its prototypical appearance in early sources such as the Dead Sea Scrolls and the targum, suggests that it was known at least by the first century C.E., and perhaps earlier. It could even have developed in that period when Hebrew was no longer the spoken language of the people. Once the Bible was translated into Aramaic, the wordplay mentioned earlier in this chapter became too obvious to ignore. It seems quite possible that this midrashic tradition, or at least some very early echo of it, identifies a Second Temple listener's response to Psalm 118:22, "The stone which the builders rejected."

Suspicion, Messianism, and Jesus

Earlier in this chapter we examined the manner in which the Jewish literary tradition has employed the catenic piyyut to illustrate typological parallelism. In the search for Second Temple listener response, we may be further assisted by the construction of a hypothetical piyyut to illustrate the adumbration occurring in the minds of first-century Jews confronted with the charismatic Galilean teacher. Although the following piyyut has no historical roots, its structure illustrates the value of typological parallelism in teaching a received tradition, and the uniqueness of continuing revelation unfolding in the present:

PIYYUT: THE MESSIANIC REVELATION

"The deeds of the parents are prophetic signs to the children." You find whatever is stated of David is also stated of Jesus:

David was born of a royal line, as it is said: *A star rises from Jacob, and a scepter comes forth from Israel* (Num. 24:17).	Jesus was born of a royal line, as it is said: *And Jacob the father of Joseph the husband of Mary, of whom Jesus was born* (Matt. 1:16).
David was born in Bethlehem, as it is said: *I am sending you to Jesse the Bethlehemite* (1 Sam. 16:1).	Jesus was born in Bethlehem, as it is said: *In Bethlehem of Judea, for so it has been written by the prophet* (Matt. 2:5).
David was born of a suspicious pregnancy, as it is said: *Whose son is that boy?* (1 Sam. 17:55).	Jesus was born of a suspicious pregnancy, as it is said: *He was the son, or so they thought, of Joseph* (Luke 3:23).
David was born to an eternal destiny, as it is said: *Your house and your kingship shall ever be secure before you* (2 Sam. 7:16).	Jesus was born to an eternal destiny, as it is said: *a light for revelation to the Gentiles, and for glory to your people Israel* (Luke 2:32).
David was not recognized as an exceptional child, as it is said: *the stone the builders rejected has become the head* (Ps. 118:22).	Jesus was not recognized as an exceptional child, as it is said: *Where did this man get all this?* (Matt. 13:55).
David was a shepherd, as it is said: *You shall shepherd My people Israel* (2 Sam. 5:2).	Jesus was a shepherd, as it is said: *I am the good shepherd* (John 10:14).
David was elevated by God, as it is said: *And the spirit of the Lord gripped David from that day on* (1 Sam. 16:13).	Jesus was elevated by God, as it is said: *This is my Son, with whom I am well pleased* (Matt. 3:17).

David had no earthly home, as it is said: *I shall dwell in the house of the Lord my whole life long* (Ps. 23:6).	Jesus had no earthly home, as it is said: *the Son of Man has nowhere to lay his head* (Matt. 8:20).
David was a prophet, as it is said: *The spirit of the Lord has spoken through me; his message is upon my tongue* (2 Sam. 23:2).	Jesus was a prophet, as it is said: *A great prophet has arisen among us* (Luke 7:16).
David was anointed, as it is said: *Samuel took the horn of oil and anointed him* (1 Sam. 16:13).	Jesus was anointed, as it is said: *She has anointed my feet* (Luke 7:46).
David reigned over the twelve clans, as it is said: *He preferred to make me king over all Israel* (1 Chron. 28:4).	Jesus reigned over the twelve clans, as it is said, *You who have followed me will also sit on twelve thrones* (Matt. 19:28).
David wept, as it is said: *The king went up to the upper chamber of the gateway and wept* (2 Sam. 18:33).	Jesus wept, as it is said: *Jesus wept* (John 11:35).
David survived from the showbread, as it is said: *So the priest gave him the consecrated bread of the Presence* (1 Sam. 21:6).	Jesus learned from the showbread, as it is said: *Have you not read what David did when he and his companions were hungry?* (Matt. 12:3).
David was saved by God, as it is said: *The Lord said to my lord, "Sit at my right hand"* (Ps. 110:1).	Jesus was saved by God, as it is said: *The Lord said to my lord, "Sit at my right hand"* (Matt. 22:44).

With this exploration of adumbration and the catenic piyyut, we have discovered one more way in which Jewish sources illuminate the New Testament, this time not through source materials but through typological parallelism. This method also strongly suggests a form of listener-response association, in that the specific details of the manner in which the parallelisms complement and redefine each other is never made very explicit. However, because the qualities that make each parallel powerful are themselves so listener-specific, and because the gospel records are necessarily as vague as they are about the suspicions raised by Jesus' birth and infancy, we are left here with only the broadest strokes of a painting, the details of which we can no longer supply.

"The stone the builders rejected" speaks to us of society's rejection of suspect origins, particularly when they are attached to persons of power. But the phrase also reminds us once again, as in the case of the Fish Who Paid Taxes, that power and truth often lie hidden in corners outside the pale of societal expectations and definitions. The children of God are often unrecognized as such; even more so the building stones of the kingdom. Like the treasure hidden in the field, the leaven in the lump, the grain of mustard seed growing invisibly, the kingdom proclaimed by Jesus was one that had little to do with temporally accepted structures of power and authority. For this reason we need to recognize the nuclear mashal of "The stone the builders rejected" as a proclamation not of Jesus' messianic character, but of the invisible and contradictory power of God at work deep within the spiraling cycles of human history.

Chapter 9

Listener Response:
Wedding Feasts and Wineskins

(Matthew 9:14–17)

Some years ago a priest friend of mine confessed to me his suspicion that Christians misunderstood the parable of New Wine in Old Wineskins (Matt. 9:14–17; Mark 2:18–22; Luke 5:33–39). His hunch struck me as worth exploring, for indeed all cultures that we know of, from Greek and Roman through European and American, value aged or mature wine over young or new wine, almost without exception. Certainly the Second Temple culture within which Jesus lived and taught appreciated the value of mature wine, as will be shown through citations from rabbinic literature. I then found my own suspicion—that Jesus' parable is not intended to affirm the value of young or new wine—supported in an article by David Flusser, in which he asks: "why should Jesus, the 'glutton and drinker' (Matt. 11:19), who knew the value of an old wine, have used a simile, according to which the new wine is better than the old? Such an unnatural comparison does not fit the way in which Jesus explained his doctrines."[1]

Christian tradition has frequently understood this parable as an argument for supersession and displacement: the fragile and temporary vessels of the Old Covenant cannot tolerate the exciting vitality, the fresh sparkling wine of the New, and so the old is destabilized and eventually destroyed. Henceforth no Christian will drink anything but new beaujolais![2]

---

1. David Flusser, "New Wine," 27; see also 28 and 31. Crossan (*Parables*, 95) denies any dominical connection to this statement of enological sophistication, understanding it rather as a free-floating proverb, as does Bultmann, 102. Bultmann, 98, says it is impossible to tell from any of the three gospels whether new wine or old wine is preferable.

2. For example, Allen observes (93): "To graft Christianity on to Judaism would not only increase the rents in the latter, and ultimately destroy its forms and ordi-

Obviously something is wrong here with the traditional exegesis: once again as in so many examples we have already seen, a facile homiletic interpretation of the text is possible only when the details of the text itself are ignored. Rather, the saying of Jesus about new patches on old garments, and new wine in old wineskins, is intended as an argument against certain innovations in the face of inherited tradition. On an exoteric level, the parable functions as an argument from practicality, not unlike a helpful household hint: one who attempts to repair a worn garment with inappropriate materials will ruin the garment, and one who stores drink in the wrong containers will wind up losing everything. But on an esoteric level, Jesus' listeners find themselves confronted with a teaching about the preservation of their received Jewish traditions and the dangerous instability of indiscriminate innovation.

Similarities and Differences in the Transmitted Text

The Gospel of Thomas transmits the pericope under consideration as though it were two totally unrelated sayings. According to Thomas, Logion 104:[3]

> They said [to Jesus], "Come, let us pray today and let us fast."
>
> Jesus said, "What is the sin that I have committed, or wherein have I been defeated? But when the bridegroom leaves the bridal chamber, then let them fast and pray."

Much earlier in Thomas, we read the second half of the synoptic pericope, but transmitted in reverse order from the synoptics. In Matthew 9:14–17, patches are spoken of first and wine second; in Thomas wine is spoken of first and patches second. Thomas also connects the parable to the Servant

---

nances; it would also be disastrous for Christianity itself which, confined in the forms of Judaism, would burst them asunder and be dissipated like wine poured on the ground. Forms such as fasting could not hold the wine of the new Christian spirit. The last clause, 'and both are preserved,' can only give expression to the thought that if Christianity be allowed to develop independently of Jewish modes, both Christianity and Judaism are preserved. But the thought of the preservation and continuance of Jewish modes of religion is foreign to the context. The clause is doubtless due to the editor, who is thinking rather of completing the literary parallelism than of the meaning underlying the words which he records." Cf. Green, *Matthew*, 104; Hill, 177; Newman and Stine, 273–74.
3. Funk, *New Gospel*, 51.

of Two Masters (Matt. 6:24; and see Chapter 5), though in Matthew the parable of the wineskins and the parable of two masters are completely unrelated. According to Thomas, Logion 47:[4]

> Jesus said, "It is impossible for a man to mount two horses or to stretch two bows. And it is impossible for a servant to serve two masters; otherwise, he will honor the one and treat the other contemptuously. No man drinks old wine and immediately desires to drink new wine. And new wine is not put into old wineskin, lest they burst; nor is old wine put into a new wineskins, lest it spoil it. An old patch is not sewn onto a new garment, because a tear would result."

In the synoptic gospels, a number of similarities can be observed in the parallel versions transmitted by Matthew, Mark, and Luke. The text in all three cases is short: in Matthew, four verses, in Mark, five verses, and in Luke, seven verses. Five points of similarity between the three versions of the text are significant:

1. The question of why Jesus' disciples do not fast in the same manner as do those who come to inquire of Jesus. Specifically, Jesus' disciples are contrasted with the disciples of John the Baptist and the disciples of the Pharisees, both of the latter apparently having an accepted fasting discipline.

2. The image of a joyous wedding feast attended by at least the groomsmen, and possibly the groom. No mention is made of bridesmaids or a bride (as I have already noted in Chapter 5 in relation to the Wise and Foolish Maidens), nor do any of the three gospels suggest either that the wedding has taken place or that it will take place in the future. In fact, all three texts hint that the groom will be gone before the wedding occurs.

3. The image of a new patch sewn on an old garment and the additional harm that the new patch subsequently brings to the old garment.

4. The image of young wine poured into worn wineskins and the regrettable damage the wine causes to the skins, in addition to the loss of the wine itself.

5. The derivatory question of whether "new" is a regrettable addition to the "old," or whether some sort of carefully constructed harmony can be negotiated between them.

Along with these five common points, there are also significant differences among the three versions of the same pericope—differences that not

---

4. Id.

only reveal the historical vagaries of textual transmission but also suggest the gospel editors' attempt to adapt Jesus' original saying to the needs of the later Christian community and its developing tensions with Judaism. To recapture any possible dominical intention within the pericope, these differences must be addressed as well.

First, Matthew's initial question reveals significant disagreement over the practices of piety between the followers of John the Baptist and the followers of Jesus. The gospels do not even agree who asks the challenging question: "Why do the disciples of John fast and your disciples do not?" Matthew states it was the followers of John, Luke infers the scribes and Pharisees,[5] and Mark identifies the questioners as both John's disciples and the Pharisees. The struggle between the Baptist community and the Jesus community reflected in Matthew's and Mark's versions could have been contemporaneous with Jesus' ministry, but also could have continued into the early church for two hundred years or more, thus influencing the gospel redactors.

Loisy, Bauer, Goguel, and others believe that the text of John 3:25 read originally: "This led to a controversy about purification between John's disciples and Jesus." Their interpretation is based on the struggle they identify between the two communities. Flusser supports this interpretation:

> Jesus stayed for a while in the company of John the Baptist, and then founded his own separate community. The reason for this separation was apparently Jesus' view of the Kingdom of Heaven as being realized here and now, as against the view of John the Baptist, which regarded the realization of Jewish Messianic aspirations as a future event. . . . When [John] was executed on the orders of Herod Antipas, the belief that [John] had come back to life was born (Matt. 14:1–2; 16:14). It is reasonable to assume that the belief in the resurrection of John the Baptist also influenced the belief in Jesus' resurrection, since Jesus' disciples included former disciples of John.[6]

---

5. Luke says that "they" (*hoi*) came to Jesus with a question. The closest reference in the text is Luke 5:30: "the Pharisees and their scribes," *hoi Pharisaioi kai hoi grammateis autōn*. The followers of John are not suggested as part of the confronting party.

6. On the tension between the followers of Jesus and John the Baptist, see R. Brown, *Gospel of John*, 1.lxvii–lxx (extensive information here) and 150–52; Hill, 175, Bultmann, 19–20, 23–24; Flusser, *Meqorot*, 81–112 and *JOC*, 140–48; Crossan *Historical*, 259–60, referring to Matt. 11:16–19. Howard, 11 to Matt. 3:10, brings the text as "And all the people were thinking and reckoning in their circumcised heart: John is Jesus"; and see Howard, 205. See also Acts 18:5–19:7; Justin,

Second, Matthew and Mark suggest that Jesus' disciples simply do not fast at all. Luke says that rather than fasting, the disciples of Jesus openly feast. The topic of controversy is not the annual fast days of the Jewish calendar but practices of ascetic piety on a daily or weekly basis, as shaped by individual and competitive schools of thought within Second Temple Judaism.[7]

Third, the three gospel versions differ as to the frequency of the discipline of fasting by the Johannites (the community of John the Baptist, not John the evangelist) and the Pharisees, thus implying as well a difference of intent. Matthew says that the Johannites and Pharisees fast frequently.[8] Luke says that the Johannites fast constantly,[9] combining fasting with prayer, and that the Pharisees do likewise.[10] The difference of intent is implied in the distinction between "frequently" and "constantly."

Fourth, Matthew suggests that the time for fasting will come at some indefinite point in the future. Mark says that the groomsmen will fast on the day that the bridegroom is taken away from them. Luke suggests an extended fast that will begin when the bridegroom leaves.[11]

Trypho 80 (Williams, 171); *Pseudo-Clementine Recognitions* 1.54–60 (ANF 8.91–92).

7. Fasting twice a week was an important discipline in some parts of the early church, as witnessed by the Didache 8:1; compare, however, the attitude in Luke 18:12. On such ascetical practices in the Second Temple period, see Alon, *Mekhkarim*, 1.291, 2.18:12.

8. Greek: *polla*. Peshitta: *tenan sagi* meaning "over and over again." See Jastrow, 954 and 1679–80, "much repeated."

9. Greek: *pukna*. The adverb is missing from the Peshitta text. Tetraevangelion Latin: *jejunat perseverauter*.

10. The disciples of John may well have fasted frequently, given the connection between repentance and fasting. That the Pharisees would fast "constantly" seems extremely doubtful, as at least according to Neusner, they were bound together by rite and rituals of table fellowship including rigorous tithing of all food and drink. In fact, Neusner (*Judaism in the Beginning*, 55) claims that fasting played no part in the Pharisaic tradition as we know it through rabbinic Judaism.

11. Not all Greek texts of the three gospels make the distinction concerning "will be taken away." However, Matt. 9:15 and Luke 5:35 have *aparthē* (Latin: *auferetur/fuerit*). According to Allen, 163, *aparthē* appears only here in the New Testament but is found frequently in classical Greek, to indicate the movement of fleets and armies (see Liddell and Scott, 175 *apairō*). The Peshitta makes a distinction, as does the Tetraevangelion, between Matthew and Mark who have *nishtaqel/ashtaqel* (Jastrow, 1623; Latin: *quum ablatus fuerit*), and Luke who has *nitaterim* (Jastrow, 945; Sokoloff, *Dictionary*, 363; Latin: *quum attolletur*). Thus, in Matthew and Mark the bridegroom seems to be taken away; in Luke he is driven away. The distinction is tantalizing but perhaps impossible to resolve.

Fifth, Luke identifies the verses that follow—on the garment and the wineskins—as a parable; the other two gospels include no such literary transition.

Sixth, Matthew and Mark suggest, in an obfuscating explanation, that the new patch will restrict the "fullness" of the original garment, causing an even worse tear in the very garment someone was trying to save by adding a patch. Luke suggests that the new patch (rather than the original garment) will tear, and that the mismatch between the new patch and the original garment will appear absurd or offensive to aesthetic taste.

Seventh, all three gospels agree that no one places (pours? stores? puts?) new wine in old skins. The new wine will burst the wineskins and spill out, resulting in the regrettable loss of the wineskins. None of the synoptics appear overly concerned with the new wine itself except for its function as an agent of destruction for the storage vessels:

1. Mark says simply that new wine belongs in fresh skins, like to like.

2. Matthew and Luke state that by putting new wine into fresh skins, the damage caused by the new wine can be minimized, saving the old skins for a better use.

3. Luke attaches a final addendum, praising the virtues of aged wine over the less desirable young wine. In essence Luke says: "After tasting mature wine, no one in his right mind would want to drink new wine!"[12]

In its original setting we have a confrontation of Jesus concerning the failure of his disciples to fast. Jesus responds to the challenge with an image of feasting groomsmen, and then with a bipartite parable about old clothes and used wineskins so as to make some point about the relationship between new and old, young and mature, fresh and worn. The logic by which the four subjects—fasting, groomsmen, old clothing, and wineskins—connect with each other is not immediately apparent. Unravelling the puzzle requires that each subject be approached from at least three angles: a study of the Greek words in relation to Hebrew and Aramaic; the identification of other texts that illuminate the synoptic parable; and the symbolism suggested by each of the parable's subjects in parallel litera-

---

12. Flusser argues ("New Wine," 26, 28, 30) that the Lukan version is the closest to the original, that Mark depends on Luke, and Matthew on Mark. Though he begins with the argument for the priority of Luke given by Lindsey, Flusser adds his own argument that Luke's version makes the most logical sense, is most sympathetic to tradition, is an integral part of the text, and that Marcion and certain other church fathers particularly rejected Luke's praise of old wine ("New Wine," 27 and elsewhere), perhaps fearing it could be understood as approving of the Jewish covenant. See also Plummer, 164–65; Metzger, ad loc.

ture. By so doing, innovations in the practice of piety and the formulation of doctrine condemned by the Matthean parable move to the foreground of the text.

Patching Damaged Garments

The Hebrew root Q-R-ʾA, in the sense of tearing or rending garments, appears frequently in the Hebrew Scriptures, particularly in relationship to mourning.[13] The act of rending, or ripping, a garment as a sign of mourning and of sorrow is called *qeriʾah*, and, although such an act is frequently referred to in the literature as a "custom" (*minhag*), it is also carefully regulated by legal opinion (*halakhah*). The symbolic act of rending is given various interpretations: the rending of the heart (by rending one's clothing "over the heart"; see Joel 2:13);[14] the rending of a relationship, particularly at the death of one's parents; or even the rending of the fabric of creation. Of particular note in regard to the gospel parable is the opinion that one is obliged to rend one's garments upon hearing of the death of one's teacher. According to BT Moed Qatan 26a:

> Our sages taught: These are rends that are not [to be] sewed up: One who rends [his clothes] for his father or mother or his teacher who taught him wisdom [*torah*]. . . *The chariots of Israel and the horsemen*

---

13. The rending of garments (*qeriʾah*) appears with frequency in Scripture; see Gen. 37:29 and 34; Josh. 7:6; Job 1:20 and 2:12; Qoh. 3:7, and most important, Joel 2:13 (cf. *Trei Asar* to Joel, 11 esp. n40). According to halakhah, one is obliged only to rend on occasion of national disaster or death, but all other uses (e.g., repentance) are optional, not required (cf. BT Shabbat 105b, and Steinsaltz thereto, 460–61; *Enc. Talmudica*, 3.337). The term also appears as a sign of despair or distress unrelated to death, e.g., 1 Kings 21:27; 2 Kings 5:7 and 22:19. On the word meanings, see Qimḥi, 336; Kohut, 7.210; Ben-Yehudah, 6202–5; Jastrow, 1424.

14. To rend the clothes over one's heart is a symbol of rending the heart. See BT Moed Qatan 26b: "To what extent does he rend [his garment]? To [exposing his breast down to] the [region of the] navel; some say [only] down to the [region] of the heart. Although there is no [authentic] proof of this point, there is some [scriptural] allusion to it, as it is said: *And rend your hearts and not your garments* (Joel 2:13)." Here is an example of how the same metaphor can mean two opposite things, depending on the culture in which it is delivered. In classical Greek culture, to rend someone's garment means to retain a guest with eagerness, or to invite him with urgency; people who do this lay hands on the traveling-cloak as if trying to force someone to stay; see Cicero, *Epistles to Atticus*, 1.18.70 (Winstedt, 1.81), where Pompey wraps his cloak tight so that no one can get him to stay; and Erasmus, *Coll. Works*, 31.142; cf. 1 Sam. 15:27.

thereof (2 Kings 2:12), that is, for a master who taught the Torah. How exactly does it convey this meaning?—As R. Joseph rendered it [in Aramaic]: "My master, my master, who was better protection to Israel with his prayer than chariots and horsemen could be."

We also find the common connection between the death of one's teacher and the rending of garments in JT Moed Qatan 3:

Who is one's master [*rabo*]?

It is the one who has taught him wisdom [rather than the master who has taught him a trade].

It is anyone who started him off first—the words of R. Meir.

R. Judah says, It is anyone who has enlightened his eyes in his repetition of traditions, even in one thing only. . . .

R. Eliezer would even make a tear in mourning on the demise of someone who had begun teaching him at the outset [but was not his principal teacher].

R. Samuel removed his phylacteries on the news of the demise of one who had enlightened his eyes in his learning of Mishnah.

Thus it is that the rending of a garment would have been a natural expression of the disciples' grief over Jesus' having been taken away from them. This rend would then have resulted in a garment in need of later patching.

A rend was to be made immediately upon learning of the death of the one being mourned, and the rend could later be repaired or patched only in specific manners. Accordingly, the above passage from BT Moed Qatan, citing an ancient authority, goes on to say: "For all the dead, everyone bastes[15] after seven [days] and mends completely[16] after thirty [days]. For one's father and one's mother [and one's teacher][17] one bastes after thirty

---

15. *Shalal*; see Jastrow, 1585.

16. *Aḥah*; see Jastrow 40 (*aḥi*); Ben Yehuda, 142–43.

17. Omitted in some texts, but because it follows the previous text—"These are rents that are not to be sewed up"—it is safely presumed to be original. Note that JT Moed Qatan sometimes includes all three, and sometimes only mother and father; and compare Ginsberg, *Palestinian*, 1.390. Both Jewish and Christian traditions count one's teacher as one's "true" father. According to Irenaeus (*Adv. Haer.* 4.41, 2 in Quasten, 1.9), "For when any person has been taught from the mouth of another he is termed the son of him who instructs him, and the latter is called his father." However, another form of argument also justifies grieving the death of a non-blood relative, particularly one who has been as formative as one's teacher.

[days] and never mends completely."[18] To mend a rent garment was considered a desecration of the memory of one's teacher or parent. The requisite tearing of a garment was not done on personal, spontaneous impulse but in specific ways, fulfilling specific requirements. However, as happens with well-worn garments, rends or tears sometimes turned out worse than intended, and when it came time to close the rend, repairs could not be made to the garment without adding an additional piece of material. Ritually torn garments were required to be repaired, except in the above-noted cases, so one went to great lengths to make sure such repair was accomplished. At times, when the tear was particularly bad, a patch (*tala*) was needed.[19] The garment torn as a sign of mourning was always a used one; to tear new clothes was not permitted, for it would signal waste.[20] The patch that was used needed to be chosen carefully. The garment itself could not have been laundered during the period of mourn-

---

According to the traditional reading of Lev. 21:2–3, one is to mourn only the seven degrees of direct blood relationship. However, *Qohelet Rabbah* Proem 7 (Buber, 4a and notes), based on Isa. 3:26, distinguishes between mourning (*avelut*) as formal and external, and grieving (*aninut*) as internal and substantive. At M. Berakhot 2.7, R. Gamliel grieves for his servant Tobias as though he had been a blood relative. Other pertinent texts include M. Sanhedrin 6.6; Nahmanides, *Kitvei*, 2.156; Steinsaltz, *Berakhot*, 72; Higger, *Semahot* 1.10 (p. 100); Ginzberg, *Palestinian*, 1.187; Shelomo Adret to Berakhot, 73. Mourning provides a public means of support and condolence; those who grieve are not provided with such assistance and hence may be in even greater need of comfort by those who are sensitive enough to perceive the deep grief.

18. BT Moed Qatan 22b; see also JT Moed Qatan 3.7 and Tractate Semahot 9:6 (Higger, 170).

19. On *tala*, see Ben-Yehuda, 1875 and 1878; Kohut, 4.32; Jastrow, 536. Alternative spellings include *matlit, tilah, telai, tilyah*. The Greek text to our pericope uses *epiblēma*, a word that appears only once in the Septuagint, with a doubtful translation (Isa. 3:22); see also Sym. to Josh. 9:5 (11). Various texts of the Vulgate use *commissura, insumentum, immissura, assumentum*. Obviously the Latin does not comprehend the Greek, which in turn seems not to comprehend the Hebrew or Aramaic, given the confusion in semitic forms. In classical Greek, *epiblēma* is a "tapestry for hangings"; see Plummer, 162–63. On *reqi'a*, see Targum Job 37:18 (Jastrow, 1497); Targum Josh. 9:5; *Midrash Tehillim* to Ps. 146:3; and JT Sanhedrin 4,22b top (Jastrow, 847); BT Baba Batra 20a; *Aikhah Rabbah* 1.1,4; JT Ma'aser Sheni 4, 55b bottom.

20. It is forbidden halakhically to rend any garment that is in good shape, or that could be of use to someone else, particularly when giving vent to anger and frustration. Such rending is considered wanton destruction and vandalism. See 1 Kings 1:1; 1 Sam. 24:4; Deut. 20:19; BT Berakhot 62b (Steinsaltz, 272) and Shabbat 105b; and *bal tashhit* in *Enc. Talmud.*, 3.345–47, esp. n86.

ing, so were a new patch added of materials that had not been preshrunk,[21] it would shrink upon laundering, making an even worse tear in the older garment. A patch from another old garment might not match well, creating a lack of "harmony"[22] and making the newly repaired garment look even worse.[23] In short, even were the patching of a garment torn on the occasion of grieving a teacher to be allowed, such patching would be extremely difficult and, unless done with care, likely to result in the garment's being damaged even further.

Here it seems is the correct context of Jesus' charge to his disciples. Using his pending departure as an opportunity for didactic instruction, Jesus first creates a parable concerning a patch (*tala*) and the repair of garments rent in mourning. To repair a garment rent in mourning for one's teacher is a desecration of the teacher's memory. Even should one try to repair such a garment, it would be extremely difficult. Should an unshrunk patch (Matthew and Mark) or a patch torn from a brand-new garment (Luke) be used, it would shrink away from the old garment, creating more damage. An old patch on an old garment would be unlikely to match, publicly shaming the disciples and further desecrating the teacher's memory. In such cases, better that the torn garment be left torn, without repair, commemorating for the disciples the memory of their teacher and continuing for them a kind of public memorial.

The disciples, already criticized by outsiders for their failure to fast, are then cautioned by the parable of the patches not to violate public standards of mourning. The theme of public discipline as a form of witness to the received tradition is common in rabbinic literature. For example, according to *Tractate Derekh Eretz* 4.5:

> One should not be alert among the sleepy nor sleepy among the alert; one should not weep in the presence of those who are joyous nor be joyous in the presence of those who weep; one should not be seated among those who are standing nor stand among those who are sitting; and one should not study the scriptures among those who study the oral Torah nor study the oral Torah among those who study the scriptures. As

---

21. Greek: *agnaphos*, i.e., "uncarded" in Matthew and Mark (Liddell and Scott, 11); in Luke it is *kainon*, "new."

22. Greek: *sumphoneō* at Luke 5:36. See Liddell and Scott, 1689–90, and Gregory of Nazianzus, "Concerning Himself and the Bishops" 652–708 (Meehan, 69).

23. Patches were considered to reflect negatively on one's dignity, particularly of scholars or of students of a great teacher. See BT Shabbat 114a and Berakhot 43b, in which six specific items are called a "disgrace" to educated persons, including old, worn-out shoes. See also Derekh Eretz Zuta 5:3 and 7:2. Patches also raise the possibility of *sha'atnez*; see Deut. 22:11; M. Kelim 26:2 and 28:6.

a general rule, no one should act differently from his fellow men in company.[24]

Further, near the end of Tos. Berakhot, chapter 2, Hillel is quoted as saying: "Among those who stand, do not sit, and among those who sit, do not stand. Among those who laugh, do not weep; and among those who weep, do not laugh." From the mouth of a teacher two generations before Jesus, one is called upon not to draw attention to oneself in public but to affirm social convention.

The disciples, appearing as mourners among mourners after Jesus' departure, are to create no public scandal by rejoicing. They are to keep alive the memory of their teacher by wearing a public memorial to him of unpatched garments. This first parable is followed immediately by a parable about wine and wineskins. The two parables are forged together associatively by the coincidence of the words patch (*tala*) and wine (*tila*).

New Wine in Old Wineskins

The interpretive principle determining the exegesis of Matthew's particular version of the parable of the wineskins is set forth in the Talmud. According to BT Baba Batra 91b:

> Our sages taught: [It is written], *you shall eat old grain long stored* (Lev. 26:10). This teaches that the older the produce, the better it should be. From this principle, one may make inferences in relation to things which are commonly stored away. But whence may one also make inferences concerning things which are not commonly stored away? It is explicitly stated: *Old store long kept*, which implies "in all cases". . . . R. Papa said: All things are better when they are aged, except dates, beer, and small fishes.

The parable attached to the parable of the patches employs the rich associative imageries of new wine and old wine, new wineskins and old wineskins. Each of these terms deserves careful exploration, while bearing in

---

24. *Tractate Derekh Eretz* 4:5, in Higger, 1.115 and 2.46–47, and see his *Zeirot*, 139; *Toledot Izhak* on the Torah by Yitzhak Caro, beginning of parashat va-Yeshev; and in *Yesh Nohalin* of R. Abraham b. R. Shabtai Shaftil Horowitz HaLevi, 39:2; *Devar Hokhma* of Haim Satanover, Second Article, 53:1; *Sedeh Haim* at 111; *Sefer ha-Yir'a* of Rabennu Yonah 11:2; *Eliyahu Zutta* 1 and 15; *Mishnat Hakhamim* of R. Moshe Hagiz, par. 466. See also Paul in Rom. 12:15: "Rejoice with them that do rejoice, and weep with them that weep."

mind that the emphasis in the parable is not upon wine but upon the fate and value of the wineskins.

Several types of wine are known from the Hebrew Scriptures and many more types are known from the intertestamental writings and the early rabbinic literature. In Jewish culture of the Second Temple period, the use of wine was both copious and highly regulated.[25] Wine was regarded as one of God's special blessings upon creation, but was in almost all circumstances to be taken in moderation.[26] Among the types of wine that we find mentioned in Scripture and the early rabbinic literature are dark wine, red wine, white wine, clear or pure wine, new or fresh wine, old wine, sweet wine, bitter wine, sour wine, boiled wine, wines named for specific provinces, mixed wine, wine for idolatrous libations, tithed wine, untithed wine, undiluted wine, spiced wine, a young wine called *tirosh*, and several wines difficult to identify.[27] Among this last category is *tila*, an

---

25. Wine was being made and consumed as early as 3500 B.C.E. in the Fertile Crescent (Wilford, B1). See *IDB*, "Wine," 849–52; id. in *Enc. Talmudica* and *Enc. Miqrait*; an excellent summary remains Goodenough, 6.126–222.

26. On wine as a blessing, see Ps. 104:15; Prov. 9:2; Song 8:2; Ben Sirah 31:28–29 and many other places; see also BT Taanit 11a. Matt. 11:18–19 and Luke 7:33–34 describe Jesus as one who was reputed to enjoy his wine very much. See also Cohen, *Parables*, 87: a Nazirite had to bring a sin-offering because to abstain by vow from wine was a refusal of one of God's gifts. Wine was also a medium of healing; the Talmud contains many recipes for medicines made with wine. On moderation in use, see, e.g., BT Berakhot 29b; Yoma 76b; Taanit 17a; Sanhedrin 70a; in the Hebrew Scriptures, Hos. 4:11; Prov. 23:29–35; Hab. 2:15; Mic. 2:11; Isa. 28:7; Ben Sirah 19:2.

27. Some of the sources mentioning these types of wine are: Dark wine: M. Niddah 9:11, BT Baba Batra 97b and the targumim to Esther 1:9. Red wine: Gen. 49:11, Deut. 32:14, Ben Sirah 39:26, M. Niddah 9:11, JT Shabbat 8.1, 11, BT Shabbat 129a, Gittin 70a. White wine: BT Yoma 18a, Zebahim 78b, Keritot 6a, Baba Batra 97b, *Yalqut Shimeoni* to Esther 1:9. Clear/pure wine: Tos. Terumah 4:3, BT Shabbat 109a and 139a, Gittin 69a, and Rashi thereto. New wine: M. Tebul Yom 1:1, BT Gittin 67b, Qiddushin 20a, Nazir 38b. Old wine: M. Tebul Yom 1:2, Avot 4:20, Baba Batra 6:3, BT Qiddushin 20a, Keritot 6a, Avodah Zarah 66a, Rashi to Pesahim 42b; in particular see also Ben Sirah 9:10—"A new friend is like new wine; when it has aged, you can drink it with pleasure." Sweet wine: BT Pesahim 86b, Avodah Zarah 30a, JT Terumot 8:5, 45c. Bitter wine: JT Terumot 8:5, 45c, BT Avodah Zarah 30a. Sour wine: M. Baba Qamma 9:2; Baba Batra 6:3; BT Baba Batra 97b; JT Pesahim ch. 11, end. Boiled wine: M. Terumot 2:6, Tos. Terumot 4:4, JT Terumot 8:5, 45c, BT Avodah Zarah 30a. Provincial wine: for example, the Wine of Helbo (Ezek. 27:18). Mixed wine/wine for idolatrous libations: BT Avodah Zarah 72a. Undiluted wine: M. Berakhot 7:5. Tirosh: Gen. 27:28 and 37, Num. 18:12, Deut. 28:51, 33:28, Isa. 24:7 and 36:17, Hos. 4:11, 2 Kings 18:32, Jer. 31:12, and many others. See

apparently cheap sharp wine (and the connecting word to the previous parable about the patch, or *tala*). According to BT Avodah Zarah 30a:

> R. Joshua b. Levi said: "There are three kinds of wine to which the prohibition through being left uncovered does not apply, namely strong, bitter and sweet. Strong is the acrid tila, *which makes the wine skins burst.*[28] Bitter is the wine of unripe grapes; sweet is the wine made of grapes sweetened [by the heat of the sun]."

Tila (or *tilia*) was not highly favored, apparently because it was strong, dry, bitter, and explosive. According to BT Gittin 70a, Mar Uqba said: "If a man drinks white tilia, he will be subject to debility." R. Hisda said: "There are sixty kinds of wine; the best of all is red fragrant wine, the worst is tilia." However, *tila* appears to have had quite specific medicinal purposes: according to Avodah Zarah 28a: "An einabta[29] is a forerunner of the angel of death. What is the remedy for it? Rue in honey or parsley in tilia."

It is not known whether *tilia* was a young wine or an aged wine, though from its explosive character, one would assume it to be a young or new wine. But certainly the general categories of young or fresh or immature wine and old or aged or mature wine are the most frequently mentioned categories in the New Testament and the literature in general. In the majority of rabbinic texts in which wine is used as a symbol of social status, or even as an indicator of God's blessing, aged wine is associated with the privileged. For example, at BT Qiddushin 20a:

> It is taught [in relation to the way a Hebrew slave is treated]:
> *Because he is well with thee* (Deut. 15:16),
> [Your slave] must be [treated as an] equal to you in food and
>   drink.
> You should not eat white bread while he eats black bread.
> You should not drink old wine while he drinks new wine.
> You should not sleep in a feather-bed while he sleeps upon straw.

IDB, 849, and Murray, 285–86. Tur Sinai to Job, 279–80 n1, says that *tirosh* is the new wine of which Matthew speaks, and such an understanding is supported by Rashi to Job 32:19 in *Miqraot Gedolot*; see also Bolle, 385. However, it seems much more likely that Matthew's wine is the unstable *tila*. On the word "wine," see Kutscher, *Milim*, 31–35.

28. *Had tille harifa de-metzarei ziqi*. Note the similarity to the Peshitta of Mark 2:22—*metzarei le-ziqa*.

29. Specific definition unknown; Jastrow (1091) and BT Avodah Zarah 28a (Soncino, 140) describe it as being a "berry-like excrescence."

Or at BT Ketubot 67b we read the story of someone's careful biblical exegesis shot down by a surprise family visitor:

> A man once applied to Raba for financial assistance.
>
> Raba asked him: "What sort of food are you accustomed to?"
>
> The man replied: "Plump chickens and well-aged wine."
>
> Raba exclaimed: "Have you no consideration for the burden under which our community suffers, [that you should eat so well while they are in want]?"
>
> The man replied: "Do I eat food which belongs to them? Of course not! I eat the food [apportioned me by] the All-Merciful. It is written: *The eyes of all wait for Thee, and Thou givest them their food in [his] due season* (Ps. 145:15). It does not say 'in *their* due season' but 'in *his* due season,' which teaches us that the Holy One, blessed be He, provides each individual with the food which accords with his own habits."
>
> Just then, Raba's sister, whom he had not seen for thirteen years, walked in, bearing a plump chicken and a jug of well-aged wine.
>
> Raba exclaimed: "Look what has just been set in front of me!"
>
> And then he said to the man: "I am humiliated! Come; sit down and we will eat."

At the same place, we read how a tiny clue revealed a poor man's past history of better days:

> Mar Uqba was accustomed to sending a sum of money to a certain poor neighbor before Yom Kippur. Once his son, who delivered the charity, reported: "When I walked in, I noticed that the man was indulging in old wine, so I did not give him the money." His father retorted: "If he has such delicate taste, it is a sign that he must once have known better days. Therefore, I will double the amount of my gift."

Texts such as these make clear that from the point of view of associative symbols, old wine is always preferable to new. If one is seen drinking new wine, one is either a maltreated servant or a once-wealthy man now fallen on hard times.

The Hebrew generic term for new wine is ordinarily *yayin ḥadash*, or in Aramaic *ḥamra ḥadata*. Old wine is usually *yayin yashan*, though sometimes *yayin miyushan* or *yayin atiq*. On the basis of the Septuagint text, one can identify the Greek parallels to these respective generic terms as being *oinos neos* (new wine)[30] and *oinos palaios* (old wine). These Greek parallel terms are the ones used in all three versions of the pericope under consideration, but their generic character destroys the punch of the parable as told in Hebrew or Aramaic translations, which surely refer to the unstable and explosive character of the specific type of wine known as *tila*. However, there is still something to be learned from the generic terms. The Greek word *palaios* is used to describe the "old" garments that have been rent or torn, the "old" wineskins into which the new wine is put, and the superior "old" wine which is preferred to the new wine. Obviously then, *palaios* does not have a completely negative meaning, as is so frequently assumed by Christian exegetes, for it is the *oinos palaios*, the aged or mature wine, which is superior to the new in Luke 5:39: "No one after drinking mature wine will wish to drink new wine, for he will say, 'the old is the best.'"[31] From an enological point of view, the truth of the statement is beyond question and the plain meaning of the text is clear. However, as cautioned earlier, the point of the parable is not wine—new or old—but the containers in which the wine is stored.

The Transport and Storage of Wine

It is difficult to determine what "wineskins" the New Testament is talking about, for the Greek term *askos* seems to be used indiscriminately in the LXX for any number of storage vessels of stone, clay, or skin. The usual meaning of *askos*, however, is an animal skin made into a bag, such as those the Beduin still make.[32] However, the Septuagint uses *askos* indiscriminately to translate three different Hebrew words: *ḥeimat, nevel,* and *nod*.[33] In addition, these three Hebrew words have common synonyms in-

---

30. Acts 2:13 ("Others sneered and said, 'They are full of new wine'") uses *gleukos*. The word appears only once in the LXX, at Job 32:19: "Behold my belly is like wine [*gleukos*] which has no vent; it is ready to burst like new wineskins." Murray (286 n5) says that *gleukos* is a "new *sweet* wine," certainly different from bitter *tila* under consideration here.

31. Best = *chrēstoteros*. On *chrēstos*, see Liddell and Scott, 2007: "useful, good of its kind, serviceable." The Peshitta gives *basim*; see Jastrow, 178—"sweet, pleasing, well-prepared." The Hebrew equivalent would be *taim*: Jastrow, 543—"pleasant, consoling, wise."

32. See Liddell and Scott, 258. The common English translation—"bottle"—is incorrect, as Newman and Stine, 273–74, make clear.

33. Hatch and Redpath, 172; in general on the subject of containers, see the excellent treatment by Brand.

cluding *ov, qanqan*, and possibly *pitus*. To figure out why one cannot put new wine into a well-worn *askos*, we must determine as closely as possible what sort of vessel is being referred to.

A Greek *askos* must be differentiated from a Greek *kados*, a clay vessel.[34] Prior to the development of sturdy storage vessels, wine and other liquids were carried and stored in small skins, the most common being the skins of camels, bears, fish, goats, or even human beings.[35] The most common form seems to have been a whole goatskin, with the feet tied together and the neck functioning as a spout. It is perhaps this sort of wine-carrying vessel that we find referred to in at least a dozen places in the Hebrew Scriptures, though by various names.[36] It is probable that in considering the parable of the wineskins, all storage vessels for liquids (wine, water, milk) that are not made out of leather can be ruled out. The exclusion is supported by the Greek text's description of the manner of "bursting."[37] Even so, we are left with six Hebrew words that may indicate skin vessels.

The pitus. Pitus is obviously related to the Greek *pithos*. The *pitus* was at times large enough to trap an animal in,[38] and was probably made of brittle clay, needing therefore to be lined carefully for the storage of wine.[39] Though it is sometimes understood as a cheap version of the *qanqan* (discussed a little later), it was not a skin vessel and so could not burst from pressure, as in the parable. However, there is also a Hebrew root *p-t-s* meaning "to expand," suggesting the fermentation process.

The ov. An *ov* is quite possibly an animal's belly in which liquid could be stored. The word *ov* can also mean necromancer, or in Greek *eggastrimanotis*, "one who prophesies from the belly," and indeed, "belly"[40] is the most common meaning of *ov* in the Hebrew Scriptures. However, the

---

34. Greek: *kados*; the Hebrew is *kad* and the Aramaic is *kaddan*.
35. Murray, and elsewhere; *IDB*, 850–51.
36. *Heimat*—Gen. 21:14, 15, 19; *nevel*—Jer. 13:12, 1 Sam. 10:3; *nod*—Josh. 9:4, 13, Judges 4:19, 1 Sam. 16:20, Pss. 119:83; *ov*—Job 32:19a and others.
37. So also thought Jerome, for at Matt. 9:17 the Latin for *askos* is *uteres*, "bellies." Jastrow (531) cites *tila* as particularly likely to burst wineskins. The words associated with this type of bursting of skins are explosive words, rather than implying a slow leak; see Jastrow, 1301 *tz-r-y*; 153 *b-z-a*; 1517 *sh-b-r*; and 186 *b-q-'a*.
38. On the *pitus* as a place to hide, see M. Rosh ha-Shanah 3.7; E. E. HaLevi, *ha-Historit*, 351 n2 on R. Eliezer.
39. See Jastrow, 1161.
40. See Liddell and Scott, 467. Hatch and Redpath omit *ov* under the heading for *askos*. The IDB correctly includes them all (458). The LXX also says *gaster*, "belly" instead of heart—literally: my belly is like a wineskin of sweet wine (*gleukos*) without a vent, like a . . . For an alternative interpretation of *ov*, see Jaynes, 310.

"wineskins" that burst in Job 32:19 are *ovot*, a less common but still acceptable usage: something made of skins in which a liquid is stored.

The nevel. A *nevel* is also a skin of some kind,[41] though the word can also mean a timbrel, a musical instrument. The definition of a timbrel is unsure, but it may be a tambourine, with skins stretched across a frame and then hit, in turn indicating a common origin with *nevel* as a storage skin. *Nevel* in the sense of a wineskin appears only three times in the Hebrew Scriptures (Jer. 13:12, 1 Sam. 10:3, and 25:18); all other uses of the word mean something different from storage skin, and most frequently the musical instrument. The infrequent use of the word *nevel* for a wineskin makes its specifics more difficult to determine.

The ḥeimat. A *ḥeimat* is also a skin container for liquids and, like *nevel* and *ov*, tends to be identified by lexicographers as a synonym for *nod*.[42] Apparently a *ḥeimat* contained a specific amount of wine and could therefore be used as a measure, perhaps equivalent to seven kab.[43] Rabbinic literature understands *ḥeimat* as a synonym for goatskin.[44] Apparently the skin of the goat was removed without making a single cut in the hide; even the intact skin of the scrotum could function as part of the fermentation process.[45] A *ḥeimat* also fits the description of *askos* we are seeking.

Ibn-Ezra to Genesis 21:14 defines a *ḥeimat* as a vessel made either of skin or wood(!) and then refers to Habakkuk 2:15. The *ḥeimat* in Genesis 21:14 surely is not wooden, for Hagar empties it and tosses it under a bush, returning later to fill it up. This sequence of events suggests skins rather than wood, which might break, not to mention the problem of its weight when being carried on a journey. David Qimḥi to Genesis 21:14 describes it more as a backpack that could be strapped on one's shoulders; however, he also says that Hagar carried the *nodot* on her shoulders the way that slaves carry jars of water (*qadim*). According to *Bereshit Rabbah* 53:14, a *ḥeimat* is a *nod* made from leather; the midrash's definition de-

41. See Qimḥi, 205–6; Kohut, 5.301–2; Ben-Yehuda, 3486–87, calls it a jug, implying that it is made of pottery. This certainly is not its use in Hebrew Scriptures. Jastrow, 869–70, says clearly that it is leather.
42. See also Qimḥi, 110, and Kohut, 3.440. The Vulgate uses *utres* for *ḥeimat* as well as for *ov*, *nod*, and *nevel*.
43. So Qimḥi understands Hosea 7:5, Hab. 2:15, and Deut. 32:33. On the amount of liquid it would hold, see Kohut, 3.440; see also Ben-Yehuda, 1642–43, though *pace*, it is not a bottle.
44. Jastrow, 480; but one exception is Tos. Kelim Baba Qamma 6:13. The Aramaic parallel to *ḥeimat* is *ruqba*, which, according to Jastrow (1463), means "a goat-skin made into a bag, bottle."
45. M. Kelim 19:8. In BT Ḥullin 107b, pieces of *ḥeimat* are used as gloves.

rives from Psalm 56:8, playing on the tension between the roots *n-a-d* and *n-d-d*: "You have kept count of my wanderings [*nodi*]. Put my tears in your flask [*nodekha*]. Are they not in your record?"[46]

The qanqan. Though the word *qanqan* does not appear in Scripture, it was in frequent use in rabbinic literature by the time of the Mishnah. At times it seems to be a temporary vessel for wine, at other times a cask, yet other times a pitcher.[47] It is around this word *qanqan* that most of the rabbinic sayings that have bearing upon the parable of the wineskins are organized. For example, we read at Avot 4:20: "Rabbi said: Look not at the pitcher but at that which is in it. There is a new pitcher [*qanqan*] which is full of old wine and an old pitcher [*qanqan*] which has not even new wine in it."[48] *Avot de Rabbi Nathan*, Version B, has a more scatological reading: "Rabbi says: Do not look at the jug [*qanqan*] but at its contents. There are new jugs filled with old wine, and old ones without even a drop in them; they are merely filled with urine!"[49]

Although a *qanqan* does not fulfill the definition of askos, in that it is not a supple leather vessel but rather one made of some form of clay, it is a vessel form deserving attention, in that more images having a relation-

---

46. Theodor and Albeck, 2.572 and notes. The passage continues: "Its simple meaning [*peshuto*] is that You know and have counted *all my wanderings. Put my tears in your flask* [nod], in your skin [*heimat*] so that these too will be secured in your memory and remembered among your counting and your inscribing in the book. Its homiletic meaning [*midrasho*]: in your flask—David makes this allusion: 'as for she who was the owner of the flask.' This means Hagar, who wandered in the wilderness with a waterskin on her shoulder and You received her tears. Thus [I know that] You will receive my tears, 'among Your reckonings'—*are they not in Your record?*—in the Torah—that You received the tears of Hagar and of Ishmael." Compare *Sekhel Tov*, 1.54; *Yalqut Shimeoni* Genesis (94a) and Ps. 56, at 774.

47. See Jastrow, 1394.

48. Avot 4:20 (Herford, *Ethics*, 121–22). Parallel usages can be found in the non-canonical Gospels. For example, the Gospel of Thomas, Logion 97 (Layton, 396): "Jesus said, [What] the kingdom of the [father] resembles [is] a woman who was conveying a [jar] of meal. When she had traveled far [along] the road, the handle of the jar broke and the meal spilled out after her [along] the road. She was not aware of the act; she had not understood how to toil. When she reached home she put down the jar and found it empty." See also the Gospel of Truth with two other related images (Layton, 257 and 261–62).

49. ARN-B 34 (Schechter, 75; Saldarini, 201). Hebrew: *maimei raglayim*. Hence a *qanqan* can be mistaken for a chamber pot; cf. *Bereshit Rabbah* 19.11 (Theodor and Albeck, 180); *Pesiqta de Rav Kahana* 25 on Jer. 22:28 (Buber, 163a; Mandelbaum, 367).

ship to the New Testament pericope are organized around *qanqan* than around other semitic parallels to the Greek *askos*.

The nod. The Hebrew word that most often seems to bear a direct Septuagintal relationship to *askos* is *nod*.[50] A *nod* is identified in several sources as a whole goatskin, used for the storage of many things, including wine, milk, and flour. It is of particular note that a *nod* appears in several rabbinic stories addressing both symbolism and parable, as is explained later. *Nod* carries with it the associative connotations of movement, wandering, flexibility, adaptability. Virtually all commentators understand it as the easiest way to transport liquids, a sort of soft-sided canteen functioning at times as a saddlebag, and with the potential for changing its form and shape while safeguarding its contents.

An early rabbinic catena counsels: "Be like a leather bottle [*nod*], which does not allow for wind, like a deep garden bed which retains its water, like a vessel [*qanqan*] coated with pitch, which preserves its wine, and like a sponge, which absorbs everything."[51] The statement counsels those who would preserve tradition and be teachers of others in deed and in word, to be flexible rather than rigid, receptive to innovation and yet traditional; adaptable and yet conserving. The same sort of description could be applied to a valuable, well-worn wineskin.

Wineskins in general were used only for transport rather than storage. Once wine had aged, it was stored in various types of clay vessels and sealed with a clay stopper.[52] If new wine were put into clay vessels, an escape method for the gases of fermentation needed to be provided. If aged wine was put into wineskins, no provision need be made for fermentation gases, for it was a stable liquid. It is difficult to imagine new wine being put in wineskins at all, for its fragility and instability made it an unlikely candidate as a beverage to take on a journey. Though the evidence is not clear, it is presumed that wineskins were not sealed with clay, but rather tied in some fashion. To make the skins more leak-proof, they were some-

---

50. See Qimḥi, 211; Ben-Yehudah, 3461 and 3564; Kohut, 5.312; Jastrow, 884; and Kiel, 64–65, to Josh. 9:4. As in the case of previous words, the LXX makes no distinction between *nod* and other types of vessels, using *askos* for all. The Vulgate generally uses *utres* for *nod*, except at 1 Sam. 17:20 (*lagoenam*).

51. *Tractate Derekh Eretz* 1.2 (Higger, 1.57–58 and 2.33). A very similar saying appears again at 1.20.

52. See BT Shabbat 66b (*sia de-dana*); Taanit 6b; and JT Taanit 1:3 (Neusner, 154), in which it is stated that a rainfall from which it is satisfactory to conclude that a drought is broken is to be determined by whether the soil is left fit to be used for sealing the mouth of a cask; and *Pesiqta de Rav Kahana*, Pisqa 9 (Braude and Kapstein, 168).

times lined with pitch (*mezufaf*).[53] Such pitch lining retained the fermentation gases even more, thus creating greater pressure that threatened to burst the skin unless released. It may be that the reference in Matthew is originally to putting new wine into skin-bags which, having been used previously, were lined with pitch, in turn generating the explosion described in the parable.

Wine, Doctrine, and Innovation

Well before the time of Jesus, wine had become a parabolic symbol for Torah or doctrine.[54] According to Tractate Soferim, "It is said that we shall compare Scripture to water, Mishnah to wine, and Talmud to spiced wine. It is impossible to live without water; it is impossible to live without wine; and it is impossible to live without spiced wine. Blessed is the one who is supported and sustained by the three of them."[55] This saying appears to complement the words of *Avot de Rabbi Nathan*, cited earlier in part:

> Rabbi Dosa ha-Bavli says: He who learns from youngsters is like unripe grapes and [new] wine from the vat. He who learns from the old is like ripe grapes and old wine. Rabbi says: Do not look at the jug [*qanqan*] but at its contents—there are new jugs filled with old wine, and old ones without even a drop in them; they are merely filled with urine.[56]

The same sentiment is echoed in *Sifrei Devarim* 48:

> As it is said: *For your love is more delightful than wine* (Song 1:2). What is this wine? That which gladdens the heart, that is, the words of the Torah which gladden the heart. And it is said: *The precepts of the Lord are just, rejoicing the heart* (Ps. 19:9). [How is it with] wine? As you taste it the taste gets even sweeter, and the longer that it matures in the pitcher [*qanqan*] the better it becomes. So with the words of Torah: the longer they grow old in the body, the better they become. And it is said: *Is wisdom in the aged, and understanding in the long-lived?* (Job 12:12)

---

53. BT Avodah Zarah 33a.
54. On wine as a metaphor for Torah or doctrine, see for example Isa. 55:1; Prov. 9:2 and 5; BT Taanit (Malter, 84); Feldman, 140–44.
55. *Tractate Soferim* 15:6 (Higger, 278–80), and see *Shir ha-Shirim Rabbah* 8.2,1; al-Naqawa, 5.144.
56. ARN-B 34 (Schechter, 75, Saldarini, 201). The same two sayings are found in M. Avot 4:20. See also *Shir ha-Shirim Rabbah* 8.5, 1 and *Midrash Shemuel* 16 to Qoh. 8:1 (Buber, 47a–b).

[How is it with] wine? It is impossible to preserve in vessels of silver or gold; rather it is preserved in vessels of little value such as those made of clay. So it is with the words of the Torah: they are not preserved in him who thinks of himself as a vessel of silver or a vessel of gold, but in him who thinks of himself as a vessel of little worth, such as one of clay.[57]

Wine is so connected with Torah and sustenance that it is ultimately pictured, in an altogether too-mixed metaphor, as the bread of life.[58]

It is only when wine, as Torah or doctrine, is aged in human beings that later new lessons can be learned.[59] Rabbinic commentators to Deuteronomy 11:13 understand the phrase *And it will come to pass that if hearkening you will hearken* to mean that if one has absorbed and processed the old, the tradition, the mature wine of doctrine, only then will one be able safely to add new lessons to one's growing comprehension of God's revelation.[60] The emphasis within this understanding is one of inherent continuity between tradition and innovation. Only in terms of continuity does innovation have any meaning; only in terms of a carefully preserved tradition is new insight possible or given a context.[61] Doctrine remains doctrine and piety remains piety only insofar as they flow from the past and tradition. Severed from tradition, innovation loses all sense of self-correction, doctrine loses its sense of renewal, and both are destroyed.

While affirming the necessity of repeated renewal and of responsiveness to contemporary situations, at the same time tradition cautions in favor of moderation. The line between conservation and renovation or renewal is a delicate one, and moderation is the only attitude that respects both. Exaggeration and overreaction are the enemies, then, of both con-

---

57. *Sifrei Devarim* 48 to Eqev 11 (Finkelstein, 111; Hammer, 103). A similar exegesis is found in BT Taanit 7a, Nedarim 50b, and Berakhot 57a. See also Feldman, 141–47.

58. *Shemot Rabbah* 47:5. Compare John 6.

59. A paradigm for the precedence of the old over the new can be found in M. Sheqalim 6:5; see also Tos. Sheqalim 1:9 and 3:1. The point there is that the new is not to be accepted until all obligation in relation to the old has been taken care of. The practices concerning old and new sheqels were in effect during the time of the Second Temple, and would have been familiar to Jesus. Nothing new is to be accepted until all debts are paid to the old and the account adjudged to be in good order.

60. Rashi to Deut. 11:13, in Silbermann, 59–60; cf. *va-Yiqra Rabbah* 22.1 (M. Margulies, 496 and notes); *Midrash ha-Gadol Devarim* (Fish, 177).

61. For a fuller development of the theological role of innovation when referring to the doctrine of humanity, and the maintenance of received religious tradition, see chap. 2 of my *New Adam*.

servation and renovation. Fidelity to one's past and one's heritage are the anchors that allow renovation, and even innovation, to retain vitality and power in the present. For example, although the Second Temple period was in itself a fairly chaotic and explosive period in the history of Judaism, nothing prepared the faithful for the shattering despair felt at the destruction of the Second Temple by the Roman armies in 70 C.E. The struggle at that moment to be faithful to tradition and yet face a radically new situation is documented at BT Baba Batra 60b:

> Our rabbis taught: When the Temple was destroyed for the second time, large numbers in Israel began to withdraw from the joys of the world, vowing to abstain from eating meat and from drinking wine.[62]
>
> R. Yehoshua joined up with them and said: "My children, why are you refusing to eat meat and drink wine?'
>
> They said to him: "How can we eat meat, when it was the source of the Temple sacrifices at the altar and now those sacrifices have ceased? How can we drink wine, when it was the source of the libation offerings at the altar and now those offerings have ceased?"
>
> He replied to them: "If that is your logic, then you should not eat bread, for the meal-offerings too have ceased."
>
> They said: "[You are right, and so] we will attempt to manage with just fruit."
>
> He said, "But the first-fruit offerings have ceased also!"
>
> They said, "Then we will manage with other kinds of fruit."
>
> He said, "But [by your logic], you won't even be able to drink water, for the water libations have ceased!"
>
> To this, they could find no answer.
>
> He then said to them: "My children, come near and let me tell you something. It is inconceivable that you should not enter into deep mourning, for indeed such mourning has been decreed. But for you to grieve in such an exaggerated manner is out of the question, for it is forbidden that a decree be made upon the public which is beyond the level of endurance of the majority of people. Rather, this is what the sages have decided: Every one who plasters his house shall leave one small corner unplastered [as a continuing remembrance of the destruction]; when you are making the preparations for a sumptuous banquet,

---

62. On asceticism in Judaism of the Second Temple and early rabbinic period, see "Askesis in the World of the Sages," in Urbach, *World of the Sages*, 437ff.

you shall omit a few items; when a woman adorns herself with her jewelry, she shall leave off a few pieces, as it is said: *Should I forget you, O Jerusalem . . . may my tongue be deprived of its cunning* (Ps. 137:5–6). And all who mourn over Jerusalem should desist and instead seek out her gladness, as it is written: *Rejoice with Jerusalem . . . rejoice for joy with her, all you that did mourn her* (Isa. 66:10).[63]

No one can doubt that change is ever necessary, even to such venerable and staid institutions as Judaism and Christianity. In both cases, too, the faith is transmitted from one generation to the next by keeping it pure from faddish adulteration and undue "fermenting," all the while renewing its vitality and power to speak to the problems of each generation as it succeeds the one before. Through the power of renovation and innovation, faith continues to make sense. Through renovation and innovation, God continues to call out for service and covenant. Yet so as not to quench the voice of God as it speaks through history, the tradition must be conserved by respecting what has been received and practiced by the forebears who have gone before. As a faithful Jew, Jesus would have rejected anything so radically new as to be unrecognizable by the received tradition, and he would have rejected whatever jeopardized the authority and rich power of the faith he had inherited from the generations that nourished him in a variety of Judaisms. A corner may need to be left bare but the house had still to be plastered. A portion may be missing, but the faithful were still called to come from east and west in order to sit at the banquet table, rejoicing, as Matthew 8:11 puts it, "in the company of Abraham, Isaac and Jacob."

Understanding the Parable of Jesus

This chapter began with Flusser's hypothesis that the parable of the patches and the wineskins is a dominical caution against the innovative fasts of the Johannites and the Pharisees.[64] It may be that the Johannites

---

63. Compare Tos. Sotah 15:11 (Lieberman, 242, Zuckermandel, 322); BT Baba Batra 60b; Bialik, *Sefer ha-Aggadah*, 150 #21.
64. See Flusser, "New Wine" and *Die rabbinischen*, 217ff. Flusser limits Jesus' teaching to one against special and specific fasts, a limitation without justification. He bases his entire argument concerning Pharisaic innovation of fasts on Luke 18:12 but can produce no evidence from rabbinic literature. Given the anti-Pharisaic character of Luke 18, this is probably a Lukan interpolation reflecting fasting practices of some later group of Jews, as confirmed by the Didache's opposition (Lake, 1.321); and see Alon, *Mekhkarim*, 1.291ff. On fasting in the Geonic period, see M. Margulies's "Festivals and Fasts in the Geonic Period."

instituted special fasts in connection with their philosophy of repentance, but we have no evidence that new fasts were instituted by the Pharisees before 70 C.E., aside possibly from Luke 18:12. However, once the question of fasting had been raised, Jesus recognized an opportunity to teach, beginning with the images of a bridegroom and his groomsmen. The subject of fasting in turn led to images of repairing garments that have been rent, and of the storing of an unstable wine in an appropriate container. We have seen how these associations proceed logically out of the halakhic and aggadic context in which Jesus lived. But how are we to understand the message Jesus is giving to his disciples in this situation, free from the subsequent centuries of supersessionist assumption?

In his article "The Old Coat and the New Wine," Howard Clark Kee writes:

> It is often said that Jesus had a way with ordinary folk. Let us put the new interpretation to the test. If Jesus spoke the double parable to village people, how would they hear it? If the village tailor heard the first part, what would his reactions be? Would he think of the new patch versus the old coat? Would he think that a piece of *un*shrunk cloth was more valuable than a coat with a tear in it? What kind of calculation would that be? No, as he heard the first words, "a piece of unshrunk cloth . . . " he would call out, Stop! He would already know, with a dreadful certainty, how the whole thing would end. If a shopkeeper heard the parable of the unfermented wine, his reaction would be as spontaneous. And that is the way of Jesus with ordinary folk. The shopkeeper would not mentally calculate whether new wine is better than old wineskins. As he heard the situation described he too would be beside himself. Stop, you will lose everything! Both wine and skins.[65]

Given the parable's obvious concern with venerable garments and time-tested wineskins, we must assume that a critical part of Jesus' message is the maintenance and explication of the received tradition, in light of the dual temptations to forget and to innovate. The parable of the patches speaks to the disciples' human tendency to forget their teacher, and particularly to forget the care with which he interpreted Torah. The disciples would be tempted to patch, to repair the rent garment in such a manner that Jesus' absence would mean less and less over time, and his teachings lose their force. Jesus counsels his disciples instead to leave the rend where it is, to sustain his memory, yet cherishing the garment itself, the tradition of Judaism in which Jesus was so carefully schooled and out of which he delivered his own halakhic rulings. Should the disciples

---

65. Kee, "Old Coat," 20.

choose to do otherwise, they would be as bridegrooms among mourners, or as mourners among bridegrooms, strangers in their own society and the source of constant scandal.

According to *Seder Eliyahu Rabbah* 11:[66]

> *There shall they rehearse the righteous acts of the Lord, even the righteous acts of those who disperse [gifts] in Israel* (Jdgs. 5:11). [In regard to Israel's rehearsal of the righteous acts of the Lord, consider] a small town in Israel where people proceeded to build themselves a synagogue and an academy. For the latter they engaged a sage, for the former they engaged teachers of little children. Thereupon, when the people of another city nearby saw [what their neighbors had done], they, too, proceeded to build a synagogue and an academy, and they, too, engaged for themselves teachers of little children, and in this manner there came to be many houses of study in Israel, as is said, *Then the people of the Lord went down to the gates [of learning]* (Jdgs. 5:11). Blessed is one whose mouth gives new interpretation and meaning to the words of Torah within academies grown numerous in Israel. It is as though such a man is given to hear the Holy One saying to him from heaven, "My son, My great academy is yours," as it is said, *God chooses the new which is brought forth out of the give-and-take of discussion in gates of learning* (Jdgs. 5:8).

In the parable of new wine in time-tested wineskins, Jesus cautions his followers not to get drunk on innovation. Innovation and tradition do not combine easily, and when they do, they combine only from the position of utmost respect for tradition.[67] The vessels of Judaism as it was known in the Second Temple period were fragile already, because of the many factors that played upon Judaism and caused its contentiousness. Yet it was just this Judaism that Jesus held dear, however it was interpreted and whatever battles threatened its own sense of self-understanding.

---

66. Trans. adapted by the author from Braude and Kapstein, 165; Friedman, 54–55.

67. The rabbinic term *torah ḥadashah* ("new torah") must be approached with caution. The term is found in a number of sources—see, for example, *Seder Eliyahu Rabbah* (10)11 (Friedman, 55, Braude and Kapstein, 165) and 18 (Friedman, 93); *va-Yiqra Rabbah* 13.3 (M. Margulies, 2.378, esp. n4)—but it is always understood to mean "innovative explication of ideas inherent in the received tradition." The biblical source text is Qoh. 1:10, "Is there a thing of which it is said, 'See, this is new'? It has already been, in the ages before us," and see Rashi thereto; and see Scholem, "Revelation and Tradition" in *Messianic Idea*. Such an idea is closely related to the notion of *matir issurim* (the permitting of the impermissible; see *Midrash Tehillim* to Ps. 146, Buber, 535). On "innovatio-phobia" and "traditio-phobia," see Gaventa.

The vessels of Judaism were structures to hold the mature and aged wine of Torah doctrine. These vessels were to be preserved in spite of the temptation to innovate. When the instability of innovation, the ferment of discontinuity, would threaten the memory of the teaching of Jesus within its traditional Jewish context, this innovation was to be kept far away from the wineskins. Jesus himself had provided his disciples with enough innovation inherent in the tradition, employing normative rabbinic methods of argumentation and explication. The challenge that lay ahead of the young Christian community was not to add more innovation, but to preserve and live out the adequate innovations that Jesus had provided within traditional Judaism, to respect the vessels even at the cost of the new wine, how to keep the correct tension between old and new. New was not to be categorically preferred, for the old meant too much to Jesus. He, like anyone else in his right mind, knew that "the old wine is better."

Epilogue

Our definition and explorations of various gospel parables have emphasized both that they are context specific—"fitted to particular times and particular things"—and that they contain multiplex meanings that were available not only to the listeners of those times but are, for the most part, still available to us today if we will take the trouble to comprehend the contexts in which these "dominical" parables were originally taught.

Whether we believe that the words of the parables come from Jesus or from the various gospel redactors, in either case what has long been neglected in the history of Christian interpretation is the strong repeated concern and care for all the traditions and practices received from Judaism. For example, Daniel Harrington emphasizes that Matthew, as a committed follower of Christ, is equally concerned that the Jewish character of developing Christianity not be obscured or lost:

> If we assume that "the old" relates to pre-A.D. 70 Judaism (the Hebrew Bible, Israel's history, the Temple, the land, and so forth), the addition [Matt. 9:17b, "so both are preserved"] may reflect Matthew's conviction that the tradition of pre-70 Judaism is best preserved by the movement centered around Jesus. For him and other Jewish Christians the only way to move into the future without the Temple and without direct control of the land of Israel was to take Jesus and his teaching as the guide. What appeared to some Jews as a scandalous novelty was in fact the way in which "both (old and new) are preserved."[1]

Too often the history of Christianity, and of New Testament exegesis in particular, has denigrated the Jewish character of Christianity, wallowing in triumphalism and supersessionism, missing few opportunities to denigrate rabbinic thought or theology or even the presence of God's revelation in any system outside of Christianity. Such a negative attitude is so

---

1. Harrington, *Matthew*, 129.

entrenched in Christianity that the last hundred years of research attempting to reclaim Christianity's Jewish character have been largely ignored, until perhaps our recent decade. Whether or not such a search has any importance to the masses of the Christian faithful is at times a subject of debate. Recently, John P. Meier has observed: "The historical Jesus, while not the object or essence of *faith*, must be an integral part of modern *theology*."[2] However, historical and dogmatic theology, at their most vital, have never been concerned with the abstract, but with the incarnate, the practical, the tangible interface between religious philosophy and the practicality of daily life and social intercourse—in short, "the object and essence of faith."

Our search for meaning within the parables and stories of Jesus necessitates our recognition of the truth and value of particularism and contextuality as opposed to the abstract or universal. Every parable or story originates in a particular situation from the mouth of a particular teacher, but comes to us only through the memory of a particular hearer as recorded in a particular text. It is subsequently interpreted for us by particular individuals with particular agendas and shaped by the particular historical and religious culture within which they speak. To seek universal truth in parables is an exercise in frustration, for the various messages of any given parable are in its particulars. One key to unlocking the complexities of these particulars, and thus recapturing the lessons and values of an ancient teacher, is through careful work in listener-response theory.

---

2. Meier, *Marginal Jew*, 198–99.

Appendix I

Proverbs 25:11: A Word Fitly Spoken

At the same time that the canon of Scripture was developing, the text itself was very much alive, already yielding a variety of possible interpretations within the broadly distributed community of faith. The limits of the canon of Scripture were narrowing, but the variety of possible meanings for a particular text was widening within the broadly distributed community of faith which acknowledged that canon. Although a range of meanings for texts was generally accepted, the precise limits of that range— beyond which, in the community's eyes and ears, lay falsehood—became a hotly debated subject.[1] The conceptual trajectory, predating the Second Temple period, which suggested that all Scripture has more than one meaning, was a predictable and even necessary development; but, with the rise of schisms and heresies, the question of limitation had necessarily to be raised. For example, could Acts 4:32—which recorded that early Christians held all things in common—actually be interpreted to include free sex within the faithful community, as the Carpocratians insisted,[2] or was this exegesis such a stretch of the text's meaning that it could not be deemed responsible to the received tradition?

Among the various attempts to limit the exegetical possibilities of Scripture was the insistence upon each passage's remaining tied in an

---

1. The rabbinic discussion of this issue is complicated, and is often found under the rubric of *bittul Torah*—whether or not the biblical text can cancel itself out, or be canceled out by later extenuating circumstances (see for example Bialik, *Halachah and Aggadah*, 10, on Daniel the Tailor). The issue is discussed at length in Saadya Gaon's *Beliefs and Opinions*, Treatise 3, chaps. 7–9 (Rosenblatt, 157–73); see also ibn-Janaḥ, *Riqma*, 58 notes; Abramson, *Inyanot*, 269–70 and *Nissim Gaon*, 5, 527. Some would charge that the continuing development of scholarly criticism, particularly of the New Testament, is nothing more than a sophisticated form of canceling out the biblical text.

2. See for example Clement, *Stromateis* 3.2 (ANF 2.382–83); Justin Martyr, *First Apology* 26.7 (ANF, 1.171); Origen, *Contra Celsus* 5.62–63 (Chadwick, 312–13); Wilken, esp. 17–22; P. Brown.

identifiable way to its textual context. In the process of attempting to pin down a phrase's "plain meaning," reference was made at times to the confusing passage in Proverbs 25:11—"An idea well-expressed is like a design of gold, set in silver" (TEV). The difficulty with the Hebrew original, particularly with the last word, *ofanav*, is illustrated by comparing a few of its subsequent translations into English, sometimes further confused along the way by intermediary translations into Latin, Greek, Aramaic, or Syriac:

Raymond Martine	Apples of gold in silver filigree are fecund words spoken at the fitting moment.[3]
Targums Aquila and Jonathan	Like apples of gold inside of [reflected in?] silver salvers [mirrors?] [misreading filigree as *diskarin*][4] is a spoken word which like a wheel shows its face to every side.
Delitzsch Commentary[5]	Like apples of gold in settings of silver is a word spoken according to circumstances.
Jerusalem Bible	Like apples of gold in a silver setting is a word that is aptly spoken.
Jewish Publication Society (1985)	Like golden apples in silver showpieces is a phrase well turned.
King James; Revised Standard Version	A word fitly spoken is like apples of gold in pictures of silver.
McKane Commentary	Like apples of gold in settings of silver is a phrase well-turned.
New American Standard Bible	Like apples of gold in settings of silver is a word spoken in right circumstances.
Septuagint	As an apple of gold in a necklace of sardius [chalcedony]—thus [it is] to speak a [wise] word [misreading "silver filigree" as "stone latticework," hence stone = sardius]. (Compare Lev. 26:1.)
The English Version	An idea well-expressed is like a design of gold, set in silver.

---

3. Raymundi Martine, *Pugio Fidei*, 428.
4. See *Bereshit Rabbah* 93, Theodor and Albeck, 932, note.
5. Commentary on Proverbs, 155–59.

New American Bible	Like golden apples in silver settings are words spoken at the proper time.
Revised English Bible	Like apples of gold set in silver filigree is a word spoken in season.
R. Menahem ha-Meiri	Like apples of gold in silver filigree is a word spoken at the proper moment in time [kairos].[6]
Vulgate	Golden apples in silver couches is the one who speaks a word in his own time.[7]
Ahikar Papyrus	Like golden apples in a silver filigree is a word spoken to the listening ear.[8]
Weinfeld Commentary	Like apples of gold in settings of silver is a decision which settles a matter of dispute.
Faur, *Golden Doves*	Like golden apples in silver mesh is a word spoken on its two circles [faces].
Peshitta Syriac	Apples of gold inside silver salvers is a word spoken according to its true nature [physis].[9]

An understanding of the purpose and use of Proverbs 25:11 is dependent upon the correct dissection of the Hebrew word *ofnav*. The word is a hapax legomenon in Hebrew (it appears in this particular form only once in the Bible), and hence its meaning must always remain conjectural at some level. Some commentators[10] understand the root of the Hebrew

6. Perush ha-Meiri to 25:14, 238; see also Zer-Kavod and Kiel, loc. cit., 197, esp. n24a. Meiri may have been influenced by the Vulgate.
7. See Kahane, *Perush Madda'i: Sefer Mishlei*, 118–19.
8. According to Torczsyner (Tur-Sinai), *Mishlei Shelomo*, 53 and 120. This unusual reading is the result of transposing Prov. 25:11b and 12b.
9. This version of the Peshitta text is according to Melamed, *Mifarashei*, 360, and *Mekhkarim*, 284 (43/60) #324; it differs from the UBS Syriac, which reads "An apple of gold in an engraved piece of silver, that is speaking a word." On *physis*, see Wolfson, *Philo*, 2.170–80; Melamed, *Mekhkarim*, 284; Levy, part 2, 276 *fysayah*.
10. Including LXX; *Bereshit Rabbah* 93.3 (Theodor and Albeck, 1152–53); *Midrash ha-Gadol Bereshit* loc. cit. (M. Margulies, 1.755); *Yalqut Shimeoni* and *Yalqut ha-Makhiri* to Prov. loc. cit.; Qimhi, *Shorashim*, 25; Kohut, 1.219; and Melamed as noted above. Admittedly, it is difficult to distinguish between something that shows many faces because it is rolling and something that shows many faces because it is

ofnav to be *ofan*, meaning something that revolves to show various sides, such as the wheels of the chariot (Isa. 28:27).[11] Indeed, the scriptural example most frequently cited in definitions of *ofnav* is first found at *Bereshit Rabbah* 93.3: "What is the meaning of *ofan*? It is [like a wheel] which shows its face to all sides [as it turns]. Similarly were the words of Judah discernible from many sides at the moment he spoke with Joseph [Gen. 44:18]; they could be seen from every side." Rashi explains:[12]

> Judah meant to imply: "I esteem you a man of royal station." This is its plain meaning. At its face value, this reference sounds like an expression of courtesy, complimentary to Joseph. However, in the secondary overtones of this courtesy, it contains a verbal threat [in diplomatic language]—to wit, that "as a peer of Pharaoh, you will share the same Pharaonic fate which befell the Egyptian king who abducted our own ancestress Sarah" [see Gen. 20:3].

Saadya Gaon offers a closely related interpretation, that *ofan* indicates a trajectory, ever revolving, ever driving toward a goal, perhaps like a corkscrew or helix.[13] Thus for many commentators, the multifaceted character of a revolving wheel is the apt analogy for an utterance that can be understood in a variety of ways, not unlike Ben Bag Bag's famous description of Scripture: "Turn it and turn it, for everything is in it."[14]

But certain commentators offer a differing analysis of *ofnav*. Menahem ben Sarukh Hispaniensi[15] writes "*Ofnav* is not derived from *ofan*, 'a wheel,' as some have supposed, on account of the *vav* in the latter, but from *panim*, face, front or ways." Sokoloff distinguishes four meanings in Jewish Palestinian Aramaic of the related *apin*: (1) face, countenance; (2) surface; (3) way, manner; and (4) side, party to an agreement.[16] Precedent

---

round. According to Pokorney, 639 on *kwel-*, the same etymological root yields the English words "wheel" (something that shows many faces because it is rolling) and "collar" (something that shows many faces because it is round.).

11. See Segal, Ben Sirah 50:27, where *mishlei ofenayim* is often understood as "smooth-running parables," again emphasizing the sense of "wheel."

12. See Rashi to Genesis, Silbermann, 1.221, and my article on Moses Mendelssohn, "Multiplexity in Biblical Exegesis," esp. n10.

13. Saadya, *Proverbs*, 198. See also Rotenberg, 94.

14. Avot 5.25, in Herford, *Ethics*, 145.

15. Menahem ben Sarukh Hispaniensi, Eng., 4, Heb., [30]. The same explanation is referred to in *Shorashim* of Qimhi, 25, where he attributes it to ibn-Janah; see also *Pesiqta Rabbati* 100b; ibn-Janah, *Shorashim*, 44; ibn-Ezra ad loc.; and Yalon, 87 and 89.

16. Sokoloff, *Dictionary*, 70–71.

for the prefixed *alef* is found in ibn-Janah and confirmed by David ben Avraham the Karaite.[17]

Still others understand *ofnav* as indicating the dynamism between overt and covert senses.[18] Yet others, often connecting the phrase to Exodus 14:27, see in *ofnav* a sense of *kairos*, of the proper moment in time, the "due season" of a word spoken at some choice moment.[19] Another commonly accepted meaning (chosen by most English translations) is "propriety, fitness, astute perception of what is needed."[20] R. Elazar ha-Kallir, the sixth-century Jewish author of liturgical hymnody, connects *ofen* with the Urim and Thumim in an acroamatic poem.[21] Finally, certain unusual translations should be noted, such as the Ahikar Papyrus and Faur.

The Hebrew phrase is essentially untranslatable, but its accurate sense can be understood by way of Kahane's distinction between the *prima facie* and those meanings that lie behind it.[22] Just as a human face indicates the character that lies behind it, so the face of a word indicates the deeper meanings that lie below. The value of identification of a human face lies in the other character traits that are associated with one's particular identity. That is why a death-mask is a frightening thing: the deeper meanings that make the face identifiable have been erased. *Ofnav* is perhaps best understood as "the indicating face-value," that is, the opening to deeper meaning.[23] In proto-Semitic, *davoor* means "a drive, a push, a

---

17. Ibn-Janah, *Shorashim*, 44 line 65; ibn-Parhon, 3a middle; and many of the other commentators mentioned above. To David ben Avraham, see *Likkutei Qadmoniot*, "On the History and Literature of the Kairites," by Pinsker, 198. See also Jastrow, 86, *apna*.

18. Ibn-Shu'eib, 17a; Immanuel of Rome to loc. cit.; *Pugio Fidei* of Raymond Martine, though obviously parroting Maimonides; Mishlei HaGR"A (Elijah Vilna Gaon) ad loc. The distinction is based on reading *ófen* ("fashion, manner"; see Ben Yehudah, 352) instead of *ofán* ("wheel"; see Ben-Yehudah, 108–9).

19. Symmachus, Vulgate, and ibn-Janah, acc. to Gesenius, 71; Liddell and Scott, 859; ha-Meiri to loc. cit., 238; and Kohut, 6.379, all seemingly supported by Segal, *Ben Sirah* 50:27.

20. Reider to Aquilas, 31; LXX *physis*; Joseph Kaspi in *Asarah Kelei Kesef* to loc. cit.; Levi ben Gershon to loc. cit. (*Miqraot Gedolot*); Kahane, *Perush Madda'i*, 119; Ben-Yehudah, 352; BDB, 67; and Banitt, *Rashi*, 48. Zer-Kavod and Kiel, ad loc., 197 also speak of propriety, but in terms particularly of mitzvot and halakhah. Jastrow (1194) is related here, giving "persuasive."

21. Mirsky, *ha-Piyyut*, 478–79, ref. to Goldschmidt, *Mahzor*, 1.248 line 25.

22. As a face lies behind a mask; see "persona" in the dictionaries: an actor's mask (Hebrew cognate, *partzuf*); by transfer, the role or character one plays in life. See Kohut, 6.444b.

23. In Murray Bowen Family Systems Theory, this would be understood as the entry point at which one dives into a complex system. See Edwin Friedman, 36–39 and elsewhere.

rush." In this understanding, the phrase is best translated, "Like apples of gold in silver filigree settings, so is the drift of what is being spoken behind the words." We therefore return to the Maimonidean interpretation from Chapter 1, that the apertures in the silver filigree lead the eyes of the wise to peek through the *prima facie* to discover the deeper meanings, the true intent behind what is said.[24] The meanings of an utterance are available only to those who make the effort to seek the "polyglossia"[25] behind and within the plain meaning.

Once additional meanings have been deduced within the polyglossia of Proverbs 25:11, it is possible to derive behavioral expectations or halakhah from the verse, firmly grounded in these interpretations beyond the plain meaning. Two such points of halakhah illustrate the power of combining listener-response theory with an esoteric scriptural exegesis related to this verse from Proverbs.

In his treatise on the laws of personality development, Maimonides writes:[26]

> There are certain matters which are considered to have "the whiff of *lashon harah* [slander]." What is implied? [For example, a person says:] "Who will tell so and so to continue acting as he does now," or "Do not talk about so and so; I do not want to say what happened," or the like. Similarly, it is also considered the "whiff of *lashon harah*" when someone speaks favorably about a colleague in the presence of his enemies, for this will surely prompt them to speak disparagingly about him. In this regard, King Solomon said: *One who greets his colleague early in the morning, in a loud voice, curses him* (Prov. 27:14), for his positive [act] will bring him negative [repercussions]. Similarly [to be condemned] is a person who relates *lashon harah* in frivolity and jest as if he were not speaking

---

24. This sense is further confirmed by an analysis of the use of *dover* in the Bible. When the word is followed by a noun, the noun needs to be understood in the evaluative sense. For example, a *dover emet* is a speaker of truth; a *dover kazav* is a speaker of lies. No speaker sets out to tell blatantly obvious lies, but the words are subsequently evaluated as falsehoods. So *dover* and its cognate *davoor* indicate that an evaluation of what is spoken is appropriate, as in the evaluation: "There's a deeper meaning behind the surface impression."

25. This is a critical concept in the work of Bakhtin. He uses a wonderful phrase as synonym, "Galilean linguistic consciousness," by which he means that Galilean Jews in the time of Jesus were so comfortable in Hebrew, Aramaic, and Greek that they could speak in one language and simultaneously convey a message in another; see Bakhtin, 65, 327, 366, 431.

26. Hilkhot Deot, chap. 7, part 4 (*la-Am*, 2.81) on *lashon ha-ra* (trans. in Abramson and Touger, 140–42). Maimonides, *Madda* (Rabinovitch 1.335), lists the relevant source materials.

with hatred. This was also mentioned by Solomon in his wisdom: *As a madman who throws firebrands, arrows and death and says, "I am only joking"* (Prov. 26:18, 19). [Also to be condemned is] someone who speaks *lashon harah* about a colleague slyly, pretending to be innocently telling a story without knowing that it is pernicious. When he is reproved, he excuses himself by saying: "I did not know that the story was harmful or that so-and-so was involved."

Maimonides deduces the halakhic ruling that one should not speak with deliberate innuendo about a person, nor praise that person in front of his enemies, for such words are not "fitly spoken." False words suggest apples of gold behind the silver filigree that are as damaging to a person as though he or she had been murdered.[27] Innuendo encourages hearers to jump to negative conclusions; to praise in front of someone's enemies encourages an exaggerated adverse reaction (compare the sarcasm implicit in Marc Antony's speech, "for Brutus is an honorable man"). In either case, listener response is so predictable that a halakhic prohibition is deemed appropriate.

Yosef Yosspe Hahn Nortlingen, in his early-seventeenth-century work *Sefer Yosef Ometz*, cites an anonymous medieval book known as the *Orhot Tzadiqim*.[28] Though the *Orhot* does not identify Maimonides as a source, the author builds his remarks around the phrase "vessels of silver and gold in a very fine filigree." He cautions the reader not to assume that the first glance through the silver filigree will necessarily reveal the true golden apple, but rather that the more one matures, the more penetrating one's look becomes. Those who seek to understand must come back again and again to the source of knowledge, for each time, with increased maturity and wisdom, they will see even better the truth of the golden apple contained therein. *Yosef Ometz* then uses this observation of the *Orhot* as the foundation for a halakhic opinion concerning the behavior between two people who are discussing a matter. Nortlingen writes:

> If someone wants to share a new insight that you are sure you already know, be quiet anyway. Perhaps he may have some new insight which has not yet occurred to you. Even if he apparently has nothing new to teach you, be quiet anyway, until he has finished talking. Even if he does not open your eyes to new levels of meaning, he has the right to celebrate his own excitement of discovery and explanation.

---

27. Rabbinic thought includes "gossip" as a form of murder, under the rubric *lashon ha-ra*. Etymologically, the word "gossip" is derived from "God-sib," a god-parent, godchild, god-kinsman, possibly because people who have the same god-parents gossip about them with each other.

28. Nortlingen, 358, citing *Orhot Tzadiqim*, Shaar Hazkirah #24.

Ometz's halakhic opinion, then, emphasizes that in the course of exchanging ideas, one is to relate to another in a qualitative manner rather than a quantitative. The qualitative always holds out the possibility that one will discover he has not grasped the golden apple at all, but has become ensnared somewhere in the silver filigree. Suddenly his eyes are opened in wonderment, whether at the other's insight or the other's delight in learning. The halakhic opinion is designed to create a silence in which the joy and the beauty of a word fitly spoken can be truly appreciated.

Appendix II

Selections from Ḥaim bar Bezalel's
Iggeret ha-Tiyyul

In 1568 Ḥaim bar Bezalel, the brother of Rabbi Loewe (Judah the Lion), the "Maharal" of Prague, was driven out of Friedberg by an epidemic. He fled, leaving everything including his library. In the course of his travels over the next several months, he penned a delightful book entitled *Iggeret ha-Tiyyul* ("Excursionary Missive"), in which he explains Peshat, Remez, Derash, and Sod through a series of literary delicacies, organized under each category according to the Hebrew alphabet. Not only are the stories entertaining, they also help clarify the distinction between the four categories.

Peshat

Page 2b, letter *alef*:

If you look for it like searching for silver and seek it as if for treasure, then you will understand the fear of the Lord (Prov. 2:4–5). If only people would ask for the Torah with the same intensity that they ask for their fleeting fancies such as wealth and other things! When all the rest of the world is already thinking them rich, they seem to regard themselves as being poor, and race after their fancies. If only they would behave similarly about the mitzvot and their good deeds, they would no doubt be blessed thereby. *And search for it as for treasures.* I believe they are truly humble who conduct themselves well without regard to their deeds being known in order to bring themselves honor, as do those who look for treasures. Those who do their good deeds in secret without self-promotion are those who praise the King, *and they will understand the fear of the Lord*.

Page 2b, letter *bet*:

The righteous eats to his heart's content, but the belly of the wicked shall feel want (Prov. 13:25). The wicked are those who gorge their appetites all day long, and when they have completely satiated their stomachs with delicacies and all sorts of rich food, they say "Who will give us another stomach?" This is why it says: "The wicked shall want for a belly."

Remez

Page 6 a–b, letter *gimmel*:

The word "gemara" is a notarikon for Gabriel, Michael, Raphael and Uriel, which tells us that everyone who is occupied with the study of gemara [the Talmud]—lo! the angels of God surround him in order to guard him from all evil. Michael stands at his right hand, and Gabriel stands at his left; Uriel stands before him, and Raphael behind him.[1]

Page 7a, letter *yod*:

If you abandon me one day, two days will I abandon you . . . . (Sifrei Devarim, pesiqta 48).[2] Those who abandon the Torah and go off to waste even one day, likewise the Torah will abandon them and they will need two days for every one in order to recover that which they forgot of their studies. The clue to this is that the covert meaning of יום is the same as the overt meaning of יום.[3] As well the covert meaning of

---

1. Compare Singer, *ADBP*, 297 and note ccxv; Baer, 576 and note, on *malakhei elyon*. The talmud was known by that name until the beginning of printed texts. However, this name was anathema to Christian censors, so Jews were forced to choose a different name—*gemara*—which simply means "transmission of memorized oral teaching." The numerical value of *GMRA* ($3+40+200+1=244$) indicates the Jewish year of the first printing of the talmud, $[5]244 = 1484$ c.e., in Soncino, Italy. Ḥaim bar Bezalel's explanation is intended to comfort his readers, for the Jewish community was originally resistant to this new name for their beloved talmud.

2. Hammer, 104; Finkelstein and Horowitz, 112.

3. These sorts of "games" are quite difficult to explain in English translation, concerning doing arithmetic with the numerical values associated with the Hebrew letters (aleph to yod $= 1$–10; yod to qoph $= 10$–100; and tav $= 400$). In these cases here, for each word, the value of each Hebrew letter equals the sum of the values of the rest of the letters in its name. (This is somewhat like our "perfect numbers," which are equal to the sum of their lesser divisors: $6 = 3+2+1$; $28 = 14+7+ 4+2+1$; etc.) So yom is spelled yod-vav-mem. The letter 'y' $= 10$, and its name, y-o-d, gives the formula $10 = 6+4$. The letter 'v' $= 6$, and its name 'v-v,' gives $6 = 6$. Similarly with the letter 'm,' 40, and its name, m-m, and so on. Hence י-וד [10–10], ו-ו [6–6], מ-ם [40–40].

the letters ממון is also ממון,[4] which reveals to us that he who gives money in secret will find that the gift is doubled.[5] And as well the covert meaning of the letters סיום is also סיום;[6] this tells us that every uneducated lay person, who does not enjoy the fame of a Torah scholar yet supports anonymously those who do study Torah, has just as much right to share in the celebration every time a tractate is completed as do the scholars themselves, [for those who support covertly have just as much value as those who study overtly].

Page 7b, letter *kaf*:

For the vineyard of the Lord is the House of Israel (Isa. 5:7). All the trees are named according to the name of the fruit they bear except for the grape.[7] The significance of this is that [if the fruit of all other trees is ruined, the tree itself is still of use, but] if the grapes are ruined so that they cannot produce wine, the vine itself is not good for anything else but casting into the fire. [Nimshal] So it is with Israel: When they are not doing the will of their Creator—lo! their inner nature becomes as corrupt as the nations' [and they are therefore of no worth at all except to be destroyed], as it is written, *Thus says the Lord, Like the wood of the grapevine among the trees of the forest, which I have consigned to the fire for fuel, so I will treat the inhabitants of Jerusalem* (Ezek. 15:6).

Derash

Page 10a, letter *nun*:

In the midrash it is told that at the moment that Noah planted his vineyard, Satan came to him in human form.

Satan said, "I want to work with you in your efforts."

Noah replied, "All right."

What did Satan do? He brought a lamb and slaughtered it under the vine, and then he brought a lion and slaughtered it also, and then he

---

4. מ–מ [40–40], מ–מ [40–40], ו–ו [6–6], נ–נ [50–50]. On Mammon in the New Testament, see Matt. 5:24 and Luke 16:9–13.

5. The preferred way to give charity is in secret, for the recipient feels twice as good not knowing where it came from; the double מ–מ indicates this. See Maimonides, Hilkhot Matnot Aniyim 10:7–14 (*la-Am*, 5.130–31) on the graduations of charitable gifts, *mattan ba-setter* (cf. Prov. 21:4).

6. ס–מך [60–60], י–יד [10–10], ו–ו [6–6], מ–מ [50–50].

7. Compare M. Berakhot 6:1; Kehati, 1.46–47 and note.

brought a monkey, and then a pig. He mixed together the blood of the four animals, and poured it on the ground under the vine.

The intention of Satan was to reveal to Noah that everyone who decides to get drunk on wine will behave after the fashion of the animals.

For at the beginning, they sit docilely without opening their mouths, just like *lambs*;

a while later when they begin to be more affected by the wine they begin to brag about their conquests and imagine themselves to be brave as *lions*;

still later when the wine has gotten the best of them, they begin to dance like *monkeys*;

finally they are so drunk that they vomit, and wallow in their own filth like *pigs*.[8]

Sod

Page 12b, letter *hey*:

I have discovered that the letter ה, itself from the Sacred Tetragrammaton, is the letter of pregnancy [compare Gen. 47:23, in which bar Bezalel finds his inspiration[9]]. The meaning of the letter ה is "a seed" [sperm], which explains why Leah, Bilhah and Zilpah were seen to be pregnant, for there is a ה in each of their names, whereas Rachel, who does not have the letter ה in her name, was barren. And Rachel thought to have children by way of Bilhah, an idea which came to her mind when she realized that Bilhah had an extra ה, since there are two in her name.

---

8. See also *Tanḥuma*, Noah 13 (where the description of the pig is even more graphic!); see also the poem of David Samoscz, "When Noah Planted," in his *Aggadot Shoshanim*, 6, in Haberman, *Mivḥar*, 2.194.

9. הא-לכם זרע .

Appendix III

The Half-Sheqel Offering in the
Second Temple Period

The extracts that follow are translated from the introduction to Mishnah Tractate Sheqalim by Chanok Albeck, *Shishah Sidrei Mishnah* pp. 181–186.

The Sources

The Lord spoke to Moses: "When you take a census of the Israelites to register them, at registration all of them shall give a ransom for their lives to the Lord, so that no plague may come upon them for being registered. This is what each one who is registered shall give: half a sheqel according to the sheqel of the sanctuary (the sheqel is twenty gerahs), half a sheqel as an offering to the Lord. Each one who is registered, from twenty years old and upward, shall give the Lord's offering. The rich shall not give more, and the poor shall not give less, than the half sheqel, when you bring this offering to the Lord to make atonement for your lives. You shall take the atonement money from the Israelites and shall designate it for the service of the tent of meeting; before the Lord it will be a reminder to the Israelites of the ransom given for your lives (Ex. 30:11–16).

* * *

Some time afterward Joash decided to restore the house of the Lord. He assembled the priests and the Levites and said to them, "Go out to the cities of Judah and gather money from all Israel to repair the house of your God, year by year; and see that you act quickly." But the Levites did not act quickly. So the king summoned Jehoiada the chief, and said to him, "Why have you not required the Levites to bring in from Judah and Jerusalem the tax levied by Moses, the servant of the Lord, on the congregation of Israel for the tent of the covenant?" For the children of Athaliah, that wicked woman, had broken into the house of God, and

297

had even used all the dedicated things of the house of the Lord for the Baals.

So the king gave command, and they made a chest, and set it outside the gate of the house of the Lord. A proclamation was made throughout Judah and Jerusalem to bring in for the Lord the tax that Moses the servant of God laid on Israel in the wilderness. All the leaders and all the people rejoiced and brought their tax and dropped it into the chest until it was full. Whenever the chest was brought to the king's officers by the Levites, when they saw that there was a large amount of money in it, the king's secretary and the officer of the chief priest would come and empty the chest and take it and return it to its place. So they did day after day, and collected money in abundance. The king and Jehoiada gave it to those who had charge of the work of the house of the Lord, and they hired masons and carpenters to restore the house of the Lord, and also workers in iron and bronze to repair the house of the Lord. So those who were engaged in the work labored, and the repairing went forward at their hands, and they restored the house of God to its proper condition and strengthened it. When they had finished, they brought the rest of the money to the king and Jehoiada, and with it were made utensils for the house of the Lord, utensils for the service, and for the burnt offerings, and ladles, and vessels of gold and silver. They offered burnt offerings in the house of the Lord regularly all the days of Jehoiada (2 Chron. 24:4–14; compare 2 Kings 12:4–16).

* * *

We also lay on ourselves the obligation to charge ourselves yearly one-third of a sheqel for the service of the house of our God: for the rows of bread, the regular grain offering, the regular burnt offering, the sabbaths, the new moons, the appointed festivals, and sacred donations, and the sin offerings to make atonement for Israel, and for all the work of the house of our God (Neh. 10:32–33; compare 2 Kings 22:3–7, 2 Chron. 34:8–13).

Citing Exodus 30:12–16 as a Biblical precedent, Temple authorities revived the custom of the payment of an annual "Moses tax" to the Temple in Jerusalem during the reign of Hasmonean Queen Shelomzion and president of the Sanhedrin Shimeon ben Shatakh.[1] Called "the half-sheqel" (*mahatzit ha-sheqel*), the "tax" was an annual levy upon every Jewish man, adult or adolescent, slave or free, above the age of thirteen. Nearly all Christian commentators muddle their statistical information because they base their understanding of the half-sheqel too literally on Exodus 30, ignoring the fact that most of the customs concerning the half-sheqel in

---

1. Bar-Droma, 44.

effect at the time of Jesus were the product of subsequent oral Torah rather than an application of the Biblical directive. In the Exodus passage, men above the age of twenty (at which point they qualified for combat duty, and thus needed to be numbered by the census takers) were required to pay the one-time contribution. These conditions, however, did not apply to the Second Temple half-sheqel. Between the periods of the Exodus and the Second Temple, the tax was not paid consistently. Under Ezra and Nehemiah it was paid, though in a form different from the half-sheqel as begun in the Hasmonean period. After Queen Shelomzion, the half-sheqel was understood as a religious obligation, binding upon all above the age of bar mitzvah.[2]

> The pericope pertaining to half-sheqel offering, as it is related in the Pentateuch, does not appear at a surface reading to bind future generations to the annual donation of a half-sheqel for the Temple services. Rather, it applies to a particular situation in the days of Moses: *When you take a census of the Israelites to register them . . . each one who is registered shall give a half a sheqel according to the sheqel of the sanctuary.* But according to the report in 2 Kings: *All the money offered as sacred donations that is brought into the house of the Lord, the money for which each person is assessed—the money from the assessment of persons—and the money from the voluntary offerings brought into the house of the Lord, let the priests receive from each of the donors* (2 Kings 12:4). We must remember that three different types of donations were brought to the Temple during the period of Jehoash: monies for the civil purpose of mustering the population [i.e., taking a census based on the number of contributors], that being the half-sheqel offerings; monies for the religious purpose of ransoming each human life, and so consecrating it to God [see Lev. 27:1f and parallels]; and moneys which were simple voluntary donations. These three distinctions are spelled out clearly in the Targum Jonathan, and are remarked upon by a variety of commentators. The matter is made even more explicit at 2 Chron. 24, where it speaks in terms of the "Moses tax". This was also the way in which Josephus understood the scriptures.[3] From this it is argued that the half-sheqel offering is commanded as well to future generations, as Saadya Gaon, ibn-Ezra, and Naḥmanides make clear in their commentaries to Ex. 30:12. This interpretation is confirmed by the author of *She'eltot,*[4] that all of Israel is obligated to observe the half-sheqel offering, and as such it has been listed in the roster of the 613 command-

2. See Meshorer, 176.
3. *Antiquities* 9.161ff. (Marcus, 6.86ff.).
4. Mirsky, *She'eltot* 73, 3.201 and bottom note; compare Maimonides, *Sefer ha-Mitzvot* #171 (*la-Am*, 1.136–37).

ments.[5] Josephus does not understand the half-sheqel offering as a form of census-taking, but claims that Moses commanded all of Israel to pay a per capita tax of a half-sheqel.[6] He also relates that the Jews of Babylon used to contribute their drachmons, since all Jews were obligated to contribute in order to consecrate themselves to God, and these would be sent to Jerusalem.[7] Because the half-sheqel was understood as a contribution rather than as a token by which a census of Israel might be taken, the sages taught that the levites and priests (who otherwise would not have been included in a census) were also obligated to offer the half-sheqel. Every male from the age of thirteen was obligated to pay the half-sheqel, though the scriptural requirement is age twenty and up.

However, several groups apparently were exempted from the tax. Others were not officially exempted, but the tax still was not collected from them. Women and minors were not required to pay the tax, but if they chose to pay, it was accepted; the payment of the tax was not to be accepted from non-Jews. Priests (*kohanim*) were in theory required to pay but whole-heartedly refused.[8] Because they themselves were the recipients, they could argue that there was no reason to pay taxes to themselves, and so in the interests of keeping peace their tax was not collected.[9] In addition, various factions within Judaism disagreed over the conditions of the obligation. Essenes believed the tax should be paid only once.[10] Sadducees felt that the obligation should be taken care of by the wealthy alone, suspecting that the poor would try to claim sacerdotal powers if they became contributors to the Temple administration.[11] The Pharisees held that because all benefited equally from the continued daily offerings of the sacrifice in the Temple, which this tax helped to fund, all should be held

5. See Albeck, *Sha"S Moed*, 183 n2; all other notes there should also be read thoroughly.
6. *Antiquities* 3.193ff. (Thackeray, 4.408ff.).
7. *Antiquities* 18.310ff. (Feldman, 9.178ff.).
8. See M. Sheqalim 1.3, in Albeck, *Sha"S Moed*, 188; Kehati, Sheqalim, 405 notes; and Maimonides, Hilkhot Sheqalim 1.7 (*la-Am*, 3.504).
9. M. Sheqalim 1.4; JT Sheqalim 1,46a; see also Zevin, 236, and Kasher, 21.169.
10. Allegro, 71–73; Liver, 190–95.
11. On this bitter quarrel between the Sadducees and the Pharisees in the Hasmonean period, see *Megillat Taanit*, chap. 1 and references; and *Avot de Rabbi Nathan* 5 (Goldin, 39). Lichtenstein ("Die Fastenrolle," 290–91) refers to the discussion of Jacob Lauterbach on the identity of "sages" (*hakhamim*) with Pharisees (*perushim*) in "The Sadducees and Pharisees, a study of their respective attitude towards the Law" (*Studies in Jewish Literature*, Kohler, 1913). See also BT Menaḥot 65a; Finkelstein, *Pharisees*, 282–83, and Kohut, 7.305 in the text at n1, where he reads *tzaduqin*.

equally responsible for payment. This viewpoint became normative, as can be seen from M. Sheqalim.

> At 2 Kings 12:4–16 we are told that in the days of Jehoash money was collected for the Temple, and with this money the repairs to the Temple were furthered, and from a portion of it the vessels of the Temple were made, *and they offered the burnt offering in the house of the Lord* (2 Chron. 24:14). Then we are told that in the period of Nehemiah, the half-sheqel offerings were also designated for the public expense of *the showbread, the meal offering, the animals for the daily burnt offering, the sabbaths, the new moons*, etc. (Neh. 10:33). The Mishnah, at Sheqalim, chap. 4, itemizes the various objects which were funded from the donated sheqalim. It was the responsibility for maintaining the budget from which the daily public offerings were paid, which became a controversial issue between the Pharisees and the Sadducees. The Sadducees were of the opinion that an individual was entitled to donate a public offering, but the Pharisees insisted that a public offering could only be purchased from the funds of the general treasury, in which every member of the public had an equal share, since all paid the same half-sheqel. It is possible that the whole decreed system for the payment of the half-sheqel, including the local points of collection and the restrictions on the high-priest's access to the treasury, was designed as an anti-Sadducean measure. The regulations lay down criteria which were more than the situation warranted, as JT Sheqalim 1.1 explains: "in order to make a conspicuous fuss about things."

The half-sheqel was given "voluntarily" in fulfillment of religious obligation, not only by Jews in Palestine but by Jews throughout the entire diaspora. It was obligatory, and even commandeered, but everyone was assumed to be "giving" it rather than having it collected.[12] As has been

---

12. See Maimonides, Hilkhot Sheqalim 1.1 (*la-Am*, 3.502). This is the only mitzvah in the Torah that requires one to exceed one's financial means; people even were required to mortgage their homes, if necessary, to pay the half-sheqel. In general, it was assumed that God would provide whatever means necessary for the fulfillment of a particular mitzvah. In this case, even if God had not provided, the half-sheqel was required from everyone equally, since the ongoing public sacrifices in the Temple, supported by the half-sheqel, required the participation of all kosher males, in order that the public be fully and completely represented. On a directly related quarrel between the Pharisees and the Sadducees, see Lichtenstein, "Die Fastenrolle," 323, on how the Tamid sacrifice would be funded, aristocratically or democratically; and see Moskovitz, 344–45, esp. n3gimmel. Subsequently two non-Torah-based mitzvot were also made universally binding: the showing forth of the Hannukah lights, and the four cups of the Passover Seder.

stated, it was not connected with Exodus 30 except as a source of authority, nor was it connected in any way during the Second Temple period with the civil administration or the civil census.[13] Duress made the payment of the tax invalid (see above in relation to the *kohanim*), so the half-sheqel was not collected by civil or even religious "tax collectors." Rather, in the month of Addar (roughly equivalent to February), collection booths staffed by the local citizenry were set up in the provinces, to which Jews came from the area to pay their tax.[14] Thus far, archaeologists have found no evidence that rolls were kept of these payments, as they were after 70 C.E. when the Romans converted this religious tax to a civil tax.

The first two chapters of the Mishnah Tractate Sheqalim are concerned with the mitzvah of offering the half-sheqel, and the manner of its collection. The sheqel was collected at a fixed time of the year, the month of Addar, an appointed time which was determined in relation to the first day of Nissan, the "new year" of the offering of sheqels. The public sacrifices had to be purchased from this new fund, which was composed of the half-sheqel offerings collected during the previous month of Addar, according to biblical injunction. The half-sheqel offerings were given and received in the following manner: on the first of Addar, proclamation was made concerning the half-sheqel offerings and concerning the sowing of mixed seeds (Lev. 19:19, Deut 22:9). On the fifteenth of Addar, the bet din repaired the roads and *miqvaot*, and carried out various public needs. The collection tables, staffed by money changers, were set up in all the provinces, in order to exchange the various local currencies for the requisite Temple coinage. On the twenty-fifth of Addar, tables were set up in the Temple, and they began to exact pledges from all those who had not made their offerings in the provinces. Levites and priests as well were obligated to offer the half-sheqel, but not women, slaves, or boys below the age of 13. However, if these latter wished to donate, their offering was received.

Offerings were not received from gentiles or Samaritans. Sacrificial offerings were not received from them either, though oath-offerings and free-will offerings were. Anyone who offered the half-sheqel was obligated to add a surcharge to it. R. Meir argued with the sages over the number of the surcharges. The half-sheqels were changed into darics, and were sent on to Jerusalem, in order to ease the burden of the journey. Half-sheqel offerings which were stolen or lost during transport, but were found after half-sheqel offerings had been sent on to Jerusalem, were not credited to the offering for the coming year, but were added to the funds

13. See Nahmanides to Ex. 30:12 (Chavel Eng., 517–18), and see Albeck's introduction to M. Sheqalim, *Sha"S Moed*, 183ff.
14. Bar-Droma, 46: *benei ha-ir*.

are sent ahead. The School of Shammai disagreed with the School of Hillel over the status of individual donations over and above the half-sheqel. Then comes a discussion of how the surplus half-sheqel offerings and various charitable funds were to be used. And along the way, R. Judah the Prince remarks upon the history of the various coins which were used for the half-sheqel offering at differing times.

One of the most troubling aspects of scholarly work in this area is the question of exactly how the half-sheqel was paid. The term "sheqel" at times refers to a coin, but in origin it refers to a weight (Hebrew: *lishqol*, to weigh). A half-sheqel originally was a specific weight in silver, or its equivalent. Beginning in 19 B.C.E. at the order of Herod, the Temple began to produce its own special coinage for the payment of the tax, called the Tyrian sheqel.[15] The tax had to be paid in these Tyrian sheqels only, for they were among the few coins available that did not carry an image or inscription offensive to the sanctity of the Temple. Jews wishing to pay had to change other currencies into the Tyrian sheqel, for which purpose money changers (Hebrew: *shulḥanim*; Greek: *kollubistoi*) were connected with the Temple. In the provinces, Jews did not purchase the half-sheqel itself, but paid an equivalent amount in whatever coinage, which was then transported as a lump collection to Jerusalem where it was converted to Tyrian sheqels. The sheqel itself was not used only for this tax. Apparently these sheqels circulated among the population (making the Jerusalem Temple not only one of the most important minters of currency but also the largest bank in the world during the Second Temple period), and were used for both civil and religious purposes. Hence it is a grave error to assume that any mention of the sheqel in the New Testament (as Matt. 17 is assumed to do) refers automatically to the Temple tax. In fact, the sheqel itself is not an exact term; for example it is clear from the letters of Bar-Kokhba (c.132 C.E.) that in his period a sheqel equaled one drachma, not a didrachma, as is assumed by exegetes of Matthew 17.

Half-sheqels as well as full sheqels were minted, but two half-sheqels did not equal a full sheqel in terms of payment of the tax, as the payment was according to silver-weight. Because it took more effort to mint half-sheqels, and thus more profit was necessary, the amount of silver was reduced in the half-sheqel as compared with the sheqel. Therefore it be-

---

15. Such a coin indeed had been minted in Tyre, but was not produced there after 20 B.C.E., when Herod shifted the permission to mint it from Tyre to the Jerusalem Temple; see Meshorer, 172ff. It was minted in Jerusalem from 19 B.C.E. to 65 C.E., when production was stopped by the First Jewish Revolt. According to Stevenson, this was probably the coin with which Judas was paid for the betrayal.

came customary for two Jews to go together and pay in one full sheqel, rather than two half-sheqels, since in fact a half-sheqel coin did not contain enough silver to pay the half-sheqel tax, whereas a full sheqel did contain enough to pay two people's taxes. A sheqel equaled approximately two and one-half half-sheqels.

The word *didrachma* in Matthew 17 is confusing. There is no evidence available that during the Second Temple period the half-sheqel tax was ever called in Greek "the didrachma." In fact a didrachma would not qualify to pay the tax, not only because of the reduced silver-weight, but also because an extra eight percent surcharge was needed for the purpose of converting the didrachma into a Tyrian sheqel. Further, didrachmas were often defective in their silver content, so one could not be sure without weighing them whether they were at all sufficient for the tax.

A *stater*, as in Matthew 17:27, is not used to refer to a tetradrachma, so the equality of terms suggested by Matthew 17—didrachma, stater, and sheqel—and assumed by most Christian exegetes, in fact has no basis either in the literature or in the numismatics of the period.[16] In addition, archaeological finds have revealed that a tetradrachma (given the mathematics, the only possible point of reference for "stater" in Matt. 17:27) was of such poor silver content that it would have been clearly insufficient for the payment of the half-sheqel for two people.[17]

> In truth, there never was any particular coin which held the exact same worth as the half-sheqel, and even the full sheqel at the time of the Mishnah was not equivalent to two of the half-sheqels mentioned in the Torah, but rather equaled two dinars, which was a half a sela.

The rest of the structure of the Mishnaic tractate is also pertinent to our exploration:

> Chapters three and four of Mishnah Tractate Sheqalim explain how funds were removed from the treasury chamber into which they had been placed, and what they did inside the chamber. Three times a year, funds would be removed: half a month before Passover, half a month before Shavuot (Weeks), and half a month before Sukkot (Booths). They were taken out in a particular manner: in three baskets, each holding three seahs in weight, and the baskets were numbered in Hebrew (though R. Ishmael insisted they were numbered in Greek). The high priest entered the treasury in the following manner: The Passover withdrawal was withdrawn in honor of all the inhabitants of the Land of Israel; the Shavuot

---

16. Mandel, 57.
17. Meshorer, 176.

withdrawal was withdrawn in honor of the Jewish communities geographically adjacent to Israel; and the Sukkot withdrawal was withdrawn
in honor of the Jews of Babylon and other distant lands. The withdrawn
funds were used to pay for the daily sacrifices, additional offerings, the
burnt offerings on behalf of the public, the showbread, and other such
items. Whatever funds remained in the treasury after these sacrifices
were paid for, were used to pay for the red heifer offering, and other
religious needs of the city. A difference of opinion is recorded as to the
use of other surplus funds. Certain other monies were deconsecrated, and
used to pay the salaries of the craftsmen employed by the Temple. R.
Eliezer and R. Yehuda disagreed over the use of privately donated cattle.
Once every thirty days, surplus donations such as wine, oil, flour, and
fowl, were sold to the public at prices set by the Temple officials.

Chapter five begins with the names of the appointed sanctuary officers, such as those in charge of the seals, the singing, or the vestments.
No fewer than three revenuers and seven supervisors were appointed at a
given time. The method of purchasing a sacrifice was as follows: there
were four seals, upon them written in Hebrew "calf, male ram, kid, sin-
ner" (but Ben Azzai insisted there were five, written in Aramaic). One
who wished to purchase a sacrifice went to the appropriate officer, paid a
fee, then took the appropriate seal to the officer in charge of dispensing
that specific sacrifice. At the end of the day, all officers had to account for
their seals, and for the day's income. There was a special chamber in the
Temple for secretly donated gifts, and another for charitably-donated vessels. Into the first, people who wished to keep their sins secret could
make donations, and from it, the poor of good families were anonymously
supported.

According to chapter six, there were thirteen shofar chests for collecting moneys, including the half-sheqel offerings; thirteen sacrifice-re-
lated worktables; and thirteen stations for liturgical prostration in the
Temple. The followers of R. Gamliel recognized a fourteenth prostration
station, where by their own tradition, the ark had been stored. The thirteen prostration stations were oriented toward the thirteen gates of the
Temple. The composition and use of the thirteen work-tables is described. Among the thirteen shofar chests, was one marked "new
sheqels," in which the half-sheqel offering for the current year was received, and another marked "old sheqels" in which half-sheqel offerings
still owed from previous years could be placed. Six of the thirteen chests
were for freewill offerings. Jehoida the High Priest determined the usage
of these freewill offerings, based on his own exegesis of Lev. 5:15 and 18,
and 2 Kings 12:16.

The seventh chapter begins with a discussion of the disposal of
money found to have fallen between the chests for half-sheqel offerings
and the chests for the freewill offerings, or between the chest for new
sheqels and the chest for old. This is followed by a discussion of what to
do with meat which is found in Jerusalem or in the provinces, and what

to do with cattle found wandering loose. Then follows a list of seven court rulings related to various offerings.

The final chapter of Mishnah Tractate Sheqalim opens with a discussion of how drops of spit found in the streets are determined to be clean or unclean. The same discussion is applied to found utensils, and then whether a knife found on the day before Passover can be used for slaughtering at the feast. Methods for the weaving of the veil in the Temple [*parokhet*] are described (made by 82 young girls, and immersed by 300 priests), as well as how to cleanse it from contracted impurity. Next comes a discussion of how to dispose of certain kinds of consecrated meat, or the limbs of the daily sacrifices. The tractate concludes by ruling that while many other sacrifices continue to apply after the destruction of the Temple, the firstfruit tithes and the half-sheqel offerings apply only when the Temple in Jerusalem is standing.

Since the half-sheqel was a religious tax, completely unconnected to the civil authorities, in theory it ceased with the destruction in 70 C.E. However:

> According to the decree of the Emperor Vespasian, the Jews were obligated to make their half-sheqel offerings in the form of two drachmas to the Capitolium, in the same fashion that they made their contribution to the Temple while it was standing.[18] R. Yohanan ben Zakkai complained: "You did not want to make your sheqel offering, but now you will have to bust your butt to pay fifteen sheqels to the enemy government."[19]

A significant source of confusion in the issue at hand is that after the destruction of the Temple in 70 C.E., the Roman government required that all Jews continue to pay a tax equivalent to the half-sheqel, but this time to the civil authorities themselves. This seems to result in a shifting of names in the sources, so that the former *mas gilgolet* disappears, and the former half-sheqel, now termed the *capitolina*, begins to be referred to in post-70 sources as the *mas gilgolet*. This *capitolina*, sometimes erroneously called the *fiscus judaicus*, was collected by civil tax collectors and extensive records of annual payments by Jews have been found in Rome.[20] The latest textual evidence for the payment of this civil didrachmon is in Origen, *Epistle to Africanus* 14, in 240 C.E.[21]

---

18. Josephus, *Wars* 7.216 (Thackeray, 3.566ff.).
19. *Mekhilta*, Bahodesh 1 (Lauterbach, 2.194).
20. See Carlebach.
21. ANF 4.392; Quasten 2.74; and see de Lange, 34, and see 162 n56 for additional references.

In the meantime, evidence from the Copper Scroll suggests that between 70 and the mid-90s C.E., Jews continued to give donations dedicated to the Temple in anticipation of its being rebuilt. These voluntary funds were duly recorded and a list of them forms the contents of the Copper Scroll. According to this theory, the funds were discovered during the reign of the Emperor Nerva, between 96 and 98 C.E., who responded to these unexpected spoils of war by issuing a magnificent coin inscribed "Fisci Judaici Calumnia Sublata" (the insult [to the Romans] of the Jewish [continued self-taxation system] has been annulled).[22]

---

22. See Lehmann.

Bibliography

Aarne, Antti. *The Types of the Folktale: A Classified Bibliography*. Translated and enlarged by Stith Thompson. Helsinki: Folklore Fellows Communications, 1961.

Abelson, J. "Maimonides on the Jewish Creed." *JQR*, (October, 1907): 24–58.

Aberbach, Moses, and Bernard Grossfeld. *Targum Onkelos to Genesis*. N.p.: Ktav Publishing House and Center for Judaic Studies, University of Denver, 1982.

Aberbach, Moshe. "Did Rabban Gamaliel II Impose the Ban on Rabbi Eliezer ben Hyrcanus?" *JQR* 54:3 (1964), 201–7.

Abrahams, Israel. *Studies in Pharisaism and the Gospels*. New York: Ktav, 1917, 1967.

Abramson, Shraga. "Divrei HaZa"L be-Shirat ha-Naggid." In *Papers of the First Congress of Jewish Studies, 1947*, 274ff. Jerusalem: World Congress of Jewish Studies, 1952.

———. *Inyanot be-Sifrut ha-Geonim* (Studies in Geonic Literature). Jerusalem: Mossad ha-Rav Kook, 1974.

———. *Rav Nissim Gaon* (R. Nissim Gaon: Five Books). Jerusalem: Meqitze Nirdamim, 1965.

———. *Tractate 'Abodah Zarah of the Babylonian Talmud*. New York: Jewish Theological Seminary, 1957.

———. *Tractate Baba Batra*. Jerusalem: Devir and Masada, 1958.

Abravanel, Don Isaac. *Commentary on Bereshit*. Jerusalem: Benai Arabel, 1979.

Abu-Zimra, David. *Responsa*. 3 vols. Reprint. New York: Solomon Goldman, 1967.

Adler, Nathan b. Mordecai (HaCohen). *Netinah la-Ger*, 1875, in *Otzar Mifareshei ha-Torah*. 2 vols. Jerusalem: n.p., 1973.

Adret, Solomon ben Abraham. *Responsa*. Vol. 1. Bnai Brak: Gittler, Sifriyati, 1958.

Agnon, Shemuel Yosef. *Days of Awe*. New York: Schocken, 1948.

al-Harizi, Judah. *Tahkemoni*. Edited by Israel Zemora. Tel Aviv: Mossad ha-Rav Kook, 1952.

al-Naqawa, Israel. *Menorat ha-Maor*. 6 vols. Edited by Hillel Gershom Enelow. New York: 1929-32, reprint, Jerusalem: Maqor, 1972.

al-Qumsi, Daniel. *Commentarius in Librum Duodecim Prophetarum*. Edited by I. D. Markon. Jerusalem: Meqitze Nirdamim, 1957.

Albeck, Chanok, ed. *Shishah Sidrei Mishnah* (The Six Orders of the Mishnah). 6 vols. plus introductory volume. Jerusalem: Devir, 1973.

Albeck, Shalom. *Dinei ha-Mammanot ba-Talmud* (The Law of Property and Contract in the Talmud). Tel Aviv: Devir, 1976.

Albo, Joseph. *Sefer ha-Ikkarim* (The Book of Principles). 4 vols. Translated by I. Husik. Philadelphia: Jewish Publication Society, 1946.

Albright, William Foxwell. *From Stone Age to Christianity*. 2nd ed. Garden City, N.Y.: Doubleday, 1940, 1957.

———. "Zabul Yam and Thapit Nahar in the Combat Between Baal and the Sea." *JPOS* 16 (1936), 17–20.

Albright, William Foxwell, and C. S. Mann. *Matthew*. Anchor Bible. Garden City, N.Y.: Doubleday, 1971.

Alciphron. *The Letters of Alciphron, Aelian and Philostratus*. Translated by Allen Rogers Benner and Francis H. Fobes. Loeb Classical Library, 1949.

Alexander, P. S. "Rabbinic Judaism and the New Testament." *ZNW* 3 (1983):237–46.

Alfasi, Isaac of Fez. *320 Responsa of Isaac of Fez*. Edited by Anton Schmidt. Vienna, 1794.

Allegro, John M. "An Unpublished Fragment of Essene Halakhah (4Q Ordinances)." *Journal of Semitic Studies* 6 (1961): 71–73.

Allen, Willoughby C. *A Critical Commentary on the Gospel According to Matthew*. International Critical Commentary. Edited by Charles A. Briggs, Samuel R. Driver, and Alfred Plummer. New York: Scribner's, 1907.

Alon, Gedalyahu. *Jews, Judaism and the Classical World*. Jerusalem: Magnes, 1977.

———. *The Jews in Their Land in the Talmudic Age*. 2 vols. Jerusalem: Magnes, 1984.

———. *Mekhkarim be-Toledot Israel* (Studies in Jewish History). 2 vols. N.p.: Hakibbutz Hameuchad, 1958–67.

Alter, Robert. *The World of Biblical Literature*. New York: Basic Books, 1991.

Altmann, Alexander. "God and the Self in Jewish Mysticism." *Judaism* 3:2 (1954): 1–5.

Aminah, Noah. "Em le-Miqra ve-Em la-Massoret ke-Bituiim Normativiim." *Te'uda: Studies in Bible, Memorial Volume to Yehoshua Meir Grintz* 2 (1982): 43–56.

Anderson, Gary. "The Interpretation of the Purification Offering in the Temple Scroll (11QTemple) and Rabbinic Literature." *JBL* 111:1 (1992):17–35.

Argyle, A. W. "Wedding Customs at the Time of Jesus." *Expository Times* 86:7 (1975):214–15.

Aristotle. *The "Art" of Rhetoric*. Translated by John Henry Freese. Loeb Classical Library, 1947.

———. *The Basic Works of Aristotle*. Edited by Richard McKeon. New York: Random House, 1941.

———. *The Metaphysics*. 2 vols. Translated by Hugh Tredennick. Loeb Classical Library, 1956.

———. *The Nicomachean Ethics*. Translated by H. Rackman. Loeb Classical Library, 1968.

———. *Poetics*. Translated by W. Hamilton Fyfe. Loeb Classical Library, 1932.

Arnim, Ioannis ab. *Stoicorum Veterum Fragmenta*. 4 vols. Lipsiae: B. G. Teubneri, 1938.

Ashkenazi, Bezalel. *Shittah Mequbetzet to Baba Metzia* (Analecta of the Rishonim). Tel Aviv: Avraham Tsioni, 1954.

Athanasius. "The Life of Anthony." *Early Christian Biographies*. Edited by Roy DeFerrari. Washington: Catholic University of America, 1952.

Auerbach, Erich. *Mimesis: The Representation of Reality in Western Literature*. Translated by Willard Trask. Garden City, N.Y.: Doubleday, 1957.

Augustine. *The City of God, Books 17–22*. Translated by Gerald Walsh and Daniel Honan. Fathers of the Church. Washington: Catholic University of America, 1954.

———. *The Confessions*. Translated by Edward B. Pusey. New York: Modern Library, 1949.

———. *Confessions and Enchiridion*. Translated by Albert C. Outler. Library of Christian Classics. Philadelphia: Westminster, 1965.

———. *The Letters of Saint Augustine*. Translated by J. G. Cunningham. Edinburgh: T. & T. Clark, 1875.

Aus, Roger David. "Luke 15:11–32 and R. Eliezer ben Hyrcanus's Rise to Fame." *JBL* 104:3 (1985): 443–469.

Austin, J. L. *How to Do Things with Words*. 2nd ed. Cambridge: Harvard University Press, 1975.

Avineri, Izhak. *Heikhal Rashi*. 2 vols. Jerusalem: Mossad ha-Rav Kook, 1985.

Avi-Yonah, Michael, ed. *The World History of the Jewish People: First Series: Ancient Times, Volume Seven: The Herodian Period*. New Brunswick, N.J.: Rutgers, 1975.

Babylonian Talmud. Toronto and New York: n.p., 1919.

Bacher, Wilhelm. *Agada der Palestinischen Amoräer*. 4 vols. Reprint. Hildesheim: Georg Olms Verlagsbuchhandlung, 1965.

———. *Aggadot ha-Tannaim*. 4 parts in 2 vols. Edited by A. Z. Rabinowitz. Berlin: Devir, 1922.

———. "Das Merkwort פרדס in der jüdischen Bibel-exegese." *ZAW* 13 (1893): 294–305.

———. *Erkei ha-Midrash*. 2 vols. Translated by A. Z. Rabinowitz. Tel Aviv: n.p., 1923.

———. "Le Mot 'Minim' dans le Talmud." *REJ* 38 (1899):38–46.

———. "L'Exégès Biblique dans le Zohar." *REJ* 22 (1891):37–46, 219–29.

Baer, Seligman. *Seder Avodat Israel*. Roedelheim: n.p., 1868.

Bagatti, B. "Ricerche su Siti Giudeo-Cristiani." *Studii Biblici Franciscani, Liber Annuus XI (1960–1961)*. Jerusalem: Aedem Flagellationis, 1961, 302–3.

Bahye Halawi. *Rabbenu Bahye Halawi: Commentary on the Torah*. 3 vols. Edited by Charles B. Chavel. Jerusalem: Mossad ha-Rav Kook, 1971.

Bakhtin, Mikhail Mikhailovich. *The Dialogic Imagination: Four Essays*. Edited by Michael Holquist. Translated by Caryl Emerson and Michael Holquist. Austin: University of Texas Press, 1981.

Bamberger, Seckel. *Lekach Tob zu Megillat Ruth von Rabbi Tobia ben Elieser*. Mainz: Oscar Lehmann, 1887. (Bound with Greenup on Canticles.)

Banitt, Menahem. "Exegesis or Metaphrasis." *Creative Biblical Exegesis: Christian and Jewish Hermeneutics through the Centuries*. Edited by Benjamin Uffenheimer and Henning Graf Reventlow. Sheffield, England: JSOT, 1988.

———. *Rashi: Interpreter of the Biblical Letter*. Tel Aviv: Tel Aviv University, 1985.

Banks, J., ed. *The Works of Hesiod, Callimachus, and Theognis*. London: G. Bell & Sons, 1914.

Bar-Droma, Joshua. *Ha-Mediniut ha-Finansit shel Medinat-Yehudah biYmei ha-Bayit ha-Rishon ve-ha-Sheni* (The Financial System of the State of Judah in the Periods of the First and Second Temple). Jerusalem: Israel Taxation Museum, 1967.

Bar-Hayya (bar Chijja), Abraham. *The Meditations of the Sad Soul*. Edited by Geoffrey Wigodor. Jerusalem: Mossad Bialik, 1971. Also published in English, New York: Schocken, 1968.

Bar Hebraeus, Mar Gregory John. *The Laughable Stories: The Syriac Text Edited with an English Translation*. Translated by E. A. Wallis Budge. London: Luzac and Company, 1897.

Barnabas, Epistle of. *The Apostolic Fathers*. Translated by Kirsopp Lake. Loeb Classical Library, 1930.

Barnard, Leslie W. "The 'Cross of Herculaneum' Reconsidered." In *The New Testament Age: Essays in Honor of Bo Reicke*, vol. 1, edited by William C. Weinrich. Macon, Ga.: Mercer Press, 1984, 14–27.

Baron, Salo Witmayer. *A Social and Religious History of the Jews*. 2nd ed. 15 vols. Philadelphia: Jewish Publication Society, 1952.

Barr, James. "Abba Isn't Daddy." *JTS* 39:1 (1988):28–47.

———. "The Hebrew/Aramaic Background of 'Hypocrisy' in the Gospels." In *A Tribute to Geza Vermes*, edited by Philip Davies. Sheffield, England: JSOT, 1990, 307–26.

———. *The Semantics of Biblical Language*. Oxford: Oxford University Press, 1961.

Beare, Francis W. *The Earliest Records of Jesus*. New York: Abingdon, 1962.

———. *The Gospel According to Matthew*. 2 vols. San Francisco: Harper & Row, 1982.

Beavis, Mary Ann. "Ancient Slavery as an Interpretive Context for the New Testament Servant Parables with Special Reference to the Unjust Steward (Luke 16:1–8)." *JBL* 111:1 (1992):37–54.

ben Menaḥem, Naphtali. *Zemirot shel Shabbat*. Jerusalem: Moetzah le-Ma'an ha-Shabbat, 1949.

ben Sarukh Hispaniensi, Menaḥem. *Mahberet Menaḥem* (Hebraicae et Chaldaicae Lexicon). Edited by H. Filipowski. London and Edinburgh: H. Filipowski, 1854.

ben Yatzliaḥ, Chafets Aluf. *Sefer "ve-Hizhir" le-Seder Shemot*. 2 vols. Reprint. Israel, 1964.

Ben-Yehudah, Eliezer. *Millon ha-Lashon ha-Ivrit* (Thesaurus of the Hebrew Language). 16 vols. plus introductory volume. Jerusalem: Maqor Publishing Ltd., 1980.

Ben-Amos, Dan. *Narrative Forms in the Haggadah: A Structural Analysis* (Diss.). Bloomington, Ind., 1966.

Benko, Stephen. *Pagan Rome and the Early Christians*. Bloomington: Indiana University Press, 1984.

Bennett, Robert A., and O. C. Edwards. *The Bible for Today's Church*. New York: Seabury, 1979.

Bergson, Henri. *The Creative Mind*. Translated by Mabelle Andison. New York: Philosophical Library, 1946.

Berkovits, Eliezer. *God, Man and History*. New York: Jonathan David, 1959.

————. *Man and God: Studies in Biblical Theology.* Detroit: Wayne State University, 1969.

Berlin, Adele. *Biblical Poetry through Medieval Jewish Eyes.* Bloomington: Indiana University Press, 1991.

Berlin, Yeshayah Pick. *Omer ha-Shikhehah.* Johannesburg, 1866.

Berliner, Abraham. *Targum Onkelos.* Berlin: Gorzelanczyk, 1884.

Berner, Ulrich. "The Image of the Philosopher in Late Antiquity and Early Christianity." In *Concepts of Person in Religion and Thought,* edited by Hans G. Kippenberg, Yme B. Kuiper, and Andy F. Sanders, 125–36. Berlin and New York: Mouton de Gruyter, 1990.

Bernstein, Leonard. *The Unanswered Question: Six Talks at Harvard.* Cambridge: Harvard University Press, 1976.

Besdin, Abraham. *Man of Faith in the Modern World: Reflections of the Rav [J. B. Soloveitchik].* 2 vols. Hoboken, N.J.: Ktav, 1989.

Bettenson, Henry, ed. and trans. "The Didache." *The Early Christian Fathers.* London: Oxford, 1956.

Betz, Otto. "The Death of Honi-Honio in Light of the Qumran Temple Scroll." In *Jerusalem in the Second Temple Period: Abraham Schalit Memorial Volume,* edited by A. Uffenheimer, U. Rappoport and M. Stern, 84–97. Jerusalem: Yad Izhak Ben-Zvi, 1980.

Bezalel, Haim bar. "Iggeret ha-Tiyyul." *Amaroth Tehoroth.* Jerusalem: Abraham Aaron Sonnenfeld, 1884.

Bialik, Hayyim Nahman. *Halachah and Aggadah* (The Law and the Lore of the Talmudic and Post-Biblical Literature). Translated by Leon Simon. London: Education Department of the Zionist Federation of Great Britain and Ireland, 1944.

Bialik, Hayyim Nahman, and Yehoshua Hana Rawnitzky. *Sefer ha-Aggadah.* Tel Aviv: Devir, 1973.

————. *Sefer ha-Aggadah: The Book of Jewish Folklore and Legend.* Edited and translated by Chaim Pearl. Tel Aviv: Devir, 1988.

Black, Matthew. *An Aramaic Approach to Gospels and Acts.* 3rd ed. Oxford: Clarendon Press, 1967.

————. "Rabbula of Edessa and the Peshitta." *John Rylands Library Bulletin* 33 (1950–51):203–10.

Blackman, Philip. *Mishnayot.* 7 vols. Gateshead, England: Judaica Press, 1983.

Blank, Sheldon. "LXX Renderings of Old Testament Terms for Law." *HUCA* 7 (1930):221–37.

Blankstein, Lazar. *Hebrew Proverbs and Their Origin.* Edited by Shemuel Ashkenazi. Jerusalem: Kiryat Sefer, 1964.

Blau, Ludwig. "Early Christian Epigraphy Considered from the Jewish Point of View." *HUCA* (NS) 1 (1924):125–49.

Böhlig, Alexander, and Frederik Wisse, trans. *Nag Hammadi Codices III.2 and IV.2: The Gospel of the Egyptians*. Grand Rapids, Mich.: Eerdmans, 1975.

Bolle, Mena_hem, commentator. *Sefer Yirmiyahu* (The Book of Jeremiah). The Daat Miqra Series. Jerusalem: Mossad ha-Rav Kook, 1983.

Bondi, Roberta. *To Love as God Loves*. Philadelphia: Fortress, 1987.

Borsch, Frederick Houk, ed. *Anglicanism and the Bible*. Wilton: Morehouse-Barlow, 1984.

Bosniak, Jacob. *The Commentary of David Qimchi on the Fifth Book of the Psalms*. New York: Jewish Theological Seminary and Block Publishing, 1954.

Boswell, John. *The Kindness of Strangers: The Abandonment of Children in Western Europe from Late Antiquity to the Renaissance*. New York: Pantheon, 1988.

Boucher, Madeleine. *The Mysterious Parable: A Literary Study*. CBQ Monograph Series. Washington, D. C.: Catholic Biblical Association, 1977.

Bowker, John. *The Targums and Rabbinic Literature: An Introduction to Jewish Interpretations of Scripture*. Cambridge: Cambridge University Press, 1969.

Boyarin, Daniel. "Analogy vs. Anomaly in Midrashic Hermeneutic: Tractates Wayyassa and Amaleq in the Mekhilta." *JAOS* 106:4 (1986):659–66.

————. *Intertextuality and the Reading of Midrash*. Bloomington: Indiana University Press, 1990.

————. "Rhetoric and Interpretation: The Case of the Nimshal." *Prooftexts* 5 (1985):269–80.

————. "Voices in the Text: Midrash and the Inner Tension of Biblical Narrative." *Revue Biblique* 93:4 (1986):581–97.

Brand, Yehoshua. *Kelei _Heres be-Sifrut ha-Talmud (Ceramics in Talmudic Literature)*. Jerusalem: Mossad ha-Rav Kook, 1953.

Brandon, S. G. F. *The Trial of Jesus of Nazareth*. New York: Stein and Day, 1968, 1979.

Brann, Ross. *The Compunctious Poet: Cultural Ambiguity and Hebrew Poetry in Muslim Spain*. Baltimore and London: Johns Hopkins University Press, 1991.

Braude, William G. *The Midrash on the Psalms*. 2 vols. New Haven: Yale University Press, 1959.

————. "A Rabbinic Guide to the Gospels." *Scripture* 19:26 (1967):33–45.

Braude, William G., and Israel J. Kapstein, trans. *Pesiqta de-Rab Kahana*. Philadelphia: Jewish Publication Society, 1975.

―――. *Tanna DeBe Eliyahu: The Lore of the School of Elijah*. Philadelphia: Jewish Publication Society, 1981.

Brickenstein, Israel Nathan. *Perush he-Arokh al Tehillim mi-RaDa"Q* (R. David Qimchi's Systematic Commentary on the Psalms). Tel Aviv: Mossad ha-Rav Kook, 1946.

Brock, Sebastian. "Jewish Traditions in Syriac Sources." *JJS* 30:2 (1979):233–44.

Brody, Haim, and Meir Wiener. *Anthologia Hebraica*. Leipzig: Insel-Verlag, 1922.

Broner, Esther M. *A Weave of Women*. Bloomington: Indiana University Press, 1978, 1985.

Bronznick, Norman. "Qabbalah as a Metonym for the Prophets and Hagiographa." *HUCA* 38 (1967):285–95.

Brooke, George J. *Exegesis at Qumran: 4QFlorilegium in its Jewish Context*. Sheffield, England: JSOT, 1985.

Broshi, Magen. "The Role of the Temple in the Herodian Economy." *JJS* 38:1 (1987):31–37.

Brown, Francis, S. R. Driver, and Charles A. Briggs. *A Hebrew and English Lexicon of the Old Testament*. Oxford: Clarendon, 1906, 1951.

Brown, John Pairman. "The Mediterranean Vocabulary of the Vine." *VT* 19 (1969): 146–70.

Brown, Peter. *The Body and Society: Men, Women, and Sexual Renunciation in Early Christianity*. New York: Columbia University Press, 1988.

Brown, Raymond E. "Does the New Testament Call Jesus God?" *Theological Studies* 26:4 (1965):545–73.

―――. *The Gospel According to John: Volume 1, I–XII; Volume 2, XIII–XXI*. Anchor Bible. Garden City, N.Y.: Doubleday, 1966.

―――. *The Sensus Plenior of Sacred Scripture*. Baltimore: St. Mary's University, 1955.

Brown, Robert McAfee. *Unexpected News: Reading the Bible Through Third World Eyes*. Philadelphia: Westminster, 1984.

Brownlee, William. *The Midrash Pesher of Habakkuk*. Missoula, Mont.: Scholars Press, 1979.

Bruckstein, Almut Sh. "Hermann Cohen's 'Charakteristik der Ethik Maimunis': A reconstructive reading of Maimonides' ethics." Unpublished doctoral dissertation, Temple University, 1992. University Microfilms 9227440.

Brueggemann, Walter. *The Land: Place as Gift, Promise, and Challenge in Biblical Faith*. Philadelphia: Fortress, 1977.

Buber, Martin. *Israel and the World: Essays in a Time of Crisis.* New York: Schocken, 1963.

Buber, Shelomo, ed. *Leqaḥ Tov (Pesiqta Zutrati) of R. Tovia ben Eliezer.* 2 vols. Reprint. Jerusalem, 1960.

———. *Midrash Aggadah.* Vilna: Abraham Panta, 1893.

———. *Midrash Aikhah and Midrash Zutta.* Vilna: Romm, 1915.

———. *Midrash Aikhah Rabbati.* Vilna: Romm, 1899; reprint Hildesheim: Georg Olms, 1967.

———. *Midrash Mishlei.* Vilna: Romm, 1893; reprint Jerusalem, 1965.

———. *Midrash Sekhel Tov*, to Genesis and Exodus. Berlin: Itzkowski, 1900.

———. *Midrash Shemuel.* Jerusalem: Krakow, 1893; reprint Jerusalem.

———. *Midrash Tanḥuma.* 2 vols. Vilna; reprint Jerusalem, 1964.

———. *Midrash Tehillim (Shoḥer Tov).* Reprint. Jerusalem: C. Vaqshal, 1977.

———. *Pesiqta de Rav Kahana.* Lyck: Meqitze Nirdamim, 1868.

———. *Sefer Shibbolei ha-Leqet ha-Shalem of R. Tzidkiya b. Avraham ha-Rofe.* Vilna, 1887; reprint New York, 1959.

———. *Yalqut ha-Makhiri to Psalms.* Berditchev: Haim Yaakov Sheftil, 1900; reprint Jerusalem, 1964.

Büchler, Adolph. "Learning and Teaching in the Open Air in Palestine." *JQR* 4 (1913–14):485–91.

———. *Studies in Jewish History.* Edited by I. Brodie and J. Rabbinowitz. London: Oxford University Press, 1956.

———. *Studies in Sin and Atonement in the Rabbinic Literature of the First Century.* New York: Ktav, 1967.

Bultmann, Rudolph. *History of the Synoptic Tradition.* Translated by John Marsh. Oxford: Basil Blackwell, 1968.

Burckhardt, Jacob. *Force and Freedom: Reflections on History.* New York: Pantheon, 1943.

Burrows, Millar. *The Dead Sea Scrolls.* New York: Viking Press, 1955.

Buttenweiser, Moses. *The Psalms Chronologically Treated.* New York: Ktav, 1969.

Campbell, Edward F., Jr. *Ruth.* Anchor Bible. Garden City, N.Y.: Doubleday, 1975.

Carlebach, A. "Rabbinic References to Fiscus Judaicus." *JQR* 66:1 (1975):57–61.

Caro, Joseph. *Codex Shulḥan Arukh.* Vol. 1, Oraḥ Ḥayyim; Vol. 2, Yoreh Deah. Jerusalem: El ha-Meqorot, 1954.

Carroll, Lewis. *More Annotated Alice*. Notes by Martin Gardner. New York: Random House, 1990.

————. *Through the Looking Glass and What Alice Found There*. New York: Heritage Reprints, 1941.

Cassidy, Richard J. "Matthew 17:24–27—A Word on Civil Taxes." *CBQ* 41 (1979):571–80.

Cassuto, Umberto. *Biblical and Oriental Studies*. 2 vols. Translated by Israel Abrahams. Jerusalem: Magnes, 1973.

Cato, Marcus Porcius Censorius. *Roman Farm Management*. Edited by A Virginia Farmer. New York: Macmillan Company, 1913.

Catullus. *Poems*. Translated by F. W. Cornish. Loeb Classical Library, 1968.

Cave, C. H. "The Parables and the Scriptures." *NTS* 11:4 (1965):374–86.

Chadwick, Owen, ed. "Sayings of the Egyptian Fathers." *Western Asceticism*. Philadelphia: Westminister Press, 1968.

Chajes, Hirsch Peretz. *Markus-Studien*. Berlin: C. A. Schwetschke und Sohn, 1899.

Chajes, Tzvi Hirsch, commentator. *Sefer Tehillim*. Midrash Madda'i. Edited by Avraham Kahane. Kiev: Kahane, 1908.

Charles, R. H. *The Apocrypha and Pseudepigrapha of the Old Testament*. 2 vols. Oxford: Clarendon Press, 1913, 1978.

Charlesworth, James H. *Jesus Within Judaism: New Light from Exciting Archaeological Discoveries*. New York: Doubleday, 1988.

————. "From Jewish Messianology to Christian Christology: Some Caveats and Perspectives." In *Judaisms and Their Messiahs*, edited by Jacob Neusner, William S. Green, and Ernest Frerichs, 225–64. Cambridge: Cambridge University Press, 1987.

————. *The Old Testament Pseudepigrapha*. 2 vols. Garden City, N.Y.: Doubleday, 1983–85.

————. *The Old Testament Pseudepigrapha and the New Testament*. Cambridge: Cambridge University Press, 1985.

————. "Research on the Historical Jesus Today: Jesus and the Pseudepigrapha, the Dead Sea Scrolls, the Nag Hammadi Codices, Josephus and Archaeology." *Princeton Seminary Bulletin* 6:2 (1985):98–115.

Chavel, Chaim Dov (Charles B.), ed. *Sefer ha-Ḥinnukh*. Jerusalem: Mossad ha-Rav Kook, 1960.

Chazan, Robert. *Church, State and Jew in the Middle Ages*. New York: Behrman House, 1980.

Childs, Brevard. *Old Testament Theology in a Canonical Context*. Philadelphia: Fortress, 1985.

Chilton, Bruce. *A Galilean Rabbi and His Bible: Jesus' Use of the Interpreted Scripture of His Time*. Wilmington, Del.: Michael Glazier, 1984.

————. *Targumic Approaches to the Gospels: Essays in the Mutual Definition of Judaism and Christianity*. Lanham, Md., and London: University Press of America, 1986.

Chrysostom, John. *In Inscriptionem Altaris*, in Migne, *Patrilogia Latinae*, vol. 51.65ff.

————. *In principium Actorum*. Unpublished translation by Arthur Bradford Shippee.

Churgin, Pinḥas. *Targum Jonathan to the Prophets*. New Haven: Yale University Press, 1907, 1927.

Ciardi, John. *Dialogue with an Audience*. Philadelphia and New York: J. B. Lippincott, 1963.

Cicero. *De Natura Deorum*. Translated by H. Rackham. Loeb Classical Library, 1933.

————. *De Senectute, de Amicitia, de Divinatione*. Translated by William Armistead Falconer. Loeb Classical Library, 1946.

————. *In Catilinum I–IV, Pro Murena, Pro Sulla, Pro Flacco*. Translated by C. Macdonald. Loeb Classical Library, 1977.

————. *Letters to Atticus*. 3 vols. Translated by E. O. Winstedt. Loeb Classical Library, 1970.

————. *Tusculan Disputations*. Translated by J. E. King. Loeb Classical Library, 1966.

Clarke, E. G. *Targum Pseudo-Jonathan to the Pentateuch: Text and Concordance*. Hoboken, N.J.: Ktav, 1984.

Clement of Alexandria. *Clement of Alexandria*. Translated by G. W. Butterworth. Loeb Classical Library, 1982.

Clifford, Gay. *The Transformations of Allegory*. London and Boston: Routledge & Kegan Paul, 1974.

Cohen, A., ed. *The Minor Tractates of the Talmud*. 2 vols. London: Soncino, 1965.

Cohen, Chaim. "New Akkadian Evidence Concerning the Meaning and Etymology of the Word 'Mashal' in the Bible." *Te'uda: Studies in Bible, Memorial Volume to Yehoshua Meir Grintz* 2 (1982):315–24.

Cohen, Gershon. "The Song of Songs and Jewish Religious Mentality." In *The Canon and Mesorah of the Hebrew Bible*, edited by Sid Z. Leiman, 262–82. New York: Ktav, 1974.

Cohen, Naomi. "Philo's Tefillin." *Proceedings of the Ninth World Congress of Jewish Studies 1985: Division 1, The Period of the Bible*. Jerusalem: World Union of Jewish Studies, 1986, 199–206.

Cohen, Norman. "Structural Analysis of a Talmudic Story: Joseph-Who-Honors-the-Sabbaths." *JQR* 72 (1982):161–77.

Cohen, Rev. A. *Ancient Jewish Proverbs*. London: John Murray, 1911.

Cohen, Shaye J. D. *From the Maccabees to the Mishnah*. Philadelphia: Westminister Press, 1987.

———. "Jacob Neusner, Mishnah, and Counter-Rabbinics: A Review Essay." *Conservative Judaism* 37:1 (1983):48–63.

Cohn, Haim. *The Trial and Death of Jesus*. New York: Harper & Row, 1967.

Cohn, Joseph. "Zu 'Splitter und Balken'." *Jeschurun* (Berlin) 17:1–2 (1930):92.

Common, Thomas, trans. *Friedrich Nietzsche: The Joyful Wisdom*. Vol. 10 of *The Complete Works of Friedrich Nietzsche*, edited by Oscar Levy. New York: Russell and Russell, 1964.

Cowley, Arthur Ernest. *Aramaic Papyri of the Fifth Century B.C.* Oxford: Clarendon Press, 1923.

Cronbach, Abraham. "Unmeant Meanings of Scripture." *HUCA* 36 (1968):99–123.

Crossan, John Dominic. *The Historical Jesus: The Life of a Mediterranean Jewish Peasant*. San Francisco: Harper & Row, 1991.

———. *In Parables: The Challenge of the Historical Jesus*. New York: Harper & Row, 1973.

———. "Parable." *Anchor Bible Dictionary*, 5.146–52.

Culbertson, Philip. "Changing Christian Images of the Pharisees." *Anglican Theological Review* 64:4 (1982):539–61.

———. "Known, Knower, Knowing: The Authority of Scripture in the Anglican Tradition." *Anglican Theological Review* 74:2 (1992):144–74.

———. "Multiplexity in Biblical Exegesis: The Introduction to Megillat Qohelet by Moses Mendelssohn." *Cincinnati Journal of Judaica* 2 (1991):10–18.

———. *New Adam: The Future of Masculine Spirituality*. Minneapolis: Fortress Press, 1992.

———. "New Christian Theologies of Covenant." *The Reconstructionist* 51:3 (1985):15–19, 32.

———. "The Pharisaic Jesus and His Gospel Parables." *The Christian Century*, January 23, 1985:74–77.

———. "Reclaiming the Matthean Vineyard Parables." *Encounter* 49:4 (1988):257–83.

———. "Teaching the Gospel of the Incarnate Pharisee." *Religious Education* 79 (1984):279–93.

———. "What's Left to Believe in Jesus After the Scholars Have Done With Him?" *Journal of Ecumenical Studies* 28:1 (1991):1–17.

———. "Who Splashed on Whom? Textual Equivocality and Rabbinic Exegesis." *Proceedings of the Tenth World Congress of Jewish Studies, Division C, Volume 1.* Jerusalem: Magnes Press for the Hebrew University, 1990, 17–24.

Culbertson, Philip, with Megory Anderson. "The Inadequacy of the Christian Doctrine of Atonement in Light of Levitical Sin Offering." *Anglican Theological Review* 68:4 (1986):305–30.

Culbertson, Philip, and Arthur Shippee. *The Pastor: Readings from the Patristic Period.* Minneapolis: Fortress Press, 1990.

Dahood, Mitchell. *Psalms.* 3 vols. Anchor Bible. Garden City, N.J.: Doubleday, 1968.

Dan, Joseph. "Midrash and the Dawn of Kabbalah." In *Midrash and Literature*, edited by Geoffrey H. Hartman and Sanford Budick, 127–39. New Haven: Yale University Press, 1986.

———. "The Religious Experience of the *Merkavah*." In *Jewish Spirituality from the Bible through the Middle Ages*, edited by Arthur Green, 289–307. New York: Crossroad, 1989.

Danby, Herbert. *The Mishnah.* Oxford: Clarendon Press, 1933.

Dane, Perry. "The Oral Law and the Jurisprudence of a Textless Text." *S'vara* 2:2 (1991):11–24.

D'Angelo, Mary Rose. "Abba and 'Father': Imperial Theology and the Jesus Traditions." *JBL* 3:4 (1992):611–30.

Danker, Frederick. "Biblical Exegesis: Christian Views." In *The Encyclopedia of Religion*, vol. 2, edited by Mircea Eliade. New York: Macmillan, 1987.

Darr, Katheryn Pfisterer. "The Wall Around Paradise: Ezekielian Ideas about the Future." *VT* 37:3 (1987):271–79.

Daube, David. *The New Testament and Rabbinic Judaism.* Salem, New Hampshire: Ayer Company Publishers, 1984.

———. *Studies in Biblical Law.* New York: Ktav, 1969.

David, John D., and Henry Snyder Gehman, eds. *The Westminster Dictionary of the Bible.* Philadelphia: Westminster Press, 1944.

Davidson, Israel. *Otzar ha-Meshalim ve-ha-Pitgamim* (Thesaurus of Proverbs and Parables). Jerusalem: Mossad ha-Rav Kook, 1957.

———. *Thesaurus of Mediaeval Hebrew Poetry.* 4 vols. Reprint. Ktav: 1970.

Davies, W. D. *The Gospel and the Land: Early Christianity and Jewish Territorial Doctrine.* Berkeley: University of California Press, 1974.

————. *Jewish and Pauline Studies*. Philadelphia: Fortress Press, 1984.

————. "Reflections on a Pauline Allegory in a French Context." In *The New Testament Age: Essays in Honor of Bo Reicke*, vol. 1, edited by William C. Weinrich, 107–25. Macon: Mercer Press, 1984.

Davies, W. D., and Dale Allison. *The Gospel According to Matthew*. 3 vols. International Critical Commentary. Edinburgh: T. & T. Clark, 1988.

deBoer, P. A. H. "Towards an edition of the Syriac version of the Old Testament." *VT* 31:3 (1981):346–57.

DeJonge, M. *The Testament of the Twelve Patriarchs: A Critical History of Research*. Missoula, Mont.: Scholars Press, 1977.

————. *The Testament of the Twelve Patriarchs: A Study of their Text, Composition and Origin*. Amsterdam: Van Gorcum, 1975.

de Lange, Nicholas. *Origen and the Jews: Studies in Jewish-Christian Relations in Third-Century Palestine*. Cambridge: Cambridge University Press, 1976.

Delitzsch, Franz. *Biblical Commentary on the Psalms*. 3 vols. Translated by David Eaton. London: Hodder and Stoughton, 1889.

————. *Proverbs, Ecclesiastes, Song of Solomon*. 2 vols. Edited by C. F. Keil and F. Delitzsch. Translated by James Martin. Grand Rapids, Mich.: Eerdmans, n.d.

Demosthenes. *Olynthiacs, Philippics, Speech against Leptines*. Translated by J. H. Vince. Loeb Classical Library, 1970.

Derrett, J. Duncan M. "The Case of Korah versus Moses Reviewed." *JSJ* 24:1 (1993):59–78.

————. "Peter's Penny: Fresh Light on Matthew 17:24–27." In *NT* 6 (1963):1–15.

————. "The Stone that the Builders Rejected." *Studie Evangelica IV: Texte und Untersuchungen zur Geschichte der altchristlichen Literatur* 102, Berlin, 180–86; reprint Derrett, *Studies in the New Testament*. 2 vols. Leiden: E. J. Brill, 1978, 2.60–67.

————. *Studies in the New Testament*. 2 vols. Leiden: E. J. Brill, 1978.

deVaux, Roland. *Ancient Israel*. 2 vols. New York: McGraw-Hill, 1965.

Diels, Hermann. *Die Fragmente der Vorsokratiker*. 3 vols. Berlin: Weidmannsche Verlagsbuchhandlung, 1954.

Dio Cassius. *Roman History*. 9 vols. Edited by Earnest Camp. Loeb Classical Library, 1914.

Diogenes Laertius. *The Lives of the Eminent Philosophers*. 2 vols. Translated by R. D. Hicks. Loeb Classical Library, 1925.

di Ozida, Samuel. *Midrash Shemuel: Selected Commentaries on Avot*. Jerusalem: Sefarim Toraniim, 1989.

Dishon, Yehudit. *Sefer Sha'ashuim shel Rabbi Yosef ben Meir ben Zabara*. Jerusalem: Rubin Mass, 1985.

di Trani, R. Isaiah. *Tosafot*. Lernberg, 1869; reprint Jerusalem: n.p., 1968.

Dodd, C. H. *The Founder of Christianity*. New York: Macmillan, 1970.

Dodd, C. H. *The Parables of the Kingdom*. 3d ed. New York: Scribner's, 1936.

Doelger, F. J. *ICHTHUS: Das Fisch-symbol in frühchristlicher Zeit*. Vol. 1 supplement to the *Romische Quartalschrift*. Rome: 1910; vol. 2, Muenster, 1922.

Donski, Samson, ed. *Midrash Aikhah Rabbah*. Montreal: Northern Printing and Lithographing, 1956.

———. *Midrash Rabbah Esther*. Montreal: Northern Printing and Lithographing, 1962.

———. *Midrash Rabbah Shir ha-Shirim*. Jerusalem: Devir, 1980.

Draemer, David. "The Formation of Rabbinic Canon: Authority and Boundaries." *JBL* 110:4 (1991):613–30.

Drazin, Israel. *Targum Onkelos to Deuteronomy*. Hoboken, N.J.: Ktav Publishing House, 1982.

———. *Targum Onkelos to Exodus*. Hoboken, N.J.: Ktav Publishing House, 1990.

Drury, Revd Canon John. "The Sower, The Vineyard and the Place of Allegory in the Interpretation of Mark's Parables." *JTS* (NS) 24:2 (1973):367–79.

Duran, R. Simeon b. R. Tzemah. *Magen Avot*. Livorno, 1762; reprint Jerusalem: Sefarim Toraniim, 1961, 1987.

Eckardt, A. Roy. *Reclaiming the Jesus of History*. Minneapolis: Fortress, 1992.

Ehrentreu, Chanoch. *Iyyunim be-Divrei Haza"l u-vi-Leshonam* (Talmudic Studies). Jerusalem: Mossad ha-Rav Kook, 1978.

Eichrodt, Walther. *Theology of the Old Testament*. 2 vols. Translated by J. A. Baker. Philadelphia: Westminster Press, 1961.

Einhorn, Zev Wolf. *Baraita on the Thirty-Two Middot of Rabbi Ishmael*. Vilna, 1839.

Eisenstein, Judah David, ed. *Otzar Midrashim*. 2 vols. New York: E. Grossman's Hebrew Book Store, 1915.

Eliezer ben Nathan of Mayence. *Even ha-Ezer: Sefer RaAVa"N*. Edited by S. Z. Ehrenreich. New York: Grossman's, 1958.

———. *Sefer RaAVa"N*. 3 vols. in 1. Vol. 1 edited by Shalom Albeck; vols. 2 and 3 edited by A. L. Raskes. Jerusalem: Wagshal, 1913.

Elitsur, Judah, commentator. *Sefer Shofetim* (The Book of Judges). The Daat Miqra Series. Jerusalem: Mossad Ha-Rav Kook, 1976.

Eliyahu Gaon of Vilna. *Sefer Bahir*. Vilna: Romm, 1883.

――――. *Sefer Mishlei im Biur ha-GR"* A (The Book of Proverbs with Exegesis by Eliyahu Gaon of Vilna). Edited by Moshe Philips. Petah Tiqva: n.p., 1981.

――――. *Toledot ha-GR"* A. Edited by Y. L. HaCohen Maimon. Jerusalem: Mossad Ha-Rav Kook, 1970.

Elkoshi, Gedaliah. *Otzar Pitgamim ve-Nivim* (Thesaurus Proverbiorum Latinorum). Tel Aviv: Joseph Sreberk, 1959.

Emerson, Ralph Waldo. "Self-Reliance." In *Essays: First and Second Series*, 29–52. New York: Library of America, 1990.

Encyclopedia Judaica. 16 vols. Jerusalem: Keter Publication House, 1972.

Encyclopedia Talmudica. 18 vols. to date. Edited by S. J. Zevin. Jerusalem: Rabbi Herzog World Academy and Jerusalem Talmudic Encyclopaedia Institute, 1947–.

Enelow, Hillel Gershom, ed. *The Mishnah of Rabbi Eliezer, or The Midrash of Thirty-Two Hermeneutic Rules*. New York: Block Publication Company, 1933.

Englard, Izhak. "Majority Decision vs. Individual Truth: The Interpretations of 'the Oven of Aknai' Aggadah." *Tradition* 15:1–2 (1975):137–52.

Epictetus. *The Discourses as reported by Arrian, the Manual, and fragments*. 2 vols. Translated by W. A. Oldfather. Loeb Classical Library, 1926–28.

Epstein, Abraham. *Mi-Qadmoniot ha-Yehudim*. 2 vols. Jerusalem: Mossad ha-Rav Kook, 1965.

Epstein, Isidore, ed. *The Babylonian Talmud*. 18 vols. London: Soncino, 1933–45.

Epstein, Isidore, and Ezra Zion Melamed. *Mekhilta de-Rabbi Shimeon bar Yoḥai*. Jerusalem: Bet Hillel, n.d.

Epstein, Jacob Naḥum HaLevi. *Mavo le-Nusaḥ ha-Mishnah*. Jerusalem: self-published, 1948.

Erasmus. *Collected Works*. Vols. 31 and 32: Adages. Translated by Margaret Mann Phillips; annotated by R. A. B. Mynors. Toronto: University of Toronto Press, 1982–89.

――――. *Desiderii Erasmi Roterodami Opera Omnia emendatiora et auctiora*. 10 vols. Lugduni Batauorum: Peter Vander Aa, 1703.

Eusebius. *Ecclesiastical History, Books 1–5*. Translated by Roy DeFerrari. Washington, D.C.: Catholic University of America, 1953.

――――. *The Ecclesiastical History*. 2 vols. Translated by Kirsopp Lake. Loeb Classical Library, 1980.

Evans, Craig A. "On the Isaianic Background of the Sower Parable." *CBQ* 47:3 (1985):464–68.

Evans, Ernest, trans. *Tertullian's Homily on Baptism*. London: SPCK, 1964.

Even-Shoshan, Abraham, ed. *Ha-Millon he-Hadash*. 4 vols. Jerusalem: Kiryat Sefer, 1986.

———. *Qonqordantzia Hadashah le-TaNa"Kh*. 2 vols. Jerusalem: Kiryat Sefer, 1981.

Falk, Ze'ev W. *Jewish Matrimonial Law in the Middle Ages*. Oxford: Clarendon Press, 1966.

Faur, Jose. *Golden Doves with Silver Dots: Semiotics and Textuality in Rabbinic Tradition*. Bloomington: Indiana University Press, 1986.

Feinberg, Gerson, ed. *Tobia ben Elieser's Commentar zu Koheleth* (Lekach Tob). Berlin: Itzkowski, 1904. (Bound with Greenup on Echah.)

Feldman, Asher. *The Parables and Similes of the Rabbis*. Cambridge: Cambridge University Press, 1927.

Finkelstein, Louis. *Akiba: Scholar, Saint and Martyr*. Northvale, N.J.: Jason Aronson, 1990.

———. *Pharisaism in the Making*. New York: Ktav, 1972.

———. *The Pharisees: The Sociological Background of Their Faith*. 2nd rev. ed. Philadelphia: Jewish Publication Society, 1940.

———. "Pirkei Avot." *JBL* 17 (1938):13–50; reprinted *Pharisaism in the Making*, 121–58.

———. *Sifra or Torat Cohanim According to Codex Assemani #66 (The Rome Manuscript)*. New York: Jewish Theological Seminary, 1956.

Finkelstein, Louis, with Haim Saul Horowitz. *Sifrei Devarim*. New York: Jewish Theological Seminary and the Strook Publication Fund, 1969.

Fiorenza, Elisabeth Schüssler. *In Memory of Her: A Feminist Reconstruction of Christian Origins*. New York: Crossroads, 1983.

Fischel, Henry A. *Rabbinic Literature and Greco-Roman Philosophy*. Leiden: E. J. Brill, 1973.

———. "Story and History: Observations on Greco-Roman Rhetoric and Pharisaism." In *Essays in Greco-Roman and Related Talmudic Literature*, 443–472. Edited by Henry A. Fischel. New York: Ktav, 1977.

Fish, Shelomo. *Midrash ha-Gadol Devarim*. Jerusalem: Mossad ha-Rav Kook, 1972.

Fish, Stanley. *Is There a Text in This Class? The Authority of Interpretive Communities*. Cambridge: Harvard University Press, 1980.

Fishbane, Michael. *Biblical Interpretation in Ancient Israel*. Oxford: Clarendon Press, 1985.

————. "The Holy One Sits and Roars: Mythopoesis and the Midrashic Imagination." *Journal of Jewish Thought and Philosophy* 1:1 (1991):1–22.

Fitzmyer, Joseph A. *The Gospel According to Luke X–XXIV.* Anchor Bible. Garden City, N.J.: Doubleday, 1985.

Fletcher, Angus. *Allegory: The Theory of a Symbolic Mode.* Ithaca and London: Cornell University Press, 1964, 1970.

Flew, Anthony. *A Dictionary of Philosophy.* 2nd rev. ed. New York: St. Martin's, 1979.

Florsheim, Yoel. *Rashi on the Bible in his Commentary on the Talmud.* 3 vols. Jerusalem: Rubin Mass, 1981.

Flusser, David. *Die rabbinischen Gleichnisse und der Gleichniserzähler Jesus.* Bern: Peter Lang, 1981.

————. "Do You Prefer New Wine?" *Immanuel* 9 (1979):26–31.

————. "The Half-Sheqel in the Gospel and among the Dead Sea Sect." *Tarbitz* 31:2 (1962):150–56.

————. "Hillel's Self-Awareness and Jesus." *Immanuel* 4 (1974):31–36.

————. "Jerusalem in the Literature of the Second Temple." In *ve-Im Biggevurot: Presentation Volume Honoring Rubin Mass,* 263–94. Jerusalem: Rubin Mass, 1974.

————. *Judaism and Christianity: A Collection of Articles.* Jerusalem: Hebrew University Akademon, n.d.

————. *Judaism and the Origins of Christianity.* Jerusalem: Magnes Press, 1988.

————. "Scholem's recent book on Merkabah Literature." *JJS* 11:1–2 (1960): 59–68.

————. *Sefer Jossipon.* 2 vols. Jerusalem: Mossad Bialik, 1981.

————. "The Ten Commandments and the New Testament." In *The Ten Commandments in History and Tradition,* edited by Ben-Zion Segal; English editing by Gershon Levi, 219–46. Jerusalem: Magnes Press, 1990.

————. *Yahadut u-Meqorot ha-Natzrut* (Judaism and Christian Sources). Israel: Sifriyat Poalim, 1982.

Forchheimer, Paul. *Maimonides' Commentary on Pirkey Avot.* Jerusalem: Feldheim, 1974.

Fox, Michael V. *Qohelet and His Contradictions.* Sheffield, England: Almond Press, 1989.

Frank, Erich. *Philosophical Understanding and Religious Truth.* London: Oxford University Press, 1945.

Frankel, Zechariah. *Darkei ha-Mishnah.* Tel Aviv: Sinai, 1959.

Freedman, H., and Maurice Simon, eds. *Midrash Rabbah*. 3d ed. 9 vols. London & New York: Soncino, 1983.

Freud, Sigmund. *The Interpretation of Dreams*. In *The Basic Writings of Sigmund Freud*, edited and translated by A. A. Brill, 181–549. New York: Modern Language, 1938.

Freud, Sigmund, and D. E. Oppenheim. *Dreams in Folklore*. New York: International Universities Press, 1958.

Friedlander, Gerald, ed. *Pirqei de Rabbi Eliezer*. New York: Sepher-Hermon, 1916.

Friedländer, M. *The Commentary of Ibn Ezra on Isaiah*. New York: Feldheim, 1873.

Friedman, Edwin H. *Generation to Generation: Family Process in Church and Synagogue*. New York: Guilford, 1985.

Friedman, Meier (Ish-Shalom), ed. *Midrash Pesiqta Rabbati*. Vienna: Selbstverlag des Herausgebers, 1880.

———. *Seder Eliyahu Rabbah ve-Seder Eliyahu Zutta*. Jerusalem: Wahrmann Books, 1969.

———. *Sifra deBe Rav*. Breslau, 1915.

Friedman, Mordechai Akiva. *Jewish Marriage in Palestine: A Cairo Geniza Study*. 2 vols. New York: Jewish Theological Seminary, 1980.

Fromm, Erich. *The Forgotten Language: An Introduction to the Understanding of Dreams, Fairy Tales, and Myths*. New York: Grove Press, 1951.

———. *The Heart of Man: Its Genius for Good and Evil*. New York: Harper & Row, 1964.

———. *Man for Himself: An Inquiry into the Psychology of Ethics*. New York: Rinehart, 1947.

———. *You Shall Be as Gods: A Radical Interpretation of the Old Testament and Its Tradition*. New York: Holt, Rinehart and Winston, 1966.

Fuller, Reginald H. *The Foundations of New Testament Christology*. New York: Scribner, 1965.

Funk, Robert W. *New Gospel Parallels*. Philadelphia: Fortress Press, 1985.

———. *Parables and Presence: Forms of the New Testament Tradition*. Philadelphia: Fortress Press, 1982.

Funk, Robert W., Bernard Brandon Scott, and James R. Butts. *The Parables of Jesus: Red Letter Edition, The Jesus Seminar*. Sonoma, Calif.: Polebridge Press, 1988.

Garland, David E. *The Intention of Matthew 23*. Leiden: E. J. Brill, 1979.

Gaster, Moses. *Exempla of the Rabbis*. London-Leipzig, 1924; reprint New York: Ktav, 1968.

Gaston, Lloyd. *Paul and the Torah*. Vancouver: University of British Columbia Press, 1987.

Gaventa, Beverly R. "Both the New and the Old." *The Christian Century*, June 30–July 7, 1993:669.

Gavin, Frank, ed. *Liberal Catholicism and the Modern World*. Milwaukee: Morehouse, 1934.

Gerhardsson, Birger. *Memory and Manuscript: Oral Tradition and Written Transmission in Rabbinic and Early Judaism*. Lund: C. W. K. Gleerup, 1961.

―――. "The Narrative Meshalim in the Synoptic Gospels." *NTS* 34:3 (1988):339–63.

Gesenius, William. *A Hebrew and English Lexicon of the Old Testament*. Translated by Edward Robinson; edited by Francis Brown, S. R. Driver, and Charles A. Briggs. Oxford: Clarendon Press, 1951.

Gilat, Yitzhak. *R. Eliezer ben Hyrcanus: A Scholar Outcast*. Ramat Gan: Bar Ilan University, 1984.

Ginsburger, Moses. *Fragmententhargum (Thargum jeruschalmi zum Pentateuch)*. Berlin: S. Calvary, 1899.

―――. *Pseudo-Jonathan (Thargum Jonathan ben Usiël zum Pentateuch)*. Berlin: S. Calvary, 1903.

Ginzberg, Louis. *A Commentary on the Palestinian Talmud: Berakhot*. 4 vols. New York: Jewish Theological Seminary, 1941.

―――. *Ginzei Schechter* (Genizah Studies). 3 vols. New York: Jewish Theological Seminary, 1928.

―――. *On Jewish Law and Lore*. New York: Atheneum, 1981.

―――. *The Legends of the Jews*. 7 vols. Translated by Henrietta Szold. Philadelphia: Jewish Publication Society, 1968.

―――. *An Unknown Jewish Sect*. Translated by Zev Gotthold. New York: Jewish Theological Seminary, 1976.

Goldin, Judah. *The Fathers According to Rabbi Nathan*. New York: Schocken Books, 1955.

―――. "The Freedom and Restraint of Haggadah." In *Midrash and Literature*, edited by Geoffrey H. Hartman and Sanford Budick, 57–76. New Haven: Yale University Press, 1986.

―――. *The Living Talmud*. New York: Mentor, 1957.

―――. *Studies in Midrash and Related Literature*. Edited by Barry L. Eichler and Jeffrey H. Tigay. Philadelphia: Jewish Publication Society, 1988.

Goldschmidt, Daniel. *Mahzor le-Yamim ha-Noraim*. 2 vols. New York: Leo Baeck Institute, 1970.

Goldziher, Ignaz. "Matth. VII.5 in der muhammedanischen Literatur." *Zeitschrift der Deutschen Morgenländischen Gesellschaft* 31 (1877):765–67.

———. "Zwischen den Augen." *Der Islam* 11 (1921):175–80.

Goodenough, Erwin Russell. *Jewish Symbols in the Greco-Roman Period*. 13 vols. N.p.: Pantheon Books, 1956.

Gordis, Robert. *Koheleth: The Man and His World*. New York: Schocken Books, 1968.

———. *The Song of Songs and Lamentations*. Rev. and augmented ed. New York: Ktav, 1954, 1974.

———. "Studies in the Relationship of Biblical and Rabbinic Hebrew." In *Louis Ginzberg Jubilee Volume*, English vol. 173–99. New York: American Academy for Jewish Research, 1945.

Gordon, Cyrus H. *Ugaritic Handbook II*. Rome: Pontifical Institute, 1947.

Gotthold, Zev. "Le-Shanah ha-Ba'ah bi-Yerushalayim." In *Minhat Aharon: A Collection of Essays in Honor of Aaron Choueka*, edited by Yaakov Choueka and Hayim Sabbatto, 223–61. Jerusalem, 1980.

———. "Moses Our Teacher and His Prophetic Style." *Journal of Jewish Thought: Jubilee Issue*, 1985:18–41.

———. "Opvoeding tot Geloof en 'Mitsvot'." *Gesprekken in Israel* 8 (Israel: Nes Amim, 1985–86):4–22.

———. "Tarbut ha-Shalom bi-Tefilot Israel." *Mahanayim* 121 (Addar, 1969):68–89.

Gotthold, Zev, and Pau Figueras. "Baptism: Part II." *Christian News From Israel* 26:2 (1977):75–80.

Goulder, M. D. *Midrash and Lection in Matthew*. London: SPCK, 1974.

Grant, Robert. *The Bible in the Church: A Short History of Interpretation*. New York: Macmillan, 1948.

Green, H. Benedict. *The Gospel According to Matthew*. Oxford: Oxford University Press, 1975.

Green, William Scott. "Otherness Within: Towards a Theory of Difference in Rabbinic Judaism." In *To See Ourselves as Others See Us: Christians, Jews, 'Others' in Late Antiquity*, edited by Jacob Neusner and Ernest S. Frerichs, 49–70. Chico, Calif.: Scholars Press, 1985.

Greenberg, Moshe. "Jewish Conceptions of the Human Factor in Biblical Prophecy." In *Justice and the Holy: Essays in Honor of Walter Harrelson*, edited by Douglas Knight and Peter Paris, 145–62. Atlanta: Scholars Press, 1989.

Greene, John T. "Jesus of Galilee and Judas the Maccabee: Hero Worship or Messianic Machinations?" In *New Perspectives on Ancient Judaism, Volume II:*

Religion, Literature, and Society in Ancient Israel, Formative Christianity and Judaism, edited by Jacob Neusner, Peder Borgen, Ernest S. Frerichs, and Richard Horsley, 67–76. New York: New York University Press, 1987.

Greenup, A. W., ed. *The Commentary of Rabbi Tobia ben Eliesar on Canticles*. London, 1909. (Bound with Bamberger on Ruth.)

———. *The Commentary of Rabbi Tobia ben Eliezer on Echah* (Lekach Tob). London, 1905. (Bound with Feinberg on Koheleth.)

———. *The Yalkut of R. Makhir bar Abba Mari on Hosea, Zechariah, Joel, Zephaniah, Haggai and Malachi*. London: St. John's Hall, Highbury, 1913.

———. *Yalqut ha-Makhiri on Amos, Ovadia, Yonah, Micah, Nahum, and Habakkuk*. London, 1909; reprint Jerusalem, 1967.

Gregory of Nazianzus. *Three Poems: Concerning His Own Affairs, Concerning Himself and the Bishops, Concerning His Own Life*. Translated by Denis Molaise Meehan. Washington, D. C.: Catholic University of America Press, 1987.

Gregory of Nyssa. *Enconium in Sanctum Stephanum protomartyrem*. Edited by Otto Lendle. Leiden: E. J. Brill, 1968.

Grintz, I. M. *Mevoei ha-Miqra*. Tel Aviv: Yavneh, 1972.

Gross, Moshe David. *Otzar ha-Aggadah*. 3 vols. Jerusalem: Mossad ha-Rav Kook, 1986.

Gruenhut, Elazar Halevi. *Yalqut ha-Makhiri al Mishlei* (Proverbs). Jerusalem, 1902; reprint Jerusalem, 1964. (Bound with Kahana-Shapira on Isaiah.)

Gruenwald, Ithamar. "On Applied Gematria in Jewish Literature." In *Rabbi Mordechai Breuer Festschrift*, vol. 1, 823–32. Jerusalem: Academon, 1992.

———. "The Jewish Esoteric Literature in the Time of the Mishnah and Talmud." *Immanuel* 4 (1974):37–46.

Guillaumont, A., Henri-Charles Puech, Gilles Quispel, Walter Till, and Yassah 'Abd al Masih. *The Gospel According to Thomas*. Leiden: E. J. Brill, and New York: Harper & Brothers, 1959.

Gutman, Tobi. *Ha-Mashal bi-Tequfat ha-Tannaim*. Jerusalem: Abir Yaakov, 1949.

Guttmann, Alexander. "Eliezer ben Hyrcanus—a Shammaite?" In *Ignace Goldziher Memorial Volume*, 2 vols., edited by Samuel Löwinger, Alexander Scheiber, and Joseph Somogyi, 2.100–10. Jerusalem, 1958.

———. "Hillelites and Shammaites—A Clarification." *HUCA* 28 (1957):115–26.

Haas, Lee. "Bibliography on Midrash." In *The Study of Ancient Judaism 1: Mishnah, Midrash, Siddur*, edited by Jacob Neusner, 93–103. Hoboken, N.J.: Ktav, 1981.

Haberman, Avraham Meier. *Ketav Sefer Lashon: Reflections on Books, Dead Sea Scrolls, Language and Folklore*. Jerusalem: Rubin Mass, 1973.

————. *Mivḥar ha-Shirah ha-Ivrit*. Jerusalem: Rubin Mass, 1965.

————. "Two Poems of R. Saadya Gaon." *Tarbitz* 13:1 (1941):52–59.

————. *Mivḥar Peninim*. Attributed to Shelomo ibn-Gavirol. Translated by Yehuda ibn-Tibbon. Jerusalem: Sifriyat Poalim, 1947.

Hagiz, Moshe. *Mishnat Ḥakhamim*. Venice, 1733.

Hailperin, Herman. "Nicholas de Lyra and Rashi: The Minor Prophets." In *Rashi Anniversary Volume*, 115–48. New York: American Academy for Jewish Research, 1941.

Ḥakham, Amos, commentator. *Sefer Iyyov* (The Book of Job). The Daat Miqra Series. Jerusalem: Mossad ha-Rav Kook, 1984.

————. *Sefer Tehillim* (The Book of Psalms). 2 vols. The Daat Miqra Series. Jerusalem: Mossad ha-Rav Kook, 1987.

————. *Sefer Yeshayahu* (The Book of Isaiah). 2 vols. The Daat Miqra Series. Jerusalem: Mossad ha-Rav Kook, 1984.

HaLevi, Abraham b. R. Shabbatai Shaftil Horowitz. *Yesh Noḥalin*. Yossipof: n.p., 1878.

HaLevi, Elimelekh Epstein. *Aggadot ha-Amoraim*. Tel Aviv: Devir, 1977.

————. *Erkei ha-Aggadah ve-ha-Halakhah*. 4 vols. Tel Aviv: Devir, 1979–82.

————. *Ha-Aggadah ha-Historit-Biografit*. Tel Aviv: University of Tel Aviv Press, 1975.

————. *Olamah shel ha-Aggadah*. Tel Aviv: Devir, 1972.

————. *Shaarei ha-Aggadah*. Tel Aviv: Devir, 1982.

HaLevi, Yehuda. *Sefer ha-Kuzari*. Edited and translated by Hartwig Hirschfeld. New York: Schocken, 1964.

————. *Sefer ha-Kuzari*. Translated by Yehudah ibn-Shemuel. Tel Aviv: Devir, 1973.

Halivni, David Weiss. *Midrash, Mishnah, and Gemara: The Jewish Predilection for Justified Law*. Cambridge: Harvard University Press, 1986.

————. *Peshat & Derash: Plain and Applied Meanings in Rabbinic Exegesis*. New York and Oxford: Oxford University Press, 1991.

Halperin, David. *The Merkabah in Rabbinic Literature*. New Haven: American Oriental Society, 1980.

HaMeiri, Menaḥem. *Perush Rabbenu ha-Meiri to Tehillim and Mishlei*. Edited by Menaḥem Zahav. Jerusalem: Otzar ha-Poseqim, 1969.

Ḥamesh Meggilot (The Five Scrolls). A Commentary on Ruth, Song of Songs, Ecclesiastes, Lamentations and Esther. The Daat Miqra Series. Jerusalem: Mossad ha-Rav Kook, 1987.

Hammer, Reuven, trans. *Sifre: A Tannaitic Commentary on the Book of Deuteronomy*. New Haven and London: Yale University Press, 1986.

ha-Nasi, Abraham bar Chijja. *Sefer Ḥegion ha-Nefesh*. Edited by E. Freimann. Leipzig: C. W. Voolrath, 1860.

HaNaqdan, Beraḥiya ben Neturnai. *Mishlei Shualim*. Edited by A. Goldschmidt. Berlin: Erich Reisse Verlag, 1921.

Handford, S. A, trans. *Fables of Aesop*. Baltimore: Penguin Books, 1954.

Hanson, R. P. C. *Allegory and Event: A Study of the Sources and Significance of Origen's Interpretation of Scripture*. London: SCM Press, 1959.

Haran, Menachem. "Midrashic and Literal Exegesis and the Critical Method in Biblical Research." In *Scripta Hierosolymitana*, vol. 31 of *Studies in Bible*, edited by Sara Japhet, 19–48. Jerusalem: Hebrew University Press, 1986.

Harkavy, A. *Studien und Mittheilungen: Teshuvot ha-Geonim*. Berlin: Itzkowski, 1887.

Harrelson, Walter. "Christian Misreadings of Basic Themes in the Hebrew Scriptures." *Quarterly Review* 2:2 (1982):58–66.

Harrington, Daniel J. "The Jewishness of Jesus: Facing Some Problems." *CBQ* 49 (1987):1–13.

———. *Matthew*. Sacra Pagina. Collegeville, Minn.: Michael Glazier for Liturgical Press, 1991.

Harrington, Daniel J., and Anthony J. Saldarini. *Targum Jonathan of the Former Prophets*. Wilmington, Del.: Michael Glazier, 1987.

Hartman, David. *A Living Covenant: The Innovative Spirit in Traditional Judaism*. New York: Free Press, 1985.

———. *Joy and Responsibility: Israel, Modernity and the Renewal of Judaism*. Jerusalem: Ben-Zvi Posner, 1978.

———. *Maimonides: Torah and Philosophic Quest*. Philadelphia: Jewish Publication Society, 1976.

Har-Zahav, Zvi. *Diqduq ha-Lashon ha-Ivrit*. Seven vols. Tel Aviv: Maḥberet le-Sifrut, 1952.

Hatch, Edwin, and Henry A. Redpath, eds. *A Concordance to the Septuagint*. 2 vols. Grand Rapids, Mich.: Baker Book House, 1983.

Ḥazzan, Ḥaim David. "Sha'arei Teshuvah." In *Teshuvot ha-Geonim*. Livorno, 1869; reprint, Cyprus: Eliyahu ben Amozag, n.d..

Heinemann, Isaak. *Darkei ha-Aggadah*. Jerusalem: Magnes, 1954.

―――. "Die Lehre vom Ungeschriebenen Gesetz im Jüdischen Schrifttum." *HUCA* 4 (1927):149–71.

―――. "Le-Hitpathut ha-Munahim ha-Miqtzoayim le-Ferush ha-Miqra." *Leshoneinu La-Am* 14 (1946):182–89.

―――. "Scientific Allegorization during the Jewish Middle Ages." In *Studies in Jewish Thought: An Anthology of German Jewish Scholarship*, edited by Alfred Jospe, 247–69. Detroit: Wayne State University Press, 1981.

Heinemann, Joseph. *Prayer in the Period of the Tannaim and the Amoraim: Its Nature and Patterns*. Jerusalem: Magnes Press, 1966.

―――. *Prayer in the Talmud: Forms and Patterns*. Berlin and New York: Walter de Gruyter, 1977.

Hellwig, Monica. "Bible Interpretation: Has Anything Changed?" In *Biblical Studies: Meeting Ground of Jews and Christians*, edited by Lawrence Boadt, Helga Croner, and Leon Klenicki. 172–89. New York: Paulist Press, 1980.

Herford, R. Travers. *Christianity in Talmud and Midrash*. New York: Ktav, 1903.

―――. *The Ethics of Talmud*. New York: Schocken Books, 1962.

Herodotus. *The Persian Wars*. Translated by George Rawlinson. New York: Modern Library, 1942.

Herschler, Moshe, ed. *Ginzei Rishonim on Tractate Sukkah*. Jerusalem: Yad Herzog, 1962.

Hertz, Joseph H. *The Authorised Daily Prayer Book*. Rev. ed. with notes, 12th printing. New York: Bloch, 1948.

Herzog, Isaac. *The Main Institutions of Jewish Law*. 2 vols. London and New York: Soncino Press, 1936, 1980.

Heschel, Abraham Joshua. *Man's Quest for God*. New York: Scribner's, 1954.

Hesiod. "Works and Days." In *The Homeric Hymns and Homerica*. Loeb Classical Library, 1926.

Higger, Michael. *Masekhet Semahot*. New York: Bloch, 1931.

―――. *Masekhtot Kallah*. New York: Debe Rabbanan, 1936; reissued Jerusalem: Maqor, 1970.

―――. *Masekhtot Ze'irot*. New York: Bloch, 1929.

―――. "Pirqei Rabbi Eliezer." *Horeb* 8:15–16 (1944):82–119; 9:17–18 (1946):94–166; 10:19–20 (1948):185–294.

―――. *The Treatises Derek Erez*. 2 vols. New York: Debe Rabban, 1935.

Hildesheimer, Ezriel. *Sefer Halakhot Gedolot*. 3 vols. Jerusalem: Meqitze Nirdamim, 1971–88.

Hill, David, ed. *The Gospel of Matthew*. London: Oliphants, 1972.

Himmelfarb, Martha. "Heavenly Ascent and the Relationship of the Apocalypses and the *Hekhalot* Literature." *HUCA* 59 (1988):73–100.

Hirsch, Eric Donald. *The Aims of Interpretation*. Chicago: University of Chicago Press, 1976.

Hirsch, Samson Raphael. *Horeb*. 2 vols. Translated by Isidore Gruenfeld. London: Soncino Press, 1962.

———. *The Pentateuch*. 2nd ed. 5 vols. Translated by Isaac Levy. New York: Judaica Press, 1971.

Hoffman, David Tsevi. *Midrash Tannaim*. 2 vols. Berlin: n.p., 1908/9.

———. *Sefer va-Yiqra* (The Book of Leviticus). 2 vols. Jerusalem: Mossad ha-Rav Kook, 1954.

Hopcke, Robert H. *Men's Dreams, Men's Healing*. Boston and London: Shambhala, 1990.

Horace. *The Complete Works of Horace*. Translated by Charles E. Passage. New York: Frederick Ungar, 1983.

Horowitz, Chaim Shaul. *Sifre ba-Midbar*. Leipzig: Gustav Fock, 1917; reprint Jerusalem: Wahrmann, 1966.

Horowitz, Chaim Shaul, and Israel Avraham Rabin, eds. *Mekhilta de-Rabbi Ishmael*. Jerusalem: Wahrman, 1970.

Horowitz, Shimeon HaLevi, ed. *Maḥzor Vitry le-Rabbenu Simḥah*. Nuremburg: 1923, and Jerusalem: Alef, 1963.

Houlden, J. L. "Lord's Prayer." In *Anchor Bible Dictionary*, 356–62.

Howard, George. *The Gospel of Matthew According to a Primitive Hebrew Text*. Macon, Ga.: Mercer University Press, 1987.

Huntington, William Reed. "Revision of the American Common Prayer." *American Church Review* 33 (April 1881):11–31.

Hyamson, Moses, ed. *Maimonides' The Book of Knowledge: Mishnah Torah*, vol. 1. Jerusalem and New York: Feldheim Publishers, 1981.

ibn-Aqnin, Yosef b. R. Yehuda. *Sefer ha-Mussar*. Edited by W. Bacher. Berlin, 1911; reedited Jerusalem: Meqitze Nirdamim 1967.

ibn-Ezra, Abraham. *Commentary to Torah*. 3 vols. Edited by Asher Weisser. Jerusalem: Mossad ha-Rav Kook, 1976.

———. *Yesod ha-Diqduq hu Sefat Yeter*. Edited by Neḥemiah Aloni. Jerusalem: Mossad ha-Rav Kook, 1984.

ibn-Ezra, Moses. *Sefer Iyyunim ve-Diyyunim (Kitab al-Muhadara wal-Mudhakara)*. Edited by A. S. Halkin. Jerusalem: Meqitze Nirdamim, 1975.

ibn-Gikatilia, Moshe HaCohen. *Ginat Egoz*. Reprint. Jerusalem: Yeshivat ha-Haim ve-ha-Shalom, 1989.

ibn-Habib, Yaakov. *Ain Yaakov*. Vilna, Romm, 1899.

ibn-Janah, Yonah (Abulwalid Merwan ibn-Ganah). *Sefer ha-Riqmah*. 2 vols. Translated by Yehudah ibn-Tibbon; edited by Michael Wilenski. Berlin: Academy Publishers, 1929; reprint, Jerusalem: Academy of the Hebrew Language, 1961.

———. *Sefer ha-Shorashim*. Translated by Yehuda ibn-Tibbon; edited by Wilhelm Bacher. Berlin: Itzkowski, 1896; reprint, Jerusalem, 1966.

ibn-Nahmias, Yosef. *Perush al Sefer Mishlei* (Commentary to Proverbs). Edited by Moses Bamberger. Berlin: Meqitze Nirdamim, 1912.

ibn-Paquda, Bahye b. Yosef. *Sefer Hovot ha-Levavot* (The Book of the Duties of the Heart). Translated by Yehudah ibn-Tibbon; edited by A. Tzifroni. Tel Aviv: Mossad ha-Rav Kook, 1949.

———. *The Duties of the Heart*. 2 vols. Translated by Moses Hyamson. Jerusalem: Feldheim, 1962, 1970.

ibn-Parhon, Shelomo. *Mahberet ha-Arukh*. Edited by Salomon G. Stern. Pressberg: Anton Edlen von Schmidt, 1844.

ibn-Shu'eib, Joshua. *Sefer Derashot al ha-Torah*. Cracow, 1573; reprint, Jerusalem: Maqor, 1969.

ibn-Zabara, Joseph b. Meir. *The Book of Delight by Joseph ben Meir Zabara*. Translated by Moses Hadas. New York: Columbia University Press, 1932.

———. *Sefer Sha'ashuim shel Rabbi Yosef ben Meir ben Zabara*. Edited by Israel Davidson. Berlin: Eshkol, 1928.

Ibrahim, Youssef. "Divided Iranians Seem Unable to Settle on Firm Policy Course." *The New York Times*, October 10, 1989, 1.

Idel, Moshe. "Infinities of Kabbalah." In *Midrash and Literature*, edited by Geoffrey H. Hartman and Sanford Budick, 141–57. New Haven: Yale University Press, 1986.

Idelson, A. Z. *Jewish Liturgy and Its Development*. New York: Henry Holt, 1932.

Immanuel of Rome. *Sefer Mishlei with the Commentary of Immanuel of Rome*. Naples, 1487; reproduced Jerusalem: Magnes, 1981.

Interpreter's Dictionary of the Bible. 5 vols. Edited by George A. Buttrick. New York and Nashville: Abingdon, 1962.

Irenaeus. *The Treatise of Irenaeus of Lugdunum Against the Heresies*. 2 vols. Translated by F. R. Montgomery Hitchcock. London: SPCK, 1916.

Isaac of Corbail. *Sefer Amudei ha-Golah (Sefer ha-SMa"Q)*. New printing, Jerusalem: Mefitzi Or, 1959.

Israeli, Isaak ben Salomon. *Sefer ha-Yesodot* (The Book of Elements). Translated by Abraham ben Samuel he-Levi ibn-Chasdai; edited by Salomon Fried. Frankfort a/Main: 1900; reprint, Jerusalem: Maqor, 1968.

Jacobson, B. S. *Meditations on the Torah*. Translated by Zev Gotthold. Tel Aviv: Sinai Publications, 1956.

Jaeger, Werner. *Early Christianity and Greek Paideia*. London: Oxford University Press, 1961.

Japhet, Sara, ed. *Scripta Hierosolymitana: Volume 31: Studies in Bible, 1986*. Publications of the Hebrew University, Jerusalem. Jerusalem: Magnes, 1986.

Jastrow, Marcus, ed. *A Dictionary of the Targum, the Talmud Babli and Yerushalmi and the Midrashic Literature*. New York: n.p., 1903.

Jaynes, Julian. *The Origin of Consciousness in the Breakdown of the Bicameral Mind*. Boston: Houghton Mifflin, 1990.

Jellinek, Aaron. *Beit ha-Midrash*. 6 bks. in 2 vols. Jerusalem: Wahrmann Books, 1967.

———. *Perushim al Esther, Ruth, ve-Aikhah*. Lipsia: Leopold Schnauss, 1865.

Jeremias, Joachim. "κεφαλη γωνιας—Αχρογωνιαιος (Der Eckstein)." In *ZNW* 29 (1930): 264–80.

———. *The Parables of Jesus*. New York: Scribner's, 1954.

Jerome. *Sancti Eusebii Hieronymi epistulae*. 3 vols. Edited by Isidorus Hilberg. Vindobonae: F. Tempsky, 1912; reprint, Johnson Reprint Corp., 1961.

Johnson, Luke Timothy. *The Gospel of Luke*. Sacra Pagina. Collegeville, Minn.: Michael Glazier for Liturgical Press, 1991.

Johnson, Marshall D. *The Purpose of the Biblical Genealogies*. 2nd ed. Cambridge: Cambridge University Press, 1988.

Josephus. *The Jewish Antiquities*. 6 vols. Vols. 4 and 5 translated by Henry St. John Thackeray, vols. 6 and 8 by Ralph Marcus, vol. 9 by Louis Feldman. Loeb Classical Library, 1930, 1934, 1937, 1963, 1965.

———. *The Jewish Wars*. 2 vols. Translated by Henry St. John Thackeray. Loeb Classical Library, 1928.

———. *The Life/Against Apion*. Translated by Henry St. John Thackeray. Loeb Classical Library, 1976.

Jülicher, Adolf. *Die Gleichnisreden Jesu*. 2nd ed. 3 vols. in 1. Darmstadt: Wissenschaftliche Buchgesellschaft, 1963.

Justin Martyr. *The Dialogue with Trypho*. Translated by A. Lukyn Williams. London: SPCK, 1930.

Juvenal. *Juvenal and Persius*. Translated by G. G. Ramsay. Loeb Classical Library, 1957.

Kahana, Kalman. "Aggadah she-hi Halakhah." _Heqer ve-Iyyun_ 5. Jerusalem: n.p., 1986, 324–28.

Kahana-Shapira, Y. Z. _Yalqut ha-Makhiri al Yeshayahu_ (Isaiah). Berlin: 1893, reprint, Jerusalem, 1964. (Bound with Greenhut on Mishlei.)

Kahane, Avraham, ed. _Perush Madda'i_ (Scholarly Commentaries on the Bible): _Torah, Neviim u-Ketuvim_. Tel Aviv: Meqorot, 1930.

Kahle, Paul. _Der masoretische Text des Alten Testaments_. Hildesheim: Georg Olms Verlagsbuchhandlung, 1966.

Kahler, Erich. _Man the Measure: A New Approach to History_. New York: Pantheon, 1943.

Kamin, Sarah. _Rashi's Exegetical Categorization in Respect to the Distinction between Peshat and Derash_. Jerusalem: Magnes Press, 1986.

Kaminka, Aharon. _Mekhkarim be-Talmud_. 2 vols. Tel Aviv: Devir, 1951.

Kaplan, Aryeh, trans. _The Bahir: Illumination_. York Beach, Maine: Samuel Weiser Inc., 1979.

Kasher, Menachem M. _Torah Sheleimah_. 49 vols. to date. New York: American Biblical Encyclopedia Society, 1949–.

Kaspi, Joseph. _Asarah Kelei Kesef_. 2 vols. Jerusalem: Maqor, 1970.

————. _Mishneh Kesef_. Edited by Isaac haLevi Last. Pressberg: Alkalai, 1905.

————. _Perush ha-Sod_. Edited by Isaac haLevi Last. Pressberg: 1905 (in _Asarah Kelei Kesef_.).

Kassovsky, Chayim Yehoshua. _Otzar Leshon ha-Mishnah_. 4 vols. Tel Aviv: Massada Publishing Company, 1957, 1967.

————. _Otzar Lashon Targum Onkelos_. 2 vols. Jerusalem: Magnes Press, 1933–40, 1986.

Katan, Moshe. _Otzar ha-La'azim_. Jerusalem: Gitler Bros., 1984.

Katz, Saul. "Splitter und Balken." _Jeschurun_ (Berlin) 16:9–10 (1929):482–84.

Katzenellenbogen, Shaul, with Abraham Abeli, Shemuel Strashon, and Mattiyahu Strashon. _Netivot Olam_. Vilna, 1859.

Kautsch, E., ed. _Gesenius' Hebrew Grammar_. 2nd ed. Oxford: Clarendon Press, 1910, 1985.

Kee, Alistair. "The Old Coat and the New Wine: A Parable of Repentance." _NT_ 12:1 (1970):13–21.

————. "The Question About Fasting." _NT_ 11:3 (1969):161–73.

Kehati, Pinhas, ed. _Mishnayot_. 12 vols. Jerusalem: Heikhal Shelomo, 1977.

Kehillot Moshe (Rabbinic Commentaries on the Bible). Amsterdam: Ephraim Cohen, 1727.

Keil, H, ed. *Grammatici latini*. 8 vols. Hildesheim: G. Olms Verlagsbuchhandlung, 1961.

Kelly, J. N. D. *Early Christian Doctrines*. New York: Harper and Row, 1958.

Kelner, L. "Shakespeare and Pirkei Avot." *D'vir* 1 (1923) Berlin: 285–88.

Kermode, Frank. "The Plain Sense of Things." In *Midrash and Literature*, edited by Geoffrey H. Hartman and Sanford Budick. New Haven: Yale University Press, 1986, 179–94.

Kiel, Judah, commentator. *Sefer Shemuel* (The Book of Samuel). 2 vols. The Daat Miqra Series. Jerusalem: Mossad ha-Rav Kook, 1981.

―――. *Sefer Yehoshua* (The Book of Joshua). The Daat Miqra Series. Jerusalem: Mossad ha-Rav Kook, 1970.

Kierkegaard, Søren. *Fear and Trembling: Repetition*. Edited and translated by Howard V. and Dena H. Hong. Princeton, N.J.: Princeton University Press, 1983.

―――. *Philosophical Fragments, or A Fragment of Philosophy by Johannes Climacus*. Translated by David F. Swenson. Princeton, N.J.: Princeton University Press, 1962.

―――. *Philosophical Fragments/Johannes Climacus*. Edited and translated by Howard V. Hong and Edna H. Hong. Princeton, N.J.: Princeton University Press, 1985.

King, George B. "The Mote and the Beam." *HTR* 17 (1924):395–404.

Kirchan, Elhanan. *Simḥat ha-Nefesh*. Edited by Yaakov Shatzky. New York, 1928.

Kister, Menachem. "The Sayings of Jesus and the Midrash." *Immanuel* 15 (1982/83): 39–50.

Klausner, Joseph. *Jesus of Nazareth: His Life, Times and Teaching*. New York: Menorah Publishing Co., 1925.

Klein, Michael L. "Converse Translation: A Targumic Technique." *Biblica* 57:4 (1976):515–37.

Klein, Shemuel. *Eretz ha-Galil*. Jerusalem: Mossad ha-Rav Kook, 1946.

Kloppenborg, John S. *The Formation of Q: Trajectories in Ancient Wisdom Collections*. Philadelphia: Fortress Press, 1987.

Kloppenborg, John S., Marvin Meyer, Stephen Patterson, and Michael Steinhauser. *Q-Thomas Reader*. Sonoma, Calif.: Polebridge Press, 1990.

Klosterman, Erich. *Das Matthäusevengelium*. Tübingen: Mohr (Siebeck), 1938.

Koester, Helmut. *Ancient Christian Gospels: Their History and Development*. Philadelphia: Trinity Press International, 1990.

Kohen, Shabbatai. *Siftai Kohen*, commentary to Yoreh Deah.

Kohut, Alexander, ed. *Sefer he-Arukh me'et Rabbenu Natan ben Rabbenu Yeḥiel ha-Romi*. 9 vols. New York: Academic Vindobonensis, 1955.

Kosmala, Hans. "The Parable of the Unjust Steward in the Light of Qumran." *Annual of the Swedish Theological Institute* 3 (1964):115–21.

Krauss, Shemuel. *Paras ve-Romi be-Talmud u-ve-Midrash* (Persia and Rome in Talmud and Midrash). Jerusalem: Mossad ha-Rav Kook, 1948.

Kugel, James L. *The Idea of Biblical Poetry: Parallelism and Its History*. New Haven: Yale University Press, 1981.

Kugel, James L., and Rowan A. Greer. *Early Biblical Interpretation*. Philadelphia: Westminster, 1986.

Kümmel, Werner Georg. *New Testament: The History of the Investigation of Its Problems*. Nashville, Tenn.: Abingdon, 1972.

Kutscher, Eduard Yechezkel. *A History of the Hebrew Language*. Edited by Raphael Kutscher. Jerusalem: Magnes Press, 1984.

———. *Millim ve-Toledoteihen*. Jerusalem: Kiryat Sefer, 1974.

Lachs, Samuel Tobias. *A Rabbinic Commentary on the New Testament*. Hoboken, N.J.: Ktav, 1987.

———. "Rabbinic Sources for New Testament Studies." *JQR* 74:2 (1983):159–73.

Lake, Kirsopp, trans. *The Apostolic Fathers*. 2 vols. Loeb Classical Library, 1930.

Lampe, G. W. H. *A Patristic Greek Lexicon*. Oxford: Clarendon Press, 1961.

Landes, G. M. "Jonah: a MAŠAL." In *Israelite Wisdom: Theological and Literary Essays in Honor of Samuel Terrien*. Edited by J. G. Gammie, Walter Brueggemann, W. Lee Humphreys, James M. Ward, 137–58. New York: Scholars Press, 1978.

Lapide, Pinchas. "Hidden Hebrew in the Gospels." *Immanuel* 2 (1973):28–34.

Lasine, Stuart. "Melodrama as Parable: The Story of the Poor Man's Ewe-Lamb and the Unmasking of David's Topsy-Turvy Emotions." Edited by Reubn Aharoni. *Hebrew Annual Review* 8:101–24. Columbus: Ohio State University, 1984.

Lauren, Paul Gordon. *Power and Prejudice: The Politics and Diplomacy of Racial Discrimination*. Boulder, Colo.: Westview Press, 1988.

Lauterbach, Jacob Z. *Mekhilta de-Rabbi Ishmael*. 3 vols. Philadelphia: Jewish Publication Society, 1935.

———. "The Sadducees and Pharisees: A Study of Their Respective Attitudes towards the Law." In *Studies in Jewish Literature in Honor of Kaufmann Kohler*, 176–98. Berlin: Georg Reimer, 1913.

Layton, Bentley. *The Gnostic Scriptures*. Garden City, N.Y.: Doubleday, 1987.

Lazarus-Yafeh, Hava. *Intertwined Worlds: Medieval Islam and Bible Criticism*. Princeton, N.J.: Princeton University Press, 1992.

Le Bas, Edwin E. "Was the Corner-Stone of Scripture a Pyramidion?" *Palestine Exploration Quarterly* (1946):103–15.

Lehmann, Manfred R. "Where the Temple Tax Was Buried." *Biblical Archaeology Review* 19:6 (1993):38–43.

Lerner, Myron B. "Enquiries into the Meaning of Various Titles and Designations: I. Abba." *Te'uda: Studies in Judaica* 4 (1986):93–113.

Levi ben Gershon. *Commentary of RaLBa"G on the Torah*. Venice: Bomberg, 1547; reprint, Jerusalem, 1968.

Levin, Israel. *Abraham ibn Ezra Reader*. New York: I. Edward Kiev Library Foundation, 1985.

Levine, Amy-Jill. "Ruth." In *The Women's Bible Commentary*. Edited by Carol Newsom and Sharon Ringe. Louisville, Ky.: Westminster/John Knox Press, 1992, 78–84.

Levine, Lee L. *The Rabbinic Class of Roman Palestine*. Jerusalem: Yad Izhak Ben-Zvi, 1989.

Levita, Elias. *Meturgeman* (Lexicon Chaldaicum). Eisen: n.p., 1501.

———. *Sefer ha-Tishbi*. Basel, 1601; reprint, Benei Berak, Israel: Kaufman and Sons, 1976.

Levy, J. *Chaldäisches Wörterbuch über die Targumim und einen Grossen Theil des Rabbinischen Schrifttums*. Leipzig: Baumgärtner, 1867–68.

Lewin, B. M. *Otzar ha-Geonim*. Vol. 1: Berakhot. Haifa: Otzar ha-Geonim, 1920.

Lewis, Charleton T., and Charles Short. *A Latin Dictionary*. Oxford: Clarendon Press, 1879, 1955.

Lichtenstein, Hans. "Die Fastenrolle, eine Untersuchung zur Jüdisch-Hellenistischen Geschichte." *HUCA* 8–9 (1931–32):257–317.

———. "The Fastday Scroll: Megillat Taanit." *HUCA* 8–9 (1931–32):318–51.

Liddell, Henry G., and Robert Scott. *A Greek-English Lexicon*. 9th ed. Oxford: Clarendon Press, 1968.

Lieberman, Saul. *Greek in Jewish Palestine*. New York: Jewish Theological Seminary, 1942.

———. *Ha-Yerushalmi ki-Feshuto*. Part 1, vol. 1. Jerusalem: Darom, 1935.

———. *Mekhkarim be-Torat Eretz-Israel*. Jerusalem: Magnes Press, 1991.

———. *Midrash Devarim Rabbah*. Jerusalem: Bamberger & Wahrmann, 1940.

———. "Roman Legal Institutions in Early Rabbinics and in the Acta Martyrum." *JQR* (NS) 35 (1944):1–57; reprint, *Texts and Studies*, 57–111.

———. *Texts and Studies*. Jerusalem: Ktav, 1974.

———. *Tosefta*. 5 vols. to date. New York: Jewish Theological Seminary, 1962–.

———. *Tosefta ki-Feshutah*. 10 vols. to date. New York: Jewish Theological Seminary, 1962–.

———. "A Tragedy or a Comedy?" *JAOS* 104:2 (1984):315–19.

Lightfoot, J. B. *A Commentary on the New Testament from the Talmud and Hebraica*. 4 vols. Grand Rapids, Mich.: Baker Book House, 1979.

Lindars, Barnabas. "Slave and Son in John 8:31–36." In *The New Testament Age: Essays in Honor of Bo Reicke*, vol. 1, edited by William C. Weinrich, 271–86. Macon, Ga.: Mercer University Press, 1984.

Lindbeck, George. *The Nature of Doctrine: Religion and Theology in a Postliberal Age*. Philadelphia: Westminster Press, 1984.

Lindsey, Robert Lisle. *A Hebrew Translation of the Gospel of Mark*. Jerusalem: Dugith, 1969.

———. "'Verily' or 'Amen': What Did Jesus Say?" With a supplementary note by Ze'ev Gotthold. *Christian News from Israel* 25:3 (19), 1975:144–50.

Lipiner, Elias. *The Metaphysics of the Hebrew Alphabet*. Jerusalem: Magnes Press, 1989.

Liver, J. "The Half-Shekel Offering in Biblical and Post-Biblical Literature." *HTR* 56:3 (1963):173–98.

Livy. *Books*. 14 vols. Translated by B. O. Foster. Loeb Classical Library, 1967.

Loew, Judah ben Bezalel. *Sefer Perush Maharal le-Aggadot ha-Shas* (The Commentary of the Maharal on the Talmudic Aggadot). Edited by M. S. Kasher and Y. Y. Bilbrovitz. 4 vols. Jerusalem: Torah Sheleimah, 1959.

Loewe, Raphael. "The 'Plain' Meaning of Scripture in Early Jewish Exegesis." In *Papers of the Institute of Jewish Studies, London*, vol. 1, edited by J. G. Weiss, 140–85. Jerusalem: Magnes Press, 1964.

Loewe, W. H., ed. *The Fragment of Talmud Babli Pesachim of the Ninth or Tenth Century in the University Library, Cambridge*. Cambridge: Deighton, Bell, 1879.

Lohfink, Norbert. *The Covenant Never Revoked: Biblical Reflections on Christian-Jewish Dialogue*. Translated by John J. Scullion, S.J. New York and Mahwah, N.J.: Paulist Press, 1961.

"Longinus." *On the Sublime*. Translated by W. Hamilton Fyfe; edited by T. E. Page, E. Capps, and W. H. D. Rowe. Loeb Classical Library, 1932.

⎯ Lowe, Malcolm. "From the Parable of the Vineyard to a Pre-Synoptic Source." *NTS* 28 (1982):257–63.

Lowe, Malcolm, and David Flusser. "Evidence Corroborating a Modified Proto-Matthean Synoptic Theory." *NTS* 29:1 (1983):25–47.

Lowth, Robert. *Lectures on the Sacred Poetry of the Hebrews.* 2nd ed. London: S. Chadwick, 1753, 1847; reprint in two vols., New York: Garland, 1971.

Luria, Shelomo. *Yam shel Shelomo.* Stettin: Schrentzel, 1861; reprint, Israel, 1969.

Luzzato, Samuel David. *Betulat Bat Yehudah.* Prague, 1840.

⸻. *The Commentary of Shemuel David Luzzato on Jeremiah, Ezekiel, Proverbs and Job.* Lemberg: Aharit Tov, 1876.

Maarsen, Isaac. *Parschandatha: The Commentary of Raschi on the Prophets and Hagiographa, Part 1: The Minor Prophets.* Amsterdam: Menno Hertzberger, 1930.

Mack, Hananel. *The Aggadic Midrash Literature.* Tel Aviv: MOD Books, 1989.

⸻. "'Seventy Aspects of the Torah': Concerning the Evolution of an Expression." In *Rabbi Mordecai Breuer Festschrift,* vol. 2, 449–62. Jerusalem: Academon Press, 1992.

Maier, Johann. *The Temple Scroll: An Introduction, Translation and Commentary.* Sheffield, England: JSOT, 1985.

Maimon, Yehudah Leib ha-Kohen, ed. *Sefer Rashi.* Jerusalem: Mossad Ha-Rav Kook, 1956.

Maimonides, Moses. *The Book of Judges.* Translated by Abraham Hershman. Yale Judaica Series. New Haven: Yale University Press, 1949.

⸻. *The Book of Knowledge from the Mishneh Torah of Maimonides.* Translated by H. M. Russell and Rabbi J. Weinberg. New York: Ktav, 1983.

⸻. *The Book of Temple Service.* Translated by Mendel Lewittes. Yale Judaica Series. New Haven: Yale University Press, 1957.

⸻. *Guide to the Perplexed.* Translated by M. Friedlander. New York: Dover Publications, 1956.

⸻. *Guide of the Perplexed.* Translated by Shlomo Pines. Chicago: University of Chicago Press, 1963.

⸻. *Iggerot ha-RaMBaM.* Edited by Yosef Kafih. Jerusalem: Mossad ha-Rav Kook, 1972.

⸻. *Iggerot ha-RaMBaM.* 2 vols. Edited by Izhak Shilat. Jerusalem: Birkat Moshe, 1988.

———. *Mishneh Torah, Hilkhot De'ot* (The Laws of Personality Development). Translated by Za'ev Abramson and Eliyahu Touger. New York: Moznaim, 1989.

———. *Mishneh Torah, Yad ha-Ḥazaqah.* Jerusalem: Chaim Wagshal, 1982.

———. *Mishneh Torah, Yad ha-Ḥazaqah.* Vol. 1: Madda. Edited by Moshe Katzenellenbogen, Yaakov Cohen, and Saul Lieberman. Jerusalem: Mossad ha-Rav Kook, 1964.

———. *Moreh Nebukhim* (Guide to the Perplexed). 3 vols. Edited by Yosef Kafiḥ. Jerusalem: Mossad ha-Rav Kook, 1977.

———. *Perush ha-Mishnah* (Commentary on the Mishnah). 3 vols. Edited by Yosef Kafiḥ. Jerusalem: Mossad ha-Rav Kook, 1963.

———. *Rambam la-Am.* 10 vols. Edited by Y. Kafiḥ, M. Rabinowitz, M. Goshen-Gottstein, M. Leib. Jerusalem: Mossad ha-Rav Kook, 1987.

———. *Sefer ha-Madda.* 2 vols. Edited by Naḥum Eliezer Rabinovitch. Jerusalem: Yeshivat Birkhat Moshe, 1990.

———. *Teshuvot ha-Rambam* (The Responsa of Maimonides). 4 vols. Edited by Yehoshua Blau. Jerusalem: Meqitze Nirdamim, 1958–86.

MaLBYM (Meir Loebish ben Yeḥiel Michael Weisser). *Commentary on the Latter Prophets.* Krotoschin, 1849; reprint, Jerusalem, 1975.

Malter, Henry, trans. *Tractate Taanit.* Philadelphia: Jewish Publication Society, 1978.

Mandel, Avraham. *Ha-Missim ba-Meqorot* (Taxation in Jewish Sources). Jerusalem: Israel Taxation Museum, 1987.

Mandelbaum, Bernard. *Pesiqta de Rav Kahana According to an Oxford Manuscript.* 2nd augmented ed., 2 vols. New York: Jewish Theological Seminary, 1987.

Mantel, Hugo. *Studies in the History of the Sanhedrin.* Cambridge: Harvard University Press, 1961.

Manuel, Frank E., and Fritzie P. Manuel. "Sketch for a Natural History of Paradise." In *Myth, Symbol and Culture,* edited by Clifford Geertz, 83–127. New York: W. W. Norton, 1971.

Maori, Yeshayahu. "The Approach of Classical Jewish Exegetes to *Peshat* and *Derash* and Its Implications for the Teaching of Bible Today." Translated by Moshe J. Bernstein. *Tradition* 21:3 (1984):40–53.

Marcuse, Herbert. *One-Dimensional Man: Studies in the Ideology of Advanced Industrial Society.* Boston: Beacon Press, 1964.

Margulies, Mordecai. "Festivals and Fasts in the Geonic Period." In *Areshet: Sefer Shanah Shel Iggud Soferim Datiim,* edited by Izḥak Raphael, 204–17. Jerusalem: Mossad ha-Rav Kook, 1944.

————. *Midrash ha-Gadol Bereshit*. Jerusalem: Mossad ha-Rav Kook, 1975.

————. *Midrash ha-Gadol Shemot*. Jerusalem: Mossad ha-Rav Kook, 1983.

————. *Midrash va-Yiqra Rabbah*. 4 vols. plus introductory vol. Jerusalem: Academy of Jewish Studies, 1960.

Margulies, Reuven. *Ha-Miqra ve-ha-Massorah* (Scripture and Tradition). Jerusalem: Mossad ha-Rav Kook, 1989.

————. *Mekhkarim be-Darkei ha-Talmud*. Jerusalem: Mossad ha-Rav Kook, 1989.

————. *Sefer ha-Bahir*. Jerusalem: Mossad ha-Rav Kook, 1978.

————. *Sefer ha-Zohar*. 3 vols. Jerusalem: Mossad ha-Rav Kook, 1984.

————. *Sefer Zohar Hadash*. Jerusalem: Mossad ha-Rav Kook, 1978.

Marino, Luis Diez. *Targum de Salmos: Edicion Principe del Ms. Villa-Amil n. 5 de Alfonso de Zamora*. Madrid: Instituto "Francisco Suarez," 1982.

Martine, Raymundi. *Pugio Fidei*. Edited by J. de Voisin. Lipsiae, 1687, republished Farnborough, Hants.: Gregg Press, 1967.

Marx, Alexander. "The Correspondence between the Rabbis of Southern France and Maimonides about Astrology." *HUCA* 3 (1926):311–58.

Marx, Tzvi. *Halakha & Handicap: Jewish Law and Ethics on Disability*. Jerusalem and Amsterdam: self-published, 1992–93.

Masnut, Samuel b. R. Nissim. *Bereshit Zutta*. Edited by Mordecai HaCohen. Jerusalem, Mossad ha-Rav Kook, 1962.

————. *Midrash Daniel and Midrash Ezra*. Edited by I. S. Lange and S. Schwartz. Jerusalem: Meqitze Nirdamim, 1968.

Mattingly, Harold. *Roman Coins from the Earliest Times to the Fall of the Western Empire*. Rev. ed. Chicago: Quadrangle, 1960.

McKane, William. *Proverbs: A New Approach*. Philadelphia: Westminster Press, 1970.

————. *Prophets and Wise Men*. London: SCM, 1965.

McNally, Robert. *The Bible in the Early Middle Ages*. Westminster, Md: Newman, 1959; reprint, Atlanta: Scholars Press, 1986.

Meier, John P. *A Marginal Jew: Rethinking the Historical Jesus*. Vol. 1. New York: Doubleday, 1991.

————. *Matthew*. The New Testament Message. Wilmington, Del.: Michael Glazier, 1980.

Melamed, E. Z. *Mekhkarim be-Miqra be-Targumav u-bi-Mefarashav (Biblical Studies in Texts, Translators, and Commentators)*. 2 vols. Jerusalem: Magnes Press, 1984.

———. *Mifareshei ha-Miqra (Biblical Commentators)*. 2 vols. Jerusalem: Magnes Press, 1975.

Menachem, R. "Epitropos/Paqid in the Parable of the Laborers in the Vineyard." *Immanuel—The New Testament and Christian-Jewish Dialogue: Studies in Honor of David Flusser* 24/25 (1990):118–31.

Meshorer, Yaakov. "One Hundred Ninety Years of Tyrian Shekels." In *Studies in Honor of Leo Mildenberg*, 171–79. Belgium: Editions Wetteren, 1984.

Metzger, Bruce M. *A Textual Commentary on the Greek New Testament*. London and New York: United Bible Societies, 1971; corrected edition, 1975.

Meyer, Ben F. "A Caricature of Joachim Jeremias and His Scholarly Work." *JBL* 110:3 (1991):451–62.

Meyer, Marvin, trans. *The Secret Teachings of Jesus: Four Gnostic Gospels*. New York: Random House, 1984.

Meyers, Carol L. *The Tabernacle Menorah: A Synthetic Study of a Symbol from the Biblical Cult*. Missoula, Mont.: Scholars Press, 1976.

Meyers, Eric M. "The Cultural Setting of Galilee: The Case of Regionalism and Early Judaism." *Aufstieg und Niedergang der romischen Welt* 2.19.1 (1979):686–702.

———. "Galilean Regionalism as a Factor in Historical Reconstruction." *BASOR* 220/221 (1976):93–103.

———. "Galilean Regionalism: A Reappraisal." In *Approaches to Ancient Judaism. Volume 5: Studies in Judaism and Its Greco-Roman Context*, edited by William Scott Green, 115–32. Atlanta: Scholars Press, 1985.

Meyers, Eric, and James F. Strange. *Archaeology, the Rabbis and Early Christianity*. Nashville, Tenn.: Abingdon Press, 1981.

Midrash Rabbah. 2 vols. Vilna: Romm, 1887.

Midrash Rabbah Mevoar. 13 vols. to date. Jerusalem: Makhon ha-Midrash ha-Mevoar, 1983–91.

Midrash Tanhuma (commonly referred to as "Vulgar"). Jerusalem: Levin-Epstein, 1953.

Mielziner, Moses. *Introduction to the Talmud*. New York: Bloch Publishing Company, 1968.

Migne, Jacques Paul. *Patrologiae cursus completus, series graeca*. 161 vols. Paris, 1857–66.

———. *Patrologiae cursus completus, series latina*. 221 vols., including 4 vols. of indexes. Paris, 1844–55.

Milavec, Aaron. "The Pastoral Genius of the Didache." In *Religious Writings and Religious Systems*, edited by J. Neusner, E. Frerichs, and A. J. Levine, 89–125. Atlanta: Scholars Press, 1990.

————. *To Empower as Jesus Did: Acquiring Spiritual Power Through Apprenticeship*. New York and Toronto: Edwin Mellen Press, 1982.

Miller, Robert J. *The Complete Gospels*. Sonoma, Calif.; Polebridge Press, 1992.

Milne, A. A. *The World of Pooh*. London: Methuen, 1926.

Milton, John. *The Complete Poetical Works of John Milton*. Edited by Harris Francis Fletcher. Boston: Houghton Mifflin, 1941.

Miqraot Gedolot: The Prophets. 2 vols. New York: Shulsinger Brothers, 1945.

Mirkin, M. A., ed. *Midrash Rabbah*. 11 vols. Tel Aviv: Yavneh, 1977.

Mirsky, Aharon. *Ha-Piyyut: The Development of Post Biblical Poetry in Eretz Israel and the Diaspora*. Jerusalem: Magnes Press, 1990.

————. *Mahatzavtan shel Tzurot ha-Piyyut*. Tel Aviv: Schocken, 1968.

Mirsky, Samuel Kalman. "Meqorot ha-Halakhah be-Midrashim (Sources of Halakhah in Midrashic Literature)." *Talpiot* 1 (1944):40–71, 218–247, 498–532; 2 (1945):29–48, 348–74; 3 (1947):113–38.

Mirsky, Samuel, ed. *She'eltot de Rab Ahai Gaon*. 4 vols. Jerusalem: Mossad ha-Rav Kook, 1963.

Mitchell, Stephen. *The Gospel According to Jesus: A New Translation and Guide to His Essential Teachings*. New York: HarperCollins, 1991.

Montefiore, Hugh. "Jesus and the Temple Tax." *NTS* 10 (October 1964):60–71.

Morray-Jones, C. R. A. "Heikhalot Literature and Talmudic Tradition: Alexander's Three Test Cases." *JSJ* 22:1 (1991):1–39.

Morrey, C. R. "The Origin of the Fish-Symbol." *Princeton Theological Review* 7 (1910):93–106, 231–46, 401–32; 9 (1911):268–89; 10 (1912):278–98.

Morris, William, ed. *The American Heritage Dictionary*. Boston: American Heritage Publishing Company, 1969, 1970.

Moskovitz, Yehiel Tzvi. "Lamentations." In *Hamesh Megillot*. The Daat Miqra Series. Jerusalem: Mossad ha-Rav Kook, 1973.

————. *Sefer ba-Midbar* (Commentary to Numbers). The Daat Miqra Series. Jerusalem: Mossad ha-Rav Kook, 1988.

Murphy, Charles Theophilus, Kevin Guinagh, and Whitney Jennings Oates, eds. *Greek and Roman Classics in Translation*. New York: Longmans, Green, 1947.

Murray, Robert. *Symbols of Church and Kingdom: A Study in Early Syriac Tradition*. New York: Cambridge University Press, 1975.

Musafia, Yaakov. *Teshuvot ha-Geonim*. Edited by Shelomo Buber. Lyck: Meqitze Nirdamim, 1865; reprint, Jerusalem 1967.

Nahmanides, Moses ben Nahman. *Kitvei de-Rabbenu Moshe ben Nahman*. 2 vols. Edited by Charles B. Chavel. Jerusalem: Mossad ha-Rav Kook, 1963–64.

———. *Perush ha-Torah*. 2 vols. Edited by Charles B. Chavel. Jerusalem: Mossad ha-Rav Kook, 1959–60.

———. *Ramban: Commentary on the Torah*. 5 vols. Translated by Charles B. Chavel. New York: Shilo, 1971.

Nauck, August. *Tragicorum Graecorum Fragmenta*. Supplementum adiecit Bruno Snell. Hildesheim: Georg Olms Verlagsbuchhandlung, 1964.

Neusner, Jacob. *Eliezer ben Hyrcanus: The Tradition and the Man*. 2 vols. Leiden: E. J. Brill, 1973.

———. *The Fathers According to Rabbi Nathan*. Atlanta: Scholars Press, 1986.

———. *Invitation to Midrash: The Workings of Rabbinic Bible Interpretation*. San Francisco: Harper & Row, 1989.

———. *Judaism in the Beginning of Christianity*. London: SPCK, 1984.

———. *Judaism and Scripture: The Evidence of Leviticus Rabbah*. Chicago: University of Chicago Press, 1986.

———. *A Life of Yohanan ben Zakkai, Ca. 1–80 C.E.* Leiden: E. J. Brill, 1970.

———. *Sifre to Numbers: An American Translation and Explanation*. 2 vols. Atlanta: Scholars Press, 1986.

———. *The Talmud of the Land of Israel*. Chicago and London: University of Chicago Press. 1982–.

———. *Tosephta*. New York: Ktav, 1981.

Neusner, Jacob, William S. Green, and Ernest Frerichs, eds. *Judaisms and Their Messiahs at the Turn of the Christian Era*. Cambridge: Cambridge University Press, 1987.

Neusner, Jacob, and Richard Sarason, eds. *The Tosefta*. Hoboken, N.J.: Ktav, 1986.

Newman, Barclay, and Philip Stine. *A Translator's Handbook on the Gospel of Matthew*. London: United Bible Societies, 1988.

Nissim Gaon. *Hibbur Yafe mi-ha-Yeshuah*. Jerusalem: Mossad ha-Rav Kook, 1954.

Norden, Eduard. *Agnostos Theos*. Darmstadt: Wissenschaftliche Buchgesellschaft, 1950.

Nortlingen, Yosef Yosspe Hahn. *Sefer Yosef Ometz*. Frankfort-on-Main, 1928; reprint, Jerusalem, 1965.

Noth, Martin. *Leviticus*. Philadelphia: Westminster Press, 1965, 1977.

O'Day, Gail. "John 7:53–8:11: A Study in Misreading." *JBL* 3:4 (1992):631–40.

Odo of Chariton. *The Fables of Odo of Chariton*. Translated by John C. Jacobs. Syracuse, N.Y.: Syracuse University Press, 1985.

Oesterley, William Oscar Emil. *The Gospel Parables in the Light of Their Jewish Background*. London: SPCK, 1936.

Ogden, Schubert M. *The Point of Christology*. San Francisco: Harper & Row, 1982.

Origen. *Contra Celsum*. Translated by Henry Chadwick. Cambridge: Cambridge University Press, 1953.

Orlinsky, Harry M. "The Biblical Prepositions Tahat, Ben, Ba'ad and Pronouns Anu or Anu, Zotah." *HUCA* 17 (1942–43):267–92.

Ortega y Gasset, José. *Concord and Liberty*. Translated by Helene Weyl. New York: W. W. Norton, 1946.

Oxford Dictionary of Quotations. 3d ed. Oxford: Oxford University Press, 1979.

Padua, Aharon Moshe, and Mordecai Gumpel, commentators. *Midrash Shoher Tov, Midrash Tehillim*. Warsaw: Chaim Kalter, 1865.

Pagels, Elaine. *The Gnostic Gospels*. New York: Random House, 1979.

Parsons, Mikael. "The Critical Use of the Rabbinic Literature in New Testament Studies." *Perspectives in Religious Studies* 12:2 (Summer 1985):85–102.

Patterson, L. "Origin of the Name Panthera." *The Journal of Theological Studies* 19 (1918):79–80.

Paul, S. M. "Classifications of Wine in Mesopotamian and Rabbinic Sources." *IEJ* 25 (1975):42–44.

Peake's Commentary on the Bible. Edited by Matthew Black and H. H. Rowley. Surrey, England: Nelson, 1962, 1980.

Pei, Mario. *What's In a Word? Language—Yesterday, Today, and Tomorrow*. New York: Hawthorn Books, 1968.

Perry, Ben Edwin, trans. *Aesopica: A Series of Texts Relating to Aesop or Ascribed to Him or Closely Connected with the Literary Tradition that Bears His Name*. Vol. 1. Urbana: University of Illinois Press, 1952.

———. *Babrius and Phaedrus*. Loeb Classical Library, 1965.

Persius. "Satires." In *Juvenal and Persius*, translated by G. G. Ramsay. Loeb Classical Library, 1969.

Peshitta to the New Testament. Jerusalem: Ha-Hevra le-Kitvei ha-Qodesh, 1986.

Petuchowski, Jacob J. "The Theological Significance of the Parable in Rabbinic Literature and the New Testament." *Christian News From Israel* 23:2(10), 1972:76–86. Followed by "A Panel Discussion on Petchowski's Discussion of the Parable." *Christian News From Israel* 23:3(10), 1972:144–51.

Philo. *Philo*. 10 vols. plus 2 supp. vols. Translated and edited by F. J. Colson and G. H. Whitaker. Loeb Classical Library, republished 1968–81.

Pines, Shelomo. "The Jewish Christians of the Early Centuries of Christianity According to a New Source." *Proceedings of the Israel Academy of Sciences and Humanities* 2, 237–310. Jerusalem: Israel Academy of Sciences and Humanities, 1968.

Pirqei Rabbi Eliezer. Edited by David Luria. Warsaw, 1852; reprint, Jerusalem, 1963.

Plato. *Laws.* Translated by R. G. Bury. Loeb Classical Library, 1967.

———. *Phaedrus.* Translated by Harold North Fowler. Loeb Classical Library, 1977.

———. *Symposium.* Translated by W. R. M. Lamb. Loeb Classical Library, 1932.

———. *Symposium.* Translated by Alexander Nehamas and Paul Woodruff. Indianapolis & Cambridge: Hackett Publishing Company, 1989.

———. *The Republic.* 2 vols. Translated by Paul Shorey. Loeb Classical Library, 1970.

———. *Theatetus.* Translated by Harold North Fowler. Loeb Classical Library, 1928.

Pliny the Younger. *The Letters of Pliny the Younger.* Translated by Betty Radice. New York: Penguin, 1963, 1969.

Plummer, A. *The Gospel According to Saint Luke.* International Critical Commentary. 5th ed. New York: Scribner's, 1902.

Plutarch. *Moralia: Quaestionum convivalium.* 16 vols. Translated by Frank Cole Babbitt, W. C. Helmbold, Phillip H. DeLacy, Benedict Einarson, E. L. Minar, F. H. Sandbach, L. Pearson, and H. Cherniss. Loeb Classical Library, 1927, 1969.

Pokorny, Julius. *Indogermanisches Etymologisches Wörterbuch.* 2 vols. Bern and Munich: Francke, 1959.

Pool, David de Sola. *The Book of Prayer According to the Custom of the Spanish and Portugese Jews.* 2nd ed. New York: Union of Sephardic Congregations, 1960.

———. *The Kaddish.* New York: Union of Sephardic Congregations, 1964.

Pope, Marvin. *Song of Songs.* Anchor Bible. Garden City, NY: Doubleday, 1977.

Porten, Bezalel, and Jonas C. Greenfield. *Jews of Elephantine and Arameans of Syrene: Aramaic Texts with Translation.* Jerusalem: Hebrew University Press, 1976.

Pritchard, James B. *Ancient Near Eastern Texts Relating to the Old Testament.* 3d ed. Princeton, N.J.: Princeton University Press, 1969.

Pusey, Philippus Edwardus. *Tetraevangelium Sanctum.* Edited by Georgius Henricus Gwilliam. Oxford: Clarendon Press, 1911.

Qimḥi, R. David. *Sefer Mikhlol*. Edited by Izḥak b. Aharon Rittenberg. Fürth, 1793; new printing, Jerusalem, 1966.

―――. *Sefer ha-Shorashim*. Berlin: G. Bethge, 1847; reprint, Jerusalem, 1967.

Qimron, Elisha, and John Strugnell. "An Unpublished Halakhic Letter from Qumran." *Israel Museum Journal* 4 (Spring 1985):9–12.

Quasten, Johannes. *Patrology*. 2 vols. Westminster: Newman Press, 1950.

Quintilian. *The Institutio Oratoria*. 4 vols. Translated by H. E. Butler. Loeb Classical Library, 1920, 1989.

Rabbinowicz, E. N., ed. *Midrash ha-Gadol on Leviticus*. New York: Jewish Theological Seminary, 1932.

Rabbinowicz, R. N. H. *Diqduqei Soferim* (Variae Lectiones). 2 vols. New York: Shulsinger, 1976.

Rabbinowicz, Zvi Meir. *Midrash ha-Gadol ba-Midbar*. Jerusalem: Mossad ha-Rav Kook, 1978.

Rabinowich, Nosson Dovid. *M. Mielziner's Talmudic Terminology*. Jerusalem: Moznaim, 1988.

Rabinowitz, Louis. "The Talmudic Meaning of *Peshat*." *Tradition* 6:1 (1963):67–72.

Reider, David. *Targum Jonathan ben Uziel on the Torah*. 2 vols. Jerusalem: privately published, 1985.

Reider, Joseph. *Prolegomena to Greek-Hebrew and Hebrew-Greek Index to Aquila*. Revised by Nigel Turner. Leiden: E. J. Brill, 1966.

Reines, Alvin Jay. *Abrabanel and Maimonides on Prophecy*. Cincinnati: Hebrew Union College Press, 1970.

Reines, Ch. W. *Be-Aholai Shem* (Essays in Jewish Law and Ethics). Tel Aviv: Neumann, 1963.

Remus, Harold. "Outside/Inside: Celsus on Jewish and Christian *Nomoi*." In *New Perspectives on Ancient Judaism, Volume II: Religion, Literature, and Society in Ancient Israel, Formative Christianity and Judaism*, edited by Jacob Neusner, Peder Borgen, Ernest S. Frerichs, and Richard Horsley, 133–50. New York: New York University Press, 1987.

Richardson, Cyril C., et al. *Early Christian Fathers*. Library of Christian Classics. Philadelphia: Westminster Press, 1953.

Rivkin, Ellis. "What Crucified Jesus?" Nashville, Tenn.: Abingdon, 1984. Reprinted in *Jesus' Jewishness: Exploring the Place of Jesus in Early Judaism*, edited by James H. Charlesworth, 226–57. New York: Crossroad, 1991.

Rivlin, Asher. *Munaḥon le-Sifrut*. Tel Aviv: Sifriyat Poalim, 1990.

Roberts, Alexander, and James Donaldson, eds. *Ante-Nicene Fathers*. 10 vols. Edited by A. Cleveland Doxe. New York: Christian Literature Company, 1896; reprint, Grand Rapids, Mich.: Eerdmans, n.d.

Robinson, James M., ed. *The Nag Hammadi Library in English.* 3d rev. ed. San Francisco: Harper & Row, 1988.

Rofe, Alexander. *The Prophetical Stories.* Jerusalem: Magnes Press, 1988.

Rokeah, David. "Ben Stara is Ben Pantera: Towards the Clarification of a Philological-Historical Problem." *Tarbiz* 39:1 (1969):9–18.

Rose, H. J. *A Handbook of Greek Literature.* 3d rev. ed. London: Methuen & Co., 1948.

Rosenberg, Alfred. *The Myth of the Twentieth Century: An Evaluation of the Spiritual-Intellectual Confrontations of Our Age.* Torrance, Calif.: Noontide Press, 1982.

Rosenblatt, Samuel. "The Crucifixion of Jesus from the Standpoint of Pharisaic Law." *JBL* 75:4 (1956):315–21.

Rosenthal, E. S., ed. *Yirushalmi Nezekin.* Saul Lieberman, commentator. Jerusalem: Israel Academy of Sciences and Humanities, 1983.

Rosenzweig, Franz. *The Star of Redemption.* Translated by William Hallo. New York: Holt, Rinehart and Winston, 1971.

Ross, J. F. "Wine." In *Interpreter's Dictionary of the Bible,* 4.849–52. New York and Nashville: Abingdon, 1962.

Rotenberg, Meir. *Ha-Pitgamim she-be-Sefer Mishlei.* Tel Aviv: Reshafim, 1983.

Roth, Leon. *Religion and Human Values.* Jerusalem: Magnes Press, 1973.

Saadya Gaon. *The Book of Beliefs and Opinions.* 2 vols. Translated by Samuel Rosenblatt. New Haven: Yale University Press, 1948.

———. *Commentary on the Torah.* Edited and translated by Yoseph Kafih. Jerusalem: Mossad ha-Rav Kook, 1963.

———. *Perush le-Sefer Yetzirah.* Edited by Yosef Kafih. Jerusalem: American Academy for Jewish Research, 1972.

———. *Proverbs.* Edited by Yosef Kafih. Jerusalem: Academy for the Publication of Saadya Gaon, 1966.

———. *Tehillim.* Edited by Yosef Kafih. New York: American Academy for Jewish Research, 1966.

Sadan, Dov. "Avi Avi." In *Publications of the Society for Biblical Research in Israel, in Memory of Zvi Karl* 10, 90–99. Jerusalem: Society for Biblical Research in Israel, 1972.

Safrai, Shemuel. "The Correct Interpretation of Sanhedrin 17a." *Tarbitz* 34 (1964–65):40–42.

———. "Hassidim ve-Anshei Maaseh." In *Zion Jubilee Volume 50: 1935–1985,* 133–54. Jerusalem: Historical Society of Jerusalem, 1985.

Safrai, Shemuel, and David Flusser. "The Slave of Two Masters." *Immanuel* 6 (1976):30–33.

Safrai, Shemuel, and Menachem Stern, eds. *The Jewish People in the First Century: Historical Geography, Political History, Social, Cultural and Religious Life and Institutions*. 2 vols. Philadelphia: Fortress Press, 1974–76.

Saldarini, Anthony J. *Avot de Rabbi Nathan: Version B*. Leiden: E. J. Brill, 1975.

Samoscz, David. *Aggadot Shoshanim*, Breslau, 1827. In *Anthologia Hebraica: Poemata Selecta*. Vol. 2. Edited by A. M. Haberman. Jerusalem: Rubin Mass, 1965.

Samuel, Maurice. *The Great Hatred*. New York: Knopf, 1941.

Sanders, E. P. "Defending the Indefensible." *JBL* 110:3 (1991):463–77.

———. *Jesus and Judaism*. Philadelphia: Fortress Press, 1985.

———. *Jewish Law from Jesus to the Mishnah: Five Studies*. Philadelphia: Trinity Press International, 1990.

———. *Judaism: Practice and Belief 63 BCE–66 CE*. Philadelphia: Trinity Press International, 1992.

Sanders, James A. *The Dead Sea Psalms Scroll*. Ithaca, N.Y.: Cornell University Press, 1967.

———. *From Sacred Story to Sacred Text*. Philadelphia: Fortress Press, 1987.

———. "A Multivalent Text: Psalm 151:3–4 Revisited." In *Hebrew Annual Review* 8, edited by Reuben Aharoni, 167–84. Columbus: Ohio State University Press, 1984

Sandler, Peretz. "On the Problem of PRD''S and Quadrilateral System." In *Sefer E. Urbach*, edited by A. Biram, 222–35. Jerusalem: Kiryat Sefer, 1955.

Sartre, Jean Paul. *Being and Nothingness: An Essay on Phenomenological Ontology*. Translated by Hazel E. Barnes. New York: Philosophical Library, 1956.

Sassoon, Suleiman David, ed. *Sefer Moshav Zeqenim al ha-Torah*. London: self-published, 1959.

Satanover, Haim. *Devar Hokhma*. Lemberg, 1835.

Savar, Moshe. *Mikhlol ha-Ma'amarim ve-ha-Pitgamim*. 3 vols. Jerusalem: Mossad ha-Rav Kook, 1980.

Schalit, Abraham. *Hordus ha-Melekh: ha-Ish u-Paolav* (Herod the King: The Man and His Achievements). Jerusalem: Mossad Bialik, 1964.

Schechter, Solomon. *Aspects of Rabbinic Theology*. New York: Schocken Books, 1909, 1961.

———. *Avot de-Rabbi Natan*. Frankfort: ha-Motzia Leor, 1887.

———. *Studies in Judaism.* 2nd series. Philadelphia: Jewish Publication Society, 1908.

Schiffman, Lawrence. "New Light on the Pharisees." *Bible Review* (June 1992):30–33, 54.

Schillebeeckx, Edward. *Jesus: An Experiment in Christology.* New York: Seabury, 1979.

Schiller, Friedrich. *Essays Aesthetical and Philosophical.* London: George Bell and Sons, 1905.

Schneemelcher, Wilhelm, ed. *New Testament Apocrypha.* Volume I: *Gospels and Related Writings.* Translated by R. McL. Wilson. Louisville, Ky.: Westminster/John Knox, 1991.

Scholem, Gershom. *Das Buch Bahir.* 2nd ed. Darmstadt: Wissenschaftliche Buchgesellschaft, Leipzig, 1923, reprint 1980.

———. *Jewish Gnosticism, Merkavah Mysticism, and Talmudic Tradition.* New York: Jewish Theological Seminary, 1965.

———. *Major Trends in Jewish Mysticism.* New York: Schocken, 1965.

———. *The Messianic Idea in Judaism and Other Essays on Jewish Spirituality.* New York: Schocken, 1971.

———. *On the Kabbalah and Its Symbolism.* New York: Schocken, 1965.

Schreiber, Moses. *Responsa.* 6 vols. New York: Grossman's, 1958.

Schwarz, Robert C. "What the Thunder Said: The Desert Fathers and Mothers on Compassion." *Sewanee Theological Review* 35:2 (1992):139–57.

Schwarzbaum, Haim. *The Mishle Shu'alim (Fox Fables) of Rabbi Berechiah ha-Naqdan.* Kiron: Institute for Jewish and Arab Folklore Research, 1979.

———. "Talmudic-Midrashic Affinities of Some Aesopic Fables." In *Essays in Greco-Roman and Related Talmudic Literature,* edited by Harry Fischel, 425–42. New York: Ktav, 1977.

Schweizer, Eduard. *The Good News According to Matthew.* Translated by David Green. Atlanta: John Knox Press, 1975.

Scolnicov, Samuel. *Heracliti et Parmenides.* Jerusalem: Mossad Bialik, 1988.

Scott, Bernard Brandon. *Hear Then the Parable: A Commentary on the Parables of Jesus.* Minneapolis: Fortress Press, 1989.

———. *Jesus, Symbol-Maker for the Kingdom.* Philadelphia: Fortress Press, 1981.

Scott, R. B. Y. *Proverbs/Ecclesiastes.* Anchor Bible. Garden City, N.Y.: Doubleday, 1965.

Sefer Ben-Sirah: Text, Concordance and Analysis of Vocabulary. Jerusalem: Academy for the Hebrew Language, 1973.

Segal, Alan F. *Two Powers in Heaven: Early Rabbinic Reports about Christianity and Gnosticism.* Leiden: E. J. Brill, 1977.

Segal, Ben Zion. *The Ten Commandments as Reflected in Tradition and Literature Throughout the Ages.* Jerusalem: Magnes Press, 1985.

Segal, Moshe Zvi. *Sefer Ben-Sirah ha-Shalem.* Jerusalem: Mossad Bialik, 1959.

Sellin, Ernst, and Georg Fohrer. *Introduction to the Old Testament.* Nashville, Tenn.: Abingdon, 1968.

Seneca. *Ad Lucilium Epistulae Morales.* 3 vols. Translated by Richard Gummere. Loeb Classical Library, 1979.

————. "On Anger." *Moral Essays.* 3 vols. Translated by John W. Basore. Loeb Classical Library, 1970.

Setton, Kenneth M., ed. *A History of the Crusades.* 2 vols. to date. Madison: University of Wisconsin, 1969–.

Sextus Empiricus. *Against the Mathematicians (Against the Physicists).* Vol. 3. Translated by R. G. Bury. Loeb Classical Library, 1935.

Shapira, Judah Loew (Frankfurter). *Ha-Rekhasim le-Viq'ah* ("The Steep Shall Be Made Accessible"). Vilna: Romm, 1888.

Shaw, George Bernard. *Androcles and the Lion/Overruled/Pygmalion.* London: Constable & Co., 1930.

Sherwin-White, A. N. *Roman Society and Roman Law in the New Testament.* Oxford: Clarendon Press, 1963.

Shilat, Izhak. *Haqdamot ha-Rambam la-Mishnah.* Jerusalem: Birkhat Moshe, 1992.

Shinan, Avigdor. *The World of the Aggadah.* Tel Aviv: MOD Books, 1990.

Siker, Jeffrey. "First to the Gentiles: A Literary Analysis of Luke 4:16–30." *JBL* 3:1 (1992):73–90.

Silbermann, A. M., ed. *Chumash with Targum Onkelos, Haphtoroth and Rashi's Commentary.* 5 vols. Jerusalem: Silbermann Family, 1934.

Silverman, Morris, trans. *High Holiday Prayer Book, for Rosh ha-Shanah and Yom Kippur.* Hartford: Prayer Book Press for the United Synagogues of America, 1951.

Simcox, Carroll E. *The First Gospel: Its Meaning and Message.* Greenwich, Conn.: Seabury, 1963.

Simon, Ernst. "The Neighbor (*Re'a*) Whom We Shall Love." In *Modern Jewish Ethics*, edited by Marvin Fox, 29–61. Columbus: Ohio State University Press, 1975.

Simon, Uri. *Four Approaches to the Book of Psalms: From Saadiah Gaon to Abraham ibn Ezra.* Albany, N.Y.: State University of New York Press, 1991.

Simon, Uriel. "The Religious Significance of the *Peshat*." Translated by Edward L. Greenstein. *Tradition* 23:2 (1988):41–63.

Singer, Simeon, trans. *The Authorised Daily Prayer Book of the United Hebrew Congregations of the British Empire*. 15th edition. Revised by J. H. Hertz; notes by Israel Abrahams. London: Eyre and Spottiswodde Ltd., 1935.

Smith, Agnes Lewis. *A Translation of the Four Gospels from the Syriac of the Sinaitic Palimpsest*. London: C. J. Clay and Sons, 1896.

Smith, Morton. *Tannaitic Parallels to the Gospels*. Philadelphia: SBL, 1951.

Sokoloff, Michael. *A Dictionary of Jewish Palestinian Aramaic*. Ramat Gan: Bar-Ilan University Press, 1990.

———. *The Targum to Job from Qumran Cave XI*. Ramat Gan: Bar-Ilan University Press, 1974.

Solomon, Ann M. Vater. "Fable." In *Saga, Legend, Tale, Novella, Fable*, edited by George W. Coats, 114–25. Sheffield, England: JSOT, 1985.

Solomon, Norman. *The Analytic Movement: Hayyim Soloveitchik and His Circle*. Atlanta: Scholars Press, 1993.

Soloveitchik, Joseph B. "The Lonely Man of Faith." *Tradition* 7:2 (1965):5–67.

Span, Salomon. *Aesopi Fabulae*. Jerusalem: Mossad Bialik, 1984.

Spanier, Arthur. "Stilkritisches zum juedischen Gebet." *MGWJ* 30 (1936):339–50.

Sperber, Alexander, ed. *The Bible in Aramaic Based on Old Manuscripts and Printed Texts*. Vol. 1: *The Targum of Onkelos to the Torah*. Leiden: E. J. Brill, 1959.

———. *The Bible in Aramaic Based on Old Manuscripts and Printed Texts*. Vol. 2: *The Former Prophets According to Targum Jonathan*. Leiden: E. J. Brill, 1959.

———. *The Bible in Aramaic Based on Old Manuscripts and Printed Texts*. Vol. 4-B: *The Targum and the Hebrew Bible*. Leiden: E. J. Brill, 1973.

———. *The Prophets According to the Codex Reuchlinianus*. Leiden: E. J. Brill, 1969.

Sperber, Daniel. *Dictionary of Greek and Latin Legal Terms in Rabbinic Literature*. Tel Aviv: Bar-Ilan University Press, 1984.

Sperber, Shemuel. *Ma'amarot*. Jerusalem: Mossad ha-Rav Kook, 1978.

Sperling, Harry, and Maurice Simon, trans. *The Soncino Zohar*. 5 vols. London: Soncino Press, 1933, reprint 1956.

Spiegel, Shalom. "On Medieval Hebrew Poetry." In *The Jews: Their Religion and Culture*, 4th ed., edited by Louis Finkelstein, 82–119. New York: Schocken, 1949, 1971.

Stein, Menachem (Edmond). *Ben Tarbut Israel ve-Tarbut Yavvan ve-Roma* (The Relationship between Jewish, Greek and Roman Cultures). Ramat Gan: Massada, 1970.

———. *Philo the Alexandrian*. Warsaw: Stiebel, 1937.

Stein, Siegfried. "The Concept of the 'Fence': Observations on its Origin and Development." In *Studies in Jewish Religious and Intellectual History*, edited by Siegfried Stein and Raphael Lowe, 301–29. University, Ala.: University of Alabama Press, 1979.

Steinberg, Milton. *As a Driven Leaf*. New York: Behrman House, 1939.

Steinsaltz, Adin. *The Essential Talmud*. Translated by Chaya Galai. N.p.: Bantam Books, 1976.

———. *Midrash ha-Gadol va-Yiqra*. Jerusalem: Mossad ha-Rav Kook, 1976.

———. *Talmud Bavli*. 23 vols. to date. Jerusalem: Israel Institute for Talmudic Publications. 1984–93.

———. *The Talmud: The Steinsaltz English Edition*. 6 vols. to date. New York: Random House,1989–91.

Stendahl, Krister. *The School of St. Matthew and Its Use of the Old Testament*. Philadelphia: Fortress Press, 1968.

Stern, David. "Midrash and the Language of Exegesis: A Study of Vayikra Rabbah, Chapter 1." In *Midrash and Literature*, edited by Geoffrey H. Hartman and Sanford Budick, 105–24. New Haven: Yale University Press, 1986.

Stern, Menahem, ed. *Greek and Latin Authors on Jews and Judaism:* Vol. 1: *From Herodotus to Plutarch*. Jerusalem: Israel Academy of Sciences and Humanities, 1976.

Stevenson, Jed. "When Jesus Was Betrayed, What Coins Did Judas Iscariot Receive?" *The New York Times*, April 15, 1990.

Strack, Hermann L. *Introduction to the Talmud and Midrash*. New York: Atheneum, 1983.

Strashun, Matityahu. *Selected Writings*. Jerusalem: Mossad ha-Rav Kook, 1969.

Suetonius. *The Lives of the Caesars*. 2 vols. Translated by John C. Rolfe. Loeb Classical Library, 1970.

Tabor, James D. *Things Unutterable: Paul's Ascent to Paradise in its Greco-Roman, Judaic, and Early Christian Contexts*. Lanham, Md.: University Press of America, 1986.

Talmage, Frank. "Apples of Gold: The Inner Meaning of Sacred Texts in Medieval Judaism." In *Jewish Spirituality from the Bible through the Middle Ages*, edited by Arthur Green, 313–55. New York: Crossroad, 1989.

———. "Christian Exegesis in the Middle Ages." In *Encyclopedia Miqrait*, 8.714–22. Jerusalem: Mossad Bialik, 1982.

———. *The Commentaries on Proverbs of the Kimhi Family*. Jerusalem: Magnes Press, 1990.

Talmon, Shemaryahu. *The World of Qumran from Within*. Jerusalem: Magnes Press, 1989.

Talmud Yerushalmi. Venice ed. of 1520. Jerusalem: Hotza'at Sefarim, 1969.

Tanner, Kathryn E. "Theology and the Plain Sense." In *Scriptural Authority and Narrative Interpretation*, edited by Garrett Green. Philadelphia: Fortress Press, 1987.

Taubes, Chaim Zvi, ed. *Otzar ha-Geonim on Sanhedrin*. Jerusalem: Mossad ha-Rav Kook, 1966.

Taylor, Charles. *Sayings of the Jewish Fathers*. 2 vols. Cambridge: Cambridge University Press, 1897.

Tertullian. *Adversus Marcionem*. 2 vols. Translated by Ernest Evans. Oxford: Clarendon Press, 1972.

———. *Apologetic Works*. Translated by Rudolph Arbesmann, Sister Emily Joseph Daly, and Edwin A. Quain. New York: Fathers of the Church, 1950.

———. *Tertullian's Treatise on the Incarnation*. Translated by Ernest Evans. London: SPCK, 1956. (Also cited as "De Carne Christi," Migne, *Patrologiae cursus completus*, Patrologiae latinae 2.806.)

Theodor, J., and Chanok Albeck. *Midrash Bereshit Rabbah*. 3 vols. Jerusalem: Wahrmann, 1965.

Third Jubilee Bible of the British and Foreign Bible Society. Great Britain: British and Foreign Bible Society, 1954.

Thirty Nine Articles of Religion. *The Book of Common Prayer* (1979), 867–76.

Thoma, Clemens, and Michael Wyschogrod, eds. *Parable and Story in Judaism and Christianity*. New York: Paulist Press, 1989.

Thomas, D. M. *The White Hotel*. New York: Viking, 1981.

Thompson, Stith. *Motif-Index of Folk-Literature: A Classification of Narrative Elements in Folktales, Ballads, Myths, Fables, Mediaeval Resources, Exempla, Fabliaux, Jest-books, and Local Legends*. Rev. and enl. ed. 6 vols. Bloomington: Indiana University Press, 1955–58.

Throckmorton, Burton H., ed. *Gospel Parallels*. 2nd ed. Toronto, New York, and Edinburgh: Thomas Nelson & Sons, 1966.

Tigay, Jeffrey H. "On the Term Phylacteries (Matt. 23:5)." *HTR* 72 (1979):45–53.

Torah Temimah. 5 vols. Edited by Baruch HaLevi Epstein. Vilna, 1904; reprint, Tel Aviv, 1955.

Torcszyner (Tur-Sinai), Harry. *Mishlei Shelomo* (The Proverbs of Solomon). Tel Aviv: Yavneh, 1947.

——. "The Riddle in the Bible." *HUCA* (NS) 1 (1924):125–49.

Townsend, George Fyler, trans. *Aesop's Fables*. Garden City, N.Y.: Doubleday, 1968.

Townsend, John. "How Can Late Rabbinic Texts Inform Biblical and Early Christian Studies?" *Shofar*, 6:1 (1987), 26–32.

——. *Midrash Tanhuma Translated into English with Introduction, Indices and Brief Notes*. Vol. 1. Hoboken, N.J.: Ktav, 1989.

Toy, Crawford H. *A Critical and Exegetical Commentary on The Book of Proverbs*. New York: Scribner's, 1899.

Trei Asar (The Twelve Minor Prophets). Vol. 1: A Commentary on Hosea, Joel, Amos, Obadiah, and Jonah. Vol. 2: A Commentary on Micah, Nahum, Habakkuk, Zephaniah, Haggai, Zachariah, Malachi. The Daat Miqra Series. Jerusalem: Mossad ha-Rav Kook, 1970–73.

Trench, Richard Chenevix. *On the Lessons in Proverbs, Being the Substance of Lectures Delivered to Young Men's Societies at Portsmouth and Elsewhere*. New York: Redfield, 1858.

Tsaferis, B., E. Melidonis, and E. Kessin. "What Became of Ancient Capernaum?" *Christian News From Israel* 27:2 (1979):74–77.

Tur-Sinai (Torcszyner), Naphtali H. (Harry). *Sefer Iyyov* (The Book of Job). Jerusalem: Rubin Mass, 1972.

Twersky, Isadore. *Introduction to the Code of Maimonides (Mishneh Torah)*. New Haven: Yale University Press, 1980.

——. "Joseph ibn Kaspi: Portrait of a Medieval Jewish Intellectual." In *Studies in Medieval Jewish History and Literature*, edited by Isadore Twersky, 231–57. Cambridge: Harvard University Press, 1979.

——. *A Maimonides Reader*. New York: Behrman House, 1972.

Tzintz, David Leib. *Gedulat Yehonatan* (The Greatness of R. Jonathan Eybeshuetz). Petrokov, 1934.

Ullendorf, Edward. "Thought Categories in the Hebrew Bible." In *Studies in Rationalism, Judaism and Universalism In Memory of Leon Roth*, edited by Raphael Loewe, 273–88. London: Routledge and Kegan Paul, 1966.

Urbach, Ephraim E. "Ha-Derashah ki-Yesod ha-Halakhah u-Ba'ayat ha-Soferim." *Tarbitz* 7 (1958):166–82; reprinted in *The Period of the Second Temple, The Mishnah, and the Talmud*, vol. 2, 598–606. Jerusalem: Hebrew University Akademon, 1982.

——. *Pitron Torah*. Jerusalem: Magnes Press, 1978.

――――. *The Sages: Their Concepts and Beliefs*. 2 vols. Jerusalem: Magnes Press, 1979.

――――. *The World of the Sages: Collected Studies*. Jerusalem: Magnes Press, 1988.

van der Heide, A. "PARDES: Methodological reflections on the theory of the Four Senses." *JJS* 34 (1983):147–59.

Van Leeuwen, Raymond C. *Context and Meaning in Proverbs 25–27*. Atlanta: Scholars Press, 1988.

Van Voorst, Robert E. *The Ascents of James: History and Theology of a Jewish-Christian Community*. Atlanta: Scholars Press, 1989.

VanderKam, James. "The Dead Sea Scrolls and Early Christianity: Part Two, What They Share." *Bible Review* (February 1992):17–23, 40–41.

Vaugh, John, ed. *Francis and Clare: The Complete Works*. New York: Paulist Press, 1982.

Vermes, Geza. *The Dead Sea Scrolls in English*. Middlesex, England: Penguin Books, 1962.

――――. *Jesus the Jew: A Historian's Reading of the Gospels*. London: SCM Press, 1973.

――――. "Jewish Literature and New Testament Exegesis: Reflections on Methodology." *JJS* 33:1–2 (1982):361–76.

――――. "Jewish Studies and New Testament Interpretation." *JJS* 31:1 (1980):1–17.

Via, Dan Otto. *The Parables: Their Literary and Existential Dimension*. Philadelphia: Fortress Press, 1967.

Visotzky, Burton L. *Midrash Mishle*. New York: Jewish Theological Seminary, 1990.

von Campenhausen, Hans. *The Formation of the Christian Bible*. Philadelphia: Fortress Press, 1972.

von Rad, Gerhard. *Old Testament Theology*. 2 vols. Translated by D. M. G. Stalker. New York: Harper & Row, 1962.

Wacholder, Ben Zion. "David's Eschatological Psalter 11Q Psalms." *HUCA* 59 (1988):23–72.

Wallach, Luitpold. "The Textual History of an Aramaic Proverb." *JBL* 69 (1941):403–15.

Ward, Benedicta. *The Desert of the Heart*. London: Darton, Longman and Todd, 1988.

――――. *The Sayings of the Desert Fathers: The Alphabetical Collection*. London and U.S.: Mowbray and Cistercian Publications, 1975.

Watkins, Calvert. "Indo-European and the Indo-Europeans." In *The American Heritage Dictionary of the English Language*, 3d ed., 2081–89. Boston: Houghton Mifflin, 1992.

Weiler, Gershon. *Mishlei Filosofim* (Philosophical Parables). Tel Aviv: Nahar, 1985.

Weinfeld, Moshe. "The Counsel of the 'Elders' to Rehoboam and Its Implications." *Ma'arav* 3:1 (1982):27–53.

———. *Deuteronomy 1–11*. Anchor Bible. N.Y.: Doubleday, 1991.

Weiser, Alfons. *Die Knechtsgleichnisse der Synoptischen Evangelien*. Munich: Kösel-Verlag, 1971.

Weiss, Isaac Hirsch. "Halakhah, Midrash, Aggadah." In *Dor Dor ve-Doreshav*, 2.173–84. Jerusalem and Tel Aviv: Ziv, n.d..

Werner, Eric. *The Sacred Bridge: Liturgical Parallels in Synagogue and Early Church*. New York: Schocken, 1970.

Wertheimer, Shelomo Aharon. *Batei Midrashot: Twenty Five Midrashim Published for the First Time from Manuscripts Discovered in the Genizoth of Jerusalem and Egypt*. 2nd ed. 2 vols. Jerusalem: Mossad ha-Rav Kook, 1954.

White, Carolline. *Christian Friendship in the Fourth Century*. Cambridge: Cambridge University Press, 1992.

Wilford, John Noble. "The Earliest Wine: Vintage 3500 B.C. and Quite Robust." *The New York Times*, April 30, 1991, B1, B9.

Wilken, Robert. *The Christians as the Romans Saw Them*. New Haven: Yale University Press, 1984.

Williams, James. *Gospel Against Parable*. Sheffield, England: Almond, 1985.

Winter, Paul. *On the Trial of Jesus*. 2nd ed. Edited by T. A. Burkill and Geza Vermes. New York and Berlin: Walter de Gruyter, 1974.

———. "The Trial of Jesus and the Competence of the Sanhedrin." *NTS* 10:4 (1964):494–98.

Wischmeyer, W. "Die Aberkiosinschrift als Grabepigramm." *Jahrbuch für Antike und Christentum* 23 (1980):22–47.

Wolf, Arnold J. "Maimonides on Immortality and the Principles of Judaism." *A Maimonides Reader*, edited by Isidore Twersky. New York: Behrman House, 1972.

Wolfson, Harry Austryn. *Crescas' Critique of Aristotle*. Cambridge: Harvard University Press, 1929.

———. *Philo: Foundations of Religious Philosophy in Judaism, Christianity and Islam*. 2 vols. Cambridge: Harvard University Press, 1947.

Xenophon. *Memorabilia and Oeconomicus*. Translated by E. C. Marchant. Loeb Classical Library, 1953.

Yadin, Yigael. *Tefillin from Qumran (XQ Phyl 1–4)*. Jerusalem: Israel Exploration Society, 1969.

————. *The Temple Scroll*. 3 vols. Jerusalem: Israel Exploration Society, 1983.

Yalqut Shimeoni. Attributed to Shimeon Ashkenazi of Frankfort on Main. 2 vols. Saloniki, 1521–27.

Yalon, Ḥanoch. *Pirqei Lashon*. Jerusalem: Mossad Bialik, 1971.

Yarden, L. *The Tree of Light: A Study of the Menorah, the Seven-branched Lampstand*. London: East and West Library, 1971.

Yaron, Tzvi. *Mishnato shel Rav Kook* (The Philosophy of Rabbi Kook). Jerusalem: Jewish Agency, 1974.

Yedidya Shelomo of Nortzi. *Minḥat Shai*. Vienna, 1824.

Yeḥiel min ha Anavim. *Sefer Ma'alot ha-Middot*. Jerusalem: Eshkol, 1978.

Yellin, David. *Ketavim Nivḥarim: Torat ha-Melitzah be-Tanakh*. Vol. 2 of *Kitvei David Yellin*. Jerusalem: Rubin Mass, 1939.

Yonah ben Avraham of Gerondi. *Perush al Sefer Mishlei* (Commentary to Proverbs). New York: Shulsinger, 1946.

————. *Sefer ha-Yir'a*. In *Arba'a Sifrei Mussar*. New York: Shulsinger, 1943.

Young, Brad H. *Jesus and His Jewish Parables: Rediscovering the Roots of Jesus' Teaching*. New York and Mahwah, N.J.: Paulist Press, 1989.

Zaharopoulos, Dimitri Z. *Theodore of Mopsuestia on the Bible: A Study of His Old Testament Exegesis*. New York: Paulist Press, 1989.

Zeitlin, Solomon. "Bouleuterion and Parhedrion." *JQR* 53 (1962):169–70.

————. "A Life of Yohanan ben Zakkai: A Specimen of Modern Jewish Scholarship." *JQR* 62 (1972):145–55.

Zer-Kavod, Mordecai. "Ḥiddot be-Sefer Mishlei." *Bet Miqra* 64:1 (1976):7–11.

Zer-Kavod, Mordecai, and Judah Kiel, commentators. *Sefer Mishlei* (The Book of Proverbs). The Daat Miqra Series. Jerusalem: Mossad ha-Rav Kook, 1983.

Zevin, Shelomo Yosef. *Ishim ve-Shitot* (Personalities and Approaches). Jerusalem: Bet Hillel, 1979.

Zimmer, Eric. *Rabbi Ḥaim b. R. Bezalel mi-Friedberg*. Jerusalem: Mossad ha-Rav Kook, 1987.

Zlotnick, Dov. *The Tractate "Mourning" (Semaḥot)*. New Haven: Yale University Press, 1966.

Zlotnik, Judah Loew. *Research of the Hebrew Idiom: Sayings of the Wise and of the Commons*. Jerusalem: Darom, 1938.

Zuckermandel, Saul. *Tosephta*. Jerusalem: Wahrmann, 1965.

Zulai, Menachem. *Piyyutei Yannai*. Berlin: Schocken, 1938.

Zunz, Leopold. *Die synagogale Poesie des Mittelalters*. 2 vols. Berlin: Julius Springer, 1855.

———. *Gesammelte Schriften*. 2 vols. Berlin: Louis Gerschel Verlagsbuchhandlung, 1876.

Name Index

Aarne, Antti and Stith Thompson, 153n. 8
Aberbach, Moses and Bernard Grossfeld, 67n. 31
Abrahams, Israel, 45n. 44, 104, 106n. 42
Abramson, Shraga, 13n. 29, 202n. 31, 211n. 53, 285n. 1
Agnon, S. Y., 32n. 15
Albeck, Chanokh, 155n. 14, 208, 297, 300n. 5, 302n. 13
Albright, William Foxwell, 209n. 49
Albright, William Foxwell and C. S. Mann, 63n. 20, 176n. 64, 185n. 92
Alexander, P. S., xii
Allegro, John, 300n. 10
Allen, Willoughby, 257n. 2, 261n. 11
Alon, Gedalyahu, 32n. 16, 74n. 49, 75, 157n. 18, 261n. 7, 279n. 64
Altmann, Alexander, 144n. 40
Aminah, Noah, 92n. 16
Arbuthnot, John, 149
Argyle, A. W., 135n. 25
Auerbach, Erich, 15
Aus, Roger David, 66n. 26
Austin, J. L., 98, 122

Bacher, Wilhelm, 35n. 20, 36n. 21, 37n. 24, 47n. 48, 55n. 3, 58n. 9, 63n. 20, 65n. 26, 79n. 62, 82n. 70, 92n. 16, 101n. 31, 122n. 5, 190n. 6, 200nn. 21, 23, 205n. 40, 211n. 51
Baer, Seligman, 105n. 40, 106n. 42, 294n. 1
Bagatti, B., 58n. 7
Bakhtin, Mikhail, 290n. 25
Banitt, Menahem, xv, 4n. 4, 90n. 11, 102n. 33, 289n. 20
Bar-Droma, Joshua, 180n. 75, 298n. 1, 302n. 14

Barnard, Leslie, 151n. 2
Barr, James, 4n. 6, 177n. 68
Beare, Francis, 175n. 59, 178n. 69, 182n. 85, 221n. 4, 226n. 11
Beavis, Mary Ann, 8n. 17, 15, 183n. 86
Bell, James, 93
Ben Yehudah, Eliezer, 102n. 32, 155n. 13, 176n. 62, 201n. 29, 211n. 51, 246n. 53, 251n. 61, 263n. 13, 264n.16, 265n. 19, 273nn. 41, 43, 275n. 50, 289nn. 18, 20
Bennett, Robert and O. C. Edwards, 11n. 24
Bergson, Henri, 15n. 30
Berkovits, Eliezer, 169n. 43, 184n. 90
Berlin, Yeshayah Pick, 32n. 16
Berner, Ulrich, 62n. 18
Bernstein, Leonard, 37n. 25, 129n. 16
Betz, Otto, 61n. 15
Bialik, Hayyim Nahman, 27n. 4, 31, 32n. 16, 80n. 66, 87n. 6, 99–100, 116n. 67, 126n. 10, 127n. 14, 154n. 12, 202n. 32, 203nn. 33–34, 205n. 40, 279n. 63, 285n. 1
Bolle, Menahem, 268n. 27
Bondi, Roberta, 214n. 57
Boswell, John, 30n. 9
Bowen, Murray, 289n. 23
Brand, Yehoshua, 271n. 33
Brandon, S. G. F., 216n. 63
Braude, William, xi
Braude, William and Israel Kapstein, 281n. 66
Brody, Haim and Meir Wiener, 154n. 12
Broner, Esther, 130n. 20
Brooke, George, 101n. 30
Brown, Francis, S. R. Driver, and Charles Briggs, 200n. 21, 289n. 20
Brown, Peter, 33n. 17, 285n. 2

Brown, Raymond, 4n. 6, 11n. 24, 216n. 63, 260n. 6
Brown, Robert McAfee, 152n. 6
Brownlee, William, 153n. 7, 154nn. 9, 11
Bruckstein, Almut Sh., 109n. 49
Brueggemann, Walter, 6n. 12
Buber, Martin, 145
Büchler, Adolph, 42n. 33, 135n. 25, 138n. 31
Bultmann, Rudolph, 226n. 11, 257n. 1, 260n. 6
Burckhardt, Jacob, 82n. 71, 146
Burrows, Millar, 153n. 8

Campbell, Edward, 235n. 31
Carlebach, A., 306n. 20
Carroll, Lewis, 16n. 32, 47n. 50
Cassidy, Richard, 149n. 1, 162n. 30, 180n. 76
Cassuto, Umberto, 70n. 39
Cave, C. H., 19, 94n. 17
Chajes, Hirsch Peretz, 8n. 17
Charles, R. H., xvn. 6, 40n. 30
Charlesworth, James, 42n. 34, 90n. 13, 151n. 3, 240n. 46, 243n. 49
Childs, Brevard, 70n. 39
Ciardi, John, 188n. 2
Cohen, A., 98n. 23, 143n. 37, 268n. 26
Cohen, Chaim, 11n. 25
Cohen, Naomi, 35n. 19, 208n. 48
Cohen, Norman, 161n. 28
Cohen, Shaye, 72n. 43
Cohn, Haim, 216n. 63
Cohn, Joseph, 203n. 34
Cowley, Arthur Ernest, 211n. 51
Cronbach, Abraham, xiiin. 5
Crossan, John Dominic, 3, 116n. 66, 226nn. 11, 12, 257n. 1, 260n. 6
Culbertson, Philip, 3n. 3, 5nn. 7, 11, 6n. 12, 26n. 1, 47nn. 49–50, 135n. 25, 220n. 1, 277n. 61, 288n. 12

D'Angelo, Mary Rose, 4n. 6
Dan, Joseph, 37n. 24, 47n. 49
Dane, Perry, 20n. 40
Danker, Frederick, 100n. 30
Daube, David, 32n. 14, 70n. 39, 71n. 42, 79nn. 63–64, 175n. 58
Davidson, Israel, 13n. 29, 108n. 44, 197n. 16
Davies, W. D., 6n. 12, 179n. 73

Davies, W. D. and Dale Allison, 47n. 49
de Lange, Nicholas, 306n. 21
de Vaux, Roland, 135n. 25
DeJonge, M., 151n. 3
Delitzsch, Franz, 43n. 38, 286
Derrett, J. Duncan, 64n. 24, 162n. 31, 182n. 84, 221n. 3, 223n. 7, 227n. 13
Diels, Hermann, 43n. 39
Dodd, C. H., 129, 226n. 12
Doelger, F. J., 150n. 2
Donski, Samson, 37n. 24, 46n. 46, 112n. 58

Eckardt, Roy, 3, 4n. 6
Ehrentreu, Chanoch, 31n. 12, 32n. 16
Eichrodt, Walther, 70n. 39
Einhorn, Zev Wolf, 31n. 12, 111n. 57
Eisenstein, Judah David, 41n. 32
Elkoshi, Gedaliah, 77n. 59, 98n. 23, 192n. 10, 196nn. 14–15, 201n. 26
Emerson, Ralph Waldo, 119n. 1
Enelow, Hillel Gershom, 47n. 49, 111n. 57, 139n. 35
Englard, Izhak, 66n. 30
Epstein, Abraham, 61n. 15
Evans, Ernest, 159nn. 21, 23
Even-Shoshan, Abraham, 114n. 63, 201n. 28

Falk, Zev, 135n. 25
Faur, Jose, 287, 289
Feinberg, Gerson, 114n. 63
Feldman, Asher, 37n. 24, 43n. 37, 276n. 54, 277n. 57
Finkelstein, Louis, 42n. 33, 81n. 68, 168n. 43, 205n. 39, 300n. 11
Finkelstein, Louis and Haim Shaul Horowitz, 294n. 2
Fischel, Henry, 42n. 34, 81n. 69
Fish, Stanley, 98n. 25, 128
Fishbane, Michael, 70n. 39, 127n. 13
Fitzmyer, Joseph, 17n. 33, 226n. 11, 227n. 14, 228n. 20
Fletcher, Angus, 37n. 24
Flusser, David, 5nn. 8–9, 11, 32n. 16, 37n. 24, 63n. 20, 79n. 63, 83n. 72, 101n. 30, 103, 104n. 39, 119n. 1, 126, 139n. 33, 168nn. 42–43, 174, 183n. 88, 184n. 91, 221n. 3, 223n. 7, 226n. 10, 228n. 21, 230n. 25, 257, 260, 262n. 12, 279n. 64
Frank, Erich, 11n. 25, 88n. 7, 91n. 14, 119n. 1, 229–30

Frankel, Zechariah, 66n. 28
Freud, Sigmund, 130
Friedländer, M., 55n. 3
Friedman, Edwin, 289n. 23
Friedman, Meier, 281n. 66
Friedman, Mordecai, 135n. 25
Fromm, Erich, 11n. 25, 17n. 35, 59n. 10, 66n. 30, 80n. 66, 130n. 20
Fuller, Reginald, 27n. 3, 226n. 11
Funk, Robert, 228n. 20, 258n. 3, 259n. 4
Funk, Robert, Bernard Brandon Scott, and James Butts, 116n. 66

Garland, David, 176n. 64, 177
Gaster, Moses, 29n. 8, 158n. 19
Gaventa, Beverley, 281n. 67
Gavin, Frank, 27n. 3
Gerhardsson, Birger, 51n. 55, 227n. 17
Gesenius, William, 92n. 16, 289n. 19
Ginzberg, Louis, 4n. 4, 27n. 4, 31n. 12, 43n. 39, 72n. 44, 75n. 57, 101n. 30, 144n. 39, 162n. 31, 169n. 43, 196n. 14, 199n. 19, 201nn. 26, 28, 220n. 1, 223n. 30, 236nn. 32, 34–36, 237n. 37, 238nn. 38–40, 239nn. 41–42, 246n. 53, 250nn. 59–60, 264n. 17
Goldin, Judah, 146n. 43, 155n. 14, 189n. 3
Goldschmidt, Daniel, 108n. 44, 289n. 21
Goldziher, Ignaz, 207n. 45
Goodenough, Erwin Russell, 151n. 2, 268n. 25
Gordis, Robert, 97n. 21, 112n. 58, 169n. 43
Gordon, Cyrus, 209n. 49
Gotthold, Miriam, 217n. 64
Gotthold, Zev, 96n. 20, 122n. 6, 129n. 18, 131n. 21, 154n. 10
Goulder, Michael, 17n. 34, 226n. 12
Grant, Robert, 26n. 2
Green, H. Benedict, 258n. 2
Green, William Scott, 46n. 45
Greenberg, Moshe, 131n. 21
Greene, John, 74n. 49
Grintz, I. M., 69n. 36
Gruenwald, Itamar, 37n. 24, 42n. 34, 47n. 49
Guillaumont, A., et al, 228n. 20
Guttmann, Alexander, 66n. 27

Haberman, Avraham Meier, 212n. 54, 240n. 46, 296n. 8
Hailperin, Herman, 37n. 22

Hakham, Amos, 59n. 10, 203n. 34, 220n. 1, 239n. 44
HaLevi, E. E., 32n. 16, 44n. 42, 55n. 4, 61n. 15, 65n. 26, 66n. 28, 76n. 58, 81n. 70, 82n. 71, 116n. 67, 202n. 32, 272n. 38
Halperin, David, 42n. 34
Hammer, Reuven, 104n. 36, 294n. 2
Handford, S. A., 12n. 27, 126n. 10, 197n. 17, 202n. 32
Hanson, R. P. C., 26n. 2
Har-Zahav, Zvi, 92n. 16
Haran, Menachem, 11n. 25, 26n. 1, 37n. 24, 46n. 48, 65n. 25
Harkavy, A., 18n. 36, 28n. 6
Harrelson, Walter, xiiin. 5
Harrington, Daniel, xiin. 3, 95, 106, 135n. 25, 137n. 30, 178, 182n. 83, 183n. 87, 226n. 11, 227n. 13, 283
Hartman, David, 22n. 44, 66n. 30, 169n. 45
Hatch, Edwin and Henry Redpath, 95n. 19, 183n. 86, 271n. 33, 272n. 40
Heinemann, Isaak, 10n. 23, 35n. 19, 47n. 49, 229n. 23
Heinemann, Joseph, 108, 110n. 52
Hellwig, Monica, 11n. 24
Herbert, George, 45n. 44
Herford, R. Travers, xvn. 6, 44n. 42, 58n. 9, 62n. 18, 63, 72n. 43, 73n. 48, 136n. 28, 155n. 14, 169n. 44, 191n. 9, 211n. 51
Hertz, Samson Raphael, 32n. 15
Herzog, Isaac, 61n. 15, 73n. 46
Heschel, Abraham Joshua, 130n. 20
Higger, Michael, 138n. 32
Hildesheimer, Ezriel, 190n. 6
Hill, David, 136n. 26, 176n. 61, 178n. 69, 258n. 2, 260n. 6
Himmelfarb, Martha, 37n. 24
Hirsch, Samson Raphael, 99n. 26, 109n. 50, 176n. 60, 205n. 39
Hoffman, David Tsevi, 109n. 51, 249n. 57
Hopcke, Robert, 130
Horowitz, Chaim Shaul and Israel Avraham Rabin, 215n. 62
Houlden, J. L., 110n. 55, 111n. 56
Huntington, William Reed, 230n. 24

Ibrahim, Youssef, 156n. 15
Idel, Moshe, 89n. 10
Idelson, A. Z., 111n. 56

Jacobson, B. S., 35n. 20, 81nn. 68, 70, 84n. 74, 98n. 22, 108n. 45, 109n. 49, 192n. 10

Jaeger, Werner, 126n. 10
Jastrow, Marcus, 9n. 19, 36n. 21, 47n. 49,
    61n. 15, 63n. 20, 66nn. 27, 30, 75n. 53,
    76n. 57, 98n. 23, 114n. 63, 155n. 13,
    158n. 20, 160nn. 26–27, 176n. 62, 177n.
    66, 178, 181n. 80, 201n. 29, 261nn. 7,
    11, 263n. 13, 264nn. 15–16, 265n. 19,
    269n. 29, 271n. 31, 272n. 39, 273nn. 41,
    44, 275n. 50, 289nn. 17, 20
Jaynes, Julian, 272n. 40
Jeremias, Joachim, 5n. 11, 95, 116, 135n.
    25, 226n. 12
Johnson, Luke Timothy, 226n. 11
Johnson, Marshall, 235n. 31, 237n. 37,
    238n. 38, 239n. 43
Jülicher, Adolf, 94n. 17
Jung, Carl, 130

Kahana, Kalman, 31n. 12
Kahane, Avraham, 287n. 7, 289
Kahle, Paul, 87n. 5
Kahler, Erich, 82n. 71
Kamin, Sarah, 195n. 13, 199n. 20
Kaminka, Aharon, 65n. 26
Kant, Immanuel, 44n. 42
Kaplan, Aryeh, 91n. 14
Kasher, Menachem, 36n. 21, 43n. 39, 81n.
    68, 82n. 70, 83n. 73, 161n. 28, 176n. 63,
    196n. 15, 300n. 9
Kassovsky, Chayim Yehoshua, 176n. 62,
    177n. 66
Katz, Saul, 203n. 34
Katzenellenbogen, Shaul, 111n. 57
Kee, Howard Clark, 125n. 10, 280
Kehati, Pinhas, 32n. 16, 72n. 45, 75nn. 53,
    56–57, 295n. 7, 300n. 8
Kelly, J. N. D., 11n. 24
Kelner, L., 156n. 16
Kermode, Frank, 48
Kiel, Judah, 275n. 50
Kierkegaard, Søren, 30n. 9, 71n. 42, 86,
    223n. 7
King, George, 207n. 44, 211
Kipling, Rudyard, 106n. 43
Kirchan, Elhanan, 29n. 8
Kister, Menachem, xiin. 3
Klausner, Joseph, 8n. 17, 55n. 3, 57, 58n.
    9, 62n. 17, 67n. 33
Klein, Shemuel, 61n. 16
Kloppenborg, John, 228n. 18

Klosterman, Erich, 226n. 11
Koester, Helmut, 5n. 9
Kohut, Alexander, 4n. 4, 62n. 18, 75n. 53,
    92n. 16, 102n. 32, 114n. 63, 155n. 13,
    164n. 34, 170n. 47, 171n. 49, 176n. 62,
    178n. 69, 185n. 93, 196n. 14, 210n. 51,
    211n. 52, 263n. 13, 265n. 19, 273nn. 41–
    43, 275n. 50, 287n. 10, 289nn. 19, 22,
    300n. 11
Kook, Abraham Isaac ha-Kohen, 217n. 64
Kosmala, Hans, 126n. 12
Krauss, Shemuel, 154n. 10, 164n. 34, 166n.
    40, 171n. 50
Kugel, James and Rowan Greer, 26n. 1
Kugel, James, 122n. 5
Kümmel, Werner Georg, 27n. 3
Kutscher, Eduard Yechezkel, 4n. 6, 268n.
    27

Lachs, Samuel Tobias, xiin. 3, 32n. 14,
    155n. 13
Landes, G. M., 8nn. 16–17, 11nn. 25–26,
    119n. 1
Lapide, Pinchas, 8n. 17
Lasine, Stuart, 31n. 11
Lauren, Paul Gordon, 183n. 86
Lauterbach, Jacob, 169n. 43, 300n. 11
Layton, Bentley, 151n. 2, 228n. 20
Lazarus-Yafeh, Hava, 199n. 19
Lehmann, Manfred, 307n. 22
Lerner, Myron, 4n. 6
Levine, Amy-Jill, 235n. 31
Levine, Lee, 4n. 4
Levy, J., 287n. 9
Lewis, Charleton and Charles Short, 4n. 4,
    70n. 40, 134n. 23, 201n. 28, 251n. 61
Lichtenstein, Hans, 300n. 11, 301n. 12
Liddell, Henry and Robert Scott, 42n. 36,
    71n. 42, 75n. 53, 114n. 63, 164n. 34,
    176n. 65, 261n. 11, 266nn. 21–22,
    271nn. 31–32, 272n. 40, 289n. 19
Lieberman, Saul, 31n. 12, 35n. 19, 46n. 45,
    55n. 3, 68n. 35, 72n. 43, 73n. 47, 75,
    102n. 34, 108n. 47, 123n. 7, 143n. 37,
    157n. 18, 190n. 6
Lindars, Barnabas, 183n. 86
Lindbeck, George, 48
Lindsey, Robert, 129n. 18, 262n. 12
Liver, J., 176n. 63, 300n. 10
Loewe, Raphael, 7n. 15, 48n. 51

Loewe, W. H., 36n. 21, 55nn. 3–4, 57n. 6, 62n. 18, 63n. 20
Lohfink, Norbert, 221n. 2
Lowe, Malcolm, 221n. 3

Maarsen, Isaac, 138n. 33, 200n. 24
Mack, Hananel, 13n. 28, 36n. 21, 69n. 37, 89n. 10, 90n. 13
Maier, Johann, 76n. 57
Mandel, Avraham, 166n. 39, 304n. 16
Mantel, Hugo, 216n. 63
Manuel, Frank and Fritzie, 42n. 35
Margolis, Max, 200n. 21, 201n. 28
Margulies, Mordecai, 111n. 57, 158n. 20, 171n. 50, 172n. 52, 176n. 63, 178n. 69, 279n. 64
Margulies, Reuven, 36n. 21, 48n. 51, 67n. 31, 91n. 14
Marino, Luis Diez, 242n. 48
Marx, Tzvi, 87n. 6
Matheson, P. E., 139n. 34
Mattingly, Harold, 170n. 46
McKane, William, 11n. 25, 286
Meier, John, 3, 54n. 2, 55n. 3, 178n. 70, 226n. 11, 284
Melamed, Ezra Zion, 36n. 21, 122n. 5, 287nn. 9–10
Meshorer, Yaakov, 181n. 79, 182n. 81, 299n. 2, 303n. 15, 304n. 17
Metzger, Bruce, 262n. 12
Meyer, Ben, 5n. 11
Meyer, Marvin, 119n. 1
Meyers, Carol, 65n. 25
Meyers, Eric and James Strange, 182n. 83
Meyers, Eric, 63n. 21
Mielziner, Moses, 41n. 33, 69n. 37, 79n. 62
Milavec, Aaron, 4n. 4, 126n. 10, 174n. 55, 221n. 3, 225n. 9
Miller, Robert, 215n. 62, 223n. 7
Milne, A. A., 16n. 32
Mirsky, Aharon, 220n. 1, 230–1, 232n. 28, 233n. 29, 289n. 21, 300n. 4
Mirsky, Samuel Kalman, 31n. 12
Mitchell, Stephen, 114–7, 129
Montefiore, Hugh, 160n. 25
Morray-Jones, C. R. A., 37n. 24
Morrey, C. R., 151n. 2
Moskovitz, Yehiel Tzvi, 301n. 12
Murray, Robert, 269n. 27, 271n. 30, 272n. 35

Neusner, Jacob, 7, 46n. 47, 55n. 3, 56n. 5, 58n. 9, 66nn. 26, 29, 72n. 43, 97nn. 21–22, 102n. 32, 121n. 4, 197n. 16, 261n. 10
Newman, Barclay and Philip Stine, 116n. 66, 258n. 2, 271n. 32
Nietzsche, Friedrich, 60n. 13
Norden, Eduard, 108

O'Day, Gail, 215n. 62
Oesterley, William Oscar Emil, 226n. 11
Ogden, Schubert, 6n. 13
Orlinsky, Harry, 207n. 46
Ortega y Gasset, José, 21, 134, 137

Pagels, Elaine, 68n. 34
Parsons, Mikael, xiin. 3
Patterson, L., 55n. 3
Pei, Mario, 90n. 11, 98n. 23, 112n. 58, 227n. 14
Perry, Ben Edwin, 8n. 17, 123n. 7, 126n. 10
Petuchowski, Jacob, 8n. 17, 82n. 70
Pines, Shelomo, 5n. 9, 63n. 20
Plummer, A., 262n. 12, 265n. 19
Pokorny, Julius, 72n. 44, 176n. 65, 288n. 10
Pool, David de Sola, 79n. 63, 227n. 13
Porten, Bezalel and Jonas Greenfield, 211n. 51
Pritchard, James, 209n. 49
Pusey, Philip Edward, 135n. 25

Qimron, Elisha and John Strugnell, 169n. 43
Quasten, Johannes, xiin. 2, 26n. 2, 159nn. 21, 23, 306n. 21

Rabbinowicz, R. N. H., 62n. 18, 91n. 15, 154n. 12, 203n. 34
Rabinowitz, Louis, 48n. 51
Reider, Joseph, 289n. 20
Reines, Ch. W., 81n. 70
Ricoeur, Paul, 97
Rivlin, Asher, 100n. 28
Robinson, James, 119n. 1
Rofe, Alexander, 71n. 41
Rokeah, David, 55n. 3
Rose, H. J., 10n. 23
Rosenberg, Alfred, 55n. 3
Rosenblatt, Samuel, 216n. 63
Rosenthal, E. S., 116n. 67
Rosenzweig, Franz, 109
Roth, Leon, 81n. 70, 82n. 72, 168n. 43

Sadan, Dov, 4n. 6
Safrai, Shemuel, 4n. 5, 61n. 15, 68n. 36,
    82n. 71, 126–7, 181n. 78
Saldarini, Anthony, 155n. 14, 157n. 17
Samoscz, David, 296n. 8
Samuel, Maurice, 81n. 70
Sanders, E. P., 5n. 11, 32n. 14, 58n. 8, 68n.
    36, 74n. 49, 216n. 63
Sanders, James, 5n. 10
Sanders, James, 152n. 6, 241n. 47
Sandler, Peretz, 37n. 24
Savar, Moshe, 13n. 29, 98n. 23
Schalit, Abraham, 162n. 29, 181n. 77, 182n.
    83
Schechter, Solomon, 8n. 17, 169n. 43,
    183n. 86
Schiffman, Lawrence, 43n. 39
Schillebeeckx, Edward, 4n. 6
Schiller, Frederick, 14–5
Schneemelcher, Wilhelm, 119n. 1
Scholem, Gershom, 42n. 34, 46nn. 46, 48,
    47n. 49, 89n. 9, 91n. 14, 104n. 39, 281n.
    67
Schüssler Fiorenza, Elizabeth, 73n. 46
Schwarzbaum, Haim, 12n. 27, 13n. 28, 29n.
    7, 123n. 7, 158n. 19
Schweizer, Eduard, 136n. 27, 182, 183
Scott, Bernard Brandon, 17n. 34
Segal, Alan, 42n. 34
Segal, Moshe Zvi, 39n. 27, 40n. 30, 63n. 20,
    240n. 46, 288n. 11, 289n. 19
Sellin, Ernst and Georg Fohrer, 70n. 39
Setton, Kenneth, 85n. 1
Shapira, Judah Loew (Frankfurter), 22n. 43
Shaw, George Bernard, 126n. 11, 136n. 27
Sherwin-White, A. N., 216n. 63
Shippee, Arthur, 37n. 23, 38n. 26
Siker, Jeffrey, 196n. 15
Silverman, Morris, 108n. 44, 220n. 1
Simcox, Carroll, 179n. 73
Simon, Ernst, 82n. 70
Simon, Uri, 49
Singer, Simeon, 29n. 8, 104n. 39, 105nn.
    40–41, 106n. 42, 109n. 51, 110n. 54,
    120n. 2, 191n. 8, 294n. 1
Smith, Agnes, 177n. 66
Sokoloff, Michael, 261n. 11, 288–9
Solomon, Ann, 29n. 7
Solomon, Norman, 73n. 46
Soloveitchik, Joseph, 83, 169n. 45

Span, Salomon, 124, 196n. 14
Spanier, Arthur, 108, 109n. 51
Sperber, Alexander, 87n. 5
Sperber, Daniel, 56n. 5, 110n. 53
Sperber, Shemuel, 31n. 12
Spiegel, Shalom, 50
Stein, Menachem (Edmond), 10n. 23, 143n.
    37, 203n. 33
Stein, Siegfried, 18n. 37, 43, 44n. 42, 45n.
    43
Steinberg, Milton, 4n. 4
Steinsaltz, Adin, 42n. 34, 46n. 46, 122n. 5,
    136n. 28, 160n. 27, 227n. 13, 243n. 50,
    264n. 17
Stern, David, 84n. 74, 221n. 3
Stern, Menahem, 39n. 29, 74n. 49, 160n.
    25
Stevenson, Jed, 303n. 15
Strack, Hermann, 41n. 33, 69n. 37, 79n.
    62, 111n. 57, 155n. 14, 191n. 8, 249n. 57
Strashun, Matityahu, 42n. 33

Tabor, James, 42n. 34
Talmage, Frank, 22n. 44, 37n. 24
Talmon, Shemaryahu, 240n. 46
Tanner, Kathryn, 48n. 51
Taubes, Chaim Zvi, 28n. 6
Taylor, Charles, 32n. 16, 102n. 32, 155n.
    14, 169nn. 44–45, 191n. 9, 211n. 51
Theodor, J. and Chanokh Albeck, 46n. 46,
    81n. 70, 196n. 14, 199n. 20
Thirty Nine Articles of Religion, 27n. 5
Thoma, Clemens and Michael Wyschogrod,
    5n. 11
Thomas, D. M., 130n. 20
Thompson, Stith, 29n. 7, 123n. 7, 153n. 8,
    158n. 19
Tigay, Jeffrey, 208n. 47
Torczsyner, Harry. *See* Tur-Sinai, Naphtali
Townsend, George Fyler, 124
Townsend, John, xiin. 3
Trench, Richard Chenevix, 18–9
Tsaferis B. et al., 182n. 83
Tur-Sinai, Naphtali H., 268n. 27, 287n. 8
Twersky, Isadore, 104n. 37, 122n. 5
Tzintz, David Leib, 59n. 13

Ullendorf, Edward, 169n. 43
Urbach, E. E., 31n. 12, 58n. 9, 82nn. 70–
    72, 102n. 32, 146n. 43, 166n. 40, 200n.
    22, 278n. 62

van der Heide, A., 37n. 24
van Voorst, Robert, 58n. 9
Vermes, Geza, xi, xii, 4n. 5, 153n. 7
Voltaire, 143
von Campenhausen, Hans, 26n. 1
von Rad, Gerhard, 70n. 39

Wacholder, Ben Zion, 240n. 46
Wallach, Luitpold, 62n. 18, 64n. 22
Watkins, Calvert, 87n. 4
Weiler, Gershon, 39n. 29
Weinfeld, Moshe, 35n. 19, 183n. 86, 287
Weiser, Alfons, 224n. 8
Weiss, Isaac Hirsch, 31n. 12
Werner, Eric, 89n. 9
White, Carolline, 203n. 32
Wilford, John Noble, 268n. 25
Wilken, Robert, 285n. 2
Williams, James, 15n. 30
Wischmeyer, W., 159n. 23

Wolfson, Harry Austryn, 10n. 23, 38n. 27,
    51n. 55, 287n. 9

Yadin, Yigael, 76n. 57, 208n. 48
Yalon, Hanoch, 32n. 16, 33n. 17, 46n. 45,
    70n. 40, 288n. 15
Yarden, L., 65n. 25
Yaron, Tzvi, 217n. 64
Yellin, David, 98n. 22
Young, Brad, xiin. 3, xiiin. 4, 5n. 11, 55n.
    3, 116n. 66, 221n. 3, 226n. 11

Zeitlin, Solomon, 72n. 43, 75n. 53
Zer-Kavod, Mordecai, 189n. 4
Zer-Kavod, Mordecai and Judah Kiel, 287n.
    6, 289n. 20
Zevin, Shelomo Yosef, 300n. 9
Zlotnick, Dov, 138n. 32
Zlotnik, Judah Loew, 196n. 15
Zulai, Menachem, 106n. 42
Zunz, Leopold, 205n. 40, 250n. 59

Subject Index

"A word to the wise," 97–8, 142–3, 290

Abba, 4, 55, 61n. 15, 109, 128–9, 214, 217; Father in Heaven, 4n. 6, 55, 109, 172, 183–5

Absurdity, 187–8, 193–4, 213, 262

Admoni (ruddy), 247, 250–1

Aggadah, 5, 27, 31–3, 146, 189n. 3

Agrapha, 54

Aim le-miqra, 92. *See also* Massoret

Alef, prefixed, 90n. 12

Aleinu le-Shabeah, hymn, 104–5

Allegory (ke-min homer), 10, 12, 26, 36, 37n. 24, 39, 41, 48, 79, 102, 119, 135, 219, 224–5, 228–9. *See also* Typology

Alphabet, 86–92

Amen, 129

Ariadne's Thread, 112n. 59

Aron (coffin, ark), 232–3

Asseh doheh lo-ta'asseh (directive supercedes prohibitive), 36

Automaton, 142–3

Banquet, 133–4, 136–40, 143, 278–9

Bar-Kokhba revolt, 68, 139n. 33, 157, 166n. 39, 303

Baraita, 41n. 33, 205

Be-dibbur ehad (simultaneous contradictory revelation), 36n. 21

Bet Hillel, 51n. 55, 66n. 27, 87, 156–7, 167n. 41, 267, 303; Bet Shammai, 66n. 27, 87, 167n. 41, 303

"between your eyes," location of, 207–10

Binyan av (archetype), 92

Bittul Torah (invalidation of Torah injunction), 285n. 1

Blasphemy, 216n. 63

Body—as analogy for consonants, 91; as

analogy for words, 121; use in parable, 126n. 10; goof, 91n. 15. *See also* Soul

Bonei hayitz (builders of the wall), 43n. 39

"But I say to you," 31–2, 44

Catena, 100–3, 115–8, 230, 246, 275; Authenticating Catena, 106n. 42, 105–7; Forensic Catena, 108–11; Metaphorical Catena, 107–8; Parabolic Catena, 111–4; Topical Catena, 103–5; of suspicion, 235; Matthean catena, 114–8

Census, 164, 166, 176, 297, 299–302

Charity, 295n. 5

Children as deposit (piqadon), 29–31

Circumcision, 58, 166n. 39; circumcised heart, 260n. 6

Coins, 169–73; rattling, 143n. 37, 181n. 80

Confusion between "eyes" and "teeth," 211–2

Contextuality, 1–24, 54, 83, 92–4, 98, 121, 128–33, 213, 283–4

Covenant, 32, 36, 99, 154n. 10, 221, 224–5, 241, 257, 262n. 12

Culture of the ear, of the eye, 88–9, 92, 98

David, King, 198–9, 231–2, 237–9, 253–4

Death penalty, 215n. 63

Derash (homiletic meaning), 36–7, 47, 49, 64, 190, 274n. 46, 295–6; darshan (homilist), 49

Derekh eretz, defined, 169n. 44

Dimus (dismissed), 55n. 5

Dover (speaker), 290n. 24

Dreams, 114–5, 130

Eighteen Benedictions, 110n. 52

Epicurianism, 142n. 36, 143n. 37

Esoteric (nistar), 4, 9–10, 38–41, 47n. 48, 65, 97–8, 173, 177, 290; gnosis, 11n. 24, 3

Essenes (Dead Sea Sect), 5n. 8, 73, 75n. 57, 103, 127, 152–4, 169n. 43, 300

Etnan zonah (fee of a whore), 72, 78, 236n. 33

Exegetical Rules of R. Eliezer, 111n. 57

Exoteric (nigleh), 4, 9–10, 38–41, 47n. 48, 97–8, 258

Fasting, 12, 258–62, 279–80

Fence, 12, 17–9, 43–5, 221

Fish, 117, 122–3, 126n. 11, 149–61, 180, 182, 184–5; ichthys, 150n. 2, 159n. 23; Jesus Christ as, 159

"Fishers of men," 155n. 13

"Flee from ki'ur (the hideous)," 32, 44n. 41

Followers of Jesus, tension with followers of John the Baptist, 260n. 6, 261n. 10; Johannites, 260–1, 279–80

Fox-fables, 18n. 36, 28

Friend, 65, 84n. 74, 123, 192n. 10

Galilean linguistic consciousness, 290n. 25

Gematria, 47, 90n. 13, 144–5, 294–5

"Go out and see" (empirical teaching), 72. *See also* Maieutic Method

God—actional attributes, 109–11; bound by same norms as humanity, 34–5, 44; adding to words of, 44n. 41; Divine ego, 144n. 40; Yode'ai shimkha, 109n. 51; husband as metaphor for, 34–36, 135–6. *See also* Abba

Golden apple in silver filagree, 9–10, 19, 42n. 37, 46n. 45, 90n. 12, 285–92

Golden Rule, 81n. 69

Golgotha, 164n. 33

Gordian Knot, 113n. 60

Gossip, 291n. 27

Gradus ad parnassum, 228

Greatest principle in the Torah (kelal gadol ba-Torah), 80–4

Hada hu dekativ (this is what is meant when it is written), 107

Halakhah, 4–6, 27–37, 53, 57, 68–72, 77–9, 82–4, 99–100, 146n. 43, 173–9, 212–6, 236–7, 248, 263, 289n. 20, 290–2; as aggadah, 33–6; midrash halakhah, 8, 21,

31n. 12, 68–72; halakhah of Jesus not preserved, 5, 58, 68n. 36

Hasmonean corruption, 65, 73–4, 77

Hassidim, 4, 32n. 16, 61n. 15, 66

Hear: nishm'ah (hear, obey), 96, 98–9; izzen, 113–4; Shema, 125, 143

Heftsa ve-gavra (in rem, in personam), 73, 79–80

Hellenistic drama, 243n. 49

Heresy (minut), 55, 68, 142–3, 208

Herod, King, 164, 166–7, 303; Herod Antipas, 260

Herodians, 173–4

Hiddah (enigma), 11n. 26

Hiddush (innovative insight), 79–80, 277–82

Holy Spirit, 244, 247, 253–4

Hypocrite, 176–7, 193

Idols, idolatry, 154, 172–3, 178–9, 212n. 54

Jesus Seminar, 3

Jesus: as parabolist, xiii, 1n. 2, 8, 14–5, 93; as halakhist, 4–6, 53, 77–9, 173–9, 212–6, 280; called "ben Patera," 55n. 3

Joseph (patriarch), 233–4, 288

Joseph-who-honors-the-Sabbath, 160–1, 185

Justice (middat ha-din), 138n. 33, 179n. 73

Kairos, 287, 289

Ke-min homer. *See* Allegory

Kefar Nahum (Capernaum), 180, 182, 197

Kittim, identity of, 153n. 8

Koah nedivah (urge to donate), 73n. 47

Korah, rebellion against Moses, 162

Lashon harah (slander), 290–2

Law, apodictic and casuistic, 27n. 4, 69–71

Letter and spirit, 50, 53–4, 83, 88–92

Leviathan, 155n. 13

Listener response theory, 2–3, 7, 13–5, 20–3, 39–40, 71, 78, 88, 92–100, 119, 150, 187, 212–3, 219, 222, 252–5, 283–4, 290

Lord's Prayer, 38, 100, 109–11. *See also* Abba

Love Your Neighbor, 19n. 38, 81, 191, 200, 234

Luke, priority of, 262n. 12

Ma'asei avot siman le-banim (deeds of the parents as sign to the children), 229
Maieutic method, 71, 230
Majority opinion, 60–1, 66–7, 176n. 60
"Man the measure," 82n. 71
Marketplace, 59
Marriage (nissuin), 134–6, 259, 261; as metaphor, 33–6
Martyrdom (qiddush ha-Shem), 117, 172
Mashal, 8, 11–13, 36, 69–72, 77–9, 119–20, 189n. 4, 194–5, 219, 224–7, 255; person treated as, 119n. 1
Mask, 289n. 22
Massora, 88–9, 91, 93
Matir issurim (permitting the impermissible), 281n. 67
Matthean geneaology, 47n. 49, 235–9
Melitzah, 22n. 43
Mem, originative and comparative, 66n. 28, 67n. 32, 144n. 40
Menorah, 65, 74
Mercy (middat ha-rahamim), 179n. 73
Merkabah mysticism, 41
Metaphor, 28, 33–6, 39, 46–8, 53, 92, 94, 102–3, 107–8, 112–8, 133, 136n. 26, 137, 181, 188–90, 193, 220; meaning two opposite things, 263n. 14
Metaphrasis, xv. See also Translation
Mezuzah, 75n. 54
Mi-pi soferim (from the mouth of tradents), 50
Minyan, 135n. 24
Mitzvah, mitzvot, 99–100, 179n. 74, 293, 300–2
Mnemonic, 47, 243, 248
Moses, 152, 162, 167, 232–3, 297–8
Mourning vs. grieving, 263–7
Multiplexity of meaning. See PaRDeS
Mysterion, 39n. 28

Neumes, 89–90, 248
Nimshal, 8, 13–17, 22n. 43, 36, 95, 116–7, 136n. 27, 138n. 33, 189n. 4, 194–5, 219n, 224–7; freefloating, 137n. 30; as proverb, 257n. 1; pseudo-, 15
Noah, 46n. 47, 295–6
Notarikon, 46n. 48, 47, 151n. 2, 159n. 23, 294

Ofen, ofan, 9n. 20, 287–90; facets, 9n. 20
Old and New, 277n. 59

Oral Torah, 20n. 40, 50n. 55, 87, 175, 266, 299
Ot (sign), 154n. 10
Oven of akhnai, 66

Palhedrin, 56, 74–5
Parable, x, 6–13, 19, 21, 25–8, 48, 54, 95, 111–4, 120, 126, 135–6, 178, 194, 262, 283–4; abbreviated, 189n. 3, 204; nuclear, 196n. 15; person as, 119. See also Mashal
Paraclete, 110
PaRDeS (exegetical methodology), 36–7, 41–3, 46–7, 49, 64–5, 98, 202; paradise, 113n. 62
Paronomasia (al tiqre), 90; puns, 227n. 13; banim/bonim interchange, 226–7, 237, 252; yetzer/yotzer interchange, 127, 227n. 14
Patching, 263–6
Pearls, 102n. 33, 160n. 26; stringing pearls (haruzin), 101, 105n. 41, 230
Peshat (plain meaning), 9, 11n. 24, 36–7, 46–9, 64, 90, 191, 204, 274n. 46, 286, 288–90; pashtan, 49
Pharisees, 5, 43n. 39, 166–9, 173–5, 176n. 60, 208, 260–1, 279–80, 300–1; seven types of, 169n. 43
Phylacteries (tefillin), 190n. 6, 207–10, 264
Physician, 183–4, 195–7; "Doctor, Cure Yourself," 195–7
Physis, 287
Polyglossia, 290
Pomegranate, 42n. 37
Prayer, 104, 108–10, 142–3, 261, 264. See also Eighteen Benedictions, Lord's Prayer, and God, actional attributes of
Prophet, prophecy, 50–2, 68n. 36, 130–3, 152, 196–7, 231–4, 253–4, 272; false, 151n. 4; parables of, 10
Publican, 164. See also Tax-collector
Puns. See Paronomasia

Qal va-homer (argument a fortiori), 79
Qatan, meaning "least," 247n. 54
Qedoshim ("saints"), 168–9

Rabban, 61n. 15
Rabbis' knowledge of Greek, 123n. 7
Ras Shamra (Ugarit), 209–10

Remez (allusive meaning), 37, 47, 64, 90n. 13, 127n. 13, 294–5. *See also* Gematria, Mnemonic, and Notarikon
Rending garments, 263–7
Resurrection, 188, 226, 260

Sabbath, 28, 30, 120, 160–1, 201, 234
Sadducees, 208, 225, 300–1
Sakhnin, 57–8, 246
Samaritans, 302
Samuel, 264
Sanhedrin, 61n. 15, 80, 201n. 28, 215n. 63, 246–7, 250; synhedrion [criminal court], 214–5
Second Temple, destruction of, 278–9
Sermon on the Mount, 1n. 2, 32, 38, 192, 202
"Seventy faces of the Torah," 90, 190n. 6, 191
Sha'atnez, 266n. 23
Shammaite, 66
Shofar chests, 305
Signon (individual speaker's style), 131–3
"Society of the Orchard," 42n. 33
Sod (secret meaning), 9, 37, 47, 49, 64, 90n. 13, 296
Solomon, King, 231–2
Sons vs. strangers, 151, 180, 183
Soul: contrasted with body, 91n. 14; as analogy for vowels, 121; vowels compared to mothers, 92
Stock figures, 17–20, 219–21
Symbol, 46, 59, 64, 130, 149–50, 152, 168, 172, 263, 269, 276; agglutinate, 17, 43, 54, 150; associative, 219–20, 270
Synonyms, 121–122; dibberah torah bi-leshon benei adam, 122n. 5

Tannaitic midrashim, 69n. 37
Tax, taxation, 154n. 11, 161–9; capitation tax (mas gulgolet), 162, 164–9, 172–9, 183; pecunia non olet (the tax which has no smell), 76–7; obligatory religious gifts and offerings, 162–3; Temple Tax, 180; half-sheqel tax, 154n. 11, 180–2, 297–307; surcharge on, 302; exemptions from, 300–1; Tyrian sheqel, 181n. 77, 185n. 92, 303–4; fiscus judaicus, 306
Tax-collector, 164. *See also* Publican
Teacher, x, 2–6, 23, 31, 51–2, 56, 67, 71–2, 81, 93, 174, 180, 197, 263–7, 280–1, 284
Ten Commandments (Decalogue), 233–4
Textual transmission, 187–218
"The ass has kicked over the menorah," 64–5, 74
"The king's word is law," 35n. 19, 198n. 18
"This was to fulfill the words," 44
Three crowns, 73n. 48
Timeah (Roman treasury), 185n. 93
Toilets in the temple, 56, 75–7
Toothpick (qisam), 203, 205–7, 211–2
"Topsy turvy world", 184n. 91
Torah, 99n. 26; Torah Hadashah ("new torah"), 281n. 67
Translation, principles of, xii–xiii, 129–30, 188–92, 200–2. *See also* Metaphrasis.
Two Ways, Doctrine of, xiin. 2, 125–8
Typology, 26, 224, 229, 253

Vespasian, 76–77, 306
Vowels, 53, 83, 87–92

"What would you do?" 71
Wine, 268–79; types of wine, 268–9; storage containers for, 271–6; tila, 268–9
Winnie the Pooh, 15–6, 18, 54, 146
"With a bared head, with a raised hand," 189, 210–1
Witnesses, 91, 215n. 62; disqualified, 215; consonants as, 91n. 15

Yoke, 44n. 42, 153–4, 167–9, 172, 176, 178–9, 183–4, 216
"You have heard it said," 32n. 14
"Your" Torah, 58–9

Zippori (Sepphoris), 56, 61

Biblical and Apocryphal Citations

1 Chronicles 2:13, 247n. 54
2:15, 249
7:27, 158n. 20
15:25, 232
27:18, 247n. 54
28:2, 231
28:4, 231
29:11, 111n. 56
29:14, 173

1 Corinthians 1:23, 194
2:9, 40n. 30
3:16, 81n. 68
12:12–26, 126n. 10

1 John 2:1, 110
4:1, 151n. 4

1 Kings 1:1, 265n. 20
1:6, 131
2:11, 231
4:20, 231
4:31, 9
8:1, 232
8:12, 232
8:13, 231
9:7, 119n. 1
11:36, 246
12:7, 35n. 19
13:6, 59
14:21, 238
14:31, 238
21:27, 263n. 13
22, 133n. 22
22:5, 131

1 Maccabees 1:11, 157
4:36–40, 73

7:33–42, 73
14:47, 73

1 Peter 2:4–8, 228n. 21
2:23, 55n. 4

1 Samuel 1:14–15, 213n. 56
1:24, 116n. 65
2:1–10, 152
6:5, 178n. 72
9:18, 249
10:3, 272n. 36, 273
12:2, 201
15:27, 263n. 14
16, 235–52
16:12, 251n. 61
16:20, 72n. 44, 272n. 36
17:8, 211n. 51
17:20, 275n. 50
17:26–29, 246n. 53
17:55, 237, 253
21:6, 254
24:3, 75n. 57
24:4, 265n. 20
24:13, 232
25:18, 273
25:18–31, 198
25:23, 171
25:28, 232

1 Thessalonians 5:21–22, 32n. 17

1 Timothy 3:16, 39n. 28

2 Baruch 44:15, 137n. 29

2 Chronicles 7:20, 119n. 1
9:30, 231

12:13, 238
13:22, 69n. 37
15:6, 106n. 42
18, 133n. 22
24, 299
24:4–14, 298
24:14, 301
24:27, 69n. 37
34:8–13, 298

2 Corinthians 3:6, 53, 83
12:1–7, 42
12:7, 193n. 11

2 Enoch 30:15, 125n. 10

2 Esdras (4 Ezra) 8:3, 137n. 29
4, 40n. 30

2 Kings 2:12, 264
4:10, 65n. 25
5:7, 263n. 13
12:4, 299
12:4–16, 298, 301
12:16, 305
18:32, 268n. 27
22:3–7, 298
22:19, 263n. 13
25:7, 210n. 50

2 Peter 2:1, 151n. 4

2 Samuel 5:2, 253
7:16, 253
11, 238
12:1–15, 71
12:7, 31n. 11

13:8, 210n. 50
18:33, 254
19:43–44, 200
22:1, 232
22:25, 210n. 50
23:1, 231
23:2, 254
24, 176n. 63

2 Thessalonians 2:11, 40n.
    30

Acts 1:11, 60n. 13
1:13, 58n. 9
2:13, 271n. 30
4:32, 285
4:32–37, 63
11, 58
12:17, 58n. 9
13:6, 151n. 4
15, 58
15:13, 58n. 9
18:5–19:7, 260n. 6
21, 58
21:18, 58n. 9

Amos 9:1, 138

Ben Sirah, prologue, ix
3:8(9), 63n. 20
3:21–22, 46n. 45
3:21–25, 40n. 30
4:31, 246n. 53
6:30, 168
7:17, xivn. 6
9:10, 268n. 27
15:11–20, 125n. 10
18:19(20), 201
18:20, 196n. 14
19:2, 268n. 26
31:28–29, 268n. 26
36:30, 43
39:26, 268n. 27
40:1, 168
47:17, 39n. 27
50:27, 288n. 11, 289n, 19
51:17, 168
51:26, 168

Colossians 1:26, 39n. 28
4:3, 39n. 28

Daniel 3:14, 171n. 50
7:9, 144
10:3, 245

Deuteronomy 1:1, 205
4:11, 101
4:28, 171
4:32, 144
6:4, 103–5
6:4–5, 82
6:8, 109n. 50, 207
6:16, 109
6:22, 210
6:25, 210n. 50
9:28, 108n. 45
10:17, 177
11:13, 277
11:18, 207
11:26–28, 125n. 10
15:16, 269
15:19, 163
17:7, 215
17:13, 228n. 19
17:14–20, 73
18:3, 163
18:4, 163
19:4–13, 71
20:19, 265n. 20
22:5, 32n. 16
22:9, 302
22:10, 162
22:11, 36n. 21, 266n. 23
22:23, 70
22:25, 70
23:2, 237
23:3–4, 237
23:3–6, 236
23:7, 237
23:10–14, 76n. 57
23:13, 75n. 57, 90
23:18, 56, 71, 72, 77
24:1–4, 33–4
25:5–10, 36n. 21
26:3, 59
27:26, 64n. 22
28:37, 119n. 1
28:46, 165
28:50, 177
28:51, 268n. 27
29:22, 183n. 86
29:24, 45

29:25–26, 45
29:29, 40n. 30
30:15, 125n. 10
30:19, 144
30:20, 158
32:9, 224
32:14, 268n. 27
32:15, 95n. 19
32:27, 189n. 6
32:31, 109n. 50
32:33, 273n. 43
32:47, 99n. 27
33:3, 167, 168
33:5, 106, 233
33:28, 268n. 27
33:29, 233

Ecclesiastes. *See* Qohelet

Ecclesiasticus. *See* Ben
    Sirah

Ephesians 3:9, 39n. 28
5:32, 39n. 28

Esther 1:9, 268n. 27

Exodus 2:14, 213n. 55
3:5, 211n. 51
4:12, 99n. 26
5:12, 200
12:26, 59n. 11
13:2, 246
13:9, 207
13:16, 207
13:19, 233n. 30
14:8, 130, 189n. 6, 210
14:27, 289
15:2, 105n. 41
15:4, 99n. 26
15:18, 104, 106
15:22–26, 43n. 39
16:5, 234
19:13, 99n. 26, 201
20:2, 233
20:3, 234
20:7, 234
20:8, 234
20:12, 234
20:13, 70, 234
20:14–17, 234

20:21, 246
21, 70
21:12–13, 70
22:7, 30n. 10
23:1, 215n. 62
23:2, 60
23:19, 163
24:7, 96
25:2, 246
25:8, 82, 83n. 73, 246
25:10, 99n. 26
26:28, 145
30:11–16, 176n. 63, 297
30:12, 299
30:12–16, 298
30:18, 143
30:31, 246
32:12, 108n. 45
40:15, 246

Ezekiel 7:25, 246n. 53
8:14, 209
14:8, 119n. 1
15:6, 295
16:33, 72
17:3–10, 8n. 16
18:2, 28
20:35, 90
20:45–48 [Heb. 21:1–4], 8n. 16
20:49 [Heb. 21:5], 8n. 17
24:3–5, 8n. 16
27:18, 268n. 27
34:31, 247
36:19–23, 108n. 45
47:8–10, 150

Galatians 1:19, 58
2:9, 58n. 9
3, 63
3:28, 62n. 19
4:6, 4n. 6
4:8–9, 168n. 42
4:24, 39n. 28

Genesis 1:26, 154
1:27, 178n. 71
1:28, 154, 196
2:7, 127n. 13
4:11–12, 121

4:14, 121
4:23–25, 195–6
4:25, 199
7:22, 153n. 7
8:11, 206n. 42
9:6, 178n. 71
9:19, 151
11:7, 109n. 50
14:1, 106n. 42
14:19, 100n. 29
16:5, 99n. 26
17:27, 251
18:6, 116n. 65
18:9, 238
18:15, 108n. 48
18:25, 108n. 45
19:20, 177n. 66
20:3, 288
20:7, 109n. 50
21:14, 273
21:14–19, 272n. 36
22:2, 99n. 26
24:17, 121
24:43, 121
24:63, 109n. 50
25:25, 247
25:27, 224
26:8, 9
27:28, 268n. 27
27:37, 268n. 27
28:22, 246
31:15, 183n. 86
37:13, 234
37:29, 263n. 13
37:34, 263n. 13
38, 235
38:14, 144n. 39
38:17, 72
40:13, 177n. 66
42:15, 234
42:18, 234
43:16, 234
44:18, 288
47:12, 234
47:14, 234
47:23, 296
48:11, 109n. 50
48:16, 151n. 2
49:11, 268n. 27
50:19–21, 233–4
50:25–26, 233

Habakkuk 1:14–16, 150, 153
2:6–19, 11n. 26
2:15, 268n. 26, 273
3:17, 171n. 50

Hebrews 3:1–2, 230

Hosea 2:16, 136
4:11, 268nn. 26–27
6:5, 138n. 33
7:5, 273n. 43
14:9, 127

Isaiah 1:22, 203–4
3:22, 265n. 19
3:26, 264n. 17
5:1–7, 18, 220, 221n. 4
5:5, 45n. 43
5:7, 295
5:24, 108
6:9–10, 7, 95
10:21, 247
11:6, 247
12:2b, 105n. 41
12:5–6, 244
14:4b-21, 119n. 1
22:12–14, 133
23, 79n. 62
24:7, 268n. 27
28:7, 268n. 26
28:27, 288
29:21, 201
33:22, 184n. 90
36:17, 268n. 27
38:12, 246n. 53
40:6–7, 107
40:21–26, 124
40:25, 122n. 6
40:26, 144–5
44:6, 107
51:1, 230n. 26
53:5, 245
53:6, 100n. 29
54:5, 136
54:11–13, 227n. 13
55:1, 276n. 54
56:3–6, 183n. 86
60:22, 247
61:5, 183n. 86
61:10, 136n. 26

62:5, 136
63:16, 184n. 90
64:8, 184
65:13–14, 137
66:10, 279

James 3:1, 40n. 30

Jeremiah 2:27, 184
3:1–5, 33–34
21:8–14, 125n. 10
24:9, 119n. 1
29:7, 155n. 14
31:4, 100n. 29
31:12, 268n. 27, 272n. 36,
   273
31:29, 28
31:31–34, 221n. 2
31:32, 136
31:33, 83n. 73
39:6, 210n. 50
52:10, 210n. 50

Job 1:20, 263n. 13
1:21, 31
2:12, 263n. 13
3:3, 99n. 26
3:19, 126
4:16, 210n. 50
7:9, 107
12:12, 201n. 28, 276
14:2, 107
17:6, 119n. 1
20:8, 108
28:14, 90
31:1, 32
32:19, 268n. 27, 271n. 30,
   272n. 36, 273
37:18, 265n. 19
38, 125

Joel 2:13, 263

John 3:25, 260
4:7ff., 213
6, 277n. 58
7:53–8:11, 80
8:7, 214–6
8:11, 80n. 67
8:15, 80n. 67
10:14, 253

10:34, 59
11:35, 254
11:49, 74
11:51, 74
15:25, 59
18:13, 74
18:31, 215n. 63
18:36, 149, 177
19:17, 164n. 33

Joshua 2, 236
5:15, 211n. 51
7:6, 263n. 13
7:9, 108n. 45
9:4, 272n. 36
9:5(11), 265n. 19
9:13, 272n. 36
24:15, 125n. 10
24:17, 210n. 50
24:32, 233

Judges 3:20, 76n. 57
3:24, 76n. 57
4:19, 272n. 36
5:8, 281
5:9, 190n. 6
5:11, 281
14:5, 32n. 16
14:12, 22
14:12–14, 217n. 65
16:14, 245

Lamentations 2:13, 144–5
2:15, 145
4:22, 247
5:9, 107

Leviticus 5:15, 305
5:18, 305
16:32, 74
18:6, 32n. 16, 36n. 21
19:2, 168n. 43
19:9–10, 163
19:17, 199, 202, 204, 212–
   3, 234
19:18, 19n. 38, 81, 191,
   200, 234
19:19, 163, 302
19:36, 29
21:2–3, 264n. 17
22:28, 35

25:23, 246
25:36, 234
25:55, 246
26:1, 286
26:10, 267
27:1f., 299
27:32, 163

Luke 1:46–55, 152
2:32, 253
3:23, 253
4:23, 196–7
5:30, 260n. 5
5:33–39, 257
5:35, 261n. 11
5:36, 266n. 22
5:39, 271
6:26, 151n. 4
6:37, 80n. 67
6:37–38, 41–42, 192
7:16, 254
7:31–35, 122
7:33–34, 268n. 26
7:46, 254
8:9–10, 39n. 28
11:2–4, 109
12:13–14, 62n. 19
12:14, 213
12:16–20, 17n. 33
14:11, 156, 184n. 91
15:5, 100n. 29
15:11ff., 114
16:9–13, 295n. 4
16:13, 126
18:12, 261n. 7, 279n. 64,
   280
18:34, 39n. 28
19:11–27, 30n. 10
20:3–8, 175n. 58
20:9–16, 225
20:18, 227n. 14
20:20–25, 174
23:2, 174
24:44ff., 38

Malachi 1:6, 183n. 86
1:6–10, 73–4
2:9, 177n. 67

Mark 1:22, 1
2:17, 197

2:18–22, 257
2:22, 269n. 28
2:27, 161n. 28
3:18, 58n. 9
4:10–13, 39n. 28
4:11–12a, 7
4:24, 80n. 67
4:29–33, 175n. 58
4:33, 6
6:3, 58
12:1–9, 225
12:13–16, 174
12:28–34, 80–81, 84n. 74
12:41–44, 80
13:22, 151n. 4
14:36, 4n. 6
15:39, 4n. 6
15:40, 58n. 9

Matthew 1:1–16, 235, 239,
    253
2:5, 253
3:10, 260n. 6
3:17, 253
4:19, 155n. 13
5:3–11, 152
5:14–16, 64
5:17, 63
5:24, 295n. 4
5:27–28, 32, 44
5:40, 180n. 76
6:9–13, 109
6:24, 5, 126, 259
6:28, 172n. 52
7:1, 80n. 67
7:1–2, 216
7:1–5, 192–3
7:15, 151n. 4
7:29, xiii, 1, 8n. 17
8:11, 279
8:20, 254
9:9, 182n. 83
9:14–17, 257
9:15, 261n. 11
9:17, 272n. 37, 283
9:23, 192
10:10, 192
10:37, 126n. 11
11:16–19, 122, 260n. 6,
    268n. 26
11:19, 79n. 61, 257

11:29–30, 169n. 45
12:3, 254
12:3–9, 93
13:10–17, 95
13:10–23, 39n. 28
13:18–23, 95
13:24–53, 114–8
13:55, 58, 253
14:1–2, 260
15:14, 207n. 45
15:27, 213
16:14, 260
17, 303
17:24–27, 21, 149, 160,
    179–84
19:28, 254
19:29, 126n. 11
20:1–16, 223
21:1–9, 64
21:24–27, 175n. 58
21:28–32, 223
21:33–41, 221
22:1–14, 137n. 30
22:15–21, 173–9
22:44, 254
23:5, 207n. 47
23:12, 184n. 91
23:14, 159n. 21
24:11, 151n. 4
24:24, 151n. 4
25:1–12, 134–6
25:14–30, 30n. 10

Micah 1:7, 56
2:11, 268n. 26
7:14, 247

Nahum 1:15, 247

Nehemiah 2:8, 42
10:32–33, 298
10:33, 301

Numbers 3:12, 246
5, 79
6:3, 120
6:24–26, 177
11:16, 246
12:7, 230
14:15, 108n. 45
15:30, 190n. 6, 210

15:32, 201, 206n. 41
15:38ff, 36n. 21
16, 162
18:12, 268n. 27
18:14, 163
18:15, 29n. 8
19:5, 210n. 50
21:30, 99n. 26
23:21, 106
24:17, 253
25:3, 206n. 41
27:8, 62
28:2, 246
28:4, 82
28:7, 121
31:52, 178n. 72
32:22, 32n. 16
33:3, 130, 189n. 6, 210
33:55, 193
36:8, 62

Obadiah 1:21, 105, 107

Proverbs 1:1, 114, 232
1:6, 22, 189n. 4
2:4–5, 293
3:17, 189n. 4
5:5, 32n. 16
5:8, 57
8, 201n. 28
8:22, 100n. 29
9:2, 268n. 26, 276n. 54
9:5, 246, 276n. 54
9:7–8, 212n. 54
9:8, 205
11:5, 29
13:25, 293
15:7, 142
15:12, 212
21:4, 295n. 5
23:29–35, 268n. 26
23:32, 159n. 22
24:31, 45n. 43
25:11, 9, 285–92
25:11b and 12b, 287n. 8
25:14, 189n. 5
25:16, 41
25:28, 43, 45n. 43
26:18–19, 291
27:10, 84n. 74
27:14, 290
31:10, 30

Psalm 1:1–2, 233
1:2, 59
1:4, 107
1:5, 142
2, 11n. 24
2:6, 245
2:7, 252
5:5, 210n. 50
8, 11n. 24
18:2–3, 247
18:24, 210n. 50
19:9, 276
22:15, 107
22:28, 105–6
23, 112n. 58
23:1, 100n. 29
23:6, 254
24:7, 107
25:14, 90n. 13
25:15, 185
26:3, 210n. 50
26:8, 100n. 29
32:8, 202
36:19, 59
36:2, 210n. 50
37:14, 106n. 42
39:6, 231
44:14, 119n. 1
45, 11n. 24
45:13, 238
48, 112n. 58
49, 13n. 29
51:5, 250
56:8, 274
60:2, 233
62:12, 36n. 21
65:4, 245
69:4, 59
69:11, 119n. 1
73:7, 95n. 19
73:20, 178n. 72
77:2, 183
78:2, 11n. 26, 116
78:25, 90
79:10, 210
79:11, 100n. 29
82:6, 59
92:7–9, 106n. 42
92:8, 125
92:10, 246

92:13, 111
93:1, 107
101:3 and 7, 210n. 50
103:15, 107
104, 125
104:15, 268n. 26
105:40, 90
110, 11n. 24
110:1, 254
116:15, 41
116:16, 239
118, 219–55
118:14, 105n. 41
119:83, 272n. 36
119:99, 67
119:176, 100n. 29
122:3, 145
124:2–3, 156
126, 112n. 58
126:2, 232
131:2, 46n. 45
133, 112n. 58
133:2, 252
135:4, 224
137:5–6, 279
139:15, 100n. 29
144:4, 107
145:15, 270
150:1, 248
151, 240–2

Psalms of Solomon 4, 177n. 66

Qohelet 1:1, 231
1:2, 231
1:7, 209
1:10, 229, 281n. 67
2:5, 42
3:7, 263n. 13
3:20, 107
5:6, 41
5:14, 13
5:15, 13n. 29
8:2–5, 174n. 54
9:8, 136
9:12, 150
12:2, 97
12:9, 112, 113n. 61

Revelation 1:20, 39n. 28
13:17–18, 47n. 49
16:13, 151n. 4
19:20, 151n. 4
20:10, 151n. 4

Romans 2:1, 80n. 67
3:31, 63n. 20
8, 63
8:15, 4n. 6
8:16–17, 62n. 19
9:32–33, 228n. 21
11:25, 39n. 28
12:9–10, 32n. 17
12:15, 267n. 24
13:8, 81n. 70
14:10, 80n. 67

Ruth 1:1, 203
2:4, 236n. 35
4:2, 135n. 24
4:12, 237

Song of Songs 1:1, 232
1:2, 276
1:4, 41
1:10, 101
2:2, 172
2:15, 18
4:13, 42
7:3, 44n. 41
8:2, 268n. 26

Test. of Asher 1:3, 126n. 10

Test. of Isaac 4:53, 32n. 15

Test. of Issachar 7:2, 32n. 15

Test. of Judah 21, 151
21:7–9, 151n. 3, 153n. 7

Thomas, 226, 228
7 and 8, 228n. 20
20 and 21, 228n. 20
31, 196n. 15
47, 259
63, 17n. 33, 228n. 20

64, 17n. 33
65, 222n. 5, 228n. 20
66, 228n. 20
73–76, 228n. 20
75, 136n. 27
97, 274n. 48
100, 174n. 54

104, 258
109, 116n. 66

Wisdom of Solomon 6:21–
    25, 38n. 27

Zechariah 3:3–6, 138n. 31
8:4, 247

9:7, 211
9:9, 64
14:5, 69n. 36
14:9, 104–5, 107

Zephaniah 2:1, 199–200
3:9, 104

Classical and Early Christian References

1 Clement 37:5, 126n. 10
Abercius Marcellus, 159n. 23
Aesop, 12, 15, 123–4, 144n. 38
Alciphron, 206n. 42
Apostolic Constitutions 7:1, 126n. 10
Aquinas, 109n. 49
Aristotle, 14, 37n. 24, 50n. 55, 86n. 2, 88n. 7, 91n. 15, 177
Athanasius, 160n. 24
Augustine of Hippo, 20–1, 47n. 50, 100n. 29, 113n. 60, 149, 159n. 23, 230
Augustinus of Dakia, 47n. 49
Aulus Gellius, 134n. 23

Babrius and Phaedrus, 8n.17, 12n. 27, 15, 29n. 7, 39n. 28, 60n. 13, 124, 126n. 10, 153n. 8, 195, 197, 202

Catullus, 202n. 32
Cicero, 42n. 33, 51n. 55, 91n. 15, 205n. 37, 263n. 14
Clement of Alexandria, 10n. 24, 33n. 17, 37n. 23, 43n. 38, 47n. 50, 86n. 2, 126n. 10, 181, 285n. 2

Dante, 37n. 22
Demosthenes, 32n. 17
Desert Fathers, 134n. 23, 160, 202n. 32, 205n. 38, 214, 217–8
Didache, xiin. 2, 32n. 17, 109n. 51, 126n. 10, 136n. 27, 261n. 7, 279n. 64
Dio Cassius, 76–7
Diogenes Laertius, 32n. 17, 43n. 39, 51n. 55, 60n. 13, 192n. 10, 198n. 17

Epictetus, 30n. 9, 139
Epicurus, 142

Epiphanius, 27n. 5, 64n. 22
Epistle of Barnabas, xiin. 2, 10n. 24, 39n. 28, 47n. 49, 126n. 10
Erasmus, 48, 51n. 55, 126n. 10, 201n. 25, 202n. 32, 207n. 43, 228n. 17, 263n. 14
Eusebius, 51n. 55, 58n. 9, 74n. 50

Francis of Assisi, 54

Gospel of Truth, 37n. 23, 274n. 48
Gregory of Nazianzus, 125n. 9, 143n. 37, 169n. 45, 266n. 22
Gregory of Tours, 12n. 27

Heraclitus of Ephesus, 43
Herodotus, 123n. 7
Hesiod, 125n. 10
Horace, 202n. 32, 207n. 43

Irenaeus, 264n. 17
Inscription of Pectorius, 159n. 23

Jerome, St., 51n. 55, 202n. 32, 207, 272n. 37
John Chrysostom, 37–8, 74n. 50, 98n. 23
Josephus, 162n. 30, 300; —Antiquities, 40, 58n. 9, 73n. 48, 78, 164n. 32, 166, 167n. 41, 171n. 50, 238n. 38, 250n. 59, 251n. 61, 299n. 3, 300nn. 6–7; —Life, 58n. 7; —Wars, 30n. 9, 58n. 7, 73n. 48, 164n. 32, 306n. 18
Justin Martyr, 68n. 34, 205n. 38, 260n. 6, 285n. 2
Juvenal, 201n. 26

Lactantius, 142n. 36
Livy, 126n. 10

Longinus, 39n. 29, 143n. 38
Luther, Martin, 193

Marcion, 262n. 12
Martine, Raymond, *Pugio Fidei*, 55n. 3, 228n. 21, 239n. 41, 286, 289n. 18
Methodius, 135n. 25

Nicholas of Lyra, 37n. 22, 47n. 49

Odo of Chariton, 29n. 7, 47n. 49, 144n. 38
Optatus, Bishop of Milevis, 150n. 2
Origen, 38n. 26, 42n. 34, 47n. 49, 229n. 22, 285n. 2, 306

Paulus Fagius, 156n. 16
Persius, 202n. 32
Philo of Alexandria: *De Confusione Linguarum*, 44n. 40; —*On Abraham*, 30n. 9; —*On Joseph*, 13n. 29; —*Special Laws*, 35n. 19, 38n. 27, 78–9; —*Virtues*, 35n. 19
Pico della Mirandola, 47n. 49
Pinax of Cebes, 126n. 10
Plato, 51–2, 86; —*Laws*, 198n. 17; —*Phaedrus*, 52n. 56, 97n. 17; —*Symposium*, 1n. 1; —*Theatetus*, 71n. 42, 82n. 71, 86n. 2; —*The Republic*, 143n. 38

Plautus, 98nn. 23–24
Pliny the Younger, 51n. 55
Plutarch, 32n. 17, 89n. 9, 198n. 17
Porphyry, 35n. 19
Protagoras the Sophist, 82n. 71
Pseudo-Clementine Homilies, 126n. 10
Pseudo-Clementine Recognitions, 260n. 6
Ptolemy (Christian Gnostic), 27n. 5

Quintilian, 51n. 55, 91n. 15

Secret Book of James, 119
Seneca, 51n. 55, 198n. 17
Sextus Empiricus, 82n. 71
Shakespeare, 13n. 29, 156n. 16
Suetonius, 77n. 59

Terence, 98n. 23
Tertullian, 64n. 24, 159, 166n. 40, 187
Thales, 159n. 21
Theodore of Mopsuestia, 11n. 24
Theognis, 126n. 10

Venerable Bede, 47n. 49

Wycliff, 207n. 44

Xenophon, 42, 125n. 10

Rabbinic References

Abravanel, Don Isaac, 130–1
Abu-Zimra, David, 89–90
Adler, Nathan b. Mordecai (HaCohen), 190n. 6
Adret, Solomon b. Avraham, 91n. 14, 122n. 5, 265n. 17
Aḥer (Elisha ben Abuyah), 41, 45–6
Ahikar Papyrus, 286, 289
Aikhah Rabbah, 35—Proem 34, 153n. 7—1.1,4, 265n. 19—3.5-8, 165n. 37—3:40, 201n. 26—3.41, 200n. 23
Aikhah Rabbati, 126n. 10
Ain Yaaqov, 211n. 52
al-Ḥarizi, Judah, 29n. 8
al-Naqawa, Israel, 29n. 8, 102n. 32, 117n. 68, 139–42, 158n. 19, 276n. 55
al-Qumsi, Daniel, 200
Alfasi, Isaac of Fez, 92
Alpha Beta of Ben Sira, 98n. 23
Altschuler, David, 239n. 44
Anan the Kara'ite, 50n. 55
Aqiba, R., 41, 46, 56, 67n. 33, 82, 101, 113n. 62, 157–8, 183n. 87, 205–6, 213
Ashkenazi, Bezalel, 66n. 30
Avot de Rabbi Nathan A, 57n. 6—A-1, 44—5—A-2, 89n. 9—A-2.9, 32n. 16—A-5, 300n. 11—A-12, 156—A-14, 29n. 8, 72—A-15, 136n. 28—A-20, 165—A-25, 126n. 10
Avot de Rabbi Nathan B, 155n. 14, 157n. 17, 274—B-1, 45n. 43—B-3, 32n. 16—B-29, 136n. 28—B-34, 274n. 49, 276—B-35, 110n. 53
Azzulai, Ḥaim Yosef David, 250n. 59

ba-Midbar Rabbah 3.1, 111n. 57—10.8, 32n. 16, 44n. 41—20.14, 18—22.4, 227n. 15

Baḥye Halawi, 51n. 55, 90n. 13, 229n. 22
Ben Azzai, 41, 45, 82, 101, 305
Ben Bag Bag, 288
Ben Zoma, 41, 45, 82, 113n. 62
ben Sarukh Hispaniensi, Menaḥem, 288
ben Yatzliaḥ, Chafets, 13n. 29
Bereshit Rabbah, 111n. 57—11.4, 160n. 25—12.1, 112n. 59—19.3, 44n. 41—19.11, 274n. 49—23.4, 195–6, 199—24, 81n. 68—36, 46n. 47—36.2, 151—36.7, 171—40, 229n. 22—45.2, 227n. 13—50.10, 239n. 41—53.14, 273—59, 201n. 28—71, 4n. 6—85.7, 144n. 39—93, 286n. 4—93.3, 287n. 9, 288—973, 158n. 20
Beruria, 30–1
Bezalel, Ḥaim bar, 293
BT Arakhin 15b, 44n. 40—16b, 203, 204–6, 212
BT Avodah Zarah, 156n. 16—3b, 123n. 7—3b-4a, 158n. 19—4a, 156—8b, 216n. 63—16b-17a, 55n. 3—28a, 269—30a, 268n. 27, 269—33a, 276n. 53—50a, 172n. 51—66a, 268n. 27—72a, 268n. 27
BT Baba Batra 8a, 168—10a, 183n. 87—10b, 184n. 91—15b, 203, 206, 212—20a, 265n. 19—60b, 201, 202n. 31, 278–9—89b, 127—91b, 267—97b, 268n. 27—134a, 18n. 36
BT Baba Metzia 49b, 67n. 31—59b, 66nn. 26, 30, 201n. 25—85b, 142, 181n. 80—107b, 201n. 31
BT Baba Qamma 79b, 128—97b, 170n. 49
BT Berakhot 12a, 102n. 32—20b, 177n. 67—28b, 126n. 10—29b, 268n. 26—31a–b, 213n. 56—32b, 168—33b, 102n. 32—35b, 168—43b, 266n. 23—55a, 76n. 57—57a, 277n. 57—61a, 127n. 13—61b,

385

BT Berakhot (*cont.*)
157—62b, 76n. 57, 265n. 20—64a, 227n.
  13
BT Betzah 17a, 161n. 28—33a–b, 206n. 41
BT Eruvin 13b, 66n. 27—18a, 127n. 13—
  54b, 190n. 6—69a, 211n. 51
BT Gittin 67b, 268n. 27—69a, 268n. 27—
  70a, 269
BT Hagigah 14b, 35n. 19, 41n. 32—15b,
  42n. 37
BT Hullin 11a–b, 176n. 60—44b, 32n.
  16—62b, 237n. 37—89a, 114n. 63—
  107b, 273n. 45
BT Keritot 6a, 268n. 27
BT Ketubot 5a, 90n. 12—7b, 135n. 24,
  237n. 37—14b–15a, 60n. 14—50b, 179n.
  73—63a, 229n. 22—67b, 270—110b,
  170n. 48
BT Makkot 10a, 67n. 32
BT Megillah 9a, 91n. 15—14a–b, 170n. 49
BT Menahot 65a, 300n. 11—99a–b, 63n. 20
BT Moed Qatan 22b, 265n. 18—24a, 36n.
  21—25b, 154, 172n. 51—26a, 263—4—
  26b, 263n. 14
BT Nazir 38b, 268n. 27
BT Nedarim 50b, 277n. 57
BT Niddah 31a, 92n. 16
BT Pesahim 42b, 268n. 27—50a, 184n.
  91—50b, 4n. 4—54b, 170n. 49—66b,
  227n. 13, 246n. 53—86b, 268n. 27—
  104a, 172n. 51—119a, 153n. 7, 243–4
BT Qiddushin 20a, 268n. 27, 269—22b,
  102n. 33—30b, 92n. 16—32b, 201n.
  28—67b, 237n. 37—70a, 201n. 26
BT Rosh ha-Shanah 3b, 108n. 48
BT Sanhedrin, 184n. 91—18a and 19a,
  202n. 31—18a and 19b, 201n. 29—
  25b-26a, 164n. 35—32b, 61n. 16—38a,
  171—38b–39a, 28—39a, 18n. 36—41a,
  216n. 63—70a, 268n. 26—89a, 131–3—
  92b, 7n. 15—99b, 211n. 51—101b,
  190n. 6—109b–110a, 162n. 31
BT Shabbat 15a, 215n. 63—20b, 32n. 15—
  25b, 76n. 58—31a, 51n. 55, 82n. 72,
  84n. 74, 87n. 6—33b, 165n. 38, 171n.
  49—40b, 4n. 4—66b, 275n. 52—105b,
  263n. 13, 265n. 20—109a, 268n. 27—
  114a, 266n. 23—115b–116a, 88n. 8—
  116a, 62nn. 17—18—119a, 160—129a,
  268n. 27—139a, 268n. 27—148a, 102n.
  33—153a, 136—7—178a, 96n. 20

BT Shevuot 6b, 171n. 49
BT Sotah 15a–b, 80n. 65—34a, 229n. 22—
  42b, 211n. 51—49a, 65n. 26
BT Sukkah 18b, 4n. 4—30a, 171
BT Taanit, 276n. 54—6b, 275n. 52—7a,
  67n. 32, 277n. 57—11a, 268n. 26—17a,
  268n. 26—23b, 4n. 6—25b, 184n. 90
BT Tamid 27b–28a, 76n. 57—32a, 116n. 67
BT Temurah 29a–30b, 72n. 45
BT Yevamot, 237–9—63a, 239n. 41—63b,
  35n. 19—69a, 237n. 37—76b–77a, 237n.
  37—77a, 239n. 41
BT Yoma 9b–10a, 75—10a, 75n. 53—10b,
  75—18a, 268n. 27—22b, 203n. 32—76b,
  268n. 26—85b, 161n. 28—86b, 35–6
BT Zebahim 78b, 268n. 27

Copper Scroll, 307

David ben Avraham the Karaite, 289
Devarim Rabbah 3.3, 116n. 67
di Ozida, Samuel, 51n. 55
Duran, Simeon b. R. Tzemah, 13n. 29, 32n.
  16, 168n. 42

Edels, Samuel, 184n. 90
Elazar ha-Kallir, 106n. 42, 289
Eleazar ben Azariah, 80, 205–6
Eliezer ben Hyrkanos, 49, 55, 58n. 9, 61,
  65–8, 109, 136, 264, 272n. 38, 305
Eliyahu Vilna Gaon, 91n. 14, 168n. 42,
  250n. 59, 289n. 18
Eliyahu Zutta 1 and 15, 267n. 24
Esther Rabbah 7, 152—7.10, 227n. 14—
  7.11, 152n. 5
Eybeshuetz, R. Jonathan, 59

Fidanki, Jacob, 32n. 16

Gamaliel (Gamliel), 61–3, 67n. 32, 79–80,
  128, 205, 214–5, 265n. 17, 305

ha-Azovi, Joseph ben Harran, 51n. 55
ha-Nasi, Abraham bar Chijja, 96n. 20
Hagiz, Moshe, 267n. 24
Hai Gaon, 28n. 6, 46n. 48
HaLevi, Abraham b. R. Shabtai Shaftil
  Horowitz, 267n. 24
HaLevi, Yehuda, 21n. 42, 51n. 55, 91n. 14,
  143n. 37
HaMeiri, Menahem, 287, 289n. 19

HaNaqdan, Berahiya ben Neturnai, 18n. 36
Hazzan, Haim David, 18n. 36

ibn-Aqnin, Yosef b. R. Yehuda, 211n. 51
ibn-Ezra, Abraham, 51n. 55, 79n. 62, 90n.
13, 91n. 14, 122, 196n. 15, 201, 229n.
22, 239n. 44, 273, 288n. 15, 299
ibn-Ezra, Moses, 51n. 55, 189n. 3, 205n. 39
ibn-Ezra, pseudo-, 189n. 4
ibn-Gikatilia, Moshe HaCohen, 89n. 10,
91n. 14, 200n. 21
ibn-Habib, Yaakov, 81n. 68
ibn-Hasdai, Abraham b. Samuel ha-Levi,
50n. 54
ibn-Janah, Yonah (Abulwalid Merwan ibn-
Ganah), 9n. 20, 92n. 16, 201, 285n. 1,
288n. 15, 289
ibn-Merwan al-Jaziri, 207n. 45
ibn-Nahmias, Yosef, 189n. 4
ibn-Paquda, Bahye b. Yosef, 188
ibn-Parhon, Shelomo, 10n. 23, 51n. 55,
90nn. 12–13, 190–1, 289n. 17
ibn-Shu'eib, Joshua, 289n. 18
ibn-Tibbon, Samuel, 188n. 3
ibn-Tibbon, Yehuda, 9n. 21, 90n. 13, 188,
190n. 6, 210
ibn-Zabara, Joseph ben Meir, 13n. 29, 18n.
36, 196n. 15
Imma-Shalom, 61–3
Immanuel of Rome, 212n. 54, 289n. 18
Isaac of Corbeil, 13n. 29
Ishmael, R., 49, 58
Israeli, Isaak b. Salomon, 50—2

Jacob Sicili, 250n. 59
Jerusalem Talmud, Tractate Avodah Zarah,
172—Baba Metzia, 116n. 67—Betsah,
227n. 15—Hagigah, 41n. 32, 46n. 46,
67n. 32, 101n. 31, 102n. 32, 126n. 10—
Ma'aser Sheni, 265n. 19—Maaserot, 4n.
6—Moed Qatan, 67n. 31, 264, 265n.
18—Nedarim, 81n. 68, 227n. 13—Peah,
99n. 27, 211n. 51—Pesahim, 76, 211n.
51, 268n. 27—Qiddushin, 4n. 6—Rosh
ha-Shanah, 35n. 19—Sanhedrin, 4n. 6,
170–1, 215n. 63, 265n. 19—Shabbat, 4n.
6, 268n. 27—Sheqalim, 178n. 69, 300n.
9, 301—Taanit, 201n. 29, 275n. 52—Terumot, 32n. 16, 268n. 27—Yevamot,
237n. 37—Yoma, 64nn. 22—23, 74,
161n. 28

Joseph Ya'avets he-Hassid, 51n. 55, 196n.
15
Judah the Prince, 246, 274, 276, 303

Kaspi, Joseph, 51n. 55, 289n. 20
Kehillot Moshe, 241n. 48
Kohen, Shabbatai, 32n. 16

Leqah Tov (Pesiqta Zutrati), 127n. 13
Levi ben Gershon, 289n. 20
Levi, R., 97, 246–7
Levita, Elias, 188n. 3, 201
Luria, Shelomo, 32n. 16
Luzzato, Samuel David, 33n. 18, 91n. 14

M. Baba Batra 6:3, 268n. 27
M. Baba Qamma 9:2, 268n. 27
M. Berakhot 2:7, 264n. 17—6:1, 295n. 7—
7:5, 268n. 27
M. Betzah 4:6, 206n. 41
M. Eduyot 1:4–6, 176n. 60
M. Hullin 9:4, 206n. 41
M. Kelayim 9:8, 4n. 6
M. Kelim 19:8, 273n. 45—23:1, 208n. 47—
26:2 and 28:6, 266n. 23
M. Ketubot 4:5, 135n. 24—13:11, 170n. 48
M. Makkot 1:10, 80, 205n. 40, 214, 215n.
63
M. Megillah 4:8, 208
M. Middot 5:3–4, 76n. 57
M. Negaim 2:5, 203n. 32—10:10, 209
M. Niddah 9:11, 268n. 27
M. Parah 2:3, 72n. 45
M. Pesahim 10:7, 120n. 2
M. Pirqei Avot, xvn. 6—1:1, 18n. 37, 44—
1:10, 157—1:13, 156—2:1, 32n. 16,
126n. 10—2:5, 168n. 43—2:8, 66n. 28—
2:10, 65, 136—2:14, 191—3:2, 155—3:5,
169—3:7, 173n. 53—3:12, 190n. 6,
211n. 51—3:14, 190n. 6—3:15, 178n.
71—4:1, 67—4:2, 268n. 27—4:13, 110n.
53—4:20, 274, 276n. 56—5:23, 123—
5:25, 288n. 14—6:1, 32n. 16
M. Rosh ha-Shanah, 4n. 6—3:7, 272n. 38—
4:6, 104
M. Sanhedrin 6:6, 264n. 17—7:10, 4n. 6
M. Shabbat 6:2, 208n. 47—6:6, 206n. 41
M. Sheqalim, 297—307—1, 182n. 81—1:1,
180n. 75—1:3, 180n. 75, 300n. 8—1:4,
300n. 9—1:5, 182n. 84—1:6, 185n. 92—
2:4, 178n. 69—3:2, 32n. 16—6:5, 277n.
59

M. Sotah 9:15, 4n. 6
M. Taanit 1, 67
M. Tamid 1:1, 76n. 57
M. Tebul Yom 1:1—2, 268n. 27
M. Temurah 2:1, 72—3, 67—6:2, 72n.
    45—6:3, 78n. 60
M. Terumot 2:6, 268n. 27
M. Yadaim 2:2, 206n. 41
M. Yoma 3:2, 75—3:3, 75, 76n. 57—3:6,
    76n. 57—4:5, 75—7:4, 76n. 57—8:9, 4n.
    6
Maimon, Yehuda Leib ha-Kohen, 45n. 43
Maimonides, 104n. 37, 109n. 49, 188n. 3,
    290—1
Maimonides, Commentary to the Mishnah,
    9n. 20—Avot, 169n. 45, 192n. 10—
    Miqvaot, 9n. 18—Pereq Heleq, 22n. 44
Maimonides, Epistle to Yemen, 9n. 18
Maimonides, Iggeret ha-Shemad, 55n. 3
Maimonides, Mishneh Torah: Hilkhot Deot,
    45n. 44, 290n. 26—Hilkhot Edut, 215nn.
    61—62—Hilkhot Evel, 82n. 70—Hilkhot
    Klei ha-Miqdash, 75n. 55—Hilkhot Mat-
    not Aniyim, 295n. 5—Hilkhot Mezuzot,
    75n. 54—Hilkhot Sheqalim, 300n. 8,
    301n. 12—Hilkhot Talmud Torah, 76n.
    57—Hilkhot Yom ha-Kippurim, 74n. 52,
    76n. 58
Maimonides, Moreh Nebukhim (Guide of
    the Perplexed), 9–10, 42n. 37, 46n. 45,
    90n. 12
Maimonides, Sefer ha-Mitzvot, 9nn. 18, 20,
    299n. 4
Maimonides, Teshuvot, 51n. 55
MaLBYM, 131n. 21
Masnut, Samuel b. R. Nissim, 171n. 50
Megillat Taanit 1, 300n. 11
Meidani, 207n. 45
Meir Aldabi, 250n. 59
Meir, R., 30–1, 42n. 37, 79–80, 137, 138,
    264, 302
Mekhilta de Rabbi Ishmael, 4n. 6, 59n. 11,
    126n. 10, 144n. 38, 153n. 7, 161n. 28,
    190n. 6, 233n. 29, 306n. 19
Mekhilta de Rabbi Shimeon Bar Yohai, 4n.
    6, 59n. 11
Menahem Azariah of Fano, 250n. 59
Midrash Aggadah, 126n. 10, 162n. 31—
    Bereshit 4.25, 196n. 14
Midrash ha-Gadol ba-Midbar, 210n. 51

Midrash ha-Gadol Bereshit, 47n. 48, 66n.
    26, 111n. 57, 158n. 20, 196n. 14, 227n.
    13, 287n. 10
Midrash ha-Gadol Devarim, 32n. 16, 55n. 3,
    99n. 27, 237n. 37, 249n. 57, 277n. 60
Midrash ha-Gadol Shemot, 146n. 43, 176n.
    63, 178n. 69
Midrash ha-Gadol va-Yiqra, 168n. 43, 179n.
    74
Midrash Mishlei, 29–30, 98n. 23
Midrash Sekhel Tov, 274n. 46
Midrash Shemuel (di Ozida), 196n. 15
Midrash Shemuel, 170n. 49, 199n. 19,
    245n. 52, 276n. 56
Midrash Tanhuma (Buber), 59n. 12, 111n.
    57, 177n. 67, 195n. 13, 201n. 28, 202n.
    30, 229n. 22, 296n. 8
Midrash Tanhuma (vulgar), 29n. 8, 126n.
    10, 196n. 14
Midrash Tannaim, 4n. 6, 32n. 16, 249
Midrash Tehillim (Shoher Tov), 59n. 12,
    102n. 32, 111, 126n. 10, 143n. 37, 162n.
    31, 181n. 80, 199n. 19, 201n. 29, 202n.
    30, 232n. 28, 237n. 37, 244, 265n. 19,
    281n. 67
Miqraot Gedolot to Psalms, 241n. 48
Mishnat Rabbi Eliezer, 47n. 48
Moses de Leon, 46n. 48
Moshav Zeqenim to Deut 23:19, 55n. 3
Musafia, Yaakov, 18n. 36, 28n. 6

Nahman, R., 112–3
Nahmanides, 102n. 32, 192n. 10, 229, 264n.
    17, 299, 302n. 13
Nahum bar Simai, 172, 178
Naphtali ben Menahem, 160n. 25
Nissim Gaon, 18n. 36, 29n. 8
Nortlingen, Yosef Yosspe Hahn, 291—2

Orhot Tzadiqim, 291—2
Otiyot de Rabbi Aqiba, 90n. 13

Pesher Habakkuk, 153
Pesiqta de Rav Kahana, 64nn. 23—24, 74n.
    51, 274n. 49, 275n. 52
Pesiqta Rabbati, 202n. 30, 288n. 15
Pirqei de Rabbi Eliezer, 111n. 57, 136n. 26,
    250n. 58

Qimhi, David, 9n. 21, 96n. 20, 122n. 5,
189n. 4, 201, 251n. 61, 263n. 13, 273n.
43, 275n. 50, 287n. 10, 288n. 15
Qimhi, Joseph, 189n. 4
Qohelet Rabbah, 12–3, 17–8, 67n. 32—
Proem 7, 264n. 17—1.10, 160n. 27—
1.8,3, 55–57—1.8,4, 64n. 23—5.14, 13n.
28—9.7,1, 171—9.8, 137n. 30

Raayah Mehemna, 90n. 13
Rabbeinu Gershom, 204n. 35
Rabbi Loewe (Judah the Lion) "Maharal" of
Prague, 160nn. 25, 27, 293
Rashi, 18n. 36, 28n. 6, 63n. 20, 84n. 74,
91n. 15, 96n. 20, 102, 104, 127n. 13,
168n. 42 190n. 6, 195n. 13, 199, 200n.
24, 202nn. 30–31, 208–9, 237n. 37,
239n. 44, 243, 268n. 27, 277n. 60, 281n.
67, 288
Rotenberg, Meir, 288n. 13
Ruth Rabbah, Proem 2, 69n. 36—Proem 3,
165n. 37—1, 203n. 33—2.9, 237n. 37—
3.1, 126n. 12—8.1, 238n. 38

Saadya Gaon, 37n. 24, 91n. 14, 122n. 5,
189n. 4, 243, 285n. 1, 288, 299
Samuel bar Nahman, 172, 243, 246, 248,
252
Satanover, Haim, 267n. 24
Schreiber, Moses, 196n. 15
Scroll 1QM 7.6, 76n. 57
Seder Eliyahu Rabbah, 4n. 6, 40n. 30, 281n.
67
Sefer ha-Hinnukh, 33n. 18
Shapira, Judah Loew (Frankfurter), 46n. 47,
189n. 4
She'eltot de Rab Ahai Gaon, 299
Shemot Rabbah 3.15, 99n. 26—15, 170n.
49—25.5, 43n. 39—30, 35n. 20—30.9,
46—37.1, 243—41.1, 224n. 8—46, 183–
4—46.4, 184n. 90—47.5, 277n. 58
Shemuel ben Meir, 200n. 21, 243
Shemuel Laniado, 250n. 59
Shimeon ben Pazzi, R., 82, 126—7
Shimeon ben Shatah, R., 116—7
Shir ha-Shirim Rabbah, 102n. 32—1.1,6,
231n. 27—1.4,1, 41n. 32—1.5,3, 227n.
13—1.8, 112—1.28, 46n. 46—2.2,4,
172n. 52—4.22, 69n. 36—8.2,1, 276n.
55—8.5,1, 276n. 56

Shulhan Arukh 1, 36n. 21
Sifra, 4n. 6, 49n. 52, 81n. 68, 168n. 43,
179n. 74, 201n. 28, 205n. 40
Sifrei ba-Midbar, 4n. 6, 64n. 24, 74n. 51,
120, 121n. 4, 190n. 6, 210n. 51
Sifrei Devarim, 103, 223–4—1, 205n. 40—
31, 104n. 36—48, 4n. 6, 276–7, 294—
49, 146n. 43—232, 4n. 6—257, 76n.
57—306, 4n. 6—312, 224n. 8—344,
168n. 42—352, 4n. 6—354, 165

Talmidei R. Yonah Gerondi, 32n. 16
Tarfon, R., 80, 205—6, 213
Tobia ben Eliezer, 67n. 32
Toledot Izhak (Yitzhak Caro), 267n. 24
Tos. Berakhot 2, 267—3:7, 65n. 26—4:25,
168n. 43
Tos. Betzah 2:10, 4n. 4
Tos. Hagigah 2, 126n. 10—2:1, 4n. 6, 35n.
19—2:3–4, 41n. 32
Tos. Hullin 2:24, 32n. 16, 55n. 3
Tos. Kelim Baba Qamma 1, 76n. 57—6:13,
273n. 44
Tos. Neziqin Baba Batra 5, 127n. 14
Tos. Shabbat 3:3, 4n. 4—15:9, 166n. 39—
15:17, 179n. 74—16:18, 4n. 4
Tos. Sheqalim 1:9, 277n. 59—2:2, 32n.
16—2:13, 170n. 47—3:1, 277n. 59
Tos. Sotah 15:11, 279n. 63
Tos. Terumot 4:3 and 4, 268n. 27—4:6,
72n. 45
Tos. Yevamot 4:7, 32n. 16
Tos. Yoma 1:1—2, 75n. 53—1:7, 74—1:20,
76n. 57—1:23, 73n. 47—2:2–3, 73n. 47
Tractate Derekh Eretz (Higger), 126n. 10—
1.2, 275n. 51—1.12, 32n. 16—1.20,
275n. 51—1.26, 32n. 16—7.2, 32n. 16
Tractate Derekh Eretz Zuta (Higger) 4, 32n.
16—4.5, 266, 267n. 24—5.3 and 7.2,
266n. 23
Tractate Kallah Rabbati (Higger) 3.21, 32n.
16
Tractate Kallah (Higger), 42n. 33
Tractate Semahot (Higger) 1.10, 264n. 17—
3.3, 13n. 29—8.10, 138—9—9.6, 265n.
18
Tractate Soferim (Higger), 276
Tractate Yir'at Het 1—2 (Higger), 32n. 16
Travis, Naftali Hertz, 250n. 59

va-Yiqra Rabbah, 4n. 6, 97—4.6, 59n. 13—
5.6, 197n. 16—11.7, 224n. 8—13.3,
281n. 67—16.4, 102n. 32—18:1, 92n.
16—21, 74n. 51—21.9, 64n. 23—22.1,
277n. 60—23, 179n. 74—23.2, 32n.
15—23.5, 172, 185—28.2, 18n. 36—
29.2, 165n. 37—33.6, 171—2—36.2,
220n. 1

Yalqut ha-Makhiri, to Micah, 55n. 3; to
Proverbs, 29n. 8, 287n. 10; to Psalms,
202n. 30, 250–2; to Zephaniah, 199n. 19
Yalqut Shimeoni, to Esther, 268n. 27; to
Genesis, 160n. 25, 195n. 13, 250n. 58,
274n. 46; to Isaiah, 64n. 23; to Jeremiah,
200n. 25; to Micah, 55n. 3; to Proverbs,

29n. 8, 55n. 3, 184n. 91, 287n. 10; to
Psalms, 220n. 1, 244n. 51, 274n. 46; to
Ruth, 203n. 33, 211n. 52
Yannai, 64n. 24, 106n. 42
Yedidiya Shelomo of Nortzi, 88n. 8
Yehiel min ha-Anavim, 32n. 16
Yohanan ben Zakkai, R., 18n. 36, 66, 67n.
33, 72, 127, 136, 306
Yohanan, R., 28, 35, 203, 237, 243
Yonah ben Avraham of Gerondi, 189n. 4,
267n. 24
Yosef Habiba, 250n. 59

Zohar Hadash, Midrash Ruth, 43n. 37
Zohar, 81n. 68, 90n. 13, 144–5